Artefacts from Wrecks

Dated Assemblages from the Late Middle Ages
to the Industrial Revolution

edited by Mark Redknap

Oxbow Monograph 84

Published by Oxbow Books
on behalf of the Nautical Archaeology Society and
Society for Post-Medieval Archaeology

© Oxbow Books and the individual authors 1997

ISBN 1 900188 39 2

This book is available direct from
Oxbow Books, Park End Place, Oxford OX1 1HN
(Phone: 01865–241249; Fax: 01865–794449)

and

The David Brown Book Company
PO Box 5111, Oakville, CT 06779, USA
(Phone: 860–945–9329; Fax: 860–945–9468)

Front cover: scarlet jacket, hat, dress accessories and wooden chest from the wreck of the *Kronan* (1676).
(Photograph: Kalmar Läns Museum)

Back cover: gold *San Vicente* of John III of Portugal (1521–57);
reverse, showing the saint holding a martyr's palm and a three-masted carrack – an allusion to Portuguese
discoveries and colonial expansion. Found on Margam Beach, South Wales (see Chapter 16).
(Photograph: National Museums & Galleries of Wales)

Printed in Great Britain at
The Short Run Press, Exeter

Contents

Introduction *by Mark Redknap* v

Part I Artefact Integration and Potential
1. Ships as integrated artefacts: the archaeological potential   *by Colin J.M. Martin* 1
2. The IJsselmeerpolders: a 'source book' for late medieval and early post-medieval wreck inventories
   by Karel Vlierman 15
3. Material culture research of Canadian historic shipwrecks: the *Machault* legacy   *by Stephen Davis* 37

Part II Artefact Groups from the Age of Discovery
4. The material culture of the *Mary Rose* (1545) as a fighting vessel: the uses of wood   *by Alex Hildred* 51
5. Reconstructing 16th-century ship culture from a partially excavated site: the Cattewater wreck   *by Mark Redknap* .. 73
6. Form, function, ownership: a study of chests from Henry VIII's warship *Mary Rose*, 1545   *by Maggie Richards* 87

Part III An Interdependence of Disciplines
7. Arms and armour from wrecks: an introduction   *by Ruth R. Brown* 101
8. Piecing together the past: footwear and other artefacts from the wreck of a 16th-century Spanish Basque galleon
   by Stephen Davis 110
9. Rhenish stoneware from shipwrecks: the study of ceramic function and lifespan   *by David R. M. Gaimster* 121
10. The identification, analysis and interpretation of tobacco pipes from wrecks   *by David A. Higgins* 129
11. Coinage from post-medieval wrecks   *by Edward Besly* 137
12. The British Museum collection of metal ingots from dated wrecks   *by Paul T. Craddock & Duncan R. Hook* 143

Part IV Shipwreck Identification and Social Structure
13. The galley, galley utensils and cooking, eating and drinking vessels from an armed '*Tjalck*' wrecked on the
    Zuiderzee in 1673: a preliminary report   *by Karel Vlierman* 157
14. The Cromwellian shipwreck off Duart Point, Mull   *by Colin J. M. Martin* 167
15. The identification of a ship's place of departure with the help of artefacts   *by Piet Kleij* 181
16. *Wreck de Mer* and dispersed wreck sites: the case of the *Ann Francis* (1583)   *by Mark Redknap & Edward Besly* ... 191
17. Artefacts from the *Kronan* (1676): categories, preservation and social structure   *by Lars Einarsson* 209
18. Family life on board: the Dutch boat people between 1600 and 1900   *by A.F.L. van Holk* 219
19. Artefacts from Wrecks: an endnote   *by Alan Aberg* 229

Index of Sites 231

List of contributors

ALAN ABERG
29 Pine Walk, Liss,
Hampshire GU33 7AT

EDWARD BESLY
Department of Archaeology & Numismatics,
National Museum & Gallery Cardiff, Cathays Park,
Cardiff CF1 3NP

RUTH R. BROWN
Hawthorne Cottage, Moorfield Road, Armley,
Leeds LS12 3SE

PAUL T. CRADDOCK
Department of Scientific Research,
The British Museum, Great Russell Street,
London WC1B 3DG

STEPHEN DAVIS
Federal Archaeology Office,
National Historic Sites Directorate, Parks Canada,
1600 Liverpool Court, Ottawa, Ontario, Canada,
K1A OM5

LARS EINARSSON
Kalmar Läns Museum, Box 104,
S-391 21 Kalmar, Sweden

DAVID R. M. GAIMSTER
Department of Medieval and Later Antiquities,
British Museum, Great Russell Street
London WC1B 3DG

DAVID A. HIGGINS
297 Link Road,
Anstey, Leicester LE7 7ED

ALEX HILDRED
The Mary Rose Trust,
College Road, HM Naval Base,
Portsmouth PO1 3LX

ANDRÉ F. L. VAN HOLK
Vakgroep Archeologie,
Department of Archaeology,
Rijksuniversiteit Groningen,
Faculteit der Letteren, Poststraat 6,
9712 ER Groningen,
The Netherlands

DUNCAN R. HOOK
Department of Scientific Research,
The British Museum, Great Russell Street,
London WC1B 3DG

PIET KLEIJ
Rijksdienst voor het Oudheidkundig Bodemonderzoek,
(ROB), Kerkstraat 1,
3811 CV Amersfoort, The Netherlands

COLIN J. M. MARTIN
Scottish Institute of Maritime Studies,
University of St Andrews,
St Andrews, Fife KY16 9AJ

MARK REDKNAP
Department of Archaeology & Numismatics,
National Museum & Gallery Cardiff,
Cathays Park, Cardiff CF1 3NP

MAGGIE RICHARDS
The Mary Rose Trust,
College Road,
HM Naval Base,
Portsmouth PO1 3LX

KAREL VLIERMAN
Netherlands Institute for Ship- and Underwater
Archaeology/ROB (NISA),
Vossemeerdijk 21
8251 PM Dronten, The Netherlands
(from mid-1998, Oostvaardersdijk, 8243 PB Lelystad).

Introduction

The growth of leisure diving over the last three decades has resulted in the discovery of an increasing number of historic shipwrecks. Diligent research, survey and, in some instances, excavation, may establish their identity and date of loss. Wreck sites form sealed microcosms and dated time-capsules, and hold the potential to stimulate research beyond the simple construction of evolutionary typologies with *termini ante quos* or descriptions of the technical capabilities of a nation's shipwrights. Artefacts from wrecks convey information on how the objects were manufactured, transported and traded, and their context or lifespan; they also relate to specific functions and the people on board, reflecting circumstance and lifestyle in a manner rarely recorded on terrestrial sites. For example, the *Batavia* (1629) carried ornately engraved silver ewers, chargers, chalices and bedposts, some destined for the Mughal Emperor Janghir, while the *Lastdrager* (1653) contained a large number of pocket sundials designed for European latitudes, but apparently destined as prestige gifts for eastern locals. The practicalities of navigation can be reassessed: the *Kennemerland* (1664) carried a crude form of backstaff or Davis quadrant supposed to be obsolete by this date, and the *Hollandia* (1743) carried an octant only a few years after its introduction, and not specified as standard equipment by the Dutch East India Company (VOC) until 1747. Navigational dividers are frequent finds from wreck sites, while the crew of the *Batavia* still used a mariner's astrolabe, and those on board the *Lastdrager* a universal or 'catholic' astrolabe. The objects found on board ships were seen by the people who used them within particular milieux, and their archaeological context provides an opportunity to record or recreate this lost setting of 'associative memory', as well as to record what was actually being carried on board at a particular time (as opposed to what was recorded in documents). Some papers presented here illustrate how it may be possible to associate particular artefacts with individuals of known status, the wrecks providing a specific context rarely preserved on land. The material culture from wrecks can be viewed as a *speculum orbis terrarum*, reflecting the political ambition, economics, industry and social context of the day.

It is not unreasonable to state that the significance of wreck sites for the study of our past has only gradually received wide recognition. With a few notable exceptions, terrestrial and maritime archaeologists rarely converge to share results. In 1994 an international conference was held at the National Museum of Wales (now National Museums & Galleries of Wales) which brought together a wide range of specialists who have been working in both fields. This conference sought to highlight the importance of contemporary studies of artefacts from wrecks, focusing on the period of transition in Europe from *c.* 1485 to 1785. This period witnessed rapid developments in naval architecture, associated with the introduction of effective fire power and improved ship performance which contributed to a widening sphere of influence of the European states around the World. The conference was organised through the Department of Archaeology & Numismatics on behalf of the Nautical Archaeology Society and the Society for Post-Medieval Archaeology, and brought together an audience from Europe and America.

This book presents most of the papers delivered at the conference. They illustrate the multitude of approaches to artefact analysis, from the foundations of dated typologies (and their reliability) to the examination of the relationship between artefact groups - contextual approaches to artefact studies *par excellence*. The editor regrets that a few papers presented at the conference have not found their way into the book, but the opportunity has been taken to incorporate one additional paper on the analysis of the dispersed artefact assemblage from a late 16th-century wreck in South Wales, which complements a number of other chapters. At least one chapter in the book has benefitted from the sound advice given by the late George Boon, who died shortly before the conference. George was a widely-read and wide-ranging archaeologist, numismatist and historian and (in the best sense of the word) antiquary, who devoted most of his career to the National Museum of Wales, becoming Keeper of Archaeology & Numismatics and Curator there. His interests included maritime matters, with articles on the Porth Felen anchor stock and finds from Margam beach. For a number of years he served on the Advisory Committee on Historic Wreck Sites, and was an early member of the CNA (Council for Nautical Archaeology). With his artefact-based interests, he expressed regret shortly before his death that he would be unable to be present; this book is dedicated to his memory.

I hope that these papers demonstrate that the study of artefacts is in no way subordinate to the technical study of ancient vessels or the terrestrial context of an assemblage, and that a number of tenets frequently cited (such as the dating of guns) are open to question. Selective publication of the main groups may serve a purpose within a summary account, but full publication of all finds to internationally acceptable standards is as important an objective as the production of a report on the non-artefactual evidence. The contributions presented here provide a positive indication of the state of artefact studies relating to shipwrecks, and an insight into the diversity of our past material culture. However, it will be clear that more comprehensive work on all aspects of artefacts from wrecks is required for the full potential of this resource to be realised. If this book instils a sense of future research possibilities within and outside the sub-discipline of maritime archaeology, and encourages a holistic approach to the subject, focusing on the integration of historical, archaeological, social, functional, technological and economic studies of our past, it will have achieved its goal.

ACKNOWLEDGEMENTS

The venue for the conference, the Reardon Smith Theatre, takes its name from Sir William Reardon Smith, the generous museum benefactor who ventured into shipping in 1905, and whose first ship the *City of Cardiff* featured as a model in the *Shipwrecks* exhibition which coincided with the conference. I would like to thank the Director of the National Museums & Galleries of Wales for supporting the event, and the Society for Post-Medieval Archaeology and Nautical Archaeology Society for their enthusiastic commitment to the proceedings. Its success was the result of effort put in by both Societies, who have generously contributed towards the cost of this publication. Many thanks are owed to the Kalmar läns museum and National Museums & Galleries of Wales for the cover photographs, and to the many organisations, institutions and individuals who have generously allowed their illustrations to appear in this book. I would like to express my gratitude to Alan Aberg, Chairman of the Nautical Archaeology Society, for his support and concluding remarks, and to colleagues who agreed to chair sessions, namely John Cherry, Chris Dobbs, Gillian Hutchinson, Dr A. J. Parker, Dr Sian Rees, Bob Smith and Ray Sutcliffe. I would also like to thank the staff of the Department of Archaeology & Numismatics for assistance on the day, in particular the former Keeper, Dr Stephen Aldhouse-Green, Elizabeth Walker, Evan Chapman, Frances Ford and Monica Cox. My final sincere thanks are to the contributors both to the conference and to this publication for their excellent presentations and prompt submission of manuscripts.

Mark Redknap
February 1997, Cardiff

Abbreviations:
The following abbreviations are used:
BAR British Archaeological Reports
EIC English East India Company
IJNA International Journal of Nautical Archaeology and Underwater Exploration
NMGW National Museums & Galleries of Wales
VOC Verenigde Oostindische Compagnie (United East India Company or Dutch East India Company)

Part 1
Artefact Integration and Potential

1

Ships as integrated artefacts: the archaeological potential

Colin J.M. Martin

> Breakfast is generally cooked in a hook-pot in the galley, where there is a range. Nearly all the crew have one of these pots, a spoon, and a knife; for all these things are indispensable; there are also basons, plates, etc., which are kept in each mess, which generally consists of eight persons, whose berth is between two of the guns on the lower deck, where there is a board placed, which swings with the ship and answers for a table. It sometimes happens that a lurch will dash all the crockery to pieces; they are then obliged to eat out of wooden utensils, until they come into harbour, when they get another supply.
>
> *Jack Nastyface (pseudonym of William Robinson), early 19th-century*

A ship, as Jack so graphically illustrates from his own experiences on the lower deck, is a self-contained entity. It carries within it and replenishes at the ports it visits all the materials, foodstuffs and artefacts needed for the survival, health, and recreation of those on board, the executive and technical skills associated with its routine management and maintenance, and the particular activities or enterprises for which it was built. It is an encapsulated society, a technological microcosm, and an expression of predatory, mercantile, or military endeavour – sometimes even of recreation or ritual – unique to its particular time and associations. If a vessel goes to wreck and so enters the archaeological record it may preserve – albeit in often dislocated, fragile, and vulnerable form – a closed, wholly associated, and sometimes virtually complete assemblage of material evidence relating to itself, to its function, and in various (though in some respects perhaps atypical) ways, to aspects of its parent culture ashore.

Nor should we forget the ultimate artefact – the ship herself. It is a commonplace, but one worth repeating, that shipbuilding is the most complex and costly technological activity that most societies have engaged in. A vessel's form and design, the ways in which materials are exploited and fashioned to build it, and the detailed carpentry of its construction, may be telling indicators of contemporary technical achievement. Modern man is frequently humbled when presented with firm archaeological evidence of such achievement – witness, for example, the superb craftsmanship and sensitive understanding of materials revealed by the recent Bronze Age boat-find at Dover. The working and management of ships, too, involves specialised artefacts which may provide insight to a continuum of practical techniques and intellectual perceptions – the business of navigation; medicine at sea; the administrative procedures of weighing, measuring and accounting; and a wide array of everyday crafts and skills, some specifically nautical, others not.

In the post-medieval period the richness of the nautical archaeological resource is complemented by what is often an overwhelmingly full documentary one. Ships usually represent a massive capital outlay to states or mercantile enterprises, and consequently generate an abundance of paperwork – building specifications; accounts relating to running, maintenance and repair; tonnage and capacity calculations; manifests of cargo, provisions, equipment and armament; crew and passenger lists; and so on. From the 16th century plans and constructional diagrams begin to emerge, though always with a bias towards state-owned warships. Should a vessel be wrecked, yet more documentation may be generated by enquiries into its loss, the fate or survival of those on board, insurance assessment, and salvage. Such material may touch on matters far beyond the immediacy of the shipwreck. Survivors of Armada ships wrecked in 1588, for example, have left detailed ethnological descriptions of life on Fair Isle and western Ireland which in other circumstances would never have been recorded (Martin 1975, 148–9; Gallagher and Cruikshank 1990), while a remarkable episode of shipwreck and salvage off Barra in the Outer Hebrides in 1728 created an archival resource of unimaginable bulk and rich historical potential at many, and often quite unexpected levels (Martin 1992).

The juxtaposition between archaeological remains, documentary sources and iconographic ones, is well illustrated by the case of the *Dartmouth*, a fifth-rate warship of 240 tons built at Portsmouth by Sir John Tippetts in 1655. In 1678 she underwent a major rebuild at Rotherhithe, for which copious accounts survive. Probably in the same year she was sketched by van de Velde the Younger (Fig. 1). In 1690, while engaged on behalf of William and Mary in anti-Jacobite gunboat diplomacy in the Sound of Mull, the ship was wrecked. Her remains were discovered in 1973, and three seasons of

Fig. 1. A fifth-rate warship, probably the Dartmouth: *wash sketch by Van de Velde the Younger,* c. *1678.*
(Photograph: National Maritime Museum)

investigation followed (Martin 1978). A substantial part of the lower hull had survived, neatly complementing the above-water elements so ably recorded by van de Velde. Close examination of the structural evidence revealed, however, that *Dartmouth's* build was unconventional, at least when set against the precepts of contemporary technical writers whose treatises modern scholars, understandably enough, have hitherto regarded as definitive sources. But academic writers – ancient and modern – tend at times to be impractical and unworldly, and few have engaged in the workaday business of building ships. The horny-handed craftsmen who did so engage rarely had much time or inclination for writing, or were illiterate – a disability which seems to have occasioned them little practical disadvantage. Consider the case of the 1200–ton first-rate *Charles*, launched at Deptford in 1668. She had been built, according to the diarist John Evelyn (who was present at the ceremony), '*by old Shish, a plain honest carpenter, master-builder of this dock, but one who can give very little account of his art by discourse, and who is hardly capable of reading, yet of great ability in his calling.*' In the hands-on business of wooden shipwrightry, vernacular tradition and family-based apprenticeship counted for much more than book-learning – and the Shishes, Evelyn shrewdly notes in conclusion, had been building ships at Deptford for more than three centuries. It follows that hull remains, like those of the *Dartmouth*, are likely to be the only reliable indicators of actual building practice until the comparatively recent past.

However, by their nature archaeological remains are rarely complete statements of the original complex structural artefact. The *Dartmouth's* surviving hull lacked all its upper parts and both extremities, and there was no clear indication of its orientation (Fig. 2). The late Keith Muckelroy, remembered here with fond respect as a colleague in the *Dartmouth* investigation and as a pioneer in the study of wreck formation processes, determined the latter through a spatial analysis of artefact categories across the site (Muckelroy 1978, 88–91). What appeared at first sight to be a random scatter of jumbled archaeological material resolved itself into a remarkably coherent statement of the original organisation of objects within the ship. Thus clay pipes could be shown to cluster around the galley remains, reflecting regulations which restricted smoking to this fire-proof area. Another cluster in what proved to be the stern region suggested that officers considered themselves exempt from the rule. The stern was itself identified by its association with artefacts which reflected the executive functions and relatively higher social standing of the captain and his officers – navigational instruments, weighing and measuring equipment, surgical instruments, and good quality personal accoutrements and tableware. Crew quarters towards the forecastle were likewise indicated by a preponderance of domestic treen and coarse pottery, equipment associated with the boatswain's store, and weaponry and munitions from the ship's armoury. Orientation was clinched by a number of mica lozenges which could be identified unequivocally in the van de Velde drawing as glazing from the stern cabin lights.

The point at which the surviving structure had lain along the ship's axis was determined by a critical comparison of the archaeological evidence with documentary sources. About 5 m of the keel was preserved, including an elegant horizon-

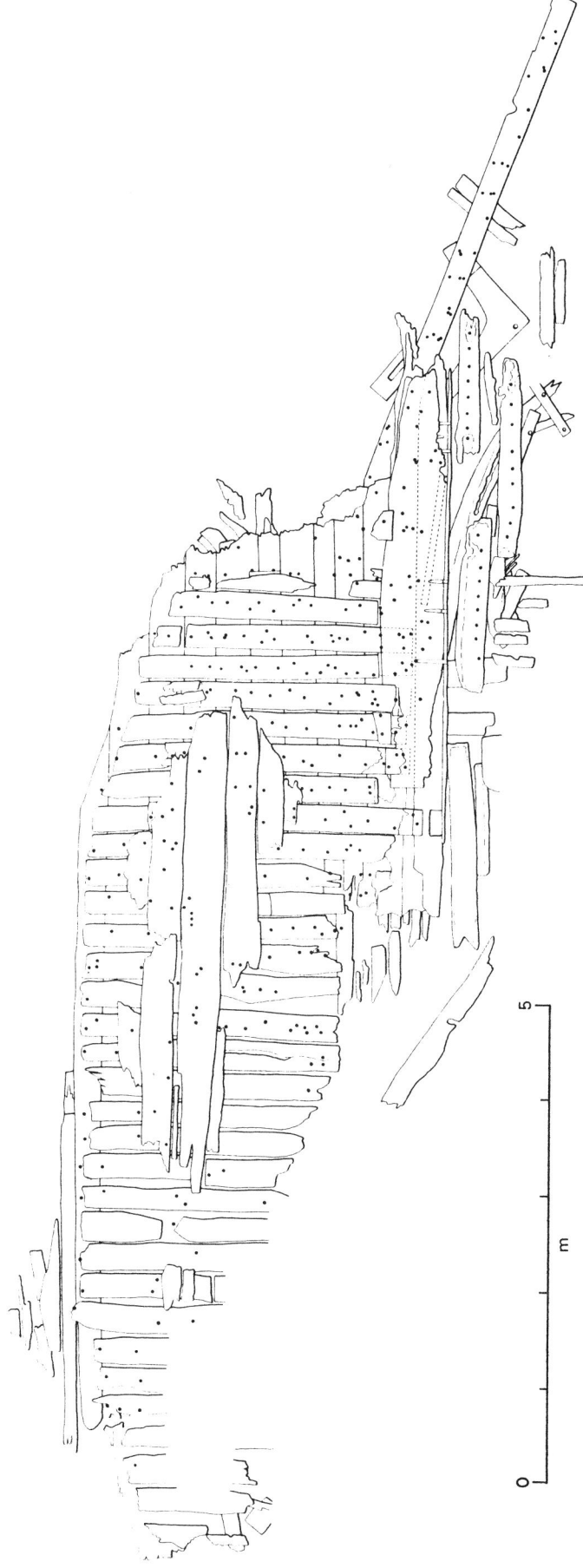

Figure 2. Surviving hull structure recorded on the Dartmouth wreck site in the Sound of Mull, 1973-5.

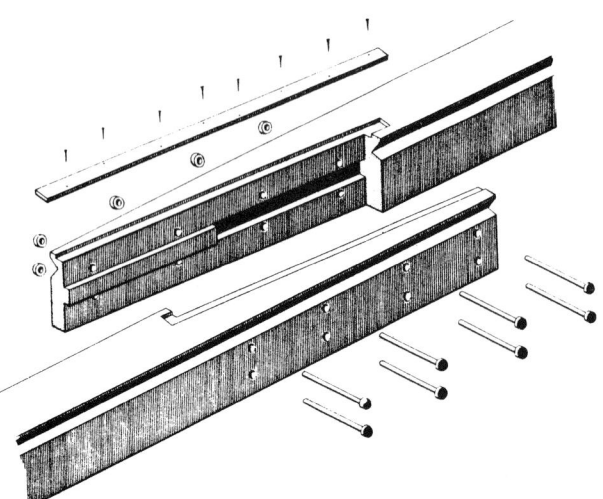

Figure 3. A diagrammatic reconstruction of a scarf joint on the Dartmouth's keel.

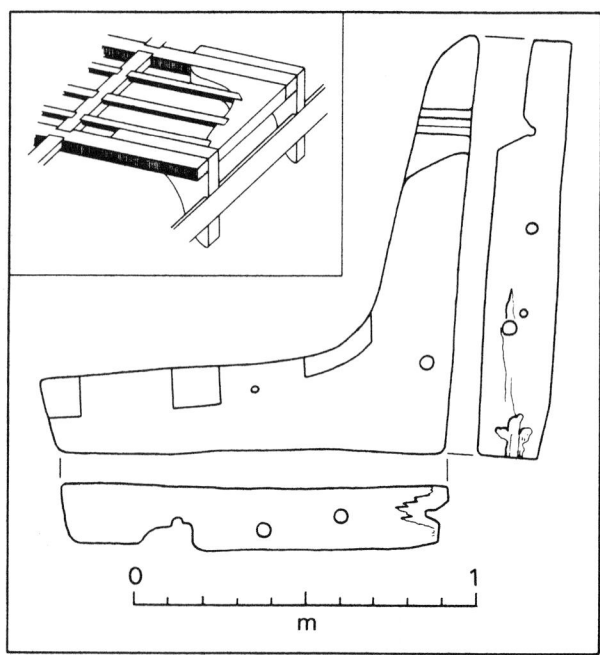

Figure 4. An oak lodging knee from the Dartmouth wreck showing (inset) its restored location within a structural module of the main deck.

tal scarf joint with a faced overlap of 4 ft 3 in (1.3m) (Fig. 3). The first item in the 1678 refitting account from Rotherhithe records a replacement of the entire keel, involving an 88 ft 6 in (27 m) linear run of 13 in (0.33 m) square elm (Martin 1978, 55). Yet the *Dartmouth's* keel, as her descriptive specification confirms, was only 80 ft (24.38 m) long (Adnams 1974, 272). The discrepancy of exactly twice the measured scarf overlap indicates that the keel was made up in three sections and so, assuming them to be equal and this to be the aftermost joint, a fixed point in the structure's longitudinal axis is obtained. The surviving timbers, and their curvature, can thus be used to project the ship's original underwater shape with some confidence.

Even displaced single components can be made to yield useful information. A lodging knee (Fig. 4) was found pinned beneath the *Dartmouth's* lower hull. It came originally from the main deck assembly, now long collapsed and – apart from this sole survivor – presumably destroyed. Yet the knee's dimensions, fastening holes, and component recesses allow a detailed reconstruction of the deck structure – apparently built in 5 ft (1.52 m) modules – to be made. Once the possibility of modular construction was recognised, moreover, it was observed that the main hull framing, though the individual widths of the futtocks varied considerably, conformed to a remarkably consistent centreline spacing of 1 ft (0.305 m).

The above does no more than touch upon the potential of even fragmentary and insubstantial structural remains such as those encountered on the wreck of the *Dartmouth*. Such studies are significant in their own right, but they may bear on wider issues too. The considerable ingenuity evident in repairing and squeezing a little more service from *Dartmouth's* ageing and ramshackle hull speaks of a navy under acute pressure from a parsimonious government (a circumstance well borne out by the documentary sources), while the use of building techniques which minimised the need for complex or wastefully-derived components undoubtedly reflects the timber-supply crisis of the mid-17th century (Albion 1952).

On account of her very ordinariness *Dartmouth* may stand as a microcosmic example of the archaeological value of shipwreck remains. But what of the smaller objects which ships contain, often in overwhelming profusion? Archaeologically such collections have two outstanding virtues. Deposition by calamity makes for a better representative survival of cultural material than the collections of discarded rubbish which characterise many terrestrial sites. This attribute is often enhanced underwater by anaerobic environments which encourage the preservation of organics. The preponderance of ceramics and, to a lesser extent, metals, on dry-land sites has tended to obscure the fact that more than 90% of most societies' material culture is organically-derived. There is almost nothing which, given the right environmental conditions, cannot survive in a waterlogged situation. Then again, wreck collections are by their nature closed groups of related finds. Everything on board a ship was in contemporary use at the moment of sinking.

These characteristics can give shipwreck assemblages a special significance, which may best be best be illustrated by examples. A bronze siege cannon (Fig.5a) from the wreck of the Spanish Armada ship *La Trinidad Valencera*, which sank off Donegal in 1588 (Martin 1979a) is clearly a significant object in its own right, but is made considerably more so by its archaeological and documentary associations. The Armada, it is known, carried a heavy siege train for the projected campaign in England, and this weapon – a 40–pounder full *canon* from the royal gunfoundry at Malines – was part of it (Martin 1988). Its weight mark – 5186 Castilian *libras* of 460 g (2904 kg) – clearly identifies it in a list of guns shipped aboard the

Valencera (two almost identical *canones* from the wreck bear weights which also match the documented figures). The description of the piece is full and explicit, and includes the interesting detail – for which the sea has removed all archaeological trace – that the royal arms had been picked out in paint. An even more striking documentary association has emerged. In 1587 a scale drawing was made of this very gun – the weight mark identifies it beyond reasonable doubt – as part of a policy submission to Philip II (Fig. 5 left). This is a rare example of early technical drawing, and since the subject itself is available for scrutiny it is possible to test the accuracy achieved by the 16th-century draftsman. That accuracy is considerable, as indeed was the precision of the 16th-century weighing which emerged when the piece was checked against a calibrated modern weighbridge (Martin 1988, note 19).

The documents reveal that each of these heavy guns was supplied with two field carriage assemblies, of which elements have been identified on the wreck. They include ten massive iron-reinforced spoked wooden wheels and five axletrees. The wheels fall into two types: Type I, which has six felloes and twelve spokes and is 1.52 m in diameter; and Type II, which is 1.3 m in diameter and has five felloes and ten spokes. These have been identified as main and limber wheels respectively. All the felloes are of ash, the spokes of oak, and the naves of elm, just as good wheelwrightry practice prescribes (Jenkins 1972, 61–71). The axletrees (of ash) were complete with iron fittings, including countersprings recessed into their lower faces and clamped to the axle stubs with iron clout-plates. There were no holes for linch-pins, indicating that these components were new and unassembled when brought aboard, a conclusion confirmed by a documentary source which notes that the siege carriages carried by the Armada had been built in 1587 (Martin 1988). A full-scale replica has now been reconstructed from archaeological and archival sources (Fig. 6).

Implements and instruments connected with the working of the guns are also included in the assemblage, each element adding, by association, to the overall significance of the group. By far the most revealing of these are a gunner's rule and three associated shot-gauges. The 22.2 cm wooden rule, calibrated on each side (to different proportional scales) with a progressive sequence of figures, was intended to equate bore diameter with the weight of the shot appropriate to it (Fig. 7). Examples of 16th-century gunners' rules are attested in contemporary literature (Cataneo 1571; Gentilini 1598; Capo Bianco 1602), and generally relate to iron shot. It is reasonable, therefore, to ascribe the larger proportional scale on the *Trinidad Valencera* example to the weights of iron spheres, which suggests that the smaller one – which must be calibrated for projectiles of greater mass – is intended for lead.

On this basis a number of simple calculations can be applied to test the thesis. Assuming a mean specific gravity for cast iron of 7.26, the value of a one-pound shot on the larger scale may be determined as 327 g – a unit closely compatible with the 'light' Milanese pound of 726.75 g (Lewis 1960, 218). Since the *Valencera* was a Venetian ship and certainly had Italian gunners aboard such a conclusion seems reasonable. Confidence in the identification is however undermined when the calculation is applied to the other figures on the scale, for which a division of the resulting shot-weight by the number concerned ought to result in the same figure as the unitary calculation. However the values range from 241 g to 367 g. The former is far too low to accommodate any known standard current in 16th-century Europe (the nearest being the 'subtile' Venetian pound of 301 g), while the latter

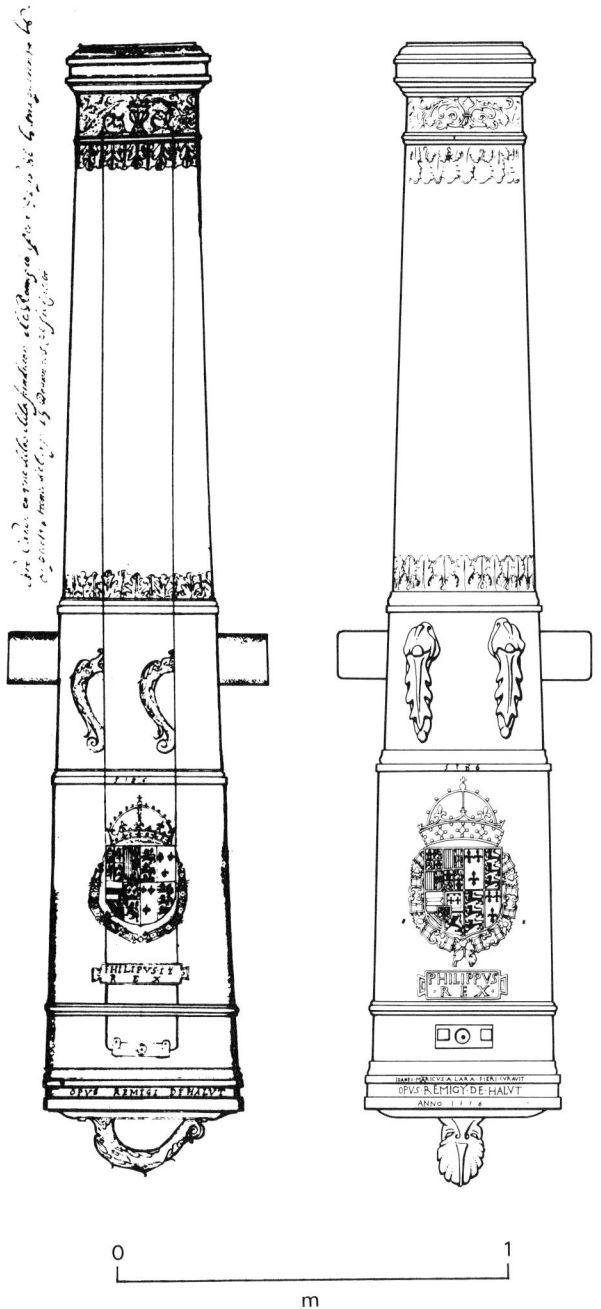

Figure 5. A scale drawing (left) of a cañón de batir *by Remigy de Halut of Malines, from a manuscript of 1587 (Archivo General de Simancas, Mapas, Planas, y Diagramas, V-8) compared (right) with the same gun, identifiable by its matching weight-mark of 5186 Castilian* libras, *which was recovered from the Armada wreck* La Trinidad Valencera.

Figure 6. One of the cañones de batir *from* La Trinidad Valencera *mounted on a replica siege-carriage built by the artificers of Devonport Naval Dockyard in 1988 to specifications recovered from documentary and archaeological sources.*

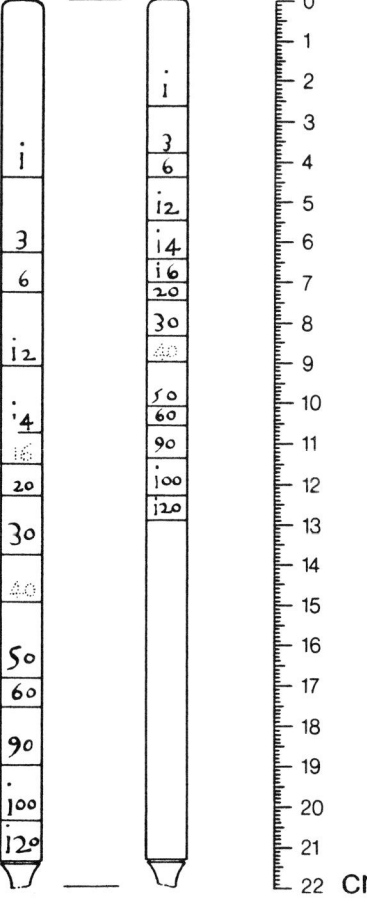

Figure 7. A boxwood gunner's rule from La Trinidad Valencera.

is tolerably close to the 'heavy' Milanese pound of 362.5 g (Lewis *op.cit.*). All that can be concluded is that whatever weight-system was intended for the scale, its internal inconsistencies are such as to defy resolution.

Even greater confusion is engendered when the reverse side of the rule is examined on the reasonable assumption that it is calibrated for lead. Here the calculations are just as diverse, and much lower, showing a range between 82 and 131 g. There is no known weight unit which remotely accommodates such values. However, it may be noted that the linear proportion of this scale in comparison with the larger calibration on the other side is approximately 6 to 10, which broadly equates with the proportional specific gravity differential of iron and lead – 7.26 to 11.37. It seems that the instrument-maker has succumbed to the fundamental arithmetical error of assuming that a proportional adjustment of the linear dimensions would result in an appropriate spherical volume/weight equation. In this case the misconception is such as to render the figures entirely meaningless.

This need not unduly have concerned the individual gunner involved, since the scale was complemented by a matching set of annular wooden templates, calibrated to the same diameters and shot-weight figures. Three examples of such gauges were found in association with the rule, and correspond to its one-, twelve-, and sixteen-pound graduations for iron. The gauges thus carry the same errors as the rule, and so at user-level they would cancel one another out. But unless we assume that every gunner and shot-manufacturer in late 16th-century Europe possessed identically misconceived instruments – which most assuredly they did not – we may postulate confusion of inestimable proportions in the apparently straightforward business of relating the manufacture and distribution of ammunition appropriate to the guns actually aboard individual ships. The problem was doubtless compounded by the multiplicity of weight standards and the general lack of standardised gun-types, prevalent throughout the fleet. This must have been a significant factor – perhaps even the most significant one – behind the Armada's abysmal gunnery performance in the Channel battles. More than that, it focuses attention on the broader question of early modern numeracy which, unlike literacy, has not yet been widely investigated (Martin 1983, 414–429).

The Armada wrecks have also yielded examples of weaponry intended for the kind of close-quarter action favoured by the Spaniards. A composite bronze and wrought iron breech-loading swivel gun was recovered from the *Trinidad Valencera* site, loaded and ready for use (Fig. 8). Such weapons, with their trunnions set on pintles which were in effect universal joints, could be reloaded speedily, elevated and traversed across wide arcs with ease, and were usually mounted on a ship's sides and upper works. The *Valencera* example remains as its gunner left it, ready for action, in 1588. It still has a stone shot in its barrel, a powder charge stoppered with a wooden plug in its interchangeable breech chamber and a twist of hemp in its touch-hole to keep the priming dry. A folded pad of leather is inserted behind the locking wedge to ensure a tight fit. Nine punch-marks set on the right-hand side of the breech stirrup match nine similar marks on the chamber, presumably to relate the one to the other. These arrangements imply a well organised firing procedure, of which some aspects can be deduced from the archaeological evidence. Marks on the left-hand side of the locking wedge suggest that it was normally struck free after discharge by the gunner with a hammer held in his left hand. His right hand would thus have been free to lay the piece by means of its extended tiller bar. But in the aiming position, with the tiller held at arm's length to ensure a safe distance between his eyes and the imperfect breech seal, the gunner would have been unable to ignite the

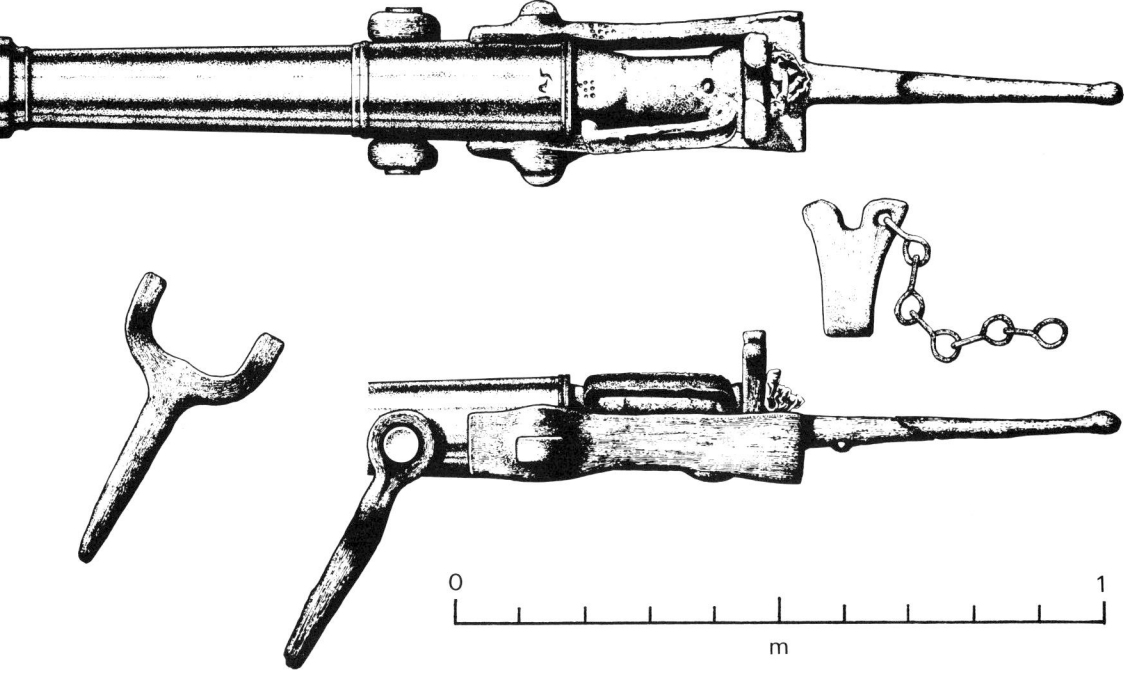

Figure 8. Composite bronze and wrought-iron swivel gun from La Trinidad Valencera.

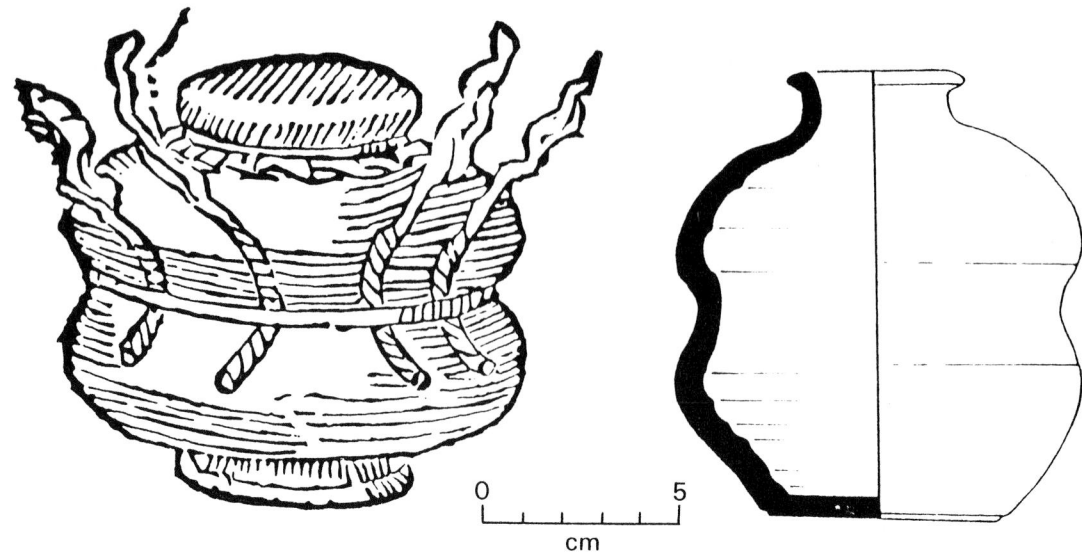

Figure 9. A ceramic firepot (alcancía) from La Trinidad Valencera compared (left, and not to same scale) with the depiction of a similar weapon by Cyprian Lucar (1588).

priming. A Number Two facing the gun on its right hand side may therefore be postulated. He would fire the piece on the gunner's word of command, extract the spent block when the gunner cleared the wedge, and insert a loaded one after a fresh projectile had been inserted into the breech (Martin 1983, 302–305).

Incendiary weapons are as old as warfare itself, but examples have rarely before been found in archaeological contexts. They are now turning up on wrecks. Among the pottery forms identified during the excavation of *La Trinidad Valencera* is a clear-glazed red earthenware bottle with a flared neck and distinctive pinched waist (Martin 1994; see Fig. 9). Its soft fabric with micaceous inclusions matches red earthenware of the so-called Merida type, which has been shown to originate in Portugal or western Spain (Williams 1979). A complete example has a capacity of 0.39 l, and contained a black sludge which, on analysis, was found to comprise mainly carbon, with slight indications of sulphur. The object may be identified with the *alcancías de barro* – earthenware firepots – listed in a 1586 planning document related to the Armada (Duro 1884, 305). They were to be supplied at a unit cost of one *real* by contractors in Lisbon. The form is well illustrated in contemporary literature, which describes various recipes for its gunpowder-based napalm-like filling, and shows how lighted fuses were tied round its pinched waist to ignite the mixture on impact (Lucar 1588; Gentilini 1598; Cataneo 1571).

Another incendiary weapon recovered from the same wreck was a wooden tube reinforced with cord bindings which contained charges designed to spew out flame and pellets over a four-episode sequential cycle lasting perhaps thirty seconds. Mounted at the end of a shaft, such weapons were used by the leading troops in storming a breach or carrying a ship by boarding (Martin 1994). It, too, is well attested in contemporary technical literature, though this is the first example, to the writer's knowledge, to have been identified in modern times. The weapon is described in Armada documents as a *bomba* (English equivalent = "trunk"), with a unit cost of 4 *reals* (Duro 1884, 305). Graphic and harrowing descriptions of *alcancías* and *bombas* in combat situations during the siege of Malta are provided by Balbi de Correggio (1568).

Cargoes make up a significant element of many wreck assemblages, and in addition to their intrinsic interest as groups of artefacts they carry significance as snapshots of mercantile enterprise frozen in transit, often preserving details of packaging and stowage. The unsympathetic salvors of the Nanking cargo unfortunately failed to record in any meaningful way the almost intact survival of a consignment of mid-eighteenth century Chinese porcelain packed in chests of tea (Hatcher 1987). More remarkable, and happily recorded to the highest archaeological standards, was the prefabricated monumental arch stowed in the hold of the Dutch East Indiaman *Batavia*, lost off the coast of Western Australia in 1629 (Green 1989, 179–190). Information relating to cargo stowage may be gleaned even on fragmentary and scattered sites by careful archaeological recording and interpretation – witness the pan-lid handles recovered from the wreck of the Dutch East Indiaman *Adelaar*, lost off Barra in 1728, whose unflattened rivet-stubs suggest that the lids and handles were shipped unassembled for ease of packaging (Fig. 10). Archae-

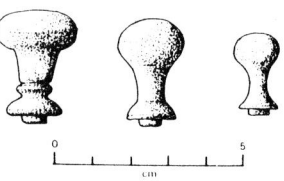

Figure 10. Copper pan-lid handles from the wreck of the Adelaar *(1728). the unbeaten rivet-studs show that they were yet to be attached to the sheet metal lids, which were presumably nested for ease of packaging in transit. Scale 1:2.*

ology may further elucidate aspects of a ship's cargo which have escaped inclusion in its formal documentation. An example is provided by the *Kennemerland*, a Dutch East Indiaman wrecked on the Out Skerries of Shetland in 1664. A small and varied group of attractive portable items from the site is best explained as part of an individual seaman's trade chest (Fig. 11). Company regulations permitted this practice, and allowed discretion in the choice of content. One of the items, a brass tobacco box, bears the same date as the shipwreck.

Metal ingots are rarely found in terrestrial contexts since they exist in that form only as a convenience for transport or use as a raw material. By their nature, however, they are often found on wrecks. The *Adelaar* has produced a number of lead ingots, of which a type-sampling is illustrated in Fig. 12, while a major collection from the *Kennemerland* site has been the subject of a major investigation (Price *et al.* 1980). In spite of a recent plea, however, the potential of shipwrecks as a key source for the study of post-medieval ingots has barely been touched upon (Craddock and Hook 1995, and this volume).

Wrecks frequently contain commonplace objects which, for one reason or another, seldom survive in other archaeological contexts. One such is the slatted wooden lantern, until recently known only from contemporary pictures (there is a fine representation in Breugel's *Gloomy Day*). Now examples are turning up with such regularity on post-medieval shipwrecks that Dr Antony Firth of Southampton University is compiling a typology of them. The *Trinidad Valencera* site has produced the component parts of one type, closely paralleled

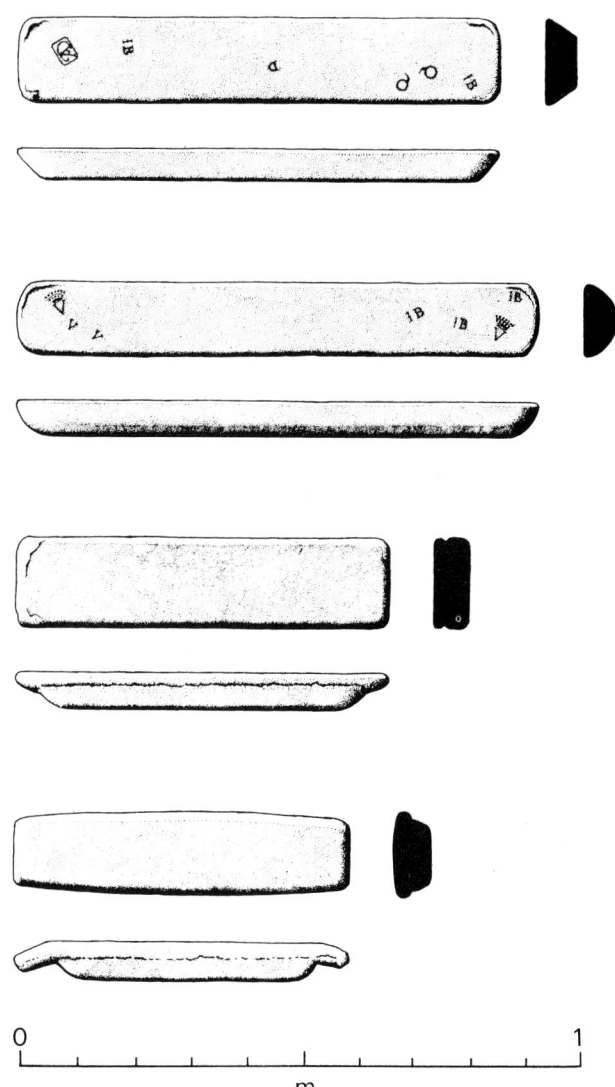

Figure 12. Lead ingots from the Adelaar *(1728).*

by finds from the *Mary Rose* (McKee 1982, 134). The only element missing is the lights, though grooves in the edges of the uprights and the ends of thin wooden glazing bars in one of them suggests a material such as rectangular panels of translucent horn. From the same wreck comes the top element of a rather different type, with a leather carrying handle. In this case the uprights, of which two stumps have survived within their pegged mortises, are ungrooved, indicating another form of lights. The answer is provided by the ship's manifest, which records the issue of eight wooden lanterns of two different sorts – the one covered with waxed linen, the other glazed with horn. Not only are the documents and the archaeology here mutually supportive, but the former provides the latter with the one element which has not survived as physical evidence (Fig. 13).

The potential for good organic survival often makes shipwreck sites rich repositories of environmental evidence. Though as yet unpublished, the *Mary Rose* material is likely to be exceptionally significant in this respect (Ian Oxley, pers. comm; Hildred, this book Chapter 4.). The assemblage in-

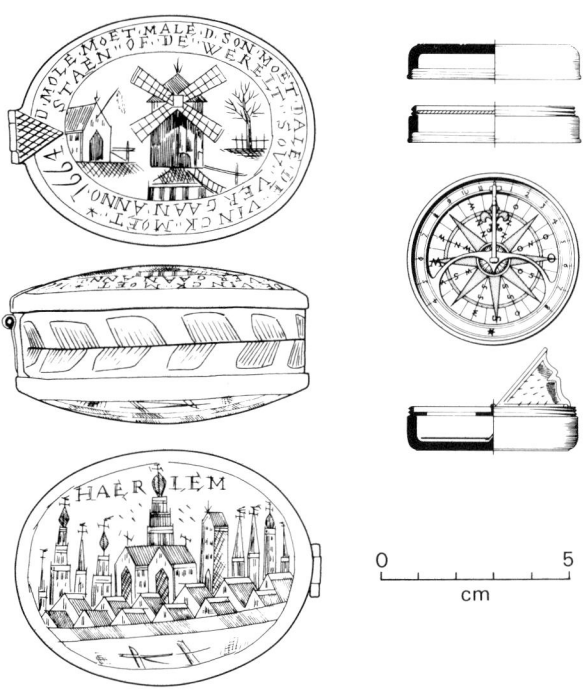

Figure 11. Items believed to be personal trade-goods, from the wreck of the Kennemerland *(1664). Left: a brass tobacco-box dated 1664 (its inscription translates "The mill must grind, the sun must sink, the finch must stand, or the world must end"). Right: a pocket combination compass/ sundial.*

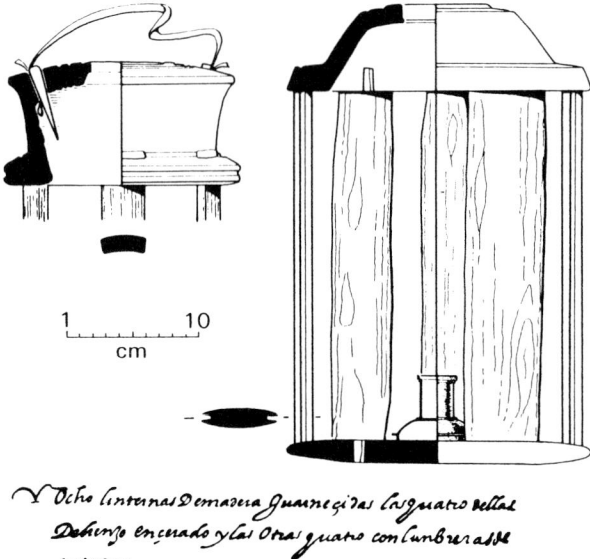

Figure 13. Wooden lantern assemblies from La Trinidad Valencera *(1588), restored from surviving components. The facsimile extract from the ship's manifest (Archivo General de Simancas, Contraduría Mayor de Cuentas, 2a 280/1472) translates "Eight wooden lanterns of which four are provided with lights of waxed linen, and the other four with lights of horn".*

cludes extensive human skeletal remains, amongst which malformations perhaps associated with archery stresses have been identified (Rule 1983, 184–5). An animal-bone assemblage from *La Trinidad Valencera* has yielded much information of diet and butchery practice aboard the Armada ships (Armitage 1995). Some of this contradicts the evidence of documentary sources, notably the unexpectedly high proportion of sheep bones identified. Since mutton does not respond well to salting and is rarely associated with ship victualling lists it is surmised that the animals may have been shipped live or obtained as fresh meat at Lisbon or Corunna. The substantial collection of pig bones undoubtedly does derive from salted cuts, with the jawbones showing evidence of longitudinal cleavage. All appear to be from young male animals, probably castrated. Some of the sheep and cattle bones are cut and smashed in ways suggestive of soup preparation, or the extraction of the last scraps of nourishment. Vermin are represented by two almost complete skeletons of black rats, and rodent tooth-marks are present on some of the other bones. A feline *ulna* attests the presence on board of a young cat.

An important area of common interest to nautical archaeologists and their terrestrial counterparts is pottery. Most land sites produce ceramics in abundance, and pottery is far and away the most common source of dating evidence, not to mention its value as an indicator of status, cultural contact and trade. Shipwrecks, too, are frequently rich in ceramics, and provide collections which have the inestimable advantage of coming in closed and often very precisely dated assemblages. This value may be enhanced by studying related groups from several wreck sites. The Armada again provides a revealing case-study, since the archaeological contexts provided by the individual wrecks are enhanced by a knowledge of the origins and subsequent itineraries of the vessels involved and by documentation of their provisioning prior to the campaign (Martin 1979b, 1995). A ceramic common denominator is provided by the olive-jar, in which the fleet's oil ration was exclusively supplied. The documents indicate that the esparto-encased jars were accounted for in half-*arroba* (6.2 l) units, a capacity confirmed by the examples found. Another type common to all the sites is Merida-type red earthenware, glazed and unglazed, which may be associated with Portugal (in general) and Lisbon (in particular; Fig. 14). It was at Lisbon

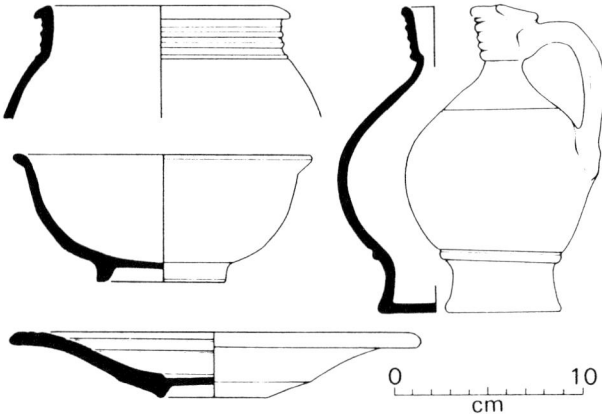

Figure 14. Mérida-type glazed earthenware from La Trinidad Valencera *(1588). These forms can be equated with the four types contracted from potteries in Lisbon in 1586 and described as "platos, excudillas, ollas y jarros de barro vidriados" (Martin 1979, 299). Scale 1:4.*

that the fleet mustered before it sailed.

Many ships also touched at Seville prior to coming to Lisbon, and this contact explains the presence on board them of Columbia Plain tin-glazed earthenwares, long associated with the area. But no Columbia Plain was identified on the wreck of the *Santa Maria de la Rosa*, a ship built at San Sebastian in 1587 before being requisitioned and taken direct to Lisbon for the Armada. The site has, however, produced a hard off-white ware with a honey-coloured glaze which is not represented in the other collections and which may therefore be ascribed with some confidence to the San Sebastian region. This supposition is reinforced by the identification of similar wares from the mid-16th-century Basque shipwreck and whaling station at Red Bay, Labrador.

Even greater potential exists for the comparative analysis of ceramic collections derived from a series of related wrecks spread (preferably at regular intervals) over a substantial period. Such a study has recently been accomplished by Marken (1994), whose work on ceramics from seventeen wreck contexts with Hispanic associations dating from 1500 to 1800 has produced a number of unimpeachable chronological type-runs, particularly of coarsewares. From this he has developed a theoretical basis for the typological analysis of olive jar and Columbia Plain forms by the identification and

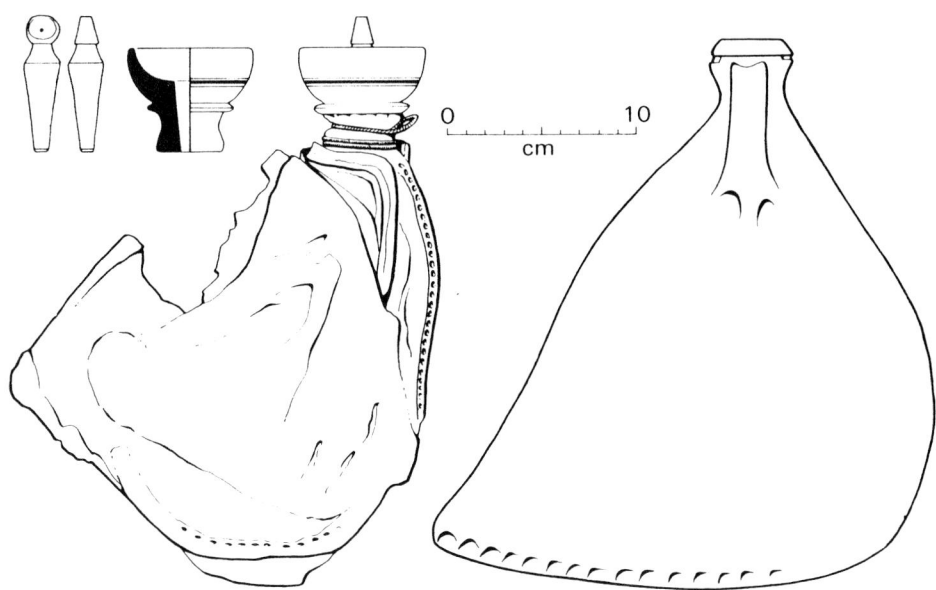

Figure 15. Goatskin wine-bag from La Trinidad Valencera *(1588), compared with a 16th-century ceramic skeuomorph from Lower Parrock, Sussex (after Freke). The latter is a reconstruction of the form, and not to scale.*

comparison of particular attributes. With such methods it is now often possible to define the typological dating of an unassociated example within a quarter-century bracket, though it has to be stressed that the variables involved, and the ever-present possibility of idiosyncrasy, makes the process complex and not always reliable. Dr Marken's research has demonstrated that simple typological characteristics are rarely in themselves dependable indicators of date, especially if derived from a single vessel or sherd. The systematic analysis of a statistically significant group must always be aimed at, and even then the answer is likely to be couched in probabilities rather than certainties. This, one suspects, has always been so with the typological dating of most coarsewares.

Wrecks, with their capacity to preserve organic materials, have on occasion produced prototypes of what have been recognised in terrestrial contexts as ceramic skeuomorphs. A type of goatskin wine bag from *La Trinidad Valencera*, complete with turned funnel-mouth and stopper, may be equated with a pottery form from the early 16th-century kiln site at Lower Parrock, East Sussex (Freke 1979, 103–104), which clearly seeks to replicate it (Fig. 15). Another example is the stave-built barrel costrel from the Duart Point wreck (see p. 174 below), a form echoed since Roman times in ceramic versions (Webster 1969, Fig.1/10).

In conclusion it must be said, with regret, that effective collaboration between nautical archaeologists and their terrestrial colleagues, especially in the field of ceramic studies, has (with a few notable exceptions) so far been somewhat disappointing. The potential is considerable, but the road ahead may be rocky, for evidence from shipwrecks will on occasion call into question long-established criteria of typological dating. The *Dartmouth* of 1690, for example, has produced a firmly associated group of clay pipes which, on typological criteria alone, would extend from the mid-17th century at one end to a decade or so into the 18th at the other (Martin P.F. 1977 and 1987). A similar discrepancy may be argued for dating criteria applied to the so-called Bellarmine forms of stoneware, of which the Dutch East Indiaman *Vergulde Draeck*, lost off Western Australia in 1656, has produced almost all the forms represented by a well-known chronological typology which – though admittedly now regarded as somewhat outdated – spans the greater part of the 17th century (Green 1977; Holmes 1951). Other important collections have been recovered from the *Batavia* (1629) and *Kennemerland* (1664) (Green 1989; Forster and Higgs 1973) (Fig. 16). These findings in no way discredit the concept of typological dating, but they do emphasise that the criteria are complex and need, in many instances, to be examined afresh. This recognition ought to have profound and far-reaching consequences, since not only the dates of the artefacts but conclusions drawn (and often subsequently further built upon) from their associations may often require fundamental revision. The danger of circular argument is often closer than we recognise, or would readily admit to.

It is beyond contention that wreck material, properly investigated and recorded, has the capacity to make a unique and substantial contribution to the discipline of archaeology as a whole. Yet with one or two shining exceptions it has so far had relatively little impact. A number of reasons may be adduced. Underwater archaeologists often adopt a somewhat blinkered approach to their sites, and fail to see the wider implications of their finds. Nor can the sub-discipline (if so it may be described) claim a particularly good publication record, though this criticism can be levelled at many terrestrial colleagues too. To cap it all, there may often be an implied association (one hopes unjustified) with the excesses of the much publicised, though happily diminishing, practice of underwater treasure-hunting. As a result 'straight' archaeolo-

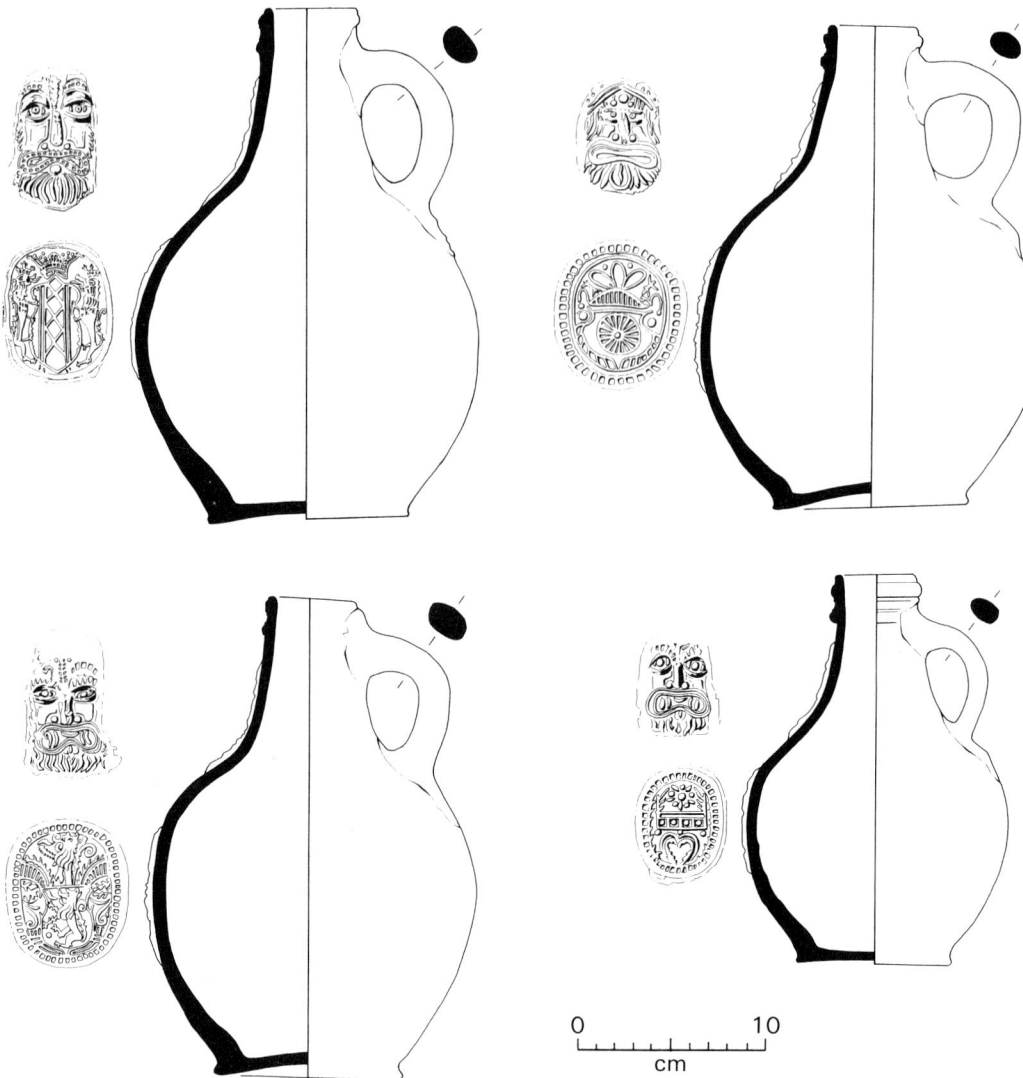

Figure 16. A group of Frechen stoneware flagons from the Kennemerland *(1664). Scale 1:4.*

gists may sometimes feel, however subconsciously, that their nautical counterparts operate in a peripheral area of limited consequence and sometimes suspect propriety.

This conference seeks to allay such fears and to promote closer collaboration – indeed full integration – among archaeologists whose only differences are those of working environment and (to some extent) subject specialisation. Those who investigate post-medieval shipwrecks underwater are urged to apply the highest standards to their investigations, to set their findings into wider archaeological contexts, and above all to publish them. Those whose business lies in the terrestrial spheres of archaeology, for their part, must apprise themselves of the findings of their nautical colleagues, even (indeed especially) when these may on occasion appear to contradict long-accepted interpretations.

A final point must be made. Shipwrecks are complex archaeological phenomena whose processes of disintegration and eventual stabilisation within the undersea environment are difficult to understand and quantify. Yet an understanding and quantification of formation processes is essential if wrecks are to become more than mere quarries of interesting artefacts. There are no short cuts. But if we can correctly interpret these processes through good archaeological practice driven by a genuine respect for this rich but vulnerable resource, tempered by intellectual rigour and more than a touch of humility, then life will be breathed into our shipwreck assemblages, turning them into the vibrant and very human realities which brought them into being.

References
Adnams, J. R. 1974 'The *Dartmouth*, a British frigate wrecked off Mull, 1690', *IJNA* 3, 269–274.
Albion, R. G. 1952 'The timber problem of the Royal Navy', *The Mariner's Mirror* 38, 4–20.
Armitage, P. L. 1995 Unpublished Level III report on the mammalian bones excavated from the shipwreck *La Trinidad Valençera*.
Capo Bianco, A. 1602 *Corona e palma militare di artiglieria*, Venice.
Cataneo, G. 1571 *Del' arte militare... con l'essamini di bombardieri*, Brescia.
Correggio, Francisco Balbi di 1568 *Relacion de toda lo que el anno MDLXV en la isla de Malta....* , Barcelona.

Craddock, P. T. and Hook, D. R. 1995 'Ingots from the sea: a coming of age', *IJNA* 24, 67–70.

Duro, C. F. 1884 *La Armada Invencible, tomo I*, Madrid.

Foster, W. A. and Higgs, K. B. 1973 'The *Kennemerland*, 1971. An interim report', *IJNA* 2, 291–300.

Freke, D. J. 1979 'The excavation of a 16th-century pottery kiln at Lower Parrock, Hartfield, East Sussex, 1977', *Post-Medieval Archaeology* 13, 79–125.

Gallagher, P. & Cruikshank, D.W. 1990, *Francisco de Cuellar: letter from one who sailed... a new annotated translation*, in P. Gallacher and D. W. Cruikshank (eds), *God's Obvious Design*, London.

Gentilini, E. 1598 *Instruttioni di artiglieri*, Venice.

Green, J. 1977 *The A-VOC Jacht* Vergulde Draeck, *wrecked Western Australia, 1656*, Part I, BAR Supplementary Series 36 (i), Oxford.

Green, J. 1989 *The A-VOC Retourschip* Batavia *wrecked Western Australia, 1629: Excavation report and artefact catalogue*, BAR International Series 489, Oxford.

Hatcher, M. 1987 *The Nanking Cargo*, London.

Holmes, M. 1951 'The so-called 'Bellarmine' mask on imported Rhenish stoneware', *Antiquaries Journal* 31, 173–179.

Jenkins, J. Geraint 1972, *The English Farm Wagon*. Newton Abbot.

Lewis, M. 1960, *Armada Guns*, London.

Lucar, C. 1588 *Tartaglia's colloquies and Lucar appendix*, London.

McKee, A. 1982 *How we found the Mary Rose*, London.

Marken, M. 1994 *Pottery from Spanish Shipwrecks, 1500–1800*, Gainesville (Florida).

Martin, C. J. M. 1975 *Full Fathom Five: wrecks of the Spanish Armada*, London.

Martin, C. J. M. 1978 'The *Dartmouth*, a British frigate wrecked off Mull, 1690. 5. The ship', *IJNA* 7, 29–58.

Martin, C. J. M. 1979a '*La Trinidad Valencera*: an Armada invasion transport lost off Donegal', *IJNA 8*, 13–38.

Martin, C. J. M. 1979b, 'Spanish Armada pottery', *IJNA 8*, 279–302.

Martin, C. J. M. 1983 *The equipment and fighting potential of the Spanish Armada*, Unpublished Ph.D thesis, University of St Andrews.

Martin, C. J. M. 1988 'A 16th century siege train: the battery ordnance of the 1588 Spanish Armada', *IJNA* 17, 57–73.

Martin, C. J. M. 1992 'The wreck of the Dutch East Indiaman *Adelaar* off Barra in 1728', in R. Mason and N. Macdougall (eds), *People and Power in Scotland: essays in honour of T C Smout*, Edinburgh.

Martin, C. J. M. 1994 'Incendiary weapons from the Spanish Armada wreck *La Trinidad Valençera*, 1588', *IJNA* 23, 207–217.

Martin, C. J. M. 1995 'Spanish Armada Ceramics', in C. M. Gerrard, A. Gutierrez & A. J. Vince (eds), *Spanish Medieval Ceramics in Spain and the British Isles*, BAR International Series 610, Oxford, 353–357.

Martin, P. F. de C. 1977 'The *Dartmouth*, a British frigate wrecked off Mull, 1690. 4. The clay pipes', *IJNA* 7, 219–223.

Martin, P. F. de C. 1987 'Pipes from the wreck of the *Dartmouth*, 1690: a reassessment', in P. Davey (ed.), *The Archaeology of the Clay Tobacco Pipe. X. Scotland*, BAR British Series 178, Oxford.

Muckelroy, K. 1978 *Maritime Archaeology*, Cambridge.

Price, R., Muckelroy, K. & Willies, L. 1980 'The *Kennemerland* site: a report on the lead ingots', *IJNA* 9, 7–25.

Rule, M. 1983 *The Mary Rose. The Excavation and Raising of Henry VIII's Flagship*, London.

Webster, G. 1969 *Romano-British coarse pottery: a student's guide*, CBA Research Report 6, London.

Williams, D.F. 1979 'Petrological analysis', in C.J.M.Martin 1979, 'Spanish Armada Pottery', *IJNA* 8, 298–299.

2

The IJsselmeerpolders: a 'source book' for late medieval and early post-medieval wreck inventories

Karel Vlierman

INTRODUCTION

Over 50% of the Netherlands is situated below sea level. Since the 10th century, this low-lying land has been gradually isolated from the influences of low and high tide by a relentless process of dike building and land reclamation, a chapter in Dutch history known as " the eternal battle against the sea".[1]

After 1932 the *Zuiderzee* was renamed the *IJsselmeer*. The *Wieringermeerpolder* was the first polder to be drained, followed by the *Noordoostpolder*, *Oostelijk Flevoland* and *Zuidelijk Flevoland*. A total of 166,000 ha of new land was reclaimed (Fig.1), and on this former sea bed, covered by thick layers of sediments, hundreds of shipwrecks have been found.

The *Nederlands Instituut voor Scheeps- en onderwater Archeologie/ R.O.B. (N.I.S.A.)*[2] has been excavating these shipwrecks since 1942. At the time of writing the remains of 435 ships, dating from the 13th to the end of the 19th century, have been registered.

A large number of these wrecks still contain their artefactual inventory. Many can be dated to within twenty-five years or less, and on occasions to the exact date of sinking (Vlierman 1983, 1). These 'time capsules' contain not only information on the daily life and work of a captain, but often also of his family or mate.

An important characteristic of the shipwrecks is that they provide information about ordinary people in circumstances for which almost no written sources are available. All the ships and their artefacts represent a form of 'source book' for late and post-medieval shipbuilding techniques, and of utensils and equipment used over a period of more than 700 years.

At the N.I.S.A. we try to publish the information about each ship and its equipment/inventory as an indivisible whole. This paper presents not only information about the nature and the preservation of the artefacts, but also outlines the ship types and their methods of construction. As only a small number of the ship finds have been thoroughly investigated and published, at this stage comparison between individual inventories is barely possible.[3]

THE DISCOVERY, INVESTIGATION AND STORAGE OF THE SHIPWRECKS

At the time of writing, 350 of the 435 registered shipwrecks have been excavated and recorded. Fifteen well-preserved ships have been protected *in situ* to preserve them for future investigation. Seven excavated and recorded medieval ships have been reburied at different locations. Three exceptional ships have been conserved. Two of these, a mid-17th century merchantman (Fig.2) and a so-called *ventjager* wrecked *c.*1700 (Vlierman 1991, 95–104; Fig.3), are currently shown in the Rijksmuseum for Ship Archaeology at Ketelhaven. The third vessel, an early 17th-century *beurtschip*, will be exhibited at the new location in Lelystad. Two Roman logboats found beyond the Zuiderzee region at Zwammerdam, are also on display.

METHODOLOGY

In the polders most of the shipwrecks were found during the first years after draining the land (by, for example, digging canals and ditches for example) and later in the course of building activities or while ploughing. Several new wrecks are still being reported each year. Once reported, a preliminary investigation of the site (lasting a few days) is conducted by a small team of two specialists. Three trial trenches are usually dug in order to gain a first impression of the nature of the remains (Fig.4). This is to evaluate:

1. the size of the ship
2. the type of ship
3. the completeness, inventory and cargo
4. the date of wreckage

After the investigation the wreck is covered up again.

The trial excavation also produces data about the soils and stratigraphy above and below the wreck (Fig.5), which may 'fix' the event in a time frame.

The number of ships in the *Noordoostpolder* and *Oostelijk Flevoland* turned out to be very high. In general, they were considered an obstacle by the development planners. The

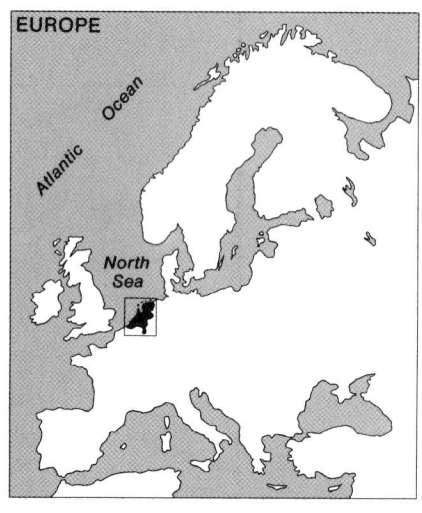
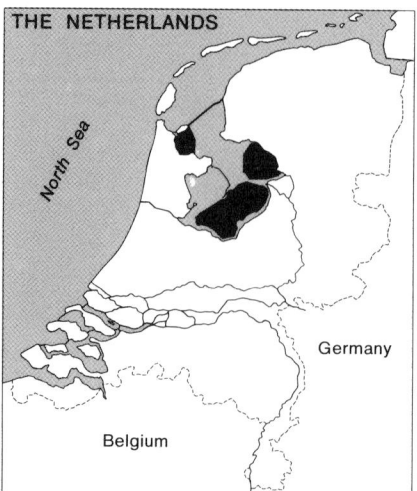
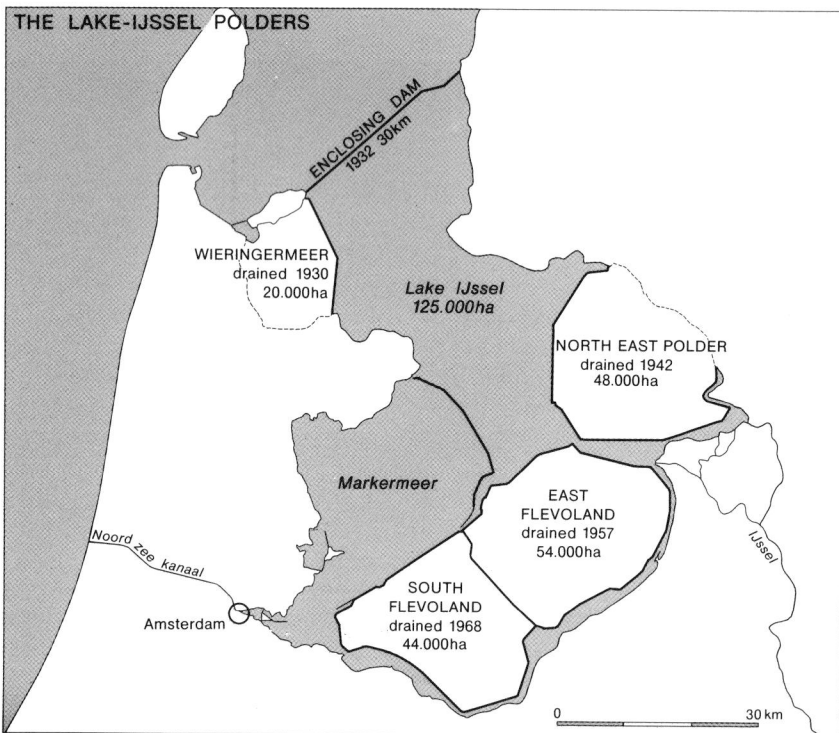

Fig. 1. The Zuiderzee water management and land reclamation project. (Drawing N.I.S.A.)

Fig. 2. The mid-17th century merchantman from lot E 81 Noordoostpolder in the Rijksmuseum for Ship Archaeology at Ketelhaven. (Photograph: R.O.B.)

Fig. 3. The ventjager *from lot H 41 Oostelijk Flevoland, coming into the Rijksmuseum for Ship Archaeology at Ketelhaven, June 1987. Preservation of the wreck was finished in the summer of 1995; final restoration will take place at the new location of the N.I.S.A. at Lelystad. (Photograph: N.I.S.A., K. Vlierman)*

Fig. 4. A survey trench on a 19th-century cargo vessel on lot K 7 Noordoostpolder. (Photograph: N.I.S.A., L. van Dijk)

Fig. 5. The geological strata and the disturbance of the soil around the 17th-century vessel on lot S 19 Oostelijk Flevoland. (Photograph N.I.S.A., J. V. Potuyt)

18   *Karel Vlierman*

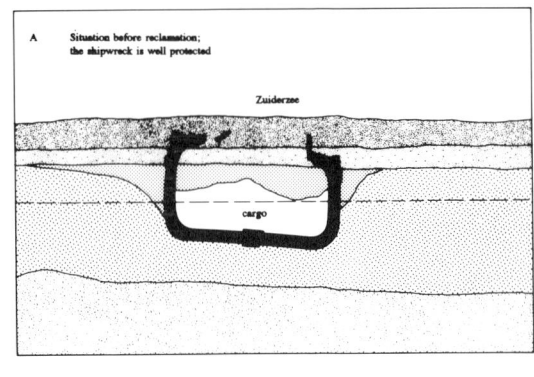

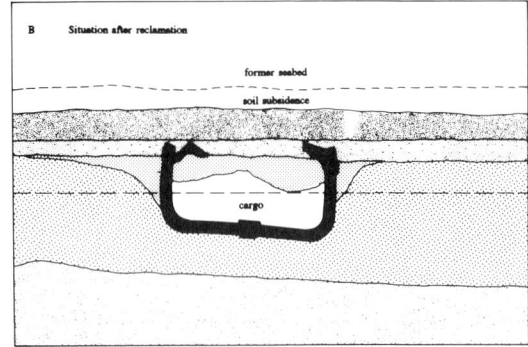

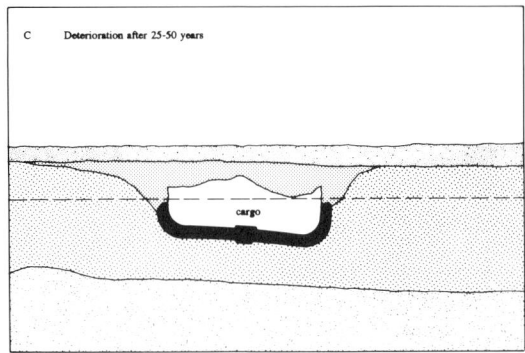

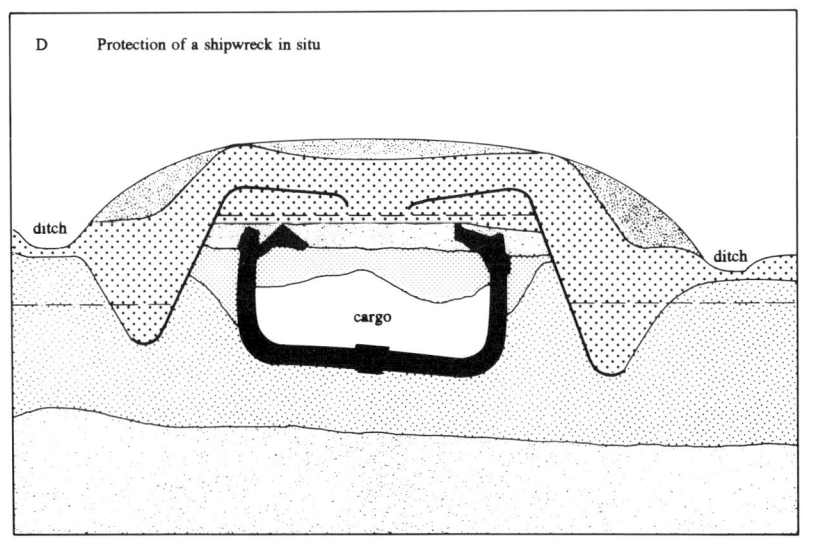

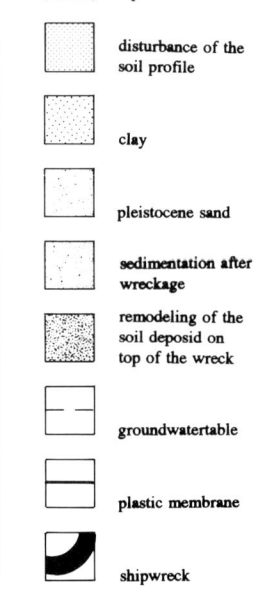

Fig. 6. Protection of a shipwreck in situ. (Drawing: N.I.S.A., G.J. Zand)

policy of the former *Rijksdienst voor de IJsselmeerpolders* was to excavate as many shipwrecks as possible before the land was farmed; the remainder were to be left for future investigation. The disadvantage of this procedure was that by this later stage large parts of the wrecks had rotted away, excavation taking place a long time after the initial draining of the polder (Reinders 1982, 12).

Since 1975 the emphasis of research has shifted away from 'excavation whenever feasible' to 'excavation only if essential'. As a result, more effort is now spent on conserving the wrecks *in situ*. Wooden remains come under threat if soil settles or if the water-table sinks: major dangers are fungus growth and damage by farming machinery.

CONSERVATION IN THE FIELD

A method has been developed to conserve shipwrecks *in situ* (De Roo *et al* 1978). If the vessel has settled in a dense body of clay, damage to the wood may be prevented. A vertical screen of plastic sheeting is installed around the wreck to prevent lateral drainage (Fig.6). Vertical drainage is prevented by the clay. A layer of soil is deposited on top of the wreck, and covered with plastic membrane to prevent evaporation. Either a small funnel-shaped opening is left immediately above the ship, or holes are made in the membrane to admit rain. The effect on the water-table can be considerable: the artificial rise above that of the surrounding field may be up over a metre.

If soil conditions preclude conservation in the field, the risk of damage by farm machinery may be reduced by applying an extra quantity of soil, though this will not prevent fungal attack.

Shipwrecks destined for full conservation and museum display are provisionally stored below the water-table. If reburial near the site of discovery is not feasible, then the wreck can be buried in a two-hectare central depot in Zuidelijk Flevoland. This currently holds seven shipwrecks found in the polder.[4]

EXCAVATION AND RECORDING

During excavation, the first stage is the partial exposure of the outside of the wreck. The interior is then excavated as far as possible without removing any fixed ship parts (Fig.7).

Once the photography and drawing has been completed, the internal elements of the wreck are removed in stages so that the lower parts of the structure can by recorded. Eventually, only the empty shell of the wreck remains in the soil. This procedure has turned out to be most practical for polder maritime archaeology. A different approach is only adopted if a ship is to be exhibited in the museum, whereby the floor timbers and frames are left *in situ*, and either the ship is cut into a number of sections for transport or the wreck is raised as one unit (Fig.8).

Until the late 1970s the various stages of excavation were drawn on one or more plans, with a longitudinal section and number of cross sections. To do this, a datum line was strung from bow to stern (overall length) and, where necessary, transverse tapes were affixed. From these, plumb-lines were used to take measurements which would be entered on drawings which were used as the only basis for reconstruction. Paper tends to buckle and distort in humid conditions, losing dimensional stability, and so in about 1980, paper was replaced by drawing film. Recording became more detailed, additional drawings being prepared to show all the various parts *in situ*, using colour coding to indicate various construction elements. However, these drawings alone still remained the basis for reconstruction work.

Since the early 1980s, drawings have been prepared of all elements of a ship, preferably on a scale 1:10. Several views are recorded, with details such as dowel/treenail holes and repair work accurately drawn in. Such drawings are referred to as *plankuitslagen* (Fig.9). Once all elements have been drawn, the drawings are used to supplement the strake diagrams to produce a reconstruction model. From this point on, these diagrams are primary sources of information for the construction of the model. The field drawings continue to serve mainly as a record of the position of the vessel in the field and sur-

Fig. 7. The partly uncovered wreck of a late 15th-century hulk on lot U 34 Oostelijk Flevoland. (Photograph: N.I.S.A., L. van Dijk)

Fig. 8. The salvaging of a 18.5 m long early 17th-century beurtschip on lot B 71 Oostelijk Flevoland. The total weight of the wreck and iron support approximately 50,000 kg. (Photograph: N.I.S.A., J.V. Potuyt)

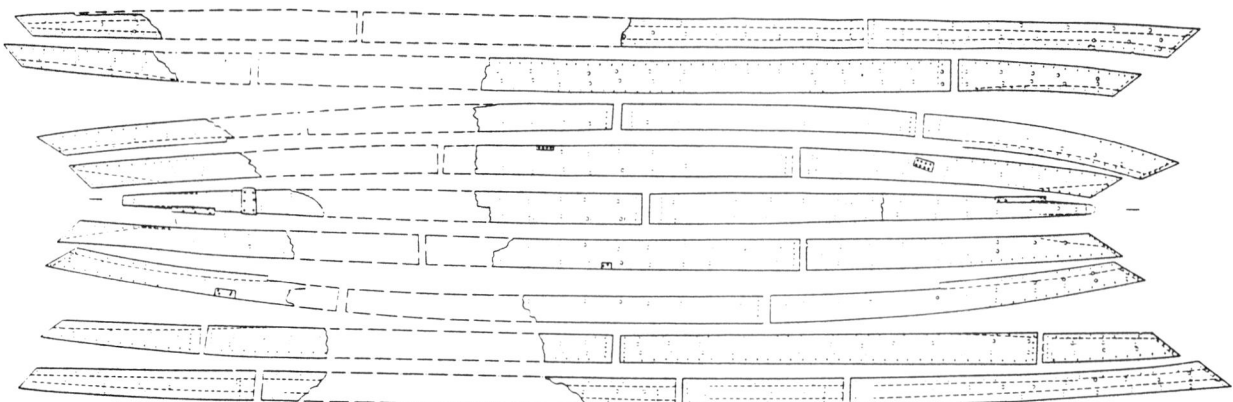

Fig. 9. The plankuitslagen *of a 15th-century cargo vessel. (Drawing: N.I.S.A., J.-M.A.W. Morel)*

vey drawings on which the reference numbers of parts may be entered.

In recent years measuring tapes and plumblines have been replaced by the pantograph. Initially, a two-dimensional field pantograph was used, but more recently a three-dimensional pantograph has been developed which can also produce plane projections of upright elements (Koehler 1994, 103–104). As the range of a pantograph is limited, a ship must be drawn in sections (Fig.10). The pantograph drawings are then combined into a single survey drawing per excavation stage. This survey drawing effectively replaces the 'old' plan views.

A study of the remains of the ship, as recorded in photographs and drawings, may indicate the degree of completeness of the discovery. Materials and techniques utilized provide an insight into the methods of construction. In all cases an attempt is made to reconstruct the wreck as a scale model. The strakes of the vessel's elements are used to reconstruct the shape of the hull. First a mock-up is made from strake shapes, transferred to special cardboard, and affixed to mock-up frames. Once this cardboard model is found to be satisfactory, a 'definitive' wooden model may be constructed (Fig.11).

Fig. 10. Use of the three-dimensional pantograph to record a late 17th-century cargo vessel on lot H 107 Oostelijk Flevoland, 1993.
(Photograph: N.I.S.A., B. Neyland)

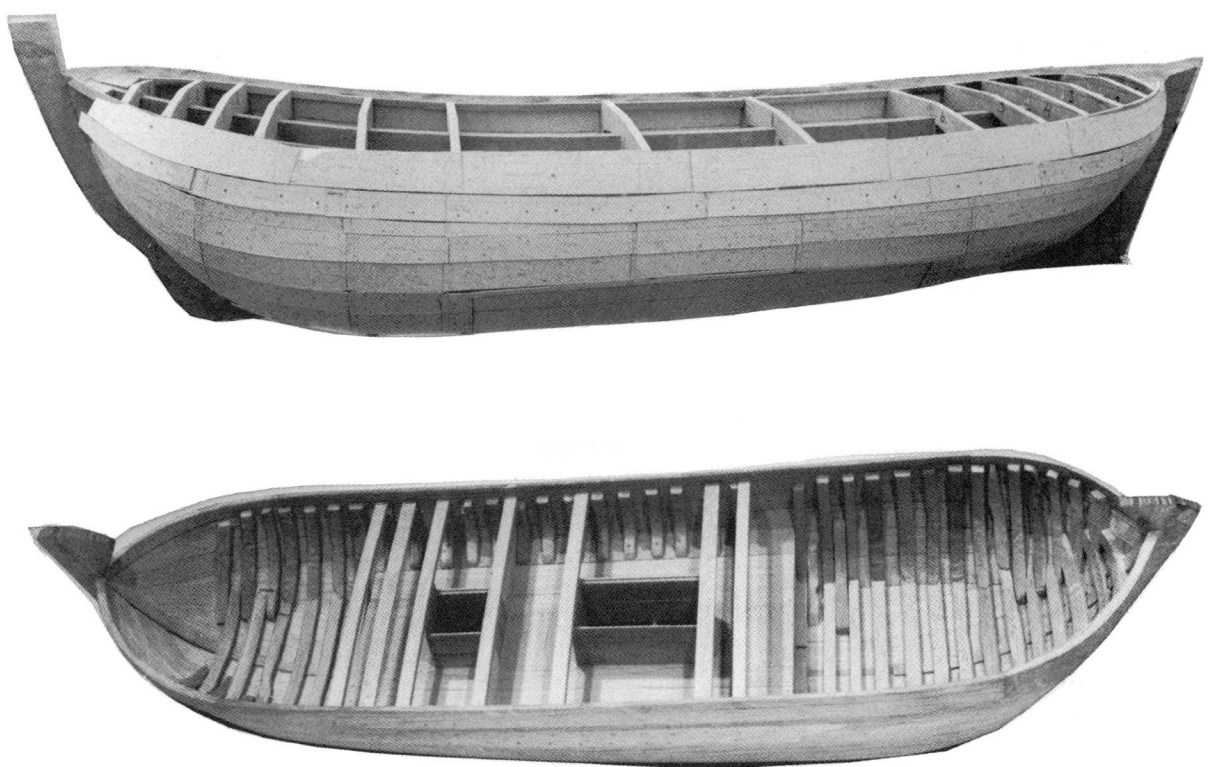

Fig. 11. A mock-up (scale 1:10) in cardboard and a wooden model (scale 1:20) of the 17th-century ventjager *from lot H 41 Oostelijk Flevoland. Made by J. van der Zee (N.I.S.A.). (Drawing: N.I.S.A., L. van Dijk)*

Ship types

Although they once sailed the Zuiderzee, most of the shipwrecks can be characterized as being inland ships. Of course, until the beginning of the 19th century, many large sea-going ships would have crossed the Zuiderzee,[5] especially on the route to and from Amsterdam. However, very few of these larger vessels sank along the main route.

The smaller, inland water vessels which have been excavated represent several types. The period up to about 1500 is represented by the remains of ten Hanseatic cogs and several small cargo vessels of various sizes which were mainly used for short coastal and river journeys. One such is the late 13th-/early 14th-century cog excavated in 1983 (Vlierman 1996A, table I). A full-size replica of the vessel is now under construction in the old Hanseatic city of *Kampen* (Fig.12). Such cogs were clinker-built, usually with flat, carvel-built bottoms, and were most commonly up to 16 m in length (except for the largest cogs and hulks which are between about 20 and 30m long).

Many changes in shipbuilding techniques occurred from the second half of the 15th century, stimulated by the fast-growing population in Europe and the search for new sources of food and other goods. Shipbuilders had to look for, and found, new ways to increase ship capacity, equipping them with more masts and sails to permit the transportation of more extensive cargos.[6] The vessel most characteristic of the *Zuiderzee*, the so-called *waterschip*, is a particularly good example illustrating changes in building techniques. The ship type is mentioned in written sources dating from 1339. It was 16 m long and clinker-built with a broad-bottomed front part and a sharp stern (Fig.13). From the mid-16th century up to the 19th century, it appears that its shape, construction and accommodation plan hardly changed, the main developments being an increase in length in the 16th century to 20 m, and a change to carvel construction (Fig.14). In the 17th century 'new look' ship types were established, which then slowly evolved during the 18th and 19th centuries. The most common ship types to have been excavated so far are the small- and medium-sized cargo vessels with a length of up to about 20 m. These types are known by the Dutch terms *tjalk*, *praam* and *boeier* (Fig.15). Besides these cargo vessels, working boats and different types of fishing boats have also been found, such as the *waterschip* mentioned above, the *schokker*, *botter* and *punter* (Fig.16).

The oldest medieval sea-going large ship excavated so far is a three-masted cargo-vessel or warship with a length of about 30–35 m, which sank *c.* 1500. The ship is most probable a *hulk* (Vlek 1987; Reinders & Oosting 1989, 118; Fig.17).

Only one ship of the *Verenigde Oostindische Compagnie*, called *Buitenzorg*, is known to have been wrecked at the point where

Fig. 12. The early 14th-century cog on lot Oz 36 Zuidelijk Flevoland in 1983 (top) and the building of the replica (scale 1:1) by De Boer & Sars in the old Hanseatic city of Kampen, June 1995 (bottom). (Photographs: N.I.S.A., L. van Dijk (top); N.I.S.A., K. Vlierman (bottom))

Fig. 13. An early 16th-century clinker-built waterschip *(length 16m) on lot K 84 Oostelijk Flevoland. (Photograph: N.I.S.A. J. V. Potuyt)*

Fig. 14. A late 16th-century carvel-built waterschip *(length 20 m) during the survey of the deck on lot Kz 47 Zuidelijk Flevoland, 1978. (Photograph: N.I.S.A., J.V. Potuyt)*

Fig. 15. A late 16th-century peat barge on lot Lz 1 Zuidelijk Flevoland (top), a mid-18th century tjalk on lot B 55 Oostelijk Flevoland (centre), and a late 18th-century boyer on lot F 34 Oostelijk Flevoland. (Photographs: N.I.S.A., L. van Dijk (top); N.I.S.A., J.v. Potuyt (centre and bottom))

Fig. 16. A 17th-century mud-barge on lot B 19 Oostelijk Flevoland (top), an 18th-century punt on lot Lz 8 Zuidelijk Flevoland (bottom left) and a mid-19th century botter on lot F 60 Oostelijk Flevoland. (Photographs: N.I.S.A., J.V. Potuyt)

Fig. 17. The excavation of a late 15th-century hulk on lot U 34 Oostelijk Flevoland in 1987. (Photograph: N.I.S.A., L. van Dijk)

Fig. 18. The stern post of the VOC-ship Buitenzorg. (Photograph: R.O.B.)

the Zuiderzee and Waddenzee meet. The ship was anchored near Texel in the winter of 1759/60, but dragged her anchors and was sunk by ice. Her remains were discovered in 1958. The lowest part of the stern [7] can be seen in the Rijksmuseum for Ship Archaeology at Ketelhaven (Fig.18). Parts of the only sea-going ship to have been completely recovered in The Netherlands (from lot E 81 Noordoostpolder) can also be seen. This is the 27 m long wreck of a mid-17th-century cargo ship, with a large, open hold and a completely closed ceiling planking, particularly suitable for timber haulage and grain transportation (Fig.2).

CONSERVATION AND INVESTIGATION OF THE SHIP INVENTORIES

Observations on the conservation applied by N.I.S.A.

The inventory, equipment and cargo found on shipwreck excavations in the *IJsselmeerpolders* provide a unique picture of shipbuilding and live on board (Fig.19). *All* objects recovered from the shipwrecks are conserved, and those not on display are stored by ship in the Museum depôt (Figs 20, 21) as well as in a computer database for study purposes. The collection currently holds about 20,000 objects of all kinds of materials,

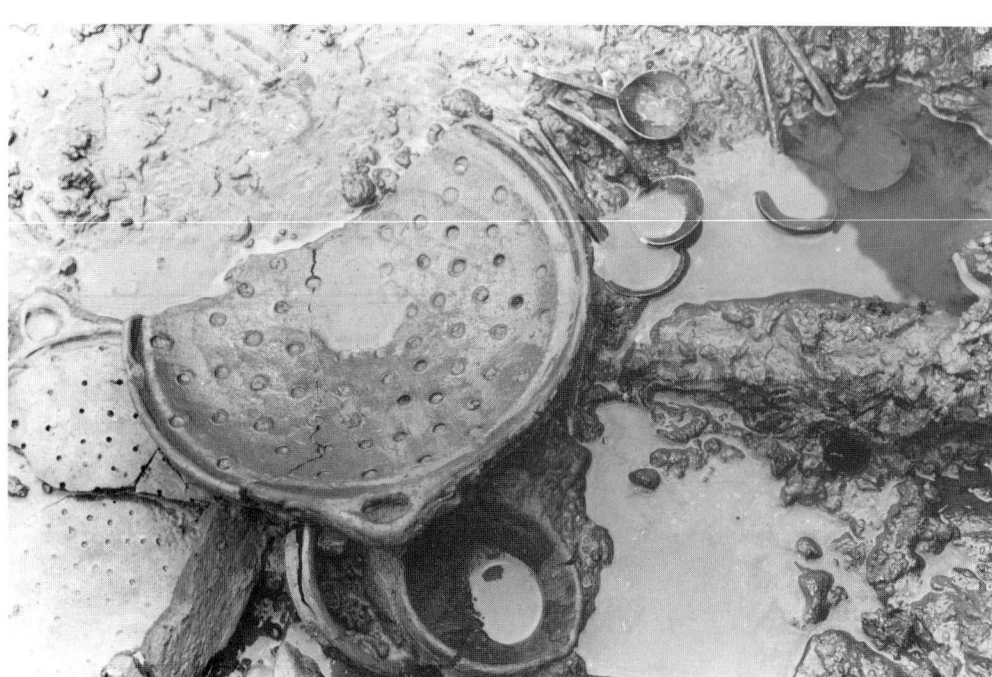

Fig. 19. Artefacts from the mid-18th century tjalk B 55 Oostelijk Flevoland in situ. (Photograph: N.I.S.A., L. van Dijk)

Fig. 20. One of the storage cases in the National Ship Archaeological Depôt.

and is growing steadily, for a few vessels are excavated each year. Depending on age and type of vessel, the number of objects recovered can vary from 50 to 500 (sometimes more).

In about 1975 aggressive conservation methods for metals were abandoned in favour of research into better or new methods (Vlierman & van Dijk, 1980). The conservation processes are always reversible, at least in principle, enabling improved techniques to be applied to objects in the future. After conservation and restoration, environmental controls in the depôt and exhibition areas prevent further wear and deterioration of the aretfacts.

About one third of all the objects found in shipwrecks are made of wrought or cast iron of greatly diverse types and qualities. The most effective method of removing the hard concretion has been found to be annealing, where the iron object is heated in a special furnace, developed in the late 1970s (Van Dijk 1986). The object is placed in a furnace, slowly heated to about 650°C (wrought iron) or over 800°C (cast iron) and then slowly cooled. The thermal expansion coefficient difference of iron and rust, the latter snaps away from the iron and is easily removed (Fig. 22). A modified version of the technique has also been used on coins (Van Dijk 1985 & 1987; Fig.23).

Once wooden artefacts have been conserved, cleaned and re-assembled, they receive treatment with linseed oil (large straightforward dried objects). For PEG-impregnated and smaller objects beeswax or furniture oil is used.

Three treatment regimes have been developed to conserve waterlogged wood:

1. Slow air drying, at a rate determined by analysis and tests. This only works for wood which is virtually rot-free.

2. Impregnation with a solidifier (polethylene glycol or PEG, a water-soluble plastic), followed by fast drying. This is done with moderately to severely deteriorated wood.

3. Freeze-drying in a vacuum. This applies in some cases to moderately well preserved wood.

A special epoxy adhesive used to re-assemble broken fragments of wood is also well-suited to glue PEG-impregnated

Fig. 21. The artefactual inventory of the Lutina *(from lot H 48 Oostelijk Flevoland), wrecked 20 November 1888. (Photograph: N.I.S.A., J.V. Potuyt)*

Fig. 22. A cast-iron cooking pot from an 18th-century praam *(Az 71 Zuidelijk Flevoland) before and after the treatment by heating. (Photograph: N.I.S.A., L. van Dijk)*

Fig. 23. The late 18th-century coin assemblage from ship L 79 Oostelijk Flevoland before and after treatment. Next to the silver and copper coins were found some lead tokens and shoe buckles and a watch and a silver watch chain. (Photographs: N.I.S.A., L. van Dijk)

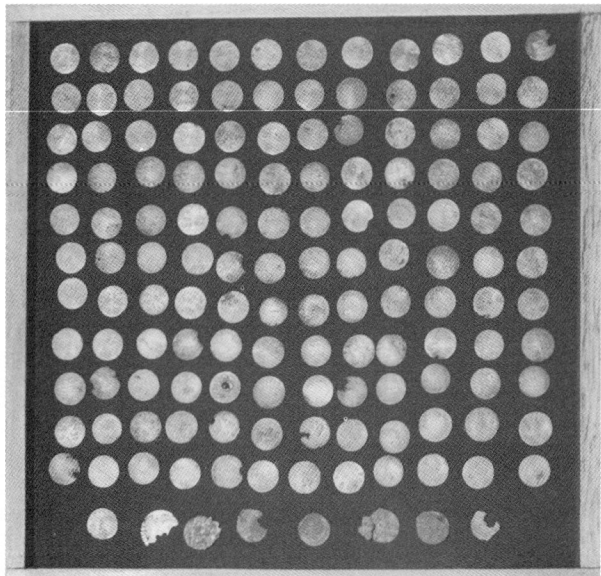

Fig. 24. Restored shoe from the early 17th-century beurtschip *B 71 Oostelijk Flevoland. (Photograph: N.I.S.A., L. van Dijk)*

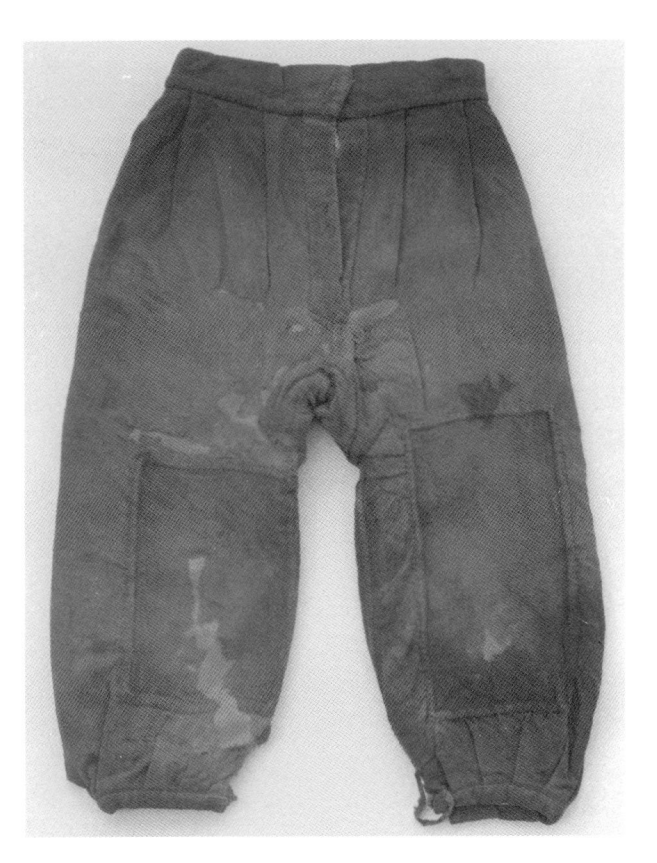

Fig. 25. Restored woollen pants found on board the botter *on lot F 60 Oostelijk Flevoland, which sunk in June 1876 (Vlierman 1994, 321). (Photograph: N.I.S.A., M.Schraal)*

wood. When mixed with a filler substance, this glue can be used to fill holes and cracks and can be painted with pigments to match the colour of the original wood. For objects in a very poor condition, a replica may be made in new material for display purposes.

Until the start of treatment, leather is kept immersed to avoid the risk of drying and distortion. After thorough rinsing the material is saturated with a soft variety of the plastic polyethylene glycol dissolved in water. If reconstruction is required following conservation treatment, the leather is rubbed with castor oil to make it supple and easy to handle. Missing parts may be replaced by other pieces of leather, using leather glue to restore the original shape (Van der Land 1982; Fig.24).

Textiles are rarely found, as most fabrics decompose rapidly. Silk, linen and cotton in moist conditions develop the first signs of decay within a short period, and are rarely found on shipwrecks more than a century old. Wool is the exception. In favourable conditions (e.g. embedded in clay, or within luting material) it may survive for long periods. Lack of specialist staff limits activities in Ketelhaven to washing textiles with traditional types of soap. After cleaning, disconnected pieces may be manually sewn together, those garments which have become too weak to carry their own weight being reinforced with supporting lining (Fig.25).

Investigation and classification

The large ships excavated so far have yielded unexpectedly detailed information. Research into the objects found on board the mid-17th-century merchantman E 81 (*Noordoostpolder*) has led to the conclusion that almost all the artefacts recovered during the excavation (except for a couple of spare blocks) were worthless at the time of of sinking (Vlierman, in prep.; Fig.26). The reason can be applied to the other large ships found in the IJsselmeerpolders. All the ships measured between 3.5 and 5 m in height, so that, when a ship sank in the shallow Zuiderzee, the deck would, for most of the time, have been at or near low-water sea level. Consequently it would still have been possible in the first days after the shipwreck to salvage the cargo and inventory (equipment for this has been found on board several ships). We may conclude that although the large ships wrecked on the Zuiderzee can provide much information on their methods of construction and shape, less can be said about their equipment and inventories.

In order to gain a better insight into the equipment and inventories found on board small inland water vessels, we have tried to classify objects by function. This has been primarily to facilitate comparison between inventories of small- and medium-sized vessels which sailed on the Zuiderzee. For this purpose we used over 700 objects recovered from the late 19th-century cargo vessel *Lutina* and classified them by function. We felt that this method was useful, in spite of the fact that similar methods have created problems when applied to ships of the Dutch East India Company (Green 1977). The following factors determined the method of classification applied to this IJsselmeerpolder wreck:

1. It is a small cargo vessel.

2. The recovered inventory appears complete.

*Fig. 26. Three old, damaged and leaky copper kettles, two cooking pots, a saucepan and ceramics (top), and an unused (spare) fiddle block with marks of the block maker's tools from the mid-17th century merchantman from lot E 81 Noordoostpolder.
Photograph N.I.S.A., J.V. Potuyt)*

3. The objects date from recent times and are easy to identify.

4. The accommodation plan of the ship was easy to reconstruct and the objects were found on or near to their original location.

5. The ship had a small crew (probably only two).

The artefacts were divided into the following main categories: equipment, inventory and personal belongings. These were subdivided into eleven groups.

The general classification of the ship as a whole is as follows (Reinders 1985):

A. Ship with standing and running rigging
B. Equipment
   1. Ship's equipment
   2. Working equipment
   3. Military equipment
C. Inventory
   4. Documents and stationary
   5. Navigational instruments
   6. Tools
   7. Household effects
   8. Kitchen utensils
   9. Eating and drinking gear
   10. Victuals

D. 11. Personal belongings
E. Cargo, Merchandise

At this point, it ought to be possible to provide an example of an inventory from the period 1500–1800, classified according to the above functional categories. Unfortunately, representative, comparable information and detailed documentation is not yet available. As stated earlier, the data from only a few shipwrecks have been completely analysed so far, and over 150 files await more detailed research and publication.

Illustrations taken from the publications of two late 19th-century inventories give an impression of the extensive range of the functional groups: the *Lutina* which sank in 1888 (Zwiers & Vlierman 1988), and a *tjalk*, *De Zeehond*, wrecked in 1886 (Oosting and Vlierman 1990). The archaeological report on *De Zeehond* includes a comparison of the equipment and inventories of both ships (see Fig.27).[8]

The inventories indicate a different crew structure, which could be checked afterwards by studying existing documentary information. The *Lutina* had two old men on board (the skipper and his mate), while *De Zeehond* carried a young family. At the museum in Ketelhaven we have organised two family reunions for the descendants of the ships' crews.

A forthcoming report will deal with two comparable late 18th-century *praams*, peat-transporting vessels used in the north-east of the Netherlands. Two students from Texas A & M University have recently analysed the data from these wrecks for their doctoral theses (McLaughlin-Neyland & Neyland 1993). The results show that the classification applied to 19th-century cargo vessels can also be extended to shipwrecks of the 18th century. The illustrations of the different functional groups of these wrecks also provide technical information (Fig.28).

During the 1994 Annual Conference of the Medieval Pottery Research Group in Southampton, I briefly compared five late medieval ships and others of the post-medieval period (Vlierman 1992, 10–22; 1993, 70). The difficulties of recording artefacts from late medieval ship inventories according to the method of classification used for the 19th-century cargo vessels of the Zuiderzee were outlined, and the following points, which are the first provisional results of the comparison, were made:

– more or less comparable cargo vessels contained 25–100 artefacts in the late medieval period, 150–300 in the 18th and early 19th centuries, increasing rapidly to 500 or more in the second half of the 19th century.

– artefacts found on medieval ships cannot easily be recorded using the eleven categories mentioned above because of their small number and multi-functional nature.

For the late medieval period, a division can only be made into three basic groups:

1. Objects associated with cooking, eating and drinking.
2. Tools.
3. Personal belongings and weaponry.

Colin Martin has already described the archaeological potential of ships as integrated artefacts (see chapter 1). Indeed these 'time capsules' are remarkable sources of information on daily life, and as such they need to be accorded the greatest attention by archaeologists dealing with late and post-medieval sites in north-western Europe. Ships often contain numerous artefacts which were in use at the same time on board, and when found elsewhere are usually undatable.

A comparison of complete inventories found on board ships of the same type but dating to different periods not only yields information as to the number of artefacts, but can also offer the opportunity to compare assemblages of (for instance) carpenters tools, and cooking, eating and drinking utensils and vessels. Kleij has discussed how the ship's inventory can be used to identify the home port (see chapter 15). The inventory can also be used to gain an insight into the presence of families and the number of people on board. Van Holk has discussed this subject for the period *c*.1600–1900, and outlined the methods used to collect information from artefacts (see chapter 18). Such methods also offer perspectives for the identification of standard objects (Vlierman 1994), groups of items or the typological development of form, such as the development of the late-medieval ship carpenter's axe (Vlierman 1985; Hocker and Vlierman 1996; Vlierman 1996B), or the development of *sintels*.[9] Sintels, small iron clamps used in the medieval period to fasten the caulking material in the seams of the hull, changed in shape through time. The large number of well-dated shipwrecks found so far in the IJsselmeerpolders has made it possible to sort the different types of sintels into groups based on short periods of use. It is consequently now possible to date shipwrecks found in north-western Europe on the basis of these clamps, without any associated finds, to within a period of 50–75 years (sometimes even less), providing an important new archaeological dating method for the late medieval period (Vlierman 1996A).

Publications

To gain further insights into the material culture present on board small and medium-sized inland vessels, it is necessary to investigate and publish the assembled data from as many shipwreck excavations as possible from the IJsselmeerpolders in the near future.

Our first excavation report on a 16th-century fishing boat was published in 1978, and followed by reports on three late medieval ships; three medieval riverboats (near Arnhem); four 17th-century working-boats; a 19th-century cargo-vessel from the province of Overijssel; a late 19th-century *tjalk* from the province of Groningen, and a cog-like vessel. Forthcoming publications in the series *Flevoberichten* will be the reports on two 18th-century peat-*praams*; sintels – a caulking-method to date medieval shipwrecks; thirteen small medieval ship (fragment) finds outside the bounderies of the Zuiderzee; lead tokens from the IJsselmeerpolder wrecks; a 15th-century cog found at Almere; a 16th-century working boat at Workum, province of Friesland; a *watership* on lot Nz 42 (I) and a late 17th-century Dutch freighter.

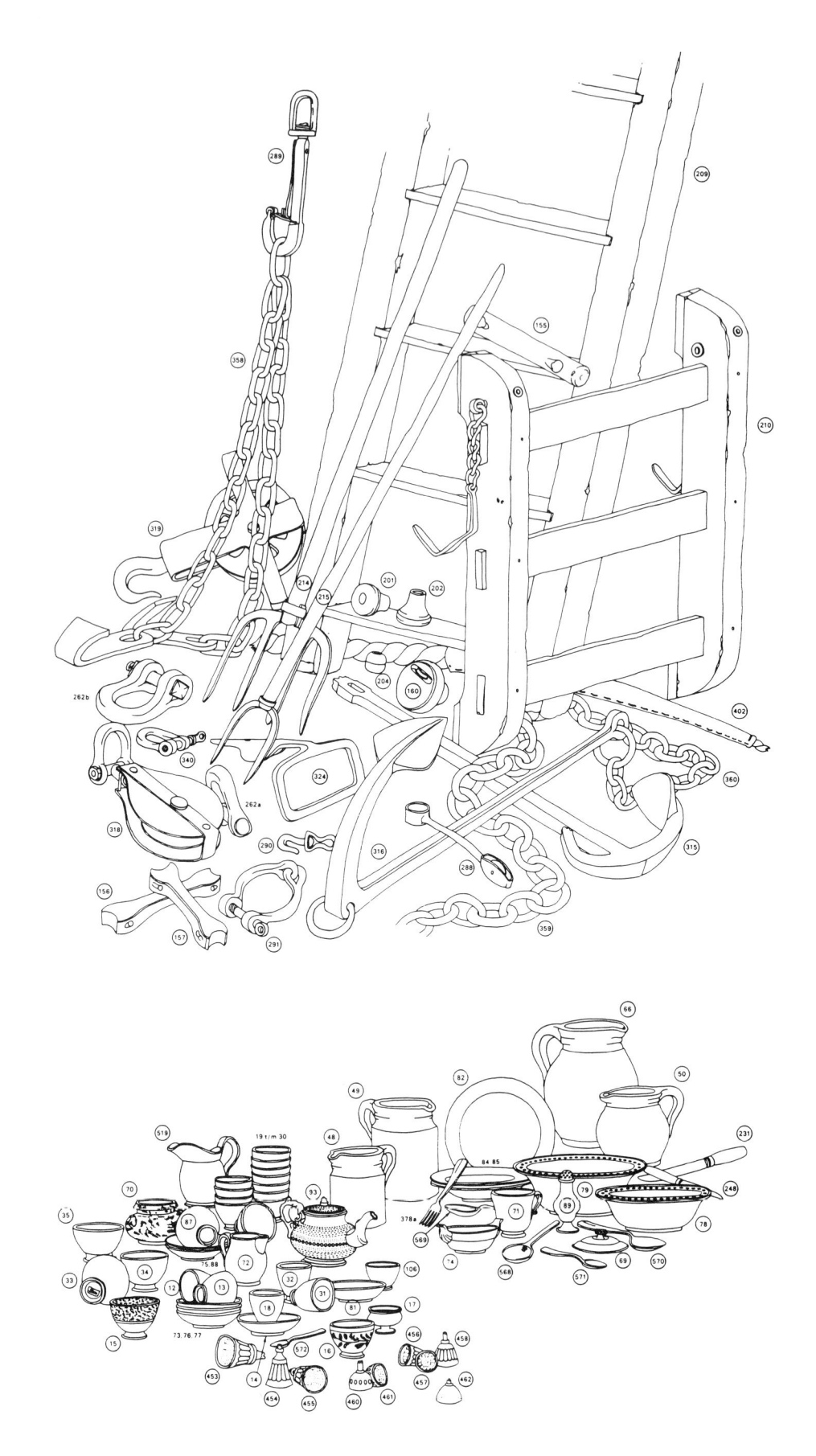

Fig. 27. ↑ → *Illustrations of groups by function: 'ship's and working equipment' (top), and 'eating and drinking utensils' of the late 19th-century cargo vessels* Lutina *(left), and* De Zeehond *(Zwiers & Vlierman 1988; Oosting & Vlierman 1990). (Drawing: N.I.S.A., K. Vlierman)*

The IJsselmeerpolders

34   *Karel Vlierman*

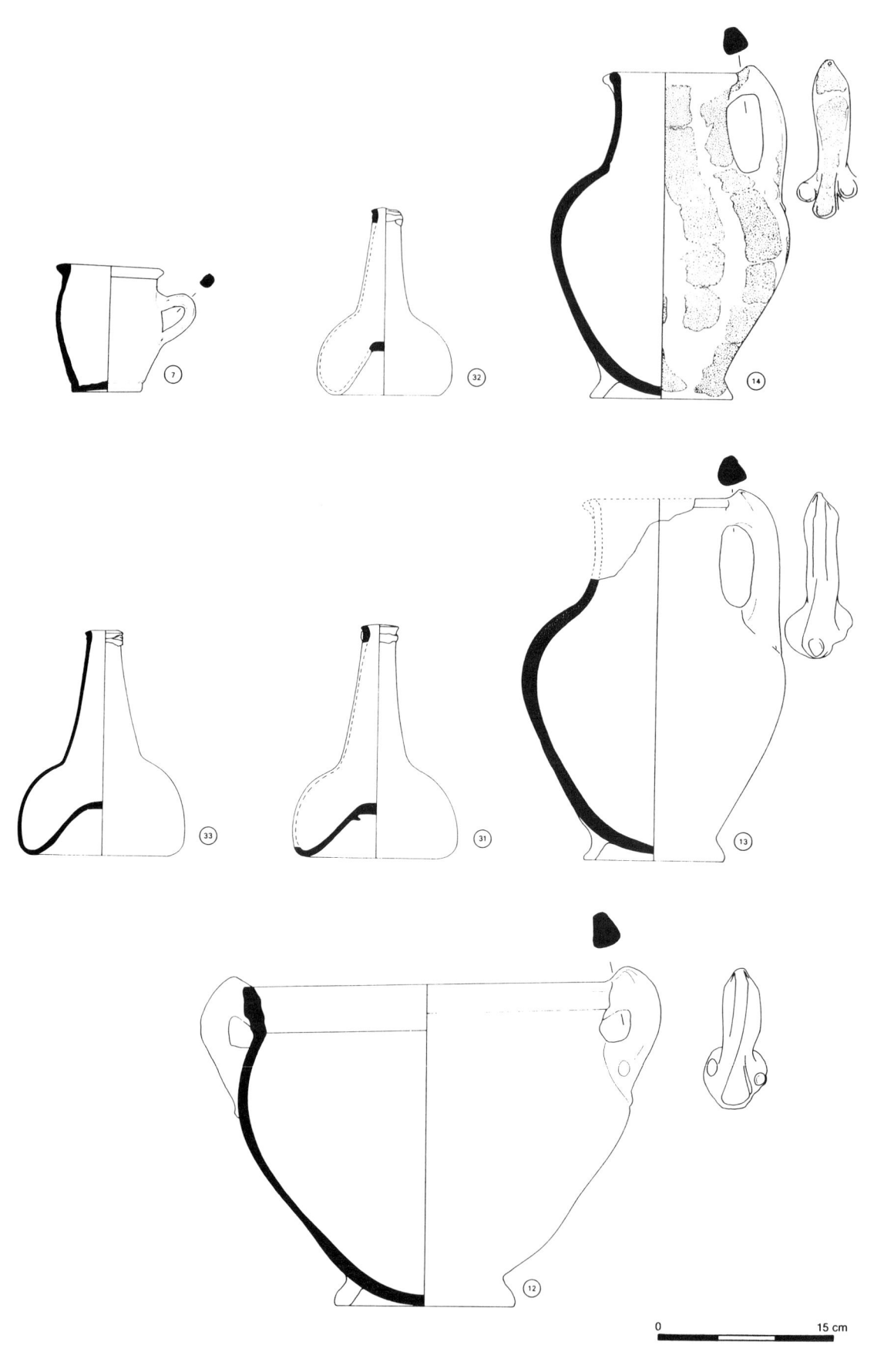

Fig. 28. The functional group 'victuals and provisions' (McLaughlin-Neyland & Neyland 1993) which forms part of the inventory of an 18th-century praam *on lot E 14 Oostelijk Flevoland. (Drawing: N.I.S.A., K. McLaughlin-Neyland)*

In 1983 we started work on the publication of ceramics found on board some late medieval and post-medieval ships in the *Corpus van Middeleeuws Aardewerk uit gesloten vondstcomplexen in Nederland en Vlaanderen (C.M.A.)* series. Our intention is to publish the ceramic assemblage of one IJsselmeerpolder wreck each year.

Acknowledgements

English translation: Rerum Antiquarum, K.E. Waugh.

Glossary

Batavia werf: Batavia wharf; wharf near the *Houtrib* lock at Lelystad, where Willem Vos built the replica of the VOC ship *Batavia* (scale 1:1), wrecked in 1629 on the west coast of Australia. The *Batavia* was launched in 1995. In the same year a start was made in building the replica of the 17th-century flag ship *De Zeven Provinciën* of Admiral Michiel Adriaansz de Ruyter.

beurtschip: market ship, regular service boat.

boeier: boyer; 1) 16th/17th-century coaster of the west and north European coasts, 2) typical Dutch pleasure boat or yacht used since the 17th century; *boeieraak*: flat-bottomed vessel of the province of Zeeland; *boeierschuit*: 19th/20th-century Dutch inland vessel of the river IJssel.

botter: typical Dutch fisherman, especially in use on the southern part of the *Zuiderzee*.

Buitenzorg: a VOC ship named after a residency north of Batavia on the island of Java in the former Dutch East Indies, which was wrecked in the winter of 1759/60 near the island of Texel in the Waddenzee.

Centrum voor Scheepsarcheologie (CSA): Centre for Ship Archaeology (C.S.A.) of the State Service for Archaeological Investigations in the Netherlands (R.O.B.) of the Ministry of Welfare, Culture and Health. Until 1 March 1992, Ship Archaeological Department of the Department of Public Works-Directorate Flevoland of the Ministry of Transport and Public Works.

Corpus van Middeleeuws Aardewerk uit gesloten vondstcomplexen in Nederland en Vlaanderen (CMA): Corpus of medieval pottery from sealed find complexes in The Netherlands and Flanders (C.M.A.).

De Zeehond: 'The Seal'; the name of a so-called *groninger tjalk*, a typical Dutch cargo-vessel built in the province of Groningen in 1878 and wrecked in 1886.

Flevoberichten: series of reports on the structure and development of the IJsselmeerpolders and other works of land reclamation.

Friesland: Province in the north of the Netherlands bordering the Waddenzee in the north and the Zuiderzee/IJsselmeer in the west.

hulk: 'hulc'; medieval merchantman of north and west Europe.

IJsselmeer: Lake IJssel; after sealing off the saltwater Zuiderzee from the Waddenzee by a 32 km long dyke (the *Afsluitdijk*) the then 'sweet' Zuiderzee was renamed the IJsselmeer.

IJsselmeerpolders: polders (= reclaimed land) in the former Zuiderzee.

Kampen: Hanseatic city near the mouth of the river IJssel and the Zuiderzee in the province of Overijssel.

Ketelhaven: former working-island for building the dykes of Oostelijk Flevoland near the mouth of river IJssel. Location of N.I.S.A. from 1971 to 1998.

Lelystad: provincial capital of the province of Flevoland.

Lutina: name of a 19th-century cargo-vessel, which was wrecked on 20 November 1888, and has been excavated on lot H48 Oostelijk Flevoland.

Nederlands Instituut voor Scheepsarcheologie (NISA): Netherlands Institute for Ship Archaeology ([N.I.S.A.]; Ship Archaeology Department, Underwater Archaeology Department, National Ship Archaeological Depot, Rijksmuseum for Ship Archaeology) of the Ministry of Education, Culture and Welfare, until 12 April 1995 Centre for Ship Archaeology. The N.I.S.A. will be relocated to near the *'Batavia' werf* at *Lelystad* in 1998.

Noord-Holland: province in the north-west of The Netherlands, bordering the North Sea in the west, and the Zuiderzee in the east.

Noordoostpolder: North-East Polder; the most northern polder of the province of Flevoland, bordering the province of Friesland in the north, and the province of Overijssel in the east. Drained in 1942, it comprises 48,000 ha of land.

Oostelijk Flevoland: East Flevoland; polder in the middle of the province of Flevoland, bordering the provinces Overijssel and Gelderland in the east. Drained in 1957, comprising 54,000 ha of land.

plankuitslag(en): shape of (a) moulded plank(s).

praam: pram; a flat-bottomed, and flat inland vessel popular in The Netherlands from the 17th century. Since the 19th century several variants are known, like *Drentse praam, Meppeler praam, Hoogeveense praam* etc.

punter: punt; typical Dutch small and flat-bottomed boat, particularly used in the shallow lakes of north-west Overijssel and particularly in the village of Giethoorn.

Rijksdienst voor de IJsselmeerpolders (RIJP): the IJsselmeerpolders Development Authority, successor of the Department of Public Works-Directorate Flevoland.

Rijksdienst voor het Oudheidkundig Bodemonderzoek (ROB): State Service for the Archaeological Investigations in The Netherlands (R.O.B.).

schokker: Dutch flat-bottomed fishing boat of the *Zuiderzee*, used in particular between the cities of Enkhuizen, Lemmer, Vollenhove and Elburg. After the evacuation of the island of Schokland (1859) also in use on the river Schelde.

sintels: *(gesinteld mosbreeuwsel)*; new name for *gesinteld werk*. A caulking method for wooden ships. The more or less triangular seams are filled up with moss. The moss is held in the seams with small wooden laths or chips of wood, which are fastened with iron clamps, so-called *sintels* (medieval Dutch and German name). The shape of the sintels developed between c. 1150 and 1550. The earliest examples date back to the 9th century. After c.1550 the method was not used in The Netherlands for the building of new ships (Vlierman 1996A).

Texel: the largest island of the Waddeneilanden, directly north of the province of Noord-Holland.

tjalk (tjalck): typical Dutch round built vessel with a flat bottom, in use for the transport of cargo over the shallow waters in the Low Countries. Probable predecessors the *wijdschip* and *smalschip*.

ventjager: fish carrier; fast sailing/fishing boat, which takes in the catch of the fleet to bring it to market. *Ventjagers* also peddle sails, rope, and food etc. to the fishing vessels.

Verenigde Oostindische Compagnie (VOC): Dutch East India Compagny (V.O.C.).

Waddenzee: sea in the north of the Netherlands between the provinces of Friesland and Groningen and the Waddeneilanden. The Waddenzee meets the Zuiderzee in the south.

Waterschip: the most characteristic fishing vessel of the Zuiderzee between the 14th and early 19th century. There were two types: one 16 m in length and completely clinker-built (before c.1550) and one 20 m in length and carvel-built.

Wieringermeerpolder: polder in the north-east part of the province of Noord-Holland, bordering the former island of Wieringen in the north. Drained in 1930, it comprises 20,000 ha of land.

Zuidelijk Flevoland: Southern Flevoland; latest and most southern polder of the province of Flevoland. Drained in 1968, it comprises 44,000 ha of land.

Zuiderzee: Zuiderzee; inland sea in the heart of the Netherlands, after 1932 renamed the IJsselmeer. From the Roman period to the late medieval period this sea was called Almere.

Zwammerdam: village in the province of Zuid-Holland. In the 1960s and 1970s the Roman fort of *Nigrum Pullum* was excavated. A total of six vessels were discovered and salvaged. All the vessels form part of the collection of the N.I.S.A.; two conserved logboats are exhibited.

Notes

1. 1932 was an important year for the security of the Zuiderzee. In its northern part, a 32 km-long dike was built connecting the provinces of *Noord-Holland* and *Friesland*, thereby sealing off the heart of the Netherlands from the North Sea.
2. Known until 12 April 1995 as the *Centrum voor ScheepsArcheologie (C.S.A.)* of the *Rijksdienst voor het Oudheidkundig Bodemonderzoek (R.O.B.)*.
3. The excavation reports published so far have been mainly descriptive.
4. It is also used by the Underwater Archaeology Department for the storage of their finds.
5. Up to 20 feet (7 m) deep.

6 Not only shipbuilding techniques changed. Contacts with different cultures and countries resulted in a demand for new goods, such as spices, Chinese porcelain, tropical wood etc.
7 Still 6 m high.
8 The illustrations do not provide an acceptable level of archaeological and technical information, and anyone who recognizes or sees an artefact of interest is welcome to visit our depot to examine it more closely.
9 An aspect of our research which has greatly enhanced our ability to date medieval wrecks.

References

Dijk, L.van 1985 'Reiniging muntvondst', *Jaarverslag Onderafdeling Scheepsarcheologie 1985*, 26–28.

Dijk, L.van 1986 'Behandelingsmethode voor bodemvondsten van gietijzer', *Jaarverslag onderafdeling Scheepsarcheologie 1986*, 40–44.

Dijk, L.van 1987 *Het reinigen van een muntvondst uit het scheepswrak L 79 Oostelijk Flevoland*. RIJP-Rapport 1987–16Cbw, Lelystad.

Green, J.N. 1977 *The loss of the Verenigde Oostindische Compagnie Jacht Vergulde Draeck, Western Australia 1656*. 2 Vol. BAR Supplementary Series 36, Oxford.

Hocker, F.M. & Vlierman, K. 1996 *A small cog, wrecked on the Zuiderzee in the early fifteenth century*, Excavation Report 9. Flevobericht NR.408, Almere.

Koehler, L. 1994 'Meten is weten, recente ontwikkelingen in het opmeten van scheepsarcheologische objecten', *in* R. Reinders & M. Bierma (eds) *Vis en visvangst. Inleidingen gehouden tijdens het zevende Glavimans symposion Vlaardingen, 23 april 1993*, 101–106.

Land, J. van der 1982 *De restauratie van vier paar schoenen uit een scheepswrak op kavel OZ 71 in Zuidelijk Flevoland*. Werkdocument 1982–92Abw, Lelystad.

McLaughlin-Neyland, K. & Neyland, B. 1993 *Two prams wrecked on the Zuider Zee in the late eigthteenth century. Excavation reports 15 and 16*. Flevobericht NR.383, Lelystad.

Oosting, R. & Vlierman, K. 1990 *'De Zeehond'. Een groninger tjalk gebouwd in 1878, vergaan in 1886*. Opgravingsverslag 13. Flevobericht nr. 323, Lelystad.

Oosting, R. & Vlierman, K. 1993 'Een 17de-eeuws vistransportschip gevonden in Swifterbant'. *Cultuur Historisch Jaarboek voor Flevoland 1993*. (eindred. G.H.L.Tiesinga), 87–106.

Reinders, R. 1982 *Shipwrecks of the Zuiderzee*, Flevobericht nr.197, Lelystad.

Reinders, R. 1985 'The inventory of a cargo-vessel, wrecked in 1888', *in* C.O. Cederlund (ed.), *Post Medieval Boat and Ship Archaeology*, BAR International Series 256, Oxford, 81–99.

Reinders, H.R. & Oosting, R. 1989. 'Mittelalterliche Schiffsfunde in den IJsselmeerpoldern', *in* W. Haio Zimmermann (ed.), *Wilhelmshavener Tage 2*. Wilhelmshaven, 106–122.

Roo, H. de, Reinders, R., Scheer, A.van der, Wevers, A., Zelhorst, L. & Zwiers, P.B. 1978 *Bescherming van scheepsresten in de grond*, Werkdocument 1978–285Abw., Lelystad.

Vlek, R. 1987 *The Medieval Utrecht Boat. The history and evaluation of one of the first nautical archaeological excavations and reconstructions in the Low Countries*. BAR International Series 382. National Maritime Museum Greenwich.

Vlierman, K. 1983 *Aardewerk uit de inventaris van twee laat middeleeuwse vrachtschepen in Oostelijk Flevoland*, Corpus van Middeleeuws Aardewerk uit gesloten vondstcomplexen in Nederland en Vlaanderen (CMA). aflevering 1 en 2, Lelystad.

Vlierman, K. 1985 *Bijlen uit laat-middeleeuwse schepen*, RIJP-Rapport 1985–55Abw., Lelystad.

Vlierman, K. 1991 'Een zeventiende eeuwse ventjager', *in* R. Reinders & R.Oosting (eds), *Scheepsarcheologie: prioriteiten en lopend onderzoek. Inleidingen gehouden tijdens de Glavimans symposia in 1986 en 1987*, 95–104.

Vlierman, K. 1992 'De uitrusting en inventaris van een kleine 15e-eeuwse kogge', in R. Reinders (ed.), *Scheepsuitrusting en -inventaris. Inleidingen gehouden tijdens het vijfde Glavimans symposion Amsterdam, 5 april 1991*, 10–22.

Vlierman, K. 1993 'Late Medieval Pottery on Dutch Shipwrecks and a Well-Dated Inventory of the Early 15th century', *Medieval Ceramics 17*, 69–76.

Vlierman, K. 1994 'A note on deck-lights, -glasses or -prisms from 19th-century wrecks in Flevoland, The Netherlands', *IJNA 23*, 319–323.

Vlierman, K. 1996A '... *Van Zintelen, van Zintelroeden ende Mossen...*'. *Een breeuwmethode als hulpmiddel bij het dateren van schepen uit de Hanzetijd*. Scheepsarcheologie I Flevobericht Nr. 386, Lelystad.

Vlierman, K. 1996B *Kleine bootjes en middeleeuws scheepshout met constructiedetails*, Scheepsarcheologie II. Flevobericht NR.404, Almere.

Vlierman, K. in prep. *De inventaris van de 17de-eeuwse koopvaarder van kavel E 81 in de Noordoostpolder*.

Vlierman K. & van Dijk, L. 1980 *Conservering en restauratie van kleine voorwerpen bij het museum voor Scheepsarcheologie te Ketelhaven*, Werkdocument WD 1980–149Abw, Lelystad.

Zwiers, B.P. & Vlierman, K. 1988 *De 'Lutina'. Een Overijssels vrachtschip, vergaan in 1888. Het onderzoek van een vrachtschip gevonden op kavel H 48 in Oostelijk Flevoland*. Opgravingsverslag 12. Flevobericht nr. 323, Lelystad.

3

Material culture research of Canadian historic shipwrecks: the *Machault* legacy

Stephen Davis

The wrecks forming the subject of this paper are those which have been investigated by the Underwater Archaeological Services Unit of Parks Canada, the Department of Canadian Heritage. Parks Canada is responsible for the national parks, an enormous amount of real estate, larger than the land mass of England and Scotland. In addition, it administers 128 national historic sites that date from the 16th to the 20th century, and one early 11th-century Viking site. Over 1200 'historic-period' archaeological sites have been recorded, of which 124 are under water.

The quantity and variety of artefacts recovered from historic sites prompted Parks Canada to establish a laboratory for artefact research. Since the mid-1960s, a group of researchers[1] have studied the material culture of historic-period Canada. This was originally concerned with the identification and dating of excavated ceramics, glass, smoking pipes, weaponry and structural hardware. Specialist fields now include domestic metal artefacts, tools, ships' rigging and fittings, blacksmithing and metalwork, toiletry equipment, electricity, lighting devices, staved containers, coins, clothing and footwear, beads and trade goods.

The detailed study of the rich artefact assemblages from some shipwreck sites was initially justified on the grounds that the knowledge gained would be applied to other Parks Canada collections, and that the specific dating of shipwrecks (in the case of the *Machault*, 8 July 1760) would be used to 'fine tune' the dates of terrestrial-site material. A wide range of organic material frequently survives in a waterlogged, anaerobic environment, particularly in the northern regions. With these advantages in mind, Parks Canada decided that the excavation of the wreck of a mid-18th-century French frigate might answer questions concerning the attribution and dating of artefacts recovered from Canadian land sites which have French occupation dates of approximately the same period.

Between 1758 and 1760 British occupation forces had succeeded French at Louisbourg, Fort Beausejour and Quebec City in very short order, so that the material culture left by both groups were very well mixed. It was rarely possible to separate French from British contexts. This was a particularly acute problem with items of everyday use, such as eating utensils and clothing. In order to resolve this, in 1969 marine archaeologists went to the Restigouche River, the final resting place of the *Machault*, and began the arduous task of excavating this vessel. The site investigation and retrieval of the ship's timbers and artefacts took four years. In contrast, the identification of the numerous artefacts is still in progress, revealing fresh insights into trade, commerce, sea navigation and domestic life aboard a French vessel in the mid-18th century.

THE WRECK

The frigate, reported to have been between 500 and 550 tons, was launched as a privateer in Bayonne in 1758. In 1760 it was hastily refitted as part of a convoy to deliver troops and supplies to save a besieged Montreal, the last city in New France still resisting the British invasion. On 8 July 1760, the *Machault* was scuttled by her crew to prevent it falling into the hands of the British, who had cornered her in the Restigouche River. Before sabotaging the ship, many of the supplies and cargo were removed. We know from contemporary accounts of the skirmish that the French had removed most of the food, munitions, tools and other supplies that France had sent for the Canadian cause, as well as the personal items related to everyday life belonging to the sailors, soldiers and officers. The investigating team anticipated finding remains of supplies destined for the colony and little else. Yet the quantity of material recovered from the wreck was enormous: the ship's cargo of merchandise, together with material which the French could not use in the land camp or what was privately owned.

The greatest portion of the cargo was private venture merchandise (mainly tableware) stowed in the lowest part of the *Machault's* hold. This included commercial goods intended either for resale in New France, or (failing a successful journey) for re-routing for sale in Santo Domingo or Louisiana. Included in the ill-fated ship's cargo were a shipment of shoes, Chinese export porcelain, English soft-paste porcelain, coarse earthenware vessels and mess supplies (including salt pork in

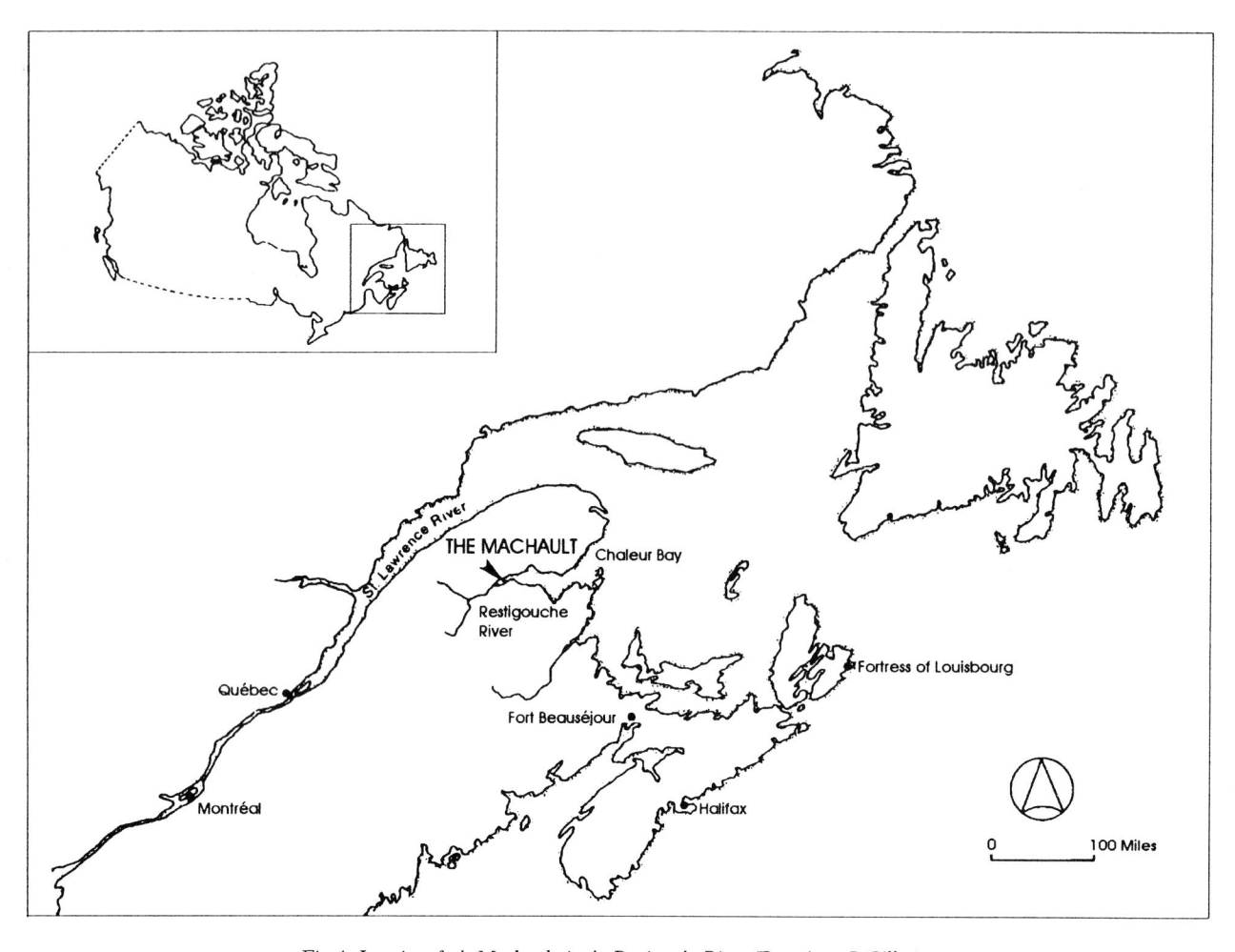

Fig. 1. Location of the Machault *in the Restigouche River.* (Drawing: C. Pillar)

barrels and an unknown beverage in English bottles). Most of the artefacts were recovered in the bow portion of the shipwreck, largely as a result of the river current and tidal flow.

Records of the suppliers and contractors of the fleet note a cargo of some '5,500 pr. shoes' (Beattie 1968, 11). It is not clear how the cargo of shoes and other merchandise was allocated between the convoy ships in preparation for the ocean crossing, or how much of the cargo was removed from the *Machault* before it was torched. The captain of one of the British ships sent to clean up the site in October and November 1760 stated that they 'brought away ... some shoes' (*ibid.* 33). Nevertheless, a large quantity of footwear was left behind. The remaining footwear cargo, worn shoes and boots and related artefacts such as shoe buckles have permitted a comprehensive study of 18th-century colonial footwear fashion and construction.

Other material found included the *Machault*'s weaponry; items lost, broken, or discarded; spare parts and tools; and mess supplies for those who stayed on board up to the ship's last moments. The artefacts from the *Machault* reveal aspects of 18th-century maritime travel, defence at sea and a variety of daily human activities. They show that Canadians during the period who could afford to pay were supplied with consumer goods from all parts of the globe.

THE ARTEFACTS

Mixing, serving and individual eating bowls and porringers formed part of the cargo. The selection was suprisingly varied: continental, French, English and Chinese ceramics (some utilitarian and undecorated, others extremely refined). The cargo shipment of Chinese export porcelain from the *Machault* is decorated with underglaze blue and overglaze Imari-style and *famille rose* colours. The presence of Chinese export porcelain for purchase in New France has dispelled the notion that inhabitants of the French colonies generally received inferior or less desirable manufactured goods than people at home.

The main cargoes were tea and tableware. Teawares predominated, reflecting the archaeological and archival records. The bulk of the porcelain was used for hot beverages (tea and coffee), and to a lesser extent for the table. All were functional items, and there were no purely ornamental items such as large decorative jars or statuettes; it appears that the *Machault* cargo

Fig. 2. The blue-painted patterns on pieces intended to compose a tea service are not the same on each item; even tea bowls and saucers do not match. Our own ideas about what constitutes a 'set' are not applicable to 18th-century sensibility. (Photograph: R. Chan, RA15106B)

is typical of the largely practical shipments exported from China. Although wares for toiletry and many other functions were made, they are rarely found on historic Canadian sites and were not found in the wreck of the *Machault*. The decoration on the porcelain reflects a partiality for floral and Chinese landscape subjects typical of the European taste of the mid-18th century. Archaeological evidence in Canada suggests that preference for Imari decoration waned in the second half of the 18th century, and the *Machault's* cargo supports this view.

A cargo of English soft-paste porcelain made at the Bow factory and tin-glazed earthenware from Liverpool was revealing, affirming that, then as now, war did not completely impede trade. The large quantity of ceramics found on the *Machault* included a relatively small cargo of tin-glazed earthenwares, comprising 157 English tin-glazed earthenware bowls in various sizes. They were recovered stacked one inside another, and were probably shipped wrapped in straw in crates, casks or rush baskets resting on myrtle branches. In addition, there were forty-three tin-glazed earthenwares of French origin

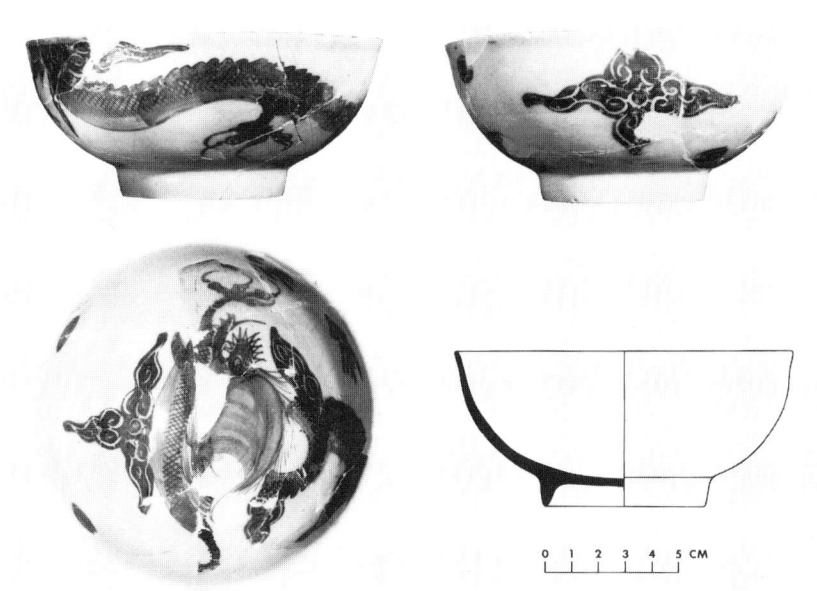

Fig. 3. Based on their manufacture and decoration, the dragon bowls were either from Lambeth or Liverpool (England). All had similar oriental shapes decorated with chinoiserie pattern dragon motifs, stylized flowers, and cloud-like elements using the sgraffito technique very common at Liverpool. These dragon bowls came in several sizes, ranging from 110 to 230 mm in rim diameter. The smallest bowls were for tea or coffee, the medium-sized ones were slop bowls, and the largest were punch bowls. (Photograph: R. Chan, RA-B)

that were probably for use on board ship. They included plates, platters, bowls, a porringer, a dish, a pitcher, a sauce-boat, tureens, basins, chamber pots and pharmaceutical pots.

Over 1,000 plain and decorated French coarse earthenware food storage, preparation and serving vessels were recovered, many still stacked in piles in the hold. The collection includes mostly green-glazed jugs, bowls, milk pans, and terrines of various sizes; plain green-glazed and decorated porringers, plates and platters; and plain unglazed two-handle cooking pots. Among the less frequent forms represented are soup tureens, a barber's bowl and two drinking-water jars. This is one of the best examples of massive importation of coarse wares from France to New France, and the variety of wares and forms reflects the assortment of culinary utensils in everyday use in the colony during the mid-18th century.

The quality of these objects is comparable to that of identical products sold in France and England. There was some degree of functional specialization or stylistic choice in the availability of coarse wares. For example, for a standard eating container one could choose between the Saintonge-style plain green-glazed bowl or a more elegant and more expensive slip-painted porringer from the Rhone Valley.

Fig. 4. Southern French plain unglazed twin-handled cooking pot. Several dozen cooking pots made of coarse earthenware were found. These pots were practical: they did not leak, they conducted heat well and they were cheap. Unfortunately, these pots tended to become brittle with use and were easily broken: fragmented coarse earthenwares are often found on French colonial sites dating from the first half of the 17th century through to the 18th century. (Photograph: R. Chan, RA-1851B)

Cooking and other household utensils of sheet copper and brass were durable and easily repairable, and when finally worn out, the recycled metal had numerous uses. These utensils were also popular trade items with the native Americans, and consequently, land sites rarely contain many intact examples in such materials. The *Machault*, however, provided us with a variety of artefacts including a number of nesting brass kettles, large copper kettles, copper lids with brass knobs, a brass colander and a brass 'frying pan'-type chamberstick.

Fig. 5. The chamberstick (candleholder) was designed to be easily carried wherever light was needed. This form takes its common name from the frying-pan shape. It is of sheet brass with simple riveted construction. (Photograph: R. Chan, RA 3146B)

A number of tools were also found aboard the *Machault*; one particularly interesting category within that group was the metal-working tools. These consisted of a vice, punch, two chisels, a punch, tongs and a bellows board (see Ross 1981, 226–237). These tools are particularly interesting because they were found in the port bow area, and this indicates a working smith aboard the vessel (*ibid*, 244; Rees 1980, 236–65).

The technology that would have allowed a smith to displace the cook from the galley with a minimum of fuss was commonplace at the time (Light 1987, 658–65). The smith attained the necessary forging and welding temperatures with charcoal and a side blast in a forge whose bed was sand. Perhaps the interchangability of the forge and the galley fire explains why the presence of a working smith (or armourer) on board naval and other vessels was rarely noted or commented upon.

Two hundred wine bottles manufactured, filled and sealed in England were probably part of the cargo. Over twenty examples have wired-down corks, demonstrating that corks were not covered and were not driven all the way into the bottle necks, contradicting conventional beliefs of how bottles were sealed in the 18th century. The necks and bases in this assemblage were used as a control sample to test the validity of a dating formula for English cylindrical wine bottles (Jones 1986). Several hundred hollow-stemmed French wine glasses recovered also formed part of the cargo (Bryce 1984, 21).

Blocks, tackles, rope and fragments of the ship provided information on the ship's rigging; navigational instruments and sailmaker's tools for caulking, cleaning and repairs provided an insight into ship maintenance. A miscellany of artefacts recovered during the excavation relate to personal hygiene, grooming and social pastimes: combs, barbers' bowls, a medical syringe, pipes and tobacco boxes, jewellery, sewing and mending tools and lighting. One artefact evokes the war then in progress. Markings on a brass wrist escutcheon, still attached to the wooden stock of a Long Land Pattern musket, record the weapon's original owners. Captured from Colonel

Fig. 6. Forging tools recovered from the Machault (left to right): vice, punch, tongs and two chisels. (Composite photograph: R. Chan, not to scale)

William Shirley's American regiment by the French under Montcalm at Fort Oswego in 1756, the musket was reissued for use on the *Machault* (Bryce 1984, 21).

Personal items such as clothing provide an insight into individual style and status. In general, items from archaeological sites which relate to this category are non-organic metal fasteners such as hooks, buttons and buckles. Small discs of punched leather, possibly used to fasten a sailor's jacket, were occasionally found, a type of mundane object that rarely appears in paintings or period documents. Their discovery during archaeological excavations is therefore important for costume historians.

Fig. 7. An example of the corking and wiring method of the Machault cargo bottles. (Photograph: R. Chan, RA-5068B)

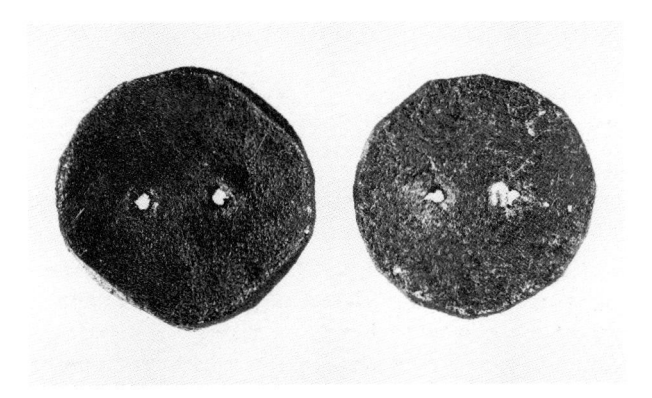

Fig. 8. Plain, unadorned clothing buttons from the Machault. These leather discs punched with holes were possibly fashioned by the wearer from materials at hand. (Photograph: R. Chan, RA-16908B)

Fig. 9. Four shoe-buckle frames recovered from the Machault *displaying both plain and decorative shapes fashionable at this time.*
(Photograph: R. Chan, RA-19090B)

Similarly, the assemblage of shoe and knee buckles recovered from the *Machault* display the range of materials available to individuals at this time. Shoe and clothing buckles were often a statement of personal taste and social position. Depending upon the individual, the buckle was as much an item of jewellery as it was a functional fastener: the shape, size and decoration of the buckle changed over time as the victims of fashion fell prey to the 'latest model'. Consequently, collections of clothing buckles that predate the last quarter of the 18th century are relatively rare in museums, because the earlier items were frequently melted down and recycled into more contemporary and fashionable objects.

It is certainly possible that the buckles on the *Machault* are English in origin, where the Midlands were renowned as the centre of manufacture and international exporter of such items. Throughout the 18th century, England was the major producer of shoe buckles, supplying 'the whole demand for America, Holland, France, Germany, Italy and Spain' (Timmins 1967, 214–5). All of the clothing fasteners found were probably left in haste or forgotten by the ship's crew and officers. Shoe buckles are a sensitive indicator of status and gender, and the *Machault* collection has proved an excellent source for comparative research by archaeologists and museum curators.

During the underwater excavation of the *Machault*, the equivalent of fifty artefact storage boxes of 18th-century shoe pieces were recovered. In terms of quantity, the footwear from the *Machault* forms the most impressive assemblage of leather in our reference collection of leather artefacts from Canadian archaeological sites. On the basis of the number of soles recovered, over 400 unworn men's shoes had formed part of the ship's cargo. This excludes twenty-nine items of worn footwear: shoes and boots left by the crew of the ship. The *Machault* shoes help to date and identify shoe parts recovered from other 18th-century archaeological sites, and have provided patterns for the individual shoe components for reproducing appropriate footwear for our costume animation programmes and site displays.

Few of the items found were complete, since the linen sewing thread had disintegrated and over time the component shoe parts had shifted and become detached. In many respects this was an advantage, for the disassembled components permitted the study of the individual pieces and display tell-tale stitch holes and tool marks. This information is extremely valuable when researching the cut and assembly methods of historic footwear (see Goubitz 1984, 187–196).

All of the *Machault* shoes have rounded toes, low heels and wide ratchets for large buckles characteristic of the period. The soles are cut symmetrically with no specific left or right shape. However, close inspection reveals differences in the construction of the shoe and in the choice of leather, and the quality of craftsmanship of the shoes become apparent.

The collection illustrates two methods of shoe construction – turned or welted – which usually determined the weight or thickness of the shoe leather. A turnshoe has a fairly thin upper and a single sole. The shoe upper and sole are stitched together while inside out. Upon completion, the assembled shoe is turned right side out. Polished, light and flexible, turnshoes were appropriate for elegant leisure wear, indoor sports or dancing. Welted shoes were the day-to-day street shoes. A welted shoe has a welt stitched to the bottom edge of the upper to which the sole is finally attached. Constructed with thick welted soles and thicker uppers than turnshoes, this type of footwear provided maximum protection and durability, important factors for military and working wear. The welt also creates a flexible yet watertight seam. Garsault was describing a welted shoe when he stated '*Lorsque les semelles sont d'une épaisseur convenable, & que tout le reste du soulier est solidement étoffé, il est ce qui s'appelle, un* soulier ordinaire....' (de Garsault 1767, 13).[2]

Eighteenth-century shoes could be made with either the grain or flesh of the hide outwards, and the choice of surface was significant. The grain of the leather is the outer surface originally bearing the animal's hair, wool or fur; the flesh is

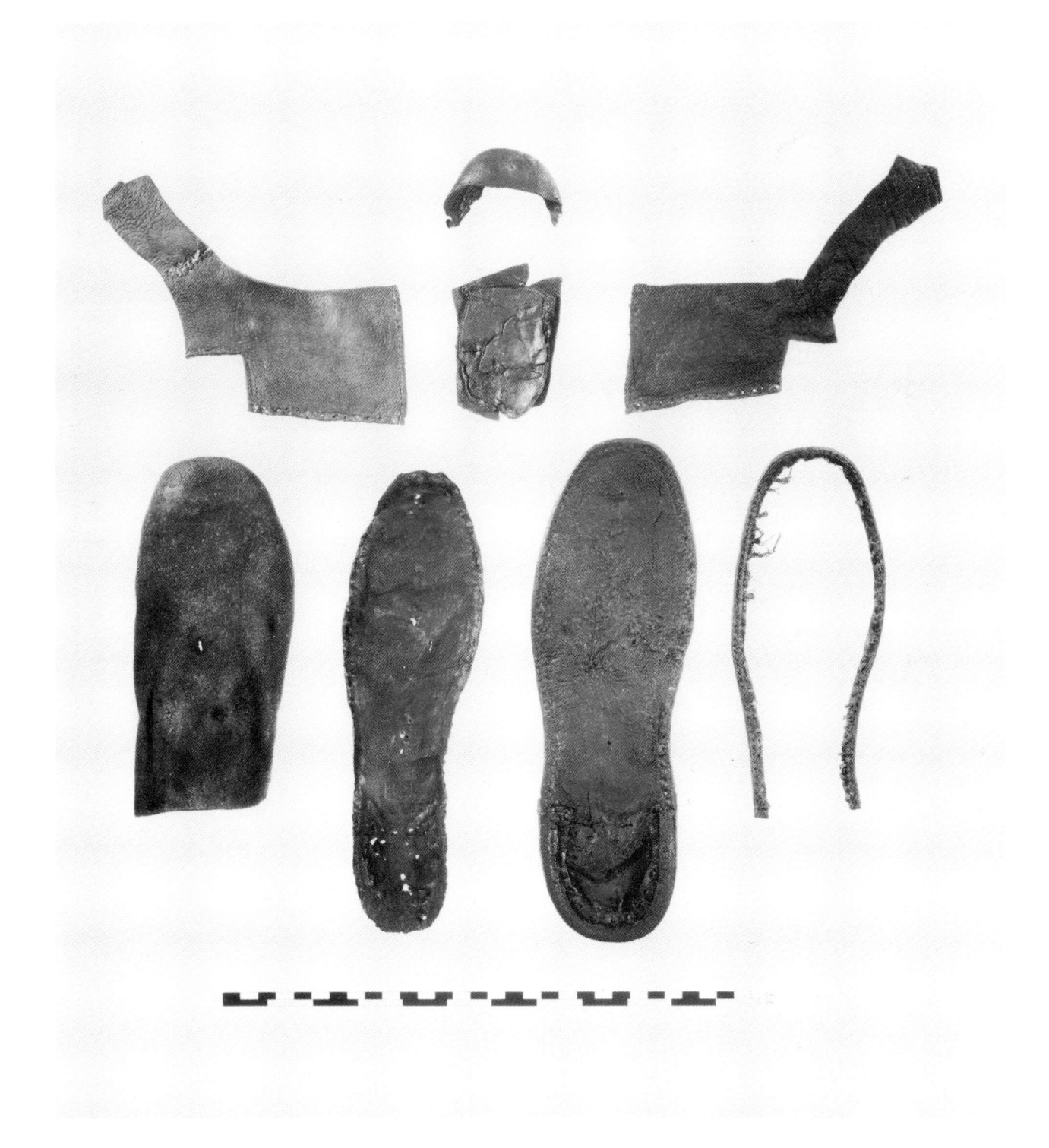

Fig. 10. Disassembled welted shoe parts laid out following conservation treatment: toe puff, two quarters, mid-sole filler, vamp, insole, sole and welt. Each shoe consists of an upper and a bottom. The upper includes a vamp and one or two quarters. During the 18th century the vamp and quarters of men's shoes were usually cut out of calfskin. The bottom or underpart of the shoe essentially comprised an insole, sole, welt, rand, heel and perhaps some mid-sole filler. The insole was cowhide, and the sole was cut from 'strong leather': oxhide treated in a particular way with lime and barley. (Photograph: R. Chan)

Fig. 11. Unworn, straight soles of men's shoes from the Machault. *During the 18th century, shoes were made over a straight last, the shoemaker's wooden model for shaping shoes. Constructed in this way, there is no left or right shoe and technically, 18th-century straight-lasted shoes could be switched to either foot. After some wear, however, the leather conforms to the wearer's feet, and one can generally discern a left or right sole shape and upper on excavated, well-worn footwear recovered from 18th-century sites. A welt seam is visible on the bottom of the left sole; there is no seam on the bottom of the turnshoe on the right.*
(Photograph: R. Chan, RA-10756B)

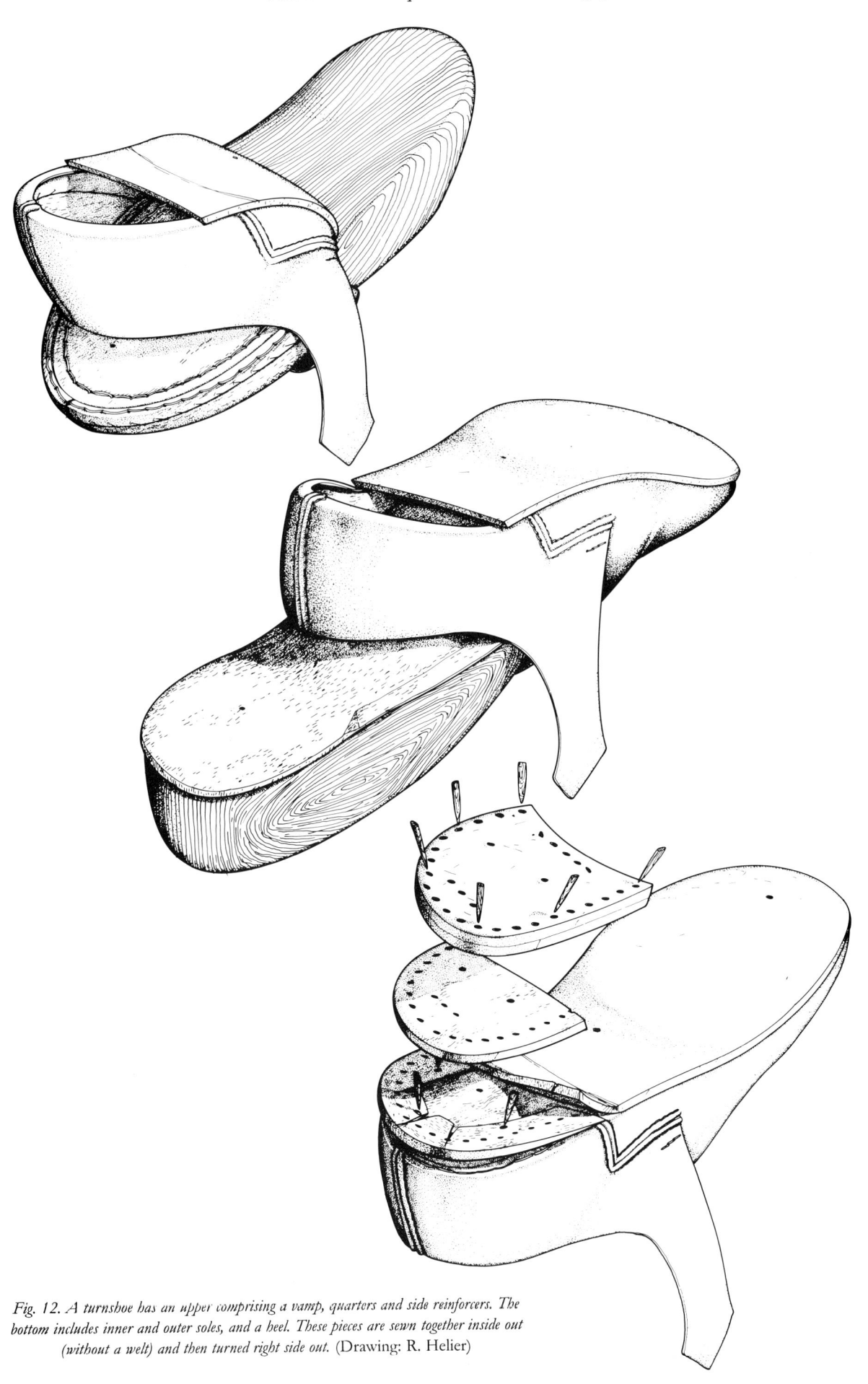

Fig. 12. A turnshoe has an upper comprising a vamp, quarters and side reinforcers. The bottom includes inner and outer soles, and a heel. These pieces are sewn together inside out (without a welt) and then turned right side out. (Drawing: R. Helier)

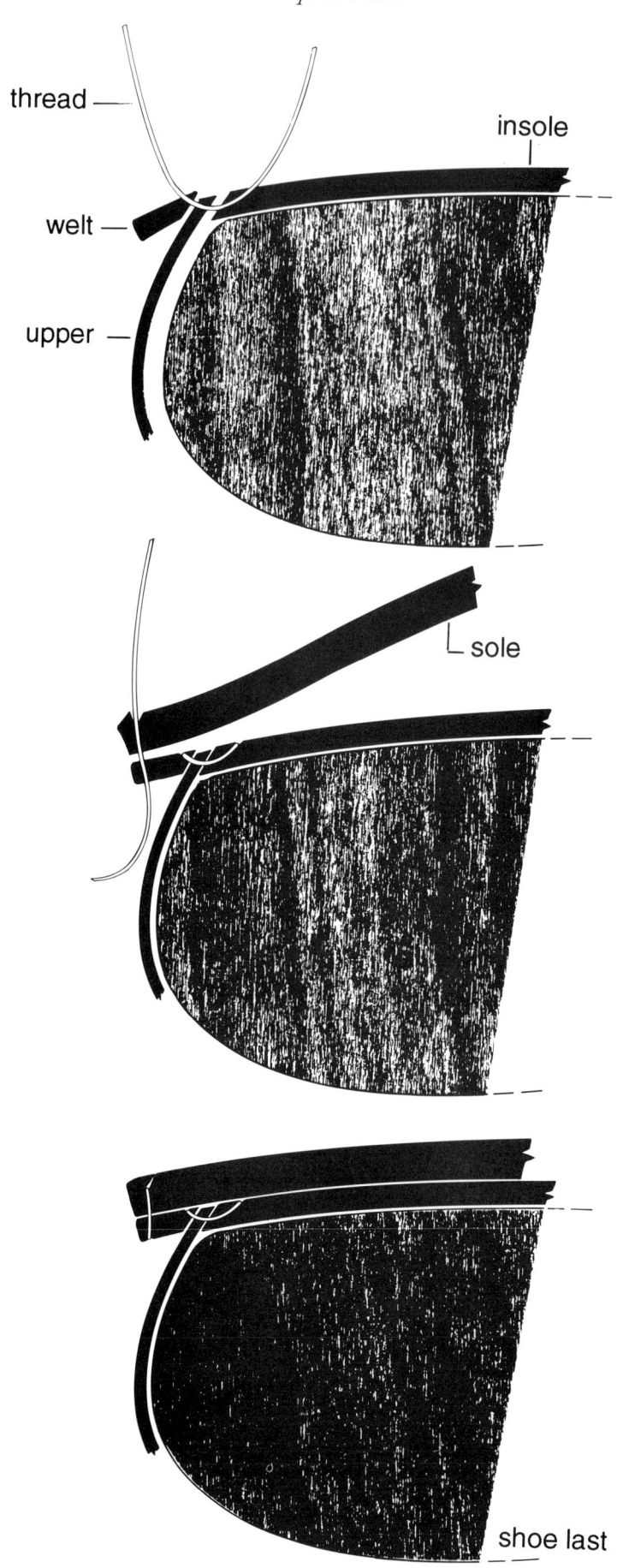

Fig. 13. *A welted shoe is made by sewing the upper to the insole and the inside edge of a welt and then attaching the sole to the welt.* (Drawing: R. Helier)

the inner surface of the hide, which was against the animal's body. The smooth grain side of the hide could be polished; shoes made flesh side out were simply blackened. All of the *Machault* turnshoes were assembled with the smooth grain of the leather outwards. Many of the welted shoes retrieved from the wreck have the rough suede-like flesh surface that was resistant to showing scuffs and scrapes, important factors for military or working wear.

Quality of craftsmanship is also reflected in the *Machault* footwear. The number of stitches per centimetre may be used to differentiate coarse from refined construction; precisely cut, matching components are another criterion. Most of the footwear specimens retrieved from the wreck of the *Machault* were heavy, welted *souliers ordinaires*. Some of these welted shoes have extremely thick uppers and bottoms in comparison with others. These are probably the heavy waxed shoes *(gros celeries cire)*, a variation of the ordinary shoe noted in Garsault's description. Heavy waxed shoes had uppers cut out of cowhide or thick calfskin assembled with the rough, flesh side out and treated with a mixture of mutton tallow, wax and lamp-black. Garsault noted that only the lower classes, particularly the labourers, wore heavy waxed shoes *(ibid*, 35). Occasionally, heavy waxed shoes were fixed with hobnails. The coarsely constructed welted shoes from the *Machault* were probably not for commercial resale in Quebec, but intended for the French military.

Examples of finer quality welted and turned shoes also survived. Although similar in shape, they are more refined in cut and in choice of materials. Assembled with a smooth, polished surface, the lighter weight, flexible shoes found aboard the *Machault* were probably worn by the ship's officers and are typical of civilian footwear in 1760. It would appear that the surface, thickness and quality of the shoe leather can reflect the wearer's social, economic or occupational status.

Summary

A wreck that produces quantities of material culture requires time and expertise, in addition to the costs of storage, curation and conservation. Yet a properly maintained collection can form an excellent 'investment': even now we continue to consult the *Machault* material with new questions and fresh ideas.

The *Machault* provided an opportunity to study a variety of material groups from a time capsule dated 1760. The unique aspect of this collection was the presence of duplicate material. The rich cargo and quantity of material culture contributed to many specialist studies on subjects ranging from English bottle glass and Chinese export porcelain to leather footwear manufacture and 18th-century weaponry.

Finally, it is appropriate to note some of the advantages of studying shipwreck material, particularly cargoes. Firstly, cargoes permit a much better idea of variety and variation of an object for any given moment, important when studying a material group not previously studied in any detail. The large numbers of similar material culture often allow comment on manufacture technology, packaging and the shipping of consumer goods.[3] The quantities of repetitive material may also provide opportunities for experimenting with innovative and potentially destructive conservation methods, and provide examples for distribution within teaching collections.

Cargoes often confirm and clarify the evidence from terrestrial archaeology and art history, since they rarely contain

Fig. 14. A man's welted shoe, part of the cargo shipment from the Machault, *following conservation and reconstruction. The latchets overlap the front of the shoe; when worn they would be fastened with a shoe buckle. This example was assembled with the smooth grain side outwards.*
(Photograph: R. Chan, RA-1603B)

old, unfashionable merchandise. They help us to understand the edges of fashion, such as the lifespan of an object's shape, and when an object was long-lived rather than 'old fashioned'.

Cargoes can be compared against written inventories, which may reveal discrepancies such as the inclusion of private cargo amongst company or government shipments. On the other hand, as company inventories are often cursory, the artefact assemblage may elucidate their sketchy descriptions.

Wrecks are frequently inaccessible for salvage at the time of sinking. Consequently objects that seldom appear in land-site assemblages – such as copper and brass pots which could be recycled – may be recovered intact. The marine environment often preserves organic material (leather footwear and even barrels of partly consumed salt pork) that may not survive well on land sites. Even valuable items, such as jewellery, money and other precious artefacts, are often inaccessible to salvagers and hence survive for archaeologists to study.

The excavation of the *Machault* has produced a rich cultural legacy: fine selection of mid-18th-century consumer goods and an 18th-century sea-going vessel. The artefacts on board have contributed significantly to the body of knowledge now possessed by Parks' material culture analysts, and subsequent underwater excavations on other sites have benefited from experience gained from the investigation of this ship.

Acknowledgements

This paper includes research conducted by a number of Parks Canada's material culture specialists, originally published in *Legacy of the Machault: A Collection of 18th-century Artefacts* by Catherine Sullivan (Studies in Archaeology, National Historic Parks and Sites Branch, Parks Canada, Environment Canada, 1986). I am grateful for the information generously shared by my colleagues: Chuck Bradley, Douglas Bryce, Phil Dunning, Gérard Gusset, Olive Jones, John Light, Virginia Myles, Catherine Sullivan and Ron Whate.

This paper from the Department of Canadian Heritage, Parks Canada, is reproduced with the permission of the Minister of Public Works and Government Services, Canada, © Her Majesty the Queen in Right of Canada, 1997.

Notes

1. Currently numbering 11.
2. "When the soles are of suitable thickness and all the rest of the shoe is solidly built, it is known as an *ordinary shoe*...." Although the reconstructions of the shoes are based wholly on the leather artefacts found during the excavation of the *Machault*, Garsault's *L'Art du cordonnier* was a particularly helpful resource. Garsault's treatise on handmade footwear preserves for readers today the many technical subtleties of the "gentle craft" as it was sometimes called.
3. For example, the assembly of 18th-century shoes, corking of English wine bottles, and packing of tin-glazed earthenware.

References

Beattie, J. 1968 'The Battle of the Restigouche', *National Historic Sites Service Manuscript Report Series* No. 19. Parks Canada, Ottawa.

Bryce, D. 1984 *Weaponry from the Machault*, Studies in Archaeology, Architecture and History, Parks Canada, Ottawa.

de Garsault, M. Francois Alexandre Pierre 1767 *L'Art du cordonnier* in *Descriptions des Arts et Metiers*, Academie Royal des Sciences, Paris.

Goubitz, O. 1984 'The Drawing of Registration of Archaeological Footwear', *Studies in Conservation* 29, 187–196.

Jones. O. 1986 *Cylindrical English Wine and Beer Bottles, 1735–1850*, Studies in Archaeology, Architecture and History, Parks Canada, Ottawa.

Light, J.D. 1987 'Blacksmithing Technology and Forge Construction', *Technology and Culture* 28, No. 3, July 1987, 658–665.

Ross, L.A. 1980 'Underwater Archaeologist Vade Mecum to the Companies, Duties, Tools and Related Supplies of 18th-century British and French Naval Vessels'. Parks Canada, *Microfiche Report Series* No. 222.

Ross, L.A. 1981 'Eighteenth-century French Naval Duties as Reflected by the Tools Recovered from *Le Machault*', Parks Canada, *Microfiche Report Series* No. 137.

Timmins, S. (ed.) 1967 *Birmingham and the Midland Hardware District: A Series of Reports*, London: Frank Cass and Company Ltd. (first published in 1866).

Part II
Artefacts Groups from the Age of Discovery

4

The material culture of the *Mary Rose* (1545) as a fighting vessel: the uses of wood

Alex Hildred

The study of artefacts from shipwreck sites can have many purposes. The assumed contemporaneity of objects afforded by a terminal date has numerous implications, particularly for the typological dating of artefacts from undated sites or from poorly defined contexts within sites. The occurrence of duplicate objects, either indentured or carried as cargo for trade, provides an opportunity for the statistical analysis of discrete artefact types. The parameters for this are manifold – the types of wood used for specific object groups, the consistency in manufacturing technique, the type of material and size of object being the most obvious. In the case of a ship provisioned by the state, by an individual or by a company, the distinction between state/personal/company property may be discerned through the study of the above. This has been demonstrated in the study of chests recovered from the *Mary Rose* (Richards, in this volume). The frequency of categories of objects from specific locations within shipwrecks can aid the identification of those areas where certain functions had been performed, and those areas reserved for personal use, storage of cargo or the provisioning and maintenance of the vessel.

This paper is based on an initial study of selected groups of wooden objects recovered from the Tudor warship *Mary Rose*, in particular of its ordnance and domestic utensils. Over 19,000 artefacts were recovered from the *Mary Rose*, of which 6,503 (36.3%) are treen. The large groups of duplicated objects include 4,000 bricks and 2,000 shot. Of particular importance are the objects of domestic treen which infrequently survive because of their fragility and lack of intrinsic value (Colour Plate 1C). Items of everyday furniture, if they survive, are difficult to date accurately. Assemblages from shipwreck sites are therefore vital in studying certain groups of object.

This study does not examine the use of specific woods for particular purposes, or detail the various methods of manufacture with reference to the inherent qualities of specific woods. These aspects will be addressed when individual groups are published.

The totals presented within the tables of wood type refer to artefacts which have undergone microscopic species identification. Any numerical difference between tables and the totals quoted within the text can be accounted for by examples lacking species identification.

To assist the reader in the location of large numbers of artefacts, a boxed representation of the site has been devised. Left to right the boxes represent sectors from bow to stern, relating to excavation trenches. Top to bottom the sectors shown include the starboard scour pit, castle deck, upper deck, main deck, orlop deck, hold and port scour pit. The area covered measures approximately 40 m by 20 m.

The *Mary Rose* was built between 1509 and 1511 to serve as a fighting platform. It is assumed, therefore, that the assemblage represents the fighting/living activities of 185 soldiers, 200 mariners and 30 gunners. Although episodes of refurbishment and rebuilding were undertaken during her 36–year life, no evidence has been found to suggest that she was ever intended for anything but warfare. By 1545 she carried seven large guns on each side of her main gun-deck (Colour Plate 1A) set at gun-bays with hinged lids which, when closed, provided a flush external surface with the carvel planks of the hull at this level. In total she carried up to thirty-nine carriage-mounted guns, positioned on three decks.

The uses of differing wood species for certain purposes is reflected within the artefacts and the hull. Although oak from the south of England is numerically the most predominant wood within the hull, substantial elements were fashioned from other woods, including elm, poplar, spruce and pine (Vine 1995).

THE ORDNANCE

Gun-port lids

All seven of the starboard main deck gun-ports had lids which were open when the ship sank. Seven portside lids were excavated from debris resulting from collapse of the portside and salvaging activities. Lid sizes vary, all providing close fits into their corresponding ports. They were manufactured from four oak elements. Two rectangular boards, butted together with the grain aligned across the port, formed the outside face;

two boards, butted together and aligned vertically, formed the inside face. Outside boards are larger and form a lip, fitting tightly against the ship. Ports are trapezoidal, the tops of the ports being 190 mm wider than the bottoms.[1]

Individual elements are held together with up to thirty nails displaying diamond-shaped heads and a central ring on the inside port face. Two iron straps with curved upper ends (forming hinges) are fixed to the outside face (Fig. 1).[2]

Fig. 1. External view of gun-port lid showing strap hinges and bolts. (Copyright: The Mary Rose Trust)

Gun Mountings

Three distinct forms of carriage for large guns were recovered, two supporting bronze guns and one supporting iron guns. Complete assemblages were often reconstructed from elements excavated nearby (see Fig.3 for distribution and unassigned individual elements).

Carriages for bronze guns

In all but one instance, carriages supporting bronze guns consist of an elm bed (either a single plank or two planks joined lengthways by three loose wooden tenons held with oak pegs); two trunnion support cheeks held onto the bed with wrought iron bolts and oak pegs; two stepped cheeks; two axles and four solid trucks (Hildred and Rule 1984) (Figs 2, 3). Bed, cheek and truck dimensions vary depending on the weight and size of their gun and shipboard location. These separate into three distinct forms; main deck, upper deck and castle deck.[3]

The two *trunnion support cheeks* are held into slots/mortises in the bed by single or double oak-pegged tenons protruding from the cheek underside. Iron brackets held with wedged iron bolts located on the front and rear help to secure these to the bed.[4] All are fashioned to accept the trunnions, sized for particular guns. Grain is aligned vertically.

Stepped cheeks are located into trunnion support cheeks by a mortise and tenon reinforced by a draw-bolt which enters the front face of the trunnion support cheek and terminates

Fig. 2. Bronze bastard demi culverin on replica carriage. (Copyright: The Mary Rose Trust)

The material culture of the Mary Rose (1545)

Guns and gun carriage elements

KEY
- ● Axle
- ○ Wheel
- ■ Tiller
- ◨ Truck
- ☐ Trail
- ▲ Stepped cheek
- △ Breech chamber wedge
- △ Trunnion support cheek
- ♣ Bed fragments

Location not known
● ○ ■ ◨ △

Bronze gun assembly

Wrought iron gun assembly

Tiller

Axle: roughout

Axle: finished

Breech chamber

Breech chamber wedge

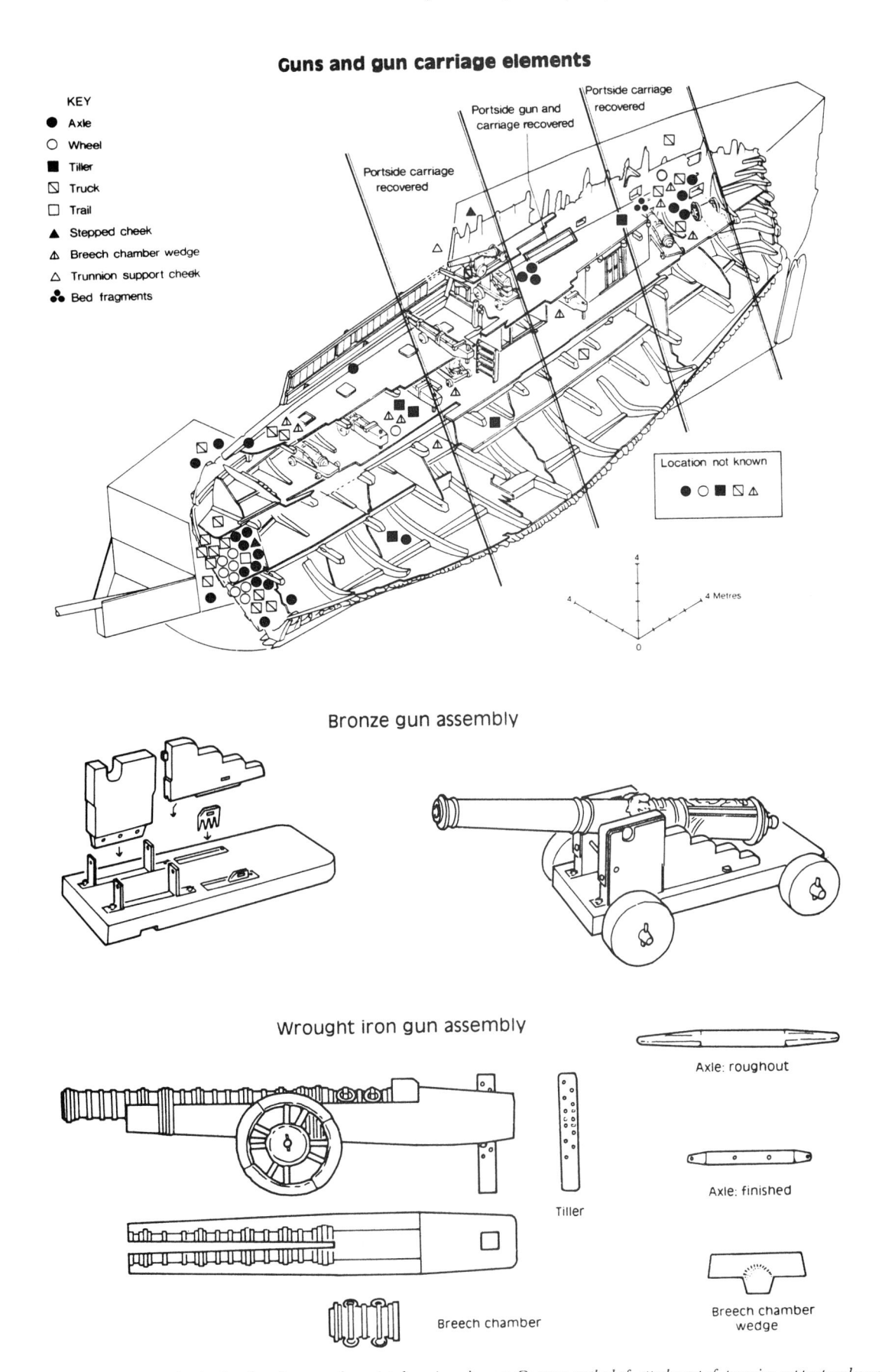

Fig. 3. Above: *isometric view showing location of guns and associated carriage elements.* Centre: *method of attachment of trunnion support and rear stepped cheeks into bed, and reconstruction of a carriage for a bronze gun.* Bottom: *elevation of wrought iron portpiece on sledge. Tiller, unfinished axle, finished axle and breech chamber wedge. Sledge with barrel and breech chamber removed (centre), breech chamber below.*(Copyright: The Mary Rose Trust)

halfway through the stepped cheek. This locates over a staple in the bed and is wedged.[5] The grain is aligned horizontally.

Axles are positioned beneath the bed except in one instance (MR 79 A 1232). The section touching the bed is square with arms tapered to accept trucks retained with iron linch pins. The squared cross-section reflects bed width and gun width at cascabel.[6]

Truck diameters differ between front and rear cheeks, and occasionally between right and left, dictated by the structure of the ship.[7]

One gun wedge (*quoin, qoyning*) was found *in situ*, supporting a cannon (MR 81 A 3003). This was made of oak, measuring 340 mm in length, and had a short handle. Two of the ten recovered were made of oak and four were made of elm.

Carriage elements have been visually identified as of elm, except for the axles, which are of ash.

Eight carriages were recovered: five supported *in situ* starboard guns, and three were attributed to portside guns. Two of these fit guns brought up by the Deane brothers, who worked the site in 1836 and 1840 (MR 79 A 1276, 1277).

Four elements cannot be assigned to carriages. Two stepped cheeks, a trunnion support cheek and one bed fragment. None are compatible, suggesting at least four more carriages (Fig. 3).

Trailing Carriage

One rear portion of a trailing carriage was recovered (Fig. 4). It has an internal width of 300 mm and may have supported a *saker* or *falcon*, both listed in the Anthony Roll, the contemporary inventory of ordnance for the King's ships completed in 1546.

Carriages for wrought iron guns

Breech-loading wrought iron guns were recovered on elm sledges, each supported by a single axle and pair of (spoked) wheels or (solid) trucks. A single piece of elm is hollowed out for the barrel, breech chamber (to contain the powder) and breech chamber wedge (*forelock*). The rear of the sledge is stepped upwards and is solid, designed to absorb the backward force upon firing of the gun. An iron wedge protects the front face of the step. A tiller (*post*, or *foot*), pierced with a number of holes to alter elevation, is located through a slot at the rear of the sledge (Fig. 3).

Sledge dimensions vary with the location of the type of gun (*portpieces, fowlers,* and *slings*).[8] Twenty-six iron guns listed in the Anthony Roll may have required sledges.

Breech chamber wedges take up the space between the breech chamber and the rear of the sledge; wedges of different widths allow flexibility in choice of chamber. The front of the bed is fashioned exactly to fit into the ring assemblies on the barrel, but the space for the breech chamber is merely a semicircular hollow.

Four gun sledges were recovered. Three others (now in the National Maritime Museum, Royal Armouries and Woolwich Rotunda) were raised by the Deanes. Those guns found *in situ* retained breech chamber wedges. The Inventory lists '*tymber for forlocke*', possibly describing the nine spare wedges recovered.[9] All have a downward projecting tang to locate in the breech chamber recess. Spare breech wedges were found close to *in situ* sledges.

Axles[10] and Trucks

Four sledges had axles bearing solid elm trucks. A sledge for a sling from the upper deck (MR 81 A 645) had one truck measuring 465 mm in diameter and the other measuring 490 mm. Both were 110 mm thick. Trucks from one main deck portpiece sledge (MR 81 A 2650) had diameters of 590 mm and were 190 mm and 200 mm thick.

Two sledges found *in situ* retained spoked wheels. Another gun-port displayed a pair of wheels and broken axle, the carriage having been extracted during previous salvaging.

All spoked wheels found *in situ* have eight oak spokes within a central elm hub.[11] Spoke ends are shouldered as they enter the felloe and each is held with an oak wedge. The four elm felloes are secured by loose oak pegs placed in pre-drilled holes between them. Wheel weight was reduced either by removing scallop-shaped pieces from the inner face of the felloes or by chamfering the rim. Linch pins of oak and iron were found. Incised broad arrows on the hubs suggest Royal ownership. Nine *elevating tillers* have been recovered: seven of oak, one of ash and one of alder.[12]

Unassigned trucks, wheels and axles

Thirty-six trucks can be attributed to guns found *in situ*. A further twenty include a group of eight from orlop deck and the hold in the bow (Fig. 3).[13] There are no signs of wear, and these may be the '*spaer truckells iiij payer*' listed in the Inventory. The other twelve recovered may reflect the positions of guns previously recovered.

Spoked wheels show a similar distribution, eight being found with the stored trucks (Figs 3, 5). Six are attributed to

Fig. 4. Portion of a trailing carriage for a bronze saker or falcon.
(Copyright: The Mary Rose Trust)

Fig. 5. Spoked wheels in store on the orlop deck in the bow during excavation. (Copyright: The Mary Rose Trust)

Fig. 6. Reel of tampions as excavated. (Copyright: The Mary Rose Trust)

guns found *in situ*; the other five were from the main and upper decks. One stored example has ten spokes.[14] The inventory lists '*spaer whelys iiij payer*'.

Many of the fifty-six axle fragments are too small to allow attribution, although twenty-three have been associated with guns. Six complete axles and four fragments were found in the same area as the spare trucks and wheels. These axles[15] are 'roughouts' distinguished by the fact that they are not shouldered, and their arms do not have holes for lynch pins.[16] The Inventory lists '*VJ spaer axtrys*'.

Tampions

Tampions were found within the muzzles of bronze guns and sealing the mouths of breech chambers. They were also found individually, or as unfinished *reels* (Fig. 6). Reels are turned and left in a semi-finished state, orientated back-to-back, the next two being aligned front-to-front. To complete them, the central spindle would have been sawn.[17]

Most reels feature tampions of uniform size, but one had three rows of tampions, aligned side by side along the length of the grain. A total of ten tampions were on this reel, each row having a different diameter.[18] This may be the method by which smaller tampions were formed.

Fifty-five tampion reels were recovered. Thirty-three % of these (eighteen) are of poplar and 2% of willow (one). The Anthony Roll lists 4,000 tampions. Most reels were stowed on the orlop deck in the bow, many within barrels. Only four were on the main, upper and castle decks close to guns (Fig. 9).

Of the 168 loose tampions recovered, thirty-nine are of poplar, with one each of elm, pine and fir. Tampions are circular with a chamfered edge so that the larger diameter provides a flush face on the outside, narrowing towards the inside. Thickness varies with diameter.[19] Although the largest concentration (forty) was found in storage with the reels, and may indeed be able to be matched with incomplete reels, individual distribution is more widespread and reflects gun stations (Figs 6, 9).

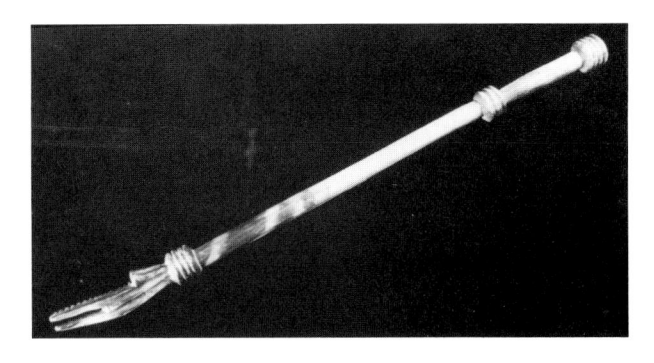

Fig. 7. Linstock carved to resemble a dragon. (Copyright: The Mary Rose Trust)

56   *Alex Hildred*

Gun furniture

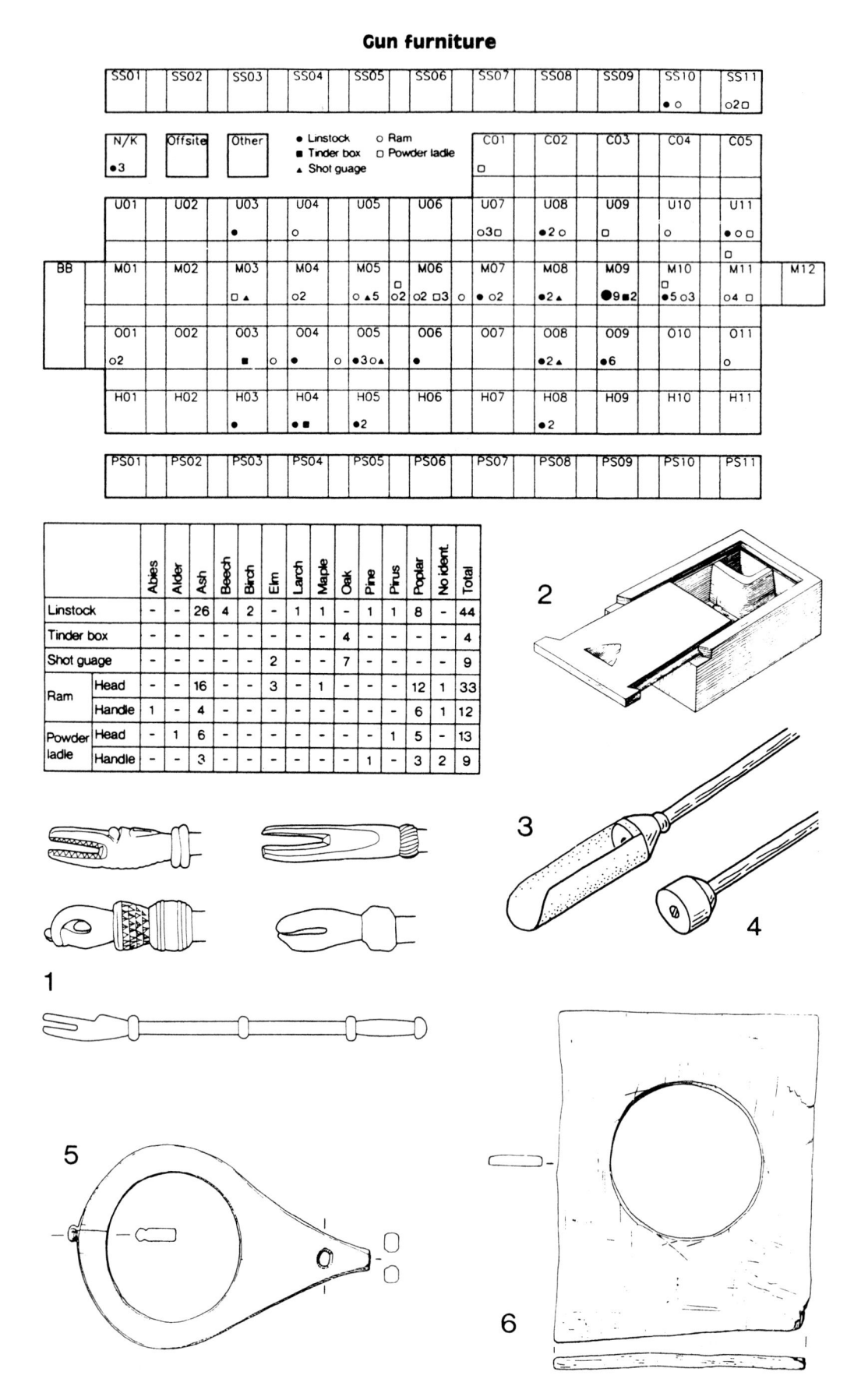

SS01	SS02	SS03	SS04	SS05	SS06	SS07	SS08	SS09	SS10	SS11
									● ○	o2 □

N/K	Offsite	Other	● Linstock ○ Ram	CO1	CO2	CO3	CO4	CO5
●3			■ Tinder box □ Powder ladle ▲ Shot guage	□				

U01	U02	U03	U04	U05	U06	U07	U08	U09	U10	U11
		●	○			o3□	●2○	□	○	●○○ □

BB	M01	M02	M03	M04	M05	M06	M07	M08	M09	M10	M11	M12
			□▲	o2	o▲5	□ o2	o2 □3 ○	●o2	●2▲	●9■2	□ ●5 o3	o4 □	

O01	O02	O03	O04	O05	O06	O07	O08	O09	O10	O11
o2		■	o ●	○ ●3o▲	●		●2▲	●6		○

H01	H02	H03	H04	H05	H06	H07	H08	H09	H10	H11
		●	●■	●2			●2			

PS01	PS02	PS03	PS04	PS05	PS06	PS07	PS08	PS09	PS10	PS11

		Abies	Alder	Ash	Beech	Birch	Elm	Larch	Maple	Oak	Pine	Pinus	Poplar	No ident.	Total
Linstock		-	-	26	4	2	-	1	1	-	1	1	8	-	44
Tinder box		-	-	-	-	-	-	-	-	4	-	-	-	-	4
Shot guage		-	-	-	-	-	2	-	-	7	-	-	-	-	9
Ram	Head	-	-	16	-	-	3	-	1	-	-	-	12	1	33
	Handle	1	-	4	-	-	-	-	-	-	-	-	6	1	12
Powder ladle	Head	-	1	6	-	-	-	-	-	-	-	1	5	-	13
	Handle	-	-	3	-	-	-	-	-	-	1	-	3	2	9

Fig. 8. Above: distribution of gun furniture. Below: detail of linstock types (1), tinder box (2), powder ladle (3), rammer (4) and shot gauge types (5–6).
(Copyright: The Mary Rose Trust)

Linstocks

Forty-four linstocks, each fashioned to hold a slow burning match, were excavated. Having about the length of a man's arm, these poles functioned to light priming powder within touch holes of the large guns. Royal Armouries inventories do not mention linstocks until 1675 (Blackmore 1976, 318). However, earlier inventories list *'Touches de ferro'* for the years 1388, 1396 and 1399 (*ibid, 254–55*). These may have been heated iron rods used to ignite guns. The non-listing of linstocks within inventories relating to *'Kings Shippes'* during the Tudor period may be due to the fact that they were the personal possessions of gunners, rather than of the King (PRO E 101/60/3; Society of Antiquaries MS 129; Anthony Roll). Individual designs within the assemblage supports this.

Linstocks conform to a general pattern: a feature carved to hold a match, a haft and a grip to form the handle. Each element can vary in size, form and surface decoration. Two basic types emerge based on the method used to clasp the lint: a 'clenched fist' (two examples) and 'animal jaws', approximating dragons (Figs 7, 8/1). Details recorded included wood type, location, length, dimensions and decoration of the linstock head, finials, haft and grip.[20] One linstock roughout (MR 81 A 3700) is of square cross-section and indicates the size of block necessary (53 mm).

Thirty of the forty-four linstocks retained terminal finials and could be studied for evidence of a heel spike. Sixteen had a hole for the insertion of a spike. Variability in total length as well as in individual parts suggests that these were not issued as a group of staves to be finished on board. The diverse woods used, which include ash, poplar, birch, *pirus*, maple, beech, pine and larch, supports this (Fig. 8).

Decoration and design were also examined in the light of dimensions, wood and location. Only three 'pairs' of linstocks were identified. Nearly identical in appearance and perhaps manufactured by an individual or to a set design, these still have different species and location.

Distribution has been studied to try to ascertain ownership and areas of storage and use (Fig. 8). Six were from the hold, thirteen from the orlop deck (with a concentration of six in one area), seventeen from the main deck and four from the upper deck.

The localized concentration on the main and orlop deck rather than beside the guns was unexpected. The large number of chests in this area (Richards, in this book) and the discovery of one empty chest lying between the main and orlop deck in a similar alignment to a number of linstocks, suggested that linstocks had been stored in one or more chests in the stern. Despite their personalised appearance, only one was found within a chest containing gunnery equipment and personal possessions. Two were recovered from inside an open 'workbox' in the carpenters cabin. Both are incomplete and may have been there for repair.

In considering possible reasons for the 'personalisation' of linstocks and yet storing them in one location, the most likely explanation may be that such areas were designated for lighting the match.

Tinder Boxes

Four small oak boxes are known from the wreck, each carved from a single block of wood. All have slots carved in their sides for sliding lids, and are divided internally into compartments, displaying cut marks inside one compartment. Two have holes through the base, filled with a wooden bung (Fig. 8/2). Two are darkened, possibly scorched. Three contained felt or soft contents which were analysed. Two samples have been identified as human hair. A substantial sample consists of bark-like wooden fragments mingled with fibrous matting. Cloth-like material was also recovered.

Two were within the galley area and one inside and another outside the carpenter's cabin. They have been provisionally identified as tinder boxes used to bring fire from the galley to designated areas. Perhaps linstocks were stored in this area and personalised for easy recognition. Lanterns were found within the next sector.

Shot Gauges

Nine wooden gauges for selection of shot were recovered. Two distinct styles exist: either square/rectangular with a circular hole, or elongated ('pear-shaped') with a circular hole and a handle (Fig. 8/5–6). Their function was to match shot diameter to gun bore. Two were made of elm, both of rectangular form. The rest were made of oak. Distribution was restricted to the main and orlop deck, with a cluster of five on the main deck amidships where shot was stored.[21]

Powder Ladles

The thirteen powder ladles are made from various woods, differences even occurring between the head and handle of the same ladle. Distribution is widespread, reflecting the gun positions (Fig. 8, 8/3). Heads are turned from one piece of wood (ash, poplar alder, *pirus*/maple) with the face showing the cross-section. A central hole is drilled through the finished head for the handle.[22] These are made of ash, poplar and pine; only seven were associated with their heads.

Ladles consist of four separate elements: head, handle, ladle formed from a sheet of either copper or brass, and a brass retaining collar. There are variations in the method of attachment of ladle to collar and head. The head is always fashioned with a band rebated around the face to receive the ladle and collar. The handle is chamfered where it fits into the head and is held with a nail and often reinforced with an oak wedge.[23]

Rammers

The thirty-three turned rammer heads show a similar variety of woods (ash, poplar, elm, maple) with distribution which complements that of ladles. Heads and handles are made from different woods (Fig. 8, 8/4).[24]

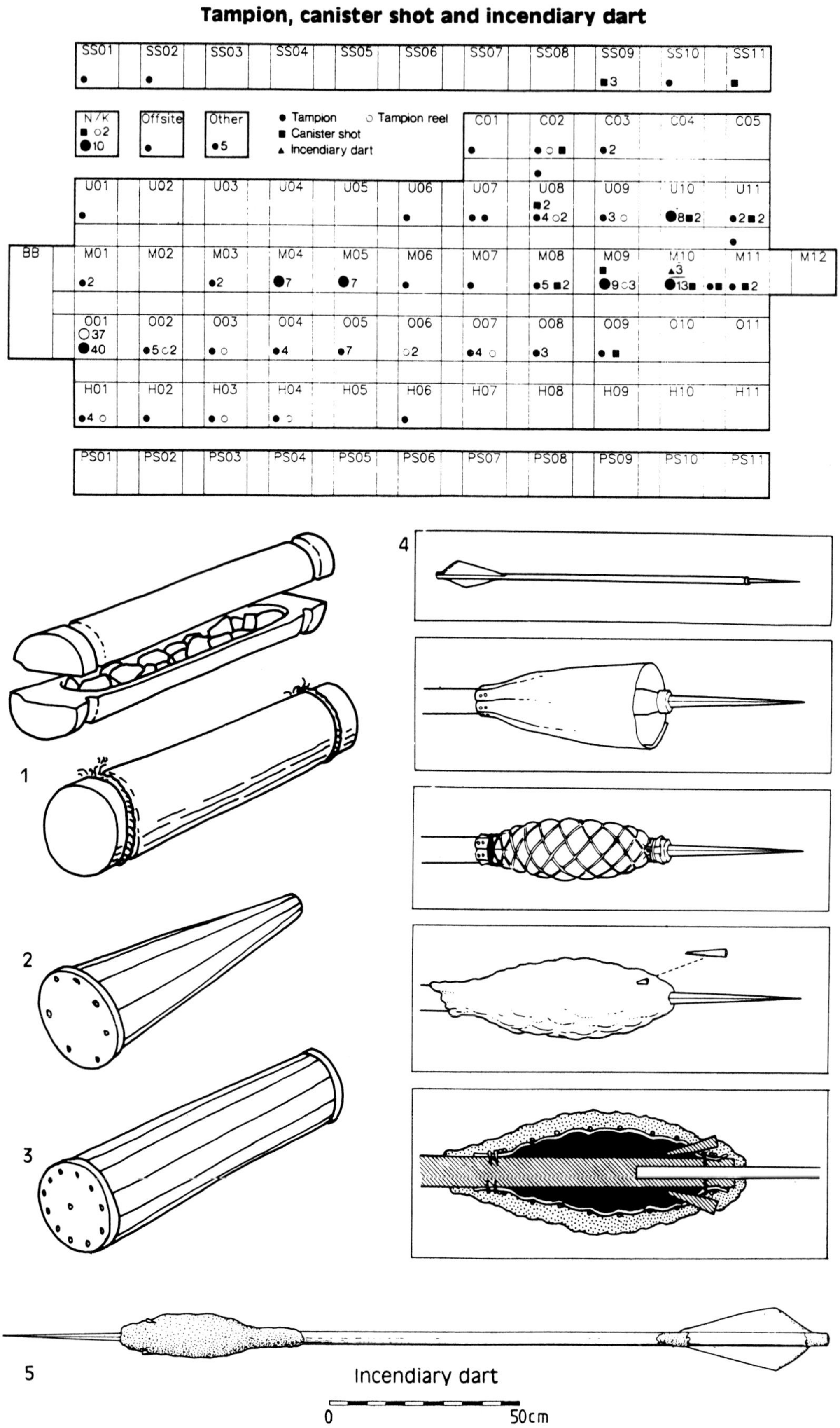

Alex Hildred

Fig. 9. Above: *distribution of tampions, canister shot and incendiary darts.*
Below: *detail of different types of canister shot (1–3), and method of manufacture of incendiary dart.* (Copyright: The Mary Rose Trust)

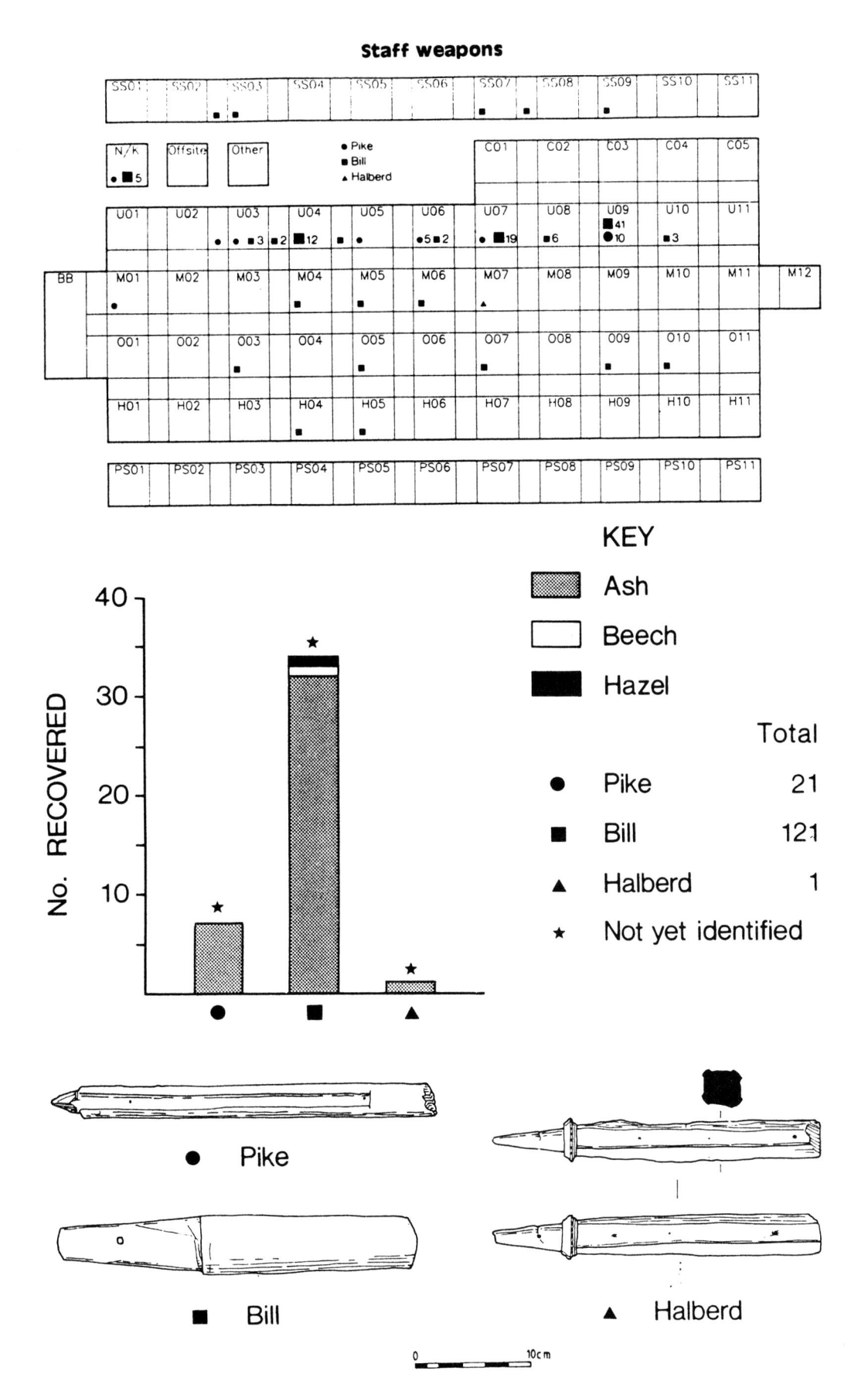

Fig. 10. Above: *distribution of staff weapons and wood types.*
Below: *illustrations of pike head, bill head and halberd.* (Copyright: The Mary Rose Trust)

Canister Shot

This category contains a maximum of twenty examples of materials placed within differing forms of canister designed to scatter upon impact. The canister is always made of wood (ash, elm, oak, Scots pine or pine). Three distinct forms exist (Fig. 9).

1. The cylindrical canister. All have lengths less than 500 mm and diameters of less than 55 mm (where identified these are pine; Fig. 9/1).

2. The conical Lanthorn shot. Formed by binding staves to form a cone and securing with a lid (Fig. 9/2).

3. The cylindrical Lanthorn shot. Manufactured in a similar manner to lanterns, the major distinction is that canister ends and staves are thinner and fitted together without gaps or grooves, resulting in additional holes in canister ends. There is also a central hole in each end of the canister, and staves display marks of binding. Nineteen ends are known; five of those identified are of oak and three each of pine, elm and ash. Staves are exclusively of pine or Scots pine.[25] Their distribution reflects positions of use rather than storage (Fig. 9/3).

Incendiary Dart

One complete incendiary dart and parts of two further examples were recovered (Fig. 9). The complete dart has a haft of silver fir (*Abies*) of 40 mm in diameter with an oak flight at one end[26] with a small rectangular (10 mm × 8 mm) hole at the opposite end for spike insertion. Just behind this is a 15 mm band forming a collar to retain a cloth bag which contained an incendiary mixture and was pierced with oak pegs and coated with tar. The bag is nailed behind the collar with the opposite end nailed 155 mm further down the haft. The flight is held in place by splitting the haft, inserting the flight[27] so that it finishes some 45 mm before the haft end, and coating the end with tar. The complete dart is 1845 mm long (Fig.9/5). These are well described and illustrated (e.g. Biringuccio 1540). It is unlikely that these are the '*Dartes ffor toppys*' mentioned in the Anthony Roll, which lists forty dozen.

Staff Weapons

Three types of staff weapon have been identified: bills, pikes and a single halberd (MR 80 A 1288). Distribution, numerical occurrence and species attributes are based on a study of stave heads. The Anthony Roll Inventory (1546) lists 150 bills and 150 pikes, with no mention of halberds.

Of the 121 bill heads recovered, thirty-two are made of ash, one of beech and one of hazel (eighty-seven remain unidentified). One complete bill haft was recovered.[28] The haft form is indicative of the others, parallel sided at its lower end and increasing in diameter to a maximum just before a chamfered shoulder which supports the iron head. The tip narrows towards the end, which is 'duck-billed'. Although cylindrical over most of its length, the head is tapered to give a flat back and more rounded front (the back having tell-tail staining indicating the iron fixing). All bills have one large hole (5 mm in diameter) to accept the bill head, and a smaller hole (3 mm) situated 25 mm from the shoulder.[29]

The major concentration of bill heads is on the upper deck in the stern (forty-four), with a further twenty-five in the adjacent sector. A second cluster of seventeen occurs on the upper deck in the bow. Five were found on the orlop deck, and two in the hold near the galley. The distribution mirrors that of the 'in use' longbows and arrows (Fig. 10).

Only twenty-one of the 150 pikes listed were recovered. They are smaller in section than bills, parallel-sided, and are recognisable by two rebates (25 mm in width and 2 mm in depth) cut into opposing flattened faces. The tip is fashioned to a point which projects 25 mm from the haft.[30] Morris pikes range in length between 4876 mm and 6096 mm (Norman and Wilson 1982). The side cheeks of iron holding the tip fit the haft rebates and are held with small pins placed equally along the rebate. Only seven have had wood identification (all are ash). Their distribution is similar to that of bills (Fig. 10).

The single ash halberd (Fig. 10) comprises a section of head measuring 301 mm in length, with a diameter of 34 mm. It has a decorative square brass collar of leaded brass (76% copper, 12.2% zinc, 9.28% lead, 1.50% tin), and a 30 mm rebate on opposite faces for metal cheek pieces.

Longbows and Arrows

The Anthony Roll inventory lists 250 bows of yew and 400 sheaves of arrows. Arrows were recovered tied in bundles or in spacers of twenty-four arrows, which if considered a sheaf, would make a total of 9,600 arrows. All longbows recovered are of yew, totalling 137 complete and thirty-five incomplete bows (Hardy 1992). The 2,497 complete arrows and 1,471 tip fragments show much variation in wood type. Of the 461 examined, 435 are of poplar, twenty are of walnut and two each are of alder and birch. Similar proportions apply to tip fragments (excepting walnut), with a bias towards poplar. Ascham (1576) decreed that ash was better than poplar, and listed the following: beech, ash, oak, birch, alder and elder.

SHIPS FITTINGS

Lanterns

Eighteen lanterns forming two distinct types were recovered, distinguished by method of access to the candle.

i. Hinged door lanterns

Eight lanterns have an outward opening door. They are of similar sizes.[31] All have six staves of 25 mm width and a thickness of 7–10 mm. Each stave is grooved on each long edge to accept horn slats, except for the two staves which form the sides of the door frame. These are bevelled towards their outer edges and grooved only on their inside edges to accept the horn door panel. Tangs of 25 mm which protrude from ei-

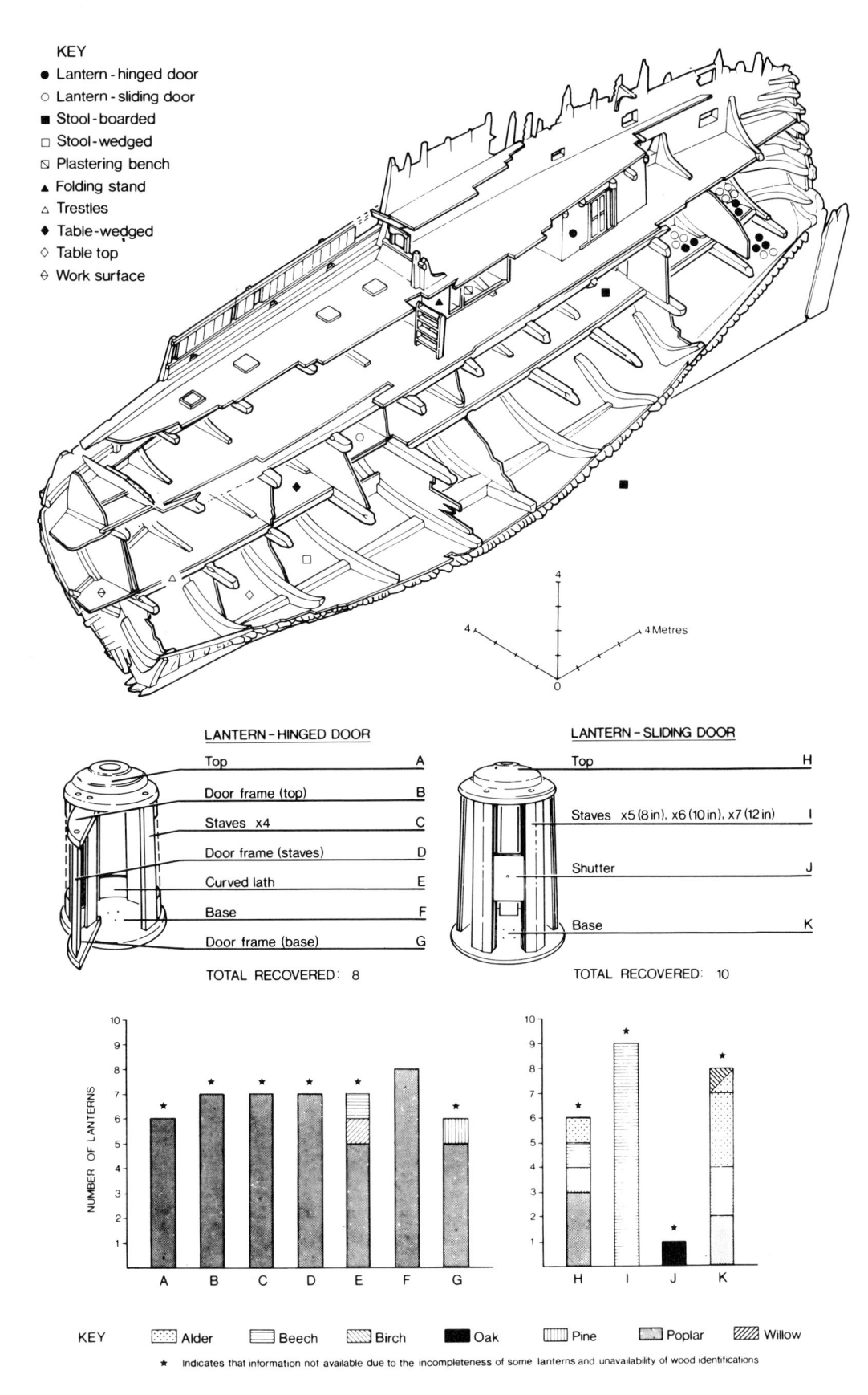

Fig. 11. Above: distribution of lanterns and furniture. Below: lantern types and wood species of particular elements.
(Copyright: The Mary Rose Trust)

ther end of each stave affix into holes in the base and top. Bases and tops have five holes, four for staves and one for the hinged door stave. Remains of a thin wooden lath band between all staves adjacent to the base and top reduces the amount of horn required. The bases have in their centres the remains of four small pin holes and iron staining. Tops are turned to form a dome. There are no holes within the top for attachment of a handle. One was excavated from the cabin containing carpentry equipment, the rest were in two adjacent sectors in the stern (Fig. 11).

Bases, tops and staves of these lanterns are of poplar. One lower door frame is of pine. Where fragments of lateral laths are present, these are of willow, with one of beech. Similarities in form, size and choice of wood indicate that their manufacture was standardised (these are unmarked).

ii. Sliding door lanterns

Ten lanterns with sliding door panels were recovered (Figs. 11, 12). The staves have tangs centrally on their ends locating into holes within the bases and tops. All staves have a single groove on each long side to accept alternate horn slats, except two which are next to each other which have two grooves on the sides which face each other. One set of grooves holds the horn panel and the other allows free movement of the door shutter. There are no laths between the staves forming a top and bottom band. These can be divided into three sizes, based on the diameter of the base.[32]

Four have incised markings on bases or lids. The individual elements for a lantern are made from a variety of different woods (although staves are exclusively of beech; Fig. 11). One oak shutter was recovered. This variety of wood type and size, together with the presence of markings, suggest that the lanterns were 'personalised'. This could relate to either ownership or their working shipboard position (as opposed to safe storage location).

Their distribution is extremely limited and may reflect those areas considered safe either for storage of items requiring fire, or as distribution points for fire (Fig. 11). All but two lanterns (one of each type – one in the carpenter's cabin and one above the galley) were restricted to two sectors.

Furniture

Six types of object have been classified as furniture (Figs 11, 13, 14). These do not include footed chests (see this book, Chapter 6), nor any elements physically attached to ship's structure.

i. Stools

A wedged stool of oak and parts of two elm stools of boarded construction were found.[33] Examination of the completed boarded elm stool suggests that the longitudinal side members are nailed to end boards, which are rebated at their outer edges and canted inwards from the base towards the seat[34] then nailed to the longitudinal members. Ends are narrower at their top and wider at the base.[35]

The two unconnected end boards are of similar construction.[36] As with the complete example, the lower edge is curved and chamfered.

The wedged stool consists of a rectangular oak seat bored with four splayed holes to receive four oak stakes. Two stakes are of round section, two are square, and none are identical. At the top of each stake is a notch for a wedge.[37] This is the earliest securely dated example of an English wedged stool, and was recovered from the hold in the bow.

ii. Bench

A four-legged oak bench was found inside the barber surgeon's cabin. Tentatively identified as a 'plastering bench', it comprises an oak plank which tapers along its length.[38] At each end the top is bored with staggered holes to receive the legs which are wedged. The angle created by the different lengths of the legs is pronounced.

iii. Folding stand

Outside this cabin was found a folding oak stand with pegged mortise and tenon joints (Figs 11, 13, 14). With the addition of a board this could have functioned as a high table. Remains of possible leather support straps over the top of the upper rail were nailed into rebates in three places. The stand is formed of two joined frames, one pivoting inside the other.[39] The uprights are chamfered and held into top and bottom rails with tenons. These are supported on each side by a carved buttress-shaped block retained with a single peg into the rails. The lower rails are chamfered on their lower edge. One of the upper rails is inscribed with the Roman numeral IV.

Fig. 12. Sliding door lantern.(Copyright: The Mary Rose Trust)

iv. Trestles

Two plain oak cross bars form the main components of three-legged trestles functioning in pairs to support a loose board or table. Each cross-bar has three rectangular mortises on its underside (two are aligned longitudinally to one end of the bar, the third is aligned laterally at the opposite end). The mortises are angled, forcing the three legs to splay outwards. One oak leg, of rectangular section, was recovered *in situ*, showing that the legs were held in place by wedges which were forced between the tenon on the leg and the mortise.[40]

v. Work surface

A loose board, tentatively identified as a 'work surface' was found on the orlop deck.[41] This may have been used with the trestles.

vi. Wedged table

A wedged oak table/ saw horse with splayed legs was recovered from the orlop deck in the bow.[42] The legs were rebated into outwardly-angled mortises and wedged. Cut marks are visible on the upper surface of the top, but it is difficult to determine whether these were made by regular use of a knife over the surface or by a saw.

Fig. 13. Folding oak stand recovered from the main deck.
(Copyright: The Mary Rose Trust)

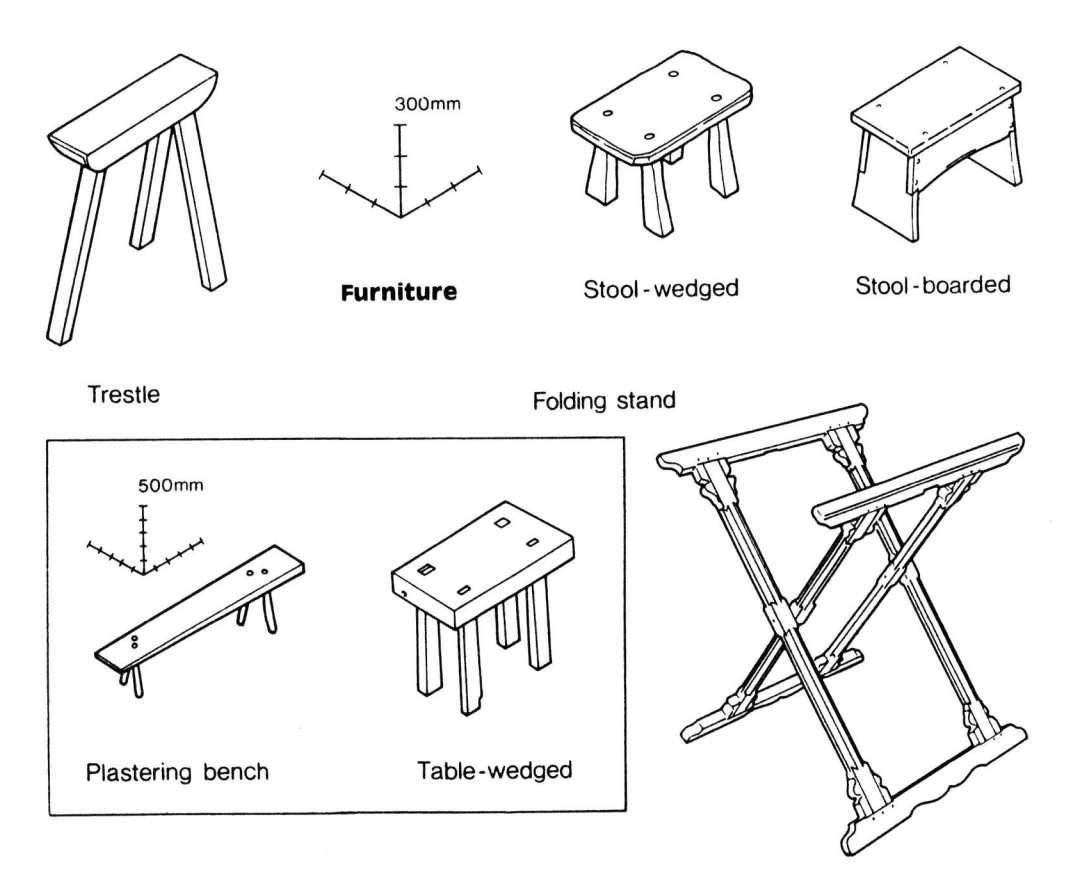

Fig. 14. Items of furniture recovered. (Copyright: The Mary Rose Trust)

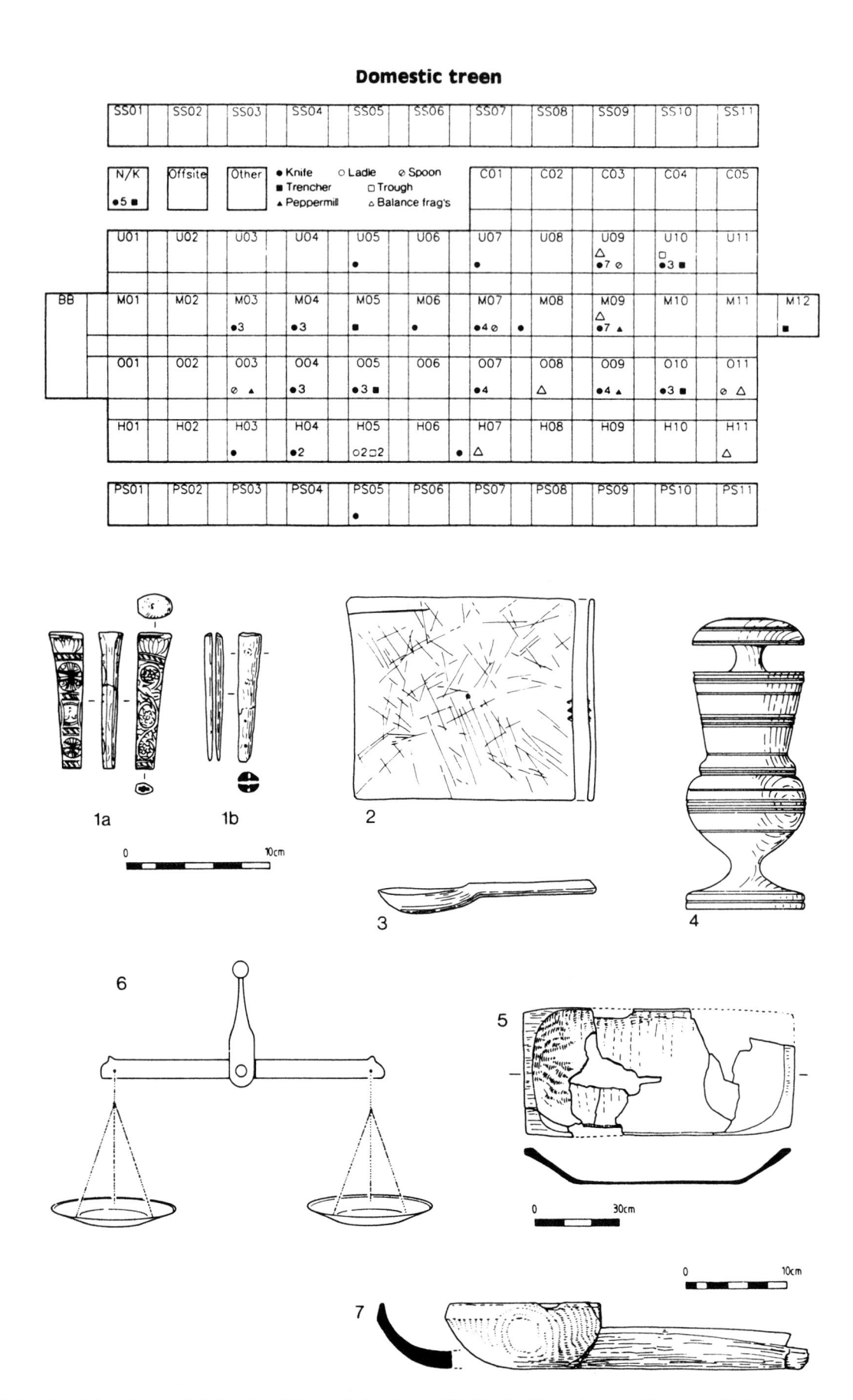

Fig. 15. Location of domestic treen. Knife handles, whittle tang (1a), scale tang (1b). Trencher (2), wooden spoon (3), peppermill (4), trough (5), balance (6), ladle (7). (Copyright: The Mary Rose Trust)

vii. Table top

One loose table top was found in the hold adjacent to the wedged stool.

Domestic Equipment

Knives

Fifty-eight knife handles have been classified as being for domestic/personal use (Fig.15/1a, 1b). Ten knives lay within their wooden sheaths, and blade morphology and size was studied from radiographs.

Knives have been divided into two basic types, based on the method adopted to attach the blade to the handle. *Whittle tang* is identified by an upward extension of the blade (the tang) tapered to fit into a solid handle with a drilled hole (Fig.15/1a). *Scale tang* is where the handle is formed of two wood 'scales' fixed to the flattened tang (Fig.15/1b). There are twenty-nine examples of each. Woods represented include ash, box, burr elm, cherry, chestnut, maple, oak, poplar, sycamore, willow and yew, with a predominance of boxwood (89.7%, twenty-six knives). Thirteen of the fifty-three from known locations were found inside chests, ten associated with human remains and the remaining thirty randomly distributed (Fig.15).

i. Whittle tang knives

The predominant woods used are box (55%, sixteen examples) and maple (31%, nine examples), with one example of each in ash, burr elm and cherry.

In fourteen examples, the tang extends through the entire length of the handle. These 'full tang' examples are predominantly of boxwood. In fifteen cases the tang terminates within the handle; these are predominantly of maple, and termed 'partial tang'.[43]

Decoration to the surface of the knives is restricted. Two full tang examples have copper alloy tops with engraved designs; one is of burr elm. A third knife in boxwood has pin pricked decoration (Fig. 15/1a).

Five maple partial tang knives display a single scored line with a varying number of lines aligned diagonally above it. One of these has an the initial 'W'. Eight styles have been observed based on handle morphology.

ii. Scale tang knives

All twenty-nine examples are different, and all have a flat tang, drilled to accept iron rivets which retain bipartite scales. Rivet number, size and decorative appearance varies.

One style emerges, consisting of five yew knives of similar size and plain form. Ten others are of box, but their shape and size varies. Wood types differ, with chestnut, oak, poplar, sycamore, willow and yew represented, the predominent being boxwood (34.5%, ten examples).

iii. Knives and sheaths

Ten knives found within sheaths vary in size, form and location. Woods represented include beech, birch, box and maple. Fifteen empty sheaths were found. Woods utilised include ash, box, elm, hawthorn, oak, pine, poplar, spindle tree and willow, with no clear preference for a particular wood. Sheaths are made either of two halves and joined centrally at the back and front, or by boring out a single piece of wood. Differences in form and surface decoration suggest that these are personal possessions.

Trenchers

Of the six small rectangular boards found, two show scratch marks suggesting repeated use of a knife (Fig. 15/2). Two are of beech, one of oak and three lack species identification. Three have notches cut out of their edges, and one has an incised letter W.[44]

Wooden spoons

Only three eating spoons were recovered. Two spoons are delicately carved in maple.[45] Both have large shallow bowls and short stems chamfered from the upper surface towards the tip. One bears an incised reversed letter N beneath the bowl (Fig. 15/3). The third example is made of birch. It has a flat stem on the underside, with a shallow thick bowl.[46]

Peppermills

One complete ash peppermill and the top of a second made of cherry were discovered inside personal chests in the stern (Fig. 15/4). The complete peppermill is made in three sections: a rounded handle forming a pestle, a central grinder, and a collecting cup.[47]

Balances

Remains of four balances were recovered, three coming from the hold in the stern (Fig. 15/6). They consist of two pans, each suspended by three equally spaced ropes to a beam which passed through a shear suspension bar and was held by a peg. The upper extension of the shear formed a handle with a knob at the end.[48] Of the three arms recovered, two were of oak and one of ash. They may have been used to measure equal portions, as no weights were found with these balances. They were found within an area containing fish bones, some within pans. Pans are all of beech and vary in diameter.[49] A pronounced rim is drilled with three equidistantly spaced suspension holes. A possible arm fragment was recovered from the main deck and a fragmentary beech pan from the hold.

Troughs

Fragments of three large troughs were recovered, two from the galley and one from the upper deck contexts (Fig. 15/5). They are cut from a single block of wood and are rectangular in shape; the wall slopes inwards to the inside of the base from both ends.[50] The one identified is beech.

Ladles

Parts of two ladles were found in the galley. The most complete example is a large turned cherry ladle with a round deep bowl.[51] Other fragments are of alder, from a similarly robust ladle (Fig. 15/7).

Tankards and Flagons

Fewer than fifty drinking vessels of any material were recovered. Thirty of these were stave-built. This total is based on the number of bases. Classification includes 'tankards', for drinking (Fig.17) and 'flagons' for serving. Twelve are gallon flagons.[52] Woods used include beech, hazel, lime, oak, pine, poplar and willow with the mixing of woods within individual examples. Staves are made from oak (eight units), pine (sixteen), spruce (one) and beech (three), with pine predominant. Bases are mainly of oak (ten); eight are pine, three beech and one Scots Pine. The eighteen lids recovered include five still unidentified, four of pine, three each of oak and beech and one each of poplar and elm. Handles are made from oak (five), poplar (five), beech (four), lime, ash and pine (one each); four remain unidentified. The hooping is predominantly willow (nine), with two instances of hazel; two remain unspeciated. No pattern of wood usage or uniformity in stave number, size or surface decoration can be identified to suggest formal naval victualling.

Fig. 17. Tankard.(Copyright: The Mary Rose Trust)

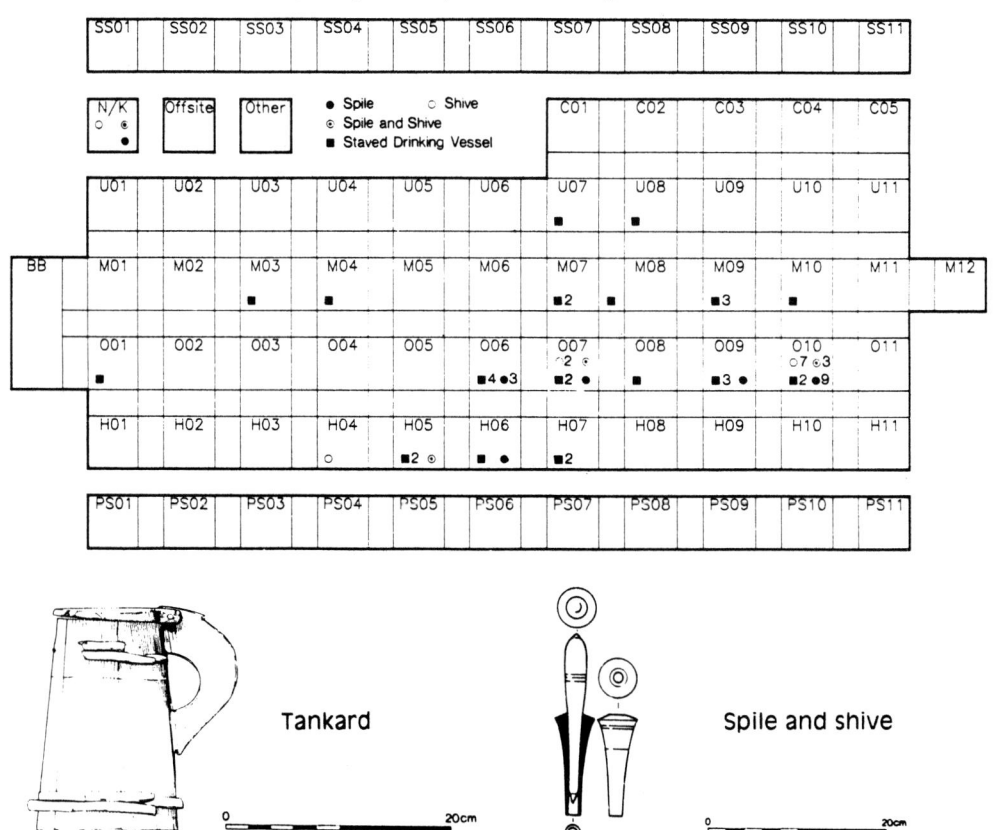

Fig. 16. Location of tankards, flagons, spiles and shives.(Copyright: The Mary Rose Trust)

Their distribution displays concentrations within access of the galley and on the main deck close to the carpenter's cabin (Fig. 16). Two complete tankards were found within the barber-surgeon's cabin.

Spiles and shives

The identification of twenty-two spiles and seventeen shives (including six found with spiles inside shives) resulted from a 'Tools and Allied Trades' meeting at the Mary Rose Trust in 1988. These artefacts functioned as a 'tap with a bung', the shive forming the tap and the spile the bung set inside the shive, and they functioned to enable access to the contents of barrels (Fig.18). Most are of poplar, but willow and alder are represented. Five sets have both components of poplar, and one set is made of willow.[53]

Their distribution concentrates on the orlop deck in the stern, with twelve spiles and ten shives within one sector, all but one of each stored in an open box, and all but one made of poplar. The area contained a large number of staved containers, but none have *in situ* spiles and shives (Fig.16).

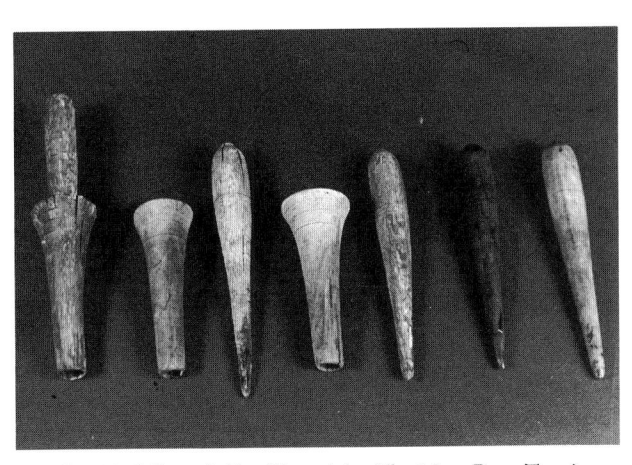

Fig. 18. Spiles and shives.(Copyright: The Mary Rose Trust)

Bowls, dishes and plates

Wooden treen primarily for eating has been subdivided according to the following criteria:

Bowl: height more than 1/3 of, but not greater than, its diameter.
Dish: height less than 1/3 of, but greater than 1/7 of its diameter.
Plate: height not greater than 1/7 of its diameter.

Using these definitions, the *Mary Rose* assemblage comprises fifty-six bowls, 116 dishes and thirteen plates (Figs 19, 20). A preliminary study suggests that visual sorting may identify further distinguishable features. Dimensions given in the endnotes record maximum diameter and height.

Bowls: these are made of alder (ninteen), beech (thirty), birch (four), elm (two) and oak (one).[54] They display a widespread distribution, principally on the main and upper decks (Fig. 19).

Alder bowls: nine out of nineteen bear some form of marking; two are branded with an "H" on the outer rim (MR 81 A 4050, MR 80 A 908). Markings, usually restricted to the inner or outer base, include arrows and incised lines.

Beech bowls: fifteen out of thirty bear decoration, two having branded "H's" on the outer rims (both from the same sector of the wreck). Two have holes in the rim, possibly for a hanger.

Birch bowls: two show incised lines on the outer base; one has notches cut into the rim (MR 82 A 2354).

Elm bowls: one of the two bears incised lines on the outer base.

The oak bowl shows no markings.

Twenty seven out of the total of fifty-six bowls bear markings. Their distribution suggests that they represent personal objects rather than stowage of bulk issue. Smaller examples may have been for drinking: hence their distribution and 'personalisation'.

Dishes

Of the 116 dishes recovered, 110 are of beech. Five are made of alder and one is of elm.[55] Five bear "H" brands on their rims, one having an additional brand on the base (MR 81 A 6611). Only twenty-three display any markings, and with the exception of the "H", this is restricted to incised lines on the base. Their distribution reveals a cluster of ninety-two forward of the galley, reflecting stowage for victualling (Figs 19, 20). Most were found in barrels. Three out of the five alder dishes are from this area, as is the elm dish; the rest are of beech.

Plates

Of the thirteen plates excavated, twelve are of beech and one is alder.[56] None bear any markings. Four were found within the galley, one in the barrel containing the bulk of the dishes, four from separate areas on the orlop deck, and one each from the upper deck and area just outside the starboard side (Figs 19, 20).

Kidney daggers/ballock daggers or ballock knives

Sixty-five kidney dagger handles were excavated. Fifty-seven (88%) were made of boxwood, five of maple (7.5%), one of *pomoideae*, one of ash and one unclassified. They can be assigned to three types, based on grip form: those having a definite medial ridge to the front and back, those of circular form and those which are faceted (Fig.21). The use of wood, location, dimensions and shape do not correspond with any identifiable style (Fig.24).

In all cases, the blade had been extended to form a tang which penetrates the entire grip and is held by an iron or copper alloy button on top of the pommel. Features studied included pommel shape, grip form, lobe form, button shape and lobe guard fixing holes (Fig.24).[57]

68   *Alex Hildred*

Blade shape has been reconstructed from the shape of the tang hole as it enters the underside of the lobes, and all but one blade is single edged.[58] Only one kidney dagger (*pomoideae*) was found inside a chest (MR 81 A 1304).

Radiographic examination of two concreted kidney daggers (MR 81 A 1845, MR 82 A 1916) revealed the presence of three knife handles within the concretion which had formed over the blade. One excavated sheath yielded three small handles slotted into it (MR 79 A 1000; Fig. 22). Post-excavation records have indicated an association between kidney daggers and forty-three knives to form sixteen *trousses* having between one and four *by-knives*. By-knives are predominantly made of boxwood (79%). Three were made of maple (7%), and six are as yet unidentified (14%; Fig. 25). By-knives

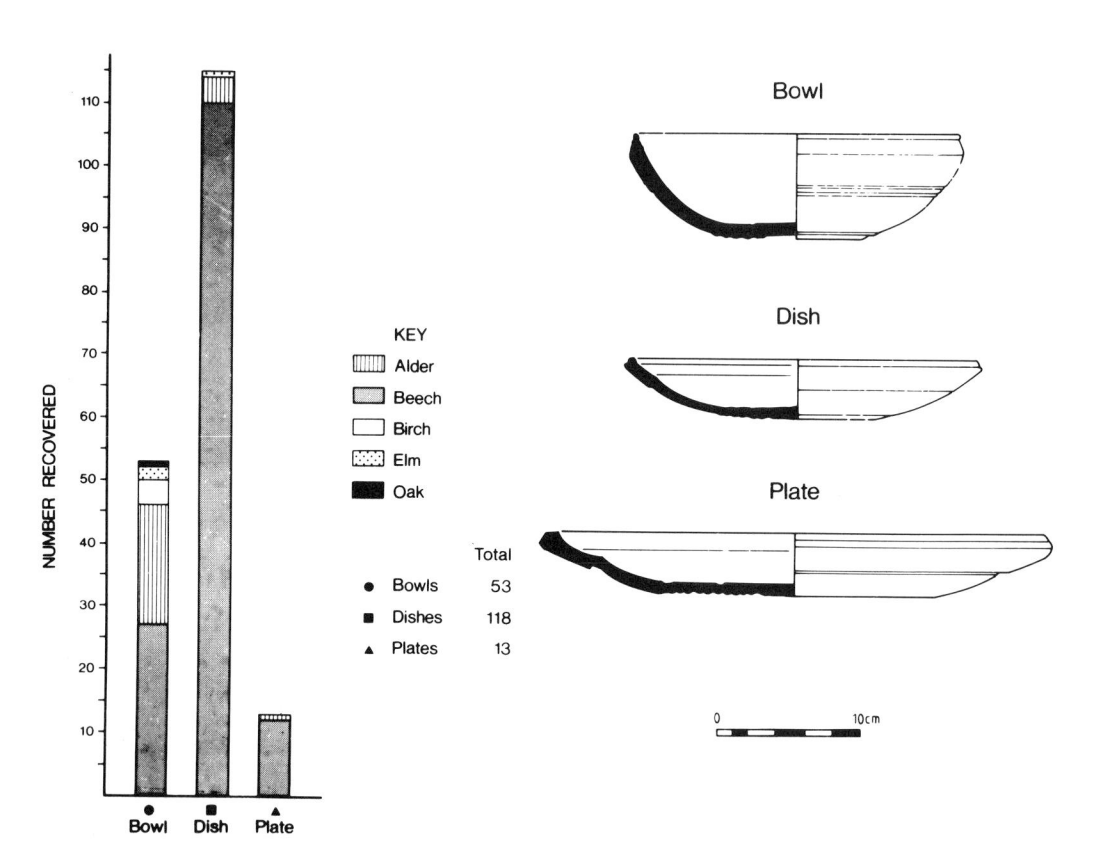

Fig. 19. Location and wood types for bowls, dishes and plates. (Copyright: The Mary Rose Trust)

Fig. 20. Bowls, dishes and plates recovered from the Mary Rose.
(Copyright: The Mary Rose Trust)

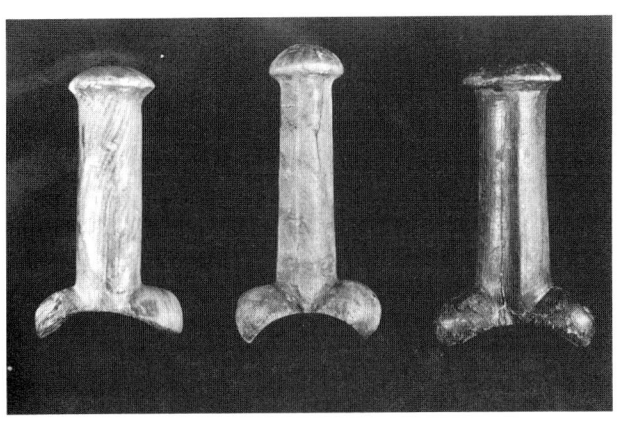

Fig. 21. Kidney dagger handles. Left – right: round form, faceted, medial ridge. (Copyright: The Mary Rose Trust)

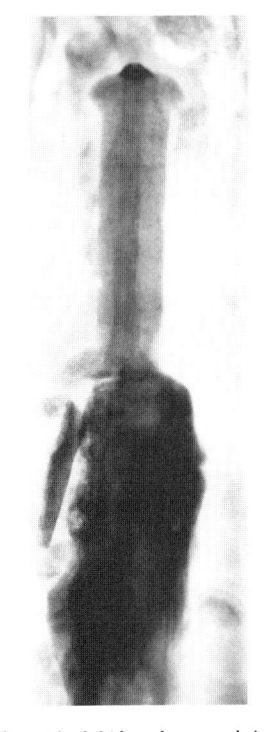

Fig. 22. Radiograph of kidney dagger and sheath with by-knives.
(Copyright: The Mary Rose Trust)

are scale tang, and where associated with a kidney dagger are of the same wood. Where two or more by-knives are associated with a kidney dagger, the by-knives have a similar shape but are different sizes. The number of rivets holding the scales varies with size.[59]

The distribution of kidney daggers and those daggers associated with by-knives reflects more than any other discernible feature the density of skeletal remains. Such daggers probably functioned as an all-purpose knives and tools, both weapons and domestic utensils (Fig. 24).

DOMESTIC HYGIENE

Combs

Eighty-one combs were excavated, three with decoration branded onto their surface and two incised. They fall into two categories: those with a single row of teeth (two were recovered, both of beech), and double-sided, with a medial bar and teeth both sides (Fig. 23). Forty-two have been microscopically identified as made of box; the remainder have been visually identified as box (S. Bickerton, pers.comm. September, 1995).

The double-sided combs display variety and have been subdivided on the basis of tooth size, the shape of medial bar and curvature of the ends.[60] There is no apparent distribution pattern reflecting type. Twelve combs were associated with human skeletal remains. Sixteen were found inside personal chests (four inside one chest; Richards, in this volume). Only two were found within the barber-surgeon's cabin (one within the chest). Two combs were found within specially manufactured cases (Fig.25).

Fig. 23. Selection of boxwood combs.
(Copyright: The Mary Rose Trust)

CONCLUSIONS

The woods represented within the assemblage form an extensive list, including alder, ash, beech, birch, box, burr elm, cherry, chestnut, cork, elm, fir, fruit woods, hawthorn, hazel, holly, juniper, larch, lime, maple, oak, pine, pomaceous woods,

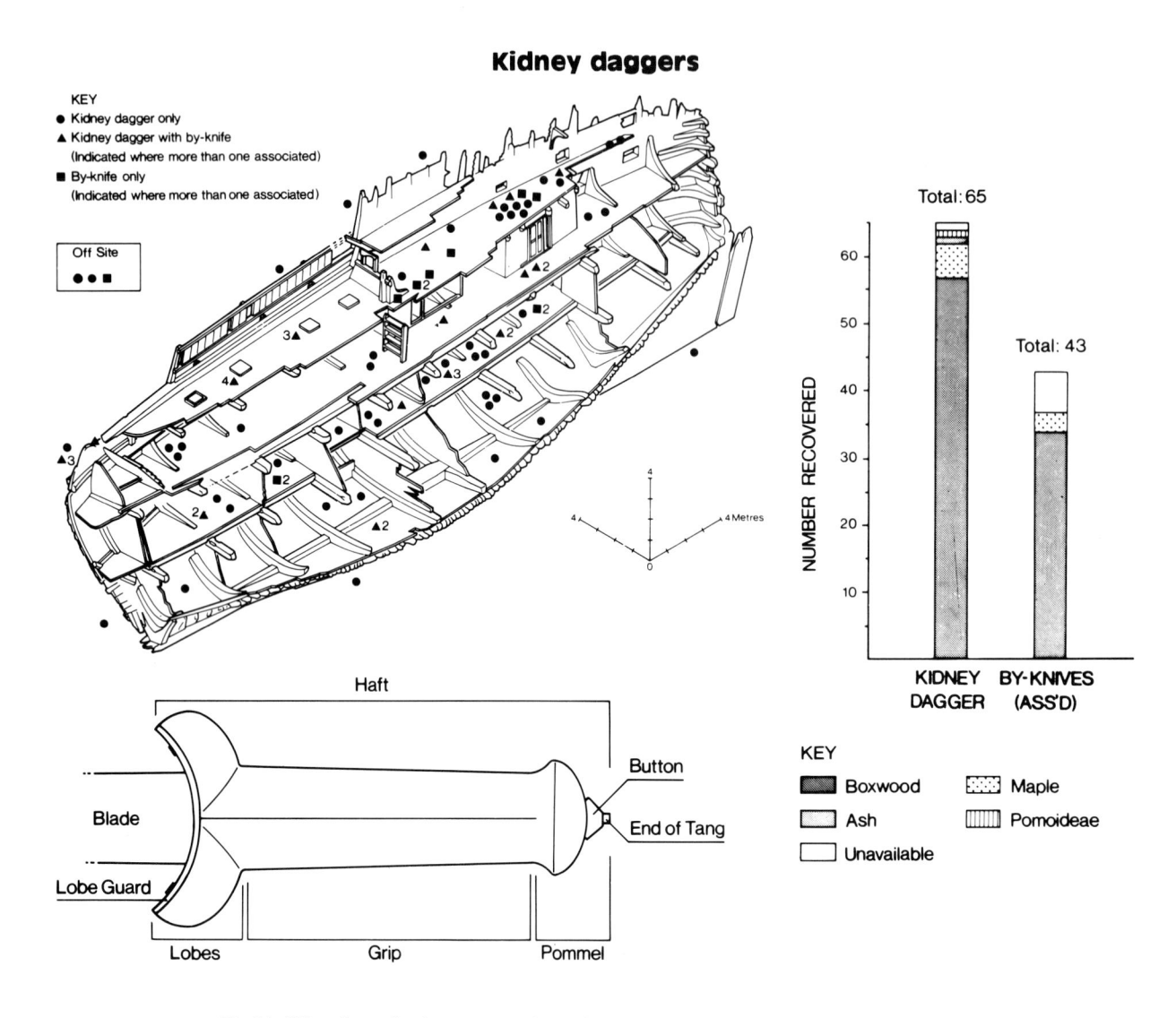

Fig. 24. Kidney dagger distribution, terminology and wood type. (Copyright: The Mary Rose Trust)

poplar, *pirus*, Scots pine, silver fir, spindle tree, spruce, sycamore, walnut, willow and yew. By percentage, the most common wood is oak, accounting for 8.24% of the total of 6,503 wooden objects found. Any conclusion resulting from the above study must be made in the knowledge that of these 6,503 artefacts, some 3,699 have still not been analysed (56.88%).

A number of observations can now be made, such as the preference of elm for gun carriages and the exclusive use of ash for axles. Yew was used for bows, while a variety of woods was used for arrows, and ash predominated for staff weapons. Perhaps more enlightening are the groups in which a preference for specific woods exists for part of the assemblage; they often lack marks which personalize the objects, suggesting the possibility of mass production – for example, the beech dishes compared with bowls; or the hinged door lanterns compared with the sliding door lanterns. The preference of certain woods for particular objects despite their personal nature (combs, kidney daggers) most probably reflects the properties required. It is even more interesting when shipboard location (i.e the enclosed distribution of dishes compared with the scattered distribution of bowls) also contrasts corporate *versus* private manufacture and ownership. Some items remain enigmatic, such as the purely functional *linstock*, with its highly decorative and individualistic choice in wood type, design and surface decoration. As the detailed study of complete groups of artefacts is completed, further enigmatic instances will no doubt be forthcoming.

Acknowledgements

Thanks are owed to Andrew Elkerton for provision of computerised information. To Peter Crossman, Nick Evans, Debby Fulford, Roger Purkis and Clare Venables for artefact illustration; Peter Crossman for specific layout, illustrations, isometrics and tables. Research on artefact groups included work by Susan Barber, Maggie Richards, Sydney Richman and Simon Ware. Many thanks to Richard Hubbard for photo-

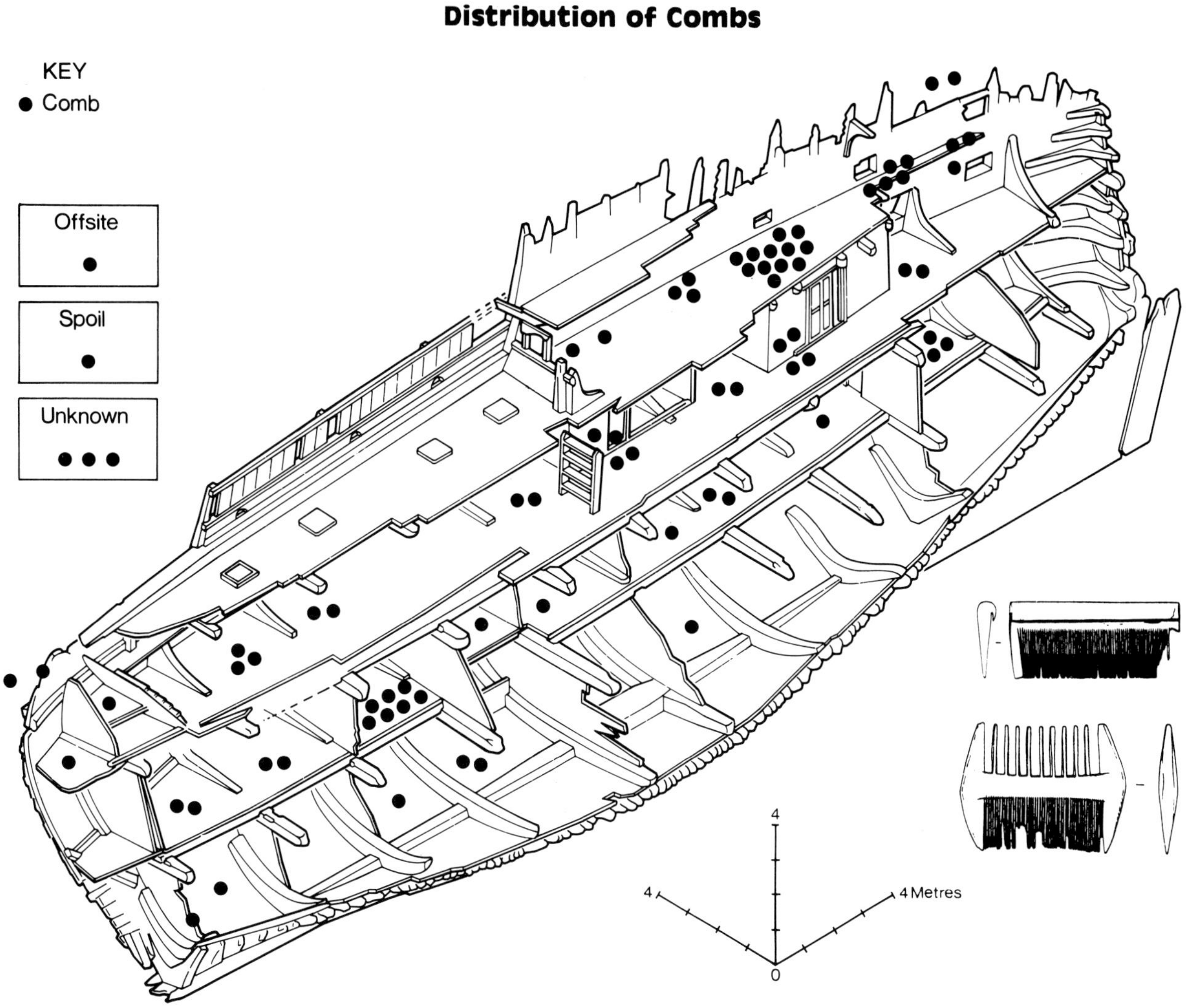

Distribution of Combs

Fig. 25. Distribution of combs. (Copyright: The Mary Rose Trust)

graphic reproduction. Wood analysis was undertaken by Susan Bickerton and Sue Cooke. For help with editing the text special thanks are due to Andrew Elkerton and Maggie Richards.

Notes
1. Thickness varies between 155 mm and 100 mm.
2. The largest gun-port lid measures 830 mm × 760 mm and the smallest lid 750 mm × 610 mm.
3. Bed lengths vary between 1760 mm and 2160 mm with widths between 635 mm and 960 mm. Thickness varies between 120 mm and 170 mm.
4. The trunnion support cheek height is related to the desired angle of elevation, and location on board the vessel, varying between 385 mm (main deck) and 790 mm (upper deck), thickness between 95 mm (castle deck) and 125 mm (main deck), and length between 475 mm and 550 mm.
5. Lengths vary between 750 mm and 900 mm; heights vary between 385 mm and 480 mm and thickness varies between 100 mm and 140 mm.
6. The longest complete axle recovered measures 1720 mm by 130 mm tapering to 90 mm (for MR 81 A 3002).
7. Diameters vary between 240 mm and 668 mm, with thicknesses ranging from 90 mm to 190 mm.
8. Lengths vary between 3000 mm and 4000 mm; widths (at wedge) between 650 mm and 900 mm; height (at wedge) between 400 mm and 450 mm.
9. Lengths vary between 840 mm and 520 mm; widths between 270 mm and 150 mm; heights between 255 mm and 160 mm.
10. The most complete axle (MR 81 A 645) is 1015 mm long, with an arm face diameter of 90 mm.
11. Wheels found *in situ* vary in diameter between 960 mm and 990 mm and in thickness between 100 mm and 110 mm.
12. The most complete example has a height of 980 mm and a width of 110 mm (MR 80 A 1364). Thickness varies between 60 mm and 75 mm.
13. Diameters range from 300 mm to 668 mm and thickness varies between 90 mm and 155 mm.
14. All have diameters of between 900 mm and 1000 mm, with a thickness of 110 mm.
15. Which measure between 1316 mm and 1937 mm in length.
16. All with a width of 130 mm or more, tapering to a minimum of 130 mm.
17. The spindle scar measures between 20 mm and 33 mm in diameter.
18. 85 mm, 80 mm and 70 mm.
19. The largest tampion recovered has an outer diameter of 160 mm, inner diameter of 145 mm and thickness of 85 mm. The smallest has an outer

20. Head lengths vary from 60 mm to 180 mm, hafts from 330 mm to 530 mm and grips from 80 mm to 141 mm. Overall length varies from 653 mm – 860 mm (i.e. between two and three feet). Haft diameters are between 26 mm and 35 mm.
21. The following diameters have been recorded: 100 mm (3×), 118 mm, 130 mm, 148 mm, 174 mm, 175 mm and 186 mm.
22. Most handles are incomplete, but recorded diameters range from 25 mm to 45 mm.
23. Diameters range from 50 mm to 168 mm. The largest complete ladle has a head diameter of 111.35 mm, head length of 129.36, handle hole of 28.23 mm and ladle length of 492.96 mm. The smallest has a head diameter of 50 mm, head length of 70 mm, handle hole of 25 mm and ladle length of 270 mm.
24. Head diameters vary between 60 mm and 195 mm, head lengths between 63 mm and 190 mm and handle hole between 30 mm and 40 mm. The only complete ram has a diameter of 160 mm, head length of 185 mm, handle hole of 34 mm and handle length of 3450 mm.
25. The largest of these is 474 mm in length, with a diameter of 171 mm and stave width of 43 mm. End thicknesses range from 10 mm to 14 mm. The smallest end diameter is 100 mm.
26. Length 345 mm; maximum width 155 mm.
27. 5 mm, increasing to 15 mm at the end.
28. This has a length of 1667 mm and a maximum diameter of 56 mm.
29. Head lengths vary from 135 mm to 150 mm, with the majority of diameters ranging from 40–50 mm.
30. Rebate length is 145 mm on those examples where it can be measured. The longest portion recovered measures 460 mm in length.
31. They have bases of 204 mm diameter with a thickness of 13 mm and stave length of 229 mm.
32. Diameters are 200 mm, 254 mm and 350 mm utilising five, six and seven staves. Stave lengths vary with increasing diameters. Base thickness varies with diameter, from 12 mm for the 200 mm diameter bases to 19 mm for the others. Heights range from 228.6 mm to 356 mm, the tallest corresponding with the largest bases.
33. The boards comprising the boarded stool are 24 mm thick.
34. 424 mm × 300 mm.
35. The stool has a height of 300 mm.
36. Height of 285 mm, a width of 140 mm at the top and 185 mm at the bottom.
37. The seat is just over 28 mm thick and has a length of 456 mm, a width of 280 mm and total height of 328 mm.
38. It measures 1400 mm in length long by 200 mm in width, with a thickness of just under 60 mm. The leg length varies between 335 mm and 430 mm.
39. With a length of 1160 mm and width of 750 mm.
40. The leg lengths range from 523 mm to 527 mm, with widths of 150 mm and 137 mm, and thicknesses of 110 mm and 90 mm. The one leg *in situ* has a length (height) of just under 568 mm.
41. This measures 1165 mm in length and has a width of just under 290 mm and a thickness of just over 110 mm.
42. The top board has a length of 1020 mm and a width of 970 mm, with a thickness of 135 mm. The rectangular legs have a length 810 mm, with a width of between 75 mm and 120 mm and a thickness of between 35 mm and 60 mm.
43. Sizes vary, the largest having a length of 108 mm and a diameter (or maximum width if ovoid) at the top of 27 mm and at the base of 16 mm. The smallest has a length of 75 mm, and diameters of 15 mm and 10 mm.
44. Sizes differ, having lengths between 105 mm and 187 mm, widths between 92 mm and 151 mm and thicknesses between 4 mm and 12 mm.
45. They have lengths of 140 mm and 150 mm, and bowl diameters of 57 mm and 60 mm.
46. Length is 185 mm.
47. The complete unit stands 210 mm high with a maximum diameter of 80 mm. The single pestle has a height of 68 mm and a diameter of 74 mm.
48. The most complete arm fragment measures 364 mm in length. The only complete pole is 254 mm long.
49. Between 280 mm and 210 mm. They have a maximum height of 60 mm.
50. The largest is 920 mm long, 173 mm wide and 12 mm deep. The second is 780 mm long and 350 mm wide, but shallower.
51. It has a length of 354 mm and diameter of 140 mm.
52. The largest complete flagon has a height 430 mm and a base diameter of 255 mm; the smallest tankard has a height of 187 mm and a diameter of 120 mm.
53. These range in size, spiles between 215 mm and 155 mm and shives between 112 mm and 93 mm. The maximum shive diameter (the largest hole which could be tapped) is 45 mm.
54. Dimensions vary, the smallest being 150 mm × 90 mm and the largest being 459 mm × 159 mm.
55. The dimensions range from 170 × 40 mm to 385 × 65 mm.
56. Diameters range from 150 to 400 mm.
57. Handles range in length from 135 mm to 126 mm; widths across the lobes vary from 64 mm to 59 mm.
58. A study of complete sheaths and interpretation of radiographs has suggested blade lengths of between 335 mm and 360 mm.
59. Sizes vary from 95 mm to 41 mm with widths of between 17 mm and 13 mm at the top of the handle to 8 mm at the base.
60. Sizes range from 60 × 40 mm to 115 × 70 mm. One subdivision shows consistency in size, 92 × 70 mm with a bar width of 13 mm and end width of 13 mm.

References

Ascham, R. 1576 *Toxophilus*. Transcription by A.W. Hodkinson (1985), The Simon Archery Foundation, Manchester.

Biringuccio, V. 1540 *Pirotechnia*. Transcription by C.S.Smith and M.T.Gnudi (1966), M.I.T. Press, Cambridge, Massachusetts and London.

Blackmore, H.L. 1976 *The Armouries of the Tower of London. Vol. I Ordnance*, London.

Hardy, R. 1992 *Longbow. A social and military history*, Patrick Stephens Ltd., Portsmouth.

Hildred, A. & Rule, M. 1984 *Armaments from the Mary Rose*, Antique Arms and Militaria, May 1984.

Norman, A.V.B.& Wilson, G.M. 1982 *Treasures from the Tower of London*, Lund Humphries Publishers Ltd, London.

Vine, S.M. 1995 'Some aspects of deck construction in the Mary Rose', *Proceedings 3rd New Researchers in Maritime History Conference*, 17–18 March 1995. Royal Naval Museum, Portsmouth.

Manuscript Sources:

Anthony Roll Manuscript 1546 The Pepys Library, Magdalene College, Cambridge.
Society of Antiquaries MS 129, Society of Antiquaries, London.
British Library Harley Manuscript 1419, British Museum, London.
PRO E101 /60/3, Public Record Office, London.

5

Reconstructing 16th-century ship culture from a partially excavated site: the Cattewater wreck

Mark Redknap

INTRODUCTION

Selective or partial excavation of a wreck site can yield a wealth of information regarding the date, vessel type and size, and perhaps the economic place of origin of the vessel and life on board, and has the advantage of leaving parts of the site untouched and available for future investigation. One such archaeological investigation took place in the late 1970s in the Cattewater, the last reach of the river Plym as it flows into Plymouth Sound (Fig.1). The discovery of timbers and early ordnance in 1973 by the dredging of deeper channels for air-sea rescue craft led to an emergency designation order; the subsequent archaeological investigation of the site undertaken between 1976 and 1979 resulted in the partial examination of a 16th-century ship and its contents.

The objectives of the investigation were i) to establish the position and extent of any surviving hull structure, ii) to establish the method of construction, iii) to establish its date. Excavation was limited to the two ends and western edge of the hull (Fig.2). The southern end was the first to be discovered, and deposits in this area were found to be intact above the hull. An area of undisturbed deposits to the north of this area was left undisturbed, and excavation resumed northwards along the western hull edge, until the northern end of the hull structure had been located. Very little of the debris field was examined. In contrast to the southern area, the northern sector had been severely damaged by dredging, and deposits only remained *in situ* between futtocks. An area of the site within a 50 m radius of the position position 50° 21' 41.4"N., 04° 07' 37.5" W. remains designated under the *Protection of Wrecks Act* 1973.[1] The hull structure represented the lowest section of hull from one end past the midships area, where dredging had caused extensive damage. Most of the artefactual evidence came from the southernmost area of the hull, from deposits which were associated with the ship's ballast.

THE CATTEWATER INVENTORY

The artefacts from the site were originally published by material type, wooden objects being grouped into ship structure, personal objects and those items assisting the working of the ship, such as wedges and staves (Redknap 1984). Following the growing practice of grouping artefacts by function, the finds are now grouped and quantified in like manner – from the ship and its working equipment to household effects, eating and drinking equipment, and stores – in order to shed some light on the social and economic aspects of her shipboard culture and times. New thoughts on some artefacts are presented.

1. Ship structure

All the main timbers within the surviving structure (keel, garboards, outer planking, floor timbers and futtocks) were of oak. Ceiling planking was of mixed species (pine, oak), and treenails of oak or elm. A total of fourteen equal-armed floor timbers (lowest elements of the frames, directly over the keel), with fish tails in way of garboard strakes and offset rectangular limber holes, were found *in situ*, each measuring about 200 mm in cross-section. The sawn outer planking (60–70 mm thick) had been fastened carvel-fashion (flush) by a combination of treenails and iron nails. Ceiling planking varied in thickness, and included one possible inspection hatch for the bilges. The keelson (the longitudinal timber located on top of floor timbers along the centreline of vessel) was notched on its lower surface to fit over floor timbers, and swelled at its centre for a main mast step, where it measured 540 mm in width by 400 mm in height; adjacent to the mast step was a tapered eliptical pump pipe hole. Filling pieces (short planks) had been fitted horizontally between first futtocks (frame timbers) at the floor timber heads to prevent material falling through to the bilges. Scantlings and profiles suggest a vessel of between 200 and 300 tons burden (see Fig.2 and below).

2. Ship equipment

Relating to the ship itself are the elements of ship's equipment: a parrel truck for the running rigging of the vessel, treenails, the ballast, a marlinspike or fid of hardwood, rope or varying diameters and small ragged fragments of vegetable fibre, possibly flax,[2] thought to be deteriorated sail cloth.

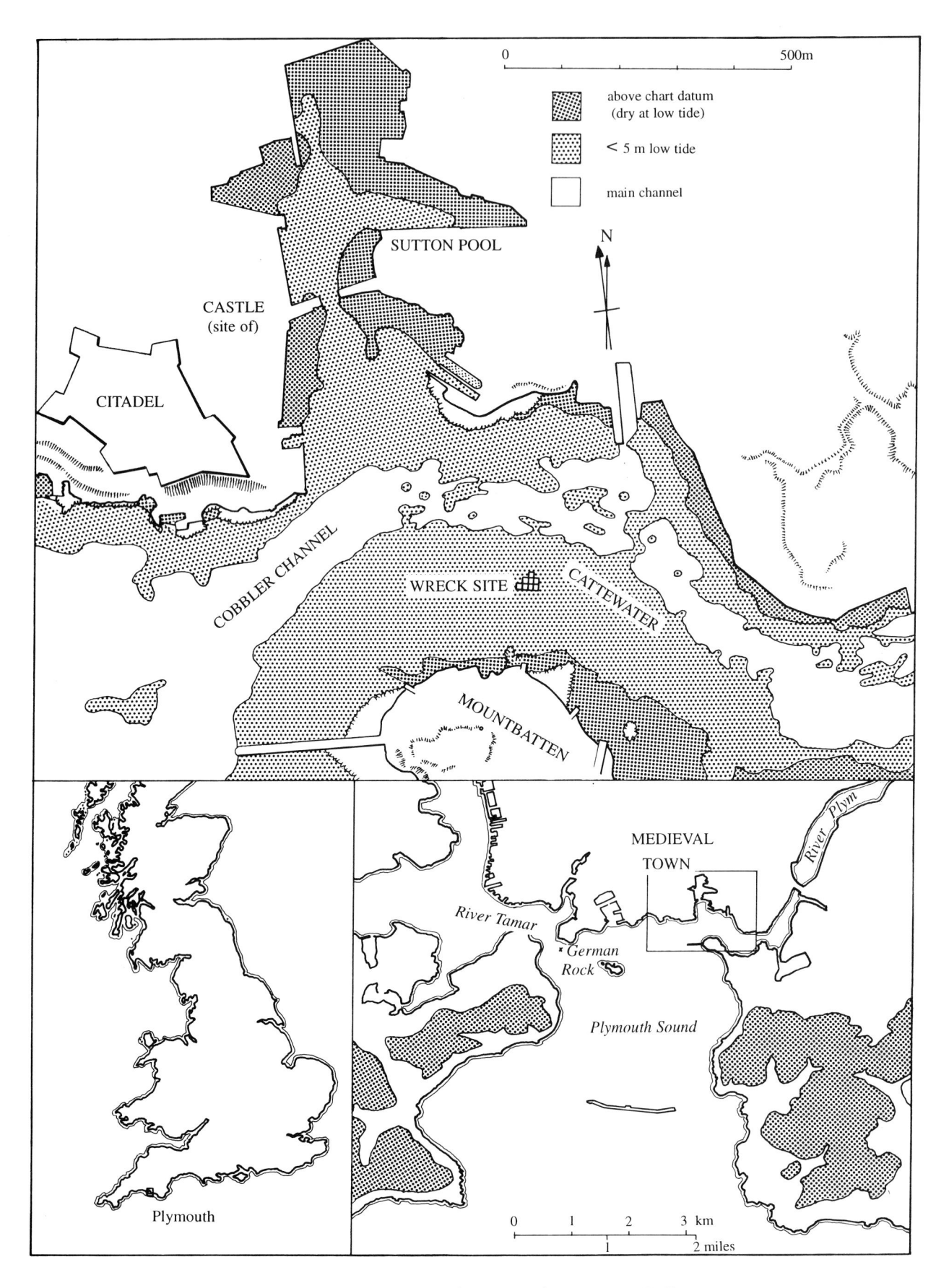

Fig. 1. Location of the Cattewater wreck, showing site grid. (Drawing: M. Redknap)

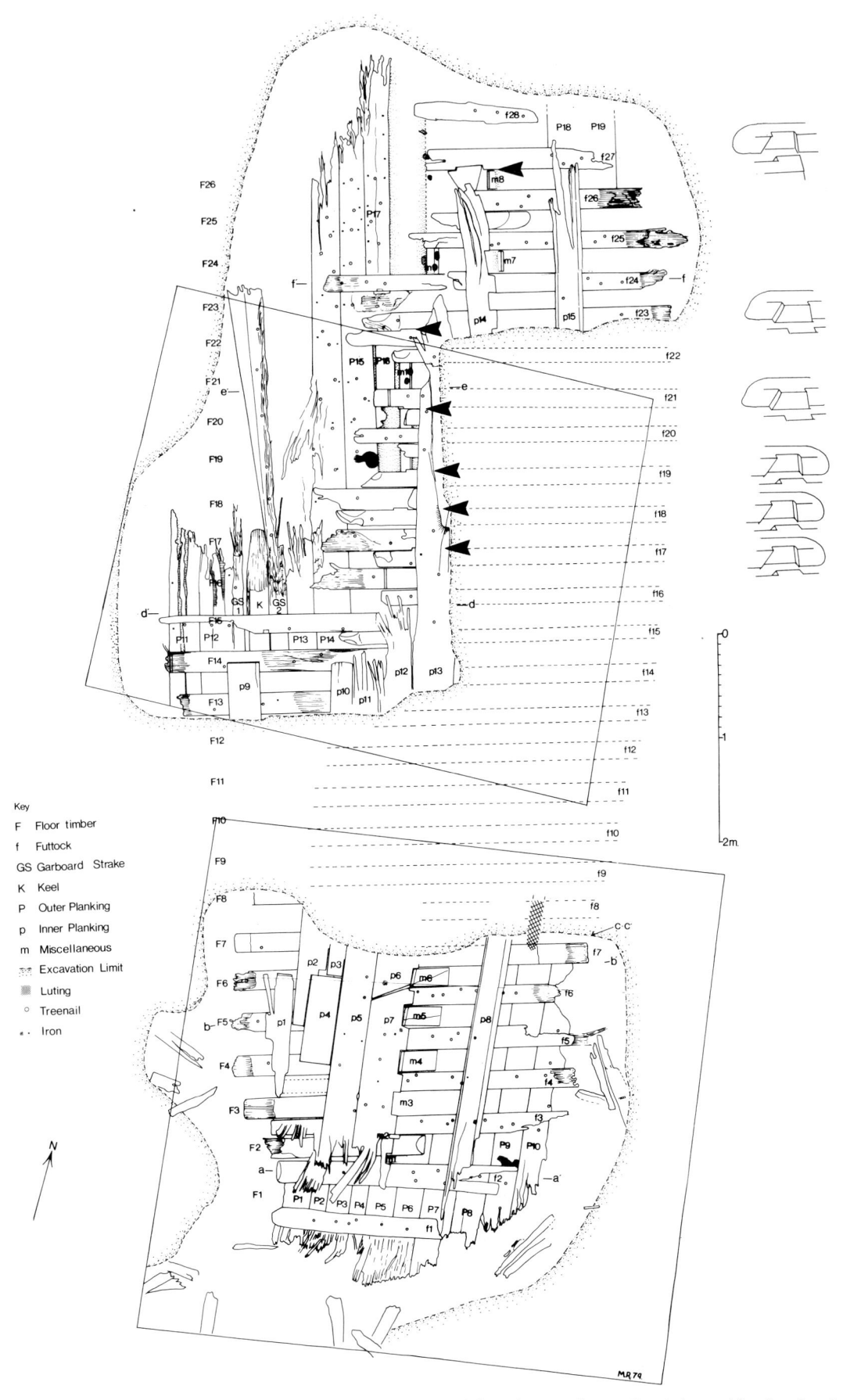

Fig. 2. The Cattewater wreck hull structure, showing position and direction of dovetail mortises between floor timbers and first futtocks, where visible.
(Drawing: M. Redknap)

No internal divisions were found in the areas examined for retaining ballast or separate work areas, and ballast may have run right through the ship as high as the upper limit of the ceiling planking. The range of ballast is indicative of frequent off-loading and incomplete replacement with fresh material. One small faced ashlar block of sandstone suggests that building material may have formed a component of the ballast. The dominant lithology of wreck ballast is important; in this case, local limestone was most common, together with granite and slate. Chalk and flint from Dorset or Kent/Cinque Ports, and Lower Carboniferous limestone from the Bristol or South Wales areas were well represented. Most ballast was left on site, though an approximate idea of the lithic source area configuration may be indicated by the proportions of main stones plotted *in situ* (chalk 6%, flint 6%, limestone 88% by stone count).[3] The ballast gravel contained only nine species of freshwater mollusc (in contrast to sixty in the Plym silts), and a complete absence of marine organisms, indicating that it came from a fairly lime rich river at or upstream from the limit of saline influence, and the present distribution of several of the species suggests somewhere east of Lyme Regis, possibly the Hampshire or Sussex areas.

3. Military equipment

'Military equipment' on board included at least three swivel guns (Figs 3,4), light guns formerly known as *serpentynes* (as defined by Smith 1995, 104) and used by merchant shipping. Their carefully trenched beds of oak have sections cut for the retaining rings of the barrel, and an abutment for the wedge (which on one is still *in situ*, securing a breech chamber). The tubes were secured to their beds by three or four iron retaining straps contoured around the assembly and securely nailed. The hole for the swivel bolt is still visible on each stock. The tube bore of 55 mm matches that of the smaller stone shot from the site (52.5 mm). Parallels to the guns are provided by two from the Riddarholmen wreck in Stockholm harbour (post-1523/4; Smith 1995, 105), two fragments of gun from Castle Rising in Norfolk, those from the Kattegat now in the Danish Royal Arsenal Museum, one example with bed and swivel now in the Nederlandsch Historisch Scheepvaart Museum, and another example with oak trenched bed and swivel found in 1986 to the west of the Goodwins (Fig.5; Redknap 1990; Smith 1995, Figs 1–2). The frequency of swivel guns on ships is indicated by documentary evidence and wrecks such as Highborn Cay which produced thirteen small swivels (albeit of a different type) and numerous breech chambers. The Cattewater wreck has produced a breech chamber, stone shot of two sizes and lead shot of several sizes (16 mm and 13 mm); gunpowder was recovered from the breech chamber. The identical construction and dimensions of the three guns indicate that they probably originated from the same workshop.

The archaeological investigation of wreck sites is of utmost importance for the study of early artillery, as such sites can provide much needed dating for certain types such as swivels, whose date and development have been difficult to establish.

4. Tools

The finds concerned with ship management are limited to one hafted iron tool of uncertain function and wedges of various sizes. One wooden artefact published originally as a 'notched length of softwood, function unknown', may be the stave from a lantern or hour-glass with thick base/top (Fig.6; Redknap 1984, fig. 24, 1). It measures 374 mm in length, the 'inner' side having a slightly tapered mortise 34 mm towards both ends, which are tapered. The width of 21.5 mm and thickness of 10 mm compares to that of staves from the *Mary Rose* (25 mm and 7–10 mm respectively; this book, Chapter 4). However, the Cattewater stave is longer than examples from the *Mary Rose* (229 mm), a length which is closer to that between mortises on the Cattewater object of 212 mm. If a lantern stave, then it must be an unused one in 'knocked down' state, as no fastenings are evident. Similar objects, or parts thereof, have been noted from other wreck sites, including the *San Juan* and Aber Wrac'h wrecks (of different form, in which the legs have end mortises tenoned into top and base discs: L'Hour and Veyrat 1989, Fig.16), *Mary Rose*, and *Trinidad Valencera*. The top of a lantern has been reported from the wreck at Yarmouth Roads, Isle of Wight, and compared to one depicted in an untitled triptych attributed to the Antwerp School, dating from 1535 (Firth 1990, 9). Another example is illustrated in *nächliches Einholen der Fischreusen in der Stadtgracht Gent/Brugge* of about 1500 (Venedig, *Bibliotecca Marciana Brev. Grimani fol.4ʳ*; Hansen 1984, Abb.305). Some wooden lanterns used wooden sticks coated in fat or resin, but most candles/tallow – some with doors, panels of glass or even parchment windows. A number of 16th-century paintings suggest that lanterns were not at all uncommon by the mid-16th century, by which time cheap versions, some with horn windows, were available (e.g. Breughel's '*The Dark (or 'Gloomy') Day*'; Verhaeghe 1992, fig.4).

5. Domestic effects

Household or domestic effects are limited to several internally glazed sherds which may come from a south-west French chafing dish (Redknap 1984, fig.39, no.57), no furniture being recognised, though straw found in the ballast may have come from bedding or packing material, as on the *Mary Rose*.

6. Galley utensils

Artefacts associated with the galley are well represented: floor and peg tile from the hearth (*ibid*, fig. 40, nos 80–83), fuel in the form of charred wood (*ibid*, fig.24, no. 15), and cooking utensils in the form of at least two (possibly three) *Grapen* tripod cooking pots (Fig.6, 1–3), a redware jar or dish (base and three body sherds; Fig.6, 6), a North Devon ware cooking pot, a wooden bucket lid with rope handle and wooden bungs of various sizes (Redknap 1984, fig.24).

7. Eating and drinking equipment (excluding knives)

Eating and drinking equipment from the ballast deposits includes a turned wooden bowl (Fig.6, 10)[4] and a fragment of

CATTEWATER WRECK.

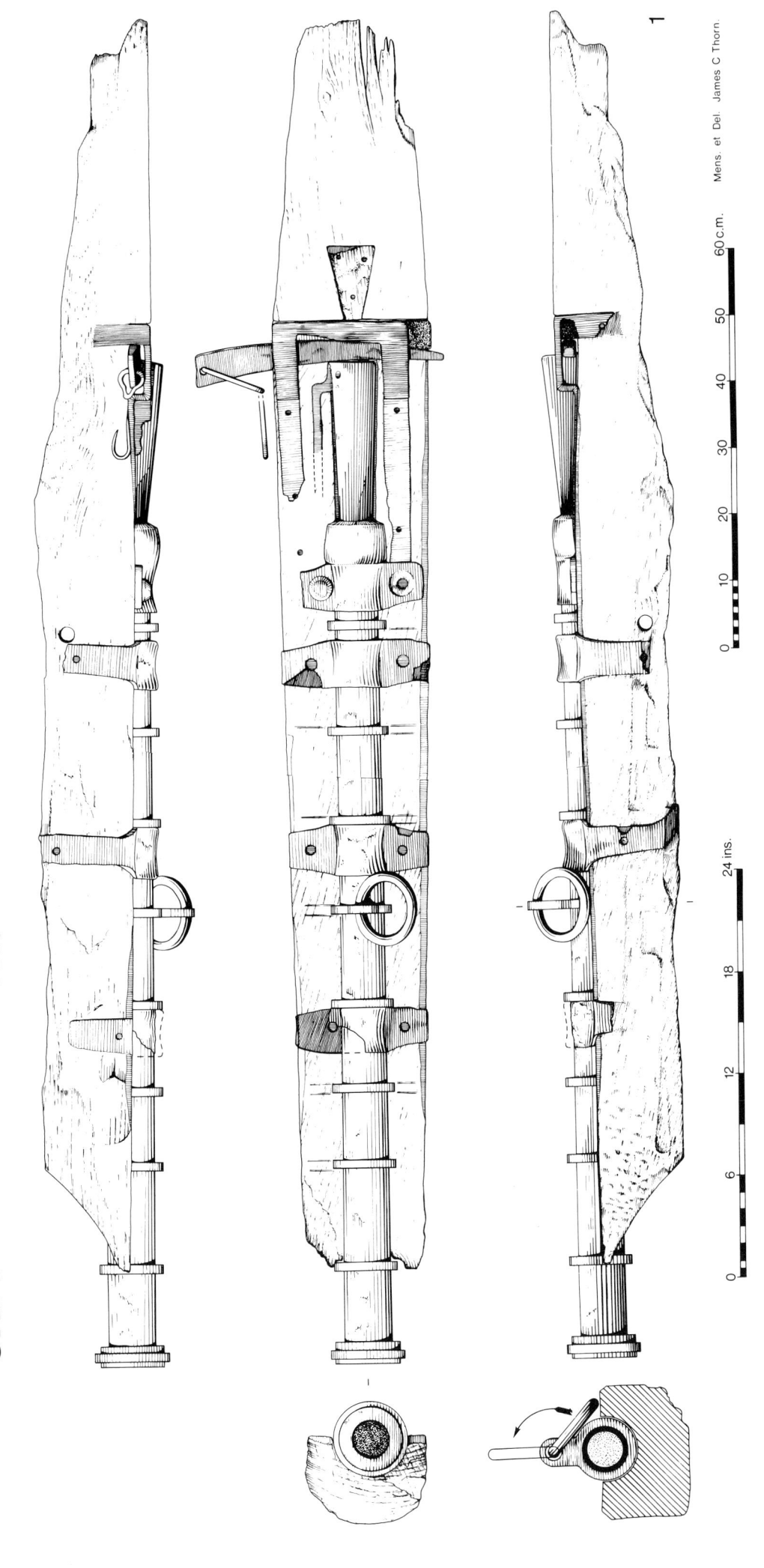

Fig. 3. *The complete Cattewater gun.* (Drawing: J.C. Thorn, Ancient Monuments Laboratory (English Heritage), Crown Copyright)

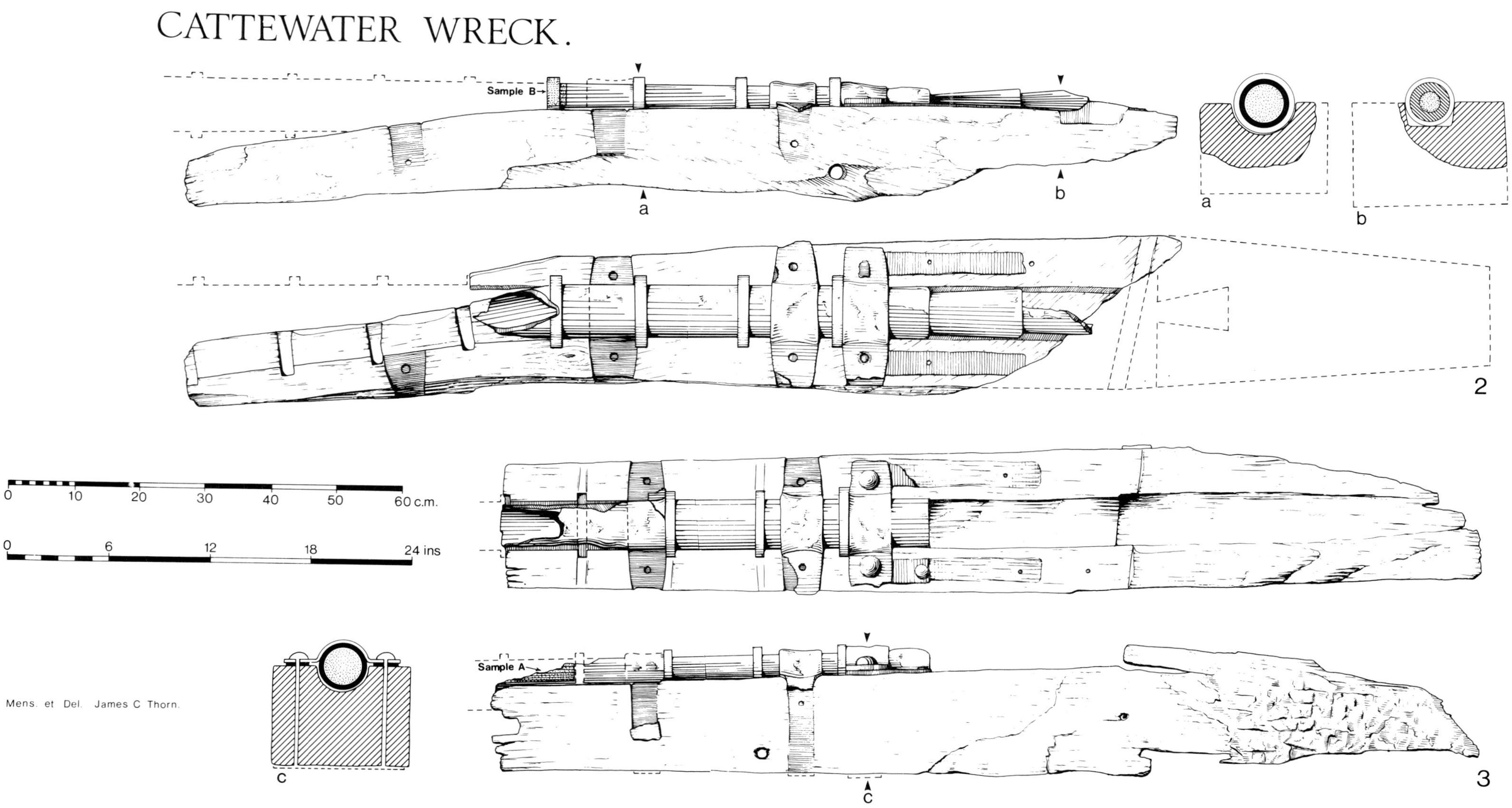

Fig. 4. *The two incomplete Cattewater guns.* (Drawing: J.C. Thorn, Ancient Monuments Laboratory (English Heritage), Crown Copyright)

Fig. 5. The complete swivel gun found just westward of the Goodwin Sands in 1986. (Photograph: H.M. Royal Armouries, Tower of London)

Siegburg ware, perhaps a funnel-necked jug or beaker (Fig.6, 4). In less secure contexts (possibly disturbed by the dredging) were found rim and base sherds from Raeren stoneware drinking mugs and Dutch Redware dish, which could originally have been associated with the wreck (Fig.6, 8–9). Stoneware is commonly found on English coastal sites, and the Raeren form is particularly common during the second quarter of the 16th century.[5] Redware dishes of this form had a long period of production, but the Cattewater profile is consistent with an early 16th-century date.

8. Victuals

Some bone was recovered – mainly cow (*Bos*), of which 59% came from the ballast deposits (Fig.7). Other species were few in number: sheep/goat (*Ovis capra/Capra hircus*), pig (*Sus scrofa*), one dog (*Canis familiaris*, possibly living on board as a pet) and codfish.[6] The beef cuts corresponded to 'peny-peece' cuts, presumably salted, while the cod remains represent a valued commodity of importance to Plymouth. Victual storage is represented by barrel/cask staves (stored in 'knocked down' state; Redknap 1984, 46), barrel parts and perhaps two unstratified sherds from Iberian olive jars (possibly post-wreck). A sample of material taken from the inside a barrel stave (CW78 426; sample no. S-7180) was found to contain fragments of seed and insects (though too small for identification); another sample (CW78 325; sample no. S-7185) contained small fragments of seed coat, most unidentifiable except for *Ranunculus sp.* present with small pieces of other higher plant remains (Dr R. W. Clarke, *in litt.*).

9. Personal belongings

Personal belongings are in the form of footwear – a pair of shoes stylistically dated to *c.* 1470–80, one right shoe to *c.*1490 (Fig.8, 6), and several shoe parts to *c.*1530; a belt or strap with the impression from a spectacle-type buckle, and a purse decorated with incised lines (Fig.8, 5), of a type which can be found depicted on late 15th-/early 16th-century sculpture (Swan 1984, 71–5). A knife in a leather sheath (Fig.8, 1) from a residual context is paralleled by an identical example from excavations at Trinity Street, Exeter (site 316, layer 17) dated to the first half of the 16th century (this site also produced shoes similar to Redknap 1984, Fig.41 no.101 from context 5). The textiles include part of an armhole or sleeve in woollen textile of light greenish-brown in colour – possibly originally light green (some indigo present), and a fragment of very fine high grade woollen fabric, possibly merino, of pinkish red colour (no dye detected). The textiles are paralleled by those from Baynard's Castle deposits, and 15th/16th-century levels from the Poole Town Hall Cellars.

A double-sided soft-wood wooden comb with fine teeth (to comb out lice; Fig.8, 4) represents hygiene, and personal tools comprise mainly knives – one hexagonal softwood handle with brass strip inlay (Fig.8, 2; Colour Plate 4D), one (fastened by rivets; Fig.8, 3) similar to an example from excavations in Amsterdam dated to the last quarter 15th/first quarter 16th century.

10. Cargo

The main cargo has not been identified – and it may have been off-loaded. One problem can, of course, be distinguishing personal property and victuals from cargo/trade items, imported foodstuffs and company property.[7] In the early 16th century Plymouth's exports included textile (woollen cloth), leather (hides) and tin. By 1500 Plymouth, Dartmouth, Barnstaple and Exeter handled some 10% of the country's cloth exports, and imported only some 11% of England's wine, along with foodstuffs (Biscayan salt, Spanish oil, wheat, rye, beans and peas according to harvests, and large quantities of salted fish), industrial raw materials (Spanish iron), and from the late 15th century an increasing amount of manufactured goods such as canvas and linen (Childs 1992, 82–3). At Plymouth, Gascon and Iberian cargoes were the most important.

Date

The main dating evidence obtained from the site can be summarised as follows (Redknap 1985):

– The uncalibrated radiocarbon date for the end of one floor timber (CW 438) is 340 +/- 80 BP (Har.-3310), or AD 1420–1600 calibrated to 1 sigma (using Ralph *et al* MASCA 73), or cal AD 1514, cal AD 1600, cal AD 1616, range cal AD 1448–1648 to 1 sigma (using Stuiver and Pearson 1986). The uncalibrated radiocarbon date for outer plank P8 (south end) is 510 +/- 50 BP (UB-2225), or cal AD 1418, range cal AD 1386–1440 to 1 sigma (using Stuiver and Pearson 1986). However this sample was not related to growth rings. Dendrochronological cross-matching, while appearing to offer a match for outer rings of AD 1454 and AD 1457, was not considered acceptable visually.

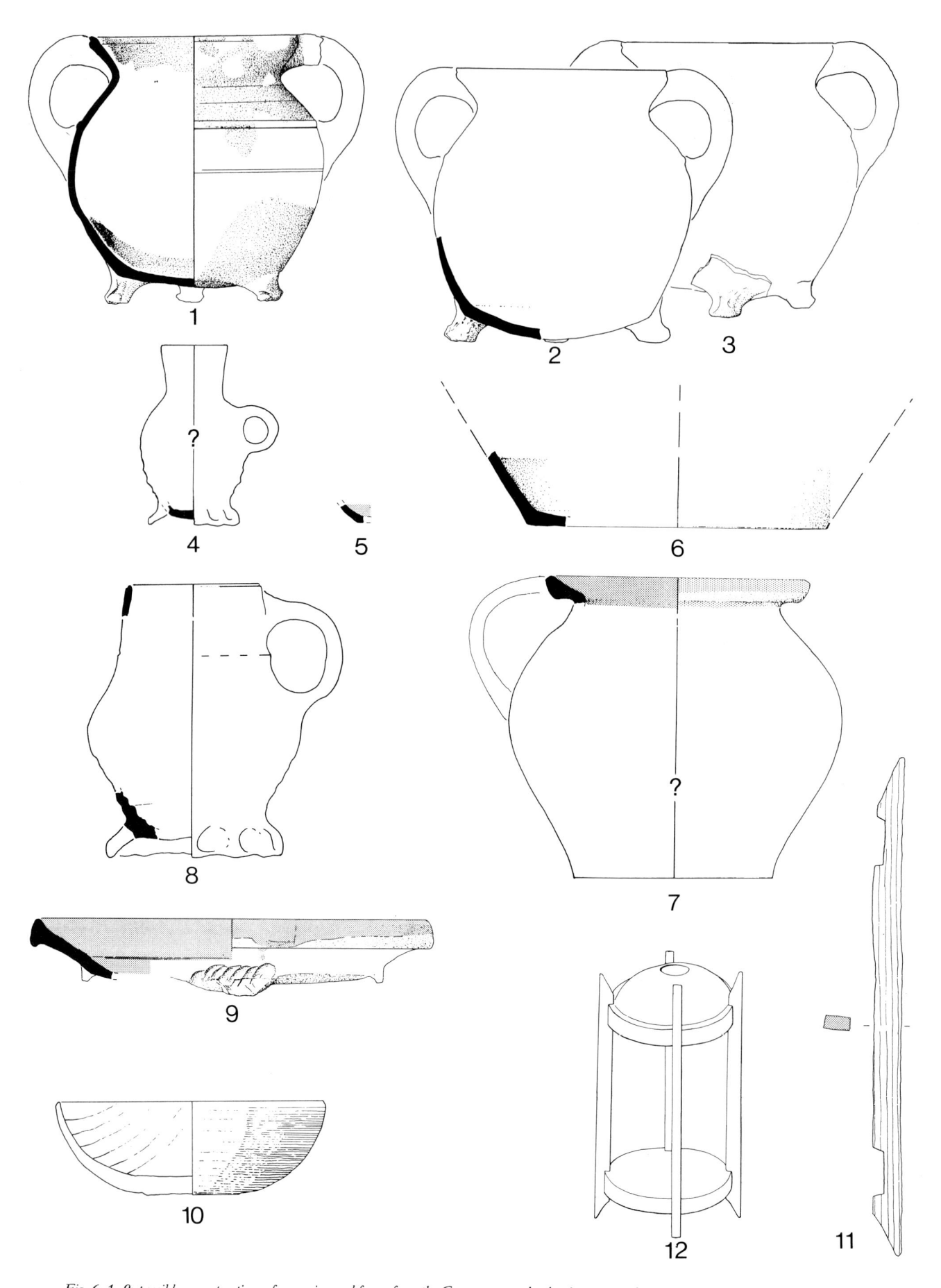

Fig. 6. 1–9: possible reconstructions of ceramic vessel forms from the Cattewater wreck, showing extent of parts found (in black). 10: wooden bowl. 11–12: wooden stave, and reconstruction as part of a lantern. (Drawing: M. Redknap)

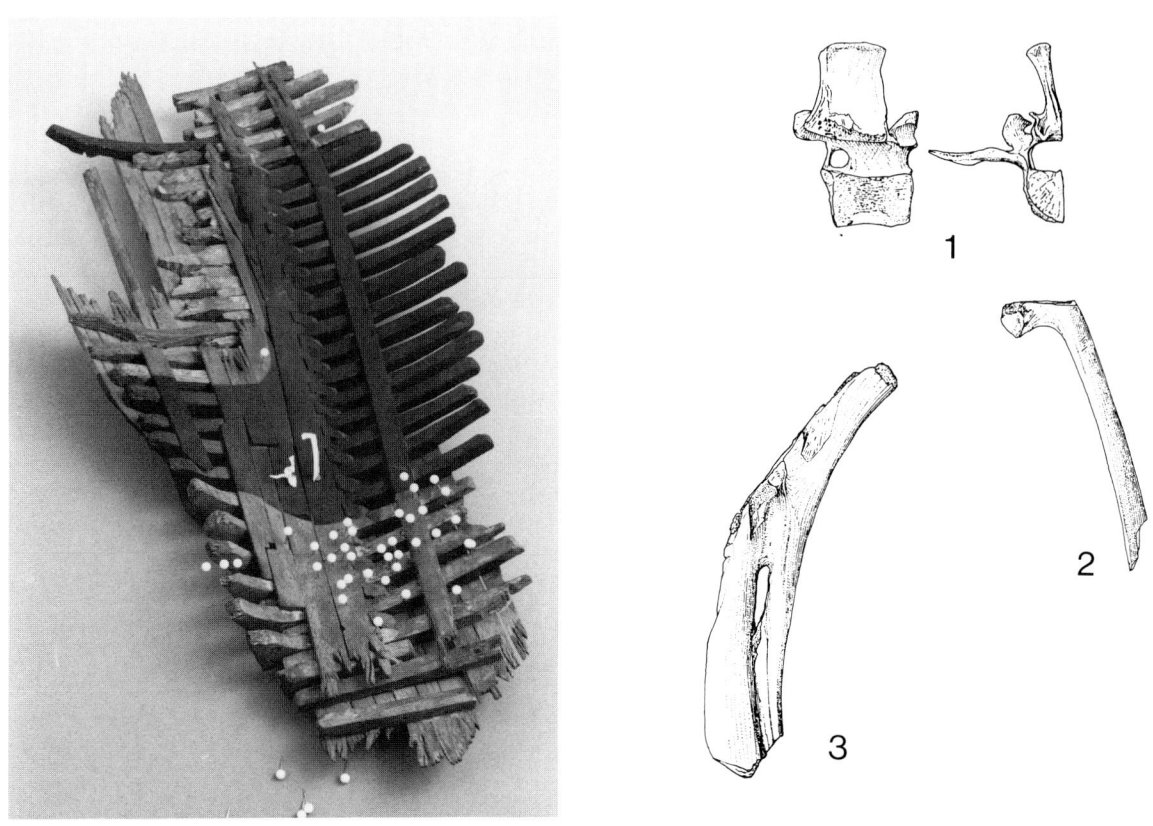

Fig. 7. Distribution of animal bone from the Cattewater wreck. 1–3: butchery to cow vertebra, rib and ulna/radius.
(Drawing: M. Redknap. Photograph: National Museums & Galleries of Wales)

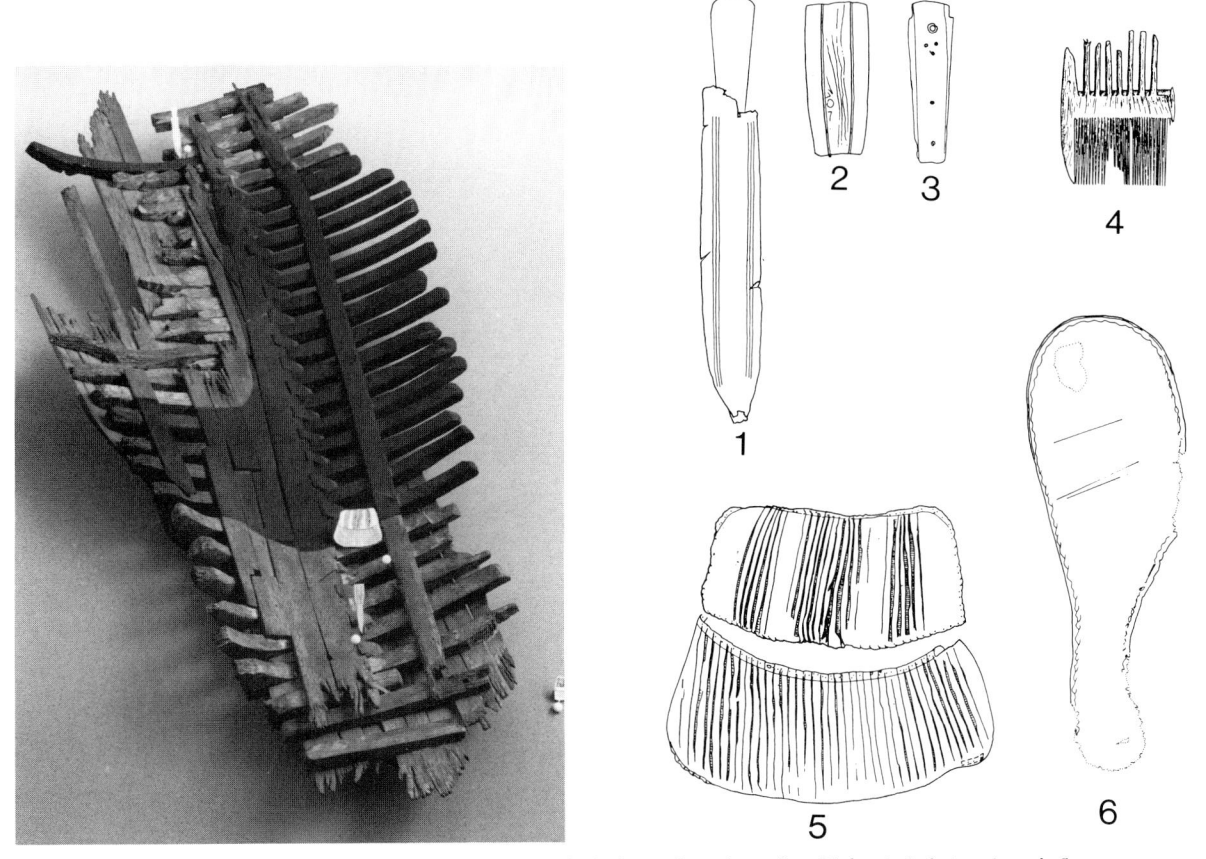

Fig. 8. Personal belongings from the Cattewater wreck. Left: findspots of certain artefacts. Right: 1–3: knives. 4: comb. 5: purse.
6: shoe sole with round toe, c.1490 style. (Drawing: M. Redknap. Photograph: National Museums & Galleries of Wales)

- The three guns recovered, all composite iron swivels, are *serpentynes* (serpentines) popular during the 16th century (Redknap 1984, 49–64); for the problems of dating such guns, see this book, Chapter 7).

- The vessel was skeleton built, with no sign of refit from clinker.

- Parallels for the keelson include Rye vessel A, *Mary Rose* and *San Juan*.

- The ceramics and leather from the wreck appear to date to about 1495–1530.

She would appear on this evidence to have sunk in the early 16th century (no clay pipes, whose earliest shipboard occurrence recorded so far is 1592; this book, Chapter 10).

Origin of the vessel: construction

Since the publication of the site, most recent debate on 16th-century ship structure has concentrated on the identification of what were provisionally termed '*lapped dovetails*', and may now be called '*dovetail mortises*' (elsewhere '*dovetail tenons*' or '*frame mortises*' : e.g. Barker 1991) fastening floor timbers to futtocks, designed to increase the resistance to racking and hull distortion and loosening of fastenings as a result of varying hydrodynamic pressure and cargo weight. They are often the only frame scarphs to survive by virtue of their low position in the hull. Similar fastenings have since been recognised on a number of Spanish and Basque ships such as the *San Juan* (1560/5; Grenier 1985; 1988), the Villefranche 1 wreck thought to be the *Lomellina* (1516; Guérout, Rieth and Gassend 1989, 40–6, Figs 12–19); the Calvi I wreck, dated to the end 16th century (*Gallia Informations* 1992-1, 57; Villié 1994, 31), the Highborn Cay wreck (c.1520–70; Oertling 1988; 1989) and possibly the Mollases Reef wreck, Turks & Caicos Islands, British West Indies (oak hull c.1500–25; Keith *et al* 1984; 1985)[8], and the 16th-century Yassi Ada wreck (Steffy 1994, Fig.5–11 a-b). It would appear that marker frames may be indicated by the direction of these fastenings.[9] In the case of the Cattewater (Fig.2), at least eleven frames were so assembled (probably more); the dovetail recesses were generally cut into the floor timbers, with the exception of one (floor timber F27) where this was reversed. The direction of the dovetail suggests that floor timber F26/futtock f27 may represent one of the marker frames,[10] the forward or aft-most frame from the central set of pre-erected frames, with a possible master or midship frame (often located beneath the forward end of the mast step, dislodged in this case by dredging) in the vicinity of floor timber F20. This is supported by the profiles of the frames at this point. The *San Juan* oak timbers indicate that she was built in a manner developed from the midships frame and batten principle; the fourteen frames with dovetail mortises were prefabricated and erected together amidships (Grenier 1994, 138). Battens were then fastened from stem to stern-post around these central fames, and the remaining frames prepared to fit the natural curve of the battens. Only further investigation of the Cattewater wreck can establish whether this procedure was followed in its case.[11]

It has been suggested that the Cattewater wreck may belong to the Iberian ('*Iberico-Atlantic*') group of wrecks on the basis of this construction (e.g. Maarleveld 1992, 128); Calvi I and Villefranche 1 are thought to have been of Mediterranean build.[12] Italian and other Mediterranean shipwrights were certainly being employed for their internationally recognised skills, but we have only a few examples from this period which have been meticulously recorded, and native English manufacture cannot be ruled out (was it adopted alongside carvel construction as another borrowed method?).[13] It has been reported that no positive evidence of such fastenings have been identified on the *Mary Rose* (Rule and Dobbs 1995, 26), and that where examination of the junction of her floor timbers and first futtocks has been possible, the shipwrights appear to have fashioned a hooked overlap at the heels of the floors, sometimes described as 'interlocked' or 'knuckled' (Steffy 1994, 134–5). These appear similar in some respects to the 'hook' at the end of floor timber F26 (Fig.2), where it joins futtock f27 on the Cattewater wreck, reducing the overlap required, but still permitting a secure fastening. Caution is needed when attempting to characterize regional shipbuilding practice on the basis of one or two details of construction. This particular joint, appearing on many late 16th-century ships, may by then have been commonplace, and only when further early 16th-century English ships are examined will it be possible to characterise English shipbuilding practices adequately.[14] Baker does draw attention to the absence of any mention of such mortises in the English sources, such as the detailed 1620 '*Treatise on Shipbuilding*' by John Wells (1991, 67). Another variation in shipbuilding practice may be the profile: each midships floor timber on the Cattewater wreck has a clear 'fish-tail' drop and central or slightly off-centre limber hole – characteristics not always evident on Iberian wrecks. Certainly the Cattewater wreck would appear on the basis of artefacts to be of English economic place of origin when lost, and the dovetail mortise one of those minor modifications in ship design to improve the construction method and accuracy, and provide additional strength. The extant ship remains are too slight to permit a convincing reconstruction of her lines. Using the earliest known English method for calculating tonnage ('*Bakers Old Rule*') and the maximum and minimum estimates for beam and depth of the vessel, estimated tonnage of minimum 186 tons burden and maximum 282 tons burden can be obtained, though such figures are unreliable (Friel 1984, 135–6).

Place of origin: the artefactual evidence

A place of origin can be attributed or suggested for a few of the artefacts recovered from the site. When the 'high,' moderate' and 'low' circulation categories described by Kleij (see Chapter 15) are applied to the finds, the following picture emerges:

Moderate rate of circulation:
– swivel guns – may have been manufactured in England.
– shot – from the local Beer/Seaton area.
– ceramics – most galley pots from London/south England, one lead-glazed redware vessel possibly from The Netherlands, one stoneware drinking vessel from the Rhineland, a possible chafing dish and jar from south-west France.
– tile: possibly east Devon.

Low rate of circulation:
– ballast stone – most from local Plymouth/Devon area, some from Bristol to south-west England.
– ballast gravel – possibly from the Sussex/Hampshire area

The range of pottery mirrors that to be anticipated at Plymouth and other sites along the seabord of the southern coast of England. The moated manor house at Acton Court near Bristol provides an interesting near-contemporary illustration of a range of imports to a high status site in the south-west of England. Much of the pottery is believed to have come to the site at one time, perhaps acquired in honour of a royal visit by Henry VIII in 1535, and is thought to have been discarded in the 1540s. The percentages of all imports are Low Countries wares 2–9%, Rhenish wares 43–79%, Iberian wares 16–25%, Italian wares 3–19% and French wares 3–23% (Vince and Bell 1992, Table 2). A preliminary account of the pottery recovered from the Alderney wreck, thought to have been lost in 1592 while carrying despatches and supplies to the English army in Paimpol, Brittany, sheds light on later 16th-century supply. In addition to tin-glazed earthenware *albarelli*, lead-glazed earthenwares were prominent, alongside some Köln/Frechen *Bartmänner* and Beauvais light holders (common in the Channel Isles). Single finds included a jug from Brittany, a North-West France chafing dish and a large Normandy stoneware storage jar (Davenport and Burns 1995, 36–9). Broad similarities with reference to vessel function (tripod cooking pot, jug, storage jars) and provenance can be recognised between this late 16th-century collection and the earlier Cattewater assemblage, which similarly reflects the available supply and perhaps vessel routings. The negative evidence is equally significant: in the case of the Cattewater wreck, the scarcity of Iberian pottery (with the exception of several unstratified sherds of olive jar and a small sherd of red micaceous 'Merida-type' ware which may post-date the wreck) contrasts with the inventories of the *San Juan*, Studland Bay and New World wrecks.

Conclusion

A condition of some artefact classifications is that the vessel has to be in a reasonable condition so that the relationship between the position of objects and the accommodation plan of the ship is still evident. On less completely preserved or selectively excavated sites, it may still be possible to retrieve data leading to a useful interpretation of layout and internal organisation: in the case of the Cattewater wreck (Colour Plate 4C), the tripod pitchers (represented by yellow pins) and the wooden bowl (red pin) were found all at one end of the hull structure, corresponding to the distribution as recorded of hearth tile. Bone was similarly distributed (Fig.7), though this may reflect in part the better survival of these deposits. In contrast, personal possessions such as knives were found at both ends of the site; while allowance must be made for differential survival of deposits and the impact of recent site disturbance, this may suggest a wide distribution of personal possessions on board (Fig.8).

A key distinction, only possible through careful survey and meticulous excavation, must be made between material found *in situ*, that found in secure but secondary wreck deposits such as dislodged ballast, those from post-wreck formations, and those from recently disturbed deposits such as dredged areas (in the latter areas, where hull structure remains, artefacts may still be found *in situ* where lodged between frames). Economic use of hold space is indicated by barrel staves between futtocks in 'knocked down' condition. The galley or cook room was probably on the ballast – in the area to the south of the site.[15]

Dutch post-excavation methodology can be applied to the study of wreck sites in British waters. The composition of inventories from wrecks in The Netherlands shows a numerical rise in artefacts represented (with allowance for vessel and crew size): the composition on comparable craft in the early 15th century ranges from 25–100 items, rising to 155–300 in the 18th/19th century and 500 by the second half of the 19th century. The partial investigation of the Cattewater wreck, in which only 50% of the identified structure and twelve square metres of its debris field were examined, and the detailed recording of all material (despite its partial nature) reflects this trend: fifty-three items from secure wreck deposits (or 63% of 16th-century artefacts recovered) and thirty-one items from insecure or unstratified contexts (37% of contemporary material from the investigation likely to have originated from the wreck). If ship's equipment, military equipment and stores are excluded, the artefact assemblage is reduced to fifty-one items, but the percentages are similar – 64% from secure wreck contexts.

The Cattewater project illustrates how selective excavation of a wreck can be a cost effective mechanism for the initial investigation of a wreck site and the assessment of its archaeological and historical importance prior to further programmes of fieldwork, while ensuring that much of the site and associated evidence remains untouched for the future (provided that threats have been realistically appraised). The drawbacks of this approach, in the case of the Cattewater, have been that i) the ship's date of loss and identity remain obscure (though future documentary research and a comprehensive programme of dendrochronological sampling may yet achieve this); ii) her size and function are understood to a limited degree; iii) the artefact assemblage is incomplete, and conclusions consequently limited and iv) the distribution of artefacts probably reflects differential survival of deposits and the extent of the excavation. The hull structure and debris field on the seabed should, of course, be the subject of regular monitoring.

The selection of areas for excavation will depend on site preservation, vessel form, operating conditions and other variables, and should always reflect the resources available for both excavation and post-excavation work. Indications of the absent inventory are indicated by surviving 16th-century inventories, such as that of the much larger *Great Bark* of 1531 (Laughton 1919, 21–2). This inventory included a *shype kettell of xxiiij gallons* (probably brass), a *pytche pott of brasse*, a *gryndyng stoen*, a *Crowe of yeron*, *iij compassys* and a *Runyng glas*; of other items listed, the Cattewater has provided examples of the *pompe* (the pump hole in the keelson), possibly the *mayne parrell* (one truck), and as discussed above, perhaps evidence for a *lantarren* (five on the *Great Bark*). On the smaller Cattewater wreck, the tripod pitchers with their sooted exteriors probably functioned as 'ship's kettle'.

Much information on the topography of early 16th-century Plymouth may be gleaned from the earliest surviving harbour chart of the Sound and coastline, made in defence against invasion about 1539. This shows the town's fortresses (some '*not yet made*'), and defence provisions around the ancient harbour the Cattewater, which, sheltered from all but prevailing south-west to westerly winds, remained the principal anchorage into the early post-medieval period for the town which developed around Sutton Pool, and was described in Leland's Itinerary *c.*1535–43 as '*a goodly rode for great shippes*'. By the early 16th century the three-masted skeleton-built ship was a standard sea-going vessel in northern Europe, and Devon ships will have shared this tradition. Skeleton-built carvel ships are generally thought to have been established on the north and south coasts of Devon by the 1480s, the ship type being thought to have developed from Portuguese caravels, first recorded trading to England in 1448 (Friel 1992, 76–7).

The nationality of the ship (in terms of where she was equipped) relies on the data supplied in part by its portable artefacts (ceramics, some local) and personal belongings, and partly by the less mobile stone ballast (mainly local, ranging in source from South Wales to Kent) and sand (Hampshire/Sussex?). The names and types of many Devon ships are known, as are the trades in which they were engaged: Gascony and Iberia were the most important overseas markets for Plymouth. Inventories of Devon ships are rare,[16] depriving us of specific information regarding their rigging and equipment. The Cattewater wreck cannot yet be identified as a Devon-built ship, but she appears to have operated in south-west England. The location of the wreck suggests a number of possible causes for the sinking – an accident or severe storm causing damage (possibly elsewhere), sinking at anchor or before she could be beached, fire or explosion (no evidence found for this), or some other cause. The only incident so far noted between *c.*1490 and 1530 which might correspond to the Cattewater wreck is the sinking of a certain ship (*quedam navis de la Croyne in partibis hispanis*) called the *St James* (*Sanctus Jacobus*), whose master and owner was one *Rolandus molis alias Rolandus morissa de la Croyne*, on 17 January 1494 *in portum de Plymouth*, and wreck on the shore with loss of all her rigging (*ibidem per infortunum magni ventus et aure horribil: predicta navis.... toto aparatu suo occider..t*) (Simon Carswylle's Book, *f.*48, Plymouth City Records Office). This account serves as a reminder of the importance of Iberian trade with Plymouth, but the description of the loss 'in the harbour' is imprecise, and until further archaeological or documentary evidence is forthcoming to confirm identity, the Cattewater wreck must remain anonymous. Other ship losses documented for the area have been listed using well known sources (Redknap 1984, 98), but no other historically documented losses have subsequently come to light.[17] The site has yielded few clues as to where she was built, though this is a consequence in part of a limited database on 16th-century ship construction. As outlined by Friel, Devon shipping in the early 16th century was much like that found in other parts of Britain and Northern Europe, for technical innovations could be transmitted rapidly. Despite the incomplete nature of the site investigation, a number of conclusions have been drawn from the artefactual evidence which cast further light on socio-economic conditions, armament, layout and lifestyle on board this early 16th-century ship, one of the very few which can be dated to within fifty years of Columbus' first Atlantic crossing, and upon which the economic fortune of south-west England depended.

Acknowledgements

I am most grateful to the H.M. Royal Armouries and the Ancient Monuments Laboratory (English Heritage) for permission to reproduce photographs; to the Department of Photography, NMGW, for new photography; to Steve Waring, RCAHM(E) for information on shipping losses on the Maritime SMR; to Dr Sian Rees and Gillian Hutchinson for their valuable comments on the draft text, and finally to the many colleagues who have provided information on sites of this type and period over the years.

Notes

1. The coordinates locate the centre of the timber obstruction encountered by the dredger in June 1973.
2. Fibre identification by H.M.Appleyard.
3. Field procedures for collecting the maximum amount of data from ballast mounds have since been published by Lamb *et al* 1990.
4. Similar example found on the Studland Bay wreck (Ladle 1993, 18).
5. The composition contrasts with that from the Studland Bay wreck, which contained Isabela Polychrome lustreware, Columbia Plain ware, and Merida-type costrels. The ship's origin is also indicated by her ballast; approximately 55% from the Basque coast (Ladle 1993, 17).
6. The Studland Bay evidence also suggests salt beef with mutton and pork, and one mallard duck (Ladle 1993, 19). For *Gadus morhua* on a late 16th-century merchantman see Brinkhuizen 1994.
7. For example, a small quantity of cod found on the Cattewater wreck was interpeted as provisions. Frequency of commodity and method of packing are important criteria for identifying cargo.
8. Horizontal treenail and mortise noted on the futtocks; T.Carrell, *in litt.*; Oertling 1989, Fig.5.
9. They have also been recorded on later wrecks off Florida, such as the *San Martin* (1618) and *Santa Margarita* (1622: D.D.Moore, *in litt.*). Barker (1991, 69) notes the Portuguese description by Manuel Fernandes (*Livro de traça de Carpintaria*, 1616) to overlaps between floors and futtocks of *3 palmas*, 'and they will mortise (*malhetar*) the floor into the futtock one dedo'. Hooked overlaps appear to have been used in the late 16th century vessel at Yassi Ada (Rosloff 1986, 127).
10. The *almogma* (Carroll *in litt.*), *emmocadura* (Lavanha), or dovetail mortises *malhete rabo-de-minhoto* (Portuguese: Barata).

11 The combination of treenail/iron nail fastenings recorded on the Cattewater wreck (in general, one treenail and one or two iron nails per strake) has also been noted on the *San Juan*, where two treenails and two iron nails were used for each strake to frame join (Grenier *et al* 1994, 139).

12 One frame with a dovetail mortise has been found on the early 16th-century Studland Bay wreck, thought to be a merchantman built in 'southern-European style', possibly Spain, and lost *c*.1520: Hutchinson 1991, 173; Ladle 1993.

13 Some of the stone and gravel from the ballast came from the southern coast of England, while most appears to be local to Plymouth.

14 The floor profiles on the *San Juan*, Molasses Reef and other sites differ to those of the Cattewater wreck floors, lacking the 'fish-tails'.

15 It has been noted that the hearth on Dutch ships was gradually moved to bow or stern part of cargo vessels from the end of the 15th century.

16 Friel has published accounts of fitting out of two late 16th-century Dartmouth ships – excluding weapons, items included lanterns, platters, items for cook rooms; provisions included biscuits, beer, beef, pork, fish, butter and pease (Friel 1992, 75–6).

17 The wrecking of the *John* on Pole Sand, Exmouth, in 1573, with the loss of 18,000 of the Newfoundland fish on board, illustrates the importance of fish to the area (Admiralty Court Miscellaneous Books and Exemplifications 1573 file 45, no.301, p.148).

Bibliography

Barker, R. 1991 'Design in the Dockyards about 1600', *in* R. Reinders and K. Paul (eds), *Carvel Construction Technique. Fifth International Symposium on Boat and Ship Archaeology* (Amsterdam 1988), Oxbow Monograph 12, 61–69.

Brinkhuizen, D.C. 1994 'Some notes on fish remains from the late 16th century merchant vessel Scheurrak SO1', *in* W. van Neer (ed.), Fish Exploitation in the Past, Annales du Musée Royal de l'Afrique Centrale, Sciences Zoologiques no. 274, 197–205.

Carpenter, A., Ellis, K.H. & McKee, J.E.G. 1974 *Interim report on the wreck discovered in the Cattewater*. Maritime Monographs and Reports 13, National Maritime Museum.

Carrell, T.L. 1993 'Western hemisphere underwater news', *IJNA* 22, 184–188.

Childs, W.R. 1992 'Devon's Overseas Trade in the Late Middle Ages', *in* M. Duffy *et al* (eds) 1992 *The New Maritime History of Devon. Vol.I. From Early Times to the late Eighteenth Century*, Conway Maritime Press in association with The University of Exeter, 79–89

Davenport, T.G. & Burns, R. 1995 'A sixteenth-century wreck off the Island of Alderney', *The Archaeology of Ships of War*, International Maritime Archaeology Series 1, 30–40

Duffy, M., Fisher, S., Greenhill, B., Starkey, D.J. & Youings, J. (eds) 1992 *The New Maritime History of Devon. Vol.I. From Early Times to the late Eighteenth Century*, Conway Maritime Press in association with The University of Exeter.

Firth, A. 1990 'Shedding light on a lantern', Nautical Archaeology Society Newsletter Autumn 1990, 8–9.

Friel, I. 1984 'Notes on the identification & reconstruction of the wreck', *in* M.Redknap (1984), 135–139.

Friel, I. 1992 'Devon Shipping from the Middle Ages to *c*.1600', *in* M. Duffy *et al* (eds) 1992 *The New Maritime History of Devon. Vol.I. From Early Times to the late Eighteenth Century*, Conway Maritime Press in association with The University of Exeter, 73–78.

Grenier, R. 1985 'Excavating a 400–year-old Basque Galleon', *National Geographic Magazine* 168.1 (July 1985), 58–68.

Grenier, R. 1988 'Basque Whalers in the New World: The Red Bay Wrecks', *in* G.F.Bass (ed.), *Ships and Shipwrecks of the Americas*, London, 69–84.

Grenier, R., Loewen, B. & Proulx, J.-P. 1994 'Basque Shipbuilding Technology *c*.1560–1580: The Red Bay project', *in* C.Westerdahl (ed.), *Crossroads in Ancient Shipbuilding*, Oxbow Monograph 40, 137–141.

Guérout, M., Rieth, E. & Gassend, J.-M. 1989 'Le Navire Génois de Villefranche, un naufrage de 1516?', *Archaeonautica* 9.

Hansen, W. 1984 *Kalenderminiaturen der Stundenbücher. Mittelalterliches Leben im Jahreslauf*, Callwey.

Hutchinson, G. 1991 'The early 16th-century wreck at Studland Bay, Dorset', *in* R.Reinders and K.Paul (eds), *Carvel Construction Technique*. Oxbow Monograph 12, 171–175.

Johnston, P.F. 1993 'Treasure Salvage, archaeological ethics and maritime museums', *IJNA* 22, 53–60.

Keith, D.H., Duff, J.A., James, S.R., Oertling, T.J. & Simmons, J.J. 1984 'The Molasses Reef wreck, Turks and Caicos Islands, B.W.I.: A Preliminary report', *IJNA* 13, 45–63.

Keith, D.H. & Simmons, J.J. 1985 'Analysis of Hull Remains, Ballast, and Artifact Distribution of a 16th-Century Shipwreck, Molasses Reef, British West Indies', *Journal of Field Archaeology* 12, 411–424.

Ladle, L. 1993 *The Studland Bay Wreck. A Spanish Shipwreck off the Dorset Coast*, Poole Museum Heritage Series Number One.

Lamb, W.R., Keith, D.H. & Judy, S.A. 1990 'Analysis of the Ballast of the Molasses Reef Wreck', *National Geographic Research* 6, 291–305.

Laughton, L.G.Carr 1919 'Documents. The Inventory of The Great Bark, 1531', *The Mariners Mirror* 5.1, 21–2.

L'Hour, M. & Veyrat, E. 1989 'A mid-15th-century clinker boat off the north coast of France, the Aber Wrac'h I wreck: a preliminary report', *IJNA* 18, 285–298.

Maarleveld, T. 1987 'Scheepsboukundige verkenning van de resten van een koopvaarder in de Waddenzee', *Flevobericht* 280, 69–74.

Maarleveld, T.J. 1992 'Archaeology and early modern merchant ships. Building sequence and consequences: an introductory review', *Rotterdam Papers* VII, 155–174.

Mortlock, B. & Redknap, M. 1978 'The Cattewater wreck, Plymouth, Devon, Preliminary results of recent work', *IJNA* 7, 195–204.

Oertling, T.J. 1988 'Elegant Remains Yield Details of Discovery Ship Construction', *INA Newsletter* 14.3/4, 8–15.

Oertling, T.J. 1989 'The Highborn Cay wreck: the 1986 field season', *IJNA* 18, 244–253.

Pomey, M.P., Long, L., L'Hour, M., Bernhard, H. & Richez, F. 1993 'Calvi a) Port de Commerce. Epave: Calvi 1, *in* 'Recherches Sous Marines', *Gallia Informations* 1992–1, 57–58.

Redknap, M. 1984 *The Cattewater Wreck. The investigation of an armed vessel of the early sixteenth century*, BAR131, National Maritime Museum Archaeological Series No.8, Oxford.

Redknap, M. 1985 'The Cattewater wreck: a contribution to 16th century maritime archaeology', *in* C.O.Cederlund (ed.), *Postmedieval Boat and Ship Archaeology*, BAR International Series 256, Oxford, 39–59.

Redknap, M. 1990 'Surveying for Underwater Archaeological Sites – Signs in the Sands', *The Hydrographic Journal* 58, October 1990, 11–16.

Rosloff, J.P. 1986 'Excavation of a 16th century vessel at Yassi Ada, Turkey, by the Institute of Nautical Archaeology 1982', *in* C. R. Cummings (ed.), *Underwater Archaeology, The Proceedings of the 14th Conference on Underwater Archaeology*, 125–128.

Rule, M. & Dobbs, C.T.C. 1995 'The Tudor Warship *Mary Rose*: aspects of recent research', *The Archaeology of Ships of War*, International Maritime Archaeology Series 1, 26–29.

Smith, R.C., Keith, D.H. & Lakey, D. 1985 'The Highborn Cay wreck: Further exploration of a 16th-century Bahaman shipwreck', *IJNA* 14, 63–72.

Smith, R.D. 1995 'Wrought-iron swivel guns', *The Archaeology of Ships of War*, International Maritime Archaeology Series 1, 104–113.

Steffy, J.R. 1994 *Wooden Ship Building and the Interpretation of Shipwrecks*, Texas A & M University Press.

Stuiver, M. & Pearson, G.W. 1986 'High-precision calibration of the radiocarbon time scale, AD 1950–500 BC', *Radiocarbon* 28 No.2B, 805–838.

Swan, J.M. 'Leather', *in* M. Redknap, *The Cattewater Wreck. The investigation of an armed vessel of the early sixteenth century*, BAR 131, National Maritime Museum Archaeological Series No.8, Oxford, 71–5.

Verhaeghe, F. 1992 'Light in the darkness: a ceramic lantern', *in* D.R.M. Gaimster & M. Redknap (eds), *Everyday and Exotic Pottery from Europe. Studies in honour of John G.Hurst*, Oxbow, 167–176.

Villié, P. 1994. *Calvi I. De l'Archéologie à L'Histoire* (Be Boccard, Paris).

Vince, A. & Bell, R. 1992 'Sixteenth-century pottery from Acton Court, Avon', *in* D. R.M. Gaimster & M. Redknap (eds), *Everyday and Exotic Pottery from Europe. Studies in honour of John G.Hurst*, Oxbow, 101–112.

Watts, G.P. 1993 'The Western Ledge Reef wreck: a preliminary report on the investigation of the remains of a 16th-century shipwreck in Bermuda', *IJNA* 22, 103–124.

Zeiler, J.T. 1993 'Zes vaten rundvlees uit het scheepswrack SCHEURRAK SO1', *Tussentijdse Rapportage* 10.

6

Form, function, ownership: a study of chests from Henry VIII's warship *Mary Rose* (1545)

Maggie Richards

INTRODUCTION

On 19 July 1545 the *Mary Rose* sailed into her final battle as the French and English fleets met in the Solent. As Henry VIII watched from the shore, she heeled over and sank in the murky waters. In 1982 the ship was successfully raised and returned home to Portsmouth, following extensive excavations (Rule 1983).

The ship produced a unique assemblage of over 19,000 artefacts, many of which are mundane objects which, in the normal course of events, are rarely cherished and handed down through time in the same way as ornate, sumptuous, superior and valuable items. The true value of much of the assemblage lies in its reflection of everyday items in use in 1545, albeit on board a warship.

Whether in a ship at sea or a house on land, there was a need for some form of container for storage. This was provided by the chest, a basic piece of furniture which could also serve as seat (Gloag 1966, 76) or table. The differences between a chest and a coffer are unclear, and furniture historians do not seem to agree on a definition. We have opted for the description by Randle Holme, a heraldic artist who argued in the 1649 '*Academy of Armory*' that a 'chest' had a *straight, flat lid* whilst a 'coffer' had a *curved, domed lid*. Using those simple criteria, only 'chests' were recovered.

Few items of furniture dated before 1600 have survived (Knell 1992, 31), and the *Mary Rose* chests provide a unique opportunity to study a large, dated contemporary group, not only with regard to form and construction, but also to function, as a number were found with contents *in situ*.

EXCAVATION

As a result of damage sustained during the sinking and the general disintegration of any iron fixings used to hold the components together, chests and their contents were usually excavated *in situ* (Colour Plate 1B). The positions of any contents and sediment samples were meticulously recorded before removal, after which the chest would be dismantled and brought to the surface. Excavation was very time consuming, particularly in areas where many chests were found to have been stowed. Some had collapsed on top of each other, making the identification of individual chests difficult (Fig.1). Not all of the chests were found unscathed, many being represented only by fragments or a single element. In four examples where chests were deemed to be still robust, valuable diving time was saved by the construction of purpose-built lifting containers. This made it possible to raise the chests undamaged, and allowed detailed recording and recovery of the contents once landed on board the recovery vessel *Sleipner* (Fig.21).

Figure 1. Model, showing the position of chests in the area outside the carpenter's cabin on the main deck and the orlop deck below.
(Copyright: The Mary Rose Trust)

THE CHEST ASSEMBLAGE

A project was undertaken during the summer of 1990, at which time over 120 artefact numbers were assigned to complete or incomplete chests, representing a total of over 400 individual components or fragments. Conserved material was retained in controlled conditions (55–60% relative humidity and temperature of 18°C) and amounted to ten complete chests: each having been dismantled for the conservation process.[1] Four of these have been reconstructed and are now on public display within the *Mary Rose* Exhibition; six were dismantled and stored flat in the 'conserved organics' storage area. The remaining complete chests, elements, and fragments were stored in an unconserved, wet condition, and wrapped in two layers of polythene sheeting. Regular repacking and retreatment with a biocide solution had precluded fungal attack. Unconserved material was kept in a wet finds area. Conserved items have been measured, photographed and drawn before and after conservation; unconserved items have generally only been measured and briefly described directly after excavation.

METHODOLOGY

Using information from the *Mary Rose* database of all artefacts identified as chest or 'chest?', it took six weeks for a team of four people (plus a photographer for one or two hours daily) to fully examine the wet material. Only the part(s) assigned to a single artefact identification number were examined at any one time. Every component or fragment was unpacked and drawn at a scale of 1:1 on polythene; detailed notes, measurements and photographs were taken before retreatment in biocide, rewrapping and relocating in the 'wet finds' storage area. Any part(s) thought not to fit in with the rest of its assigned finds number were immediately allocated a new identification number, under which it was then recorded, drawn and wrapped.

With such a large multi-part group, it was considered unwise to unwrap and examine all of the assemblage concurrently for a number of reasons – the difficulty in maintaining individual numbering integrity for over 400 similar wood boards; the large amount of space that would have been required to lay out the whole assemblage; and, most importantly, the need to prevent wet material drying out (being unwrapped for as short a period as practicable).

Various species of wood were identified within the construction of the chest assemblage (Fig.6). Their condition was generally good, with the appearance of the majority of wet material superficially unchanged from that described at the time of excavation. However, some poplar pieces had the consistency of soggy cardboard and proved difficult to handle, often fragmenting at the slightest touch.

Iron fittings such as hinges, locks, hasps and brackets did not survive, and were only indicated by staining, holes and rebates in or on the wood surface. It proved easier to identify such features on the wet material than on those items which were already conserved. Two forms of iron hinge were used: the 'strap' or the 'split ring' (Fig.2).

To complete the compilation of chest data, the conserved chests were examined and drawings checked.

Using the 1:1 drawings, the constructional data and the archaeological information on the database, it was possible to find and fit 'missing' fronts, lids and fragments for a number of incomplete chests. A minimum of fifty-one chests had been recovered, and while many were complete (or virtually so), the total also includes those represented only by a single element.

TYPOLOGY

All of the *Mary Rose* chests were of boarded[2] construction, but of varying constructional complexity, with some featuring components in addition to the basic carcass of base, ends, sides and lid (Fig.15).

A number were fitted with a till, an internal lidded shelf, suitable for keeping small valuables separate from other larger items stored within the chest. An 'L' shaped rebate was cut into the side back and the side front of the chest into which the till base and side would be fitted, and a domed depression was drilled for the pivots of the till lid. An internal partition which simply served to divide the storage space was identified in two examples. Others featured battens attached to the underside of the lid to ensure a tighter and more secure fit. Many (but not all) were fitted with handles, usually made either of wood blocks or rope (two may have had iron ring handles). Three chests had staining caused by iron brackets affixed to the corners, presumably for strengthening.

Four different methods of affixing the boards together were identified: i. iron nails, ii. iron nails in conjunction with rebates cut along the edges of some carcass elements, iii. wooden pegs or dowels in conjunction with rebates and iv. dovetailing with nails.

While many chests were unique in appearance, some were very similar. Two simple characteristics were chosen in order to create a typology: did the base of the chest rest on the deck, and was it fitted with iron hinges and a lock? From this, three types of chest could be identified:

Type 1. Base rested directly on deck. No evidence of hinges and lock to attach and secure lid.

Type 2. Base rested directly on deck. Evidence of hinges and lock to attach and secure lid.

Type 3. Base raised from deck (i.e. had legs). Evidence of hinges and lock to attach and secure lid.

Subtypes

Types 1, 2 and 3 were then subdivided using the construction method as the determining factor (Fig.3).

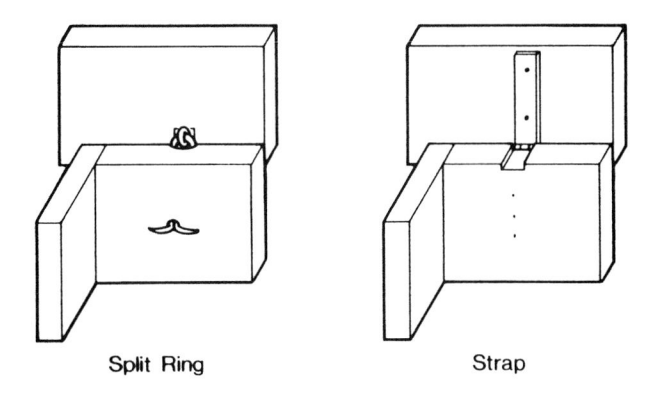

Fig. 2. The two types of hinge identified on Mary Rose *chests.* (Copyright: The Mary Rose Trust)

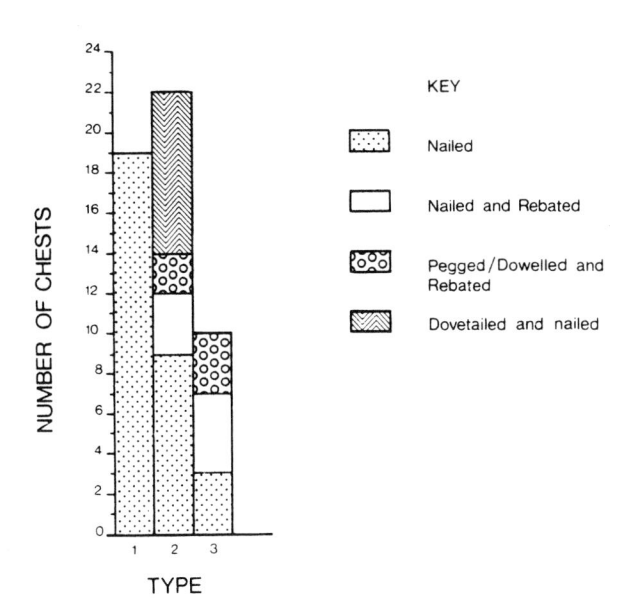

Fig. 3. Breakdown of the three Mary Rose *chest types into subtypes.*
(Copyright: The Mary Rose Trust)

Chest subtype .1 = nailed
Chest subtype .2 = nailed and rebated
Chest subtype .3 = dowelled/pegged and rebated
Chest subtype .4 = dovetailed and nailed

DETAIL OF TYPES

Type 1

Nineteen chests conform to the criteria for *type 1*. All were simply fastened together with nails, and therefore classified as *subtype 1.1* (Fig.3). However, as two groups, each of a uniform and distinct design, were present, they were further divided by form, eight falling into *subtype 1.1/1* (Fig.4) and eleven into *subtype 1.1/2* (Fig.5).

Out of the eight chests classified as *subtype 1.1/1*, seven were without lids. The eighth had a possible lid, but no clear indication of whether or not it was attached and if so how. Poplar was used in the manufacture of five examples, while the other three were made of elm. Board thickness ranged between 20–25 mm. None displayed any evidence for the attachment of handles. Finished dimensions (l × w × ht) range between 1300 × 470 × 410 mm and 1145 × 485 × 409 mm.

All eleven examples classified as *subtype 1.1/2* have a 'crate-like' appearance, and were manufactured using elm boards 19 mm in thickness. Two holes were drilled into each end for the horizontal attachment of rope carrying handles. Lids were secured by nails and were larger than the 'carcass' (by 25 mm all round), presumably to enable the lid to be levered off easily. Two uniform sizes of crate were identified, and so they were further divided by size: seven (*subtype 1.1/2.1*) having average dimensions of 1930 × 381 × 305 mm, with the remaining four (*subtype 1.1/2.2*) having average dimensions of 2235 × 381 × 357 mm.

Type 2

A total of twenty-two chests were identified as *type 2*, demonstrating four methods of fastening the elements together: nine chests belonged to *subtype 2.1*; three to *subtype 2.2*; two to *subtype 2.3*; and eight to *subtype 2.4* (Fig.3).

Type 2 chests varied in size, ranging (l × w × ht) from 765 × 305 × 245 mm to 1435 × 490 × 500 mm. Boards used in the construction of the carcass were 20–25 mm in thickness, with the exception of those used for *subtype 2.3* which were 30 mm.

All elements of the *type 2* chest carcass were generally made from the same species of wood. However, fittings such as handles, tills and battens were often manufactured from a different wood to that utilised in the carcass. Handles were generally made from oak or elm, battens from beech and tills

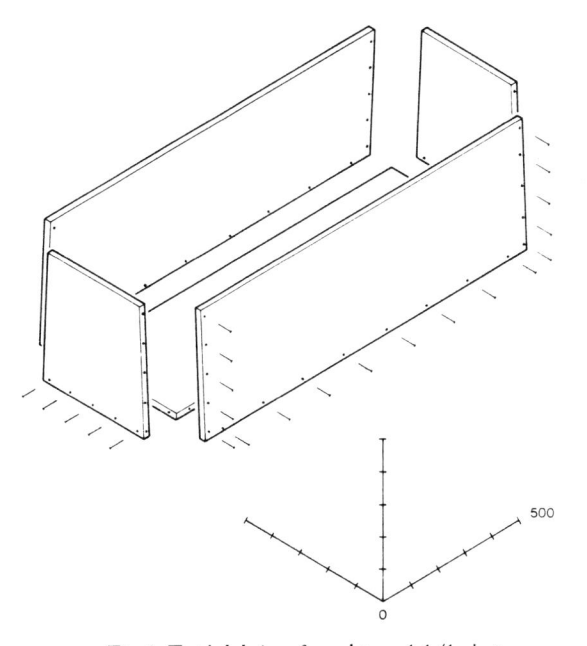

Fig. 4. Exploded view of a subtype 1.1/1 chest.
(Copyright: The Mary Rose Trust)

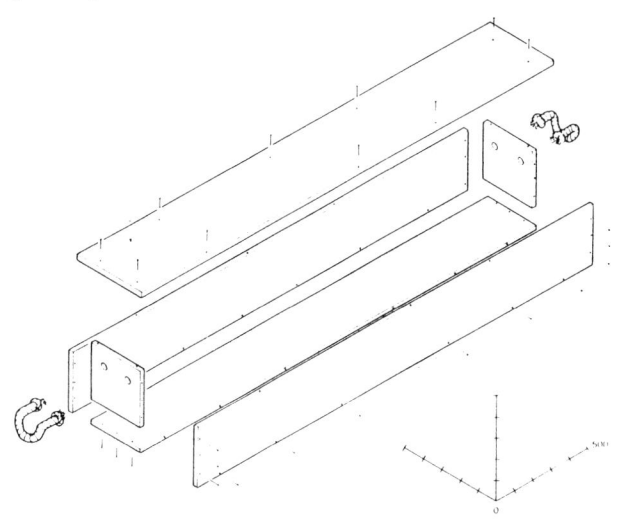

Fig. 5. Exploded view of a subtype 1.1/2 chest.
(Copyright: The Mary Rose Trust)

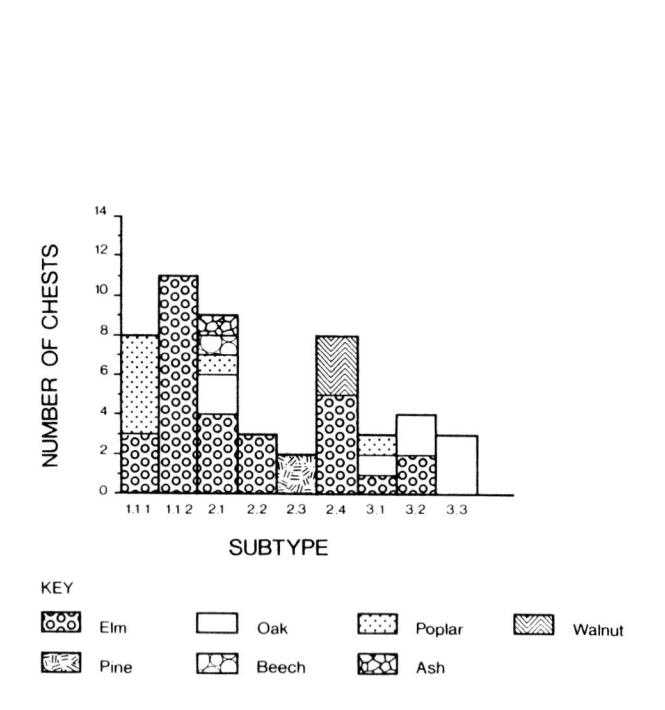

Fig. 6. Analysis of wood species utilised in Mary Rose *chest subtype carcass manufacture.* (Copyright: The Mary Rose Trust)

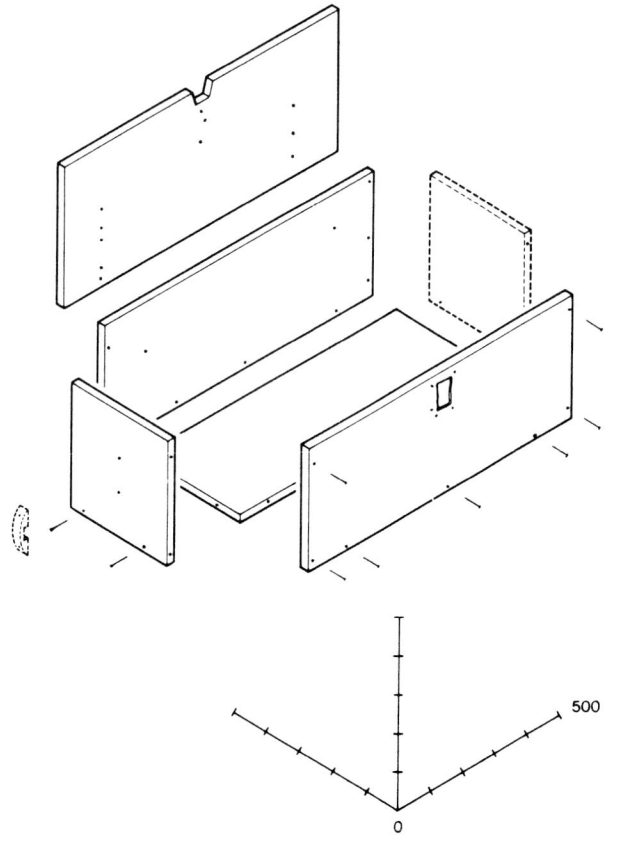

Fig. 7. Exploded view of a subtype 2.1 *chest.* (Copyright: The Mary Rose Trust)

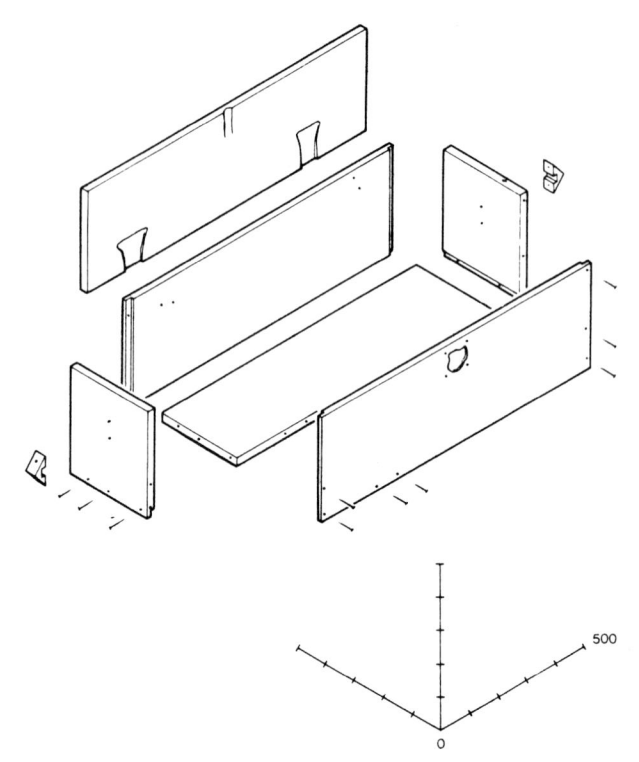

Fig. 8. Exploded view of a subtype 2.2 *chest.* (Copyright: The Mary Rose Trust)

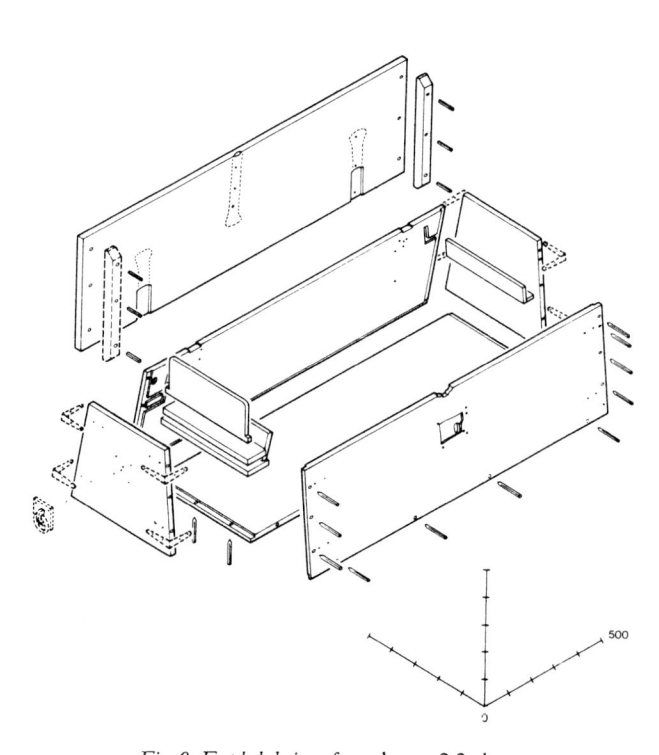

Fig. 9. Exploded view of a subtype 2.3 *chest.* (Copyright: The Mary Rose Trust)

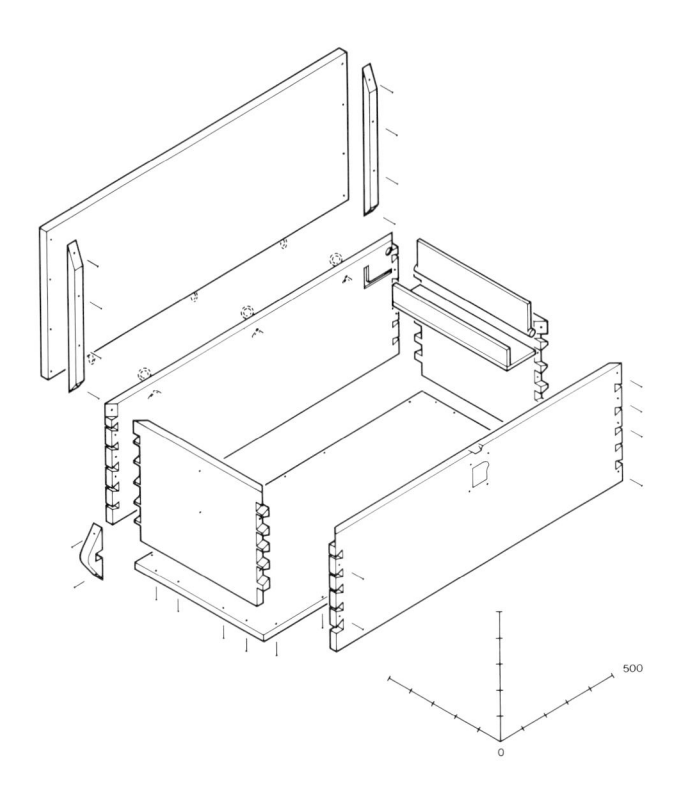

Fig. 10. Exploded view of a subtype 2.4 chest.
(Copyright: The Mary Rose Trust)

of elm or oak. Elm, oak, pine, poplar, walnut, beech and ash were found to be have been used in *type 2* carcass manufacture (Fig.6), elm being the most common. Only two *type 2* subtypes were consistent in the species of wood used for the carcass: all *subtype 2.2* chests were made of elm and all *subtype 2.3* were made of pine.

The two chests assigned to *subtype 2.3* are very similar, and unique in the context of the *Mary Rose*, for several reasons. They are the only examples manufactured from pine, the 30 mm boards are a minimum of 5 mm greater in thickness than any others used. They are both fitted with two tills, one lidded and one unlidded. They have ends which are wider at the base than at the top, and are therefore canted, producing a finished chest which closely resembles those in common use later by seamen in the 19th century. One example featured painted marks (Fig.11), which at the time of excavation could still be seen on the internal faces of the carcass elements. It would seem likely that they were applied by the carpenter as constructional marks. One chest (Fig.9) is fitted with a false base to its lidded till, creating a unique 'secret compartment' not found in any other *Mary Rose* chest. As both *type 2.3* examples are so similar in construction and dimensions, it seems likely that they were purchased from the same maker, with the 'secret compartment' a specified 'extra' requested by its purchaser.

Eight chests (*subtype 2.4*) were dovetailed, and their presence on board an English warship in 1545 may cause some surprise to furniture historians, as this method of construction has been generally associated with continental rather than English manufacturing at that date. However, it is not possible to state whether these particular chests were made in England or simply imported from the Continent.

Type 3

Ten chests were identified as *type 3* with three classified as *subtype 3.1*; four as *subtype 3.2*; and three as *subtype 3.3* (Fig.3).

As with *type 2*, the *type 3* chests varied in size, ranging from a minimum of 655 × 250 × 425 mm to a maximum of 1040 × 460 × 575 mm. The boards used in the construction of the carcass were also 20–25 mm in thickness.

Oak, elm and poplar were used in the construction of *type 3* carcasses (oak being most frequently used; Fig.6). In common with *type 2* chests, fittings were often made from a different type of wood to that used for the carcass.

Type 3 chests differed from *type 2* in two minor aspects of construction and form; not one example was fitted with handles, and the ends were made to be deeper than the sides, thereby raising the base from the deck. This created 'legs' to either end: the 'leg' height (deck to base of chest) in the examples recovered varied considerably, ranging from a mere 25 mm to a maximum of 200 mm. Leg form was created by sawing a section out from the base of the end.

Decoration

While the majority are plain and none can be regarded as ornate, a few chests (*types 2* and *3* only) carry forms of decoration. No evidence indicative of any kind of outer cover or lining was present.

A few bear simple, rough, compass-inscribed patterns. A simple geometric design of a petalled 'flower' with the outer tip of each petal touching the edge of the circle was created by first drawing a circle and then arcs within that circle from

Fig. 11. A painted carpenter's mark applied to an internal face of a chest carcass. (Copyright: The Mary Rose Trust)

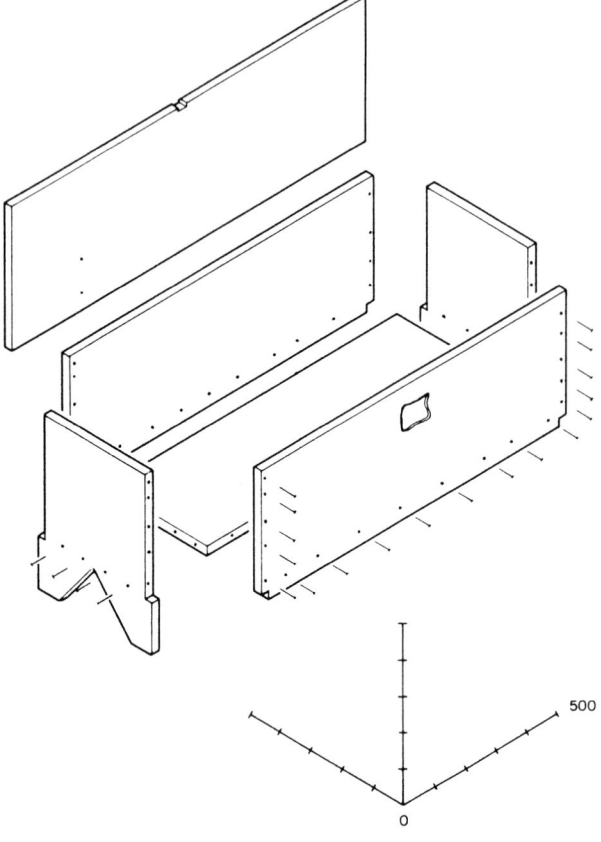

Fig. 12. Exploded view of a subtype 3.1 chest.
(Copyright: The Mary Rose Trust)

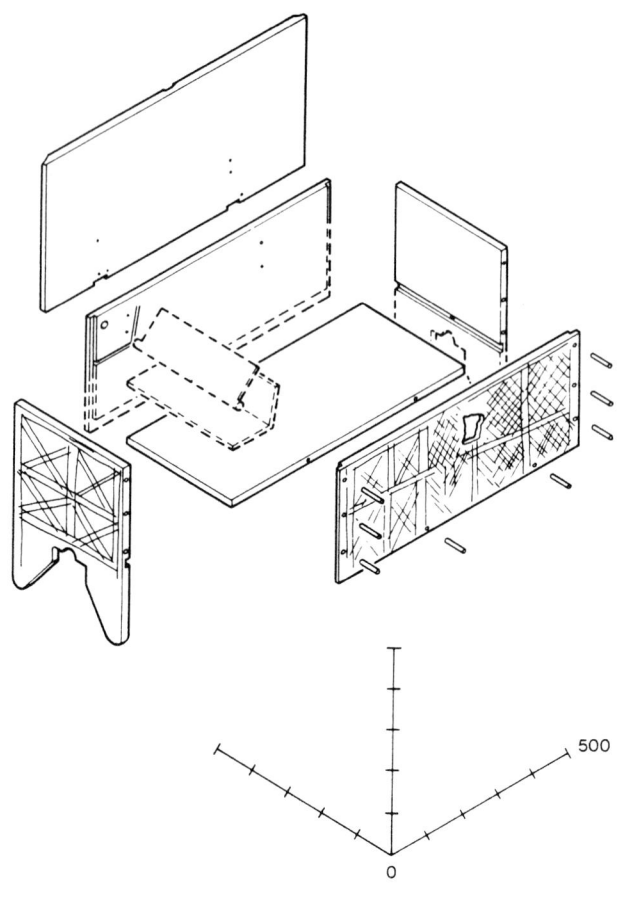

Fig. 14. Exploded view of a subtype 3.3 chest.
(Copyright: The Mary Rose Trust)

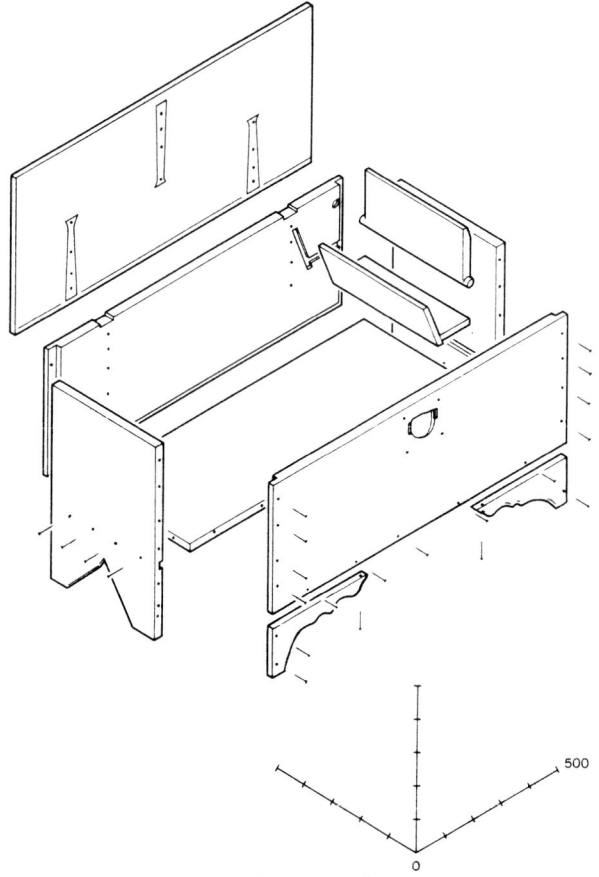

Fig. 13. Exploded view of a subtype 3.2 chest.
(Copyright: The Mary Rose Trust)

COMPONENT	SUBTYPE									
	1.1/1	1.1/2	2.1	2.2	2.3	2.4	3.1	3.2	3.3
Battens	-	-	-	-	2	7★	-	-	1
Brackets (iron)	-	-	-	-	2	-	1	-	-
Handle, block (wood)	-	-	7★	3	-	8	-	-	-
Handle, ring (iron)	-	-	-★	-	2	-	-	-	-
Handle, rope	-	11	1★	-	-	-	-	-	-
Hinge, split ring	-	-	1★	2	-	7★	-	1	-★
Hinge, strap	-	-	7★	1	2	-★	3	3	2★
Internal partition, lidded	-	-	-	-	-	1★	-	-	-★
Internal partition, unlidded	-	-	1	-	-	-★	-	-	-★
Till, lidded	-	-	-	-	2	6★	1	3	2★
Till, unlidded	-	-	-	-	2	-★	-	-	-★
Total chests, by subtype	8	11	9	3	2	8	3	4	3

Fig. 15. Analysis of components (in addition to carcass) used in construction of chest subtypes. * indicates that information is not available for every subtype example because of the incompleteness of some chests.
(Copyright: The Mary Rose Trust)

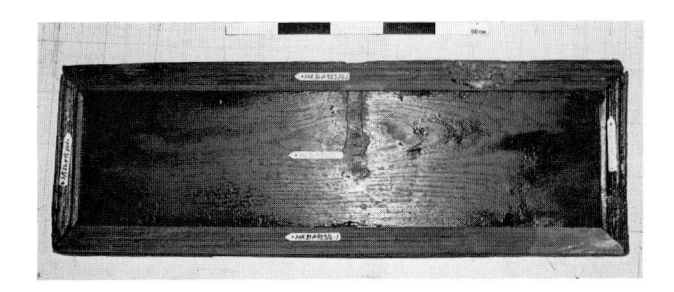

Fig. 16. Lid of a chest with decorative mouldings.
(Copyright: The Mary Rose Trust)

regularly spaced points on the circumference. In some instances this was a solitary design; in others it was repeated with overlapping circles to cause petals of one 'flower' to partially form the petals of the adjacent one in the pattern. With the exception of the back and the portion of the legs beneath the base, the outside of a small *type 3* chest is covered with a scored design of diagonal lines within squares (Fig.14). All of the incised/scored decoration is fairly crude in application, and stops clear of construction lines, suggesting that it was applied to the completed chest.

Other chests bear well-executed, carved decoration. Some lids have scallops or multiple straight lines applied to the edges. A type 2 oak chest has a beautifully carved front (Colour Plate 2B) with an inverted shield (its origins are unknown), beneath the rebate for the lockplate. To either side of the shield are fourteen vertical channels, each with a circular depression above and below. In order to explain the apparent inversion of the shield, it has been suggested that this was a reused panel, with the blank space which was originally beneath the shield now filled by the lock rebate. However, as there are no unnecessary nail holes and the carved decoration leaves well-proportioned margins around the panel, it seems unlikely that it has been reduced in size.

Three chests, all *type 3*, feature components which are purely aesthetic, serving no obvious functional or constructional purpose. Two examples have decorative mouldings dowelled around the edges of the lid (Fig.16). The third chest is fitted with shaped wooden spandrels in order to enhance its finished appearance (Colour Plate 2A).

CONTENTS AND OWNERSHIP

When complete/almost complete chests were discovered and excavated, they were allocated a unique artefact identity number, in common with all artefacts. Each chest was also given a feature number, and the sediment within was given a context number. Consequently, the record card for any artefact excavated from within a chest, or in the case of those badly damaged, any artefacts in close association with a chest were cross-referenced with the appropriate chest feature and context number.

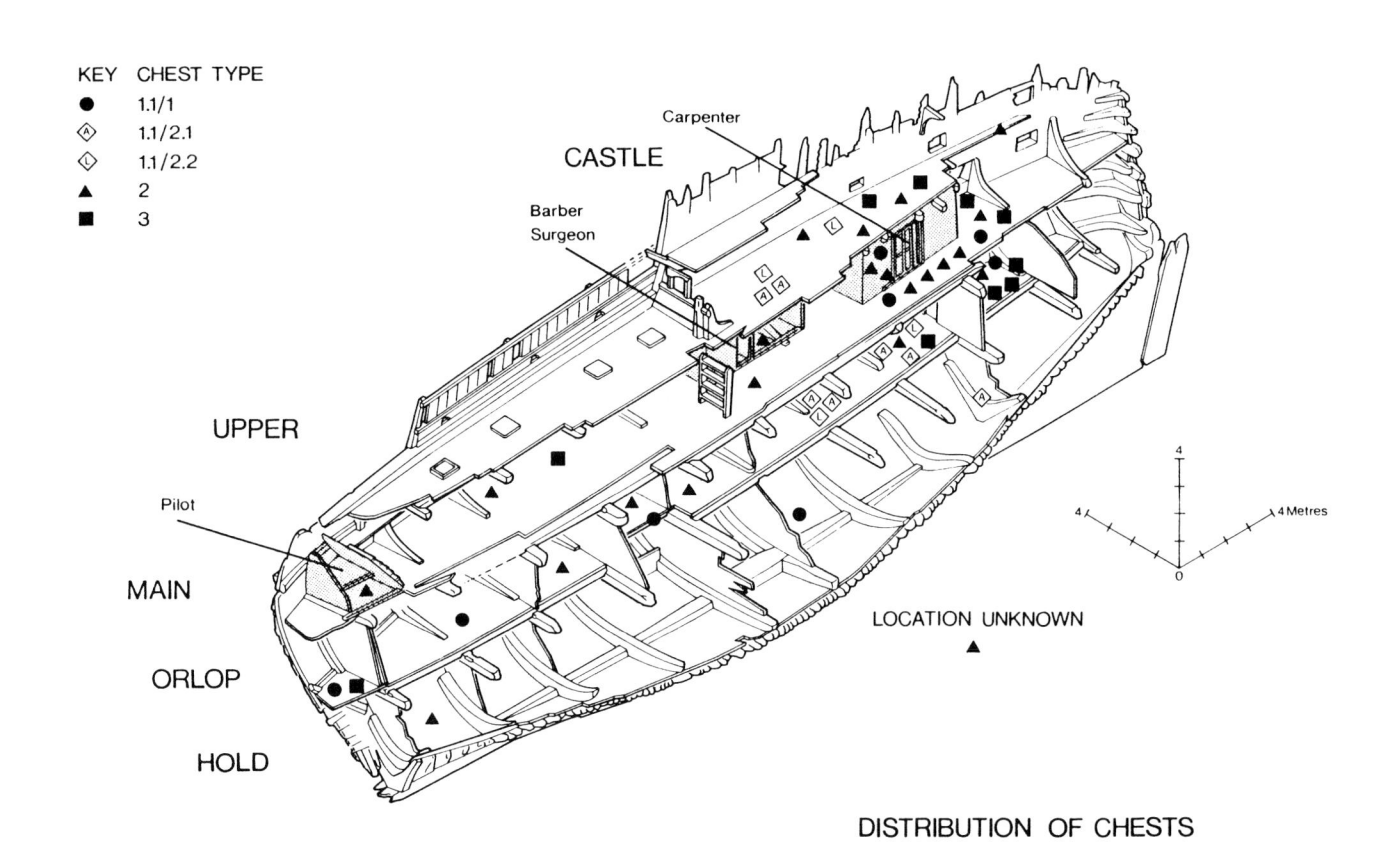

Fig. 17. Isometric of surviving Mary Rose *structure showing excavated position of chests.* (Copyright: The Mary Rose Trust)

Contents type 1

Only three of the eight *subtype 1.1/1* lidless chests (Fig.4) were found with assignable contents, because the other five were in a very poor and damaged condition. Two of the three were stowed on the main deck, one outside and one inside the carpenter's cabin (Fig.17). The contents of each had formed a mass of concretion as a result of the corrosion of metal components of various tools stored within both chests. Off-cuts of oak, fragments of lead sheet, lead ingots, rulers, planes, a tinder box, knives, numerous ash tool handles and a possible pick (Fig.18) were stowed in the chest situated inside the cabin. Rebate-, moulding-, jointing- and trying- planes, a caulking mallet, axes, ash tool handles and another tinder box were contained in the chest found outside. The third *subtype 1.1/1* chest with contents was situated on the orlop deck toward the stern. It was by no means full, but contents included a number of spiles and shives, a trencher and a bowl. Any items within a *subtype 1.1/1* were openly accessible to any member of the crew. The chests were not fitted with handles, suggesting that they were not designed for transportation and that once in position, there they remained.

It would seem possible that these chests were brought on board as empty store chests for unspecified use, and were simply convenient receptacles utilised to keep the ship tidy, stowing tools, equipment or materials. The chest depicted in a line drawing of a 16th-century tailor's shop (under the table) would seem to serve a similar function (Fig.19).

Ten of the eleven 'crate-like' *(subtype 1.1/2*, Fig.5) chests were stowed on either the upper or orlop decks toward the stern. The eleventh was found in the hold (Fig.17), but it is possible that it was originally stowed on the orlop deck and fell during the gradual collapse of the ship's structure.

Of the seven smaller chests (*subtype 1.1/2.1*), five were discovered with some contents *in situ*; all were arrows, a number of which appeared to have been tied with thin cord into sheaves of twenty-four. One apparently full chest exca-

Fig. 19. Line drawing 'The Tailor', after Jost Amman 1568.
(Copyright: The Mary Rose Trust)

vated from the upper deck in 1980 yielded 936 arrows which would equate to thirty-nine sheaves. Made of poplar, beech, ash and hazel, the arrows averaged 800 mm in length and were packed with two sheaves along the length of the chest, with the metal tips of the arrows meeting at the centre (Fig.20). It would seem likely that the two empty chests of the same dimensions also originally contained arrows. The total arrows

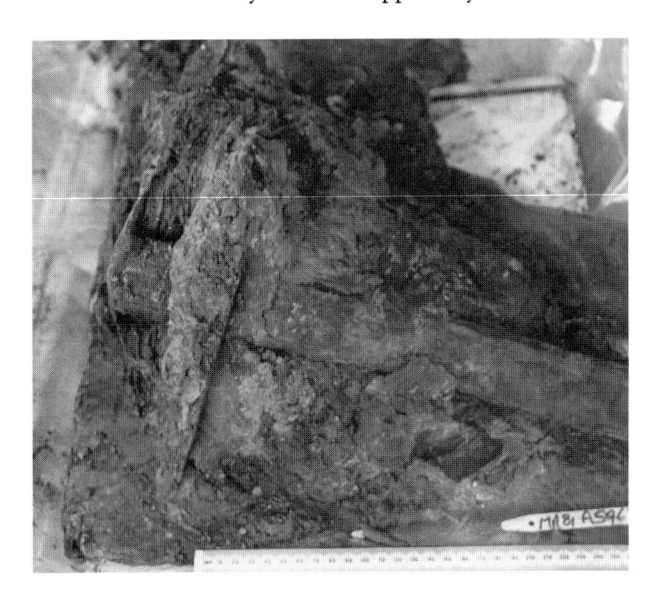

Fig. 18. The head of a pick just visible in the concreted contents of a chest.
(Copyright: The Mary Rose Trust)

Fig. 20. Stored arrows in a chest. The area of dark staining was caused by the degraded iron arrow tips. (Copyright: The Mary Rose Trust)

supplied in seven chests would total approximately 6,552, and almost 4,000 arrows were actually recovered during excavation.

Three of the four larger chests (*subtype 1.1/2.2*) had some contents *in situ*, all of which were yew longbows, averaging 1,982 mm in length. One full chest containing fifty longbows was stowed on the orlop deck, and was raised intact, facilitating excavation on the deck of *Sleipner* (Fig.21). If all four chests were originally full, they would have supplied a total of 200 bows. One hundred and thirty-seven complete and a number of bow fragments were recovered, accounting for 172 of that number. The last inventory for the *Mary Rose* (Anthony Roll 1546) lists 250 bows.

The uniform manufacture in two sizes of these 'crate-like' chests (not totally dissimilar in appearance to ammunition crates still used by the armed services today) suggests that they were perhaps standard government issue supplied from the Tower of London. Their form and dimensions were directly related to the contents, either longbows or arrows, required for supply, transportation and storage.

Contents types 2 & 3

Sixty-eight percent of *type 2* and 60% of *type 3* chests were found with contents, providing twenty-one sub-assemblages for comparison. In contrast to the *type 1* chests, there was no absolute consistency in the kinds of objects stored. This suggests that they were individually owned, storing personal and/or professional possessions.

Only three cabins were located in the surviving portion of the *Mary Rose* hull, all being situated on the main deck (Fig.17). The rôles of those who used them have been suggested by the artefacts found inside each cabin, and they have been identified as belonging to the pilot, barber surgeon and carpenter. A fine example of a dovetailed chest (*subtype 2.4*) was found within each of the cabins; in addition one *subtype 1.1/1* and one *subtype 2.1* were stowed in the carpenter's cabin.

The barber surgeon's chest (Fig.10) has been on public display in the *Mary Rose* Exhibition since 1984 (Fig.22). Made of walnut, with elm handles and beech battens, it contained approximately sixty items, including turned poplar ointment canisters, spatulas made of pine for spreading the ointment, Raeren stoneware medicine bottles with cork stoppers (Colour Plate 2D), a fragmentary glass bottle, a pear-shaped bottle made of cherry or maple with a hole through the centre of its teat-shaped removable top (virtually identical to an early 17th-century pewter feeding bottle in the Museum of London collections; Hornsby *et al* 1989, 76), the fragile remains of what may be a trepan, a pewter canister (others were found in the cabin), a brass syringe and wooden bowls and handles for surgical instruments. All of the items found stored within the chest and the majority of objects within the cabin itself appear to be tools of the barber surgeon's trade, rather than items for his own personal use. However, it would seem likely that this 'medical kit' belonged to him personally, and that he would have been required to provide his own equipment for use on whichever ship he was serving.

In contrast, an elm dovetailed chest situated in the pilot's cabin contained mainly personal items: a decorated leather pouch, a carved boxwood knife sheath, a set of typologically identical copper alloy aiglets and remnants of very degraded textile, suggesting clothing of some kind. A gimballed com-

Fig. 21. A chest containing longbows was raised intact and the contents were excavated on the deck of Sleipner. *(Copyright: The Mary Rose Trust)*

Fig. 22. The barber surgeon's chest and equipment on display in the Mary Rose *Exhibition. (Copyright: The Mary Rose Trust)*

pass (Colour Plate 2C) was the only item of navigational equipment found inside, but nearby was a pine plotting board and two pairs of dividers with their ash wood case, which may well have been stored safely within the chest when not in use.

Valuable and highly regarded items were contained in the walnut dovetailed chest situated inside the carpenter's cabin, suggesting a literate owner of some status and wealth: four pewter plates, a leather book cover, a decorated pouch, silver coins, silver rings and a sundial in a leather case (the only one of its kind recovered from the ship). Three small lead weights, a long chalk line reel, and two ash handles thought to be gimlets were the only items of carpentry equipment stored inside.

Two other chests were also stowed in the carpenter's cabin: one *subtype 1.1/1,* whose contents have already been discussed, and an elm *subtype 2.1* chest used mainly to store clothing (indicated by the large amount of degraded textile identified in sediment samples, as were small amounts of braid, thread and aiglets). Two whetstones and a small knife handle completed the contents.

In addition to those found in the three cabins, *type 2* and *3* chests were found on the upper, main and orlop decks, the majority being stowed toward the stern (Fig.17).

A damaged chest, recovered from the upper deck in the aftercastle area, contained small lead weights, another gimballed compass and two pairs of copper alloy dividers amongst its contents, suggesting the presence of another pilot on board. Alternatively, perhaps the same pilot owned both chests, one stowed in his cabin and the second used as a 'duty' chest for safekeeping of items in constant use.

Silver items – coins, rings, a pendant (Fig.23) and a call on a chain – were among valuable items stored in the *type 2.1* oak chest with a carved front (Colour Plate 2B) found outside the carpenter's cabin. An engraved copper capped knife handle, stylistically Flemish in origin, was one of only two such knife handles recovered. A kidney dagger with two by-knives was the only example of the sixty-five daggers recovered, found stored in a chest (its handle the only one to be made of *pomoideae,* the majority being manufactured from boxwood). A pair of shoes and a leather book cover, six bone dice, two whetstones, two thimble rings, a lead weight and tool handles were also among the contents. The owner of all these objects would seem to be a literate man of some wealth, and the presence of copper alloy priming wire (one of only four recovered) and a carved linstock suggest that he might have been a master gunner.

Discovery of what appears to be a personal 'grooming kit' comprising of a five piece bone manicure set (Fig.24), comb, fragments which may be a mirror, a handle thought to be for a shaving brush, razor and whetstone, presents a picture of a man fastidious with regard to his personal hygiene and appearance. The razor was one of only two which were not found in the barber surgeon's chest or cabin. The 'grooming kit' along with a leather-covered tool holder, tool handles and a leather flask were found stored inside a simple *type 2.1* chest, the only example to be fitted with rope handles which was also stowed in the area outside of the carpenter's cabin.

The equipment necessary for an individual to catch fresh fish (possibly to supplement rations on a long voyage) was found in an elm *type 2.2* chest found near the barber surgeon's cabin. Handlines, cork and willow floats, a disgorger, a single-handled ceramic pot with a pouring lip, a wooden bowl, a leather flask, knives and wood knife sheaths were all stored inside.

The only *type 2* or *3* chests that are similar in both construction and dimensions are the two pine *type 2.3* chests. Both were stowed on the orlop deck, one (with the false base to its lidded till: Fig.9) stowed toward the bow, the other toward the stern, and although their contents were not identical, they were not dissimilar. Both contained degraded textile (presumably clothing), remains of a sword and leather scabbard, bone dice

Fig. 23. A silver pendant concreted to silver rings, which may have belonged to a Master Gunner. (Copyright: The Mary Rose Trust)

Fig. 24. A bone manicure set. (Copyright: The Mary Rose Trust)

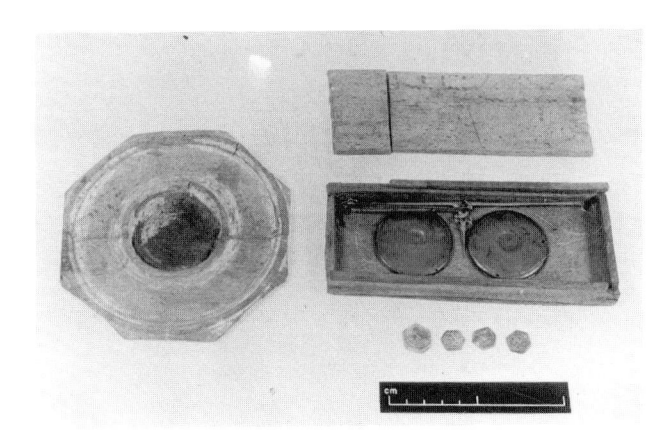

Fig. 25. Apothecary's balance, case, weights and an unidentified object found stored together in a chest. (Copyright: The Mary Rose Trust)

and beads. In addition, an unfinished shot mould, four boxwood combs and a leather comb case were in the chest from the bow, and a pair of decoratively slashed shoes in the chest toward the stern. The similarity of the contents together with the form of the chests suggest that they may have belonged to two individuals with the same status in the ships hierarchy, storing clothing and equipment appropriate to their position.

Several of the items found inside a *type 3.1* poplar chest stowed on the upper deck toward the stern suggest that it may have belonged to an apothecary (Fig.25). A small staved container approximately 110 mm tall and 65 mm in diameter showed traces of a white substance, presumably its original contents (analysis has yet to be completed). For weighing of such material, a small rectangular beech wood case with a sliding lid revealed a copper alloy balance, each pan 50 mm in diameter, plus three copper hexagonal weights of approximately 3.5 g and one of 6.8 g. An octagonal plate of beech, with traces what appears to be red paint has no clear purpose, but it may have been some kind of 'mixing' pallet. Two small tool handles made of hazel may have been used for his trade. A leather flask, a pair of square-toed shoes, degraded textile and aiglets completed the contents.

A master gunner may have owned a *type 3.2* oak chest, one of two examples with decorative mouldings affixed to the lid, stowed on the main deck toward the stern. In common with the *type 2* chest also thought to be that of a gunner, it contained a priming wire and carved linstock. However, this gunner owned two books rather than just one and a single pewter plate. Few contents were found as the chest was incomplete, and it is likely that the remainder of the original contents were displaced.

The only examples of handwear recovered from the *Mary Rose* were inside an oak *type 3.3* chest stowed on the orlop deck, toward the stern. Strangely, both are thumbed left-handed leather mittens making their exact purpose unclear, as they are obviously not a pair. Clothing in the form of degraded textile, twenty-six typologically identical aiglets and a square of silk fabric was amongst the contents. Two wicker-covered flasks (one made of glass and one of ceramic) miraculously survived intact. The owner of this chest was able to grind pepper for medicinal purposes or season to his rations, as he was in possession of peppercorns and one of only two peppermills recovered.

A number of chests were found to contain a single pair of shoes. However one individual possessed three spare pairs of the same size, stored in a *type 3.1* oak chest stowed on the main deck toward the bow. One pair was covered in decorative slashes, while the other two pairs were fairly plain. He also owned a silk-lined knitted hat with the appearance of a rimmed flat beret. A pewter flask with a left hand screw thread, a leather book cover and a leather covered balance case were also in the chest. The case was empty, but the recesses inside show that this was for a tiny balance, and the pans would have measured approximately 25 mm in diameter. A copper alloy object, tentatively identified as a candle snuffer, was also present.

The *type 3.2* elm chest with decorative spandrels (Fig. 13 & Colour Plate 2A) was stowed on the orlop deck in the stern. Containing mainly clothing in the form of red degraded textile, wool cord with knotted tassels and copper alloy aiglets, it also stored a large proportion of the total coinage found on the ship. A mineralised lump comprised of at least forty-five silver coins. Seven of the twenty-seven gold coins recovered were also inside this chest, consisting of three angels, a half angel and three half-sovereigns. The gold coins alone would have covered the pay for an ordinary mariner for over a year. The owner of this chest was certainly a well heeled individual or perhaps the ship's purser.

CONCLUSION

There were two classes of items stowed in the chests recovered from the *Mary Rose*. Ship's supplies, in the form of general tools and equipment or munitions, and individually owned valuable professional and personal items.

It would appear that the form of a *type 1* chest was directly related to its function. An open, lidless chest was designed for the storage of necessary materials, tools or equipment, thereby keeping essentials to hand and the ship tidy. The elongated 'crate-like' chests were the purpose-built means of transporting and storing the longbows or arrows supplied directly from the Tower of London.

In contrast to the *type 1* chests, there is no obvious link between form and function in *types 2* and *3*, other than they all appear to have stowed personally owned items. As all of these chests were fitted with locks, the owner could store his belongings and ensure he had sole access by means of a key.

Ordinary mariners and soldiers serving on the *Mary Rose* were likely to only have possessed the clothes they wore, in addition to any meagre items that could be carried about the person. These men would not have needed or afforded to own a chest. Only individuals with wealth and status in the shipboard hierarchy would be likely to own enough items to warrant storage, afford the purchase and transportation of a personal chest, and command the use of limited deck space on board a crowded warship.

Acknowledgements

The other members of the 1990 study team were Clare Venables, Sue George, Simon Ware and Richard Hubbard. Thanks are also due to Sue Bickerton and Glenn McConnachie for the microscopic identification of wood species; Peter Crossman and Richard Hubbard for the preparation of illustrations and photographs used in this paper; and Andy Elkerton for editing this text and for the provision of computerised data, on which the 1990 study was based.

Notes

1. Impregnation with Polyethylene Glycol (PEG) followed by freeze drying.
2. Method also described as 'planked' (Hayward 1977, 22).

References

Gloag, J. 1966 *A Social History of Furniture Design from BC 1300–AD 1960*, Cassell.
Hayward, C. 1977 *English Period Furniture*, Evans.
Hornsby, P.R.G, Weinstein, R. & Homer R.F. 1989 *Pewter. A Celebration of the Craft 1200–1700*, Museum of London.
Knell, D. 1992 *An Encyclopaedia of English Country Furniture*, Barrie and Jenkins.
Rule, M. 1983 *The Mary Rose. The Excavation and Raising of Henry VIII's Flagship* (Second Edition), London.

Manuscript Sources:

Anthony Roll Manuscript 1546 The Pepys Library, Magdalene College, Cambridge.

Part III
An Interdependence of Disciplines

7

Arms and armour from wrecks: an introduction

Ruth R. Brown

INTRODUCTION

This paper is divided into three sections: the first on different types of arms and armour, their dates and the materials they were made from; the second on the contexts in which maritime archaeologists can find them; and finally on approaches to the subject's study. The reader will find a bibliography of recent or useful arms and armour books at the end of the paper.

ARMS AND ARMOUR

Armour

There are three types of armour based on construction: mail, small plates and large plate. Mail is made from metal rings linked together to make shirts or coifs. This was the main type of armour used in the Middle Ages up to the late 14th century, when plate armour became more common. Afterwards, mail was used to make shirts worn under armour or gussets or sleeves of arming doublets. Armour made from small plates was common throughout the medieval and early modern periods. Ordinary soldiers would wear a jack or brigandine, a jacket with small iron plates sewn into a fabric base.

Plate armour developed during the 14th century and reached its apogee in the 15th century, when it clad a knight from head to toe. During the 16th century, it became more specialized, with different armours for war and tournament, three-quarter armours for heavy cavalry, half-armours for infantry and corselets for pikemen. The increasing use of gunpowder did not end immediately the practice of wearing armour, which was made thicker to withstand shot. However, as armour got heavier, soldiers began discarding parts of it. Sir Richard Hawkins on his voyage to the South Seas in 1593 claimed that, although he had obtained light armours for his men, *'they esteemed a pott of wine a better defence than an armour of proof'*. Armour in the 17th century was utilitarian, often mass-made. The cavalry troops who fought in the British Civil Wars preferred a plain breast and back, a gauntlet to protect the hand holding the reins and a helmet which protected the face and neck. Eventually they abandoned armour for leather buff coats.

Armour is made up of many components which reflected changing patterns of warfare and male fashion. Helmets were stuffed with wool, hair, moss or straw to absorb shock and make them more comfortable. Elizabethan breastplates followed the civilian fashions of the day with the peascod belly. The neck was protected by a gorget which was later used on its own as a symbol of command. Gorgets have been recovered from the *Batavia* (1629), while officers' gorgets have been recovered on the Swedish warship *Kronan* (1676) (see this book, Chapter 17, Fig. 5). Other armours protected the arm, hand and legs.

Shields were used for personal defence in the earlier Middle Ages while the 15th century soldiers, particularly archers, and sailors sheltered behind large shields called pavises during battles. Spurs and stirrups, while not much use on board ship, would be needed when it reached port as they are necessary in societies dependent on horse for transport.

Most armour was made from iron or steel. It could be decorated by engraving, etching, embossing or gilding. It was held together by leather straps and buckles, hinges and pins or hooks and eyes, usually made from iron or copper alloy. Armour does not survive well underwater. It is ironic that the leather straps, helmet-linings, brass washers and buckles have a better chance of survival than the armour itself; a few brass links are all that might remain from a mail shirt.

Edged weapons

Medieval swords are quite large, with straight, double-edged blades and simple hilts, often in the shape of a cross. In the 16th century, swords, like armour, went through major changes, and different swords evolved for different uses. Lighter swords which could be worn as part of everyday costume were introduced such as the rapier, which had a long straight blade designed for stabbing rather than slashing and a hilt of a network of bars to protect the hand. A later type was the broad sword with a wide double-edged blade for slashing and a basket-hilt, which by the later 17th century was used mainly by horsemen. An example was discovered on one of the Padre Island wrecks (1554). The small sword, a form of light rapier, was introduced about 1675, and continued in use well into the 19th century. This was worn by gentlemen in town as a fashion accessory until the late 18th century, and naval officers might wear a version of this civilian sword.

The hanger, originally used in hunting, had a short, wide curved blade and became very common on board ship in the 17th and 18th centuries. Being useful in the restricted space on deck, it was widely adopted by naval officers. It was a grander form of the cutlass issued to ships' crew. This had an iron hilt and curved blade, used against personnel and rigging.

In the 17th century, firearms and bayonets were the weapons of the infantry but cavalry were still armed with swords. Official patterns come in surprisingly late in Britain - not until 1788. Until then, cavalry swords were supplied by the colonel of the regiment rather than centrally by the government. Even then, officers had a great deal of lassitude in choosing their own swords. In 1788 official swords were chosen for infantry officers and these were widely copied by officers of the Royal Navy and marines, often decorated with naval motifs.

Swords were made up of several elements. The blade, of iron or steel, could be engraved, gilt or blued. It could be sharpened along one edge or both for slashing or at the point for stabbing. Some had a fuller or central depression to make the blade lighter and more flexible. Hilts were made from a variety of materials. The grip might be of wood, covered with skin and bound with wire, or of expensive materials such as precious metal, porcelain or horn. The guard which protected the hand was usually made of metal such as iron, steel, brass or silver (for an example from the Duart wreck, see this book, Chapter 14, Fig 19). The whole hilt could be of cast metal such as brass, silver or even gold and decorated with gilding, enamelling or precious stones. A sword was usually carried in a scabbard of leather, strengthened with wood and a metal chape, or in a scabbard of metal. These could be suspended from a waistbelt by hangers or from a baldrick worn over the shoulders. Swords like other arms and armour would be decorated with tassels, ribbons or a sword knot.

Sword-making involved several craftsmen. Large-scale blade production was concentrated in a few areas in Europe: Solingen in Germany, Toledo in Spain and in Birmingham in England. Blades were then often sent to local craftsmen to be hilted. The frequent use of hall-marked hilts made by gold- or silversmiths gives a chronology which can then be used to date hilts made of base metals. However, swords were continually being altered. A hilt might be replaced by one in a newer fashion, while blades were easily broken. There were also national styles such as the Scottish basket hilt or the Neapolitan cup-hilt rapier which survived over a long period of time.

The commonest edged weapon was the knife, which was carried for various purposes: eating, working or self-defence. There were specialized fighting knives, such as daggers or dirks. From these developed the bayonet, introduced in the late 17th century. At first it was stuck into the muzzle of infantry musket but this impractical method was replaced by attaching it to the side, enabling infantry to attack cavalry like pikemen. Bayonets, still in their scabbards, were recovered from the site of HMS *Fowey*, lost off Florida in 1748.

Edged weapons do not survive well underwater and the thin steel blades may only be represented as an imprint in concretion. Hilts of materials such as brass, silver, gold or wood might survive as might leather scabbards or their brass or silver chapes and lockets. As with armour, it is the ancillary material, such as the silk and leather hangers and baldricks which can survive better (for an example from a Dutch *tjalk*, see this book, Chapter 13, Fig. 8).

Staff weapons

In the 15th century, infantry were armed with staff weapons, such as bills, halberds, partizans or spontoons. The staff weapon which survived longest in use was the pike. This had a wooden haft of about 16 foot (often ash) and a brass or iron ferrule to stop its end from splintering. The head was of steel or iron - either long and leaf-shaped or short and diamond-shaped - and had long metal cheeks to prevent it being easily sliced off. As an infantry weapon, the pike was replaced by the musket and bayonet in the last quarter of the 17th century. Thereafter in Britain a number of the old pikes in store were cut down for use as boarding pikes and these were still issued to ships in the 19th century. The long wooden hafts are particularly vulnerable to erosion or attack by marine organisms. On the *Batavia*, for example, all that remained of a batch of pikes were the ferrules.

The axe could be used as both tool and weapon. The Royal Navy issued boarding axes with spikes on the back to ships and examples have been found aboard HMS *Fowey*.

Bows and arrows

The earliest projectile weapons were bows. There are two types: the long bow and the crossbow.

The long bow was made from wooden stave of D-shaped cross-section (usually yew, but also ash or elm). It could either be notched or have horn nocks at each end to hold the string. Arrow shafts could be made from many different woods: poplar, willow, ash, elder or hornbeam. The iron heads were made in different shapes, depending on when they were made and for what use. Arrows were kept in quivers ready for use. To prevent chafing on the wrist, the archer wore a brace, usually of leather. There are few undisputed surviving medieval long bows, and the largest surviving collection of archery material must now be that found on the *Mary Rose* (1545).

The crossbow was a more complicated weapon. It had a shorter bow and a central tiller. The bow could be made of wood, steel or from composite materials, such as horn and wood glued together, while the tiller could be made of wood such as cherry. Some crossbows were elaborately inlaid with horn or bone. Strings were made from linen, wool or sinew. The bow was shot by a simple lock, by which a nut held the string in place when spanned, which was released by pressing a trigger or lever. It needed some help to span it (that is in the position to shoot); such as belt and hook, the goatsfoot lever, the windlass or cranequin. Mechanisms of 16th-century date were more complicated. Unlike longbows, a number of medieval crossbows have survived. The crossbow shot bolts or quarrels, shorter and thicker than an arrow with a stubby iron head. The shaft was often of oak or ash.

Bows were enormously powerful weapons in the medieval period, certainly more so than the first firearms; arrows and bolts could penetrate armour. They continued to be used for warfare on land and at sea well into the 16th century. A crossbow could shoot one bolt per minute a range of 75 m, while longbows could shoot a fearsome six arrows per minute more that 200 m, feats which early firearms could not emulate. Bows could also shoot fire-arrows, particularly feared at sea. Both types of bows were superseded for war in the course of the second half of the 16th century, although they continued in use for sport and the hunt.

Documentary evidence shows that the Spaniards used crossbows in their conquest of America, and they certainly have been found on early wrecks in the New World, at Padre Island (1554) and on the Molasses Reef (c.1500–1550). Crossbow parts have also been found on the Villefranche wreck, thought to be a Genoese ship lost in the second decade of the 16th century.

The wooden arrow and bolt shafts, long bow staves, and crossbow tillers can survive underwater in the right conditions, as can leather accessories such as bracers and quivers; even bow strings have been recovered from the Padre Island site. However the horn nocks, nuts, iron heads and composite or steel bows are more vulnerable to decay.

Handguns

Gunpowder was first used in Europe about 1300, although handguns were not common until later in the 14th century. These early examples were less powerful than the bow because the powder was of poor quality and the weapons were clumsy to use since the barrels of these early guns, or hackbuts as they are often known, were made of cast bronze or very thick iron. It was not until lighter guns with reliable actions and good quality powder came into use that guns finally replaced virtually every other type of weapon in warfare.

Handguns comprise three main parts: the lock, the stock and the barrel. The lock is the 'action'; in other words, what shoots the gun. The earliest lock was a simple mechanism worked by pressing a lever which dipped a lighted match into powder. This developed into the matchlock, which was in use from about the mid-16th century until about 1700. It was simple to make and repair, but had disadvantages, being difficult to use on horseback or in the rain. The glowing match was dangerous around gunpowder and at night could gave away troop movements. Its main accessory was match - cord soaked in saltpetre. The demand for match was large: a garrison of 1,500 men besieged in Lyme went through five hundredweight a day during the 1640s.

The wheellock appeared earlier in the 16th century. It was a complicated mechanism, worked by using a key to wind up a wheel. When released, the wheel would whirr round and strike a piece of pyrites, thereby causing sparks to shower onto powder in the pan and fire the gun. It was used for prestigious weapons such as sporting guns or cavalry arms. The complicated working mechanism, made from many small parts, made it expensive to make, and it frequently went wrong and was difficult for a non-specialist to repair. Moreover, if the key was dropped or lost, the gun was useless. The wheellock was still used on sporting weapons in central Europe after it had been superceded by the flintlock on military guns. Its main accessory was the key or spanner.

The snaphance gun first appeared in the late 16th century and an improved version, the flintlock, appeared early in the 17th century. The flintlock was not as complicated or as expensive as the wheellock, nor did it have the drawbacks of the matchlock. It used flint to strike a steel to ignite the powder. It was first used on pistols and carbines, and during in the last years of the 17th century it replaced the matchlock on muskets. The flintlock was the commonest lock on all forms of handguns in the 18th century. Its main accessory was flint.

The size of the stock which holds the barrel and lock together, and the size of the barrel itself dictate the type of gun and its use. Barrel size was called calibre or bore, and was measured by the number of lead balls in a pound it fired. The higher the number the smaller the calibre; for example a gun of 24 calibre (each shot weight 1/24 pound) was smaller than a 12 calibre gun where the balls weigt 1/12 pound. Guns of different sizes developed for specific purposes. The smallest gun, needing only one hand to fire, is the pistol, which first appeared in the 16th century and was useful in a restricted space, such as on horseback or on deck or for personal defence (for an example from the Duart wreck, see this book, Chapter 14, Fig. 15). As it could be easily concealed, it was used in criminal activities. The barrel was usually between 6 and 18 inches with a calibre of about 1/2 inch or 24 bore. Pistols were often made in pairs and kept in holsters or fitted cases. A specialized form of pistol was the revolver, which contained a revolving magazine, allowing more than one shot to be fired without reloading. Although examples have survived from earlier times, it did not become common until Colt manufactured large numbers in the mid-19th century.

The arquebus, later called a carbine, had a barrel of about 18 to 30 inches with a calibre of about 2/3 to 3/4 of an inch, i.e. about 16 bore. In the 16th century this was a weapon for light infantry, but later the carbine was also used by troops who fought in a restricted space such as marines on board ship or dragoons on horseback.

The musket was the largest gun and fired the heaviest bullet. Between the late 16th century and the late 17th century it was so heavy that it was supported on a musket rest. Later the barrel was reduced from over five foot to less than four foot, making it lighter and more manageable. The calibre was about 1 inch, later reduced to about 3/4 inch, i.e. 12

bore. It remained the main infantry weapon until the mid-19th century when it was replaced by the rifled musket.

The musketoon or blunderbuss was a wide-mouthed short-barrelled gun, firing grape-shot. It was used on board ships and on coaches. It often had a brass barrel.

Most guns of this period were smoothbore, meaning the inside of the barrel is smooth. However, the inside of a barrel can be rifled, that is grooved to give the ball a spin, making it fly further and straighter. Early 16th-century guns with rifling show that it was introduced early in the development of firearms. It was used for mainly for sporting guns until the 18th century when military rifles were made for companies of sharpshooters or snipers. Rifles needed patchboxes, often set into the butt, to take the cloth patch in which the ball was wrapped. A German hunting rifle with a patch box was recovered from the *Vasa* (1628) and another a patch box was found on the *Batavia* (1629). Some later rifles were also breechloading (i.e. they were loaded at the back of the barrel), but this did not become common until the 19th century except for expensive sporting guns. Muzzleloaders need a rammer and worm to bring the charge home and clean it afterwards. Rammers are usually of wood or steel and the worm of iron.

At this period guns normally fired lead balls. These could be pre-cast and stored in barrels or could be cast as needed from lead ingots using moulds. A form of linked musket shot has been discovered on a number of ships.

For long term storage gunpowder was normally kept in barrels, but once in use, there were a variety of different containers. These include larger and smaller powder flasks, often made from horn, bandoliers, which had a dozen musket charges ready for use in lead bottles and later cartridge cases which held ball and charge together in paper cartridges.

Firearms were manufactured on a commercial scale in Liège and the Dutch Netherlands, Germany (first in Nuremburg, then in Suhl) and later in England in London and Birmingham. However, gunmaking was carried out on two levels. Most small towns had their own gunsmith who would make guns to order from pre-made components. The locks were made of forged steel and barrels usually of iron. Stocks are normally made of wood - walnut was considered the most suitable - but other materials such as ivory, brass or even iron could be used. The stocks can be carved or engraved, or have bone, horn or metal plaques or silver wire inset. Fittings include sideplate, buttplate, escutcheon plates, or rammer pipes made from brass, silver or iron.

Underwater any iron work, including barrel and lock, corrode, leaving the stock and any brass fittings. However, the woodwork may be sufficiently preserved to indicate a date, and the shape of the lock cut-out may be used to identify the type of action. Often only the butt, the thickest part of the stock, remains.

Artillery

Little is known of the first cannon to be used on ships. They were probably small breech-loaders (that is, they were loaded at the rear). The two most common breech-loaders are a tube, usually of wrought iron and separate chambers on a wooden bed, in use until the early 17th century at least (for an early 16th-century example, see this book, Chapter 5, Figs 3 and 4) and a smaller gun of wrought iron or bronze on a swivel with a saddle to hold the chamber, in use from the mid-16th to the early 18th century (for an example from *La Trinidad Valencera*, see this book Chapter 1, Fig. 8).

The shape now recognized as a muzzle-loading gun evolved in the late 15th century and was in use up to the mid-19th century. This was first made of brass and later of cast iron. Early examples can be very elaborate, but they became increasingly utilitarian as time passed (for an example from the *Kronan*, see this book Chapter 17, Fig.8; from a Dutch *tjalk* see Chapter 13, Fig. 1). At first guns were given names such as culverin, saker or fowler but the practice of calling the gun by the weight of shot it fired spread in the 17th century. Muzzle-loaders range from the largest - 42 pounder - down to the smallest − 1/2 pounder.

A special muzzle-loader was the carronade, a short fat gun invented in the 1770s and manufactured by the Carron Company of Scotland. It was first used by merchant ships but within a few years was adopted by the Royal Navy and later copied by other governments. Some foreign powers used brass carronades. Within a few years a sort of bastard carronade resembling a long cigar was being used by merchant shipping. Because its date of introduction is known, the carronade is a useful indicator of date. Other types of short guns were mortars which were mounted in bomb vessels or used in sieges to throw hollow shells inside towns or shore batteries, and howitzers, used on the battlefield.

Before the late 15th century, ships carried few guns, but by the early 16th century, great warships carried a large number of small calibre guns. By the mid-16th century ships such as the *Mary Rose* carried large and small wrought-iron breech-loaders and large brass muzzle-loaders. In the second half of the 16th century cast-iron muzzle-loading guns were introduced. From this period until the early 18th century, when small wrought-iron breech-loaders were finally replaced by cast-iron swivel guns, ships could have a mixture of brass, wrought- or cast-iron guns, either muzzle-loading or breech-loading. The *Mauritius* (1609) carried brass, wrought- and cast-iron guns from the Netherlands, England and Portugal when she was wrecked. During the 17th and 18th centuries the proportion of cast-iron to bronze guns increased on naval ships. Although bronze had a better reputation than cast iron, it was also more expensive. This practice was well advanced in Britain, as she had direct access to cast-iron guns but other navies took longer to make this change. Bronze guns were made in foundries all over Europe but only a few countries such as Denmark or France were able to make cast-iron guns for themselves, while Britain and Sweden were the only two countries able to export cast-iron guns in large numbers. Thus the presence of English or Swedish cannon does not help to identify the nationality of a ship.

Quite small merchant ships would be armed, particularly in times of war; the owners could hire guns for a specific voyage. The small breechloaders were still used on these ships long after these guns had been abandoned by state navies. Wrought-iron guns survived longest in societies where they were unable to cast iron. For example, the merchant ship lost off Tal-y-bont, Cardigan Bay, West Wales, was armed with wrought-iron guns and small cast-iron guns, probably came from North Italy, where the manufacture of such guns as late as 1700 is detailed in contemporary manuscripts.

Shot comes in different shapes and materials, and a ship would normally carry more than one type to be used against crew, rigging or hull. Iron was used to make solid round shot, the commonest type, bar shot, expanding shot, incendiary shot and hollow shells, filled with explosive or small shot. Small guns could shoot lead balls and wrought-iron guns fired stone shot. Lanthorn or cannister shot were tubes filled with broken flints and diced shot was made from iron cubes wrapped or cast within lead (for example from the *Mary Rose*, see this book, Chapter 4, Fig. 9). The gunner would use a shot gauge or gunner's rule to make sure the right shot went with the right gun (for example from *La Trinidad Valencera*, see this book Chapter 1, Fig. 7).

Powder was stored in barrels, flasks and cartridge charges. Loading and firing guns required more tools: scoops, rammers, worms and prickers. Guns were fired by linstocks, and later by portfires or gunlocks. Guns were often loaded ready for action, then sealed with a tampion at the muzzle and a lead apron over the vent.

Gun-carriages have been surprisingly little studied - early salvage having concentrated on lifting guns which were more valuable. Work is only now being focused on carriages, such as Colin Martin's recent investigations on the siege train on *La Trinidad Valencera* (1588) and on the rôle of gun-carriages in the defeat of the Spanish Armada. Other surviving carriages presently under study are from the *Mary Rose* and the *Vasa*.

Brass and wrought-iron guns and stone shot survive very well under water; cast iron however often deteriorates and needs treatment if raised. Carriage survival can be fragmentary, although in the right conditions preservation can be almost complete.

Incendiary devices

It has already been stated that fire-arrows and shells can be shot from bows and guns. Other such weapons include grenades (hollow shells usually made of iron, though they can be made of pottery or even glass). They were filled with powder and thrown by hand or fired from guns (for an example from *La Trinidad Valencera*, see this book Chapter 1, Fig. 9). Despite being among the most common finds on ships they are under-represented in the literature.

An important weapon in siege warfare was the petard: a brass pot filled with powder and attached to a gate to make a breech in fortifications. One has been found on the wreck of the *Mauritius* (1609) while records of the English East India Company show that petards were used at sea.

One last category is the harpoon, used mainly in whaling. Examples of these have been found on the Highborn Cay wreck (16th-century).

Contexts

It should be borne in mind that in the past arms and armour were a normal part of everyday life, unlike today where weapons are either used by sportsmen, armed services or criminals. Gentlemen would carry swords as part of their city clothes and take pistols on journeys, while workmen habitually carried a knife or dagger as a tool and weapon. Duelling, although frowned on by some, was ingrained in certain parts of society.

Ships' defence (ship and crew); troops

The most obvious use for armaments on board is for defence and attack of the ship itself. Medieval illustrations show ships with soldiers wearing armour, jacks and helmets shooting cannon, long bows, crossbows, and hiding behind shields and pavises. In practice it is often difficult to distinguish between soldiers, sailors and gunners and therefore to determine who was armed with what. The *Mary Rose* had soldiers and sailors on board, while the Spanish Armada was a floating army, rather than what we think of today as a fleet. The *Vasa* had 133 crew to sail the ship and about 300 soldiers and gunners aboard when she went down. The *Amsterdam* (1749) was carrying Dutch soldiers to man the VOC forts in the east. In the 18th century ships had sailors, gunners and marines attached, as well as troops being carried to conflicts or garrison duty abroad.

Some weapons were used mainly on board ship, such as boarding axes, pikes, cutlasses, musketoons and most artillery. The seven-barrelled nock gun was invented in the 1780s specifically for men in fighting tops to clear enemy marksmen. However, there are differences in firearms issued for land and sea service. In Britain, for example, the Board of Ordnance did not see the point of spending a lot of money on weapons whose use would be occasional, and consequently sea-service firearms were made as cheaply as possible, often from old parts or obsolete land patterns. Sea-Service muskets had flat buttplates so that they could stand in a rack. Early examples were not intended to take bayonets. Barrels were usually blackened in order to preserve them against rust; for the same reason, wooden rammers rather than steel were used. Sea service pistols differed from cavalry pistols, as they had wooden rammers and belt hooks and marines were issued with shorter muskets. The brass fittings might have specific naval marks such QD for quarter deck.

Even quite small ships would carry some kind of arms for self-defence, particularly in time of war. Pirates were always a threat and, of course, pirates themselves would be armed. Merchant ships could hire guns and firearms for specific voyages, while owners of large fleets often had a pool of weapons which they could issue to ships as needed.

Ships might carry service arms even when there were no troops on board, for armies, garrisons or colonists overseas.

The *Machaut* (1760) was carrying munitions to the French colonists of Quebec. This would determine the type of weapons being sent; Britain sent old-fashioned weapons to Virginia because the colonists there faced an enemy using low technology. Even old armour was sent there in the early 18th century. If, on the other hand, they were facing a strong European power, more up-to-date weapons would be issued.

Crew and passengers' property

Passengers on their way to a new life in the colonies might be carrying civilian arms, particularly firearms for self-defence and hunting. Crews and officers might have their own swords or firearms which were not officially issued.

Trophies of war; souvenirs

Captured arms could be used either for war or for display as a trophy. French cannon captured from Vigo were found aboard the *Association* (1707). During the Napoleonic wars the British Board of Ordnance would regularly buy weapons from captured ships for reuse. On a more personal scale an officer might wear a sword surrendered by an enemy officer while a sailor or soldier might have a pistol taken as a souvenir of action or even just from a foreign bazaar. Foreign weapons have been collected as curiosities or souvenirs as long as people have travelled.

Export

From an early date arms and armour production was concentrated in certain areas. In the Middle Ages Milan had first been a centre for the production of mail and then for plate armour. Bow staves for England were imported from Switzerland, the Rhine valley and Italy. In the 17th century, Dutch and Flemish firearms were in demand all over Europe. In the 18th century cast-iron cannon were exported from Britain and Sweden. Walsall, near Birmingham (English Midlands) was internationally famous for its production of spurs. The English East India Company imported saltpetre, used in the manufacture of gunpowder, from India.

Henry VIII was a purchaser on a grand scale. Between 1510 and 1513 he imported 40,000 yew staves from the Veneto and 7,000 armours from Florence and Milan. Some twenty-five years later he bought armours from Cologne and Antwerp. The musket fragments from the *Mary Rose* may be part of a consignment of guns ordered by the king from North Italy. It is interesting to reflect where all the arms and armour on the *Mary Rose* were actually manufactured.

There was also an export trade in parts; sword blades from Solingen, Klingthal and Wupperthal in Germany, from Toledo in Spain, and from Sheffield and Birmingham were sent abroad to be hilted in local styles. Gun barrels were exported from Spain to other countries for fitting up. In The Netherlands in the 18th century sword hilts made in Japan were in demand while in England there was a similar fashion for Indian swords. European blades were taken east for decorating, and then reimported into Europe, so one weapon might possess elements made over a long period of time and place.

Most countries had their own arsenals for casting bronze guns. In such cases it was the gunfounders rather than the guns who were itinerant; Flemish, Dutch and Swiss founders, in particular, were in demand across Europe. An exception was the Portuguese foundry established in Macao to take advantage of the cheap labour and copper from Japan and iron from India, run for many years by the Boccaro family. Examples being brought from Macao to Portugal were found on the *Sacramento* lost off South Africa in 1647.

Gifts

Arms and armour were frequently exchanged as gifts between heads of states. James VI and I was sent armours by the Shogun of Japan and a few years later the English East India Company sent a great bombard to a Sumatran potentate.

Smuggling and gun-running

Governments were always keen to control the export of arms and armour and deprive potential enemies of the most advanced weaponry. However, then as now, manufacturers could get round regulations in both legal and illegal ways. Such business is by its nature difficult to estimate but the number of times that the English government repeated its prohibition on the export of cast-iron guns in the late 16th and early 17th century show that it existed. Similar restrictions on trade occurred during the Napoleonic wars. Cannon and firearms were the usual objects of this trade.

Ballast

Finally guns, particularly old broken cannon and shot, were carried as ballast.

DISCUSSION

Of course, one weapon can fall into more than one category. To illustrate the problems, I will discuss two different wrecks.

The second Anholt find was discovered off Denmark shortly before the outbreak of the Second World War. On the basis of a lead seal, it was identified as a merchant ship lost in the late 16th century while carrying a cargo of iron-related items from England: iron bars, casks of steel and cast-iron guns lashed down and covered in canvas. However, the ship itself was armed with six breechloading wrought-iron guns. Moreover a colleague has recently re-identified the seal as belonging to the Commonwealth period (1649–1660) and discovered a parallel from excavations in the New World.[1] This illustrates the difficulties in trying to build a chronology of gun development dependent on the belief that wrought-iron breech-loaders became obsolete with the introduction of cast-iron guns. Wrought-iron breech-loaders continued to fulfil different purposes, either in a society in which it was still cheaper or easier to produce wrought-iron, or where breech-loading was still favoured, possibly by sailors themselves, or where wrought-iron breech-loaders and cast-iron muzzle-loaders had different but complementary uses.

The English East Indiamen, *Doddington*, lost off South Africa in 1755 *en route* to India, was rediscovered in the 1970s. By correlating the finds with the archives, we get a complicated picture. She carried forty iron guns, of which twenty-six were the ship's armament, the responsibility of the shipowners, and fourteen were being shipped, along with iron carriage wheels, to the Company forces in India. She also carried four brass guns and howitzers and carriages for the British government. There were small arms for the ship's crew, again provided by the shipowners, as well as carbines for 100 men of the Royal Regiment of Artillery, government issue. The 100 EIC soldiers were armed with muskets provided by the Company. Finally, there were trading guns to the value of £50 allowed to the captain to exchange for supplies at Madagascar. This excludes any personnel property or trading goods belonging to the crew or passengers. Moreover, in times of war, it was custom on the East Indiamen for crew, troops, and passengers to exercise the great guns and small arms, so that a number of these weapons would be in regular use during the voyage.

Study of arms and armour

The study of arms and armour has a long pedigree. Early antiquaries such as Sir Walter Scott collected pieces for their age, craftmanship or famous associations, while a few made more specialized collections. Scholarly books and articles in the 19th century concentrated on medieval arms and armour. The first serious study of medieval artillery was written by the future emperor Napoleon III while a prisoner in France. There has been increased interest during the 20th century in firearms, and much has been published on service guns and swords. More recently, interest in historical re-enactment has lead to the study of 16th- and 17th-century munition arms and armour, while nautical archaeology has been the main fillip to the research in artillery.

Arms and armour forms an international field of research. Most European countries have specialist and popular journals and related societies, and many have at least one museum dedicated to the subject, often based on their Royal Armoury or armed services. However there are drawbacks to using these collections: they are heavily biased towards fine armours, often with royal connections, certainly of higher quality than those normally found on wrecks. Items may be preserved because they are atypical or unusual, while the arms of the common soldier have often perished because they were not thought worthy of preservation. An example of this is the Almayne rivet, a type of armour which Henry VIII bought in thousands, but of which few have survived. Some parts of arms and armour have been lost: 18th-century muskets no longer have their slings, bayonets have lost their scabbards, while the flints and ammunition are rarely preserved. Therefore, while museums have an important part to play, they must be used with caution. By way of illustration three different collections which include munition arms and armour have been selected.

The first is the Royal Armouries, whose collections are now located in three centres: the Tower of London; Fort Nelson, near Portsmouth; and in the new Royal Armouries Museum in Leeds. This owes its origins to the Tower's rôle as arsenal and repository for national treasures and contains the remains of several munition collections. The earliest surviving parts are from Henry VIII's armoury and include staff weapons, firearms and armour. This material has been very useful for the study of the *Mary Rose*, leading to the identification of gun shields onboard ship. Until this discovery, the gun shields in the Tower were thought to be glorified princes' toys rather than serious weapons, so that their position has now had to be reassessed.

There are two separate collections of Civil War material: the remains of the government stores, housed in the Tower, and of Popham's troop at Littlecote House (currently under study). There are weapons from the British army and navy from the late 17th to late 19th century, much of which has been published by arms and armour scholars such as Howard Blackmore and De Witt Bailey.

The Royal Armouries also contains some rather unexpected objects, such as 16th-century munition armours from Malta, captured from the French during the Napoleonic wars, which are largely unstudied, and French armours taken during the siege of La Rochelle in 1627 and later reissued to English forces. There are also weapons seized from Paris in 1815 and artillery captured in earlier wars.

The *Musée d'Art et d'Histoire de Genève* contains an unusual and little-known collection of siege material dating from 1602 when the Duke of Savoy attempted unsuccessfully to seize the city. This is known as the *Escalade* because of the ladders used by the Savoyards. Besides arms and armour, it includes more unusual items such as a petard and what must be the biggest collection of 17th-century siege ladders and ropes in existence.

Perhaps the most important collection of munition arms is in the *Landeszeughaus* at Graz in Austrian Styria. The weapons and armour date mostly from the 16th and 17th centuries when Styria was a bulwark against the Ottoman Turks. After the last victory the arsenal was kept as a memorial and became the focus for local pride which enabled it to survive from being merely a collection of obsolete rusty armour into an object of antiquarian interest. The collection, housed in a baroque arsenal which still has many of its original fittings, includes armour, firearms, swords and staff weapons. Most of the artillery was taken by Napoleon and not returned. Much of the firearms and 16th-century armour come from Nuremburg but some 17th-century material was made locally. The collection is so large that it is largely unpublished, although a steady stream of publications on aspects of the collection is now appearing. Most papers are in German but are well-illustrated, and a few are now in English.

Makers and Marks

Many examples of arms and armour bear some kind of mark, such as makers' names. Clearly arms and armour had to be of high quality as one's life literally depended on them; if they were not up to scratch, one wanted to know who was to blame, while makers sought to protect their good reputations. Arms bear other sorts of marks. Guilds such as the Armourers' Company and the Gunmakers' Company of London inspected and stamped the work of both their members and foreigners. Sword blades made in Passau would bear the famous running wolf mark. Some arms and armour went through proof and were marked accordingly. Other were marks of ownership; the British government's broad arrow is famous; the French equivalent is the fleur-de-lys. Occasionally items are dated, such as most bronze cannon. This area is well-researched; for example there are books on Scottish weaponsmiths, London gunmakers and European gunfounders.

Assemblages

Researching the arms and armour is comparatively easy; more difficult is deciding what can be done with the information, and how far the evidence can be pushed. Some questions are obvious, such as 'were the items stored in chests or were they on deck or at least to hand'? 'Were guns ready for action or stowed below'? Detailed and critical examination of the arms and armour on a wreck can tell us about other things, such as the condition of a society's technology.

There is, for example, the archery equipment from the *Mary Rose*. Here the equipment, its position on board ship, and even the bones of the archers throw much light on the use of this weapon. There is a useful caveat; until the discovery of the equipment, conventional thinking stated that bows quickly lost favour after the discovery of gunpowder. On the contrary the *Mary Rose* evidence indicates that it took a long time for men to harness the power of the new weapon, let alone surpass established arms such as bows.

There are a number of problems in the interpretation of arms and armour from wrecks. Contemporary salvage should never be underestimated; if a wreck's location was known, attempts were often made to recover valuable items, such as brass or even iron guns. Most of the known Armada wrecks were subjected to contemporary salvage attempts. This can obviously affect interpretation since in identifying 16th-century wrecks the balance of brass, wrought-iron and cast-iron guns is often essential.

A considerable quantity of information is now being obtained from wrecks of 16th-century date, but archaeologists appear reluctant to take on board the information from these. The sequence of securely dated wrecks show ships with wrought-iron and bronze guns in use well into the second half of the 16th century. In terms of armament assemblages as a whole, there is little to make a fifty year chronology out of the American wrecks from Molasses Reef, Highborn Cay and Padre Island since they contain the same elements. Yet the Cayo Nuevo wreck with one bronze gun and four cast-iron guns has been dated as contemporary with the Padre Island wrecks, which in terms of armament it does not resemble. One problem here is the desire to find the 'earliest' example, the 'first' ship.

Another problem can be called the 'two-wreck syndrome'. This occurs early in excavation. In an attempt to identify and date a wreck, a few items are lifted and brought to different experts who give widely different dates. The confused excavators then assume they are dealing with more than one wreck on the same site. This happens surprisingly often; ships which have been identified as 'two-wrecks' at an early stage include the *Invincible*, the Bronze Bell wreck and, most recently, the Erne Bay wreck (Devon). One reason for this two-wreck syndrome is the slow acceptance that wrought-iron guns continued in use for a very long time and that one ship could carry both wrought- and cast-iron guns. Just as the invention of gunpowder does not make bows and arrows obsolete overnight, the invention of cast-iron does not make wrought-iron guns obsolescent. One of the main reasons for the continuation of small wrought-iron swivel guns is that founders had difficulties casting small guns. This was not solved until the early 18th century. There is no reason, of course, why all items from one wreck must be of the same age anyway.

Another difficult factor in using arms and armour is its 'international' nature. The different types of arms and even different parts of arms can come from quite different geographical sources, through trade or capture in war. For example, in the 17th century France and Britain would rarely be trading with each other in armaments because of their long history of hostility. However it is possible for a French or British ship to have similar weapons aboard, since they used the same sources such as the Low countries for firearms or Solingen for sword blades, while they may have cannon captured from the other country. This is particularly true of wrecks from the earlier half of the period under discussion.

Colin Martin has pushed the evidence from underwater excavations in new directions through his work on the Spanish ships, using an analysis of shot recovered and detailed work on Spanish gun carriages. This provides arguments on why breechloaders survive long after modern historians deem them useless. The paper in this volume by Alex Hildred on wooden objects relating to arms and armour is another promising field for investigation. Archaeology would benefit from critical examination of past discoveries, much as land archaeologists continually reinterpret land sites. The above-mentioned Anholt wreck is such a site, ripe for re-evaluation, with these new parallels to be investigated.

Arms and armour form an important resource for both terrestrial and nautical archaeologists. The discovery of guns often provides the first indication of a wreck's position. For this reason they deserve to be taken more seriously as a whole, as part of the ship, rather than a separate study on their own as something slightly arcane or outlandish. More can be gained by pooling our knowledge together.

Note
1   Many thanks to Geoff Egan of the Museum of London for identifying this parallel.

Further Reading
Alm, J. 1994 *European Crossbows: A Survey*, London.
Beer, C. de 1991 *The Art of Gunfounding*, Rotherfield.

Bailey, D. W. 1985 *British Military Longarms 1715–1865*, London.
Blackmore, D. 1990 *Arms and Armour of the English Civil Wars*, London.
Blackmore, H. L. 1994 *British Military Firearms 1650–1850* (2nd ed.), London.
Blackmore, H. L. 1971 *Hunting Weapons*, London.
Blackmore, H. L. 1976 *The Armouries of the Tower of London. Vol. 1: Ordnance*, London.
Blackmore, H. L. 1985 *English Pistols*, London.
Blackmore, H. L. 1986 *A Dictionary of London Gunmakers 1350–1850*, London.
Blair, C. 1958 *European Armour*, London.
Blair, C. (ed.) 1983 *Pollard's History of Firearms*, Feltham.
Bound, M. (ed.) 1995 *The Archaeology of Ships of War*, International Maritime Archaeology Series 1, Oswestry.
Boudriot, J. 1992 *Artillerie de Mer: France 1650–1850*, Paris.
Brown, R. R. 1995 'Arming the East Indiamen', *in* M. Bound (ed.).
Brown. R. R. forthcoming *British gunfounders and their marks*.
Cleere, H. & Crossley, D. 1995 *The Iron Industry of the Weald* (2nd edition), Cardiff.
Dufty, A. R. 1968 *European Armour in the Tower of London*, London.
Dufty, A. R. 1974 *European Swords and Daggers in the Tower of London*, London.
Edge, D. & Paddock, J. M. 1988 *Arms and Armour of the Medieval Knight*, London.
Godoy, J-A. 1980 *L'Escalades et ses Souvenirs*, Geneva.
Hammond, P. 1986 *Royal Armouries*, London.

Hardy, R. 1986 *Longbow*, Portsmouth.
Hoff, A. 1978 *Dutch Firearms*, London.
Journal of the Arms and Armour Society, 1953 – continuing.
Kennard, A. N. 1986 *Gunfounding and Gunfounders*, London.
Kist, J. B., Puype, J. P., van der Mark, W. & van der Sloot, R. B. F. 1974 *Dutch Muskets and Pistols*, London.
Krenn, P. 1991 *The Landeszeughaus of Graz*, Graz.
Krenn, P. & Karcheski, W. J. 1992 *Imperial Austria*. Munich. (Catalogue of the Landesmuseum, Graz).
May, W. E. & Annis, P. G. W. 1970 *Swords for Sea Service* (2 vols.), London.
Norman, A. V. B. 1980 *The Rapier and the Small-Sword*, London.
Norman, A. V. B. & Wilson, G. M. 1982 *Treasures from the Tower of London*, Norwich.
North, A. 1982 *European Swords*, London.
Oakeshott, R. E. 1981 *The Sword in the Age of Chivalry*, London.
Pfaffenbichler, M. 1992 *Armourers*, London.
Puype, J. P. 1985 *Dutch and other Flintlocks from Seventeenth Century Iroquois Sites*, Rochester, NY.
Richardson, T. 1991 'H. R. Robinson's 'Dutch Armour of the 17th Century", *Journal of the Arms and Armour Society* 13.
Robson, B. 1975 *Swords of the British Army*, London.
Smith, R. D. 1995 'Wrought-iron swivel guns', *in* M. Bound (ed.), 104–113.
Teesdale, E. B. 1991 *Gunfounding in the Weald in the sixteenth century*, London.
Whitelaw, C. E. 1977 *Scottish Arms Makers*, London.

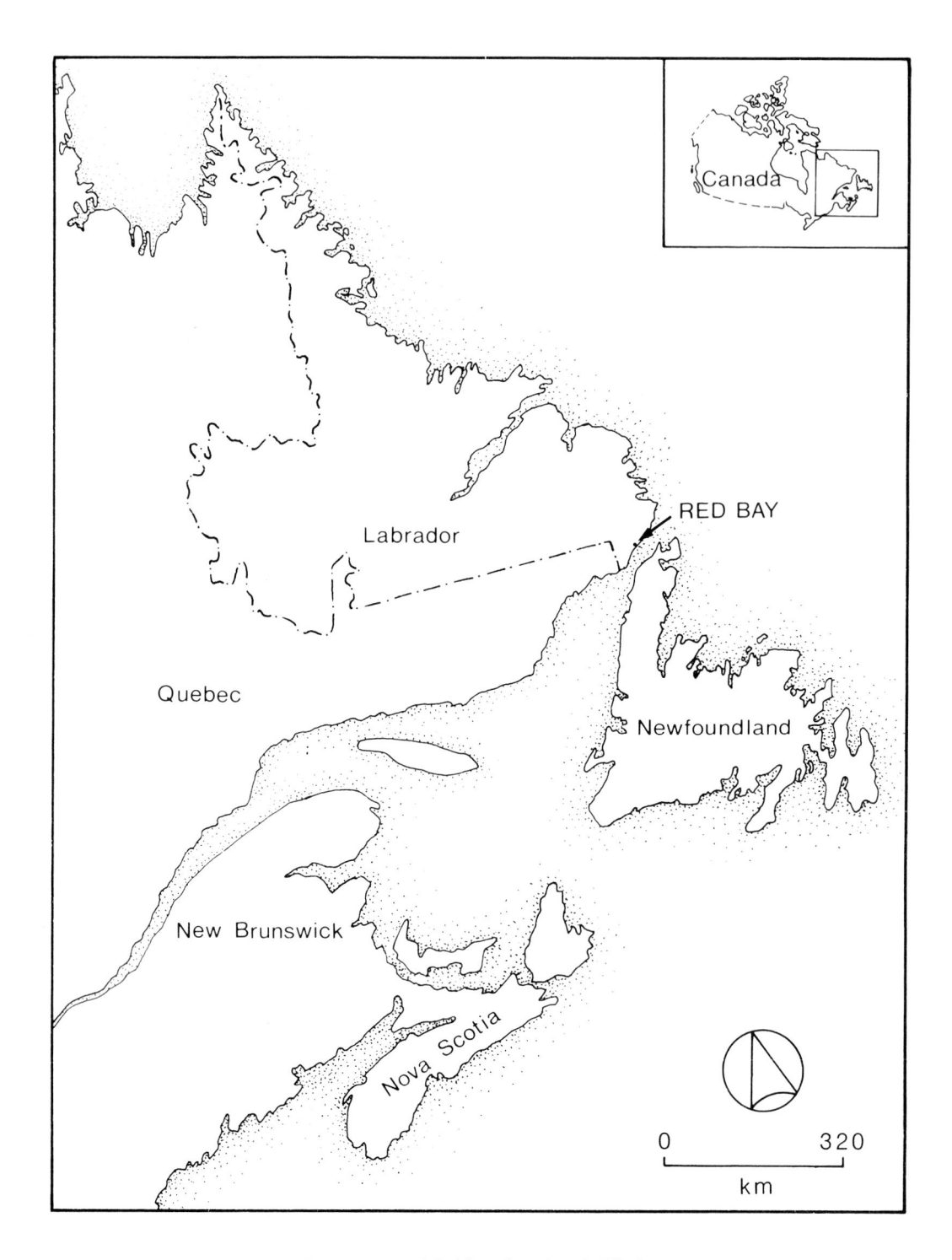

Fig. 1. *Location of Red Bay.* (Drawing: C. Pillar)

8

Piecing together the past: footwear and other artefacts from the wreck of a 16th-century Spanish Basque galleon

Stephen Davis

The second half of the 16th century was the heyday of the whaling industry in Canada. From about 1540 to 1600, Spanish Basques annually departed for Terranova to hunt the whales migrating through the Strait of Belle Isle, the body of water that separates northern Newfoundland from mainland Labrador. The hub of all the activity was Red Bay, a port on the southern coast of Labrador (Grenier 1985, 58 f.).

Arriving in the summer months and remaining as late as January, as many as 1,000 men worked in shifts around the clock to process the slaughtered whales into oil. A valuable commodity in Europe at this time, whale oil was primarily used for lamp fuel. It was also used in the cloth and leather industries, as an additive to drugs, for lubrication and for various other purposes.

In 1565 the season was drawing to a close in Red Bay when disaster befell one ship loaded for departure. According to the legal testimonies preserved in Spanish archives, the *San Juan* was struck by a gale so fierce that she severed her moorings and ran aground thirty yards from shore with her entire cargo of oil. The sinking of the *San Juan* was a commercial disaster; remarkably, there was no loss of life. It appears that most of the crew of perhaps seventy men were ashore at the time of the storm, and those aboard managed to make their way to land. According to documents relating the event, the crew also salvaged much of their sea gear and clothing after the storm.

In 1978, Parks Canada's Marine Archaeology Section located what is thought to be the wreck of the *San Juan*. The excavation of this vessel lasted eight field seasons, while the research on the ships's timbers and associated artefacts continues. Previous excavation and research on the French frigate *Machault* (1760) provided useful experience for the project.[1]

Certainly the largest and perhaps most important artefact from the excavation of the *San Juan* is the surviving hull structure, which has permitted a detailed study of her construction. Previous experience with timbers excavated from wet sites had demonstrated that mechanical treatment and conservation of a complete ship was impractical, both in terms of cost and the future stability of the wood. Consequently it was decided to rebury all of the ship's timbers once they had been individually recorded, drawn and photographed. This laborious process proved extremely profitable, for much has been learnt about the construction of Basque galleons (the 'freighters' of the 16th century).

Other types of material culture recovered during the excavation illustrate aspects of domestic activity, life on land and on board a ship, coopering, stowage, and dress of a 16th-century sailor, in particular the various types of leather footwear worn by sailors.[2]

Excavation of the Red Bay shipwreck yielded 410 cut and stitched leather fragments of footwear. Most of the shoes were incomplete or fragmentary: the thread holding the shoes together had disintegrated, and water and ice action had dispersed the pieces over the whole site, there being no concentrations indicative of bulk storage. However, a mixture of the different types and styles came from the stern area of the vessel, where the crew lived when on board the ship. Choosing only intact vamps as evidence of a single item, a minimum shoe count was calculated: at least forty-nine individual shoes went down with the ship. The volume of archaeological leather recovered suggests that the actual number of shoes lost was far greater. Piecing together these fragments, it is possible to reconstruct the shoes, revealing a variety of footwear worn in the mid-16th century.

Shoe Construction

All the footwear recovered at Red Bay share characteristics: the shoes and boots have right or left soles, rounded toes, no attached heels, and upper and bottom sections. The upper covers the top of the foot. It comprises a vamp that encloses the forepart of the foot and quarters that encase the heel. The shoe bottom is essentially the sole. Depending on the method of construction, the bottom of the shoe may comprise an insole, a sole, a welt or a rand and possibly a sole insert for increased comfort. Many of the shoes show evidence of repair, the most common being replaced soles and stitched split seams.

An upper generally had a leather toe puff to help shape the toe of the shoe, as well as side and heel stiffeners and an edge binding whip-stitched to the inside of the shoe for

112   *Stephen Davis*

Fig. 2. Scale model created from detailed drawings and measurements of ship's timbers recovered during the excavation of the Basque whaling vessel.
(Photograph: R. Chan, RD-22P)

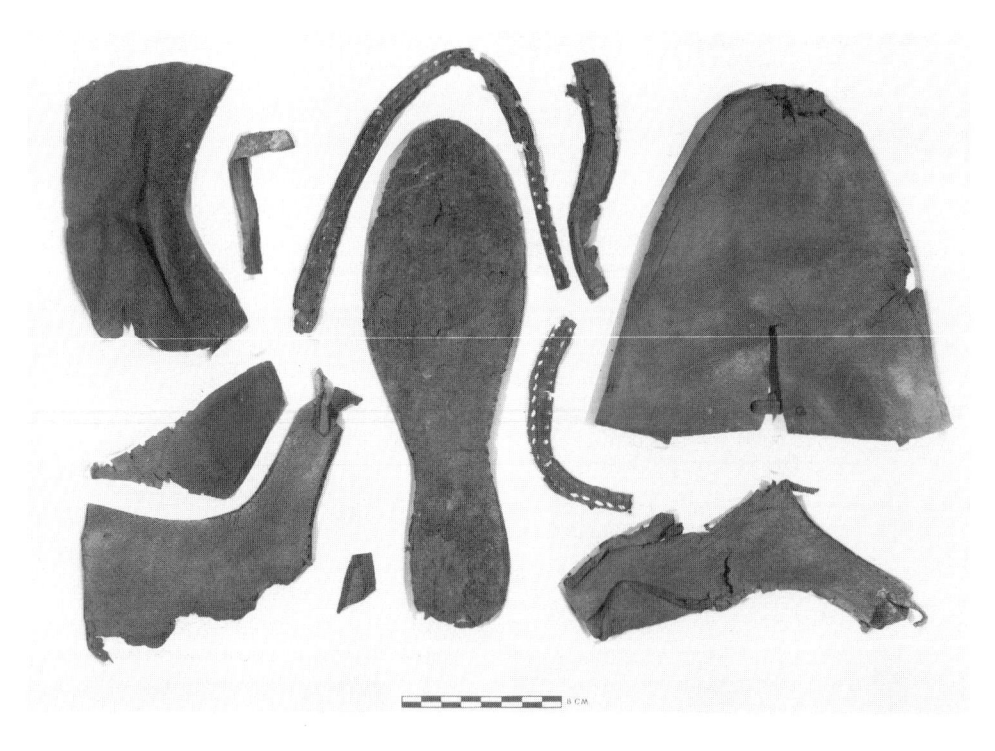

Fig. 3. Where possible, shoe parts were lifted together and recorded prior to conservation. Once conserved, the individual pieces were laid out in custom-cut ethafoam trays. Depicted here are the remains of a welted ankle shoe for the left foot. (Photograph: R. Chan, RA-16453B)

attached to the shoe with the smooth, grain side against the ground.

The main difference in the footwear lies in the way the sole or bottom was attached to the upper. By the 16th century, European footwear was turned or welted.[4] Turned and welted assembly involve different components and display identifiable construction techniques that allowed the initial sorting of artefacts into two types.

Turnshoes

Based on the number of vamps, a minimum of twenty-one shoes with no fastenings, similar in appearance to modern-day espadrilles, were recovered. The vamp of the turnshoe was cut straight across the instep, usually with no front opening. Several vamp artefacts have short, 10 to 20 mm slits at the centre fronts or at the tops of the side seams. It is likely that the wearer created these to allow more room for the foot when pulling the shoe on and off. The quarters were attached to

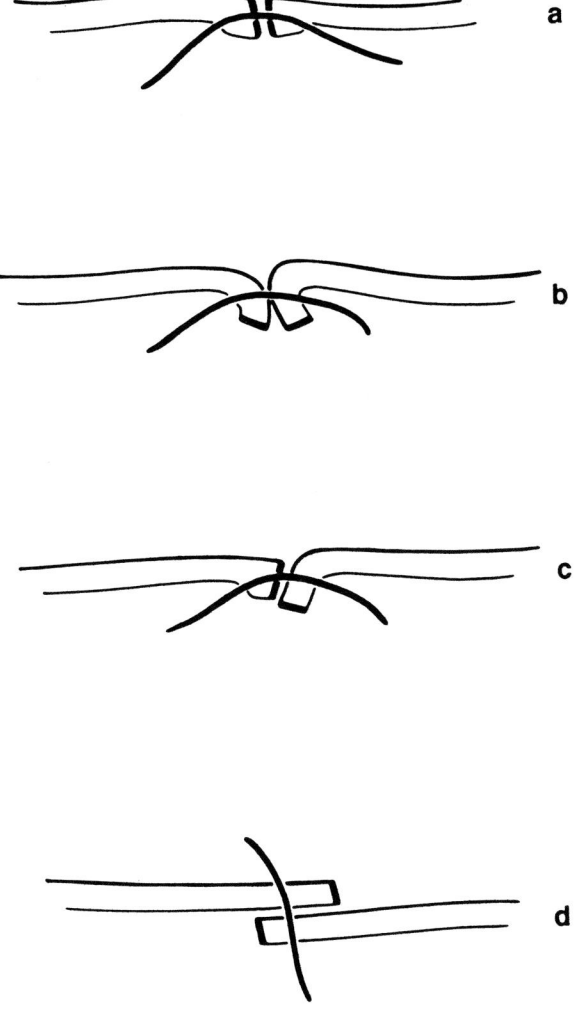

Fig. 4. As a rule the seams of the upper are inside the shoe, closed with flesh/grain stitches: the thread penetrates the flesh surface and exits the cut edge of the hide (a). Other methods of seam closure identified in the collection are butting (b), half-butting (c), and lapping (d). Half-butted seams only occurred in the Red Bay assemblage where the seams were repaired. (Drawing: C. Pillar)

additional support. Sometimes the upper was also leather lined. The stitching thread originally used to hold these components in place had disintegrated; hence pieces were often not recovered *in situ*. Nevertheless, the stitch holes are generally evident on the leather, attesting to the attachments no longer present. These tell-tale holes also reveal the method of seam closure necessary for differentiating turned and welted footwear (see Goubitz 1984 for survey).

The vamps and quarters were stitched together with the smooth, grain surface of the hide (*i.e.* the part originally bearing the hair) outwards. The rough, flesh side of the leather was always inside the shoe. If the upper was lined, the lining was also grain-side-out within the shoe. Generally the uppers were cattle hide. Goat or sheep skin was sometimes used for the linings, and in one case for a vamp. The thickness and quality of hides vary considerably, and some of the leather has split into layers. Such delamination is frequently the result of insufficient tanning.[3] The sole was also cattle hide, and it was

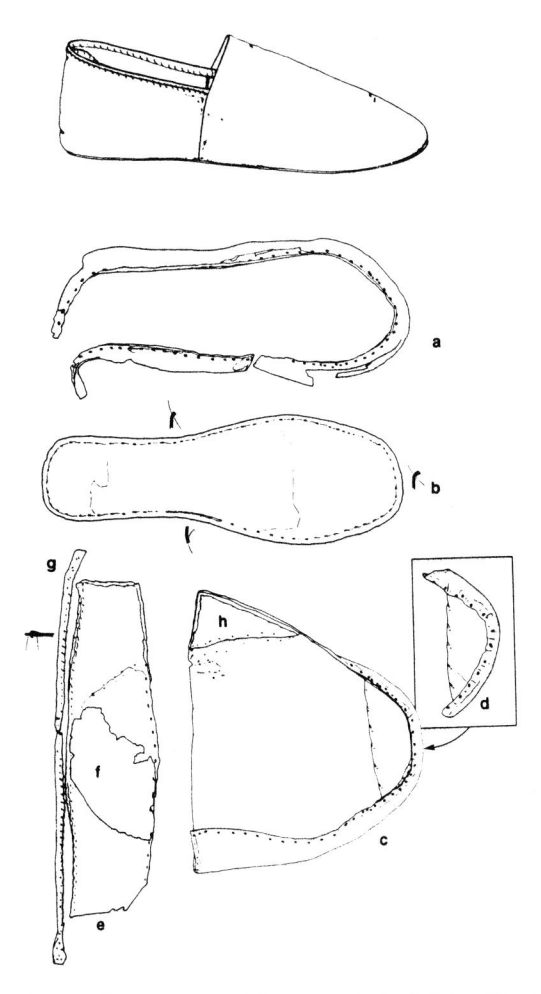

Fig. 5. The turnshoe, as reconstructed here, was made of thin leather. The upper components comprised a one-piece quarter (e) wrapping around the back of the shoe. A top band (g) was whip-stitched to the top edge of the quarters to help prevent this area from stretching, and a heel stiffener (f) supported the back of the shoe. Other reinforcers included side stiffeners (h) and a toe puff (d), also whip-stitched to the inside of the vamp (c). The shoe bottom included a rand (a) and a sole (b). (Drawing: C. Pillar)

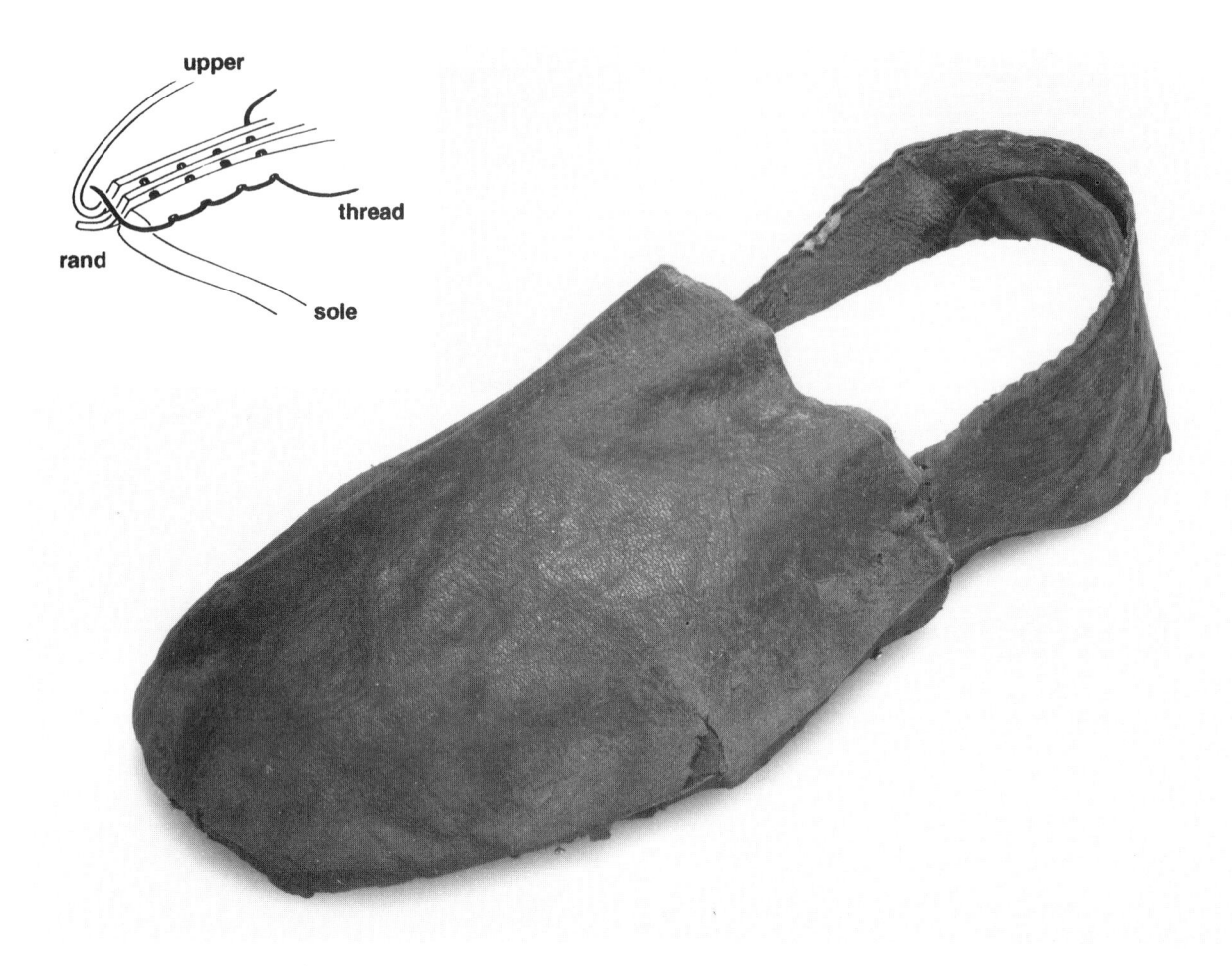

Fig. 6. The Red Bay turnshoes have narrow lengths of leather (rands) inserted between the uppers and soles. The three components, assembled and stitched together, were turned upon completion of the seam. This turnshoe upper was recovered intact and reshaped over a carved ethafoam last.
(Drawing: C. Pillar; photograph: R. Chan, RA-17896B)

the vamps along straight side seams. Since the low, almost rectangular shape of the quarters made two individually shaped quarters unnecessary, the back part was often cut as one piece with no back seam.

A semi-circular leather heel stiffener was attached inside the shoe quarter, and a strip of leather, called a top band, was stitched to the top edge of the quarter. The top band served to strengthen the back of the shoe and keep the heel quarters from stretching. Most of the top bands recovered are between 4 and 6 mm in width, stitched grain-side out to the tops of the quarter. A variation was a folded strip secured as above, with the folded edge up. In both cases, the top band was merely lapped against the inside edge of the quarter and secured with whip-stitches.

Once assembled, the upper was joined to the sole. A narrow length of leather, called a rand, was inserted between the upper and sole, and the three components were stitched together. Upon completion of the seam, the assembled shoe was turned right side out. Turnshoes recovered from late 15th-century archaeological sites sometimes have wide rands to which an additional or repair sole could be attached; there is, however, no evidence of this practice in the Red Bay assemblage. Apparently the purpose of this rand was to strengthen the seam and make it watertight.

Although flexible and watertight, it is difficult to imagine that the turnshoes found on the wreck were suitable for extended wear while working on land. With only a single, thin sole, turnshoes provided little protection from the cold, wet rocky shores. Lightweight turnshoes would be ideal to slip on aboard ship, or while at work in smaller whaleboats. It is also possible the turnshoes were worn inside heavier footwear when extra warmth or support was needed.

Welted Footwear

In this assemblage, welted shoes differed from turnshoes primarily in the shapes of the upper components and the assembly of the soles. The welted shoe was a more substantial shoe with two soles. The insole was stitched to the upper along with a strip of leather called a welt, onto which the sole was directly sewn. Assembled right side out from start to finish, these shoes could have thicker leather uppers and heavier soles than were possible with turnshoes. Such footwear with sturdy welted soles would be practical for wear while on shore cutting up whale blubber and tending fires.[5]

When a sole had become excessively worn, the damaged portion would be cut away and a new sole stitched directly to the welt. Another method for extending the wear of a worn

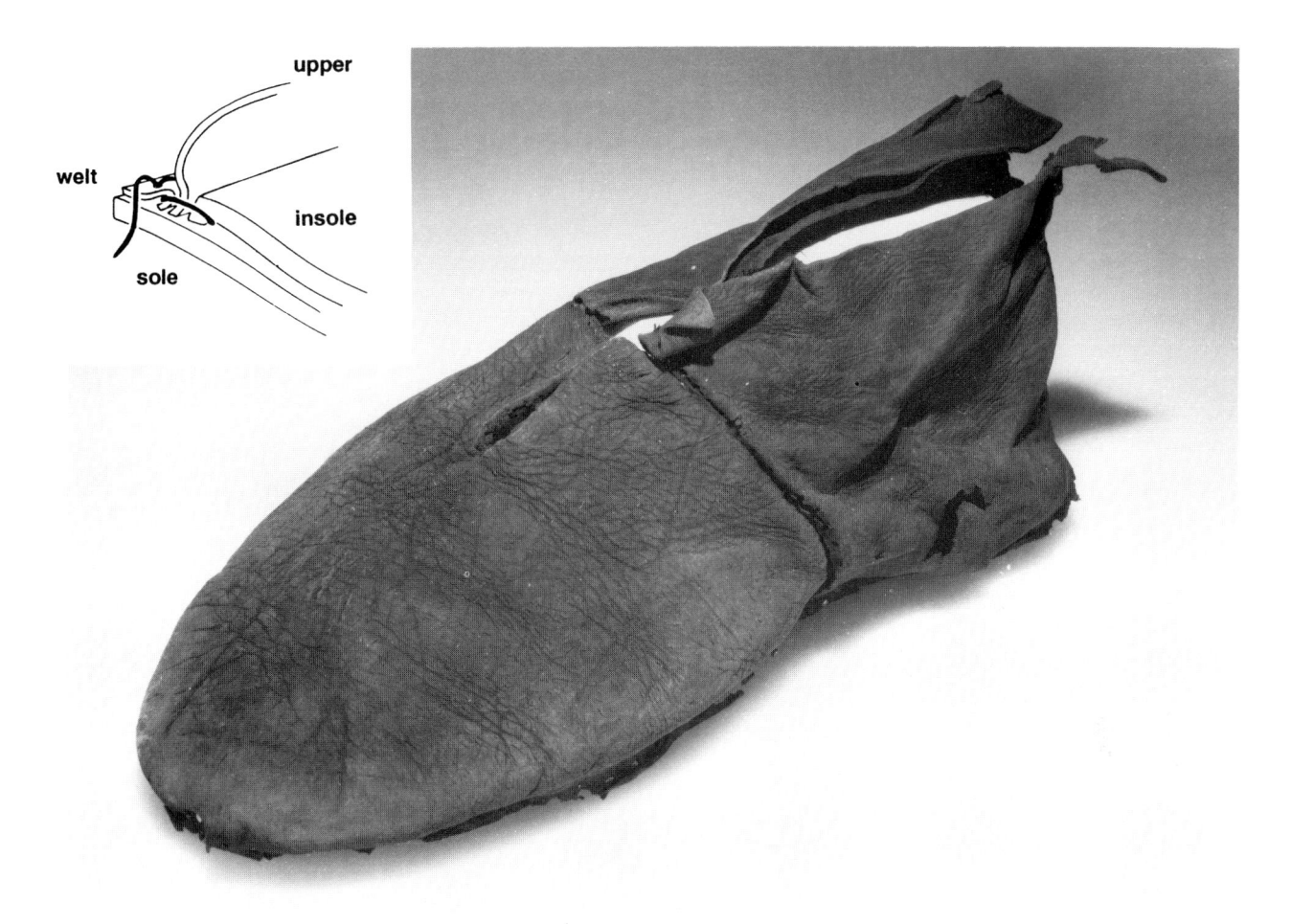

Fig. 7. The welted shoe has an insole. It is stitched together with the upper and a strip of leather (welt) which wraps around the edge of the upper. The sole is then sewn directly to the welt. Assembled right side out from start to finish, welted shoes can be made from thicker leather than possible with turnshoes. This ankle shoe was reconstructed over a carved ethafoam last for photography. (Drawing: C. Pillar; photograph: R. Chan)

sole was to tunnel-stitch a clump sole directly to the worn one; however, only one clump sole has been found in the entire collection. Seams also periodically required stitching, and to judge from some unusual combinations of stitching, the repairs were probably made by the wearer.

The turnshoes and welted shoes share a number of features. For example, many of the seam stitches are the same, and the toe puffs and side and heel reinforcers are identical. Again, the number of vamps provided a minimal object count of twenty-eight welted shoes. The types of welted footwear in the assemblage comprise ankle shoes, boots and latchet shoes.

Ankle Shoes

The majority of the welted shoe components recovered from the wreck are ankle shoes, with ankle-high uppers. Unlike the low, slip-on turnshoes, an ankle shoe had a front opening tied with a leather shoelace, and, unlike the turnshoe, most had two quarters joined together at the centre back. Often the top 20 mm of this seam was left unstitched, presumably to make it easier to pull the shoe on without splitting the seam. Given the height of the ankle shoe, no top band was necessary. The heel stiffener supported the back of this shoe. If the shoe quarters were lined, the lining and heel stiffener extended only

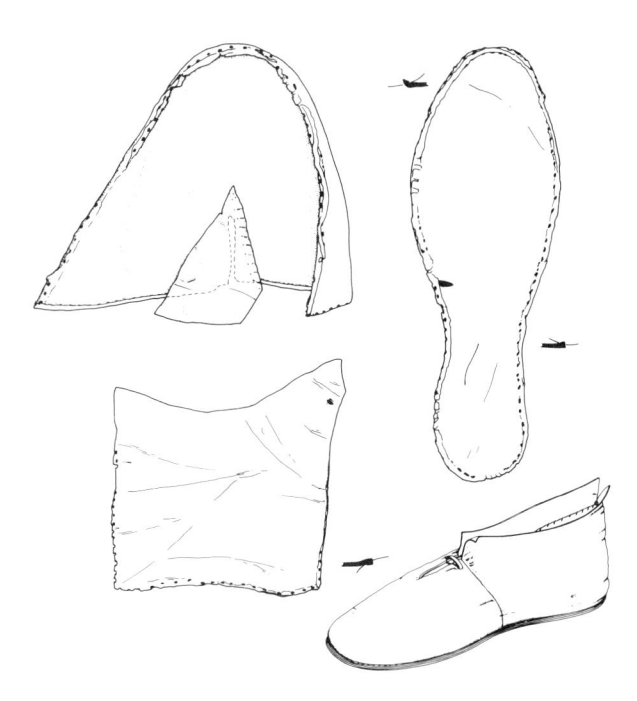

Fig. 8. The vamp, insole and quarter components illustrated here are typical of the elements which contribute to the reconstruction of a welted ankle shoe. The tongue flap was whip-stitched to the inside vamp. (Drawing: C. Pillar)

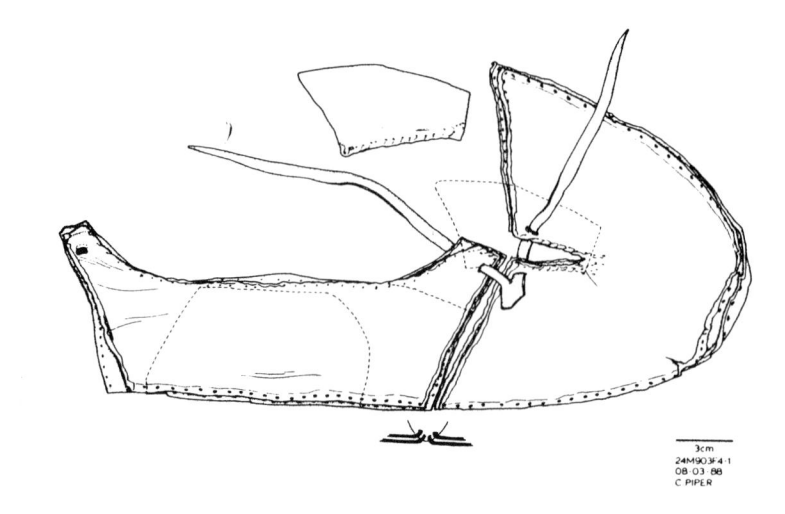

Fig. 9. The upper of this ankle shoe was completely leather lined; the heel stiffener was inserted between the two layers of the one-piece quarter, secured with whip-stitches. This artefact shows the shoelace typical of all the shoes in the collection with tied closures. The tongue flap was originally placed as indicated, whip-stitched to the edge of the front opening. (Drawing: C. Pillar)

to the height of the back opening. One shoe had a counter (similar to a heel stiffener except that it is attached to the outside of the shoe).

As with the turnshoes, the quarters were stitched to the vamp along a straight side seam. The front opening, a slit at the centre of the vamp 45 to 50 mm long, had two holes punched on either side for the shoelace. A triangular flap or tongue was attached to one edge of this opening; the opposite edge was leather bound. These features were recovered assembled together in only four instances; however, the presence of whip-stitch holes along the inside edges of the vamp openings and the fronts of shoe quarters indicate they were standard features for all the welted shoes.

Unlike modern shoelaces, the lace used to tie these 16th-century shoes consisted of a narrow strip of leather split in half lengthwise within 10 to 20 mm from one end, creating two separate strands joined at the base. The lacing of the shoe is also curious when compared with the methods we use today. Beginning on the inside of the shoe, each strand was guided through a hole on the side with the tongue attached. The laces crossed over the outside of the opening and entered the holes on the opposite side. The shoes excavated with their laces still attached show that the laces terminated inside the shoe. As this would be uncomfortable for the wearer, it is likely that the laces were pulled through the front opening to the outside of the shoe, where they could be knotted without rubbing against the foot. Several laces recovered were tied with reef knots.

Within the assemblage of welted shoes there are variations in the shapes of the individual components as well as in the methods of construction; inconsistencies in stitching and the exact shapes of components are to be expected in handmade footwear. One shoe, however, is significantly different in appearance and is therefore noted as a separate style in the collection. As with the other ankle shoes, the vamp has a front opening, tongue, edge binding, and a split-leather shoelace. The difference is the shape of the shoe's back part, which is lower and without a backseam. The wrap-around quarter was cut in two sections to economize on leather, and the entire upper was lined. In profile, this snug, low-fitting shoe with a sturdy welted sole is not unlike the appearance of today's athletic footwear, though the rigours demanded of this shoe were likely far greater.

Two welted shoes were recovered with fragments of plaited reed or straw 'soles' placed on the leather insoles. It is remarkable to have any evidence of these perishable straw soles, though it is reasonable to suggest that most of the crew took advantage of this simple device. It is likely that the straw cushioned and insulated the wearer's feet against the cold and damp ground in the same way as the cork, felt or rubber inserts used today.

Boots

A list of the clothes and footwear bought to outfit a sailor preparing for a whaling voyage to Terranova in the late 1570s includes entries for one pair of fishing boots and three pairs of shoes (Barkham 1981, 24). Other inventories consistently record one pair of boots, though the number of shoes varies from three to six pairs. If a pair of boots was standard among sailor's equipment, it is surprising that more evidence of their use was not recovered: only one pair of boots was located during the excavation of the *San Juan*: perhaps the crew escaped the storm wearing their boots.

The uppers of the boots, which have thick welted soles, are symmetrically cut and cleverly pieced together. One of the insoles was cut in two pieces. The seamed sole particularly suggests that the boot was cobbled together, for no shoemaker would compromise materials in such a critical area (J.Swan, *in litt.*). Boots illustrated in 16th-century iconography show that the upper varied in height, extending to the calf, knee or thigh. It is impossible to determine the original height of the boots recovered at Red Bay as the uppers were cut away, probably to salvage the leather for shoe repair or reconstruction. Translation – the modification of discarded footwear into new shoe parts – was common practice in the 16th century. Examples of translation often appear as cut-up components, illustrating to the cobbler's ability to recycle old shoes.

Fashion vs. Function

Several shoe fragments suggest that some items of fashionable footwear were also brought to the whaling station, such as the latchet shoe. This had two straps, called latchets, extending from the top fronts of the shoe quarters. The latchets were folded over the vamp and fastened together at the front of the shoe. Shoes with latchets were first introduced in the second half of the 16th century and remained popular through to the end of the 18th century.

The latchet shoes in the collection have welted soles. Although the quarters are low and there is no need for a front opening, the throat of the vamp has several short slits for flexibility. The top of the backseam is unstitched. A knotted leather lace inserted through two holes in one of the vamps indicates that the latchets were tied to the front of the shoe.

Pinking and slashing, two methods for clothing decoration popular in the 16th century, are also represented in the collection. Slashing was more popular in the first half of the 16th century. Broad slashes were cut into footwear and garments, often exposing rich fabric linings in contrasting colours. A complete one-piece shoe quarter lining in the collection displays the decorative slashing frequently illustrated in contemporary portraits. As the lining was inside the shoe where the slashes would not be seen, it is likely that this component was originally the vamp of a slashed shoe, cut down and transformed into a lining.

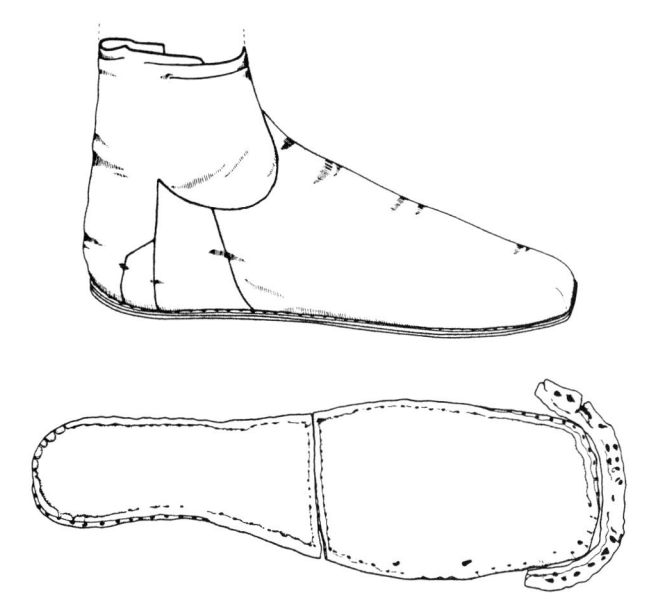

Fig. 10. Partial reconstruction of a boot: insole and welt fragments. The top leg of the boot was apparently cut away (note the horizontal slashes), making it impossible to determine its original height. The insole associated with this boot was also pieced together and joined with an edge/grain seam. (Drawing: C. Pillar)

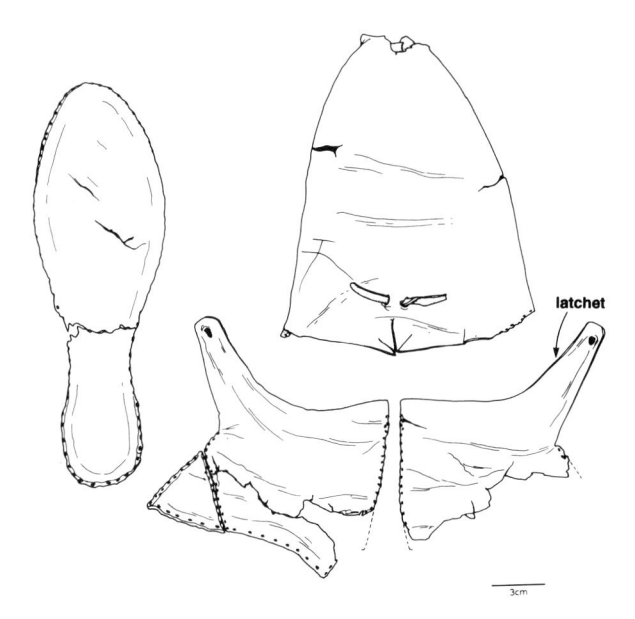

Fig. 11. Components associated with a Red Bay latchet shoe: right insole, vamp and two quarters. The fragmented leather shoelace remaining in the vamp originally extended through the latchet lace holes. This artefact has a pieced quarter, perhaps to economize on leather. Note that the centre back seam stitches terminate below the top edge, leaving approximately a 10 mm top back vent for ease. (Drawing: C. Pillar)

Fig. 12. Reconstruction of latchet shoe uppers. This item was recovered with the shoelace intact and knotted. (Photograph: R. Chan, RA-17900B)

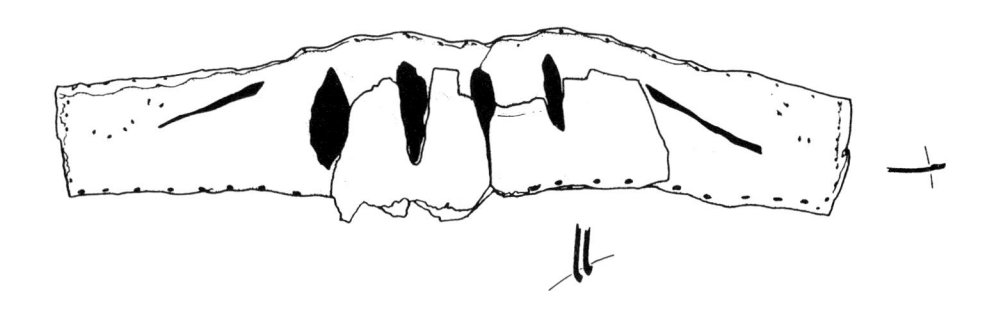

Fig. 13. A quarter lining with slashed cut-outs. The lining was inside the shoe where it would not be seen, indicating that it was probably recycled leather originally part of a fashionable slashed shoe. (Drawing: C. Pillar)

Pinked items had tiny slits, holes or stars cut or punched in all-over patterns. This practice was most popular in the second half of the century. Useless in cold and wet conditions, it is unlikely pinked footwear was worn for work. Nonetheless, at least some members of the ship's company (probably the officers) brought with them on economic grounds a few items of pinked apparel, perhaps to reflect personal status. The fragments of pinked footwear have rows of tiny 4 mm-long cuts piercing the leather.

Some of the shoes display irregular slashes and cuts are easily distinguishable from the symmetrical, fashionable slashes by the shoemaker. These are probably the result of the cobbler's (or perhaps the wearer's) crude attempts to create ease for a more comfortable fit.

Summary

While contemporary guild restrictions for shoemakers indicate that conformity to style and quality was enforced with monetary penalties during the 16th century, the archaeological evidence suggests that such punitive measures were not always successful. The Red Bay collection displays a variety of deviations in assembly contrary to the specifications stated in guild records. This may be explained as the inconsistency

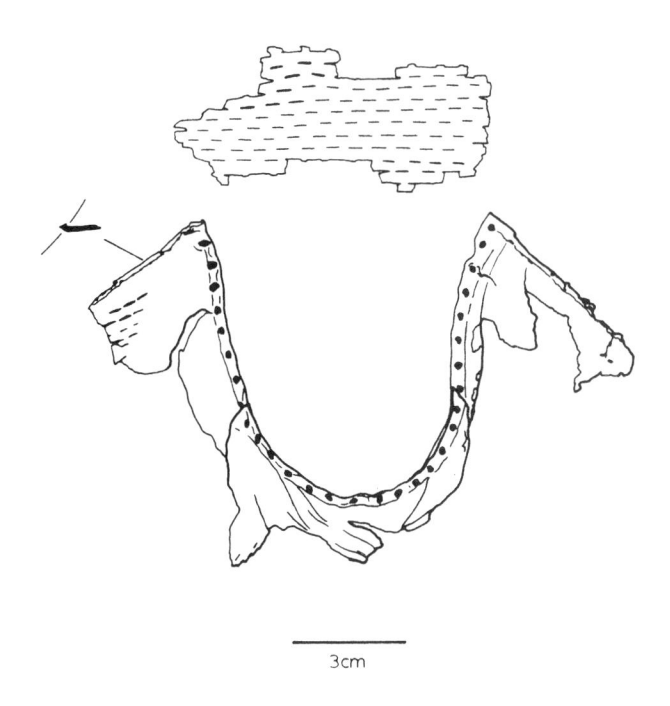

Fig. 14. Fragments of a one-piece shoe quarter display the tiny slits creating a pinked surface decoration. (Photograph: R.Chan)

to be expected in any item of handmade clothing. The shoe repairs, translations, and the unusual seamed and pieced uppers suggest second-hand or second-quality merchandise. It is likely that cost was a consideration for both the ship's outfitters and the crew. One way to curb expenses may have been to purchase cheaper repaired or rejected footwear.

We know from surviving notarial records listing the personal possessions of sailors in Terranova that a minimum of four to six pairs of shoes per labourer was not excessive, though only a single pair of boots formed part of his equipment. It appears that shoes, rather than boots, were more frequently worn or more frequently wore out. The number of spare shoes needed for a whaling season probably accounts for the quantity of footwear recovered from the shipwreck.

Sixteenth-century footwear excavated from archaeological sites in England and The Netherlands reveal similarities in cut, style and construction to the Red Bay examples. Contemporary iconography provides ample depictions of the itinerant tradesmen, labourers, farmers and peasants in the 1500s; unfortunately, there are few illustrations clearly depicting the dress of the sailors and whalers of the 16th century. While the few available engravings fail to present the footwear in great detail, they are consistent in showing the men shod in snug-fitting low shoes. It is possible that the artists were capturing

Fig. 15. Poultry Sellers, *c.1570 by Joachim De Beuckelaer and studio. In this painting of two vendors, the man on the right wears the leather turnshoe style found at Red Bay. His trousers are the baggy slops favoured by sailors in the 16th century. His male companion wears welted ankle shoes.* (From the collections of the Montreal Museum of Fine Arts, donated by Thomas O. Hecht and Madeleine Feher; photograph by C. Guest, MMFA)

the essence of the turnshoes abundantly represented in our collection.

The footwear from Red Bay forms a revealing representation of the footwear for the common man about 1565. Here we have an assemblage displaying the diversity in cut and quality, the mundane nature and the eccentricities of the shoes at that time. The absence of dated comparative collections makes the Red Bay assemblage a particularly valuable resource for archaeologists and historians.

Acknowledgements

This paper from the Department of Canadian Heritage, Parks Canada, is reproduced with the permission of the Minister of Public Works and Government Services, Canada, © Her Majesty the Queen in Right of Canada, 1997.

Notes

1. The *Machault*, also a Spanish-Basque vessel in origin, was built in Bayonne in 1758.
2. A comprehensive series of monographs addressing the excavation and material culture research associated with the Red Bay shipwreck will be forthcoming, published by Parks Canada.
3. Delamination is not uncommon with buried leather. It is a condition where the corium layer decomposes due to the incomplete penetration of the tanning liquor, and the hide or skin separates into layers.
4. The sole of a turnshoe is sewn directly to the upper and turned right side out so that the seam is on the inside of the shoe. A welted shoe has a narrow strip of leather – a welt – attached around the bottom edge of the shoe upper and insole. The outer sole is then stitched directly to this welt.
5. The ankle boot was also represented amongst the wearing apparel recovered during the excavation of a Basque grave located during excavations of the land site. The land-site excavations were conducted by Memorial University, Newfoundland, under direction of Dr. James Tuck.

References

Barkham, M. 1981 *Aspects of life aboard Spanish Basque ships during the 16th century, with special reference to Terranova whaling voyages*, Canadian Parks Service Microfiche Report Series No. 75.

Goubitz, O. 1984 'The Drawing and Registration of Archaeological Footwear', *Studies in Conservation* 29, 187–196.

Grenier, R. 1985 'Excavating a 400–year-old Basque Galleon', *National Geographic* 168. 1 (July 1985), 58–67.

9

Rhenish stonewares from shipwrecks: the study of ceramic function and lifespan

David R. M. Gaimster

HISTORICAL BACKGROUND

Salt-glazed stonewares produced in the Rhineland formed one of the region's principal international exports during the late Middle Ages and throughout the pre-Industrial period. Evidence for this prolific trade (in the form of archaeological finds from both terrestrial and maritime contexts) can be traced today across North-West Europe, the New World and the Far East (Reineking-von Bock 1980; Gaimster 1997, Chapter 3).

Fully-fused stoneware was first developed on the Continent of Europe in the middle Rhineland during the late 13th to early 14th century, the technique of salt-glazing being introduced some one hundred years later. This significant advance was largely a result of the availability of fine plastic clays which could be fired to the point of fusion at 1250°–1300°C.

During the 14th to 18th centuries, stoneware formed a regular component of the pottery imported through British ports (Allan 1984; Gaimster 1987 and 1997; Haselgrove 1989 and 1990). Pottery initially from Siegburg and Langerwehe and later from Raeren (outside Aachen) and the Köln/Frechen district dominated the cargoes of imported ceramics from the Continent. Along with the cobalt-blue-painted Westerwald wares of the 17th and 18th centuries, their robustness, impervious bodies and utilitarian forms ensured their status as staple trade-goods both in European waters and across the globe. Their utilitarian character was enhanced with the introduction of applied relief decoration during the late 15th and early 16th centuries, thereby increasing their popular appeal. Unlike contemporary earthenwares, imported stonewares fulfilled a wide range of functions at almost all levels of society. It has been found on the sites of both royal palaces and urban tenements, as well as remote rural communities. The pivotal rôle of stoneware at all levels of northern European society during the medieval and early modern period can be seen clearly in its depiction in contemporary genre and still life paintings (see below).

The listing of imported stonewares in English probate inventories of the 16th and 17th centuries confirms the archaeological picture (Haselgrove 1989, note 1). For example, at Exeter they comprise the most frequently recorded ceramic in local probate inventories during the period 1560–1640 (Allan 1984, 119–120). An indication of the intensity of the cross-Channel stoneware trade can be seen in the London Port Books of 1615 which record a peak of over 80,000 *cast* being landed that year, the equivalent of around 320,000 quart-sized vessels (Haselgrove 1989, 135).

QUESTIONS OF STONEWARE FUNCTION AND LIFESPAN

Rhenish stonewares excavated in Britain play a considerable rôle in the interpretation of post-medieval archaeological sequences (Gaimster 1987; Hurst 1988). In addition to their importance as a precise index of cross-channel trade, they are integral to the study of ceramic assemblages on the microscale: chiefly as evidence for social behaviour and as a tool for refined chronological analysis. In this historical rôle, questions of individual vessel function and lifespan (the timelag between production and deposition date) are crucial. These fundamental aspects of interpretation have been largely neglected to date (Hurst 1988). In contrast to the majority of terrestrial sites, shipwreck contexts – by virtue of their synchronic nature and unimpeachable *terminus ante quem* status – offer wide scope for the chronological and socio-behavioural study of trade ceramics (Murphy 1983, 66–68).

On the primary question of dating, it is becoming increasingly clear that historic Rhenish stoneware, by virtue of its robust nature, enjoyed a relatively long lifespan in the domestic sphere. In the archaeological record it is often the case that finds of German stoneware bear applied dates which generally predate the aggregate deposition date of a mixed ceramic assemblage. This phenomenon of the long-term *'curation'* of individual vessels in the home is illustrated most vividly in Georg Flegel's painting *Stilleben mit einem Hirschkäfer*, signed and dated 1635, which depicts a Köln *Bartmann* jug of *c.*1525 (Erichson-Firle and Vey 1973, cat. 2824; compare Gaimster 1997, cat.31 for the type; see Fig.1). It can only be assumed that Flegel, a native of Köln, must have painted either a family heirloom or, even possibly, a pot still in general circulation a century after its production date.

Fig. 1. Stilleben mit einem Hirschkäfer by Georg Flegel, dated 1635, showing a Köln stoneware jug of about 1525.
(Wallraf-Richartz-Museum, Cologne cat.2824)

To make matters more difficult, it is all too often accepted with Rhenish stoneware that applied date relates directly to production date. However, excavations on kiln-sites have produced contradictory evidence on this point. At Siegburg, for example, excavations in 1989/90 on the Knütgen family workshop at the Aulgasse 8 site revealed a destruction horizon of 11 April 1588 which contained a series of negative ceramic moulds and vessel wasters with dates ranging from 1567 to 1586, the majority clustering in the period 1570–1580 (Ruppel 1991, figs 1–2). The find confirms that it was common practice for stoneware potters in the Rhineland to re-use existing moulds for creating applied relief decoration – often, as here, for a decade or more before they were no longer serviceable. Hence, in the case of post-medieval Rhenish stoneware with applied relief ornament, there may be a five-, ten- or even fifteen-year discrepancy between actual production date and the date on the applied relief.

On the question of individual vessel use, research has been limited to typo-functional analysis and the study of contemporary graphical source material (Ruempol and van Dongen 1990; Clevis 1993). The vast majority of terrestrial archaeological deposits are composed of material which does not relate directly to the period in which an individual vessel was in use. Usually they contain 'trash materials' of variable date, divorced from their original domestic context. Shipwrecks, as with fire-deposits on land, offer unique opportunities to study ceramics in the context of their daily use (Murphy 1983, 66).

As 'synchronous snapshots frozen in time' (Murphy 1983, 74), shipwrecks provide a laboratory in which to study the question of the respective lifespan of vessels used on board ship, a line of enquiry not usually possible on land sites. Making allowances for the discrepancies between applied date and production date, maritime contexts allow an evaluation of the 'active lives' of stoneware vessels as opposed to their 'rubbish lives' (Orton 1982, 92–93). It is hoped that this small survey of published wreck assemblages will demonstrate the potential of these contexts for the study of chronological, functional and socio-behavioural questions: questions central to the interpretation of traded stonewares on terrestrial sites.

THE SITES

A growing corpus of wreck assemblages is now being made available for study by underwater archaeologists. Chronologically this survey of both open-sea and riverine finds covers the period from the first half of the 15th century to the middle of the 18th century; in terms of geographical distribution it includes wrecks from the North and South Atlantic, North

Sea, Baltic, Caribbean, South China Sea and from the coast of Western Australia. Despite the prolific documentary evidence for the international trade in stoneware as a commodity in its own right, very few of the listed assemblages can be said to represent cargo. Most were once in use aboard ship, either as ship's inventory or as personal possessions of the crew. However, it is now clear that a number of 17th-century ships were carrying stonewares as a means of packaging and transporting specialised goods over long distances, particularly those of a sensitive and volatile nature such as medicine or mercury.

Among the earliest contexts producing Rhenish stoneware within British waters is the Cattewater wreck, Plymouth. A base of a Siegburg funnel-necked jug or beaker was found among the ballast of this armed merchantman, lost about 1530 (Redknap 1984, 39 and cat.no.36 for stoneware; see also this book, Chapter 5). Further analysis of the stoneware will help to determine its age at the time the ship was lost. It may have been in circulation for some time before being broken or discarded and becoming integrated within the ballast.

The earliest documentary maritime context for Rhenish stoneware is King Henry VIII's flagship, the *Mary Rose*, built in 1509/11, which sank in action against the French off Portsmouth in 1545 (Rule 1982). Inside the barber surgeon's cabin was a large wooden chest containing a number of corked Raeren bottles which contained the residues of medicine and the possible remains of field dressings (Townsend 1983; this book, Chapter 4; see Colour Plate 2D). Typologically the forms date to the period c.1475–1525, a date-range confirmed by excavated contexts in British and Low Countries ports (Gaimster 1997, cat. nos74 & 75). However, it is possible that these bottle forms – with one or two handles – continued to be made well into the second quarter of the 16th century, as the examples from the wholesale stock of the stoneware dealers Jan Petersss and Cornelis-de-Kanneman excavated at Bergen-op-Zoom seem to imply (Vandenbulcke and Groeneweg 1988). Nevertheless, it is also possible that the stoneware bottles, by virtue of their specialised function, had been in use for a considerable time before the ship went down in 1545. The robust and non-porous stonewares made ideal *albarelli* (pharmacy jars) for use on board ship: they were far more suited to maritime life than the delicate tin-glazed earthenware of North Italy or the Low Countries which are traditionally associated with medicinal use. Moreover, their narrow necks and neck cordons would have enabled the ship's surgeon to both carefully control dosages being dispensed from the bottles and seal them again after use.

The mid-16th-century Köln/Frechen jug found on the wreck of a Portuguese ship in the Seychelles in 1976 was one of the few dating indicators on the site (Blake and Green 1986). The precise date of the wreck is unknown, and it can only be assumed that the production date of the jug and the loss of the ship are relatively close. Stoneware vessels of this type are dated to about 1550 by both excavations on production sites in the Rhineland and consumer sites in Britain and the Low Countries. This is only the second example known of a southern European ship of the 16th century carrying Rhenish stoneware: excavations between 1972 and 1975 on the wrecks of three ships, which were lost in April 1554 from a flotilla of Spanish merchant vessels off the coast of Padre Island, Florida, also produced a small assemblage of acorn and oak-leaf-applied Köln/Frechen-type stoneware of the mid-16th century (Arnold and Weddle 1978, fig.45a). The cargo of the flotilla, lost *en route* to Spain from Mexico, was made up of gold, silver, cochineal and other New Spain products; the Rhenish stonewares, on the other hand, were clearly part of the ship's inventory or were once the private possessions of members of the crew. Ironically, little is known from terrestrial sites of the distribution of medieval and later Rhenish stoneware in the Iberian peninsula, although these maritime discoveries from colonial contexts demonstrate a significant, if minor, trade in utilitarian North European ceramics to the south.

Two Frechen *Bartmann* jugs have been published from the wreck of the English ship *Sea Venture*, lost off Bermuda in 1609 (Wingood 1982, fig. 11A). Typologically both jugs date to about 1580–90 (Gaimster 1997, cat. 51). One bears the applied arms of Orange-Nassau, a common heraldic device of the period demonstrating the importance of the Lower Rhine trade route to the Channel (*ibid*, cat. 51). Assuming a relatively close timespan between applied date and actual date of firing (say a maximum of about ten years), their discovery in this sealed context of 1609 further emphasises the prolonged lifespan of Rhenish stonewares on board ship.

However, the production date of a number of other stoneware assemblages from wrecks appears to correspond more closely to the time of loss. For instance, the Commonwealth naval vessel *Swan*, wrecked in 1653 off Duart Castle, the Isle of Mull (Western Isles) was probably refitted shortly before its demise. Judging by their applied relief ornament, the Frechen *Bartmann* bottles found on the wreck site probably became part of the ship's inventory at this point (this book, Chapter 14).

Excavations on wrecks of the Dutch East India Company have produced extensive collections of Rhenish stoneware dating to the 17th and 18th centuries. These sites are scattered along the VOC route to the East Indies first established in 1611 (Zuiderbaan 1977, 5–6; Sténuit 1977, 403–407; Gawronski 1990; for the location of many of these sites, see Redknap and Smith 1990, Fig.1). These contexts are of crucial interest in terms of stoneware function: most stoneware recovered from VOC wrecks can be classed as 'ship's inventory', while a number were clearly used for specialised storage and transportation purposes, particularly for delicate or volatile exports such as mercury.

The *Witte Leeuw*, lost off St Helena on its homeward voyage in 1613, begins the sequence of documented VOC wrecks available for study (van der Pijl-Ketel (ed.) 1982). The ship was laden with Chinese export porcelain (mainly *Kraak* wares), but excavation also recovered a number of stoneware vessels. Of particular interest is a pewter-mounted Siegburg *Pulle* (pitcher) applied with an armorial medallion bearing the arms of Spain and the date 1585 (Boiten and van Vuuren 1982, cat. no. 6.2; see Fig.2). Allowing for a discrepancy of ten years

Fig. 2. Siegburg stoneware Pulle *(pitcher), applied with a medallion moulded with the arms of Spain and the date 1585. From the wreck of the VOC* Witte Leeuw, *lost off St Helena, 1613.* (Rijksmuseum, Amsterdam Inv. no. NG 1977–178W)

BAT 2136

Fig. 3. Raeren stoneware panel jug fragment applied with a frieze of the Peasants' Wedding *c.1596. From the wreck of the VOC* Batavia, *lost off Western Australia, 1629.* (Western Australian Maritime Museum BAT 2136)

between applied date and production date, it can be assumed that this vessel was in circulation for up to twenty to twenty-five years before the final episode of deposition. A number of Frechen medallions were also found, including one bearing the arms of the City of Amsterdam, another bearing the Royal Stuart arms and the date 1603 (*ibid*, cat.6.1), the latter example possibly in circulation for a decade or more before deposition.

In contrast to the *Witte Leeuw*, Rhenish stonewares were found in profusion on the site of the VOC *Batavia*, lost off the Wallabi Islands, Western Australia, in 1629 (Stanbury 1974). The assemblage, the largest maritime find of stoneware to date, contains a wide spectrum of vessels, particularly of *Bartmann* bottles of the late 16th and early 17th centuries (see Gaimster 1997 for discussion of *Bartmann* vessel type). Production sources on the Rhine are represented by Frechen, Raeren, the Westerwald and possibly Siegburg. The wreck, when published fully, will provide a base-line for the dating of stonewares from terrestrial sites of the early 17th century.

Few of the *Batavia* sherds are dated. One exception is a rather debased portrait medallion dated [16]19 (Stanbury 1974, BAT 539C). Among the collection is another example of prolonged use among the ship's company: the remains of a late 16th-century Renaissance-style panel jug from Raeren, the body applied with an arcaded frieze of the *Peasants' Wedding* (Stanbury 1974, BAT 2136; see Fig.3). This particular relief

is dated 1596 on intact vessels preserved in museum collections (Kohnemann 1994, mould type 18).

Of equal interest is the Raeren or Westerwald-type blue-and-grey pitcher moulded with the *Hausmarke* (trade-mark) medallion of the Nijmegen stoneware shipper Jan Allers alongside a medallion applied with the arms of Sebastian von Hatzfeld and Lucia von Sickingen dated [15]95 (Stanbury 1974, BAT 326; van Loo 1984, fig.18; see Fig.4). Known medallions with the Allers trade-mark bear dates covering the period 1590 to 1600 (van Loo 1984), and it would be convenient to assume that this vessel was also made during or near to the end of this decade, particularly as the vessel is also applied with a medallion bearing impaled family arms of this date. However, the date may be commemorative, and according to van Loo (1984; 1989) the Jan Allers mark continued to be used by his family well into the 1620s. On balance I would probably come down on the side of the former scenario and postulate a production date of around 1600, particularly in view of the more limited lifespan of this combination of personal arms. In this case the pitcher was probably a personal possession of a member of the crew and unlikely to have been a pot commissioned for export. The two Jan Allers medallion fragments also recovered from the wreck (Stanbury 1974, BAT 326 & BAT 2558) are possibly from Frechen *Bartmann* bottles of a more contemporary date because these vessels are far more likely to represent commissioned cargo or transport containers. A number of highly decorated blue-and-grey Westerwald jugs were recovered from the wreck with pewter lids still attached (Stanbury 1974, BAT 2303 and BAT 2358), one with an Amsterdam pewterer's mark. This discovery confirms the VOC practice of importing Rhenish stoneware from the Rhineland to the Netherlands and mounting with pewter before export for the overseas market.

The wreck of the VOC fluit the *Lastdrager*, sunk in 1653 off Yell, Shetland, is one of the many Dutch East Indiamen lost off the Northern Isles of Scotland during the 17th century (Sténuit 1974 & 1977). This particular site, however, is one of the few which have provided evidence for the specialised use of Rhenish stoneware in the packaging and transportation of volatile goods: in this case mercury destined for industrial (metallurgical) and medicinal processes in the Far

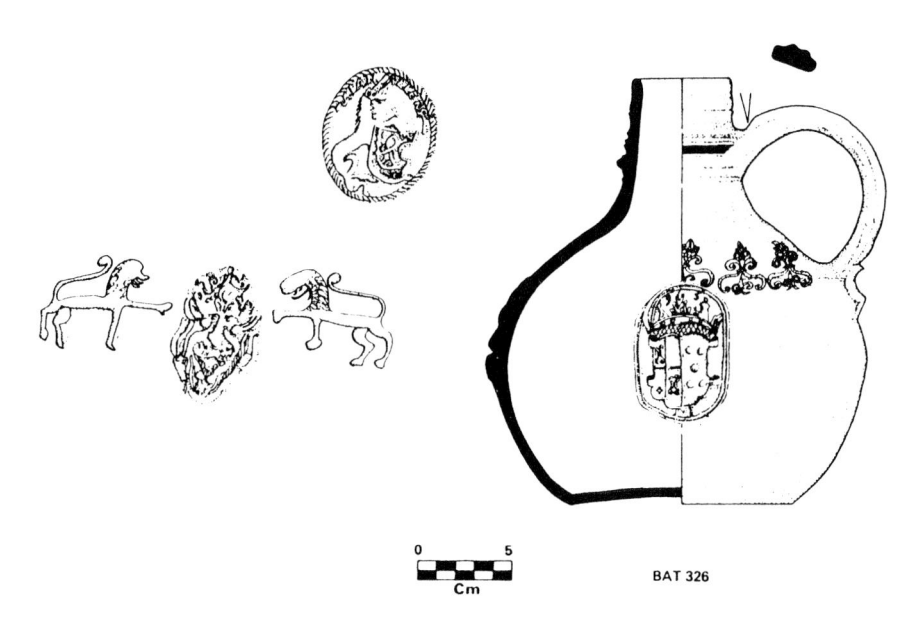

Fig. 4. Raeren or Westerwald stoneware pitcher applied with a medallion containing the trade mark of the Nijmegen stoneware dealer Jan Allers along with an armorial medallion dated [15]95. From the wreck of the VOC Batavia, lost off Western Australia, 1629.
(Western Australian Maritime Museum BAT 326)

East (Sténuit 1974, 239–243; Green 1977, 481–485). VOC archives of the early 17th century reveal that it was common practice to order Frechen-type *Bartmann* bottles for the Company's mercury export trade or for transhipment purposes (Sténuit 1974, 242; Green 1977, 481). During investigation of the wreck site metal puddles were found in association with around thirty fragments of Frechen stoneware pitchers and bottles of *Bartmann* type (around 50% of the total) and with glass bottles and their pewter caps. Another bottle containing mercury was discovered in 1881 washed up on the shore of the Isle of Fetlar, close to Yell (Reid 1884). Typologically of the same date, Sténuit (1977, 444) suggests that this jug could also come from the *Lastdrager* wreck.

A parallel discovery for this specialised use of post-medieval stoneware comes from the site of the VOC *Kennemerland*, which was also lost off the Shetlands in 1664 (Forster and Higgs 1973; see Dobbs and Price 1991 for most recent account). Two complete Frechen *Bartmann* bottles were raised, one of which was found in 1971 with its contents of 18 kg of mercury still intact (Foster and Higgs 1973, fig.8). Further investigations on the wreck in 1973 produced another Frechen *Bartmann* bottle, this time containing a cache of peach stones (Price and Muckelroy 1974, fig.8). It is impossible to say whether this find represents ship's cargo or the remains of the personal supply of a member of the ship's company. Whatever the case, the preservation of mercury and organic remains in association with Rhenish stoneware on this site demonstrates the versatility of these watertight and robust ceramic containers.

Investigations during the early 1970s on the wreck of the VOC *jacht Vergulde Draeck*, lost off Western Australia in 1656, also produced evidence for the transportation of mercury in Frechen *Bartmann* vessels. Puddles of mercury were found in reef crevices, and as droplets in fragments of concretion in half of the *Bartmann* necks, of which about eighty-eight were found (Green 1977; Elliot 1986, 89). The wreck also allows us a further opportunity of monitoring Rhenish stoneware form and ornament over the course of the second quarter to mid-17th century. Along with the *Batavia* wreck (see above), the *terminus ante quem* horizon provided by this site is proving invaluable in the establishment of manufacture and circulation dates for Rhenish stonewares found on European terrestrial sites of the period. Despite the similarity of a small number of bearded face-masks and rosette medallions, it is significant that there is no overlap in the decorative repertoire of Frechen *Bartmann* bottles recovered from either wreck. As regards form, the *Batavia* vessels are all of globular type, whereas the *Vergulde Draeck* assemblage is composed of both globular and ovoid (or biconical) bottles, the latter normally associated with mid- to later 17th-century contexts (Gaimster 1997). The absence of any mould-identical overlaps suggests a relatively close aggregate date for the *Vergulde Draeck* stonewares, a theory strengthened by the recovery of the only bottle applied with the date 1654 (Green 1977, cat. GT 830).

The medallions of imported Frechen bottles excavated from the destruction levels of the rogue stoneware kiln found at the banks of the Thames at the Woolwich Old Ferry Approach in 1974 represent the only reliably independent dating evidence for the production span of stoneware on this site. As such they hold the key to the dating of the earliest stoneware ceramics made in Britain. Alongside the locally-made products (made in the Frechen style), two sub-heraldic medallions from Frechen *Bartmann* bottles were published in the 1978 excavation report: one the crowned heart, the other a

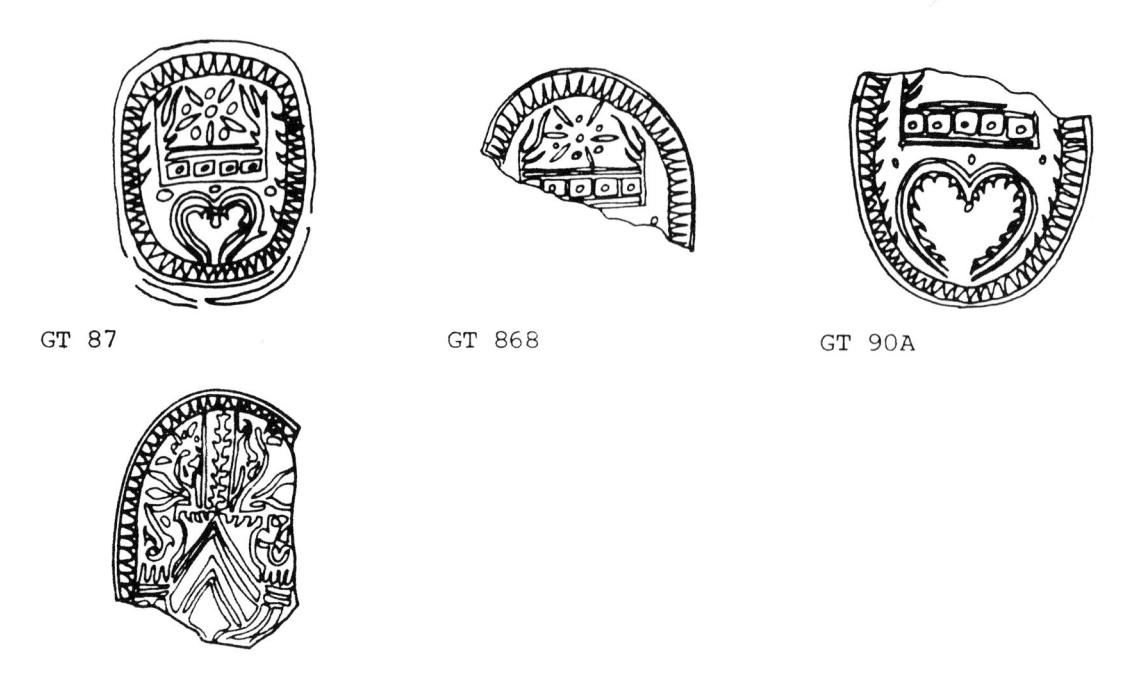

Fig. 5. Frechen stoneware bottle medallions from the wreck of the VOC Vergulde Draeck, lost off Western Australia, 1656. (Western Australian Maritime Museum GT 87, 868, 90A, 883)

simple chevron shield with a debased crest (Pryor and Blockley 1978, figs 34 & 35 respectively). Identical medallions – made from the same or very similar moulds – were recovered from the wreck of the *Vergulde Draeck* (Green 1977, cat. GT 87, GT 868 and GT 90A for the crowned rose type; and GT 883 for the chevron shield medallion; see composite Fig.5). Neither types are represented among the 1629 *Batavia* assemblage; and it is probable that they were not made before 1630. The closed contexts of the two VOC wrecks suggest that the Frechen imports at Woolwich were made at some point during the 1630s to 1650s. Although tentative at this stage, this equation pushes back the earliest date for stoneware manufacture in Britain as much as thirty to forty years – previously assumed to have only begun with John Dwight's patent of 1672 (Haselgrove 1990).

For the 18th century, the VOC *Hollandia*, lost off the Isles of Scilly in 1743, has produced a small number of Westerwald stoneware tewares (Gawronski *et al.* 1992, cat. H1682) which are only rarely found on terrestrial consumer sites (Gaimster 1997, cat. 132). Clearly a member of the ship's company thought it judicious to purchase stoneware for tea and coffee drinking aboard ship, as opposed to the more fragile earthenware or Chinese export porcelain versions which were also found on the site in large quantities. Frechen *Bartmann* bottles (e.g. Gawronski *et al.* 1992, cat. H172), Westerwald mineral water bottles and chamber pots (e.g. *ibid*, cat. H2615 and cat. H2911 respectively) and Langerwehe storage jars (e.g. *ibid*, cat. H935) constituted the remainder of the stoneware on the *Hollandia*. However, the numbers are too few to suggest that they represent anything more than ship's inventory or personal possessions. The international export trade in Rhenish stoneware had come to end by this stage except for a number of specialised forms such as these which continued to be popular abroad (Gaimster 1997). Both the VOC *Amsterdam*, which ran aground near Hastings in 1749 (Marsden 1985) and the VOC *Geldermalsen*, which sunk in the South China Sea in 1752 (Jörg 1986) have produced examples of Westerwald mineral water bottles. Once again the relatively low numbers of finds favour the impression that these vessels were personal property and were not part of the ship's cargo.

Dutch East Indiamen are not alone in providing archaeological contexts for the consumption of Rhenish stoneware during the 17th century. Finds in Scandinavian and Baltic waters provide further evidence for stoneware chronology, function and socio-behavioural analysis. Although still to be published fully, the small groups of Frechen and Westerwald stoneware from the *Vasa*, Gustavus Adolphus' 'royal ship' which sunk in Stockholm harbour in 1628 (Landström 1988), and the Swedish warship *Kronan*, which sunk off the coast of the island of Öland in 1676 (Kalmar 1986; this book, Chapter 17), demonstrate clearly the value of stoneware drinking and storage vessels for personal use aboard a warship of this date.

Stonewares from a wreck found off the island of Jutholmen in the Stockholm archipelago (Ingelman-Sundberg 1976) and from the so-called Dutch galliot which sunk in 1677 on the island of Kvitsøy off the coast of Norway (Andersen 1974) provide further evidence for both their important private rôle and their practical function as ship's equipment during the late 17th century. Alongside the typical *Bartmann* bottles of the period, the Kvitsøy site produced a number of smaller undecorated bottles from the same production source (Andersen 1974, fig.3 right). A group of these miniature vessels was excavated from the wreck of the *Vergulde Draeck* (Green 1977,

105–109). The contents of one were analysed and shown to be an ointment-like substance, with pork fat as its base. The discovery confirms the functional rôle of this particular stoneware form as a container for medicines or for valuable foodstuffs such as oil.

Other maritime contexts

This survey has concentrated on stoneware from ocean-going vessels. But it is important to remember that there are other closed maritime contexts which offer equally valuable information on the dating, lifespan and function of exported stonewares. Most notable among these are riverine contexts which range from casual finds on the shore to the cargo and inventory of wrecked vessels. From the former category, 'mudlarkers' on the banks of the river Thames in London have been collecting pewter lids of the type used in the mounting of traded stonewares during the 15th to 16th centuries (Kashden 1988). Many are still attached to their original stoneware handles while others bear Low Countries touchmarks. The publication in the Low Countries of closed ceramic assemblages in the *Corpus Middeleeuws Aardewerk* series offers further opportunities to study contemporaneous groups of post-medieval export stoneware from former inland riverine sites. Typical of this type of context is the 15th-century cog found on reclaimed land near Almere which contained a small group of Langerwehe jugs of the first half of the 15th century (Vlierman 1992, cat.1992 07/001–00; 1993, pl.6j; this book, Chapter 2). Coin evidence suggests that the ship was abandoned between c.1420 and 1440. At the other end of the chronological spectrum, the armed *tjalk* which sank in the Zuiderzee in 1673, produced a range of Frechen *Bartmann* bottles and a large Langerwehe storage jar (*Baare*) of broadly contemporary date (this book, Chapter 13).

Conclusions

Despite the wide distribution and frequency of excavated stoneware from post-medieval maritime contexts (spanning a period of over 300 years) relatively few examples can be thought with any certainty to represent cargo in its own right – despite the documentary and terrestrial archaeological evidence for this prolific international commodities trade. Most of the finds, with the exception perhaps of a percentage from the two Dutch East Indiamen the *Batavia* (1629) and *Vergulde Draeck* (1656), represent personal possessions or ship's equipment. However, a significant proportion of wrecks, including the *Mary Rose* (1545), *Vergulde Draeck* (1656), *Lastdrager* (1653), *Kennemerland* (1664) and the Dutch galliot found off Norway (1677), have supplied evidence of specialised use, namely in the storage of medicinal substances and the secure packaging and transportation of volatile cargoes, such as mercury.

Finally, we must not underestimate the importance of carefully recording stonewares from wrecks: by virtue of their chronological control these contexts offer invaluable evidence for assessing the lifespan and social 'curation' of individual wares. Dated vessels, in particular, can often be shown to have been in use for decades before the date of their final loss with the ship. With the vast majority of wrecks, it can be safely assumed that most associated artefacts were in use at the time of loss – in contrast to terrestrial sites which invariably contain large proportions of 'non-active' (residual and redeposited) artefacts. Along with the refinement of established chronologies, documented maritime sites offer the prospect of a functional and socio-behavioural context for post-medieval Rhenish stoneware. The plea, therefore, is for more detailed publication by excavators. Accurate recording of vessel profiles and applied relief decoration provides vital evidence for examining these questions.

References

Allan, J. 1984 *Medieval and Post-Medieval Finds from Exeter, 1971–1980*, Exeter Archaeological Reports, III, Exeter.

Andersen, A.B. 1974 'A Dutch galliot which struck a rock in 1677', *IJNA* 3, 91–100.

Arnold, J.Barto III & Weddle, R.S. 1978 *The Nautical Archaeology of Padre Island. The Spanish Shipwrecks of 1554*. Studies in Archaeology, New York

Blake, W. & Green, J. 1986 'A mid-XVI century Potuguese wreck in the Seychelles', *IJNA* 15, 1–23.

Boiten, A. & Vuuren, S. 1982 'European ceramics', *in* van der Pijl-Ketel (ed.), 246–249.

Clevis, H. 1993 'Juggling Jacobakannen: a quantitative analysis of measurements', *in* H. Clevis and J. Thijssen (eds), *Assembled Articles I, Symposium on medieval and post-medieval ceramics, Nijmegen 1993*, Nijmegen, 195–206.

Dobbs, C.T.C. & Price, R. 1991 'The Kennemerland site. An interim report. The sixth and seventh seasons, 1984 & 1986, and the identification of five golf clubs', *IJNA* 20, 111–122.

Elliot, G.B. 1986 'The success of Frechener flagons exported as 'Cologne Ware' in late medieval trade from the Rhine', *IJNA* 15, 85–91.

Erichson-Firle, U. & Vey, H. 1973 *Katalog der Deutschen Gemälde von 1550 bis 1800 im Wallraf-Richartz-Museum und im Öffentlichen Besitz der Stadt Köln*, Kataloge des Wallraf-Richartz-Museums, Cologne.

Forster, W.A. & Higgs, K.B. 1973 'The Kennemerland, 1971. An interim report', *IJNA* 2, 291–300.

Gaimster, D. 1987 'The supply of Rhenish stoneware to London 1350–1600', *The London Archaeologist* 5, No.13, 399–404.

Gaimster, D. 1997 *German Stoneware 1200–1900. Archaeology and Cultural History*, British Museum, London.

Gaimster, D.R.M., Redknap, M. & Wegner, H.-H. (eds) *Zur Keramik des Mittelalters und der beginnenden Neuzeit im Rheinland. Medieval and Later Pottery from the Rhineland and its Markets*, BAR International Series 440, Oxford.

Gawronski, J.H.G. 1990 'Sunken Dutch East Indiamen as a subject of underwater archaeological and historical research', *in* J.C. Besteman, J.M. Bos & H.A. Heidinga (eds), *Medieval Archaeology in the Netherlands*, Assen/Maastricht, 299–313.

Gawronski, J., Kist, B. & Stokvis-van Boetzelaer, O. (eds) 1992, *Hollandia Compendium. A contribution to the history, archaeology, classification and lexicography of a 150ft. Dutch East Indiaman (1740–1750)*, Rijksmuseum, Amsterdam.

Green, J.N. 1977 *The A- VOC Jacht* Vergulde Draeck, *wrecked Western Australia, 1656*, Part 1, BAR Supplementary Series 36(i), Oxford.

Haselgrove, D. 1989 'Steps towards English stoneware manufacture in the 17th century, Part 1, 1600–1650', *The London Archaeologist* 6, No.5, 132–138.

Haselgrove, D. 1990 'Steps towards English stoneware manufacture in the 17th century, Part 2', *The London Archaeologist* 6, No.6, 152–159.

Hurst, J.G. 1988 'Problems of Middle-Rhenish stoneware in Britain', *in* D.R.M. Gaimster *et al*. (eds), 335–342.

Ingelman-Sundberg, C. 1976 'Preliminary report on finds from the Jutholmen wreck', *IJNA* 5, 57–71.

Jörg, C.J.A. 1986 *The Geldermalsen. History and Porcelain*, Groningen.

Kalmar, 1986, *'Kronan'. Kalmar County Museum's Exhibition*, Kalmar County Museum, Kalmar.

Kashden, M. 1988 'Some notes on a collection of excavated lids', *Journal Pewter Soc.* 6.3, 88–92.

Kohnemann, M. 1994 *Raerener Bauerntänze*, Töpfereimuseum Raeren, Raeren.

Landström, B. 1988 *The Royal Warship Vasa*, Stockholm (2nd edition).

Marsden, P. 1985, *The Wreck of the Amsterdam*, London (2nd edition).

Murphy, L. 1983 'Shipwrecks as a database for human behavioral studies', in R.A. Gould (ed.), *Shipwreck Anthropology*, School of American Research Advanced Seminar Series, Albuquerque, 65–89.

Orton, C. 1982 'Pottery evidence for the dating of the revetments', in G. Milne and C. Milne (eds), *Medieval Waterfront Development at Trig Lane, London*, London & Middlesex Archaeological Society Special Paper 5, London, 92–99.

Price, R. & Muckelroy, K. 1974, 'The second season of work on the Kennemerland site, 1973. An interim report', *IJNA* 3, 257–268.

Pryor, S. & Blockley, K. 1978 'A 17th century kiln-site at Woolwich', *Post-Medieval Archaeology* 12, 30–85.

Redknap, M. 1984. *The Cattewater wreck. The investigation of an armed vessel of the early sixteenth century*, BAR British Series 131, Oxford.

Redknap, M. & Smith, R.D. 1990 'Introduction' to V.Fenwick and M.Redknap (eds), *Ships, Cargoes and East India Trade*, *IJNA* 19, 1–3

Reid, J.J. 1884 'Notice of two vessels of grey stoneware (Bellarmines or greybeards), one found full of quicksilver in Shetland, the other at Eyemouth', *Proc. Soc. Antiq.* 19, 34–38.

Reineking-von Bock, G. 1980 'Verbreitung von Rheinischem Steinzeug', *Keramos* 87, 11–50.

Ruempol, A.P.E. & van Dongen, A.G.A. 1990 *Pre-industrial Utensils 1150–1800*, Museum Boymans-van Beuningen, Rotterdam.

Rule, M. 1982 *The Mary Rose. The Excavation and Raising of Henry VIII's Flagship*, London

Ruppel, T. 1991, 'Zur Brandschatzung der Aulgasse während des Truchsessischen Krieges. Historische Überlieferung und archäologische Spuren', *Eine Siegburger Töpferwerkstatt der Familie Knütgen*, Kunst und Altertum am Rhein Nr.133, Cologne, 59–63

Stanbury, M. 1974 *Batavia Catalogue*, Western Australia Museum, Perth.

Sténuit, R. 1974 'Early relics of the VOC trade from Shetland. The wreck of the flute 'Lastdrager' lost off Yell, 1653', *IJNA* 3, 213–256.

Sténuit, R. 1977 'The Loss of the Fluit LASTDRAGER', *in* J.N. Green (ed.), 403–468.

Townsend, C.D. 1983 'Rheinisches Steinzeug aus dem Englischen Segelschiff Mary Rose', *Keramos* 102, 55–60.

Vandenbulcke, V. Lic. & Groeneweg, G. 1988 'The stoneware stock of Jan-Peterss and Cornelis-de-Kanneman: two merchants of Rhenish Pottery at Bergen-op-Zoom (NL) during the 2nd quarter of the 16th century', in D.R.M. Gaimster *et al.* (eds), 343–357.

van der Pijl-Ketel, C.L. (ed.) 1982 *The Ceramic Load of the 'Witte Leeuw' 1613*, Rijksmuseum, Amsterdam.

van Loo, J. 1984 'Jan Allers, Schipper en handelaar in aardewerk te Nijmegen en Culemborg uit de late zestiende en vroege zeventiende eeuw', *Antiek* 21, Jaarg.1, 22–29

van Loo, J. 1989 'Johann Aldersz de veer 'de Jonge', kannecooper/beytelschipper uit Dordrecht in de zeventiende eeuw', *Antiek* 23, Jaarg.7, 383–390.

Vlierman, K. 1992 'Ceramiek uit een vroeg-15e-eeuwse Kleine Kogge in Almere', *Corpus Middeleeuws Aardewerk (CMA) 7*, Amersfoort.

Vlierman, K. 1993 'Late medieval pottery in Dutch shipwrecks, and a well-dated inventory of the early 15th century', *Medieval Ceramics* 17, 69–73.

Wingood, A.J.1982 "Sea Venture". An interim report on an early 17th century shipwreck lost in 1609, *IJNA* 11, 333–347.

Zuiderbaan, L. 1977 'The historical background', *in* J.N. Green (ed.), 1–60.

10

The identification, analysis and interpretation of tobacco pipes from wrecks

David A. Higgins

INTRODUCTION

The post-medieval period has witnessed unprecedented changes in the social and economic organisation of populations; changes which have taken place on a world-wide scale. The underlying reasons and driving forces behind these changes are too numerous to describe here, but amongst them can be listed the adoption of tobacco and smoking. At first sight, smoking may seem to be no more than a trivial pastime, taken up to amuse post-medieval men and women in between bouts of inventing, exploring and colonising. However, as Goodman has recently pointed out, tobacco became a fundamental part of the global economy and influenced both the pattern and speed of western colonisation (Goodman 1993). By the 1660s, for example, tobacco duties from the Chesapeake colonies accounted for roughly one quarter of all the English customs revenues (Morgan 1975, 193). Likewise, the successes or failures of tobacco plantations were instrumental in determining the very survival of many early colonies. Tobacco itself leaves little trace in the archaeological record, but the remains of the farms, warehouses, shipping, processing plants and, above all, the pipes in which it was smoked, survive as testimony to the trade.

Despite the fact that tobacco had been 'known' since the time of Columbus, it was not until the last quarter of the 16th century that smoking appears to have been taken into western culture (Oswald 1975, 3–6). Once adopted, the habit spread rapidly through all levels of society and to almost every country in the world. In northern Europe the white clay pipe was the favoured method of taking tobacco and, over the last forty years, this class of artefact has been the subject of considerable study.

There are a number of reasons why pipes have attracted the attention of archaeologists. Firstly, they were both mass produced and extremely fragile, as a result of which they are very common on post-medieval sites. Secondly, pipes were strongly influenced by the dictates of fashion and so, given their short life expectancy, they can provide an accurate date for the contexts in which they are found. Thirdly, pipes often bear makers' marks and were made in different styles and qualities. These characteristics can be used to explore both the social status of the owner and the markets from which he or she obtained goods.

Over the last few years research on pipes has followed three main themes: identification, analysis and interpretation. A considerable amount of work has been undertaken to identify and describe both the pipes themselves and the makers who produced them. Documentary sources have been trawled to compile lists of pipemakers, and thousands of pipes have been drawn to illustrate the different styles in which they were made. Once collected, this data has been analyzed in a number of different ways. For example, graphs have been used to show fluctuations in the number of pipemakers over time, and typologies have been produced to classify and date their products. The archaeological evidence has also been interpreted to explore themes such as the differential status between sites, the movement of individuals or traded goods and the effects of the English Civil War.

Although a broad understanding of pipes has been reached, there are still many areas where particular questions remain to be answered. Typologies need to be checked and refined and regional studies carried out to define stylistic and marketing patterns in more detail. New questions are being asked of the existing evidence, and fresh material is constantly becoming available for study as post-medieval archaeology comes of age. Some of the most dynamic and exciting developments in this respect are now taking place in the field of underwater archaeology. This paper examines the contribution which pipes from wreck sites can make to existing studies, and the new avenues of exploration which they offer.

EXISTING PROBLEMS AND NEW POTENTIAL

Wrecks represent a class of site which has hitherto remained largely inaccessible to all but a few archaeologists. Technological advances combined with a growing interest in these sites have provided a completely new range of information. This data is not, however, directly comparable with land-based evidence. Wrecks produce specific collections of artefacts which were brought together for a single voyage. As outlined elsewhere in this book, the nature and range of artefacts present will be dependent on a number of factors which are peculiar to that voyage, such as the ship's destination and port of origin, the crew and the purpose of the voyage. Some ships were merchantmen which may have carried pipes as part cargoes for settlers; others will have carried pipes for trade with natives. Some ships were specially designed to carry passengers or slaves, or for military purposes. Pipes may have been carried as individual orders or as gifts for a friend or as part of the stores for the voyage. Above all, pipes would have been carried as personal possessions for use in everyday life.

The sources of the pipes on ships are likely to have been as diverse as the reasons for their presence. Some pipes may have been specially ordered to meet particular requirements; others may have simply been obtained for speculative trade. Some pipes may have travelled many miles across country as personal possessions, while others may have been purchased as last minute supplies at the final port of call. Without so much as examining the first pipe, it is clear that the material from a wreck is going to present challenges. Once a large number of wreck groups have been studied, it is likely that generalisations about the nature and organisation of them can be made. At present, however, such thoughts are in their infancy and much groundwork needs to be done. Large samples for study are needed from well documented wrecks so that relationships between the paper archive and the artefactual record can be established. It is only once this has been done that plausible hypotheses can be put forward for groups from undocumented wrecks. Despite these problems, all is not doom and gloom. There is much to be learnt during the construction of more detailed frameworks, and even small samples or isolated finds can prove to be of immense value.

Bowl form dating and typologies

One of the fundamental problems for archaeologists has been in compiling and refining pipe bowl form typologies so that pipes can be accurately identified. In order to do this a sequence of well-dated groups is needed from which typical forms can be extracted. In some areas there are many marked pipes which, once the makers have been identified, can be accurately dated. This enables a chronological sequence to be built up from stray bowl finds alone. However, pipe styles were intensely diverse both regionally and chronologically and consequently there are areas or periods where marked pipes do not occur and for which excavated groups have to be relied upon. Trying to find well-dated groups can be a frustrating task. Despite the wealth of documented events which have taken place, there are very few deposits which can be associated with them with any certainty. Even events as momentous as the English Civil War or the Great Fire of London can be hard to find in the archaeological record, and if such deposits are located, they are invariably contaminated with intrusive or residual material. All too often, a circular argument arises where a group of finds is attributed to a particular event on the basis of the pipe dates, when it is an independent date for the pipe group which is required.

The 'time capsule' nature of wreck sites has long been acknowledged as one of their most important attributes. Unlike land sites, the date of a wreck deposit can often be determined with great accuracy, and the problems of intrusive or residual material are much smaller or non-existent. Given that many ships were lost each year, it is theoretically possible that an annual sequence of artefact assemblages could eventually be recovered. The comparatively small number of wreck sites which have been systematically investigated already provide a good framework for research and offer a means of checking and refining established pipe typologies.

The importance of closely datable wreck groups is not, however, confined to merely checking established typologies. There are some periods, such as the late 16th century or the late 18th century, for which the artefactual evidence from land sites is particularly poor. The early period is a particular problem because not only is there a paucity of well-dated deposits but, where such deposits do occur, pipes are extremely rare. Documentary references to 16th-century pipes are few and far between but, collectively, they provide a patchy picture of the introduction of smoking during the last few decades of that century. Wreck groups may hold the key to understanding the introduction of smoking and defining the types of pipe which were in use. A wreck from Alderney, for example, has been tentatively dated to 1592. If this is correct, the pipes from the site are the earliest accurately dated examples yet recovered from either an underwater or terrestrial site.

Stem length and production techniques

The contribution which wreck groups can make to pipe studies is by no means limited to enhancing bowl typologies. There are many other questions about pipes and pipemaking which do not survive in contemporary records and which have been tackled from archaeological remains. The stem length of a pipe, for example, is known to have been an important factor in determining its style and price. This was because the longer the stem was, the more difficult and time consuming it was to make. The problem is that there are very few contemporary records which give details about the style or stem length of pipes, a rare example being from Bristol where, in 1710, the Company of Tobacco Pipe Makers limited production of pipes to the following lengths (Jackson & Price 1974, 83–85):

Long Pipes	16"
Dutch Pipes	14"
Jamaica Pipes	13"
Penned Heel Pipes	11½"
Gauntlet Pipes	11½"
Virginia Pipes	8½"

This document shows that six distinct patterns and lengths of pipe were recognised by the pipemakers but no record survives of their appearance, and only a handful of complete Bristol pipes of this period are known with which to compare the paper record. Until a reasonable sample of pipes has been recovered, it is impossible to identify all the bowl types or to assess how tightly the pipemakers adhered to the Company's regulations. Many of the patterns listed were clearly intended for the overseas trade, and wrecks are the obvious sites on which complete examples may be recovered. Cases of complete pipes have certainly been recovered from a number of wrecks, such as the *Adgillus* (1874) in the Irish Sea (Williams 1992) and the *Vergulde Draeck* (1656) off Western Australia (Green 1977). The Dutch pipes from the *Vergulde Draeck* had stem lengths of 350mm (13¾") – very similar to the length of the 'Dutch Pipes' produced by the Bristol makers 50 years later.

The crate of complete pipes recovered from the *Vergulde Draeck* not only provided information about stem length at that time but also allowed information about workshop practices to be deduced. This was only possible because of the large sample of identical products which were recovered (223 examples) – a sample size which is very rarely achieved on terrestrial excavations. These pipes showed that at least two different sizes of wire were being used at the same workshop to make pipes. This information may seem trivial, but it was of great importance at a time when a linear regression in stem bore was being explored as a means of dating pipes.

Other workshop practices can only be properly explored from large samples of their products. The frequency and consistency with which finishing techniques such as trimming, milling, burnishing, marking and decoration were used are factors which need to be defined. These attributes influenced the quality and price of a pipe, and so are relevant in interpreting the nature and status of domestic assemblages. Although terrestrial sites may have produced large numbers of pipes from a single workshop, these often span thirty or forty years of production, include many different styles and qualities of pipe, and encompass the products of several different employees. Only contemporary samples can be used to characterise the production at any one time and to act as a benchmark against which other periods or domestic groups can be assessed.

Trade and marketing

As well as providing information about the dating, style and production of pipes, wreck groups also offer the opportunity to study aspects of their trade and marketing. Being a generally lowly trade, conducted on a small scale in family run workshops, there is hardly any surviving documentation relating to the sale of pipes. The majority of English pipes are found no more than 10–15 miles from their place of manufacture and the surviving inventories of pipemakers often include pack saddles or carts. These pieces of information suggest that most pipes were simply sold locally by the manufacturers themselves. But in some cases different trade patterns emerge. The small town of Broseley in Shropshire, for example, became a prolific production centre which, by the second half of the 17th century, was supplying large parts of the Midlands, the Severn Valley and South Wales with pipes (Higgins 1987). There were dozens of different makers at Broseley, and yet their products are indiscriminately mixed in the areas to which pipes were sent. These makers cannot all have been travelling such distances to sell their pipes and some form of distribution involving middlemen must have been employed.

A similar situation applies to the pipemakers working in the large ports such as London, Bristol, Liverpool or Glasgow, the pipes from which are found all around the World. Did the middlemen just do business for one maker, or were mixed cargoes of pipes made up? Were all the pipes traded of the same type and quality, or were assorted shipments containing different varieties brought together? A trade advert from Bristol dated 1799 provides some tantalising clues (Fig.1). It lists a whole range of different lengths, styles and qualities of pipe which were available. These included a range of pipes for the domestic market as well as a series of types which were specifically designed for the various overseas markets. The advertisement was signed by four different pipemakers which suggests that they acted as some sort of partnership, and may well have made up orders which included the products from several different workshops. Nineteenth-century orders for Broseley pipes in the Ironbridge Gorge Museum archives show an even more complex situation. In this case, Scottish pipemakers were ordering special

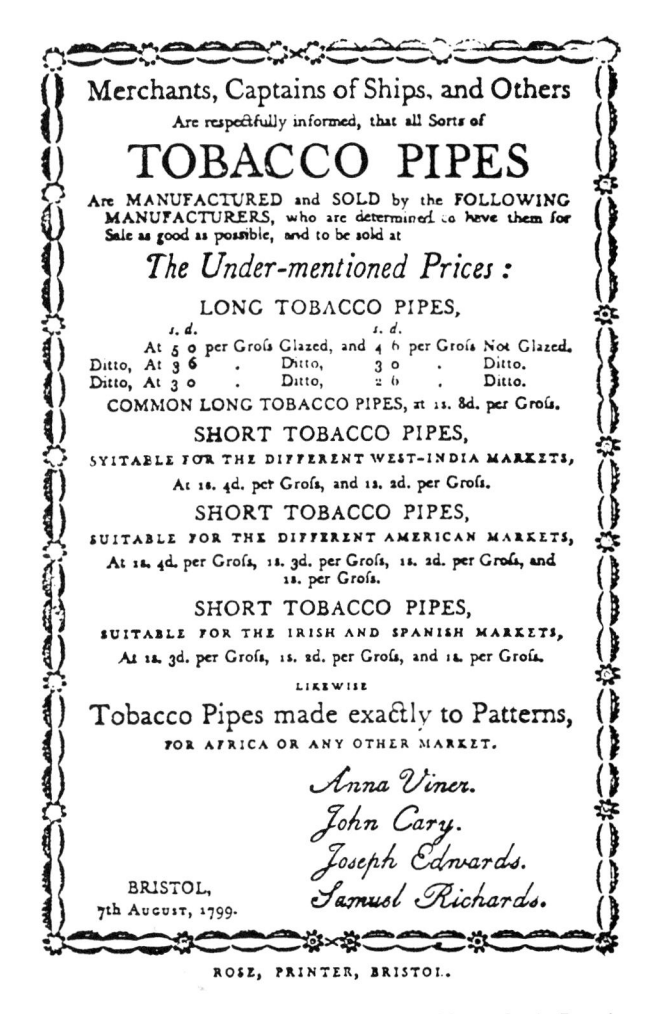

Fig. 1. An advertisement form the Bristol Pipe Makers Book (Bristol Record Office acc. no. 40241; see Jackson & Price 1974, 84).

types of Shropshire pipes to make up export orders for America. A similar practice continued into the 1980s when the Manchester pipemaking firm of *Pollock's* was making pipes for export to The Netherlands onto which they actually stuck the labels of the Dutch pipe manufacturer who had ordered them!

There is very little surviving documentary evidence for the mechanisms by which pipes were traded. The recovery of actual orders, made up and preserved on wreck sites, would shed much new light on this subject. They would show whether different styles of pipe or different makers' products were packed together, and give an idea of the range of products which were being shipped to foreign markets. Such groups would also offer the possibility of identifying the various types of export pipes, such as those listed in the 1799 advert. The recovery of pipe cargoes would also provide valuable information on the scale of the pipe trade, since it is not even known whether pipes were always listed on ships' inventories. Even if the pipes were always listed, they are usually quantified as so many boxes, barrels or crates. Until complete examples of these containers can be recovered, it is not possible to accurately measure how many each might have held and thereby work out export numbers from the various port records.

Associated artefacts

The final area in which wrecks offer new potential is the study of artefacts associated with pipes and tobacco. On terrestrial sites there has often been a continual process of recycling and decay. Metal objects were invariably recycled as scrap, while organic objects have often long since decayed. This means that much of the paraphernalia associated with smoking has been lost. The metal 'pipe kilns' in which used pipes were cleaned, the pipe tongs with which the pipes were lit or the cases in which they were kept rarely survive. Likewise there were tobacco boxes and pouches, tinder boxes, snuff bottles and rasps, pipe stands and other associated artefacts which may survive on wreck sites. The Dutch East Indiaman *Kennemerland*, for example, which was lost off the Shetlands in 1664, has produced a group of four brass tobacco boxes (Martin, C.J.M. 1987). Although these were found together and appear to have formed a part of the ship's cargo, they are all different and provide a good indication of the styles and decoration of the period.

Pipes from wrecks

Identification

Despite the recent advances in pipe studies, the identification of pipes from wrecks is not as simple as it might seem. Unlike towns which stay in one place and receive goods from regular sources, ships move about and take on supplies and cargo as they travel. Consequently, wreck groups can contain an exotic 'cocktail' of pipes from many different countries. A good example is the French privateer the *Machault*, lost in 1760, which has produced pipes attributed to makers in England, and in particular Bristol, The Netherlands and Bethabara, North Carolina (Bradley 1983). Likewise, the wreck of *HMS Sapphire*, lost in 1696, has not only produced pipes from London, various places in the West Country and Chester but also from an unidentified source in the Mediterranean (Richie 1978). Britain and The Netherlands provided the principal northern European sources of traded pipes, and products from these two areas have been quite well studied. But there are many other parts of northern Europe where systematic work has not yet been carried out and other parts of the World where even the most basic evolution of pipe types remains to be defined, a good example being the stoneware pipe found on a 19th-century British wreck in Indonesia (Higgins 1991).

Another aspect to the identification problem on wreck sites is the determination of the relationship a particular pipe bears to the wreck. In some cases large numbers of similar pipes are found, all bearing the same maker's mark, and it is likely that these pipes represent cargo. The problem is less clear cut where only small numbers of pipes are found. Sometimes the nature of the wreck or circumstances of the find can be of assistance. The warship *Vasa*, lost in 1628, produced a seaman's packet containing a pipe (Cederlund 1980, 253). In this case there is no question of cargo, and the pipe can clearly be seen as a personal possession. Conversely, the crates of pipes recovered from the *Adgillus* of 1874 were clearly cargo (Williams 1992). Pipes may also have formed part of a ship's stores, for use on the voyage.

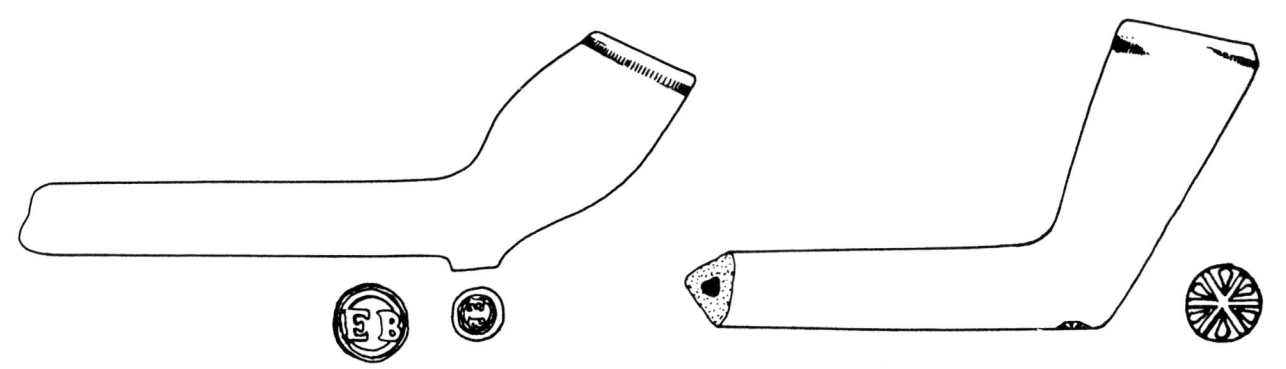

Fig. 2. Dutch pipe from the Monte Cristi 'Pipe Wreck' of c.1651–54 in the Dominican Republic, stamped EB and attributed to Edward Bird, an Englishman working in Amsterdam from c. 1630–65. Scale 1:1, with stamp at 2:1.

Fig. 3. Dutch export-style pipe from the Monte Cristi 'Pipe Wreck' of c.1651–54, stamped with a symbol mark below the bowl. Scale 1:1, with stamp at 2:1.

The condition of a pipe can be of use in determining its nature. Despite prolonged immersion in water the internal blackening of the bowl caused by use appears to survive well. Any pipes showing evidence of having been smoked must have been in use as personal possessions, rather than forming a part of the cargo or stores. Sometimes pipes were also re-used after they were broken, in which case the broken stem may have been reworked or show signs of wear. An English pipe from the *Machault*, for example, has a clearly worn groove in the broken stem where it has been clenched between the smoker's teeth (Bradley 1983, fig 8b).

It is important that this distinction between personal possessions and cargo is made, since sailors travelled widely and may have carried pipes obtained in many different ports or countries. These pipes are of immense interest in terms of social history, but cannot give a true picture of the commercial trade in pipes. This can only be determined from a study of the traded pipes themselves.

One final word of caution about the identification of pipes must be given about the context from which they were recovered. The particular significance of an assemblage of pipes from a wreck lies in the fact that they form a 'closed group', closely datable if the wreck can be identified. But the mere recovery of a pipe from a wreck site does not constitute evidence that it dates from the time of the wreck itself. Many wreck sites have been 'contaminated' with later debris dropped from passing ships. Worse still, the contents of the wreck may have been mixed and redistributed by currents, dragging anchors or the attentions of salvors, old or new.

As with any archaeological excavation, it is extremely important to determine the exact location and context of the finds and to assess the degree to which the deposit could have been contaminated. Where pipes are recovered from within seamen's packets or within cargo crates, there is no problem. Nevertheless, even apparently well-sealed contexts within the hold can pose problems, for discarded pipes may have lain amongst ballast or in inaccessible corners for some years before the loss of the ship itself. Both *HMS Dartmouth*, lost in 1690, and the *Olive Branch*, lost in 1699, have produced individual pipes which, on stylistic grounds, appear to date from well before the time of the wreck (Martin 1987, fig. 3.18; this paper, Fig. 6). In fact, the *Olive Branch* pipe of 1699 (Fig. 6) is closely comparable with a pipe lost on the Cromwellian wreck of 1653 off Duart Point, thought to be the *Swan* (Martin 1995, fig. 12, and this book, chapter 14).

Analysis

Although pipes are reported to have been recovered from many wreck sites, there appears to have been little systematic study of them. This is unfortunate, for even the simplest of questions can yield worthwhile results. The use of dated wrecks as a means of checking established typologies is an obvious case in point. The Duart Point wreck of 1653 provides an example of this. This wreck has produced at least three mid-17th-century pipe bowls (Martin 1995) which are noticeably larger than the forms dated to 1640–60 in Atkinson and Oswald's London typology (1969), which would tend to place the pipes in the 1660s or 70s, a decade or so later than the wreck. The simple checking of reliably dated bowl forms such as these can help refine typologies and provide a more secure basis for dating comparable material.

The systematic study of wreck groups can, however, provide much more detailed information about the pipes. A particularly good example of what can be achieved is provided by the *Vergulde Draeck* (1656), the pipes from which have been studied in some detail (Green 1977). A total of eight different types of pipe were identified from this wreck. Seven of the types were represented by between one and eight examples; the eighth type was represented by 233 examples, 223 of which were found packed in a box of buckwheat. The seven sparsely represented types may well have been personal possessions belonging to the crew, but there can be no doubt that the eighth type represents some form of stores or cargo. The form and marks on the pipes clearly indicate that they are Dutch and an analysis of the boxed group has provided valuable information about the pipes of this period.

In the first instance, the box and packing material provides evidence of how pipes were shipped. The pipes were all of the same form and decoration with the exception that, in three cases, the stems had been repaired during manufacture and the join disguised with a band of milling. This suggests a uniform product but one where minor defects were tolerated.

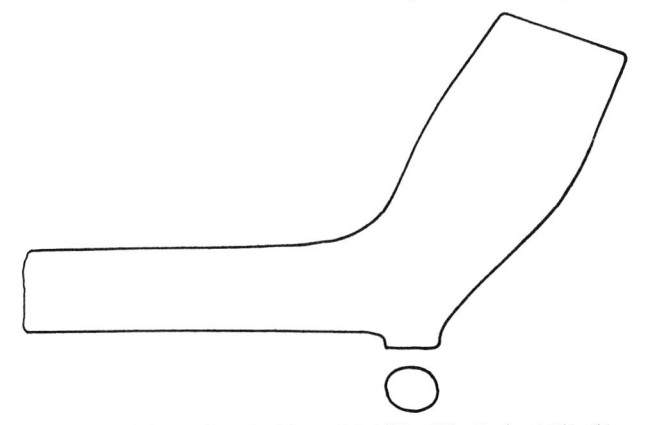

Fig. 4. English pipe from the Monte Cristi 'Pipe Wreck' of c.1651–54, possibly from Devon or Somerset, of c.1680–1710. This may well represent a late 17th-century salvage attempt on the site. Scale 1:1.

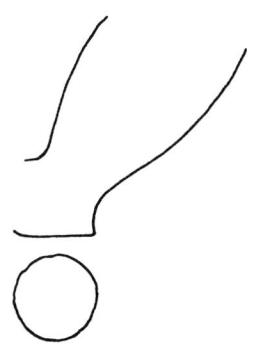

Fig. 5. Plain Scottish heel pipe (OB 85.39.19) from the Scottish ship Olive Branch, lost off Panama in 1699. Scale 1:1.

An analysis of the stem bores showed that detailed measurements with a travelling microscope were essential if subtle differences were to be detected and (as mentioned above) that a bimodal distribution of stem bores could be observed. These peaked at 2.8mm and 3.3mm, showing that two different thickness wires were being used in this workshop.

The accurate dating of the wreck meant that it could also be used to test the reliability of other dating methods, including stem bore dating. The date of the pipes, based on a Dutch typology, was about 1625–45, some twenty years earlier than the known date of the wreck. Likewise a date based on a calculation involving the bowl capacity gave a date some ten years too early. The bimodal stem bores gave dates covering a range of 50 years between 1614 and 1662, but again the average date was about twenty years too early. All these results suggested that the traditional dating of mid-17th-century Dutch pipes needed to be reviewed. In addition, the whole basis of stem-bore dating method was cast into doubt by the discovery that different sizes of wire were in contemporary use.

The *Vergulde Draeck* provides a good example of the type of analysis that is possible on wreck groups. There is no doubt that groups such as this have immense potential for contributing to the study of pipes, but that this potential remains largely under exploited (Higgins 1995).

Interpretation

The introduction and early development of smoking is poorly documented, and well-dated deposits of this period are few and far between. The fact that during the late 16th century smoking solicited comments from foreign travellers visiting Britain suggests that it was still something of a novelty elsewhere in Europe. Even where smoking did occur, it must have initially been on a small scale. Some indication of the early demand can be gleaned from the Bristol Port Books, which record the export of pipes to Ireland from as early as 1597 (Jackson and Jackson 1985, 7). In that year, and until 1603, almost all the export shipments were listed in dozens, while after 1612 the exports were usually by the gross. While these figures document a clear increase in the scale of the trade they do not provide any information about how common smoking was or how widely the habit had permeated through society.

Some information about the earliest smokers is now being revealed from wreck sites. The earliest pipes yet recovered are from the 1592 wreck off Alderney. This site has not only produced the familiar clay pipes but also a complete pewter pipe (David 1993). Metal pipes are mentioned in early references to smoking but, because they do not tend to have survived, they are rarely considered in modern literature. This example suggests that not only were metal pipes in use but that they had permeated down through society to the level of sailors by as early as 1592. Likewise, the recovery of several pipes from a partial examination of the site suggests that smoking was well established amongst the crew, perhaps more so than would have been imagined from the scant documentary references of the period.

In the case of the Alderney wreck the pipes have simply been interpreted as the belongings of the crew and used to provide a social context within which to place the early history of smoking. They provide the artefactual evidence against which to compare the documentary record. This is fine where the name and date of the wreck are known, but the situation is not always so easy. The 'Pipe Wreck' at Monte Cristi off the Dominican Republic has been so named because of the thousands of clay pipes which have been recovered from it (Hall 1989). Two basic types of pipe are prevalent on this site, a heel type (Fig. 2) and a heel-less type (Fig. 3). The forms of these pipes are typically Dutch and can be used to suggest both an origin for this unidentified wreck and to date it to the third quarter of the 17th century. The heel bowls are stamped EB and can be attributed to the Englishman Edward Bird, who moved to Amsterdam where he made pipes from about 1630–65. Bird's heel pipes are of a form that would have been smoked in Europe. The other pipes, however, are of a specific export type. Although they were made in Europe, this particular form is exceedingly rare there but very common on colonial sites in North America. In this case, the pipes can

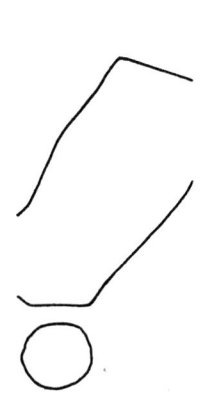

Fig. 6. Heel bowl from the Scottish ship Olive Branch *(1699), stylistically dating from c. 1650–80. Perhaps a residual artefact from within the ship (OB 85.39.19). Scale 1:1.*

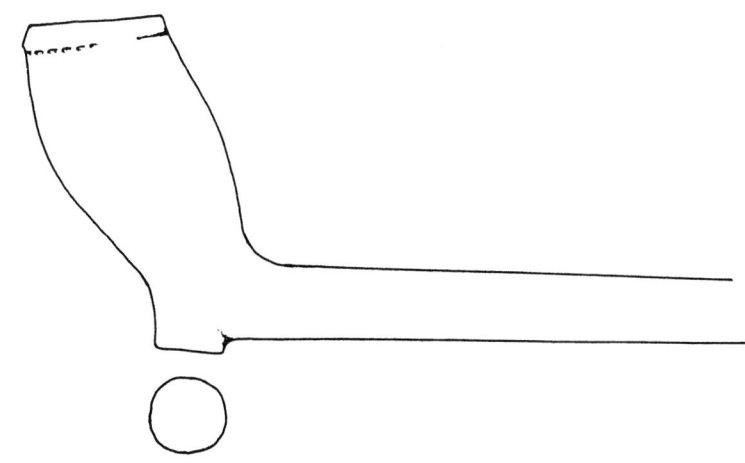

Fig. 7. Plain Scottish heel pipe (CB 79 V G29) from the Scottish ship Olive Branch *(1699). Scale 1:1.*

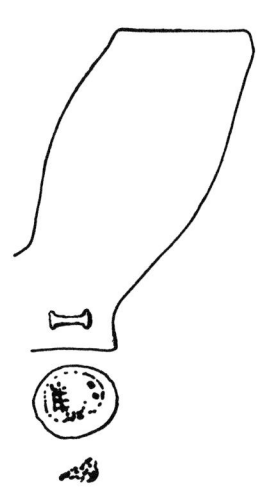

Fig. 8. Scottish pipe with moulded maker's initials (?PI) and a portcullis stamp on the heel from the Scottish ship Olive Branch *(1699). Possibly made by John or James Paterson of Stirling (OB 85.37.17). Scale 1:1.*

date from this visit and provide a reminder that wreck sites have always been of interest to salvors. The late 17th-century English pipe from the 'Pipe Wreck' may well provide the only documentation for a similar salvage attempt. As such, it provides a valuable piece of evidence and serves as a salutary lesson that all finds should be properly excavated and logged and not simply dismissed as being 'intrusive material'.

Other problems of interpretation arise when pipes of different nationalities occur together in contexts of the same date. Around English ports foreign pipes are often quite common. At Plymouth, for example, quite large numbers of Dutch pipes have been excavated alongside contemporary local products (Oswald and Barber 1969). The Dutch imports, however, are confined to deposits directly associated with the waterfront and are not so common elsewhere in the town. They can be explained as simply casual losses from visiting foreign sailors. In other cases Dutch pipes appear in closed association with British pipes. The resupply ship *Olive Branch*, lost in 1699 off the Scottish settlement in Panama, produced one Dutch pipe alongside the Scottish examples (Horton, Higgins and Oswald 1987; this paper, Figs 5–10). Dutch pipes were much more common in Scotland than in England but, even so, the records of the *Company of Scotland Trading to Africa and the Indies* clearly documents the commissioning of over 282,000 pipes for the Darien expedition (Gallagher 1987). These were all made by Scottish makers and so the Dutch pipe is almost certain to represent a personal possession brought by one of the settlers or crew.

be used to provide clues as to the origin, date, purpose and destination of the wreck.

A complication to the interpretation of the material from the 'Pipe Wreck' has been provided by the discovery of a single bowl of a slightly different type from the site (Fig. 4). Differences in this bowl's size and form clearly mark it as an English pipe of about 1680–1710. If the wreck had been located in the busy shipping lanes of the English Channel, this could easily have been dismissed as an intrusive item discarded from a passing ship. But this scenario seems unlikely in the shallow waters near to the shore of a Caribbean island. A much more likely explanation is offered by similar pipe finds from the *Nuestra Señora de la Pura y Limpia Concepción* which was lost in 1641, also off the Dominican Republic (Hall 1990). In this case the Spanish wreck produced three English pipes stamped LE and attributable to the Bristol pipemaker Lluellin (Llywelyn) Evans, who was working from about 1660–1686. The explanation for these anomalous finds is that an English salvage expedition is documented as leaving for the site in 1686 and working there in 1687. The discarded pipes must

While one stray pipe can be seen as a personal possession, it is not so easy to explain the presence of a whole group of foreign pipes. *HMS Dartmouth* was lost in the Sound of Mull in 1690. She had been resupplied in Greenock and her last port of call was at Fort William. Not surprisingly, the majority of the 58 identifiable pipe bowls recovered are of Scottish manufacture (Martin, P.F. de C. 1987). Despite this, nine of the bowls recovered (16%) are of Dutch manufacture. They are all of the same type and so must represent some form of stores or personal supply being carried on the ship. The

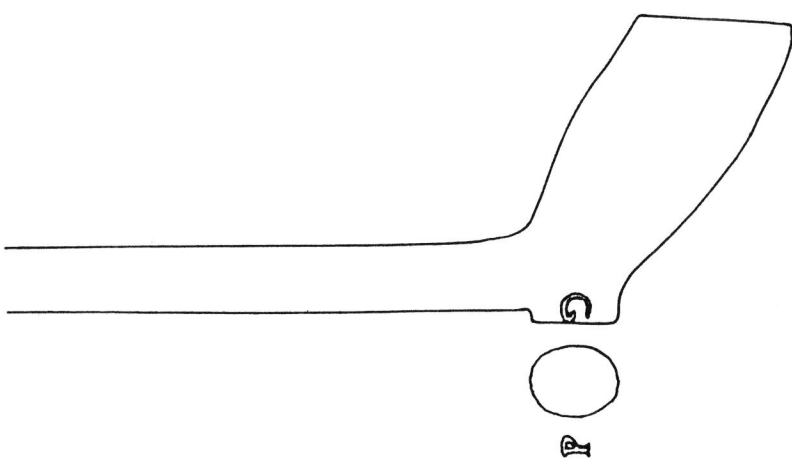

Fig. 9. Scottish pipe from the Scottish ship Olive Branch *(1699), with the moulded maker's initials PC for Patrick Crawford of Edinburgh (OB 85.35.3). Scale 1:1.*

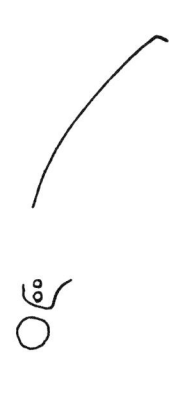

Fig. 10. Dutch pipe from the Scottish ship Olive Branch *(1699), with moulded dots on the right hand side of the heel only (OB 85.37.17). Scale 1:1.*

mechanisms by which this group of Dutch pipes came to be on an English warship may never be fully understood, but they do at least provide an example of the complexities which can be encountered when studying pipe groups from wrecks.

Conclusion

Pipe groups from wrecks offer a wide range of opportunities to gain fresh insights into post-medieval life. Pipes act as a 'marker dye' running through our record of early modern society, carrying with them information about their date, origin, quality and purpose. Being so cheap and short-lived, pipes reflect the circumstances of their loss more closely than most other classes of domestic artefact. There is an interactive relationship between the historical and documentary evidence for a wreck and the evidence carried by the pipes. When combined, these two elements offer the potential to explore avenues as diverse as the origins and social context of smoking, the manufacture and trade in pipes or the identification and dating of the wreck itself. This paper has outlined some of the ways in which pipes can be studied. It now remains for diving archaeologists to carefully collect and study these remains so that their full potential can be realised.

References

Atkinson, D. R. & Oswald, A. 1969 'London Clay Tobacco Pipes', *Journal of the British Archaeological Association* 32, 171–227.

Bradley. C. S. 1983 'Clay Tobacco Pipes from the Wreck of *Le Machault*, 1760', unpublished report prepared for Parks Canada.

Cederlund, C. O. 1980 'The Oldest Clay Pipes in the Warship Wasa', *in* P. J. Davey (ed.), *The Archaeology of the Clay Tobacco Pipe*, Vol IV, BAR International Series 92, Oxford, 253–256.

David, N. 1993 'Pewter Tobacco Pipes', *Society for Clay Pipe Research Newsletter* 38, 16–20.

Gallagher D. B. 1987 'Clay Pipes for the Company for Scotland: Documentary Evidence', *in* P. J. Davey (ed.), *The Archaeology of the Clay Tobacco Pipe*, Vol X, BAR British Series 178, Oxford, 233–238.

Goodman, J. 1993 *Tobacco in History*, Routledge.

Green, J. N. & others 1977 *The Loss of the Verenigde Oostindische Compagnie Jacht Vergulde Draeck, Western Australia 1656, Part I*, BAR Supplementary Series 36 (1), Oxford.

Hall, J. L. 1989 'The 'Pipe Wreck' at Monte Cristi', *Society for Clay Pipe Research Newsletter* 23, 6–8.

Hall, J. L. 1990 ''LE' Pipes on a Spanish Shipwreck', *Society for Clay Pipe Research Newsletter* 27, 1–5.

Higgins, D. A. 1987 *The Interpretation and Regional Study of Clay Tobacco Pipes: A Case Study of the Broseley District*, PhD Thesis submitted to the University of Liverpool.

Higgins, D. A. 1991 'An Unusual Pipe from Indonesia', *Society for Clay Pipe Research Newsletter* 31, 15–16.

Higgins, D. A. 1995 'Clay Tobacco Pipes: A Valuable Commodity', *IJNA* 24, 47–52.

Horton, M. C., Higgins, D. A. & Oswald, A. 1987 'Clay Tobacco Pipes from the Scottish Darien Colony 1698–1700', *in* P. J. Davey (ed.), *The Archaeology of the Clay Tobacco Pipe*, Vol X, BAR British Series 178, Oxford, 239–252.

Jackson, R. & Jackson, P. 1985 'Miles Casey – the Earliest Bristol Pipemaker?', *Society for Clay Pipe Research Newsletter* 5, 2–8.

Jackson, R. G. & Price, R. H. 1974 *Bristol Clay Pipes*, Bristol City Museum: Research Monograph No 1.

Martin, C. J. M. 1987 'A Group of Pipes from the Dutch East Indiaman Kennemerland, 1664' *in* P. J. Davey (ed.), *The Archaeology of the Clay Tobacco Pipe*, Vol X, BAR British Series 178, Oxford, 211–224.

Martin, C. J. M. 1995 'The Cromwellian shipwreck off Duart Point, Mull: an interim report', *IJNA* 24, 15–32.

Martin, P. F. de C. 1987 'Pipes from the wreck of the Dartmouth, 1690: a reassessment', *in* P. J. Davey (ed.), *The Archaeology of the Clay Tobacco Pipe* X, *Scotland*, BAR British Series 178, Oxford, 225–232.

Morgan, E. S. 1975 *American Slavery, American Freedom*, New York: Norton.

Oswald, A. 1975 *Clay Pipes for the Archaeologist*, BAR British Series No 14, Oxford.

Oswald, A. & Barber, J. 1969 'Marked Clay Pipes from Plymouth, Devon', *Post-Medieval Archaeology* 3, 122–142.

Richie, C. F. 1978 'Clay Tobacco Pipes from the Baybulls Wreck, Newfoundland, 1696: A Report in Support of the Preliminary Excavations', unpublished report prepared for Parks Canada.

Williams, J. 1992 'The Wreck of the *Adgillus*, 1874', *Society for Clay Pipe Research Newsletter* 36, 9–10.

11

Coinage from post-medieval wrecks

Edward Besly

INTRODUCTION

Virtually every wreck of the early modern period that is excavated produces coinage. This was a period when coinage was widely used, both in domestic economies and in international trade. The exploitation of precious metal reserves in the New World and the commercial activities of European companies in the Far East led to huge quantities of bullion, mainly in the form of coined silver, being transported long distances on a regular basis. The popular image of early modern wrecks is one of 'treasure ships', full of 'pieces of eight', and this has not been dispelled by a series of spectacular sales of coins and bullion from – to name but three – the *Atocha* (1622), the *Hollandia* (1743) and the *Nuestra Señora de la Luz* (1752). The Armada anniversary in 1988, too, drew attention to the rich finds from some of those wrecks.

For many such wrecks from the early modern period, there is of course documentary evidence – sometimes very detailed – for the identity of a ship, the date of its loss, its cargo, and so on. But this is not always the case, and the evidence of coins, particularly the personal possessions which will not be recorded on any cargo manifest, can make a useful contribution to the pictures that emerge from the study of wrecks; by the same token, the finding and recording of coins from wrecks may sometimes contribute to the understanding of questions relating to coin production and circulation. Unlike casual finds, those from a given wreck are known to have been lost on a single occasion (this may be known precisely, which is rarely true for a hoard); and whatever artificial circumstances attend the coins from a ship, they have not necessarily been selected for saving – a feature of hoards which is sometimes used to argue against their value as evidence for currency.

Coins may be present on board in several rôles. They may form part or all of the cargo; they may form the ship's funds; they may be private possessions of individuals on board. They may even be part of the fabric of the ship, as for instance the two from the Danzig area incorporated into the mast step of the late 14th-century cog from Vejby in Denmark (Crumlin-Pedersen 1979, 25) – a long-standing custom, when we remember the 1962 Blackfriars ship from the River Thames, a Roman coasting-barge with a worn coin of Domitian (AD 81–96) in this position (Marsden 1994, 49).

CARGO

Coins as cargo provide the most spectacular finds, and the three ships mentioned above will serve to illustrate this point. In chronological order: the *Atocha*, wrecked on the Florida Keys in 1622, was carrying gold and silver coinage and bullion as part of one of the regular Spanish New World treasure fleets. She has yielded over 180,000 coins, mainly of silver, packed in chests (Christie's 1988). The *Hollandia*, lost off the Scillies in July 1743, was a Dutch East Indiaman carrying coined silver in bulk to the Far East (Lane and Son 1973). The *Nuestra Señora de la Luz* sank off Montevideo in July 1752, carrying gold bars and over a million pesos in newly-minted gold coins, the old-style hand struck 'cobs' from Lima mingling with the machine-made coins of the new mint of Santiago. In this case, most of the cargo was recovered soon after the wreck. Spectacular though the 2,000 or so large gold coins recovered recently are, they represent perhaps two per cent of the original numismatic cargo, if the 200,000 pesos of contraband specie said to have been hidden in the ship's powder magazine are included (Sotheby's 1993).

There are also several examples of wrecks of ships carrying cargoes of coin from British mints, though generally of a more mundane nature. The *Admiral Gardner*, wrecked on the Goodwin Sands in January 1809, was carrying forty-six tons of copper coinage minted in Birmingham for the East India Company. She is paralleled by the *Leonidas*, lured by wreckers onto Scaterie Island, Nova Scotia, on 11 August 1832, carrying around eleven tons (about a million pieces) of the new copper coinage for Canada, or half of the total struck (Dow 1989). More recent, but at about 2,500 fathoms somewhat less accessible, are 1,240,000 silver halfcrowns and 720,000 cupronickel pennies dated 1941, en route for Southern Rhodesia, lost near the Equator when the *SS Benvrackie* was torpedoed on 13 May 1942, while somewhere in the North Atlantic there is also a substantial shipment of Faroe Islands coins dated 1941 (G.P. Dyer, pers. comm.).

Ship's money

Official ship's money is perhaps less easy to identify, but several possible examples may be quoted, again in chronological order. There is documentary reference to Spanish money taken from the looters of the King's Lynn ship *Ann Francis*, wrecked near Aberavon in Glamorgan in December 1583. The ship had left Lynn in October, and was apparently wrecked on her return voyage – the money probably representing part of the proceeds of the sale of a cargo of grain in Spain or Portugal (Blundell, forthcoming). Two barrels of copper coins, each containing about 900, were among the 4,000 coins or so found on the *Vasa* (1628) and have been suggested as being in some way 'ship's money' (Kvarning 1968, 17).

The £35 or so in mixed silver monies recovered from the English frigate *HMS Feversham*, which went down near Cape Breton in Nova Scotia in October 1711, have been interpreted as the residue of £569 drawn by the Captain and Purser in New York on 4 October, for provisioning (Christie's 1989). If this is so, the coins shed interesting light on the currency of the English New World colonies at the time, comprising a mixture of Dutch Lion Dollars, a little English money, the illegal issues of the New England settlers themselves (the Willow Tree, Oak Tree and Pine Tree shillings dated 1652), and Spanish-American coins, some of which had been adapted locally by plugging them with extra pieces of silver.

Personal possessions

The third main category of coinage, personal possessions, provides some scope for surprises. While the crew of a ship might not be paid until a voyage was over, some, particularly senior men, might be in a position to trade in a small scale on their own account; others might simply wish to keep their valuables with them. The evidence from the *Vasa* (1628) included small sums of money in purses in private sea chests, and even on the person of a sailor who was trapped below decks (Kvarning 1968, 15). The *Mary Rose* (1545) has produced several purse hangers and leather pouches or purses, one of which contained coins. So far, none of the silver coins has been identifiable, which is a little disappointing since the *Mary Rose* sank at the time of a rare period of debasement of the English coinage, and might have produced some interesting assemblages; the gold coins are dominated by the almost pure 'fine gold' issues (known as angels), rather than coins of the 22–carat 'crown gold' standard introduced by Henry VIII in 1526, though the latter are present. From the *Atocha*, small numbers of 1– and 2–escudo gold coins from the Spanish mainland mints, such as Seville, are likely to be possessions of the crew or the ship's passengers (a category not to be ignored), rather than part of the cargo of bullion bars and the huge amounts of freshly-minted New World silver coins. From just before the period officially covered by the conference, the 1963 IJsselmeer K 73/74 wreck produced a purseful of local silver coins, presumably the property of the ship's owner (Reinders *et al*. n.d., 27–8).

The situation at Needles Rock, Isle of Wight, is a little more complicated. On 24 April 1753, the 5th-rate, 44–gun *HMS Assurance* ran aground here and was lost. She was returning from the West Indies, carrying the Governor of Jamaica and nearly £60,000 in specie, almost all of which was recovered immediately (Bingeman 1980). Excavations have recovered a number of Spanish coins, predominantly 8–reales down to 1752 which might represent unrecovered cargo, but one deposit of ninety-six coins found within a limited area comprised mainly ½, 1– and 2–reales and would appear to represent a private sum of money reflecting the currency in everyday use in Jamaica in the early 1750s.[1]

A further complication is provided by the frigate *HMS Pomone*, which went down on almost the same spot in October 1811. Coins struck after 1752, which include Spanish dollars, must be from *Pomone*, but there are some surprises. The site has yielded at least twenty late 3rd-century A.D. tetradrachms from Alexandria in Egypt, mainly in the names of the Roman emperors Probus (276–82) and Diocletian (284–305). These were the currency of a closed economy, and as a general rule are rarely found outside Egypt, though a similar group was found at Jerbourg, in Guernsey, during the last century. A third, Roman, wreck on the same spot is highly unlikely, and the *Assurance* is a similarly improbable source. Here we seem to be dealing with private souvenirs, *Pomone* having spent several years in the Mediterranean. Small change from Malta, Naples, Sicily, Sardinia and Mallorca – akin to the odd foreign coins brought home from holidays abroad today – the coins of Roman Egypt, an 11th-century Byzantine copper (her last voyage had taken in Constantinople, where she picked up the retiring Ambassador to Persia) and a 2nd century BC coin from Mylasa in Caria (today Southwestern Turkey) all provide a graphic picture of *Pomone*'s Mediterranean itinerary.

Numismatic aspects

For the numismatist, wreck coins complement the evidence of hoards and single finds for coinage manufacture and currency. No one of these three categories is without its problems when one starts to ask how representative they are of contemporary monetary circulation. Ships form artificial societies, and money from them may be as unrepresentative of general circulation as hoards are sometimes claimed to be. However, the 271 silver coins from Charles II's royal yacht *Mary*, wrecked on the Skerries off Anglesey on 25 March 1675, form a remarkably normal spread of material when compared with contemporary English hoards: shillings and sixpences of Elizabeth I and James I; the same plus halfcrowns of Charles I; with a sprinkling of Charles II, Scots, Irish and continental coins, and a handful of smaller denominations (Warhurst 1977). It is possible that they derive from a limited number of deposits, and qualify as 'hoard' material; equally the paucity of small denominations among them – a characteristic of hoarded coins – may be a question of lack of survival or of incomplete recovery.

Fig. 1. Coins from the Needles, Isle of Wight (H.M.S. Assurance/H.M.S. Pomone). **Spanish America:** *1. 8 reales ('cob'), Lima 1739, assayer V; 2. 8 reales, Mexico 1751; 3. 2 reales, Mexico pre-1733; 4. 2 reales, Potosí 172X; 5. 2 reales, Guatemala (1733–c.1752);* **Roman Egypt:** *6. Aurelian (AD 270–75); 7. Probus (276–82); 8. Diocletian (284–305), billon tretradrachms, Alexandria. (Photographs: E. Besly)*

Nevertheless, wreck sites have produced new and useful information. Much relates to new varieties of coins, such as the previously unknown half plak issued by the city of Kampen in the 15th century, among the coins from the IJsselmeer K 73/74 wreck (Reinders *et al.* n.d., 27–8). The presence or absence of a category of coin in the Spanish treasure ships may help to refine the dating of coin issues or the careers of mint personnel, such as the assayers whose initials appear on the coins: it should be remembered that before the mid-17th century it was by no means usual for coins to bear an explicit date. The 1554 Padre Island wrecks in the Gulf of Mexico have made a contribution here (Arnold and Weddle 1978, 279–87). The Padre Island assemblage also allows one to observe the degree to which the 16th-century Mexican mint officials complied with the provisions of an edict of 1540 (they didn't); and the *Nuestra Señora de la Luz* illustrates the technical teething troubles of the new mechanised mint at Santiago in 1750–51.

Closer to home the wreck of the *Mary* has solved a longtime conundrum of Irish numismatics, the date of the so-called St Patrick's halfpennies and farthings. These coins, which depict St Patrick preaching and King David playing a harp, bear no ruler's name or date, but have long been recognised as Carolean; the presence of a farthing of this type on the *Mary* in 1675 finally establishes 1674 rather than 1678 of the two previously-suggested dates for its issue (Dolley and Warhurst 1977). This may seem to be a small point, but one essential strength of coins as evidence is their susceptibility to close dating and the use to which this can be put. It is therefore of some importance that their dates of issue be established as accurately as possible (in the case of the *Mary*, the St Patrick farthing is the latest coin to be found). Likewise, questions regarding the physical state, for instance of wear and clipping, of coins minted before the machine age are better understood in the context of good numbers of freshly minted examples – many of which were anything but circular or evenly struck to start with. The contrast between cob and pillar dollars from the *Hollandia* provides an extreme example (Lane and Son 1973).

COINS AND THE DATING OF WRECKS

Coins are, of course, potentially very useful pointers to the dating of wrecks of any period. For 17th- and 18th-century wrecks, documentary and historical sources will usually supply the identity of a given ship, but the coins can provide comforting confirmatory evidence. On earlier sites, from the later medieval period to the 16th century, coin evidence can assume greater importance. The 110 or so English gold nobles of Edward III place the loss of the Vejby cog around 1380

(Crumlin-Pedersen 1979). The cog excavated in 1986 at Almere, in Flevoland, yielded three coins from Gelre and Utrecht which provide a *t.p.q.* of 1420 and a *t.a.q.* of 1440 (Vlierman 1994); and the K 73/74 IJsselmeer wreck found in 1963 contained a purseful of eleven 15th-century coins closing with fresh coins issued around 1458 (Reinders *et al.* n.d.). In each case, the lack of prolific subsequent coinages – those of the Burgundian Netherlands from 1434 and the Utrecht, Deventer and Groningen issues of the later 1460s – adds a further reason for believing that the numismatic evidence is a reliable indicator of the date of the ship's loss. At Villefranche-sur-Mer in southern France, a small but varied selection of French and Italian coins helps to place the wreck of a Genoese ship in the first two decades of the 16th century (Guérout *et al.* 1989, 127 and 159–65). The ship is likely to be the *Lomellina*, lost in a mid-September storm in 1516, and the coins, which have an absolute *t.p.q.* of 1503, although one of them is a type which could have been issued until 1518, are consistent with this identification.

Table 1. Examples of coin evidence and dates of loss, 16th to early 19th centuries.

Vessel	Date of loss	Latest coin(s)	Reference/Source
Mary Rose	July 1545	1544–5	Mary Rose Trust
Girona	1588	1588	R.Heslip, pers. comm.
Atocha	September 1622	1622	Christie's 1988
Vasa	August 1628	1627?	Kvarning 1968
Mary	March 1675	1670*	Warhurst 1977
Kronan	June 1676	1676	Einarssen 1994
H.M.S. Feversham	October 1711	1705 or later	Christie's 1989
Whydah	April 1717	1716	Cembrola 1987
Hollandia	July 1743	1742	Lane and Son 1973
N. S. de la Luz	July 1752	1751	Sotheby's 1993
H.M.S. Assurance	April 1753	1752	Unpublished (author)
H.M.S. DeBraak	May 1798	'before 1797'	Hess 1987
H.M.S. Pomone	October 1811	1809	Unpublished (author)

* = excluding St Patrick farthing

As might be expected, coins from the great treasure ships give latest dates very close to those of the wrecks, where these are known. The *Atocha* was carrying coins dated 1622, the year she sank. The *Hollandia*'s cobs go down to 1739, and the Mexican pillar dollars and Dutch issues to 1742, in a ship lost in July 1743. In many other cases where the wreck can be identified, the latest coins recovered lie within one to five years of the wreck date (Table 1). In general, therefore, it would appear that coin evidence from an uncertain wreck should provide a fair indication of date of loss. However, the Glamorgan wreck of the *Ann Francis*, in December 1583, demonstrates that matters are not always so straightforward.

For many years there have been occasional chance finds of 16th-century artefacts and coins from a relatively small stretch of Margam beach, Mid Glamorgan, about two miles south of the present canalised mouth of the river Afan. In 1977, the National Museum of Wales acquired, *inter alia*, two pairs of navigational dividers and fourteen coins from Spain, Portugal and Germany which had been found in this area. The coins are very consistent in date, and none need be later than 1557. A wreck at around this date was postulated (Boon 1974). There the matter rested, but in recent years, many more coins (perhaps 200) have been found. Few have been examined professionally (see this book, Chapter 16), but it appears that 1557 remains the terminal date. The one documented wreck from the area is the *Ann Francis*, driven ashore at the mouth of the Afan in December 1583. It is not yet known exactly where this was, though there is contemporary reference to goods 'cast to land on both sides of the river Avan' (N.L.W. Penrice and Margam Mss 5728), and it is likely that subsequent coastal changes and harbour works have confused the picture. The finds may represent dispersal by coastal or human agency, but it is possible that the wreck site may be relatively close to where the concentration of finds occurs.

The *Ann Francis* was promptly looted, and was the subject of a dispute between neighbouring landowners (until, that is, the ship's true owner, Francis Shaxton of King's Lynn, got to hear of it). Here the physical evidence from Margam beach is not wholly in accord with the documentary, since of the numerous coins, apparently none was less than twenty-five years old at the time of the wreck. At the time, it was apparently normal practice for cargoes such as the *Ann Francis* had carried to be paid for in bullion silver, that is, old or foreign silver coin, and this would appear to explain the discrepancy between documentary and physical evidence (Blundell, forthcoming). However, the Museum's group includes one gold coin and three coppers, all Portuguese and all from the last few years of King John III, who died in 1557. The gold coin, allowing for some beach abrasion, is a fine example, and not worn by circulation. The coppers are less well preserved, but again not much worn. Nor, for that matter, are the Spanish and German coins, though some of the former do appear to have been clipped. The copper coins, in particular, are everyday change, and these might indicate that the ship from which they derive had visited or come from Portugal. *Prima facie*, the *Ann Francis* is the probable source of the Margam beach finds (and a pewter plate made at some time between the 1560s and the 1580s, which was found in 1989, is highly likely to have come from her). Mindful of the '*two wreck syndrome*', and in the absence of any documentary evidence (where there is plenty regarding the *Ann Francis*), the idea of a wreck c.1557 should perhaps not be pushed too far, but it may be noted that a French ship was wrecked at Oxwich, on the nearby Gower peninsula, in December 1557 (Williams 1974, 176–7), which perhaps suggests that conditions were difficult on the Glamorgan coast at that time. Whatever the case, it is important that coin finds such as these should be examined in proper detail.

The problem of interpreting beach finds surfaces again in West Wales. At Newgale, Pembrokeshire, there has been a steady trickle of coin finds over the past few years, and these are beginning to cluster into groups suggestive of single sources. Three Spanish and Portuguese copper coins all lie in the second half of the 16th century. Seven 17th-century tokens from the 1650s–1660s found since 1993 include five isued in Devon: one by a Plymouth vintner, one from

Tiverton, one from Great Torrington and two from Bideford. These are the first Devon tokens to be noted from Wales, in a series which has been carefully recorded for many years. A Youghal penny dated 1667 and a Bristol City farthing (ubiquitous in South Wales) complete this group. There are also four Spanish-American silver coins with dates around 1730. Non-numismatic artefacts from Newgale appear also to date between the 16th and 19th centuries. Identifying these with the numerous west Welsh wrecks is another matter, however. Finally, though somewhat outside the immediate brief of this paper, there are also several Roman coins. These include two unworn coins of the Roman emperor Claudius I (AD 41–54) which, in conjunction with estuarine finds of Claudian and Neronian coins from Carmarthen and Loughor, could give credence to the notion of the coastal survey of Wales in the forties or fifties AD, before the Romans occupied Wales by land, as adumbrated by the late A.L.F. Rivet in his study of Ptolemy's *Geography* (Rivet and Smith 1979, 115–17).

In conclusion, a simple point made at the 'Artefacts from Wrecks' Conference by David Higgins, is worth restating: however mundane, all artefacts deserve proper examination. In the case of coins, even though most have by now been classified (often to extremes of detail), and many handbooks exist, examination of a site assemblage by an appropriate specialist, as is normal for excavations on 'dry' land, might produce pertinent information which would otherwise be missed.

Note
1   Coins found on the *Assurance/Pomone* site in 1976–9 were summarised by J.E. Cribb in *Coin Hoards* 4 (1978), nos 400 and 404; *idem* 5 (1979), no.307; and coins found 1980–1 by E.M. Besly and J.M. Bingeman, *Coin Hoards* 7 (1985), no.573. Subsequent finds, as yet unpublished, have been identified by the writer. I am grateful to John Bingeman for permission to use this material.

References

Arnold, J. Barto III & Weddle, R.S. 1978 *The Nautical Archaeology of Padre Island. The Spanish Shipwrecks of 1554*. Studies in Archaeology, New York.

Bingeman, J. 1980 'The Needles, Isle of Wight', *IJNA* 9, 254–5.

Blundell, J. forthcoming 'A Tudor wreck near Aberavon in Glamorgan', *Maritime Wales*.

Boon, G.C. 1974 'A sixteenth-century wreck off Margam?', *Bulletin of the Board of Celtic Studies* 25, 523–4.

Cembrola, B.1987 'The Whydah is for real', *Seafarers Journal of Maritime Heritage* 1, 14–16.

Christie's 1988 *Gold and Silver of the Atocha and Santa Margarita*, Sale catalogue, 14–15 June 1988, New York.

Christie's 1989 *Coins from the Wreck of H.M.S. Feversham*, Sale catalogue, 7 February 1989, New York.

Crumlin-Pedersen, O.1979 'Danish Cog finds', *in* S. McGrail (ed.) 1979, 17–34.

Dolley, M & Warhurst, M. 1977 'New evidence for the date of the so-called 'St Patrick's' halfpence and farthings', *Irish Numismatics* 59, 161–3.

Dow, D.1989 'The lost coppers of Canada', *Coin and Medal News*, April, 27–8.

Einarsson, L.1994 'Present maritime archaeology in Sweden – the case of *Kronan*', *in* Schokkenbroek 1994, 41–7.

Guérout, M., Rieth, E. & Gassend, J.-M. 1989 *Le Navire Génoise de Villefranche: un naufrage de 1516?*, *Archaeonautica* 9.

Hess, P. 1987 'A legend found: the salvage of H.M.S. DeBraak', *Seafarers Journal of Maritime Heritage* 1, 215–22.

Kvarning, L.-Å. 1968 'The Wasa – life on board', *Wasa* (English edition), 10–17.

Lane, W.H. & Son, Penzance 1973 *The Hollandia Treasure*, Sale catalogue, 21 September 1973.

McGrail, S. (ed.) 1979 *Medieval Ships and Harbours in Northern Europe*, BAR International Series 66, Oxford.

Marsden, P. 1994 *Ships of the Port of London. First to eleventh centuries AD*, English Heritage Archaeological Report 3.

Reinders, H.R., van Veen, H., Vlierman, K. & Zwiers, P.B. n.d. *Drie schepen uit de late middeleeuwen*, Lelystad.

Rivet, A.L.F. & Smith, C. 1979 *The Place Names of Roman Britain*.

Schokkenbroek, J.C.A. (ed.) 1994 *Plying between Mars and Mercury: Political, Economic and Cultural links between the Netherlands and Sweden during the Golden Age*.

Sotheby's 1993 *The Uruguayan Treasure of the River Plate*, Sale catalogue, 24–5 March 1993.

Vlierman. K. 1993 'Late Medieval Pottery on Dutch Shipwrecks and a Well-Dated Inventory of the Early 15th Century', *Medieval Ceramics* 17, 69–76.

Warhurst, M.1977 'Tudor and Stuart coins from the wreck of the *Mary*', *British Numismatic Journal* 47, 144–6

Williams, G. (ed.) 1974 *Glamorgan County History, Vol. IV: Early Modern Glamorgan*.

Williams, P. 1974 'The political and administrative history of Glamorgan, 1536–1642', *in* G. Williams (ed.), 1974.

12

The British Museum collection of metal ingots from dated wrecks

Paul T. Craddock & Duncan R. Hook

INTRODUCTION

The purpose of this paper is twofold. Firstly, it records the British Museum's fast growing collection of post-medieval metal ingots from dated wrecks (Tables 1 to 3), updated since our previous report (Craddock and Hook 1987, recently adumbrated in Craddock and Hook 1995a).[1] Secondly, the paper seeks to illustrate the new insights and at times unexpected information which this class of material can provide, using specific examples selected from around the world, from the copper shields of the indigenous cultures of North-West Canada to the Chinese copper *cash* of the Qing dynasty.

One of the fundamental forces behind the emergence of the modern world was the huge expansion in direct maritime trade conducted over enormous distances from the late 15th century onwards. The remains of the cargoes located in wrecks are the surviving material evidence of this trade, and thus form an important document in their own right.

Metals played a significant part in every aspect of this trade, and the ingots are especially important as this is the specific form in which they were traded. The surviving ingots therefore give a physical reality and immediacy to the trade, and provide new insights and research opportunities for the continuing study of economic history. They are of importance

Table 1. Copper ingots and manillas.

Quantity	Reg. No.	Type + mark, if any	Wreck	Provenance	Date	Weight (kg)
COPPER						
5	BM MLA 1985,7-4,2 BM MLA 1985,7-4,3 BM MLA 1985,7-4,4 BM MLA 1985,7-4,5 BM MLA 1985,7-4,6	Melons	St Anthony	Off Gunwalloe, Cornwall	1527	9.2 14.7 2.9 4.2 7.6
6	BM MLA 1995,12-1,1 BM MLA 1995,12-1,2 BM MLA 1995,12-1,3 BM MLA 1995,12-1,4 BM MLA 1995,12-1,5 BM MLA 1995,12-1,6	Small bars	VOC Waddingsveen	Table Bay, Cape Town	1697	0.058 0.080 0.113 0.113 0.120 0.118
1	BM MLA 1992,12-4,2	Battery plate, MR	EIC Albion	Off East Kent	1765	9.0
1	BM MLA 1992,12-4,3	Battery plate, +	EIC Albion	Off East Kent	1765	3.5
3	BM MED 296,273,277	Granulated Copper	EIC Winterton	Off Madagascar	1792	.392
1	BM MLA 1993,6-7.2	Small bar	EIC Henry Addington	Off Isle of Wight	1798	.202
1	BM MLA 1985,7-5.1	Small bar	EIC Hindostan	Goodwin Sands	1803	.392
7	BM MLA 1985,7-5.2 BM MLA 1993,2-2,1 BM MLA 1993,2-2,2 BM MLA 1993,2-2,3 BM MLA 1993,2-2,4 BM MLA 1993,2-2,5 BM MLA 1993,2-2,6	Small bars	EIC Earl of Abergavenny	Off Weymouth	1805	.190 .200 .204 .203 .292 .221 .261
1	BM MLA 1985,7-4.8	Battery plate, ✱	EIC Admiral Gardner	Goodwin Sands	1809	14.3
3	BM MLA 1994,4-5,1 BM MLA 1994,4-4,2 BM MLA 1994,4-5,3	Battery plate 14 lb, B Battery plate 28 lb, B Battery plate 56 lb, B	EIC Carnbrae Castle	Off Isle of Wight	1829	6.5 12.7 25.5
3	BM AF 1984 N43 A,B & C	Manillas	Douro	Scillies	1843	-
2	BM MLA 1994,4-5,4 BM MLA 1994,4-5,5	Cathode	S.S. Benamain	Bristol Channel	1890	5.0 6.0

Table 2. Zinc, tin and lead ingots.

Quantity	Reg. No.	Type	Wreck	Provenance	Date	Weight (kg)
ZINC						
1	BM MLA 1990,12-4,1	Bun ingot	VOC Witte Leeuw	St Helena	1613	2.5
TIN						
1	BM MLA 1995,12-2,2	Straw	S.S. Cheerful	Off St. Ives, Cornwall	1885	
1	BM MLA 1995,12-2,1	28 lb	S.S. Cheerful	Off St. Ives, Cornwall	1885	12.7
LEAD						
1	BM MLA 1985,7-4,7	Wedge	Bartholemew	Scillies	1597	44.5
2	BM MLA 1987,6-8,1 BM MLA 1987,6-8,2	Long bars	VOC Campen	Isle of Wight	1627	72 62
1	BM MLA 1988,12-7,1	Square ended bar	VOC Hollandia	Scillies	1743	76
1	BM MLA 1993,12-4,1	Long bar	EIC Albion	Off East Kent	1765	79.5
1	BM MLA 1993,2-1,1	Long bar	EIC Fanny	Off Weymouth	1792	83
1	BM MLA 1993,6-7,1	Long bar 'Blackett'	EIC Henry Addington	Off Weymouth	1798	70
1	BM MLA 1995,2-3,1	Long bar 'Dee Bank Lead Co.'	EIC Earl of Abergavenny	Off Weymouth	1805	72
1	BM MLA 1995,2-3,2	Long bar 'Bollihope'	EIC Earl of Abergavenny	Off Weymouth	1805	75

Table 3. Silver and gold ingots.

Quantity	Reg. No.	Type	Wreck	Provenance	Date	Weight (kg)
GOLD						
3	BM MLA 1993,5-16.2 BM MLA 1993,5-16.3 BM CM 1993,7-30,1	Bars	'Tumbaga Wreck'	Bahamas Channel	mid 16th	356 519
2	BM CM 1986,9-34,1 BM CM 1988,6-6,2	10 Tael bar Half ring	Prince de Conty	South China Sea	1746	364 368
SILVER						
1	BM MLA 1985,7-4,1	Melon	St Anthony	Gunwalloe Cove, Cornwall	1527	8.000
1	BM MLA 1993,5-16,1	Bar	'Tumbaga Wreck'	Bahamas Channel	mid 16th	1.714
2	BM MLA 1989,5-5,1 BM MLA 1989,5-5,2	Bars	VOC Slot Ter Hooge	Madeira	1724	1.908 1.930
2	BM MLA 1987,1-5,1 BM MLA 1987,1-5,2	Bars	VOC Bredenhof	Madagascar	1753	1.946 1.814
1	BM MLA 1992,7-6,1	Bar	Maravillas	Bahamas Channel	1656	1.736

for studies of metal technology because they represent the metal in a transitory but crucial stage between the ore and finished artefact; the smelting processes completed but the fabrication not yet begun.

Ingots of metal are valuable, and as such were rarely discarded. Consequently, the few which have been found on land are usually from contexts devoid of dating evidence or any indication as to where they may have originated from or to where they may have been bound.

The value of material from archaeologically recorded wrecks as sealed and documented 'time capsules' has been stressed many times, not least throughout this book. The historical context of a known wreck is important for raw materials, which would only normally be in the form of an ingot for a short time. They rarely survive in this form either at their place of origin or at their destination.

Even where ingots from wrecks are marked, the information provided by the documentation can throw more light on all aspects of the metals trade, making these ingots a uniquely valuable research material.[2]

INGOTS AS BALLAST CARGOES

The British Museum's collection is specifically targeted on the ingots as cargo, exemplifying the trade in metals rather than as part of the ship's stores or fittings, for which other institutions[3] are clearly more appropriate repositories. Sometimes, however, there can be problems distinguishing between what is cargo and what is part of the vessel. This is especially true of the ballast. Some items of cargo such as the lead ingots combined both rôles as ballast cargoes. The heavy durable ingots formed convenient and necessary ballast, and consequently it was viable to send cheap and readily available materials such as lead all around the world from Europe. Similarly, during the 17th and 18th centuries, ships on the return voyage from the Far East were sometimes loaded with tin ingots as a ballast cargo, even though they were bound for Europe, which at this date still had cheap and adequate supplies of tin from the south west of Britain (Ken 1965, 3).

All but one of the lead ingots[4] in the collection were recovered from ships outward-bound from Europe. The lead was without exception from Britain, whether the vessels were English or Dutch, the latter usually belonging to the *Verenigde Oostindische Compagnie* (hereafter 'VOC'). The ingots from the VOC *Campen* (BM MLA 1987,6–8,1 & 2; Fig. 1a), wrecked on the Needles, off the Isle of Wight in 1627 (Whiting *et al* 1985) and from the *Hollandia* (BM MLA 1988,12–7,1; Fig. 1b), wrecked over a century later in 1743 off the Scillies (Willies 1985), all came from the Derbyshire mines (Fig. 2). Britain dominated the world lead trade, with Derbyshire and south Yorkshire supplying much of the Dutch requirements at least

Fig. 2. Detail of Fig. 1B, showing the EW stamp, probably to be identified with Edward Woolley of Wirksworth, Derbyshire.

until the late 18th century (Willies 1993; Blanchard 1989, 47–99; Kiernan 1989, 221–63). After that, other British lead producers came to prominence in the international markets (Burt 1984; Rowe 1983), exemplified by ingots from the famous Durham company of Blackett (such as that from the English East Indiaman (hereafter EIC) *Henry Addington*, wrecked off the Isle of Wight in 1798; BM MLA 1993,6–7,1), and Bollihope, another Durham producer (BM MLA 1995,2–3,2, from the EIC *Earl of Abergavenny*, wrecked off Weymouth, Dorset in 1805; Cumming and Carter 1990). The North Wales lead producers are represented by an ingot of the Dee Bank

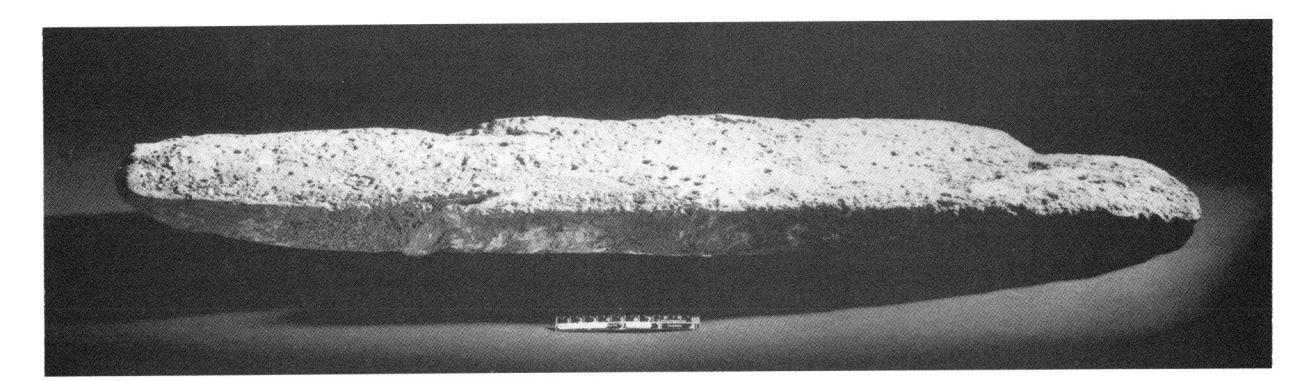

*Fig. 1. A (top) Lead ingot from the VOC Campen (1627); note the side slashes, probably intended to help lift the ingot with a noose.
B (bottom) Lead ingot from the VOC Hollandia (1743); note the square ends, typical of lead ingots of this date.*

Lead Co. (BM MLA 1995,2–3,1, also from the *Earl of Abergavenny*).

In addition to the lead ingots, the *Earl of Abergavenny* was also carrying copper and tin ingots as cargo. The excavations of the wreck have also recovered some rectangular iron blocks, about 200 mm square and penetrated by a hole running through them. Iron was certainly traded in considerable quantities, but as far as is known, always in the form of wrought iron which could be easily worked by traditional methods without recourse to a cupola furnace to melt it. One of these blocks was examined by Professor M.L. Wayman (pers. comm.), who found that it was of white cast iron with several percent of phosphorous. This made the metal extremely hard and brittle, and it proved impossible to cut a section for examination (but quite easy to shatter). The metal would have been easy to melt and cast but useless for any purpose other than as a weight, and it would seem that these blocks were made as permanent ballast, the hole being to accommodate the chain or rope used to secure them. The deliberate selection of this high phosphorus casting alloy at the beginning of the 19th century is interesting, and apparently hitherto unrecorded[5].

NEW METALS

In the post-medieval period, economies around the world were exposed to a whole range of exotic materials and crops, introduced by the new global maritime trade links. Coffee, cane sugar and cotton were sent to the Americas, whilst from the Americas potatoes came to Europe, maize to the Far East, and cashew nuts to India, the maize and cashew nuts being commercially exploited within a very short time of the discovery of the Americas[6]. Metals also feature in this category of exotic materials, which were previously unknown outside their region of production, as exemplified by zinc from India and the copper-nickel alloy, *paktong*, from China (Gilmour and Worrell 1995).

Zinc, which was certainly the most important new metal to reach Europe, was probably first produced on an industrial scale in north-west India about a thousand years ago using the principle of downward distillation into a separate collecting vessel beneath (Craddock *et al* 1990). The metal was apparently unknown in Europe before the Portuguese voyages to India in the late 15th century; thereafter progress was swift. In 1513 an Italian resident in London reported that the English had better look to their tin trade because a Portuguese vessel had just docked in London with 200 pieces of 'Indian tin'.[7] This is almost certainly a reference to zinc metal, as at this time the metal did not have a European name[8]. India has almost no tin deposits, and production was and is negligible, but the term 'Indian tin' was widely used around the Indian Ocean up to that time for zinc, where it was already traded in the early 16th century (Herbert 1984, 327–8). Similarly the famous zinc mines at Zawar in India were regularly mis-described as being tin mines in the 19th century – even by Tod, the great historian of Rajasthan, in his magisterial *Annals of Rajputana* (1829 Vol.1, 399) just after the mines had closed.

Zinc production appears to have begun in China during the first half of the 16th century (Zhou 1993). It is tempting to try and link the origins of the industry to India, having been stimulated by the arrival of Portuguese traders bringing (amongst other things) putative cargoes of Indian zinc. However, the earliest centres of production are in Yunnan and Guizhou provinces, well away from the sea (in fact, the southern Silk route would be a more pertinent route, if such a connection is to be postulated), and the technology used to produce the metal is totally different (Xu Li 1990; Craddock 1995, 316–7). The Chinese technology which is still practised is based on the long-established aqueous distillation systems using the principle of the internal condenser (Needham 1980, 81).

Although this was a completely new technology in the mid-16th century, by the end of the century Chinese zinc had already come to dominate world markets. This achievement of technical enterprise stands at variance with the traditional 'Western' view of Chinese culture as being inherently inward-looking and non-innovative; an appreciation of this and other achievements is helping to produce a more balanced perception of later Chinese technological development (Craddock 1994). The principal carriers of Chinese zinc were the Dutch, and the Museum's collection includes an ingot (BM MLA 1990,12–4,1) from the VOC *Witte Leeuw*, which sank off the island of St Helena in the South Atlantic in 1613, *en route* from Bantam in Java to Amsterdam (van der Pijl-Ketel 1982). Similar plano-convex ingots weighing between 1 and 13.4 kg were recovered from the VOC *Mauritius* which sank off the Gabon *en route* from China to Amsterdam *via* Batavia (L'Hour 1989a; L'Hour *et al* 1992). During the 17th century, the Dutch preferred to trade with the Chinese at Batavia rather than direct with the mainland. The Chinese sent large quantities of copper, lead, tin, pewter (paktong?) and zinc south (Blussé *et al* 1991), although these metals may not necessarily have all originated in China itself.

One reason for the success of Chinese zinc was its purity. The principal contaminant of zinc is lead, and the zinc from the Indian downward distillation process generally had higher lead levels than the zinc from the Chinese upward distillation process, where most of the lead stayed in the charge. The ingot of Chinese zinc from the *Witte Leeuw* has only traces of lead (Table 4)[9], but Watson writing in his *Chemical Essays* (1786) reported several percent of lead in the Indian zinc available to him[10]. This seems to have been one of the reasons that Chinese zinc production was able to survive in the face of European competition in world markets until well into this century. The traditional industry operates to this day (Craddock 1995, 316–9; Xu Li 1990).

In Europe there was a considerable demand and a keen academic interest in the new metals such as zinc (Bonnin 1924). Thus it is rather surprising that there was apparently little serious effort made to try and discover practical details of the smelting processes in order to establish rival smelting industries in Europe, and those attempts that were made rarely met with success. Thus the first commercial process, that 'discovered' by William Champion and set up in Bristol in 1739, does seem to be a modified and expanded version of the Indian process (Day 1973, 73–7; 1991). However, the process as developed by Champion was unsuccessful and soon superseded by radically different distillation technology (Almond 1990).

Similarly, attempts to establish European-style industrial metal technologies were beset by problems. This is well illustrated by the failure of the attempts to establish European-type iron smelting in India as exemplified by the Indian Steel, Iron and Chrome Co. established at Madras by J.M. Heath in 1830. This never operated profitably, but did supply much of the wrought iron for Stephenson's tubular railway bridge over the Menai Straits in North Wales, an interesting example of the reversal of usual 19th-century metal trade! Other European-financed iron-making enterprises also failed in 19th-century India, despite repeated private and even government support (Brown and Dey 1955, 176–7).

Sometimes the initial lack of European success was due to factors of local geology and topography, and could be overcome by technical innovation. Thus, the prodigious wealth of silver in the Spanish Americas was in the main contained in ore bodies that were relatively free of lead, known as dry ores, which were quite difficult to smelt by the conventional methods of the day, and with which the European metal smelters were generally unfamiliar. In addition, the mines such as Potosí in the high Andes of Bolivia, were often in very remote locations, where it was difficult to transport fuel. The answer lay in the application of mercury to the ores, in what became known as the *Patio* and the *Buryton* processes, in order to form a mercury-silver amalgam from which the silver could be easily released.[11] The process had been used on a very limited scale in Europe to recover silver from cupellation debris from the late medieval period (Craddock 1995, 215), but was adapted and developed in the 16th century in the Americas.[12] The process was essential for the treatment of the American ores, and once established, production was prodigious for the next three centuries. The mercury was initially imported from the mines of Almadén in Spain and Idria in northern Italy, but soon the mercury deposits of Huancavelica in Peru were discovered, and as Francisco de Toledo noted in 1570 *'The most important mines in the World are those of Huancavelica and Potosí'*; and in 1648 the Viceroy of Peru stated *'that Huancavelica and Potosí were the two poles which support this kingdom and that of Spain'* (Whitaker 1941).

INGOTS AS WEALTH

The precious metal of the Americas was one of the most potent driving forces of maritime trade and exploration. Obtaining gold and silver was always one of the primary objectives in the early voyages to the New World. The very first cargoes were of melted down treasures of the indigenous inhabitants, loot pure and simple, and the British Museum's collections include some of the so-called *tumbaga* bars (BM MLA 1993,5–16,1 of silver, and MLA 1993,5–16,2–3 and CM 1993,7–30,1 of gold). These were recovered recently from the bed of the Bermuda Channel (Christie's 1993). They bear the stamps of Charles V of Spain, and thus presumably came from an unknown Spanish vessel which sank in the 1520s or 1530s, before official refining facilities were established in the Americas. The bars have very variable gold, silver and copper contents, resulting from the indiscriminate melting down of Aztec and other treasures. As such they are the poignant documents of the impact of the rapacious demands of European economic civilisation on technically less developed cultures.

This source of wealth rapidly passed and deep mines were soon established, such as Potosí in Bolivia (discovered in the 1540s), particularly for silver. With the new processes outlined above, the Americas produced enormous quantities of bullion, as exemplified by the silver ingot from the Spanish treasure vessel the *Maravillas* (BM MLA 1992,7–7,1), which sank in the Bermuda Channel in 1656 *en route* from New Granada to Spain (Christie's 1992).

This bullion was in part necessary to finance the burgeoning international trade with India and the Far East, both to set up the voyages and more directly to pay for commodities purchased (Attman 1991). In the early years of trade with the Orient the movement of goods was decidedly one-sided. There was little of European manufacture (firearms and cannon apart) that was of interest to the oriental merchants. Thus, goods had to be paid for in bullion, either in coin or as ingots, much of which originated in the silver mines of the Spanish Americas. This is exemplified in the collection by the silver ingots of the *Vereinigde Oostindische Compagnie* (Dutch East India Company) from the VOC *Bredenhof* (BM MLA 1987,1–5,1 & 2), which sank off Madagascar in 1753 (Christie's 1986), and the VOC *Slot ter Hooge* (BM MLA 1989,5–5,1 & 2; Figs. 3a, 3b), which sank off Maderia in 1724 (Sténuit 1975; Christie's 1982 and 1983), both vessels *en route* to the East Indies.

Gold ingots were also used in international trade as exemplified by the ten *tael* (ounce) ingot bars made in China specifically for the European trade in the collection (BM CM 1986,9–34,1 & 1988,6–6,2). These ingots were recovered from the *Prince de Conty*, a vessel of the French *Compagnie des Indes Orientales* which sank in 1746 (L'Hour 1989b).

Table 4. *Composition of zinc ingot from the VOC Witte Leeuw (1613), with the composition of the Göteborg (1745) for comparison (Carsus 1960).*

Wreck	Museum No.	Zn	Pb	Fe	Cd	Sb
VOC Witte Leeuw	MLA 1990,12–4,1	Rem	0.4	0.07	0.04	
Göteborg		98.9		0.765		0.245

Notes: All elements are expressed as weight percent. 'Rem' = remainder. The analysis of the VOC Witte Leeuw ingot was carried out using AAS following the procedures of Hughes *et al.* 1976. The analysis should have a precision of ±10-50% for the minor and trace elements, the precision deteriorating as the respective detection limits are approached. The analysis of the Göteborg ingot was published by Carsus 1959. In addition to the zinc, iron and antimony figures quoted, copper, nickel, silver, arsenic and lead were said to be not detected. No details of the analytical method nor detection limits were given.

Fig. 3. A (left) Typical silver ingots from the VOC Bredenhof (1753). B (right) Detail of Fig. 3A showing the VOC (right) and other control stamps.

INGOTS AS DOCUMENTS OF TECHNOLOGY

As noted in the introduction, ingots occupy an especially important place in the technological record, documenting both the end of the extractive stage and the beginning of fabrication. The composition of the metal is obviously important, but the actual form of the metal can also be of interest. The copper used in the production of brass by cementation provides a good example. In this process finely divided copper was reacted with calcined zinc ore and charcoal in a closed crucible at about 1,000°C (Day 1990; Percy 1861, 612–18). Zinc vapour was formed, which dissolved in the copper forming brass directly. Clearly it was advantageous for the copper to have as large a surface area exposed to the vapour as possible, and some 18th-century accounts describe processes to granulate the copper by pouring the molten metal into cold water (Day 1973, 58–62). No such granulated copper has yet been identified from the sites of old brassworks, but several chests of granulated copper were recovered from the EIC *Winterton* which went down off Madagascar in 1792 (Table 1), another unique survival resulting from maritime preservation in a closely dated context.

COMPOSITION

Analysis of the ingots gives a good indication of the purity of the metals at a stage after the various extractive and refining processes of the smelters were complete, but before additional refining and alloying had been undertaken by the fabricators.

An enormous amount of analysis on copper alloys has been undertaken in this century. The emphasis has been very much on prehistoric metal, particularly addressing problems of provenancing the sources of the copper from the trace element content. There seems to be a perception that post-medieval copper is likely to be of a relatively high and uniform purity, and that moreover the composition is likely to be known from contemporary records. In reality, post-medieval metals could be extremely impure, with characteristic impurity patterns possibly diagnostic of specific ore bodies and processes, right up to the general adoption of electro-refining in this century. As yet, the patterns of composition are very poorly documented, resulting in part from the absence until recently of well recorded ingot material in research collections.

The economics of European copper production underwent profound change in the post-medieval period, as a result of the new conditions imposed by international maritime trade. At the start of this period the market leaders were the mines of central Europe, where the presence of silver with the copper in some mines made the copper very competitive. However, the huge quantities of silver flooding into Europe from the Spanish Americas undermined this position, and through the later 16th and the 17th centuries the central European producers faced fierce competition from a variety of other sources, including Sweden, Bengal and Japan (see below; Blanchard 1989, 32–41).

By the early 18th century, British copper, predominantly from sources in the south-west, came to dominate world markets. This was the result of a variety of technical advances, notably in the introduction of steam pumps to drain the mines, and of reverbatory furnaces to smelt the ore, allowing coal to be used as a smelting fuel (Barton 1961; Day 1991).

Analysis of British copper ingot material from the late 18th- and early 19th-century wrecks (dating from 1765, EIC *Albion*[13] to 1829, EIC *Carnbrae Castle*; Tables 1 and 5, Figs. 4 and 6)[14] has brought to light a wholly unexpected feature: a very high bismuth content. Analysis shows that the contemporary fire-refining methods were quite good at removing the sulphur and iron from the metal, but the arsenic contents remain quite high and the bismuth even more so. Even small quantities of bismuth, as little as 0.02%, cause severe embrittlement in the copper. This means that the copper in these ingots would have been very prone to crack with only moderate working, unless the metal was further refined. It seems that bismuth contents (Hook and Craddock 1988). Clearly, the problem of the bismuth was appreciated by the makers of the hammered wares, and dealt with either by further refining or by only using copper known to have produced ductile metal in the past.

This raises yet another problem. Many of the ingots analysed were cast in the form of flat sheets, known as battery plates because they were of a suitable shape for introducing to the water driven battery hammers for the production of copper sheet (Table 5). However, with their high bismuth content they certainly could not have been hammered directly without further refining; were the battery plates just a convenient general ingot shape, or were these particular ingots rejected battery copper that was being exported as inferior metal?

High bismuth contents could lie behind another problem encountered with Cornish copper in the late 18th century (Craddock and Hook 1990). One of the important new uses for copper at this time was for the cladding of hulls to protect against worm attack and fouling by barnacles and weed (Knight 1973), which necessitated that the iron fastenings used to hold the timbers of the hull together be replaced by copper bolts. While copper was considered too soft for the job, the Anglesey Mines in North Wales, which relied heavily on sales of copper cladding, developed a method of rolling and drawing the copper that left it in a highly worked and thus much hardened condition. The copper bolts produced by

Fig. 4. Detail of the upper surface of a battery plate from the EIC Albion (1765), showing the MR stamp of the then recently reconstituted Mines Royal Company.

the problem was appreciated empirically, although there was no knowledge that traces of bismuth were the cause. During the 18th and 19th centuries, vessels of hammered brass were made in Bristol, and their composition shows much lower bismuth contents than the ingots. However the contemporary cast brass standards carried in procession by local Bristol and West Country friendly societies do have the elevated

Table 5. Composition of various ingots of British copper dating from the late 18th century to early 19th century.

Museum No.	Ship	Date	Ingot	Cu	Zn	Sn	Pb	Ag	Fe	Ni	As	Sb	Bi
MED285	Albion	1765	Battery plate	99.1	<0.01	<0.15	0.034	0.087	0.015	0.088	0.86	0.04	0.17
MED286	Albion	1765	Battery plate	97.5	<0.01	<0.15	0.152	0.066	<0.01	0.167	1.64	0.09	0.12
MED287	Albion	1765	Battery plate	94.9	<0.01	<0.15	0.168	0.063	0.005	0.159	1.57	0.08	0.12
MED288	Albion	1765	Battery plate	99.3	<0.01	<0.15	0.041	0.101	0.006	0.095	0.92	0.05	0.22
MED289	Albion	1765	Battery plate	99.3	<0.01	<0.15	0.204	0.065	0.005	0.170	1.66	0.09	0.14
MED290	Albion	1765	Battery plate	99.1	<0.01	<0.15	0.054	0.095	0.008	0.107	0.95	0.06	0.23
MED 269	Winterton	1792	Granulated copper	97.7	0.03	<0.13	0.030	0.066	0.030	0.013	0.44	<0.01	0.09
MED 273	Winterton	1792	Granulated copper	98.8	0.03	<0.15	0.010	0.073	0.037	0.015	0.54	0.02	0.11
MED 277	Winterton	1792	Granulated copper	96.1	<0.01	<0.12	0.089	0.059	0.083	0.029	0.46	<0.01	0.10
1985,7-5,1	Hindostan	1803	'Cigar'	98.5	<0.01	<0.15	<0.01	0.080	0.017	0.032	0.58	0.03	0.25
1985,7-5,2	Earl of Abergavenny	1805	'Cigar'	96.7	0.01	<0.15	0.015	0.058	0.033	0.132	1.41	0.04	0.17
1985,7-4,8	Admiral Gardner	1809	Battery plate (RHS)	99.9	0.05	<0.15	0.017	0.068	0.023	0.021	0.31	<0.03	0.15
			Battery plate (LHS)	99.9	0.07	<0.15	0.020	0.074	0.038	0.021	0.34	0.03	0.17
45917V	Carnbrae Castle	1829	14 lb Battery plate	100.0	<0.01	<0.01	0.017	0.116	<0.005	0.244	0.44	0.02	1.13
45918T	Carnbrae Castle	1829	28 lb Battery plate	97.3	<0.01	<0.02	0.116	0.100	<0.005	0.088	0.35	<0.02	0.57
45919R	Carnbrae Castle	1829	56 lb Battery plate	99.5	<0.01	<0.01	<0.01	0.125	<0.005	0.185	0.37	0.02	0.98

Notes:
The analyses were carried out using atomic absorption spectrophotometry (AAS) following the procedure of Hughes et al., (1976) except for the Carnbrae Castle ingots which were analysed using inductively coupled plasma atomic emission spectrometry (ICPAES) as described by Hook (forthcoming).
The ICPAES and AAS analyses should have precisions of c. ± 1-2% for copper and ± 10-50% for the minor and trace elements, the precision deteriorating as the respective detection limits are approached.
All elements are expressed as weight percent. '<' denotes less than the value stated, i.e. the detection limit.
Manganese, cadmium, cobalt and gold were also sought but were not found to be present above their respective detection limits of c. 0.001%, 0.002%, 0.004% and 0.004%.

Anglesey Mines using copper from their mines at Parys Mountain were so superior that they replaced iron fastenings completely, and from 1780 all British naval vessels used their patent bolts.

During this period the mines were run by the redoubtable Thomas Williams, and at one stage in his protracted rivalry and disputes with the Cornish mines an agreement was reached whereby he agreed to take quantities of Cornish copper to be made into the wrought bolts (Harris 1964, 80). Almost immediately he complained that the metal was of such bad quality that '*We as contractors have been disgraced by them* (that is the Cornish suppliers) *at the Navy board insomuch it will be difficult for us ever to recover our character there*'. Williams was, of course, in very acrimonious dispute with the Cornish mines, and can hardly be considered as unbiased, but it does seem that something was seriously wrong. If the copper delivered to Williams' works had the same bismuth content as the ingot material analysed from the British Museum collection, then there would indeed have been serious problems drawing and rolling the copper.

PROVENANCE STUDIES

The distinctive trace element patterns found in trade copper can be of some assistance in provenancing the source of the metals, although extreme caution must be used in the interpretation of the results. In the 16th century, a great quantity of European copper production was centred on the mines of Central Europe, and this seems to have been the origin, *via* Antwerp, of much of the metal exported by the Portuguese at that time to West Africa (van der Wee 1963; Op der Beeck 1965; Herbert 1984, 125–132). Much of the copper produced in the 16th century at the Central European mines is characterised by substantial traces of antimony, as exemplified by a group of ingots from the Portuguese ship the *St. Anthony*, wrecked off Gunwalloe Cove, Cornwall in 1527 *en route* from Antwerp to Lisbon (BM MLA 1985,7–4,2 to 6; Craddock and Hook 1987 and 1995b; Chynoweth 1968). It must be stressed that great caution has to be used when using trace element data. All copper from Central Europe is not going to have had a uniform and distinctive trace element composition. It has been claimed, for example, that the nickel content of European copper rose through the medieval period, and that after *c.* 1300 nickel contents lay in the region of between 0.1% and 1.0% (Werner 1978). Analysis of the copper from the St Anthony shows it has the composition of apparently much earlier metal.

The metal of the ingots from known wrecks are particularly useful for building up a database for such studies, as the documentation usually includes the origin of the metal and its destination, as well as the date. In fact, it is better to have those metals which only nearly got to their destination than the metals which arrived safely and were then lost in totally anonymous deposits. The scientific value of the cargo of early 16th-century ingots in the above-mentioned St Anthony, and the few copper manillas as exemplars of the metal that was sent out to West Africa, illustrate this point very well, but have

Fig. 5. Small bars of copper from the VOC Waddingsveen *(1697) exported from Japan to Europe.*

already been discussed at some length elsewhere (Craddock and Hook 1987; 1995b).

Another example is provided by the recently acquired collection of Japanese copper ingots from the VOC *Waddingsveen* which foundered in Table Bay, Cape Town in 1697 (BM MLA 1995,11–2,1 to 6; Fig. 5)[16]. Through the later 17th and into the early 18th centuries, considerable quantities of copper were exported to Europe by Dutch vessels (Blanchard 1989, 316–39). The ingots are in the form of small cast bars weighing around 100g (Table 1 and Fig. 5). Their composition (Table 6) has some bearing on contemporary Chinese coin production. For much of the 17th century, Japanese copper imports were banned from China, and the copper of the contemporary *cash* came mainly from Yunnan province in the south-west (Burger 1976, 93). In 1683 the blockade was lifted, and Japanese copper was imported in quantity until the early 18th century, when Japan withdrew from international trade. From then on, Yunnan copper began to be used again together with the Yunnan zinc (see above) to make brass, and thereafter the mint was established in Yunnan and continued to function until the establishment of the Republic in 1912. This is reflected in the composition of the coins. The earlier 17th-century *cash* were made of quite impure copper; much purer copper was introduced in the late 17th century, and this continued into the first half of the 18th century, when once again the former patterns of impurity are observed (Cowell, pers. comm.). It seemed likely that the purer copper represented Japanese imports, but with no comparative Japanese material this remained a hypothesis. The trace element composition of the ingots is very similar to that found in the contemporary *cash* and provides additional support that the copper was indeed from Japan.

The global maritime trade in metals had significant impacts on a wide variety local economies all over the World, penetrating well beyond the usually accepted range of this trade. The inflationary effects on European economies in the 16th century caused by the import of huge quantities of gold and silver from the Americas are well known, as is to a lesser extent the knock-on effect on the whole of European non-ferrous metal production (Blanchard 1989, 3–55 and above). The effects

Table 6. Composition of ingots of Japanese copper from the VOC Waddingsveen (1697)

Museum No.	Cu	Zn	Sn	Pb	Ag	Fe	Ni	As	Sb	Co	Bi	S	Total	Weight/kg
6787-52754-W	99.9	<0.01	<0.01	1.06	0.021	0.024	0.017	0.04	0.02	0.003	<0.015	<0.015	101.0	0.058
6787-52755-Y	97.4	<0.01	<0.01	1.10	0.021	<0.006	0.017	0.04	0.02	0.003	<0.015	<0.015	98.5	0.080
6787-52756-L	98.2	<0.01	<0.01	0.49	0.013	<0.006	0.057	0.02	<0.01	0.002	<0.015	<0.015	98.7	0.113
6787-52757-N	98.3	<0.01	<0.01	1.01	0.020	<0.006	0.017	0.05	0.02	0.007	<0.015	<0.015	99.4	0.113
6787-52758-Q	96.7	<0.01	<0.01	1.51	0.020	<0.006	0.027	0.02	<0.01	0.011	<0.015	<0.015	98.2	0.120
6787-52759-T	99.2	<0.01	<0.01	0.64	0.020	<0.006	0.019	<0.02	<0.01	0.012	<0.015	0.02	99.8	0.118

Notes:
The analyses were carried out using ICP-AES as described by Hook (forthcoming). All elements are expressed as weight percent. < denotes less than the value stated, i.e. the detection limit. The analyses have precisions of about ± 1-2% for copper, ± 5% for lead and ± 10-50% for the minor and trace elements, the precision deteriorating as the respective detection limits are approached. Manganese, gold, cadmium and phosphorus were also sought but were not found to be present above their respective detection limits of about 0.0006%, 0.005%, 0.003% and 0.03%.

elsewhere from the heartlands of India to the wastes of the North American Arctic are less well documented, but just as real. Thus Boileau (1845), while on his travels in Rajputana in the 1830s, noted that English copper undercut the price of the copper from the mines of Singhana and Khetri in the markets adjacent to the mines, even though the imported copper must have been brought overland for hundreds of kilometres from the nearest port.

The indigenous cultures of the north-west coast of North America traditionally used native copper to fashion prestige items, notably shields (Wayman *et al* 1992). These were traditionally quite small and of great value. Following contact with European fur traders from the late 18th century, large quantities of metal, notably iron and copper, were traded to the the local inhabitants in exchange for furs. One consequence of this was a complete shift in the balance of economic power from the region which had access to the native copper to that which had immediate access to the traders.

The British Museum's collections of both full-size and miniature shields, together with daggers with copper decoration to the handles, were obtained in the 19th and 20th centuries, but are of unknown age. Their recent study and analysis has shown that they are all of smelted copper (Wayman *et al* 1992, 7–15, tables 2 & 3). Moreover, the distinctive bismuth content found in some of the copper strongly suggests the metal originated in the south-west of Britain. This immediately provides a useful date range for those pieces, as copper from Cornwall, and latterly Devon, dominated world markets for the period from *c*.1750 to *c*.1850 (Blanchard 1989, 39–43).

INTO THE MODERN WORLD

The highest bismuth contents we have recorded are in the battery plates (called *tiles* in the ship's inventory) from the EIC *Carnbrae Castle* which sank in 1829 off the Isle of Wight *en route* from Swansea to India (BM MLA 1994,4–5,1 to 3; Fig. 6). No one suspected at the time that this was very near the end of the century-long dominance of British copper on world markets. By the middle of the 19th century copper ore was being imported from all over the World, notably South and Central America, Australia, and Spain and Portugal, to be smelted at Swansea (Day 1991), and the British copper mining industry was all but moribund by the end of the century (Barton 1961).

At the time of the demise of the British copper mining industry, the tin mining and smelting industry was also coming under severe pressure. Tin had to a limited extent been imported into Europe from the Far East from at least the 17th century, the ingots acting as a ballast cargo, as noted above. British tin remained the world leader in international trade until new tin sources were opened up in Australia, the Dutch East Indies and above all in Malaya in the 19th century (Barton 1967). Chinese activity raised Malaya to world dominance during the late 19th century (Ken 1965). The British tin industry survived rather longer than the copper mines, as exemplified by the ingots from the SS *Cheerful* which sank in 1885 *en route* from Devon (where the tin had been loaded) to Liverpool (where it is possible that the tin was to have been transhipped for export). In addition to the standard 28lb ingots (BM MLA 1995, 12–2, 1), large numbers of thin rods or straws of tin (BM MLA 1995, 12–2, 2) were recovered which are otherwise unique in a European context, although a mould for casting similar shapes is in the Cornish Museum, Truro. Similar straws of tin were produced in Nigeria in the 19th century and widely traded as such across the Sahara (Fawns nd, 101–2), and other sticks of tin are found in South Africa and Zimbabwe (Killick 1991; Thompson 1949 and 1954). The source of the majority of the latter was probably the Rooiberg tin field, but some of the bars may have been imported trade goods (Grant 1991), and it is just possible that these British ingots were cast to this shape for the African trade. A more prosaic explanation is that they were sticks of tin ready for use in tinning operations. Whatever their true purpose, they demonstate how all knowledge of even a relatively recent artefact type can be lost quite as surely as if it belonged to prehistory.

Local tin production continued, albeit with a dramatically reduced tonnage, through most of the 20th century, although

Fig. 6. Three copper battery plates from the EIC Carnbrae Castle *(1829), weighing (left to right) 28, 14 and 56 pounds.*

smelting ended in Cornwall in 1931 (Barton 1967, 277–8), and currently (mid-1990s) ore from South Crofty, the last remaining Cornish mine is sent to Penang for smelting (A. Buckley, pers. comm.).

The copper ingots in the collection from the SS *Benamain,* which sank in the Bristol Channel *en route* from Swansea to Germany in 1889 (BM MLA 1994,4–5,4 & 5; Fig. 7), are products of a very different technology from the ingots on the EIC *Carnbrae Castle*, wrecked half a century before, and produced in a very different economic situation (Table 7). Both the *Benamain* ingots have been electrolytically refined, and the cathodes are probably the earliest surviving cathodes to have been recognised. They were destined for Germany's burgeoning electrical industry, for which the low electrical resistance of pure copper is a prerequisite.

The electrolytic refining of copper was initially developed

Fig. 7. Copper cathode from the SS Benamain *(1889). The copper was refined in Swansea and is probably one of the earliest copper cathodes to survive.*

Table 7. Composition of ingots of electrolytically refined copper from the SS Benamain (1890).

Museum No.	Ingot	Cu	Zn	Sn	Pb	Ag	Fe	Ni	As	Sb	Bi
45920U	Cathode	100.1	<0.01	<0.01	<0.01	<0.001	<0.005	<0.008	<0.02	<0.02	<0.01
45921S	Ingot	99.8	0.02	<0.01	0.116	0.008	<0.005	<0.008	<0.01	<0.01	<0.01

Notes:
The analyses were carried out using ICPAES as described by Hook (forthcoming). The analyses should have precisions of c. ± 1-2% for copper and ± 10-50% for the minor and trace elements, the precision deteriorating as the respective detection limits are approached.
All elements are expressed as weight percent. '<' denotes less than the value stated, i.e. the detection limit.
Manganese, cadmium, cobalt, gold and sulphur were also sought but were not found to be present above their respective detection limits of c. 0.001%, 0.002%, 0.004%, 0.004% and 0.02%.

by the Elkington's company in the 1860s at Pembrey in South Wales, but rapidly adopted by other firms based in nearby Swansea, to recover the small amounts of precious metal which were found in some of the imported ores, particularly those from Rio Tinto (Gore 1894, 3–6, 149–224).

Electrolytic refining of metals spread rapidly in the late 19th century as the demands of the electrical industry grew. With these ingots, we are entering the conditions of the modern World with much better documentation of the material itself and thus these ingots form the natural termination point in time (at least, at present) for the collection.

Acknowledgements

In forming this collection we have received enormous encouragement, advice, and above all ingots from many underwater archaeologists and divers. It is with great pleasure and gratitude that we acknowledge the donation of lead, copper, and glass ingots from the EIC *Albion* by Mr Tom Brown of Ramsgate; of lead and copper ingots and plates from the EIC *Earl of Abergavenny*, donated by Mr Ed Cumming of the Chelmsford Underwater Archaeology Unit; of lead and copper ingots from the EIC *Henry Addington*, by Mr Martin Woodward of the Maritime Museum, Bembridge, Isle of Wight; of a zinc ingot from the VOC *Witte Leeuw*, donated by Mr A.J. Flagg of St Helena; and of copper ingots from the VOC *Waddingsveen*, donated by Drs Bruno Werz and Duncan Miller of the Department of Archaeology, University of Cape Town, and the National Monuments Council of South Africa.

Notes

1. *Corrigenda*: since the previous report (Craddock and Hook 1987) some new, more accurate information has come to light. The VOC *Bredenhof* was misnamed the *Bredendorf*; the wreck believed at the time to be the EIC *Britannia* is now known to have been the EIC *Admiral Gardner*, and the registration number of the copper ingot from the wreck is MLA 1985, 7-4, 8.
2. The collection also includes a group of glass ingots (MLA 1992,12-4,4–14) from the EIC *Albion*, which sank off Margate in Kent in 1765 *en route* to China, together with metal ingots included in the main article. Their scientific study has also proved illuminating (Redknap and Freestone 1995).
3. Such as the National Maritime Museum, Greenwich.
4. The exception is the lead ingot from the *Saint Bartholomew* (BM MLA 1985,7-4,7), which was part of the abortive Spanish invasion fleet of 1597, and was wrecked on the Scillies.
5. As the block was clearly not part of the cargo it was not accessed to the collection.
6. Maize was being grown as a cash crop in Anhwei, eastern China by 1511 (Bray 1984, 452–9); cashew nuts were being grown in Kerala, southern India in the early 16th century AD (Bernard 1993, 91).
7. This letter is now preserved in the Public Record Office in London (*Calendar of State Papers*, Research in Foreign Archives, Italy, 1509–19). We are grateful to R. Homer and to J. Somers for pointing out this information.
8. The word 'zinc' is traditionally ascribed to Paracelsus in the early 16th century, although the word first appears in print in revised editions of Agricola's works published in the 1550s (see the editor's notes in the standard English edition of his *De Re Metallica*: Hoover and Hoover 1912, 409–10).
9. The zinc ingots from the Swedish East Indiaman *Göteborg*, which sank in Gothenburg harbour on its return from the Far East in 1745 (Carsus 1959 and Table 4) also had low lead contents, as does the metal produced now by the traditional processes in Yunnan and Guizhou provinces.
10. Zinc metal excavated from the base of a 15th-century furnace at Zawar was found to contain only about 0.35% of lead, which may suggest that the higher lead in the metal on the market was in part due to deliberate adulteration.
11. See Barba's *El Arte de los Metales* of 1640 (Douglass and Mathewson 1923) for the best contemporary history of the process in its early days; see Percy 1880, 576–656 and Bargalló 1969 for the best later descriptions.
12. See Probert 1969 for a fascinating story of the struggles of the Bartolomé de Medina to perfect the process.
13. See Redknap 1990 for an account of the wreck.
14. The battery plates from the EIC *Albion* are either stamped with a cross (unidentified) or with the letters MR (Plate 4), the latter being the mark of the revived Mines Royal Company, which obtained its ore from Cornish mines. The battery plate from the EIC *Admiral Gardner* (1809) has the rose stamp of the Rose Copper Company of Swansea, which obtained most of its supplies of ore from Cornwall. The battery plates from the EIC *Carnbrae Castle* (1829) are stamped with a capital B, which has not as yet been identified.
15. The information concerning this wreck was taken from the unpublished research proposal of B. Werz to investigate the site further, and from Werz 1992.
16. We are grateful to Roger Penhallurick for pointing this out.

References

Almond, J.K. 1990 'Zinc Production Technology 1801–1950: A Review', in P. Craddock (ed.), 151–234.
Attman, A. 1991 'The Flow of Precious Metals along the Trade Routes between Europe and Asia up to 1800', in K.R. Haellquist (ed.), *Asian Trade Routes*, Scandinavian Institute of Asian Studies, London, 7–20.
Bargalló, M. 1969 *La Amalgamación de los Minerales de Plata*, Compañia Fundidora de Fierro y Acero de Monterrey. Balderas 68. Mexico.
Barton, D.B. 1961 *A History of Copper Mining in Cornwall and Devon*, D.Bradford Barton, Truro, Cornwall.

Barton, D.B. 1967 *A History of Tin Mining and Smelting in Cornwall*, D.Bradford Barton, Truro, Cornwall.

Bernard, K.L. 1993 *Kerala and the Portuguese*, Cochin, Kerala.

Blanchard, I. 1989 *Russia's Age of Silver*, Routledge, London.

Blussé, L., Oosterhoff, J. & Vermeulen, T. 1991 'Chinese Trade with Batavia in the Seventeenth and Eighteenth Centuries', *in* K.R. Haellquist (ed.), *Asian Trade Routes*, Scandinavian Institute of Asian Studies, London, 231–45.

Boileau, A.H.E. 1845 *Miscellaneous Writing in Prose and Verse*, Thacher & Ostelle Lepage, Calcutta.

Bonnin, A. 1924 *Tutenag and Paktong*, OUP, Oxford.

Bray, F. 1984 *Science and Civilisation in China* VI 2, CUP, Cambridge.

Brown, J.C. and Dey, A.K. 1955 *India's Mineral Wealth*, OUP, Oxford.

Burger, W. 1976 *Chi'ing Cash until 1735*, Tawain.

Burt, R. 1984 *The British Lead Mining Industry*, Dyllansow Truran, Redruth, Cornwall.

Carsus, H.D. 1959 Historical Background, *in* C.H. Mathewson (ed.), *Zinc*, American Chemistry Society Monograph 142, 1–8.

Christie's 1982 Sale catalogue, 9 December 1982, Amsterdam.

Christie's 1983 Sale catalogue, 16 March 1983, Amsterdam.

Christie's 1986 Sale catalogue, 4 December 1986, Amsterdam.

Christie's 1992 *Spanish Art I: Treasure from the 'Maravillas'*, Sale catalogue, 28 May 1992, London.

Christie's 1993 *Coins, Banknotes, Commemorative Medals and Treasure from Spanish Shipwrecks*, Sale catalogue, 28 April 1993, London.

Chynoweth, J. 1968 'The Wreck of the St. Anthony', *Journal of the Royal Institute of Cornwall* 5, 385–406.

Craddock, P.T. (ed.) 1990 *Two Thousand Years of Zinc and Brass*, British Museum Occasional Paper 50, London.

Craddock, P.T. 1994 'Iron and Steel in ancient China: origins and technical change', *Antiquity* 261, 886–90.

Craddock, P.T. 1995 *Early Mining and Metal Production*, Edinburgh University Press, Edinburgh.

Craddock, P.T. & Hook, D.R. 1987 'Ingots from the Sea: The British Museum collection of ingots', *IJNA* 16, 210–6.

Craddock, P.T. & Hook, D.R. 1990 'Cornish Copper and Naval Sheathing: New Evidence for an Old Story', *in* J. Lang (ed.), *Metals from the Sea*, Historical Metallurgy Society, London, 49–50.

Craddock, P.T., Freestone, I.C., Gurjar, L.K., Middleton A.P. & Willies, L. 1990 'Zinc in India', *in* P. Craddock (ed.), 29–72.

Craddock, P.T. & Hook, D.R. 1995a 'Ingots from the Sea: a coming of age', *IJNA* 24, 67–70.

Craddock, P.T. & Hook, D.R. 1995b 'The Trade of European Copper to Africa', *in* D.R. Hook and D.R.M. Gaimster (eds), *Trade and Discovery: The scientific study of artefacts from post-medieval Europe and Beyond*, British Museum Occasional Paper 109, London, 181–93.

Cumming, E.M. & Carter, D.J. 1990 'The *Earl of Abergavenny* (1805), an outward bound English East Indiaman', *IJNA* 19, 31–3.

Day, J. 1973 *Bristol Brass*, David & Charles, Newton Abbot, Devon.

Day, J. 1990 'Brass and Zinc in Europe until the 19th century', *in* P. Craddock (ed.), 123–50.

Day, J. 1991 'Copper, Zinc and Brass Production', *in* J. Day & R.F. Tylecote (eds), *The Industrial Revolution in Metals*, The Institute of Metals, London.

Douglass, R.E. & Mathewson, E.P. (trans.) 1923 *Barba: El Arte de los Metales*, John Wiley, New York.

Fawns, S, nd *Tin Deposits of the World*, The Mining Journal, London.

Gilmour, B. & Worrell, E. 1995 'Paktong: The trade in Chinese nickel brass to Europe', *in* D.R. Hook and D.M. Gaimster (eds), *Trade and Discovery: The scientific study of artefacts from post-medieval Europe and beyond*, British Museum Occasional Paper 109, London, 259–82.

Gore, G. 1894 *The Electrolytic Separation of Metals*, "The Electrician", London.

Grant, M.R. 1991 'Trace elements in southern African tin using NAA', *in* E. Pernicka and G.A. Wagner (eds), *Archaeometry '90*, Birkhauser, Basel, 165–72.

Harris, J.R. 1964 *The Copper King*, Liverpool University Press, Liverpool.

Herbert, E.W. 1984 *Red Gold of Africa*, University of Wisconsin Press. Madison, Wisconsin.

Hook, D.R. forthcoming 'Inductively coupled plasma emission spectrometry in numismatics', in *Metallurgy in Numismatics IV* (W.A. Oddy and M.R. Cowell eds), Royal Numismatic Society, London.

Hook, D.R. & Craddock, P.T. 1988 'Analytical Appendix to J.Day, Bristol Brass', *Journal of the Historical Metallurgy Society* 22, 38–40.

Hoover, H.C. & Hoover, L.H. (eds) 1912 *Georgius Agricola: De Re Metallica*, The Mining Magazine, London.

Hughes, M.J., Cowell, M.R. & Craddock, P.T. 1976 'Atomic Absorption Techniques in Archaeology', *Archaeometry* 18, 19–36.

Ken, W.L. 1965 *The Malayan Tin Industry to 1914*, University of Arizona Press, Tucson.

Kiernan, D. 1989 *The Derbyshire Lead Industry in the 16th Century*, Derbyshire Record Society 14, Chesterfield, Derbyshire.

Killick, D.J. 1991 'A tin *lerale* from the Soutpansberg, northern Transvaal, South Africa', *South African Archaeological Bulletin* 46, 137–41.

Knight, R.J.B. 1973 'The Introduction of Copper Sheathing', *The Mariner's Mirror* 59, 299–308.

L'Hour, M. 1989a 'Naufage d'un navire 'expérimental' de l'Oost-Indische Compagnie: Le *Mauritius* (1609)', *Neptunia* 173, 14–26.

L'Hour, M. 1989b 'Le voyage inachevé du *Prince de Conty* (1746), vaisseau de la Compagnie des Indes Orientales', *Neptunia* 173, 27–33.

L'Hour, M., Long, L. & Rieth, É. 1992 *Le Mauritius*, Casterman, Le Ulis.

Needham, J. 1980 *Science and Civilisation in China* V.2, CUP, Cambridge.

Op der Beeck, R.A.E. 1965 'Flemish Monumental Brasses in Portugal', *Transactions of the Monumental Brass Society* 82, 151–65.

Percy, J. 1861 *Metallurgy*, John Murray, London.

Percy, J. 1880 *The Metallurgy of Silver and Gold: 1 Silver*, John Murray, London.

van der Pijl-Ketel, C.L. 1982 *The ceramic load of the 'Witte Leuw'*, Rijksmuseum, Amsterdam.

Probert, A. 1969 'Bartolomé de Medina', *Journal of the West* 8, 90–124.

Redknap, M. 1990 'The *Albion* and *Hindostan*: the fate of two outward-bound East Indiamen', *IJNA* 19, 23–30.

Redknap, M. & Freestone, I.C. 1995 'Eighteenth-century glass ingots from England: Further light on the post-medieval glass trade', *in* D.R. Hook & D.R.M. Gaimster (eds), *Trade and Discovery: The scientific study of artefacts from post-medieval Europe and beyond*, British Museum Occasional Paper 109, London, 145–58.

Rowe, D.J. 1983 *Lead Manufacturing in Britain*, Croom Helm, London.

Sténuit, R. 1975 'The Treasure of Porto Santo', *National Geographic Magazine*, August 1975, 260–75.

Tod, J. 1829 *Annals of Rajputana*, Smith Elder, London.

Thompson, L.C. 1949 'Ingots of native manufacture', *Native Affairs Department Annual* 26, 7–22.

Thompson, L.C. 1954 'A native-made ingot', *Native Affairs Department Annual* 31, 40–1.

Watson, R. 1786 *Chemical Essays* 4, Evans, London.

Wayman, M.L., King, J.C.H. & Craddock, P.T. 1992 *Aspects of Early North American Metallurgy*, British Museum Occasional Paper 79, London.

van der Wee, H. 1963 *The Growth of the Antwerp Market and the European Market*, The Hague.

Werner, O. 1978 'Benin-Messinge', *Baessler Archiv* 26, 333–439.

Werz, B.E.J.S. 1992 'The excavation of the 'Oosterland' in Table Bay', *South African Journal of Science* 88, 87.

Whitaker, A.P. 1941 *The Huancavelica Mercury Mine*, Harvard University Press. Cambridge.

Whiting, D., Whiting D. & Willies, L. 1985 'Lead ingots', *in* R. Larn, 'The wreck of the East Indiaman *Campen*', *IJNA* 14, 39–89.

Willies, L. 1985 'Eighteenth Century Lead Ingots from the *Hollandia*', *Bulletin of the Peak District Mines Historical Society* 9, 233–48.

Willies, L. 1993 'Development of Lead smelting techniques', *in* R. Francovich (ed.), *Archeologia delle Attivita Estrattive e Metallurgiche*, All'Insegna del Giglio, Firenze, 487–514.

Xu Li 1990 'Traditional Zinc-smelting in the Guma District of Hezhang County', *in* P. Craddock (ed.), 103–122.

Zhou, W. 1993 'A new study on the history of the use of zinc in China', *Bulletin of the Metals Museum of the Japan Institute of Metals* 19, 49–53.

Part IV
Shipwreck Identification and Social Structure

13

The galley, galley utensils and cooking, eating and drinking vessels from an armed *'Tjalck'* wrecked on the Zuiderzee in 1673: a preliminary report

Karel Vlierman

INTRODUCTION

Written sources, paintings and drawings inform us about the famous Dutch 'Trade Wars' against England in the third quarter of the 17th century, known to the Dutch as the 'First', 'Second' and 'Third' English Wars. Almost everybody in the Netherlands still knows the names of people like De Ruyter and Cromwell, and ships like *De Zeven Provinciën* and the *Brederode*.

After the raid on Chatham by De Ruyter in June 1667 and the capture and transport of Monk's flagship *Royal Charles* to Hellevoetsluis, the 'Second English War' concluded favourably for the Dutch (Braunius 1977, 353). After breaking up the *Royal Charles*, her transom decoration was retained as a trophy, and can still be seen on display in the Rijksmuseum in Amsterdam. The 'Third English War' (1672–1674) and a decisive era in the history of the Dutch fleet ended with the Second Peace of Westminster.

It is clear that considerable quantities of historical information exist about famous battles, flag- and other large warships, their commanders and crews, equipment and inventories. For a number of these ships there is also archaeological evidence. Ships like the *Mary Rose* (see this book, chapters 4 and 6), the *Vasa* and the *Kronan* (see this book, chapter 17) are well known and not only to ship archaeologists or maritime historians. Not all subjects recorded in historical sources have attracted the same degree of attention, and some of those that have need to be separated from over-nationalistic sentiments (*ibid.* 347). This may be compared with the attention given by maritime historians to the small ships used in war and everything in connection with them. Naturally researchers prefer famous subjects, but one should not neglect the, at times, unrealised and interesting information available about less famous events such as the 'Third English War' on the Zuiderzee.

Dr E.S. van Eijck van Heslinga, the adjunct director of the State Maritime Museum in Amsterdam, has confirmed that very little historical research has taken place on this matter, despite knowledge of what the archives possess from different sources (Van Eijck van Heslinga, pers.comm.).

One shipwreck situated about 10 km south-west of the mouth of the river IJssel (on lot K 45 Oostelijk Flevoland; Fig.1) was excavated by the Netherlands Institute for Ship Archaeology (N.I.S.A.) at Ketelhaven. The vessel was quite different from the more usual ship finds in the IJsselmeerpolders, displaying the following characteristics:

— it was a *tjalk-like* sailing vessel, suitable for the Zuiderzee and inland waters, with a length of about 20 m

— it was carvel-built with two wales in the sides instead of one (more common for inland water vessels), and showed evidence for leeboards

— the inner surface of the hull displayed burning marks all over the ceiling; the starboard rear section, including the stern, was completely missing

— two cast iron guns were found inside the ship, along with the remains of metal elements of the gun carriages; one cast iron gun was found outboard

— a 200 mm-thick layer of burnt fragments of wood on the ceiling of the hold floor contained several muskets, pistols, stabbing weapons, lead shot for muskets and pistols, iron shot and tools necessary for the use of the guns, three pairs of compasses and the ship's bell. The remains of a fireplace were found behind the mast

— the forward area of the hull contained a second fireplace and all the galley utensils, eating and drinking vessels, storage pots and barrels, and (carbonized) remains of food

— clusters of coins (a total of seventy-two) were found in different spots in the hold and forward area.

The condition of the ship, its equipment and artefactual inventory indicated that it was a burnt-out military vessel. The numismatic evidence suggested a date for the loss of shortly after 1670.

The Naval Defence of the Zuiderzee in the years 1672/73

The following historical review of the defence of the tidal inlets and inland waters of the Dutch Republic in the years

Fig. 1. Lifting the cast iron gun of 446 Amsterdam pounds from the starboard side of the hold, during the excavation of K 45 in August 1977. (Photograph: N.I.S.A., J.V. Potuyt)

1672/73 and the types and uses of ships within the Dutch waterways and on the Zuiderzee is based on Mioulet's thesis *Maritieme Geschiedenis en Scheepsarcheologie* ('Maritime History and Ship Archaeology': 1991).[1]

The picture commonly painted of the state of the army on the eve of attack by the Allies is quite black. The Dutch provinces had scarcely any field armies. The Republic used a system of fortifications, in which small troops were camped to defend the borders. In March 1672, King Charles II of England declared war, followed a few weeks later by France. Under pressure from the endless squabbling between sea and land provinces over financing the reinforcement of the fleet and the recruiting of troops in this 'year of disaster', the Republic appointed Willem III of Orange, the later Stadtholder and King of England, as her new Commander-in-Chief.

The efforts of Johan de Witt on behalf of the Navy during the 'First' and 'Second English War' and the attention given to the fleet in the past had led to its rational organization, and this was probably the main reason for De Ruyter's favourable result in the battle off Solebay in June 1672 (Braunius 1977, 353).

The French attacks on the Republic, together with those of their allies the Germans, had been an absolute disaster for the Dutch. In June, the first fortifications near the river Rhine and in the province of Gelderland were lost, shortly followed by those in the provinces of Overijssel, Drenthe and Utrecht (Fig.2). The remnants of the State army abandoned the IJssel line and retreated to the province of Holland, behind the water defences of inundated land.

As part of the defence of the States of Holland, after deliberation with the States General, the Admiralty of the cities of Amsterdam and Rotterdam had been recommended to act as follows: '...*met alle spoet te equiperen ende op de revieren deser landen ten voorschreven eynde te werden geemployeert, in het vaerwaeter te brengen eene goet aental der voorschreven uytleggers [bewapende schepen]...*' ('...with all speed to equip and employ to a dictated end, a right number of described armed vessels on the rivers of this country...'; Algemeen Rijksarchief, Den Haag [ARA]).

Besides the system of inundations, a naval squadron sailed out into the Zuiderzee in mid-1672 to defend Amsterdam (Doornik 1674; De Jonge 1859; Cambier 1916/17). At first this naval force consisted largely of ships recruited from the States fleet abroad.

On 19 June the States of Holland permitted the States General to appoint Lord Cornelis de Witt, deputy and attorney of the fleet, to order into action some able ships on the Zuiderzee to protect the whole sea between Amsterdam and

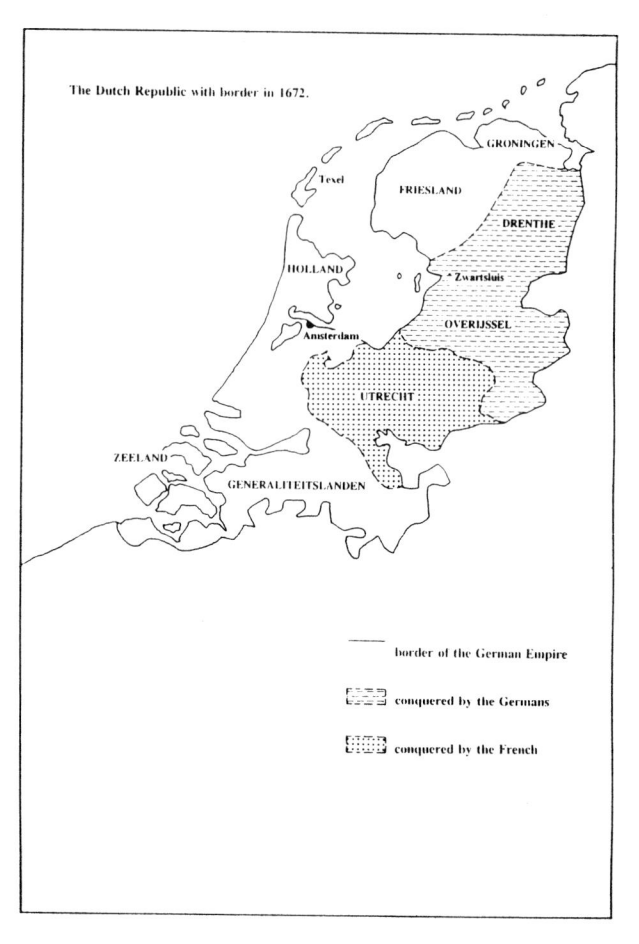

Fig. 2. The Dutch Republic of the Seven Provinces in 1672. (Drawing: N.I.S.A., G.J. Zand)

the island of Texel. Part of our understanding of the armed trade in the Zuiderzee region rests upon the account of private traders. A letter from the city of Amsterdam to the Count of Koningsmark, dated 10 November 1672 is very informative in this respect (Van Sypesteyn and De Bordes 1850, II, 83). It itemises:

- two *tjalcken*, or *platluizen* which can be rowed; one armed with three six-pounders and two of ¾ of a pound. The other vessel carried three three-pounders. Both the ships had a crew of twenty-six;
- a large *pontschip*, armed with six six-pounders and four three-pounders, with a crew of forty-one;
- five cargo vessels from Utrecht with a crew of sixteen armed only with hand weapons;
- three *pont-scheepjes* with a crew of sixteen, armed with four pigs of iron and a calibre of four pounds.

Besides these relatively small ships and vessels, the naval forces on the Zuiderzee included some taller ships. A *fluitschip* and two *katschepen* were stationed near Amsterdam and Muiden respectively, and four yachts delivered by the Admiralty of Amsterdam were stationed in front of Durgerdam. These yachts were armed with ten to sixteen guns and carried a crew of twenty-five to forty. The use of these relatively tall ships, including the two yachts supplied by the VOC and two *waddenkonvooiers* or *uijtleggers* of the Amsterdam squadron, was limited because of the shallowness of the Zuiderzee (Fig.3). All the named ships are mentioned in the report with list of crew on the Texelstrom and Zuiderzee, dated 17 July 1672 (Municipality Archive of Amsterdam).

Historical research does not yield many examples of armed vessels lost in the Zuiderzee region during the 'Third English War'. On four occasions a *vlotschuit* is mentioned, and only on one occasion a yacht. Two *vlotschuiten* were shot to pieces near Muiderberg on 5 July 1672, and were replaced by the city of Amsterdam. Three ships were lost in the attacks on the fortress Zwartsluis (Fig.4). The State's troops lost their first ship in September 1672 during the first attack against the troops of the Bishop of Münster near this fortress. Sylvius (1685, 428) wrote:

'*Op deze tijd (september 1672) voeren enige jachten en smalschepen met volk inder beleyd van eenen Muller van Amsterdam, met meeninge om een aanval op Swarte-Sluys te doen / daer in eyndelijk na veel sukkelens door tegenwint voerquamen: maar alsoo die aenslag niet te wel baleyt was / isse mislukt., waarop eenige der Staatse Troepen weder naar Amsterdam quamen / latende het jacht van Muller daar sitten / het welke **verbrant wiert**:...*' ('At this particular moment (September 1672) some manned yachts and *smalschepen*, under the command of someone called Muller of Amsterdam, with the intention of attacking Zwartsluis / sailed up ultimately, in spite of ailing by adverse wind: but the attack was not well prepared and failed, upon which a few of the State's Troops came back to Amsterdam / leaving the yacht of Muller / which **was burnt.......**'.

In a third attack, on 21 July 1673, two *vlotschuiten* were lost, scuttled by their own crew in order to prevent the enemy laying their hands on them. A letter of the same date from Jacob Lobs, Mayor of the city of Medemblik and Commander of the yachts and other craft on the Zuiderzee, to the ex-mayor of Amsterdam Hendrik Roeters (Municipality Archive of Amsterdam), provides a detailed account of what happened on that day.

The central question of Mioulet's research was whether the K 45 wreck could be placed into the context of

Fig. 3. A yacht *(left) and a* Waddenconvooier *sailing on the Zuiderzee by Reinier Nooms* (Rijksmuseum, Amsterdam)

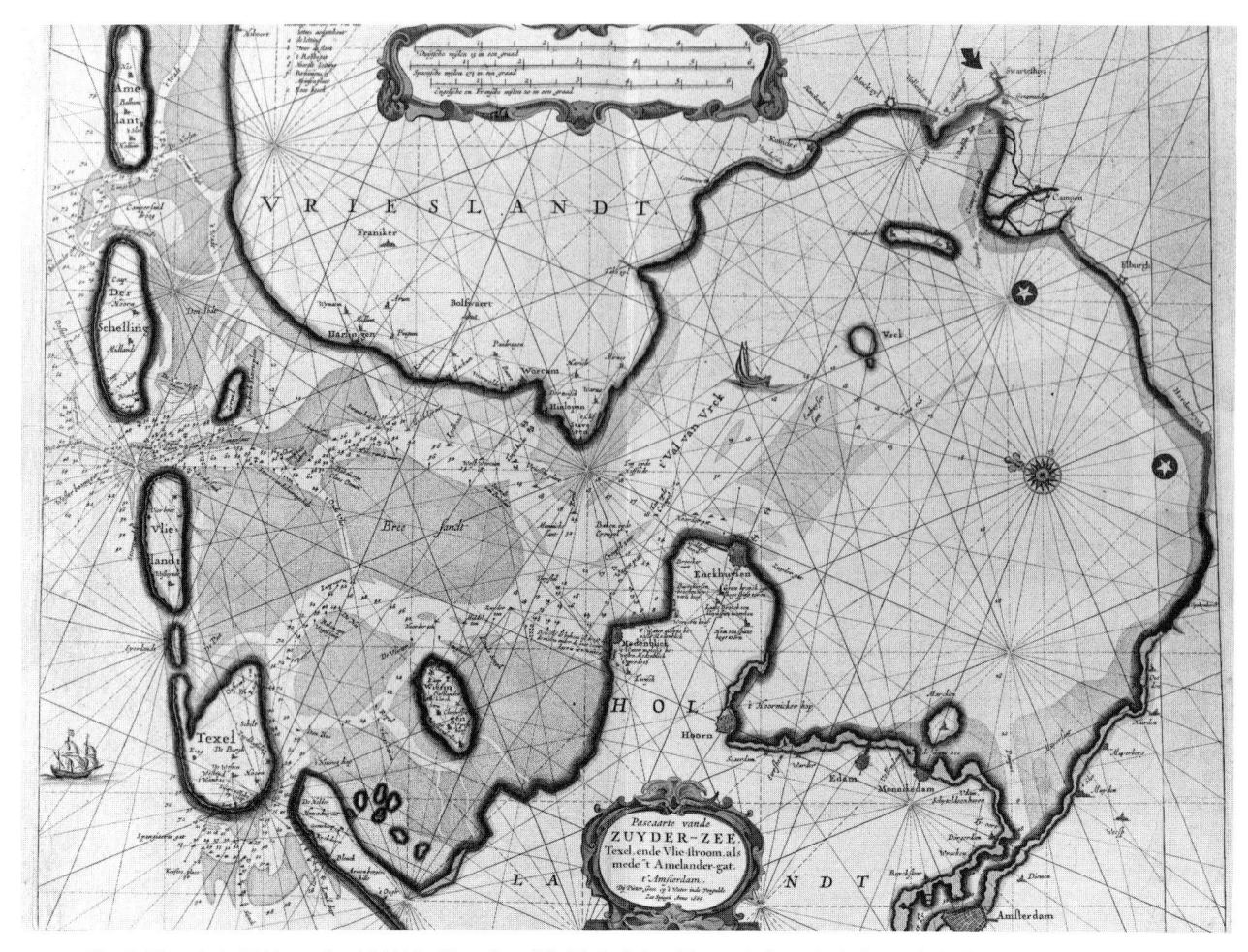

Fig. 4. Map of the Zuiderzee dated 1666 by Pieter Goos. The black circles with stars indicate the findspots of the K 45 and the stern element, found 25 km to the south. The arrow indicates the fortress Zwartsluis. (Photograph: N.I.S.A., Rijksmuseum Nederlands Scheepvaartmuseum).

the defence of the inland waters of the Republic at the time of the 'Third English War'. On the basis of the coin evidence, which indicates a wreck date shortly after 1670, the answer is yes. An *ante quem* date can also be determined historically, because neither the Admiralties of Amsterdam and the Northern Quarter (of the Republic) nor the city of Amsterdam commissioned such an armed ship as the K 45 wreck until shortly before the outbreak of the war (Mioulet 1991, 34).

It is more difficult to give a historical *post quem* date for the length of use of these ships, because they not only stayed in service until the peace of Westminster in 1674, but continued for another century. Mioulet concludes that:

– historical research does not yield much information concerning lost ships or any direct evidence for the identity of the wreck.

– the ship probably formed part of the Zuiderzee squadron

– the possibility cannot be excluded that the wreck is Muller's *yacht*, in spite of the fact that the sources yield different information concerning the armament and the findspot of the K 45, relatively far from Zwartsluis.

Mioulet suggests that further research in the archives of the Admiralties of Amsterdam and the Northern Quarter and the archive of pilotage at Haarlem may offer further possibilities for identifying the ship.

THE ARCHAEOLOGICAL EVIDENCE

As a result of the fire on board, little information survived regarding the interior, in particular the wainscot panelwork; remains of the two fireplaces and a wooden box into which the mast could be lowered were found. A roll of spare rope had been stored in this box. Some laths were found for the fastening of panelwork, and scorch marks on the ceiling planking indicated their original positions (Colour Plate 3A).

Laths on the ceiling planking some 2.7 m behind the stem, together with the absence of scorch marks in front of it made it clear that we had a partition wall or wainscot panelwork in that position and a floor around the fireplace. The only other partition was located about 7 m behind the mast. There was another straight line located 2.3 m further to the stern of the ship, set square to the ceiling, with scorch marks on the front but none on the back, indicating a 'room' partition (for comparison see Fig.5).

We may assume a roof or deck house above this 'room': perhaps a cabin, the customary quarters for the commander, officers and important passengers at this period. Three com-

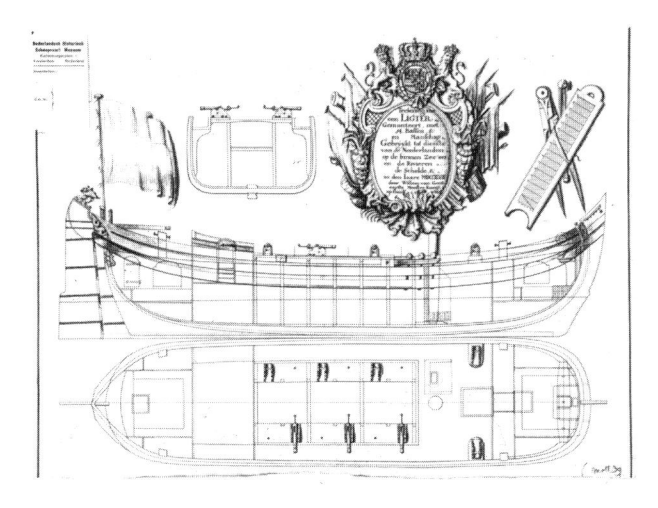

Fig. 5. An armed Ligter *from 1748*
(Rijksmuseum Nederlands Scheepvaartmuseum Amsterdam).

passes found about 7 m behind the mast appear to confirm the presence (and use?) of this proposed cabin. The external appearance may have resembled that of a *'Wijdt of Overseesz Veer'* by Witsen (1671)(Fig.6).

Turning to the evidence provided by the locations of the hand weapons, it appears that at least ten stabbing weapons, so-called *houwers*, and thirteen muskets were stored amidships (Fig. 7). One of the cleaned swords bears the inscription 'INTOLITO', probably a degeneration of 'EN TOLEDO', 'made in Toledo' (Fig.8). This weapon was probably made in Germany and the inscription indicates no more than a suggested quality standard. One pistol and the metal components of a second were also found.

Fig. 7. The badly burnt and corroded broadswords in situ.
(Photograph: N.I.S.A., J.V. Potuyt)

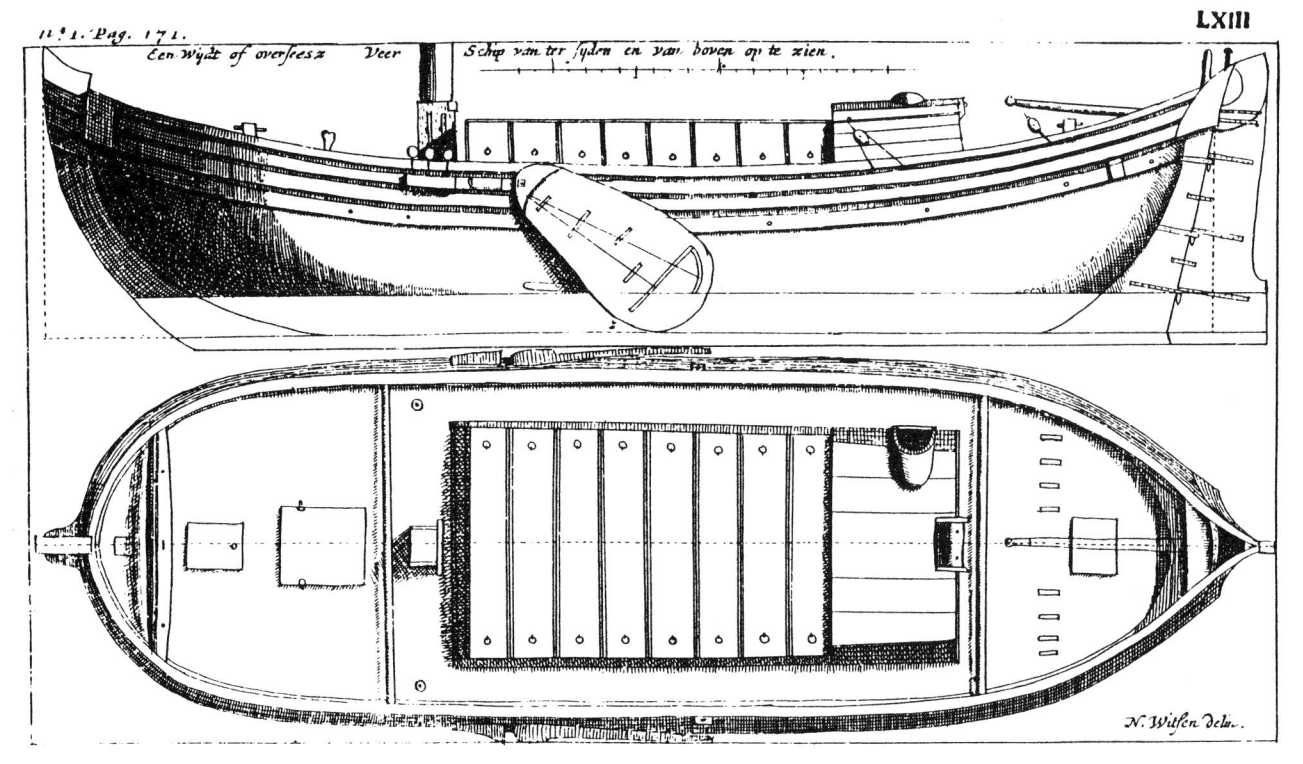

Fig. 6. A Wijdt *or* Overseesz Veer *by N. Witsen, 1671.*

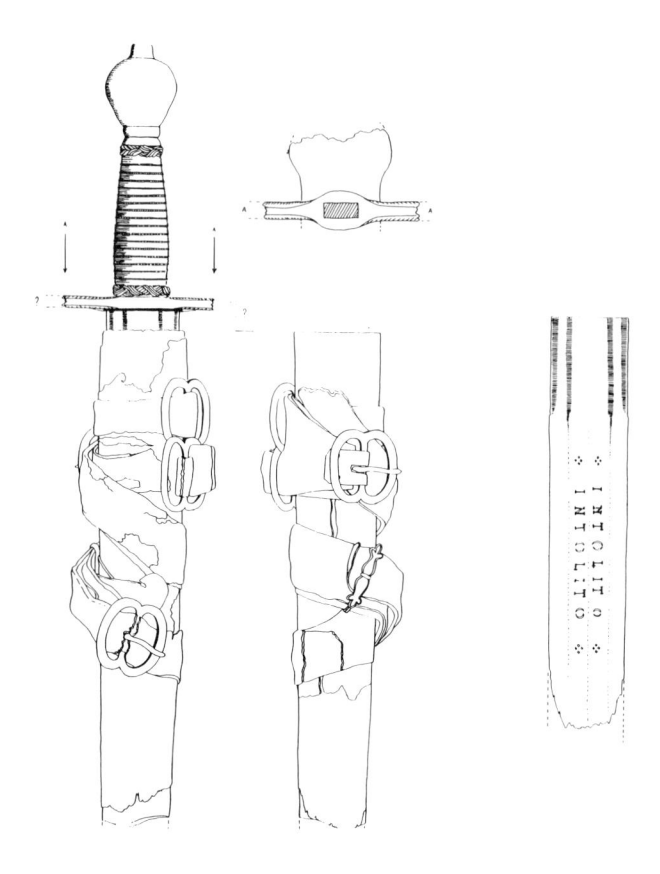

*Fig. 8. Part of one of the swords (*houwers*) bearing the inscription INTOLITO.* (Drawing: N.I.S.A., K. Vlierman)

Sleeping quarters may be assumed in the hold fore and aft of the storage location of the hand weapons, on both sides of the ship. The hearth behind the mast was probably used for activities such as the melting of lead for musket and pistol shot (no cooking pots were found around it – only the remains of a pair of bellows). Two pairs of fire tongs were found amidships on the port side in the hold.

The intensity of the scorch marks and the intact condition of the sides of the ship indicate that the fire started in or around the hearth in front of the galley and eventually spread to the stern of the ship, where most of the powder was stored. The frayed ends of the planks and the missing stern suggest that an explosion occurred, 'blowing away the aft'. The location of the gun, outside the ship, could have resulted from such an explosion.

A remarkable coincidence was the discovery five years after the excavation of most of the missing stern of the ship on lot Mz 8 Zuidelijk Flevoland, some 25 km south-west of the wreck (Fig.4).

As mentioned above, three cast iron guns were found. One lay on the portside, near to the mast, and one lay outside the stern of the ship (bearing the mark 764A on the breech band, for 764 Amsterdam pounds). The third gun was found inside in the stern of the hold on the starboard side (weighing 446 Amsterdam pounds; Fig.1). The trunnions of one of the 764 lb guns bear the mark F for Finspong, a Swedish foundry, which suggests that the gun(s) came from the dockyard of the Admiralty (of Amsterdam). The diameter of 80 mm suggests a calibre of four pounds, which means that we can classify them as four-pounders. The third gun has a diameter of 70 mm.

Hearths behind masts are to be found more commonly on late medieval ships (Vlierman 1992, 51–52). The hearth consisted of a square oak box with a thin layer of sand on the bottom, topped by bricks fixed with mortar. The box was free-standing on the keelson. The hearth in front of the galley was of a different construction and fastened onto a breast hook on the stem, about 0.5 – 0.7 m above the floor ceiling. This fire box was also made of oak, but filled with two layers of yellow bricks and topped by a cast iron plate. The hearth had a back wall of bricks set against thin planks, in front of which a half round cast-iron plate and tiles had been fixed (Fig.9).

It seems that a hearth fastened onto the stem is typical for *tjalk-* and *wijdschip-*like cargo vessels of the late 16th, 17th and 18th centuries. The oldest evidence so far for a fixed firebox on the stem dates from the 15th century and was found in a possible precursor of the typical Dutch flat-bottomed cargo vessels for inland water usage (file N.I.S.A.; shipwreck Nz 66 Zuidelijk Flevoland). No evidence has been found for a back wall on these 15th- and 16th-century fireboxes.

The Galley

The following summary presents the preliminary results of recent investigations. All the galley utensils will be described

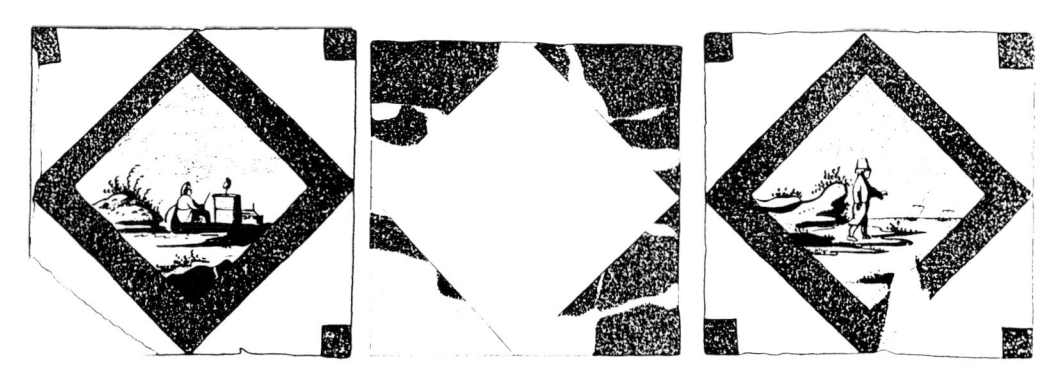

Fig. 9. Decorated tiles in tin-glazed earthenware. (Drawing: N.I.S.A., H. Testerink)

Fig. 10. Copper skimmer and lidded kettle with the cow bones found inside. (Photograph: N.I.S.A., L. van Dijk)

in detail and illustrated in a forthcoming report (Vlierman, in prep.a).

The cooking, eating and drinking vessels, storage pots, wooden barrels and most of the tools lay scattered in the front of the forward part of the ship. Their distribution indicates that these artefacts had either been stored together in the cabinets on opposite sides of the bow, or that they had been in use on the day of wreck.

Three copper kettles were found on the starboard ceiling planking (Colour Plate 3B). The largest had a capacity of 35 litres and was the standard type to be found on board vessels from the medieval period onwards.[2] Inside the kettle lay a skimmer, a wooden colander and a dead-eye (probably from the rigging, having fallen into the kettle during the fire). A 10-litre kettle with a lid contained cow bones and carbonized peas (Fig.10): presumably pea soup had been on the menu on the day of disaster. On the port side of the forward area sat the bottom of an oak barrel filled with cow bones. These were from the same half of an adult animal, and those bones found inside the soup kettle had probably been taken from this barrel. Besides these victuals were found several cod fish skeletons, all without heads, scattered in the hold: perhaps dried cod fish, so-called 'stockfish' (for 16th-century examples, see Redknap 1984, 93). A kettle with a capacity of 8 litres, the remains of a second with a similar capacity and a third smaller example complete the set of kettles "in use".

A bronze saucepan was found behind the hearth, and had been stored in a cabinet on starboard side of the bow (Fig.11). The same cabinet, or the one next to it, had probably been used to store some stoneware *Bartmann* jugs, platters, cooking pots, a milk(?) jug and a redware saucepan, since none of these artefacts display signs of burning (Fig.12). They probably fell out of the cabinet shortly before, during or after the sinking of the ship. Other stoneware jugs, including eight *Bartmänner*, were scattered in the forward area and most were found on the starboard side of the ship. Some probably contained oil or an alcoholic liquor, because they had exploded as a consequence of overheating, sherds lying scattered over an area of

Fig. 11. A bronze saucepan. (Photograph: N.I.S.A., L. van Dijk)

Fig. 12. Stoneware 'Bartmänner', redware pots, a copper kettle, a skimmer and a wooden spoon. (Photograph: N.I.S.A., L. van Dijk)

Fig. 13. One of the two North Dutch maiolica *dishes. Scale 1:4.* (Drawing: N.I.S.A., H. Testerink)

Fig. 14. Group of small redware vessels for special use, possibly medical. (Photograph: N.I.S.A., L. van Dijk)

about 5 m². The temperature had been so high that some sherds from a *Bartmann* jug and two cooking pots had warped, their glaze running. The tin-glazed earthenware was stored in a cabinet on the port side, probably directly next to the hearth.

Two North Dutch maiolica dishes, a plate with blue decoration, two small plain plates, two bowls (the sherds of one found stuck in a conglomerate of burnt material) and two pewter spoons can be classified as officers' tableware, and indicate that at least two were on board. The scattered nature of the sherds suggests that the dishes had also exploded. Some sherds still bore the fresh original colours, while others had been sooted or their tin glaze had melted.

Some of the redware cooking pots, plates, dishes and bowl-shaped saucepans have a smooth burnt glaze, indicating that they had been placed under the direct influence of, but not directly in the fire. This observation, together with their location, suggest that they were in use or stored on the starboard side of the vessel.

Two small redware bowls, a small spouted pot, a handled cup and a tankard or milk(?) jug were found on pieces of thick hawser-laid rope on the port side of the ship within the bow (Fig.14). Similar burnt surfaces indicate that they may originally have been stored together in a cabinet above the rope. The form and capacities of these relatively small objects (a quarter and half a litre) suggest a medical function. Green bottles (with and without tin screw-caps) were also heavily burnt and warped and had exploded. The fragments of at least four examples lay scattered on the starboard side of the hold.

The crew and/or soldiers on board the ship probably ate with wooden spoons directly from the kettle and used redware cooking pots or wooden dishes and plates. Some of the crew smoked. On the foredeck lay two clay pipes, while in the bow on the starboard side lay a dozen unused and used pipes, some still containing tobacco. Two broken and used clay pipes of an older type were found between the floor timbers below the ceiling planking, and give an indication of the date of construction of the ship, probably about 1650.[3] The original total numbers of wooden dishes, plates and spoons are not known, for some may have been completely destroyed by fire. The remains of at least five dishes and five spoons were found. Other objects found in the galley include a wooden ladle and a second skimmer made of latten (Colour Plate 3C).

Comparisons with other vessels

A number of observations can be made by comparing the 1673 tjalk K 45 with other ships which have crews of two to three persons:

1. The number and capacity of copper kettles is two to four times higher, but more or less comparable with the set supplied to a mid-17th century cargo vessel with a length of 27 m (Vlierman, in prep. b).

2. K 45 has the oldest complete set of latten cooking kettles.

3. The number and capacity of redware cooking pots, saucepans, bowl-shaped saucepans, platters and plates, wooden dishes, maiolica dishes, plates and bowls and stoneware jugs is three to four times higher than that found on some 16th, 17th- and early 18th-century *waterschepen*, cargo vessels and a so-called *ventjager*.

Study of the artefactual inventory of a ship through written sources such as sales lists is possible, but presents problems which result from differences in descriptions, lack of measurements, unrecorded capacities or imprecision such as '...*and some earthenware*...' – an inadequate database for proper comparison which often yields more questions than answers (Vlierman 1992, 53–55).

In conclusion, it should be emphasised that *all* the above-mentioned archaeological facts about the ship, artefacts, soil disturbance and historical information have to be seen as very small, though important, pieces of an enormous puzzle, in which each has its own part of the picture to reveal. Only very detailed documentation of all the archaeological aspects, starting on the first day of an excavation, can lead to the accumulation of a maximum number of facts that can give some answers to some of the questions. With hard work, insight, experience and combination of methods from different disciplines, it is possible to achieve worthwhile results.

Conclusions

The following conclusions concerning the K 45 and her artefacts are provisional and still open to discussion:

1. There is insufficient archaeological and historical information available to determine the ship type. There is no problem in describing the ship as *tjalk-like*, but other terms such as *wijd-* or *smalschip* could also be applied.

2. The above-mentioned historical name *pontschip* can be translated as "ferry". It is well known from 17th- and 18th-century paintings, and can mostly be related to a *wijd-* or *smalschip*.

3. The hull form and construction of a *yacht* remains unknown. Consequently it is also possible that K 45 is a yacht.

4. The number of pottery vessels from the galley, together with the presence of stabbing/piercing weapons, muskets and pistols indicates a crew of at least eight to twelve persons plus probably two officers.

5. The presence of three guns seems unusual, with consequences for the stability of the ship. The ship must have been armed with at least four iron guns.

6. The archaeological and historical date of the wreck 'shortly after 1670' is confirmed. On the basis of a comparison with other late 17th-century inventories (e.g. Schröder 1994; Vlierman and Klei 1990) we may conclude that the pottery dates to the 1670s or at latest the early 1680s.

7. Further ceramic research may yield indications for objects of an 'old inventory', and some sets of rather new pots which have been made by the same potter.

8. The proposed date of 1673 for the loss of the ship, as

mentioned in the title of this paper, indicates that this act took place in the middle of the 'Third English War'.

Acknowledgements

English translation: Rerum Antiquarum, K.E. Waugh.

Glossary

Brederode: flag-ship of Maarten Harmensz Tromp.
De Zeven Provinciën: flag-ship of Michiel Adriaensz de Ruyter.
Durgerdam: small city on the river IJ, north-east of Amsterdam.
fluit(schip): original Dutch merchantman of the 17th and 18th century.
Haarlem: city in the province of *Noord-Holland*, to the west of Amsterdam.
Hellevoetsluis: city in the province of *Zuid-Holland* on the *Haringvliet*.
katschip: cat; merchantman of the 17th and 18th century, particularly used in The Netherlands, England and Scandinavia.
ligter: lighter; general name for flat-bottomed vessels to take over and land goods and/or persons from taller ships.
Medemblik: city on the Zuiderzee in the north-west of the province of *Noord-Holland*.
Muiden: city near the mouth of the river Vecht and the Zuiderzee east of Amsterdam.
Muiderberg: small city on the Zuiderzee, east of Muiden.
platluis: see *tjalk*.
pontschip: ferry; flat(-bottomed) vessel.
tjalk, tjalck: typical Dutch round-built vessel with a flat bottom, used for the transport of cargo over the shallow waters in the Low Countries. Probable predecessors the *wijdschip* and *smalschip*.
Uytlegger: coast guard; see *Waddenconvooier*.
vlotschuit: flat-bottomed cargo vessel.
Waddenconvooier: see *Uytlegger*, used in particular on the shallow waters of the Zuiderzee and Waddenzee.
Wijdt of *Overseesz Veer (Smalschip)*: *wijdschip* or ferry; Dutch 17th-century inland ship. Also suitable for the Zuiderzee because of its size.
Zwartsluis: fortress near the mouth of the river Zwartewater, near the Zuiderzee.

Notes

1 In relation to the K 45 wreck based on collected information from the Municipality Archive of Amsterdam by Prof. dr. H.R. Reinders.

2 The only difference is the yellow copper or latten from which it is made.

3. Dendrochronological dating (one sample) provided a *terminus post quem* at 1630 AD ± 6 (Ring, August 1994).

References

Algemeen Rijksarchief Den Haag (ARA), Staten van Holland na 1572, 1404 Missive aan de Admiraliteiten van Amsterdam en de Maze d.d. 18 mei 1672.
Braunius, S.W.P.C. 1977 'Oorlogsvaart', *in* L.M. Akveld, S. Hart & W.J. van Hoboken (eds) *Maritieme Geschiedenis der Nederlanden, 2. Zeventiende Eeuw, van 1585 tot c. 1680* (Bussum) 316–354.
Cambier, J.R.J.Ph. 1916 and 1917 'Het jaar 1672', *Marineblad – orgaan der Marine -Vereniging*, 30e jaargang (1916, Den Helder), 523–536/ 617–635; *Marineblad*, 31e jaargang (1917, Den Helder), 57–77.
Doornik, Markus Willemsz 1674 *Het ontroerde Nederland*.
Jonge, J.C. de 1859 *Geschiedenis van het Nederlandse Zeewezen II*, Haarlem.
Mioulet, C.J.W. 1991 (unpublished) 'Een scheepswrak gevonden op kavel K 45. Case-study'. *Maritieme geschiedenis en Scheepsarcheologie. Een aanzet tot de studie naar een hechtere samenwerking van maritiem historisch en scheepsarcheologisch onderzoek bij het bestuderen van scheepsresten*, Leiden.
Redknap, M. 1984 *The Cattewater Wreck. The investigation of an armed vessel of the early sixteenth century*, BAR British Series 131, National Maritime Museum Archaeological Series No.8, Oxford.
Schröder, B. 1994 'Aardewerk uit de inventaris van een laat-17e-eeuwse praam in Oostelijk Flevoland', *in* K.Vlierman *et al.*, *Corpus van Middeleeuws Aardewerk (CMA), aflevering 10*, Amersfoort.
Sylvius, L. 1685 *Historiën onser tijde*.
Sypesteyn, J.W. van & J.P. de Bordes 1850 *De verdediging van Nederland in 1672 en 1673*, Den Haag.
Vlierman, K. 1992 'Koken en kookgerei op (binnenvaart-) schepen 1300–1900', *in* A. Ruempol & A. van Dongen (eds), *Quintessens. Wetenswaardigheden over acht eeuwen kookgerei* (Rotterdam), 50–59.
Vlierman, K. in prep. (a) *'Coks Commalie want' en ander 'Cocxgereetschap'. Het kook-, eet- en drinkgerei van een 'Uytlegger' vergaan op de Zuiderzee in de Derde Engelse Oorlog*.
Vlierman, K. in prep. (b) *'De inventaris van de 17de-eeuwse koopvaarder van kavel E 81 Noordoostpolder'*.
Vlierman, K. m.m.v. P. Kleij 1990 'Ceramiek uit de inventaris van een klein 17de-eeuws vrachtschip in Zuidelijk Flevoland', *Corpus van Middeleeuws Aardewerk (CMA), aflevering 5*, Amersfoort.
Witsen, N. 1671 *Aeloude En Hedendaegsche Scheeps-Bouw en Bestier*, Amsterdam (Facsimilé 1979).

14

The Cromwellian Shipwreck off Duart Point, Mull

Colin J. M. Martin

Historical background

In September 1653 a Commonwealth flotilla entered the Sound of Mull, off the west coast of Scotland. Its objective was to capture Duart Castle, the medieval seat of Clan Maclean, whose chieftains had held it since before the mid-14th century. The castle, set on a rocky headland overlooking the narrows which separate Mull from the mainland shore, dominates both the Sound and the entrance to Loch Linnhe, at whose head lie the western gateways into Highland Scotland through Lochaber and Glencoe. This vulnerable back-door to Britain was barred a year later by a Cromwellian stronghold at Inverlochy, and in 1690 by Fort William, but in 1653 London's concerns about possible Dutch designs on this unguarded route were given added urgency by a local Royalist revolt.

Scotland's situation at the close of the Civil War was confused and complex. Following the execution of Charles I in 1649 and the establishment of republican government in Britain, Oliver Cromwell had embarked upon a brutal subjugation of Ireland. In June 1650 the exiled Charles II, after signing a covenant which repudiated his father's religious policies, landed in Scotland. Cromwell responded by marching north with elements of the New Model Army and, at Dunbar on 4 September 1650, inflicted a crushing defeat on the Covenanters under General David Leslie (Lynch 1992, 279). Notwithstanding this Charles was crowned King of Scotland at Scone on 1 January 1651. Cromwell's response was delayed by illness, but in July his army crossed the Forth and decimated the Royalist forces at Inverkeithing on the 20th, before marching through Fife to capture Perth. In a desperate counter-measure Charles led his depleted army into England where, on 3 September, he was decisively defeated by Cromwell at Worcester and fled back into exile on the Continent. Scotland was placed under firm Commonwealth control, with major garrisons at Ayr, Perth and Leith, and twenty smaller strongholds gripping the rest of the country, including the Highlands.

Royalist resistance, however, continued through 1653 and into 1654 with a revolt in the west led by the Earl of Glencairn. Among his supporters were the Macleans of Duart whose chief, Sir Hector, had been killed at Inverkeithing with many of his clan. Although the revolt was sporadic and ill-organised, Cromwell was determined to nip it in the bud, and dispatched a task-force to the Western Isles. Three vessels, carrying provisions, munitions, siege equipment, and about a thousand troops sailed from Leith via Orkney and Lewis, where the garrisons were reinforced and new fortifications begun. The fleet then proceeded towards Dunstaffnage near Oban where contact was made with three vessels from the base at Ayr, including a small warship, the *Swan*. The combined force of six ships, under the command of Colonel Ralph Cobbett, then launched its attack on Mull.

When the expedition anchored in Duart Bay and came ashore on the headland, no resistance was encountered, for the Maclean chief, Sir Allan, who was a minor, had wisely decamped with his household and the Earl of Glencairn to the neighbouring island of Tiree. Seizing his opportunity, the Macleans' hereditary enemy, the Marquis of Argyll, came to Duart to assist Cobbett in rounding up members of the clan and coercing them into submission. Thus far the operation had been an outstanding success, achieved without firing a shot (Dow 1979, 93–4; Lynch 1992, 283–5).

What happened then is graphically recorded in a letter sent to Cromwell by Robert Lilburne, the senior Commonwealth commander in Scotland, from Leith on 22 September (Firth 1895, 399–400):

> 'While our men staid in this Island the 13th instant there hapned a most violent storme, which continued for 16 or 18 hours together, in which wee lost a small Man of Warre called the Swan that came from Aire, the Martha and Margrett of Ipswich, wherein was all our remayning stores of ammunition and provision, only the great Guns and Morterpeeces were saved. But that which was most sad was the loss of the Speedwell of Lyn, where all the men that were in her, being 23 seamen and souldiers (except one) were drowned. The rest of the Men of Warre and others of the fleete were forced to cutt their Masts by the board, and yet hardly escaped: wee lost alsoe 2 of our shallops; and all this in the sight of our Men att land, who saw their freinds drowning, and heard them crying for helpe, but could not save them.'

At a stroke Cobbett had lost his entire fleet: three ships sunk and the remaining three dismasted and disabled. The surviving vessels were sent south for repair while Cobbett and his men, with the help of Argyll and in considerable peril of their lives ('...*the poor men have a very sad time of it, the storms continuing daily very violent...*'), escaped overland to Dumbarton. The captain of the *Swan*, Edward Tarleton, survived the wrecking and in due course obtained the command of the 22-gun *Islip*.

THE WRECK SITE

In February 1979, John Dadd, a naval diving instructor whose duties had brought him to the area, came upon the remains of an armed wooden sailing ship at a depth of about 10 m just to the east of Duart Point (Fig. 1). A number of recoveries, including a Frechen stoneware flagon of 17th-century date, were made during this and subsequent visits, but Mr Dadd was unable to undertake extensive work on the site. In 1991, concerned that his discovery should be protected from possible depredation and investigated more thoroughly, he reported it to the Archaeological Diving Unit. This government-supported team is based at St Andrews University as part of the Scottish Institute of Maritime Studies, and is contracted to assist government agencies in matters relating to the administration of the 1973 Protection of Wrecks Act. A visit to the site that summer, accompanied by Mr Dadd, confirmed the presence of a historic wreck, while further finds reinforced the suggestion of its mid-17th century date. As a result the ADU recommended to Historic Scotland (the national regulatory agency) that the site should be designated under the Act [Designation no. 3 (Scotland), 1992].

The wreck is situated at the base of a rock face which slopes at about 45° from the Point, and the archaeological material lies on, and is contained within a seabed of gravely sand with some intrusive boulders (Fig. 2). Low Water depths vary between about 8 m and about 9.5 m, and there is a tidal range of up to 4 m. The general environment of the site, as indicated by its biological regimes (particularly of kelp species), may be categorised as including mid-energy and moderately high-energy zones (Erwin and Picton 1987, 13–15; Earll 1994). A tidal set of up to 1.5 knots, confined mainly to the ebb phase of the cycle, runs from east to west across the site.

The visible remains comprise seven heavily concreted cast iron guns up to 2.5 m in length, a wrought-iron anchor, various iron concretions and concretion complexes, two (or possibly three) concentrations of stone ballast, and considerable quantities of exposed organic material, including elements of articulated structure. The character of the ballast varies considerably between the two mounds. That to the west contains large flat slabs which have evidently been packed with

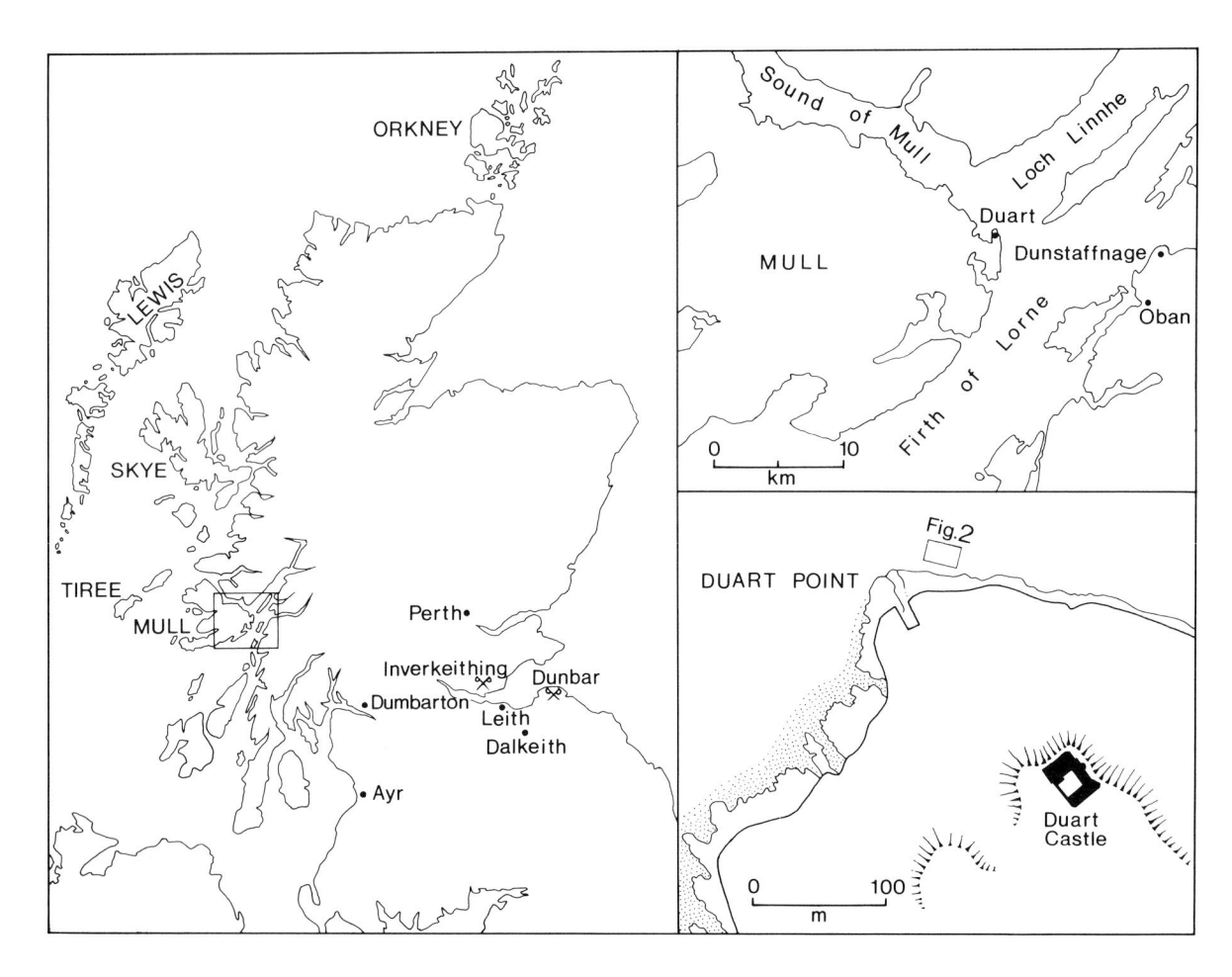

Fig. 1. Site location and places mentioned in the text.

Fig. 2. General site plan, 1994.

some care, while the central mound is made up of a tumble of smaller, more rounded boulders.

A second visit to the site by the ADU in 1992 revealed further extensive destabilisation, a condition apparently exacerbated (though evidently not caused) by its independent discovery by members of the Dumfries and Galloway Branch of the Scottish Sub-Aqua Club shortly before the Designation Order came into effect. Unaware of the wreck's prior discovery, and in good faith, the club had recovered a number of exposed and partially-buried items, including pieces of carved wooden decoration, a badly-corroded hoard of silver coins, a grindstone, various wooden objects, and the brass lock-plate of a mid-17th century Scottish snaphaunce pistol. This material was subsequently acquired by the National Museums of Scotland where it is currently undergoing conservation treatment.

In the opinion of the ADU's Director, Martin Dean, the destabilised state of the site called for immediate action if material was not to be degraded or lost. A crisis response by Historic Scotland provided resources for a week-long rescue operation by the ADU, supported by students and staff from the Scottish Institute of Maritime Studies. Further assistance was given by the Scottish Sub-Aqua Club, while conservators from the National Museums were in attendance throughout.

Eighty-three items were recovered and removed to Edinburgh for conservation.

PROJECT DEVELOPMENT

Following the wreck's designation and the rescue operation mounted by the ADU, the future of the site was uncertain. Historic Scotland, though anxious to protect and manage the site, had neither the expertise nor the resources to do so. The National Museums, on their part, were keen to acquire, conserve and curate the wreck material, but were not equipped to deal with the problems of recovering it. Under its contract to the government the ADU could not devote further time to a single site, however important. After consultation with the various interested parties the writer was granted a licence to survey and assess the wreck, determine options for its management, and take steps to mitigate the erosion. Over the winter of 1992–3 six monitoring visits were made to the site by a team from the Scottish Institute of Maritime Studies, with members of the ADU acting in a personal capacity. These visits were ably supported by members of the Dumfries and Galloway Sub-Aqua Club. Further erosion was noted, especially in the sediment-filled gully which slopes towards the shore at the eastern end of the site. Here a small but complex deposit of rope, a wooden sheave-block, rammer-heads, a shoe, wooden staves, and some fine wooden grooved and moulded panelling with applied decoration was investigated and recorded before being covered with gravel aggregate, spread to replicate the original seabed configuration. This measure proved successful, although some further erosion was later noted beyond the down-tide edge of the covered area.

Following a fund-raising campaign to develop the project, a Field Research Unit associated with the Scottish Institute of Maritime Studies was set up in 1993, and a semi-permanent field base established at Duart. By August 1995 twenty weeks of fieldwork had been completed under the writer's direction, during which more than 450 diver-hours were logged by a team of four archaeologists. A full survey and assessment of the site is now complete, and sandbagging has provided temporary protection against continuing erosion (Martin 1995a; 1995b).

Environmental assessment

It is still not clear what instigated the destabilisation episode of 1991. Seismic activity (the site lies directly on the Great Glen Fault, and has a history of minor tremors including one epicentred within 1 km of it in 1987), and the introduction about the same time of larger ferries on the Oban-Craignure run, have been considered as possible factors. It has not proved possible to quantify the effects of these inputs, but on balance they appear to have been negligible. Diver interference is the more probable primary cause. The known episodes stem from the site's discovery in 1979, when considerable interference appears to have taken place; from its independent discovery in 1992, which again led to serious disturbance; and finally by the benignly-intended but potentially destabilising rescue activities and *ad hoc* attempts at stabilisation. It is believed that other diver intrusions may have taken place, particularly in 1992. The environmental dynamics of the site are evidently complex and finely balanced, and it appears that quite small anomalies, individually or in concert, can trigger disproportionate, often unpredictable, and sometimes sequential reactions.

The main environmental input is undoubtedly the current which flows past the Point during ebb tides, caused by the draining of Duart Bay into the Sound. Though the water movement is complex and variable, it consists in essence of a smooth run across the seaward side of the site which eddies into that part closest to the shore, causing the build-up of sediments which has encapsulated the main organic deposits in drifts against the cliff base. It is these sediments, particularly at the eastern end of the site, which are now showing most evidence of destabilisation. Monitoring over the past three years suggests that the effects are most pronounced when a Spring tide coincides with a strong north-westerly wind.

The centre of Duart Bay is deep (up to 60 m) but it has a wide and shallow surround of coarse sand. When waves break in the shallows at Low Water sand is taken into suspension so that, at High Water, the bay contains a large volume of water holding considerable quantities of sand. Under such conditions the run of this distinctive sand-laden water can clearly be observed crossing the Point during the ebb tide. This brings substantial deposits of intrusive sand to the site, which tend to manifest themselves on the down-current sides of protuberances, where they form distinctive and sometimes quite substantial 'tails'. The phenomenon tends to coincide with the uncovering of organic deposits elsewhere on the site, so it appears that the one triggers the other. The sand-tails are ephemeral, and disperse when the seabed reasserts its natural stability. Organic deposits, once exposed, are however less susceptible to the process of reversal. Significant displacement usually sets in almost immediately, and is quickly followed by the onset of mechanical and biological decay. This in turn leads to the dislocation and transport of archaeological material down-tide. It seems likely that such a cycle of destabilisation had reached its critical point at the time of the ADU's intervention in 1992.

Sandbagging, although successful as a temporary palliative to such exposure, itself acts as a potentially destabilising anomaly, and certainly cannot be regarded as a long-term solution on this site. The undersides of the sandbags themselves represent inviting habitats for a diversity of burrowing fauna whose excavations – the scale of which can be impressive – add a further factor to the complex dynamics of change.

A good deal of data supporting this general picture of self-perpetuating instability has now been gathered, and it is intended that investigation into these phenomena will continue in parallel with future archaeological work on the site. The specialist studies conducted by MacLeod (1995) into the corrosion potentials of ferrous artefacts on the site, and by Gregory (1995) into the characteristics of materials degradation, have been particularly helpful in this respect. Nevertheless the most telling evidence for archaeologically destructive environmental dynamics at work have come from chance observation: the colonisation by barnacles of a carved wooden cherub as it progressively became exposed from its encapsulating sediments (Fig. 3); the transport down-tide of a large piece of pottery when the juvenile kelp plant that had adopted its surface as a hold-fast achieved a critical frond area (Fig. 4); and the incorporation into a layer of gravel laid down by ourselves as a consolidant a month earlier of a 17th-century clay pipe which, had we not known the true circumstances, might have been regarded as a wholly secure contextual association.

Evidence has also been noted for the cyclical exposure, partial destruction, and subsequent reburial of organic material. This is particularly apparent on surviving parts of the articulated structure. This phenomenon is typically characterised by the early stages of algal colonisation on timber faces which demonstrate symptoms of former episodes of mechanical and biological degradation. In some instances biological 'tide-marks' have given a clear demarcation between cyclical and first-time exposure zones.

Although the above remarks are of an interim nature their substance is likely to be refined rather than modified by

*Fig. 3. A photograph taken during the ADU's 1992 visit, showing organic material in the process of exposure. Progressive colonisation by barnacles (*Balanus crenatus*), none more than six months old, indicates a chronology of exposure from right to left. Immediately below the cherub is a human* ulna; *beneath that the partially exposed remains of a barrel costrel. Scale in cm.* (Photograph: ADU)

future investigation. The physical evidence of cyclical exposure, degradation, partial destruction and reburial is corroborated by Dr MacLeod's investigations (1995) of large iron objects *in situ*. That such episodes have occurred periodically since the wreck's deposition is clearly demonstrated by the evidence, each cycle causing a reduction in the site's overall integrity and a diminution of its archaeological content. It is unlikely, however, that many previous events – other than the shipwreck itself – have been as severe as the one recently experienced: had they been so, it might be supposed that the attrition of the site would be at an advanced or terminal stage – yet the indications are that substantial deposits remain intact or have been disturbed only recently. This reinforces the supposition that human interference has been a prime factor in bringing about the present situation.

As matters stand it is evident that a substantial part of the lower forward hull survives as articulated structure, pinned down and preserved by the two main ballast mounds. On the analogy of the nearby *Dartmouth* wreck (Martin 1978) it is likely that rich deposits of artefactual and other material will be preserved beneath it – a circumstance which would place it under little immediate threat. Much more vulnerable is material contained within the sedimentary drifts piled against the cliff base, especially at the eastern end of the site, where considerable deposits of organic material, including carved elements from the stern and what appears to be collapsed panelling from the after cabin, has been noted. At the time of writing plans are in hand to conduct a controlled rescue excavation of this area.

Fig. 4. Hebridean crogan *pot showing biological evidence of recent exposure (the area of barnacle colonisation) and subsequent down-current transport under the drag of a maturing kelp plant* (Laminaria hyperboria) *which had exploited the uncovered surface as a holdfast.*

172   Colin J. M. Martin

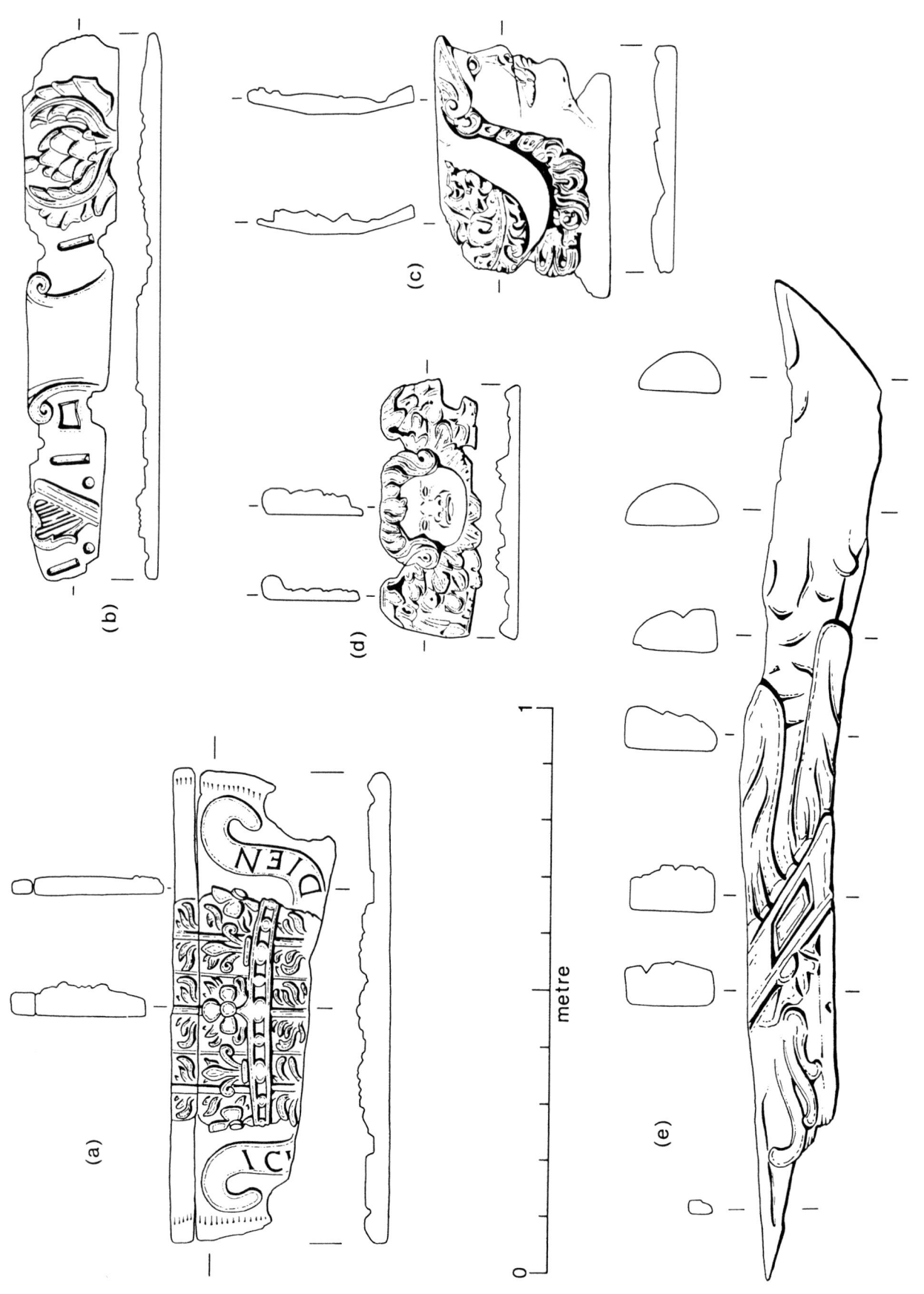

Fig. 5. The wood carvings.

DESCRIPTIVE CATALOGUE OF THE FINDS

No formal excavation has been conducted on the site, and the present corpus of finds derives from recoveries made by John Dadd in 1979, by the Dumfries and Galloway Sub-Aqua Club and others in 1992, and by exposed material rescued by the ADU and Field Research Unit. The following catalogue, though not exhaustive, includes the most significant pieces, and is generally representative of the collection as a whole.

OBJECTS OF WOOD

Carvings

All the pieces are of oak (*Quercus*)

1. *Badge of the Heir Apparent* measuring 840 × 281 mm. This fragment, made up of two conjoined pieces in low relief, shows the lower parts of three ostrich feathers enfiling a coronet with a scroll bearing the almost complete motto ICH DIEN. This symbol, often erroneously described as that of the Prince of Wales, is in fact the badge of the Heir Apparent to the English throne (Scott-Giles 1958, 218) (Fig. 5a).

2. *National symbols of Scotland and Ireland*. Two conjoining fragments of carved planking were exposed during the winter storms of 1993–4. Their combined length is 972 mm. To the right is a foliated thistle, while on the left is a seven-stringed harp of Celtic form (Scott-Giles 1958, 95–6). The two emblems are separated by scroll borders and the piece is further embellished with deeply indented nulling. The symbols are clearly intended to represent the national emblems of Scotland and Ireland (Fig. 5b).

3. *Warrior head* measuring 460 × 320 mm. This profile in low relief shows a moustachioed warrior of classical form, with curled locks emerging from beneath the neck-guard of a peaked helmet, the top of which would have been continued on an adjacent board. An acanthus scroll beyond the neck-guard suggests that the helmet had been garlanded. This motif is common in 17th-century ship decoration, and comparable examples have been recovered from the *Vasa* and *Kronan* wrecks (Figure 5c).

4. *Winged cherub* measuring 460 × 192 mm (Fig. 5d).

5. *Scrolled carving* measuring 1784 × 180 mm. This long curving piece would be appropriate to the taffrail, gallery surrounds, or beakhead of the vessel. It comprises a foliar motif with a petalled flower partly obscured by a diagonal band (Fig. 5e).

Other wooden objects

6. *Turned decorative elements*. The pieces are of black locust (*Robina pseudoacacia*). Perhaps to be associated with the carvings, or the embellishment of interior decorative panelling, are a number of turned objects, some of which are cut to a flat surface on one side (Fig. 6).

7. *Barrel costrel*. Oak with split-willow hoops (*Quercus* and *Salix*). Length 165 mm, maximum restored diameter 110 mm. This staved wooden vessel was found adjacent to the cherub carving during the rescue operation in 1992, and had suffered recent damage through exposure. Seven staves and one end survived in articulated form, as had parts (or their impressions) of eighteen split-willow hoops. The staves are of different widths, the surviving examples varying between 21 and 40 mm: three or perhaps four appear to be missing. A feature of the vessel's construction is the stave which incorporates the stoppered neck. This is monoxylous; that is, it is fashioned from the solid with the required curve worked rigidly from the parent wood. The piece would not otherwise have bent sweetly because of the intrusive neck. It thus formed a master-stave to which its straight-cut fellows were drawn by the pull of the hoops. The form is akin to the 19t-h century *bever* barrels used by farm workers (Kilby 1977, 7). Barrel costrels sometimes occur as ceramic skeuomorphs (Hurst 1977, fig.6.2; Webster 1969, fig. 1.10, and see p .11 above) (Fig. 7a).

8. *Staved bucket*. Two staves of juniper (*Juniperus*) from a small flared wooden bucket 130 mm high with a restored diameter of approximately 125 mm at the base. The piece had evidently been bound with two split hoops: a double one near the top and a single one below. Traces of a diamond pattern executed with a small punch are visible on its exterior surface (Fig. 7b).

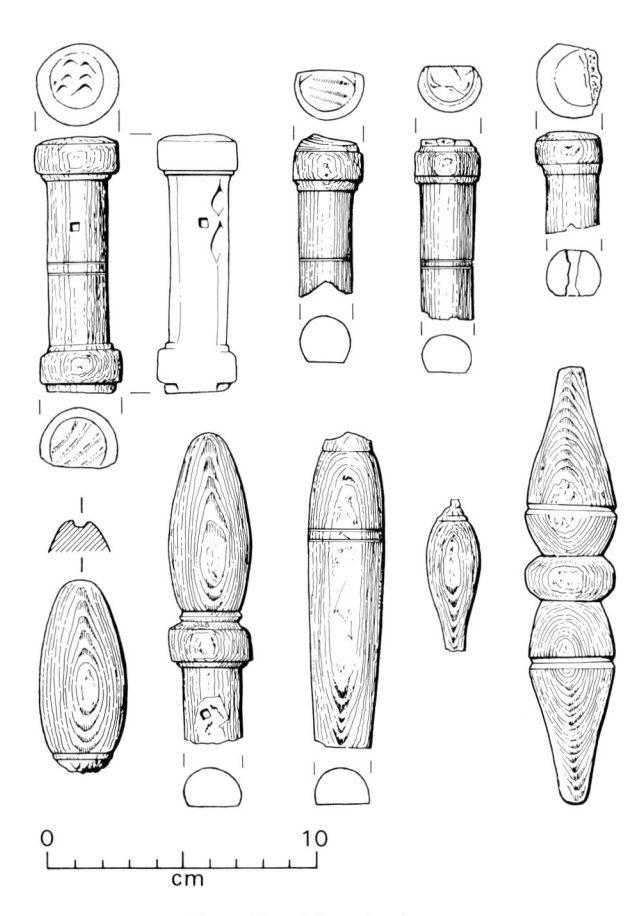

Fig. 6. Turned decorative elements.

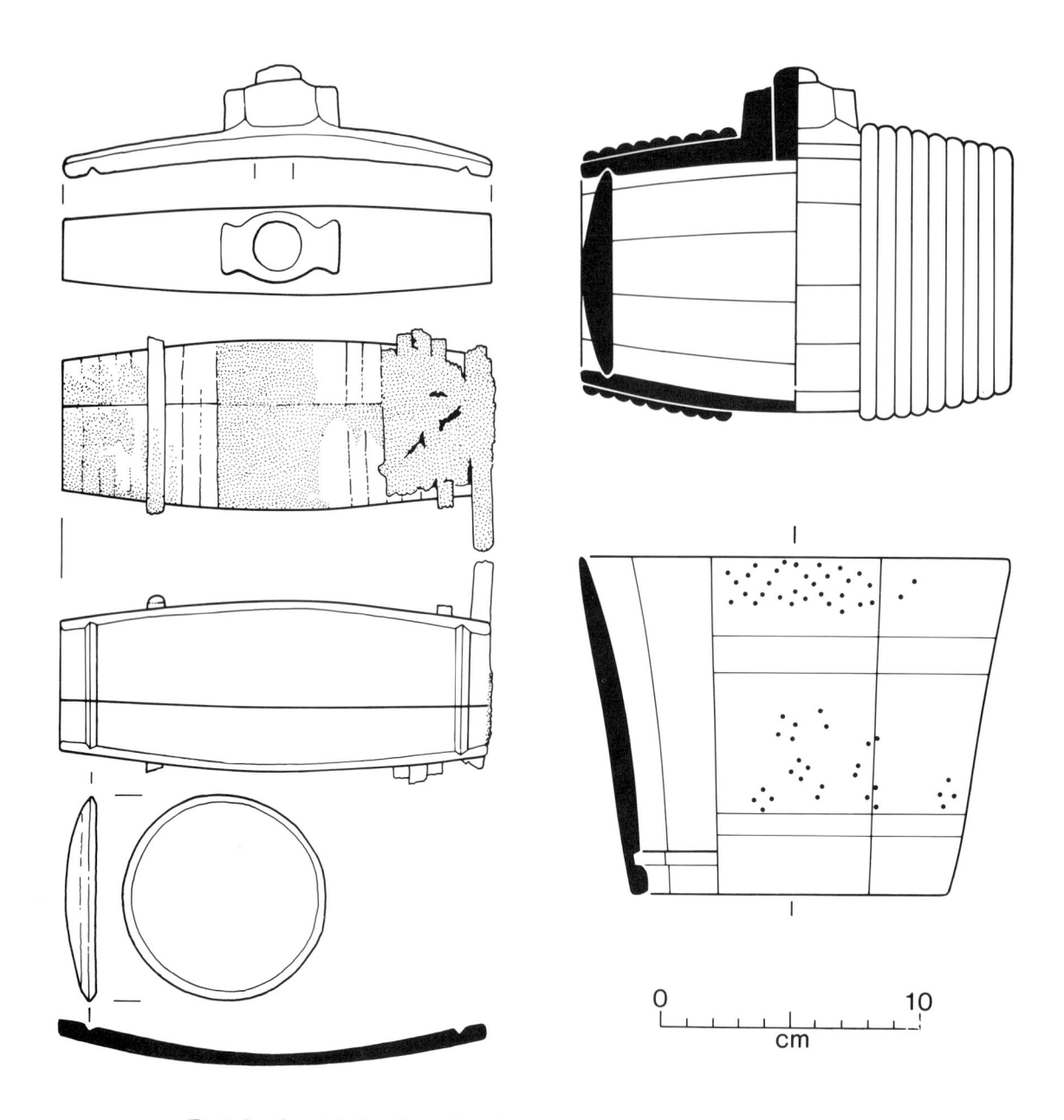

Fig. 7. Staved vessels. Left and top right: *the component parts and reconstruction of a barrel costrel;* bottom right: *a small bucket with punched decoration, reconstructed from two staves.*

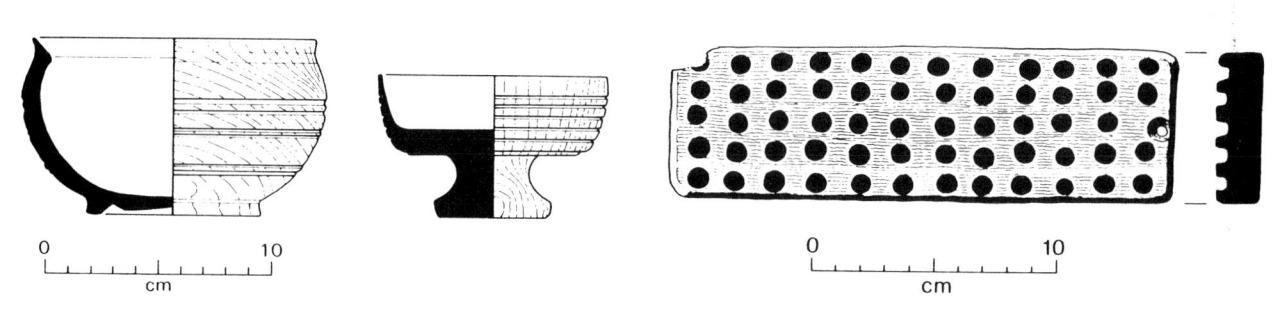

Fig. 8. Turned wooden vessels. Left: *footring bowl;* right: *pedestal cup.*

Fig. 9. Brush back.

9. *Turned wooden bowl* of maple (*Acer*). Diameter 135 mm; height 76 mm. The turning is of a high quality, with a finely tapered lip (Figure 8a).

10. *Turned pedestal cup* of maple (*Acer*). Diameter 102 mm; height 62 mm (Figure 8b).

11. *Brush back*. Oak (*Quercus*) scrubbing brush back 205 × 62 mm with 60 bristle hoes, arranged in rows of five. No trace of the bristles survives *in situ* (Figure 9).

CERAMIC OBJECTS

12. *Hebridean* crogan *pot* with rim diameter of about 200 mm; height 226 mm. This was discovered some distance down-tide of the main site, whither it had been dragged by a juvenile kelp plant which had become attached to it. About half the vessel survives, including parts of its rim and base. Marks on the base suggest that it had been placed on straw or grass while still in a plastic state. It is hand-made of buff earthenware, with a bag-shaped belly and everted rim. This distinctive form of vernacular pottery reflects a prehistoric tradition of ceramic production in the Western Isles of Scotland which continued well into the 20th century (Cheape 1988). Martin Martin, writing *c*. 1695, notes that *crogain* were always made by women (MacLeod 1934, 85–6), while the Rev. Dr. John Walker, who visited the Hebrides in 1764, describes their manufacture in some detail (McKay 1980, 171). Its association with the wreck, while not absolutely certain, is highly probable, and it may perhaps have been a container for locally acquired produce (Fig. 10).

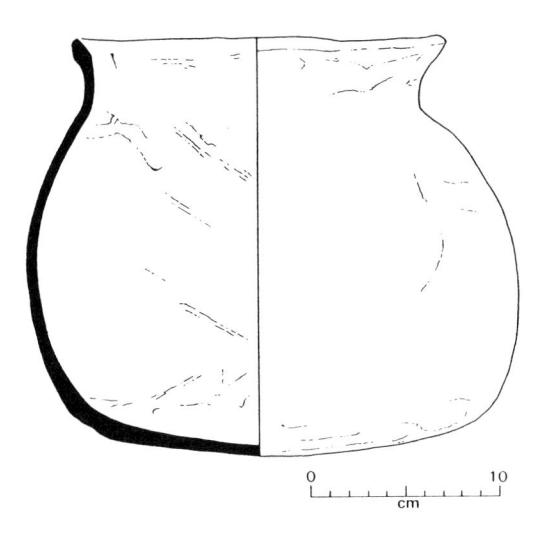

Fig. 10. Hebridean crogan *pot*.

13. *Frechen* Bartmann *jug*. Rim diameter 38 mm; height 210 mm. Reddish-grey stoneware with a mottled dark-brown salt glaze characteristic of Frechen manufacture (Hurst *et al.* 1986, 171). The sprigged face mask has a ladder-type mouth and flowing beard, while the medallion incorporates a ten-petalled double rosette, a central six-pointed star, and rouletted surround. Closely dated examples of similar medallions are known from the *Batavia* (1629) (Green 1989, 142); the *Vergulde Draeck* (1656) (Green 1977, 127 and 140); and the *Kennemerland* (1664) (personal inspection, Shetland Museum). Another group which includes the rosette motif, from Basing House, Hampshire, is though to pre-date the Civil War siege of 1645 (Moorhouse 1970, 78–82) (Fig. 11).

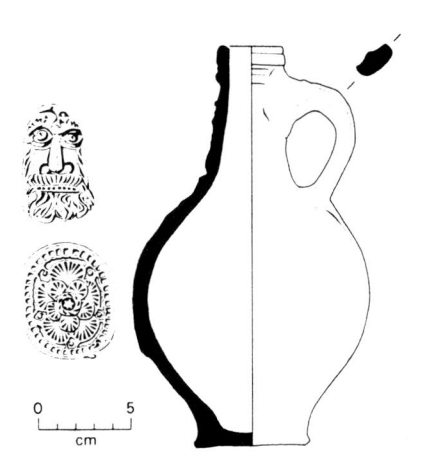

Fig. 11. Frechen Bartmann *flagon*.

14. *Clay pipes*. Three bowls have so far been recovered. All are unmarked, and undecorated except for light bottering around the rims. One is spurred, the other two flat-heeled. Their form is not inappropriate to an English origin and a mid-17th century attribution (Oswald 1975, 37–41) (Fig. 12).

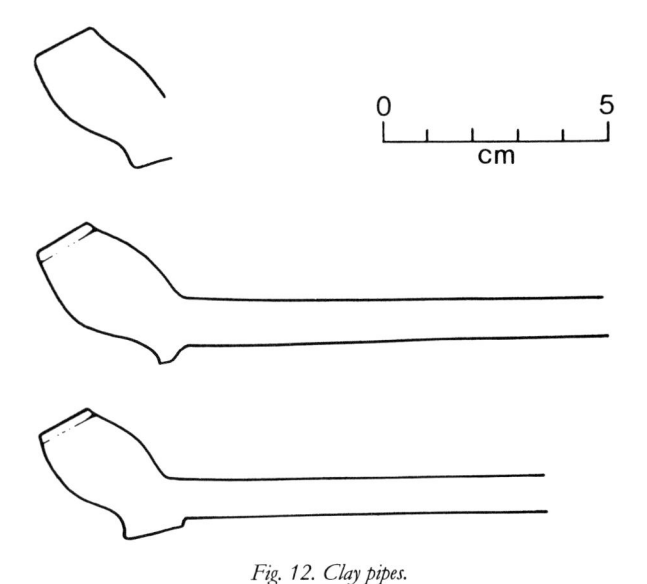

Fig. 12. Clay pipes.

15. *Brick and tile*. A complete brick of red fabric with numerous inclusions measures 9 × 4 × 2 in (229 × 102 × 51 mm), typical of the so-called Tudor brick common in the 16th and 17th centuries (Wood 1963, 275). Fragments of yellowish tile some 15 mm thick were also noted. Both bricks and tile were

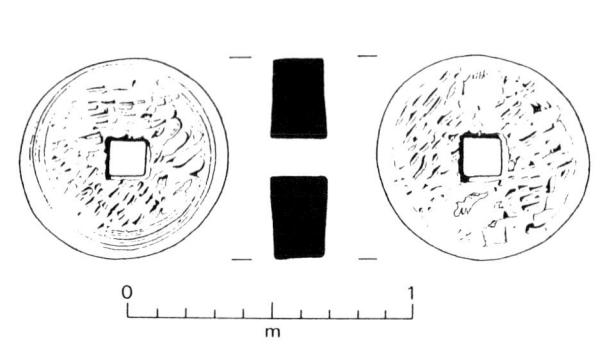

Fig. 13. Rotary grindstone.

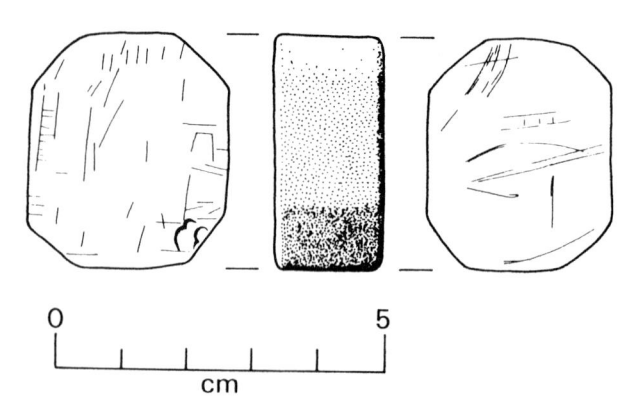

Fig. 14. Stone object of uncertain identifiction; perhaps a touchstone.

probably associated with the galley hearth and its fireproofed surround, as on the *Dartmouth* (Martin 1978, 35–6).

OBJECTS OF STONE

16. *Grindstone.* Rotary grindstone of coarse sandstone, 700 mm diameter and 200 mm thick at the centre, reducing to 185 mm at the rim, with a spindle hole 120 mm square. The piece is not quite circular, and shows evidence of use not only on its horizontal surfaces but also on its sides close to the edge (Fig. 13).

17. *? Touchstone.* A hard fine-grained stone of octagonal shape, 30 mm × 17 mm deep. Long scratch marks on both faces suggest that it may have been a touchstone (Fig.14).

OBJECTS OF METAL

18. *Snaphaunce pistol lock-plate.* Brass snaphaunce lock-plate from a left-handed pistol. Length 175 mm. The piece is chased with foliar decoration and carries the letters G T in a cartouche flanked with thistles. These are probably the initials of George Thompson (*fl.* 1639–1661), an Edinburgh gunmaker (Dr D.

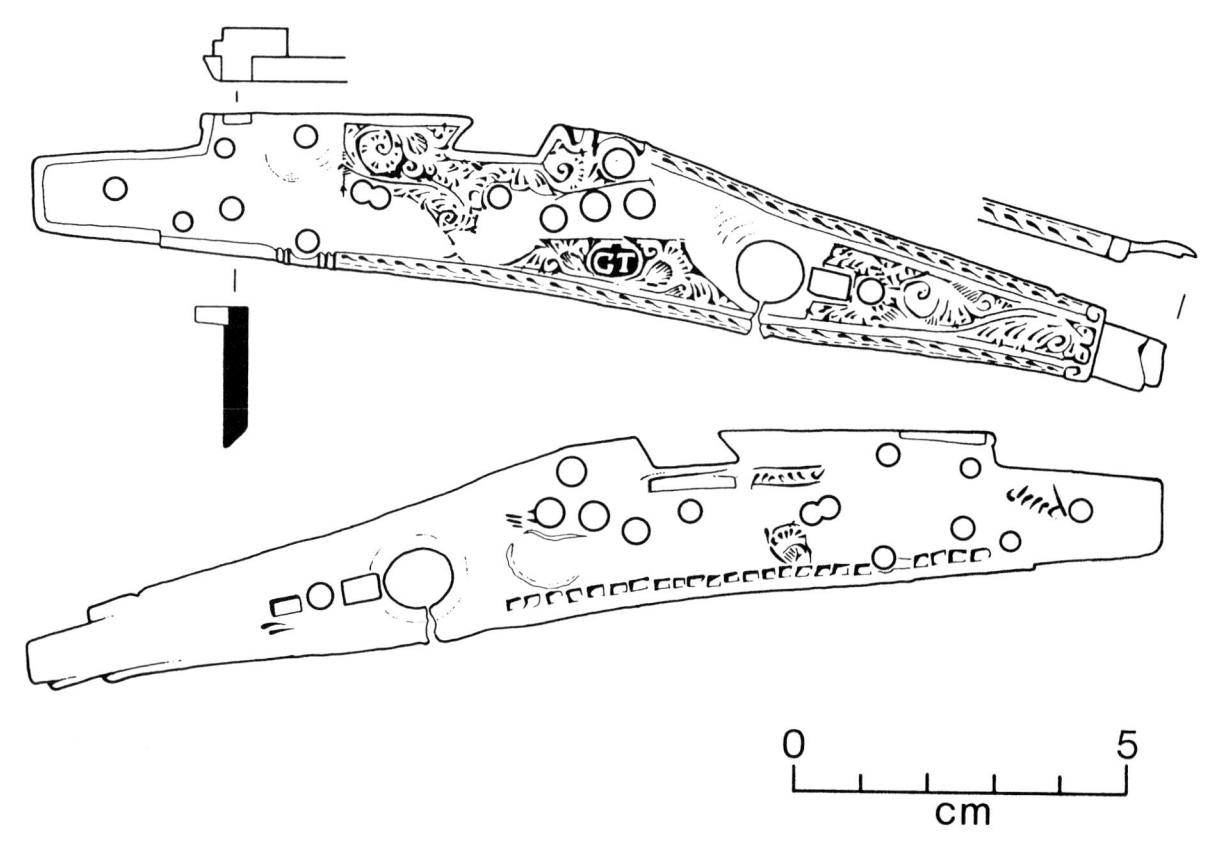

Fig. 15. Snaphaunce pistol lock-plate.

Caldwell, pers. comm.). The weapon is of distinctively Scottish type, and the tongue at its rear suggests the reception of a lemon-shaped butt terminal (Boothroyd 1981, 327–8). A pair of lemon butt pistols carrying the unidentified initials A G and the date 1634, now in the Marischal College Museum, Aberdeen, have lock-plates of similar form (Fig. 15).

19. *Copper kettle*. Diameter 400 mm; height 430 mm; approximate capacity 50 l. This is a type common on post-medieval wrecks, and may have been associated with the galley. Its body is made of a bottom piece beaten into the form of a shallow pan into which a sheet metal cylinder is attached. A shallower cylinder with a rolled rim provides the top segment, and all the elements are riveted together. Two loops provide attachments for a carrying or suspension handle (Fig. 16).

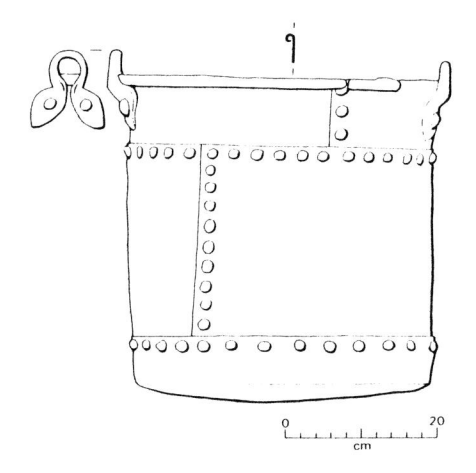

Fig. 16. Copper kettle.

20. *Pewter flagon*, measuring 250 × 130 mm; estimated capacity 0.9 l. Hinged lid with finial and thumb-piece; indecipherable touches on the handle contained within two shields. A small vessel apparently associated with the flagon when found may be a separate drinking-cup which fitted inside it (Fig. 17).

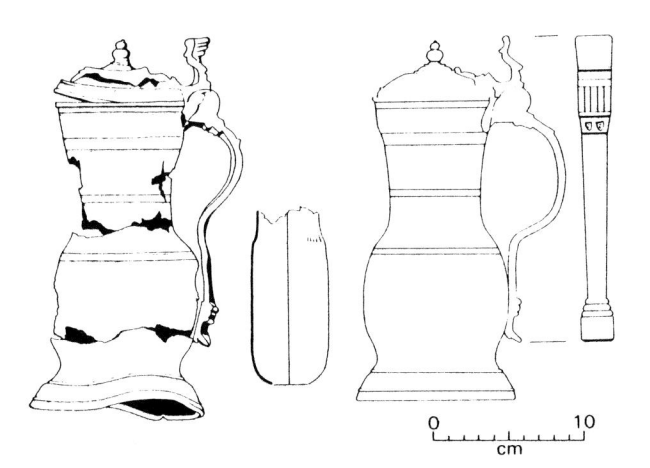

Fig. 17. Pewter flagon, as found (left), and restored (right). The small and evidently incomplete pewter vessel (centre) is said to have been inside the flagon when found.

21. *Buckles and small brass fittings*. Two spectacle-type buckles, one with the prong intact, of a form common in post-medieval contexts; one plain rectangular buckle with prong; a strap terminal paralleled by an example from the *Batavia*, 1629 (Green, 1989:175 (BAT 350)); and a brass fitting of uncertain function (Fig. 18).

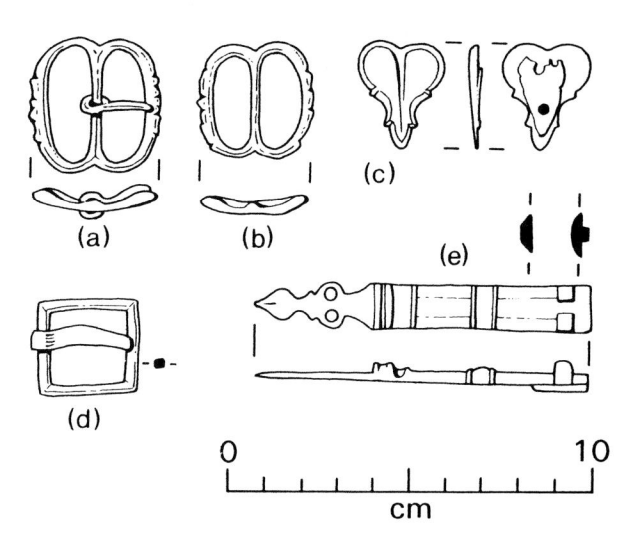

Fig. 18. Buckles and small brass fittings.

22. *Rapier hilt*. A concretion 380 mm long has been radiographed to reveal the ornate wire-wound hilt, spherical pommel, and quillons appropriate to an English rapier of the first half of the 17th century (Dufty 1974, 19–20 and plate 28). The 25 mm-wide blade, of which the top part survives, is encased within the remains of its leather scabbard (Fig. 19).

23. *Pocket watch*. A circular concretion 55 mm in diameter and 25 mm deep has been shown by radiography to contain a pocket watch. Its apparently undecorated case suggests that it may be a 'Puritan' watch – a type regarded as specifically English (Baillie *et al.* 1956, 48). The radiograph indicates that its movement, which will consist almost entirely of non-ferrous metals, is exceptionally well preserved. Its potential for restoration (and perhaps identification with a maker and owner) may equal that of the pocket watch from the *Pandora*, a Royal Naval vessel lost off the Great Barrier Reef in 1791, which was recovered in 1983 and restored to near-working condition in the laboratories of the Western Australian Maritime Museum (Carpenter *et al.* 1985) (Fig. 20).

IDENTITY AND SIGNIFICANCE OF THE WRECK

The small ceramic assemblage points unequivocally to a 17th-century origin, although it does not lend itself to a close definition of date. The Frechen flagon has parallels from dated contexts ranging from 1629 to 1664 (see chapter 9), and while the clay pipes would be appropriate to a mid-17th century attribution, recent work has shown that forms may be long-lived, with old styles overlapping newer ones, and too much

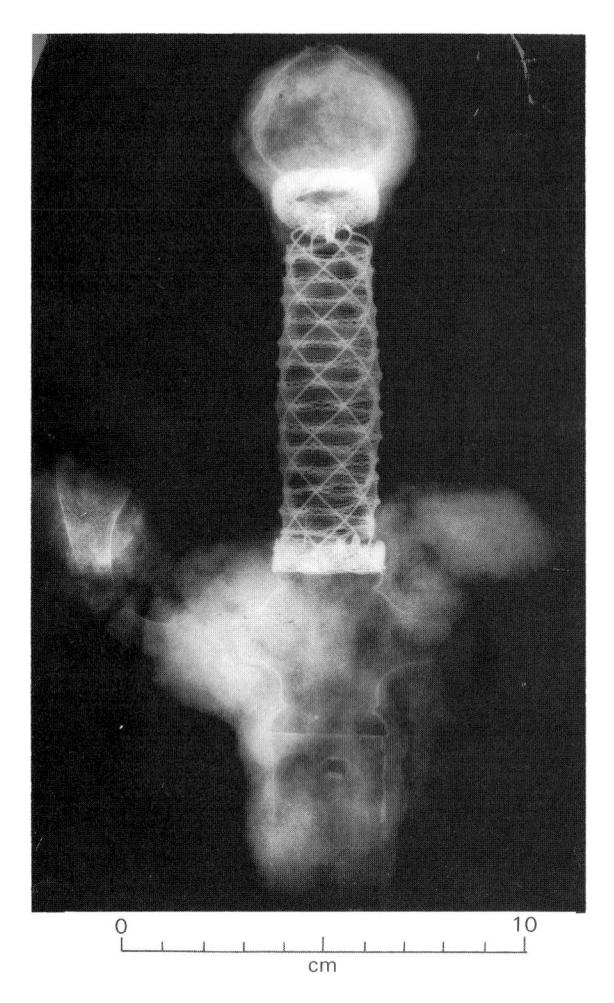

Fig. 19. Radiograph of a rapier hilt and its upper blade.
(Photograph: National Museums of Scotland)

Fig. 20. Radiograph of a pocket watch.
(Photograph: National Museums of Scotland).

reliance should not therefore be placed on so small a sample (Martin 1977; 1987). For sound museological reasons the concreted hoard of silver coins, numbering between three and four hundred, was judged too corroded for dismantling and individual examination. The few examples upon which dates could be discerned yield a *terminus post quem* of 1606, although the fragmentary lettering [R]EX CARO[on one presumably refers either to Charles I or II and must therefore post-date 1624. The snaphaunce lock-plate, however, identified as probably bearing the initials of George Thompson, whose work does not appear to pre-date 1639, reinforces the mid-17th century ascription suggested by the ceramics. Documentary searching within the period 1640–1660 subsequently identified the Cobbett expedition of 1653 as the only likely context for the wreck.

Less certainty exists as to which of the three ships it is. Consideration was given to the possibility that the remains of more than one vessel may be represented, but the pattern of articulated structural components, and the general cohesion of the site, suggest strongly that this is not the case. All the ships were apparently wrecked close inshore, and with considerable loss of life. Human remains, of which the site has produced indications, might therefore be associated with any of the wrecks. Compelling if circumstantial evidence of the ship's identity is, however, provided by the carvings of the Heir Apparent's badge and the national symbols of Scotland and Ireland. These are likely to have been associated with a warship once owned by the Crown, and this in turn points firmly towards the *Swan*.

There were two vessels of this name on the Commonwealth Navy's books. One, a fifth-rate of 200 tons and 22 guns, with a complement of 80 men, is recorded in a fleet list of 1652 (Archibald 1972, 123). This ship appears on the east coast station throughout 1653, giving convoy protection to ships sailing from Yarmouth, Hull, and Newcastle, and was still active in this capacity on 20 October (State Papers Domestic 1653–4, *passim*). She cannot therefore have been the Duart ship.

The other vessel is referred to in a warrant of 8 July 1641 which states that '*the King is pleased that his new pinnace, the Swan, now in Ireland shall be employed this year for the guard of the Irish Seas*' (Eames 1961, 49). This ship had a complement of 60 men in 1642 and, under the command of John Bartlett, operated on both sides of the Irish Sea on behalf of Charles I until 6

November 1645 when, to her captain's acute embarrassment, she was surreptitiously stolen by Parliamentary agents as she lay at anchor in Dublin Bay (Eames 1961, 53–4).

Although the term 'pinnace' usually defines a small support vessel or tender of no more than a few tons (Kemp 1979, 649), it is clear from her complement of 60 that the *Swan* was much larger than this. Indeed, if crew size is proportional to tonnage, she may have been 75% as big as her eponymous 200-ton sister on the east coast station. Charles I embarked on an ambitious and innovative programme of naval development, as his unpopular ship-money tax testifies, which included not only such leviathans as Peter Pett's *Sovereign of the Seas* but the ten identical *Lion's Whelps*, 185-ton patrol craft mounting ten or twelve guns designed to combat piracy and foreign incursion in the western approaches to British waters. Similar but nimbler vessels built by the Dutch about this time were called *pinasschips*, from which the true frigate-type later emerged (Howard 1979, 150–65). The *Swan* may well have been a pinnace in this category, displacing anything up to 150 tons and perhaps mounting ten substantial guns.

A vessel of this sort would accord well with the extent and general characteristics of the Duart wreck, allowing for the fact that some of its guns may have been salvaged by Cobbett, while others may still be buried on the site (a metal-detector contact of a size commensurate with an iron gun was recorded in 1995). Those that have been identified appear to have calibres of between six and nine pounds. That she had once been a royal ship is evident from the fact that she wore (together with, presumably, the royal arms) the badge of the Heir Apparent and the national emblems of two countries over which Charles I claimed dominion. This combination is reflected, albeit on a much grander scale, on the stern of the *Sovereign of the Seas*, as revealed in an anonymous portrait of her builder, Peter Pett, now in the National Maritime Museum at Greenwich, and by the celebrated description of the ship's lavish embellishment by Heywood (1637). The Royal Arms were placed above the rudder-head, in association with the ostrich-feathered badge of the Heir Apparent.

There are difficulties in accepting that such powerfully symbolic emblems, by their nature an anathema to republican sensibilities, could have been displayed by a Commonwealth Navy warship. Indeed, on the very day of Charles I's execution, an Act was passed against the proclamation of any successor to him, so it seems unlikely that the overt symbolism of the Heir Apparent badge could have been tolerated in the ship's decorative iconography (Davies 1959, 160). A possible explanation for its continued presence aboard the ship may, however, be advanced. When the Commonwealth was established in 1649 kingship had been declared '*unnecessary, burdensome, and dangerous to the liberty, safety, and public interest of the people*', and the Royal Arms were ordered to be removed from public places, particularly churches. Some were defaced or destroyed, but many were simply hidden, or turned around and the Commonwealth Arms painted on the back. Following the Restoration of Charles II in 1660 a statute requiring the removal of all Commonwealth heraldry, and its replacement by the Royal Arms, resulted in many of the old boards being brought out of hiding and re-erected (Friar and Ferguson 1993, 110).

That this may also have happened aboard ships which had served under the Commonwealth is implied by Samuel Pepys, whose entry for 11 May 1660 records that '*this morning we began to pull down all the State's arms in the fleet, having first sent to Dover for painters and others to come and set up the King's*'. Such a hypothesis receives support from two archaeological observations. Firstly, while nail-holes are present in the Duart carvings, no trace of the fixings themselves survives *in situ*, suggesting that they may not have been in position when lost. Secondly, this interpretation is reinforced by the apparent survival of the carvings in some quantity, evidently encapsulated with that part of the wreck formation associated with the lower hull. The implication is that they were not in their vulnerable original locations on the upper and outer parts of the hull at the time of wrecking, but stowed away safely somewhere below. If so, a substantial cache of Stuart nautical iconography may still survive on the site.

It is certain that the Duart site contains major elements of ship structure, and much associated material may be presumed. In particular, the area identified as representing the remains of the stern shows evidence that much of its content, including apparently the panelling and associated carpentry of what appears to be the after cabin collapsed in on itself, may confidently be expected to yield a rich sampling of archaeological evidence. The preservation of all types of material, especially organics, is likely to be exceptionally good.

Conclusion

Investigation of the site, although rescue-driven, has shown that the problem of erosion can be mitigated in the short term so that excavation conducted to full research standards is practicable. It is expected that those parts of the wreck considered to be most under threat will have been excavated by 1999. The historical and cultural potential of this work is considerable. Without doubt the decorative carving, dating probably to the reign of Charles I, is the most important single aspect of the find so far, for little such material survives and this is the first of its kind to be recorded on an archaeological site in British waters. Remains of the ship herself may be expected to throw useful light on 17th-century shipwrightry, while the wreck's association with the Stuart and Commonwealth navies, and New Model Army, will give further significance to its archaeological content. In more general terms, the site is likely to produce a wide range of associated artefacts which will contribute materially to the study of a wide range of contemporary technical, domestic, social and economic matters.

This paper is a revised and updated version of an interim report published in The International Journal of Nautical Archaeology *(Martin 1995).*

References
Archibald, E. H. H. 1972 *The Wooden Fighting Ship in the Royal Navy*, London.
Baillie, G., Clutton, C., & Ilbert, C. 1956 *Britten's Old Clocks and Watches and their Makers*, London.

Boothroyd, G. 1981 'The birth of the Scottish pistol', *in* D. Caldwell (ed.), *Scottish Weapons and Fortifications, 1100–1800* (Edinburgh), 315–338.

Calendar of State Papers, Domestic, 1653–4 (1879). London.

Carpenter, J., Pigott, L., & Whitewell, H. 1985 'A watch from HMS *Pandora*', *Antiquarian Horology* 15, 560–601.

Cheape, H. 1988 'Food and liquid containers in the Hebrides: a window on the Iron Age', *in* A. Fenton and J. Myrdal (eds), *Food and Drink and Travelling Accessories: essays in honour of Gösta Berg* (Edinburgh), 6–27.

Davies, G. 1959 *The Early Stuarts, 1603–1660*, Oxford.

Dow, F. 1979 *Cromwellian Scotland*, Edinburgh.

Dufty, A.R. 1974 *European Swords and Daggers in the Tower of London*, London.

Eames, A, 1961, 'The King's pinnace, the *Swan*, 1642–1645', *The Mariner's Mirror* 47, 49–55.

Earll, R. C. 1992 *The Seasearch Habitat Guide: an identification guide to the main habitats found in the shallow seas around the British Isles* (privately produced in association with the Joint Nature Conservation Committee).

Erwin, D. & Picton, B. 1987 *Guide to Inshore Marine Life*, London.

Firth, C. 1895 *Scotland and the Commonwealth*, Edinburgh.

Friar, S. and Ferguson, J. 1993 *Basic Heraldry*, London.

Green, J. 1977 *The A-VOC Jacht* Vergulde Draeck *wrecked Western Australia 1656*, Part I. BAR Supplementary Series 36 (i), Oxford.

Green, J. 1989 *The A-VOC Retourschip* Batavia *wrecked Western Australia, 1629: Excavation report and artefact catalogue*. BAR International Series 489, Oxford.

Gregory, D. 1995 'Experiments into the deterioration characteristics of materials on the Duart Point wreck site: an interim report', *IJNA* 24, 61–65.

Heywood, T. 1637 *A true Description of his Majesty's royal Ship, built this Year, 1637, at Woolwich, in Kent, to the great Glory of the English Nation, and not to be Paralleled in the whole of the Christian World*, London.

Howard, F. 1979 *Sailing Ships of War, 1400–1860*, Greenwich.

Hurst, J. 1977 'Langerwehe Stoneware of the Fourteenth and Fifteenth Centuries', *in* M.R. Apted, R. Gilyard-Beer & A.D. Saunders (eds), Ancient Monuments and their Interpretation: Essays presented to A.J.Taylor, Chichester, 219–38

Hurst, J., Neal, D. & van Beuningen, H. 1986 *Pottery Produced and Traded in North-West Europe 1350–1650*, Rotterdam.

Kemp, P. 1976 *The Oxford Companion to Ships and the Sea*, Oxford.

Kilby, K. 1977 *The Village Cooper*, Aylesbury.

Lynch, M. 1992 *Scotland: a New History*, London.

McKay, M. (ed.) 1980 *The Rev. John Walker's Report on the Hebrides of 1764 and 1771*, Edinburgh.

Macleod, D. (ed.) 1934 *A Description of the Western Isles of Scotland by Martin Martin*, Stirling.

MacLeod, I. D. 1995 '*In situ* corrosion studies on the Duart Point wreck, 1994', *IJNA* 24, 53–59.

Martin, C. J. M. 1978 'The *Dartmouth*, a British frigate wrecked off Mull, 1690. 5. The ship', *IJNA* 7, 29–58.

Martin, C. J. M. 1995a 'The Cromwellian Shipwreck off Duart Point, Mull: an interim report', *IJNA* 24, 15–32.

Martin, C. J. M. 1995b, 'Assessment, stabilisation and management of an environmentally threatened seventeenth century shipwreck off Duart Point, Mull', *in* A. Q. Berry & I. W. Brown (eds), *Managing Ancient Monuments: an integrated approach* (Clwyd), 181–189.

Martin, P. F. de C. 1977 'The *Dartmouth*, a British frigate wrecked off Mull, 1690. 4. The clay pipes', *IJNA* 7, 219–223.

Martin, P. F. de C. 1987 'Pipes from the wreck of the *Dartmouth*, 1690: a reassessment', *in* P. J. Davey (ed.), *The Archaeology of the Clay Tobacco Pipe. X. Scotland*, BAR British Series 178, Oxford.

Moorhouse, S. 1970 'Finds from Basing House, Hampshire (*c.* 1540–1645): part one', *Post-Medieval Archaeology* 4, 31–91.

Oswald, A. 1975 *Clay Pipes for the Archaeologist*, BAR 14, Oxford.

Scott-Giles, C. 1958 *Boutell's Heraldry*, London.

Webster, G. 1969 *Romano-British Coarse Pottery: a student's guide*, CBA Research Report 6, London.

Wood, E. S. 1963 *Collins Field Guide to Archaeology*, London.

15

The identification of a ship's place of departure with the help of artefacts

Piet Kleij

INTRODUCTION

Seas and rivers, often regarded today as obstacles to traffic, have formed some of the main routes of communication well into the 20th century. Road conditions in the past were poor and transportation by man or animals limited in capacity; water transport was by far the most effective way of conveying people and goods over long distances.

Most trade was conducted by ship, and new products, new ideas and new developments were distributed more easily and rapidly via the waterways, eventually reaching the hinterland by way of the ports. In his examination the obsidian trade in Ancient Greece, Renfrew rightly remarked that trade was an important means of exchanging new ideas, and therefore played a major part in economic and cultural changes (Renfrew 1969, 38–56). Much information about trade and shipping routes, and consequently economic and cultural contacts and changes, may be obtained from historical sources. Nevertheless, the amount of information differs according to the period and the place. For example, Jankuhn states in his article on early medieval Frisian trade in the Baltic that the further one goes back in time, the scarcer become the sources (Jankuhn 1956, 451–2), while according to Muckelroy more is known about 17th-century Dutch East Indiamen than about 18th-century coasters (Muckelroy 1978, 240).

In cases where the historical sources are inadequate or silent, underwater archaeology can contribute to the investigation of trade routes and contacts between peoples and places. Good wreck analysis can lead to more insight in the exchange of ideas, goods and power between various groups (Murphy 1983, 71 and 84). One precondition, however, is that the original port of departure and the destination of the ship are known. Otherwise the information obtained cannot be set in a wider context and little can be said about the contacts and influence between different places and groups. Once the origin of a wreck is known, an attempt may be made to trace its destination from its cargo or from the spot where the ship actually foundered.

Determining the port of departure of a merchantman is more difficult than would appear at first sight. Many different methods have been used for this: i. the cargo (e.g. Muckelroy 1978, 72: but that could have been loaded in any port); ii. the construction and design of a ship (e.g. Murphy 1983, 84: but a ship may have been sold to a third party or stolen, and thus have a different place of origin from what its construction might lead us to believe). What has been missing is a framework of inquiry through which the provenance of ships could be traced (Bass 1983, 97–98). This paper attempts to outline such a system, primarily applicable to merchantmen, but also to ships with other functions.

PLACE OF ORIGIN OF A MERCHANT SHIP

The term 'place of origin of a merchant ship' is vague, referring either to the place where the ship was actually built (the '*constructive* place of origin'), or the place where the ship was registered or where the owner lived (the '*legal* place of origin'), or the place where the ship was fitted out for a voyage, where the crew embarked and where it would eventually have to return to unload its cargo (the '*economic* place of origin'). Since we are attempting to trace trade routes and economic and cultural contacts, a ship's place of departure is defined here as the *economic* place of origin. This need not correspond to the ship's port of registry, or where the owner lived, or where the ship was built.

IDENTIFICATION OF ORIGIN THROUGH ARTEFACTS

If one wishes to determine the place of origin of a wreck and there are few or no historical sources available, artefacts from the findspot may provide clues (those found at the findspot but post-dating the wreck being disregarded). The sources for the artefacts provide clues to the origin of the wreck. If all objects originated from the same country or region, one may have greater confidence that the ship also came from the same place.

It is important to remember that the source of an artefact can refer not only to its place of manufacture, but also to the area in which it was used. For example, stoneware jars from Frechen (regularly found in wrecks; see this book, Chapter 9), were made in the Rhineland, but are not an indication that the wrecks in which they were found originated from either Frechen or the Rhineland. They do indicate that such vessels had contact with the much larger stoneware market area, namely the German Rhineland, The Netherlands, Belgium, Luxembourg, France, Ireland, Great Britain and parts of Scandinavia.

Different clues from a single wreck

Problems arise when artefacts from the same wreck point to different places of origin, and there may be no simple explanation. Some artefacts would have been carried on board at the beginning of a ship's maiden voyage and therefore indicate the vessel's initial place of departure. The ship may make a number of voyages and end up elsewhere as a result of being sold or stolen. In the course of time items may be laden to replace worn, lost or damaged objects from the original home port, gradually displacing those from the old port. Consequently, two or more places of origin may be found on board one vessel. Moreover, objects may be brought on board from ports reached during the various voyages, pointing to the foreign places. In other words, artefacts may be found on board a ship which reflect different places of departure and the ports called at *en route*.

In order to determine the correct indications, one must consider the relative weightings to be given to the various artefacts for the identification of the place of departure. This value may be found by considering the *rate of circulation* of the artefacts used on board.

Rate of circulation

Objects used on board a ship have a certain rate of circulation. This is the rate at which they wear, break, fall into disuse and are replaced, which varies according to the object. Those bought new at the beginning of *every* voyage have a *high* rate of circulation, indicating the last place of departure, and are therefore very important for identifying the place of origin. Objects which remain on board for years have a *low* rate of circulation and may therefore refer to an earlier place of origin which is no longer relevant. These objects are of low value in determining the origin. In short, objects with a high rate of circulation are of higher value in identifying the place of origin than objects with a low rate of circulation.

When a ship has changed its port of departure, a large number of artefacts will at first originate from the old home port, to be replaced gradually by others from the new home port. If, for example, one has a findspot from which those artefacts with a high rate of circulation point to region 'A' and those with a low rate of circulation to region 'B', there is a good chance that these are the remains of a ship which originally came from region 'B' but which changed hands and subsequently sailed for region 'A'.

One factor which might complicate any assessment has already been mentioned: during a voyage a ship may take artefacts on board in a foreign port to replace those broken *en route*. If it was a matter of only one or two things, they may stand out during the identification of the port of departure. However, in cases where there were dozens of objects, the question of whether they are to be regarded as purchase in a foreign port or not may depend on the interpretation of the whole complex.

Which artefacts have a high rate of circulation? Which have a low rate? Which lie somewhere between these rates? One ought to establish the rate of circulation of every object which might be found on board a shipwreck, but that would be impracticable. Consequently the contents of a ship have been divided into separate categories (e.g. *tableware* or *tools*).[1] A rate of circulation has been formulated according to category.

On the basis of the circulation rates of the various categories of artefact, a scheme has been drawn up starting with those categories of artefact with a high rate of circulation, and then in a descending rate. The advantage of this scheme is that it is easy to see which objects are valuable as indicators of the port of departure and which are less so. In this way it is possible to identify the home port of a wreck.

The categories

The rate of circulation of a category is determined by that of the objects within it. Differences in this rate determine the order of precedence in the scheme.

1. The ship's equipment

Ship's equipment[2] was constantly subject to heavy wear, particularly during bad weather. Many ships put out to sea with extra sails, anchors and rigging. Objects from this category had to be replaced every few voyages, and sometimes after every voyage. Ballast was sometimes discharged in the middle of a voyage, and consequently this category can have a high rate of circulation.

One disadvantage with this group is that it is often difficult to specify where the objects were made. Rigging, sails and blocks can seldom be identified with certainty as coming from a particular place. The one exception is the ballast, whose geological source can often be ascertained fairly accurately. For example, Dutch ships frequently carried yellow bricks as ballast (Sténuit 1974, 236 f.; Price and Muckelroy 1974, 260 ff.; Green 1977, 95 f.), whereas English ships had shingle, and sand/gravel and stone (e.g. Wignall 1980, 270).

2. Working equipment[3]

Objects belonging to this category were only used in unloading, loading and stowing the cargo. They were used intensively, but only on a few occasions during the voyage. They often lasted several voyages, and the category had a moderate rate of circulation. The origin of the artefacts in this category is often difficult to determine.

3. Heavy military equipment

Heavy weapons were strong, expensive and did not wear out

rapidly. They could last a long time and being expensive, were handled with care. Their rate of circulation was so low that they could still be on board long after a ship has changed its home port. For example, fifteen years after she had been given to the king of England by the Dutch, the yacht *Mary* still had two Dutch cannon on board (McBride 1973, 61 f). Cannon found on a wreck site are often found to be much older than the ship itself (Kleij in Reinders and van Holk 1993, 48); on the breaking up of a ship, they were transferred to another. Only in the case of large merchantmen were heavy weapons sometimes unloaded after a voyage and stored in an arsenal. Despite this, the rate of circulation of this category is low. It is usually possible to identify the place of origin of guns by means of their shape, inscriptions and founders' marks.

4. *Light military equipment*

Objects from this category were sturdy, did not wear out easily, and not being cheap, they were not replaced after every voyage. Apart from the occasional exception, there was often no need for them to be taken off the ship after every voyage, and so this category has a moderate rate of circulation. Such weapons may sometimes bear inscriptions, marks or distinguishing features which are easily identifiable.

5. *Documents and stationery*

Verbal and written communication was often very different (informal and formal). Writing from shipwrecks can provide another tool for ascertaining the place of origin of a ship, the evidence taking the form of i) official documentation (log books, slates), ii) private correspondence, iii) printed books. Objects from this category were often removed from the ship at the end of a voyage. The shipowners frequently wanted to check the log-book, while a bookkeeper had to make out the merchant's profit or loss accounts. At the beginning of a voyage, new books were brought on board, and so this category has a high rate of circulation.

Since the language used on board ship was often the 'national' or 'official' language, this category can assist the identification of the home port. However, the distribution of languages in the past differed from the situation today. The Spanish-, Portuguese-, English- and French-speaking areas have expanded worldwide in recent centuries, while the Dutch-speaking area has shrunk considerably.

This artefact category consists largely of paper and is therefore perishable. Nevertheless, legible text on paper may on occasions be preserved within shipwrecks (Price and Muckelroy 1977, 187 f.; Sténuit 1977, 119), and the discovery of this category is not impossible.

6. *Navigational equipment*

This category includes valuable instruments which were often taken off a ship for safe-keeping after each voyage. Large companies such as the *Dutch East India Company* even obliged captains to hand in some of the navigational equipment after a voyage to maintain secrecy. For this reason, the category has a high rate of circulation.

The origin of instruments can sometimes be traced – most obviously, if place of manufacture or the name of the maker is marked. Origin may be ascertained from the measures used. On the Continent, prior to Napoleon's weights and measures reform, each country (and sometimes even each district) had its own weights and measures. If a ship changed its port of origin, those navigational instruments which were no longer operational because of differences in measures and units of accounts of various countries were often replaced by instruments with the measures of the new country of origin.

7. *Tools*

Objects from this category could often last for several voyages, so this category has a moderate rate of circulation. Origin may not be easy to establish. Tools have shapes which are commonly found in many countries, and are seldom marked or bear the maker's name, while the type of material is often identical in all countries (iron saw, lead plumb-bob).

8. *Galley utensils*

This category comprises ceramics and wooden and metal artefacts. The more fragile objects were usually carefully stored in racks or cupboards so that they could last several voyages; since wooden and metal objects are fairly resistant to breakage, they had a moderate rate of circulation.

The sources of pottery and metal artefacts can sometimes be established accurately through their characteristic forms and fabrics, and occasional inscriptions or marks.

9. *Eating and drinking equipment*

The same considerations applied to to galley utensils apply to this category. It also has a moderate rate of circulation, and the origin may be readily identified.

10. *Furniture*

Goods in this category were usually made of wood (tables, chairs) or metal (candlesticks, lamps), but pottery or glass objects (tobacco pots, carafes) are also found. They were not subject to heavy use; the fragile goods were carefully stored and could therefore easily last several voyages. This category has a moderate rate of circulation. The source of pottery and metal objects in particular may be readily identified.

11. *Victuals*

Fresh food and drink were brought on board every voyage. The remains of food supplies have been found in shipwrecks (Dorsman in Gawronski 1986; Zeiler 1993; Reilly 1984), as has evidence of packing materials, which could last several voyages. Water barrels and bottles, for example, could be refilled when empty. For this reason, the category has a moderate rate of circulation.

The source of the victuals can be only roughly indicated, but that of the packing materials or containers such as bottles, casks or pottery storage jars may be easier to establish.

12. Personal belongings of the crew

Most crews disembarked at the end of the voyage, and only embarked again at the beginning of a new voyage, so this category has a high rate of circulation. Objects from this category (coins, tobacco boxes, medals, rings, shoes, bibles, pipes) can be easily attributed to a particular place of origin.

One disadvantage appears to be that the crew need not always have come from the same *economic* place of origin: men from other areas or countries may have signed on. Instances are known throughout the centuries: king Alfred of Wessex employed Frisians in his fleet when there was a shortage of seamen in his own country in the 9th century (Boeles 1951, 72), and the crew of a medieval Spanish ship might consist of Spaniards, French, English and Flemings (Childs 1978, 167), while the Dutch East India Company employed Asians and Americans in 1780 (*Maritieme Geschiedenis der Nederlanden* III, 1977, 152).

'Foreigners' were generally found on ships of the great trading companies which made long voyages outside Europe. This was far less the case with European trade. Captains of these ships signed on men from their own countries, and sometimes even relatives (*Maritieme Geschiedenis der Nederlanden* II, 1976, 133). In the cases where there were foreigners on board, they were usually in the minority; most of the crew usually came from the ship's place of departure or its immediate vicinity.

In the few cases where foreigners made up the majority of the crew (53% for example with the Dutch East India Company at the end of the 18th century: *Maritieme Geschiedenis der Nederlanden* III, 1977, 151), they are conspicuous because the group came from a number of different countries, whereas the crew members from the place of departure form a large homogeneous group, the latter suggesting an *economic* place of origin. Moreover, the foreigners signed on at the port of departure, where they received their earnings and may have bought some of their belongings (Van Beylen 1970, 234); consequently some of their personal possessions may point to an *economic* place of origin.

13. Cargo

The cargo may have been loaded in any port, so it need not reveal anything about the origin of a ship and for this reason is not included in the scheme (in spite of its high rate of circulation). The cargo is useful, however, for tracing (part of) the ship's last route.

14. Ship

From the method of ship construction, one can sometimes establish a *constructive* place of origin. Whether this corresponds to the economic place of origin can only be established with the help of categories 1 – 12. It may be possible to say something about the history of the ship, once the economic place of origin has been established.

Scheme for determining origin

As mentioned above, the position of a category in the scheme is determined by its rate of circulation. The higher the rate, the higher the position of the category in the scheme.

High rate of circulation
Documents and stationery
Crew's personal belongings
Ship's equipment
Navigational equipment

Moderate rate of circulation
Working equipment
Galley utensils
Tools
Light military equipment
Eating and drinking equipment
Furniture
Victuals

Low rate of circulation
Heavy military equipment

Not included
Ship
Cargo

Procedure

The first step is to determine the origin of the artefacts from the wreck: if these point to one country, this will probably be the country of origin of the ship. If they point to more than one country as place of origin, the scheme can be used to find out which place is the *last* place of origin. The artefacts and any references to place of origin can be entered under the appropriate sub-group. For example, spoons would be entered under *eating and drinking equipment*, and saws and hammers under *tools*. It will rarely be possible to fill in every category.

If all the objects within a certain category indicate the same place of origin, the group may originate from that place. If several references to different places of origin exist, attention must be paid to the *number* of objects with differing references and to the *homogeneity* of these groups. If one or more artefacts differ from the rest, it may be an exception (for example, a purchase made in a port *en route*). It becomes problematic when a large number from one category point to one area, whereas a substantial number of other artefacts from the same category indicate another. In such cases, it is impossible to establish a definite place of origin for the category, and both areas should be entered as possible places of origin.

It is clear that if the categories with the highest rates of circulation all point to the same area, while those with the lower rates of circulation point to another area, then the former should indicate the correct place of origin and the latter may be refer to an earlier place of origin. If, however, the higher categories indicate different sources, it will be necessary to check the number of times these are given (one being an exception (port *en route* etc.), two or more being suspicious).

If the lower categories produce references to different sources, frequency must be checked. For example, if the highest categories indicate place A and the lower categories indicate both place B and place C, this may imply that place A was the last home port while B and C were earlier places of departure (other explanations are possible, but it is not practical to enumerate them all here).

The ship's place of construction may be derived from the hull's method of construction. If the *constructive* place of origin corresponds to the economic one, it is likely that the ship regularly used the same home port. If they differ, the ship may have changed its home port at least once. Analysis of the cargo may indicate which ports the ship visited during its last voyage, from which port it had just sailed, or destinations for the ship (the latter may be indicated by the location of the wreck).

Quality and quantity

The degree to which the scheme can be applied with success will depend to a large extent on the manner of excavation, the number of artefacts recovered from the wreck and their distribution within the scheme. It is important not only to identify and describe all the artefacts from an excavation, but also to try to gain insight in the processes by which the wreck was formed and the finds distributed. The original location of an object on board may determine which category it belongs to: for example, a small yellow brick from the hold of a Dutch West Indiaman will usually be ballast, but a similar brick from the galley forms a component of the ship (namely the oven).

The greater the number of objects rescued from a wreck site, and the greater their allocation *across* the various subgroups, the more greater certainty will exist for correctly identifying the place of origin. It is difficult to determine the minimum number of artefacts needed for reliable results. Testing the scheme on four different shipwrecks of known origin has shown that it produces a valid result with as few as fifteen artefacts spread between five different categories (Kleij 1989, 32–60). Though statistically poor, this represents in practice a 100% score.

Research cases

Two case studies are presented here to illustrate the scheme: that of a Portuguese ship which sank off the coast of Brazil and whose name is known (Pernambuco de Mello 1979), and an unidentified ship which sank off the Dutch coast.[4] The first wreck was excavated rather crudely. The latter was discovered by scuba divers and partly ransacked. A reasonable number of artefacts whose origin could be identified were found in the wreck, and the scheme was applicable even though the ship was not excavated archaeologically.

The Sacramento

In 1668, the *Sacramento*, belonging to the *Companhia Geral do Comércio do Brazil* (Portuguese Brazil-Company) broke up on a sandbank off the Brazilian port of Bahia, with the loss of 930 people. Much has been written about the ship and the location of the foundering, with so many casualties, including several members of prominent families. The wreck was identified on the basis of cannon bearing inscriptions, the year it was lost, pottery with the coats of arms of nobility who were on board and the location of the wreck, which was recorded in documentary sources.

The Brazilian Ministry of Culture and Ministry of Defence selected this wreck for the very first Brazilian underwater archaeological excavation. If the above scheme is applicable, the place of origin derived from the objects from this wreck should correspond to the place of origin established from other sources for the *Sacramento*.

Of the many objects found at the findspot, several dozen can now be entered in the scheme, as follows:

Documents and stationery: no objects are mentioned which belong to this category.
Crew's personal belongings: five items of crockery bearing the coat of arms of the *Da Silva* family, belonging to the ship's captain, Francisco Correo da Silva: *Portugal*. Fifty small coins, mostly Portuguese: *Portugal*. Some Spanish small coins: *Spain*.
Ship's equipment: no objects are mentioned which could be classified under this category.
Navigational equipment: two Portuguese astrolabes: *Portugal*.
Working equipment: no objects are mentioned which could be classified under this category
Galley utensils: no objects are mentioned which could be classified under this category.
Tools: no objects are mentioned which could be classified under this category.
Light military equipment: dozens of Portuguese or Spanish olive jars filled with musket shot: *Portugal* or *Spain*.
Eating and drinking equipment: at least one maiolica plate: *Portugal*. Two maiolica jugs: *Portugal*
Furniture: no objects are mentioned which could be classified under this category.
Victuals: no objects are mentioned which could be classified under this category.
Heavy military equipment: thirteen cannon bearing the Portuguese coat of arms and that of the *Companhia Geral do Comércio do Brazil* (Portuguese Brazil-Company). Five of these were originally English, but the Portuguese engraved their own coat of arms on top of the English marks after 1649: *Portugal*. Four cannon bore a Dutch inscription: *The Netherlands*. One cannon bore an English inscription: *England*.
Ship: no mention.
Cargo: dozens of Portuguese lead cloth seals: *Portugal*. A few English lead cloth seals: *England*.

Of the categories with a high rate of circulation, *personal belongings* and *navigational equipment* yielded indications of place of origin: the former to Portugal and Spain (although the Spanish reference is considerably weaker than the Portuguese, being based on some small Spanish coins). *Navigational equipment* also pointed to Portugal.

Of the categories with a moderate rate of circulation, *eating and drinking equipment* referred to Portugal three times, while there were no references to other countries. *Light military equipment* indicated Spain or Portugal.

Heavy military equipment, with a low rate of circulation, pointed mainly to Portugal (thirteen cannon, including the five which were originally English), though The Netherlands (four cannon) and England (one cannon) were also represented. The latter may reflect the ship's past or the nature of the Portuguese arms industry and supply in the second half of the 17th century (see this book, Chapter 7 for a discussion on the problems of identifying the nationality of a ship from its cannon).

Three categories produced references to Portugal, and two (personal belongings and light military equipment) to Spain or Portugal. The Spanish references to 'personal belongings' are weak, and consequently this category may point to Portugal. This means that two categories with a high rate of circulation both refer to Portugal, and consequently the place of origin that can be deduced from the scheme is Portugal, which corresponds to the place of origin derived from other sources.

By far the majority of lead cloth seals were also from Portugal (the few English examples may be regarded as exceptional). The last voyage of the ship was probably from Portugal to Brazil with a cargo of Portuguese and English textile, *inter alia*. The English merchandise is not surprising in view of the very close political and commercial relationships between each other from the 17th century onwards.

The explanations for the presence of foreign weapons (failure of the Portuguese industry to produce enough, the need to purchase elsewhere, the spoils of war) cannot, however, be derived from the scheme or from the wreck.

Wreck 'TXS IV'

The above scheme was also applied to a wreck know as 'TXS IV', which lies several miles east of the island of Texel, in the Waddenzee, in the north of The Netherlands (Fig. 1). Its name and origin are unknown.[5] Since its discovery in 1985, it has been regularly investigated by divers. The objects from the wreck were examined, identified and drawn by the author as part of an inventory project of the Department of Underwater Archaeology. A small article on TXS IV has already been published (Kleij 1992).

A deep channel, the Texelstroom, runs right through the area of the wreck. This channel reaches a depth of 25 m near the island of Texel. Ships can safely anchor in this channel under the lee of the island. In the past, the Texelstroom was

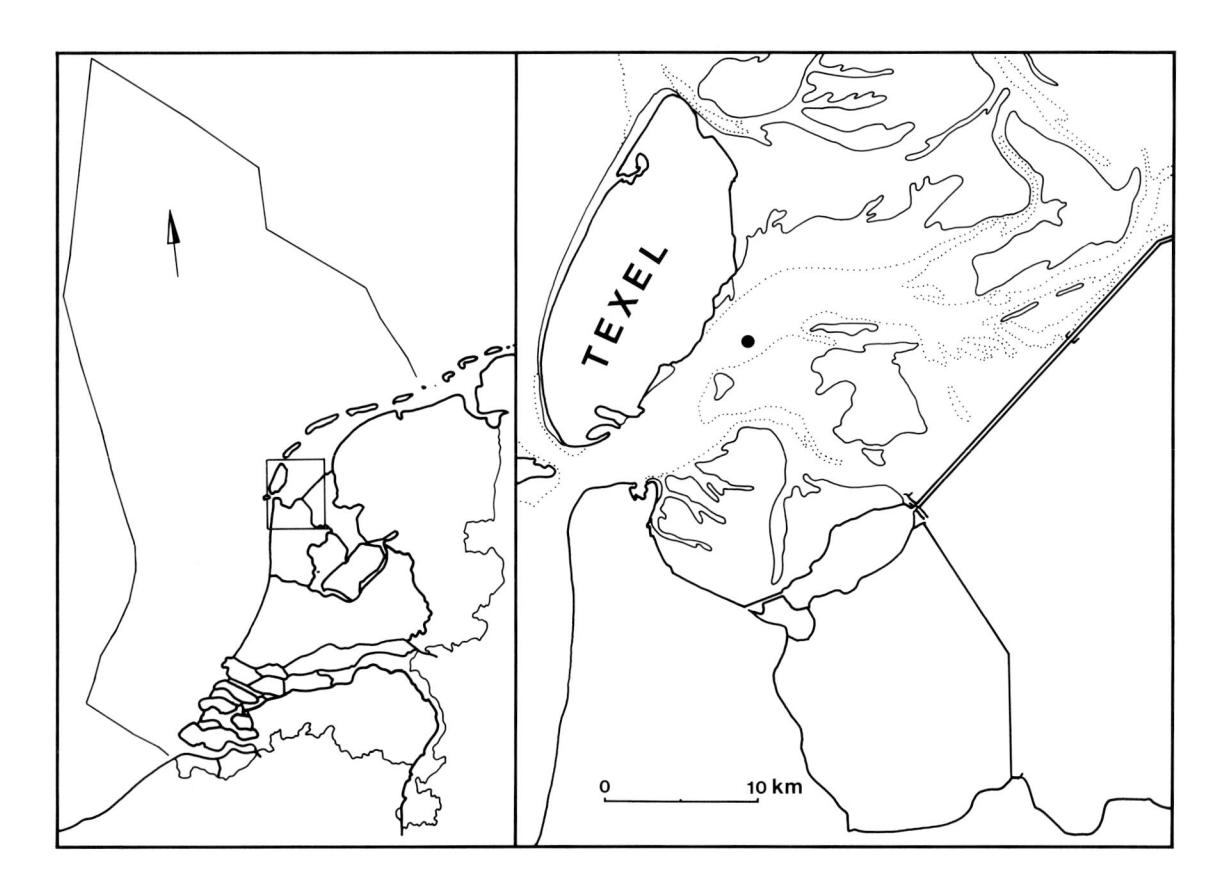

Fig. 1. The Netherlands, showing the location of the island of Texel. Black spot: position of wreck TXS IV. (Drawing: Th. J. Maarleveld)

the best road in the northern part of what is now The Netherlands. Although the Texelstroom was reasonably sheltered, it could be hazardous, and unexpected storms sent thousands of ships to the bottom during the 17th and 18th centuries. The names of a number of shipwrecks are known, but many more, such as TXS·IV remain nameless.

The seagoing ship was 30 to 35 m long, with a beam of approximately 12 m. The remains of its rudder could be seen just behind the stern. In the midships area was found a large pile of yellow and red bricks, in front of which (in the direction of the bow) lay thousands of grey and red Dutch roof tiles in neat rows. Other finds were piled around this central mound, with the larger objects (boxes and barrels) stowed in the bow and stern, and the finer items (such as jars and brassware) mainly on the port side. The starboard side was buried under stones and was therefore not accessible.

The wreck and its contents form an obstacle for the prevailing current, and water around the wreck has been gradually scouring out a channel, with increasing quantities of sand disappearing from the ship. By 1990, this channel had already reached a depth of at least four metres. If erosion was to continue at this rate, the whole find complex will have disappeared within ten to fifteen years.

As a result of excavation, a large part of the inventory has been established. Rows of Spanish olive jars, some still with their wooden stoppers *in situ*, were found on the port side of the bricks and roof tiles. Stoneware jars (small and large), some of which had been packed in wicker baskets, were also found in this area. Behind these jars were boxes and kegs with nails, hinges, axes, adzes, flenching/flensing knives for whaling, locks and keys, and also several empty casks. A large copper kettle was also recorded in this area, before it was swept away by the current.

A large whetstone and four big oars still lie partly hidden in the sand on top of the tiles and bricks. On the port side of the oars, in the direction of the bow, was found the surgeon's equipment, apparently stored in a separate chest or room. The same applies to all kinds of brassware (candlesticks, candle snuffers, a chandelier) which were found close to this equipment. A bale of skins, also nearby, is under threat of falling into the scour channel.

The forward section of the ship held even more objects: a number of barrels of coal, a stoneware vessel of fat, two boxes of candles, casks of Gouda clay pipes, odd pieces of a porcelain tea and coffee-sets and several hundred glass bottles, still partly packed in boxes. Loose bottles frequently roll off the wreck into the depths.

Four mortars and six pestles were found in front of the bottles, close to the bow section,[6] where parts of a clock were also found. Almost in the bows and in an upright position between the timbers, stood a box holding two muskets and three boxes of cartridges.

Broken and intact red earthenware lidded pans and bowls with handles were found in the vicinity of the bows, both inside and outside the wreck and in the scour channel.

A classification of the objects removed from the wreck revealed the following picture:

Documents and stationery: nothing in this category was found.
Personal belongings: surgeons usually took their own instruments with them on board, and the objects from the surgeon's chest may be regarded as personal belongings. A substantial part of his equipment was found. At least fifteen tin-glazed earthenware ointment jars, two lead-tin alloy measuring jugs (with Amsterdam marks), a lead-tin alloy inkstand (with an Amsterdam touch-mark) and five lead-tin alloy medicine bottles (with Amsterdam touch-marks): *The Netherlands*.
Ship's equipment: no objects in this category were brought up which indicated a particular country of origin.
Navigational equipment: nothing in this category was found.
Working equipment: no objects in this category were brought up which indicated a particular country of origin.
Galley utensils: a copper alloy pan from this wreck closely resembles one found in the wreck of the *Vergulde Draeck* (Green 1977, 178, fig. GT 1423) and a foot similar to one from this pan was also found in the wreck of the *Zeewijk* (Ingelman-Sundberg 1979, 50, fig. ZW 273), both Dutch wrecks. The pan may, therefore, indicate *The Netherlands*. The feet from two tripod cooking pots (so-called *grapen* or pipkins) show Dutch characteristics: *The Netherlands*. The rimsherd of a cooking pot or pipkin(Fig. 2) is also Dutch: Bergen-op-Zoom, *The Netherlands*.

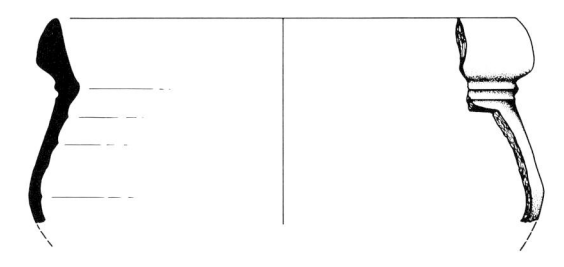

Fig. 2. Rimsherd of red earthenware (diameter about 230 mm) made at Bergen-op-Zoom, The Netherlands. From the F. Duinker collection, Oudeschild, Texel. (Drawing: P. Kleij)

Tools: nothing in this category was found.
Light military equipment: between the timbers of the bows was found a chest containing two muskets (Fig. 3) and three full boxes of cartridges. The muskets are of a type manufactured in The Netherlands, and for which many parts were used which came from Liège. They were frequently used on board Dutch ships in the 18th century. The fact that these muskets were intended for use on board and were not part of the cargo can be seen from the brass guards, which prevented the butts of the guns damaging the deck: *The Netherlands*. The boxes of cartridges show many similarities to cartridge boxes found in the Dutch East Indiamen the *Amsterdam* and the *Buitenzorg*: *The Netherlands*.
Eating and drinking equipment: a lead-tin alloy spoon of a type commonly found in The Netherlands was found within the wreck. Unfortunately the touch mark was rubbed

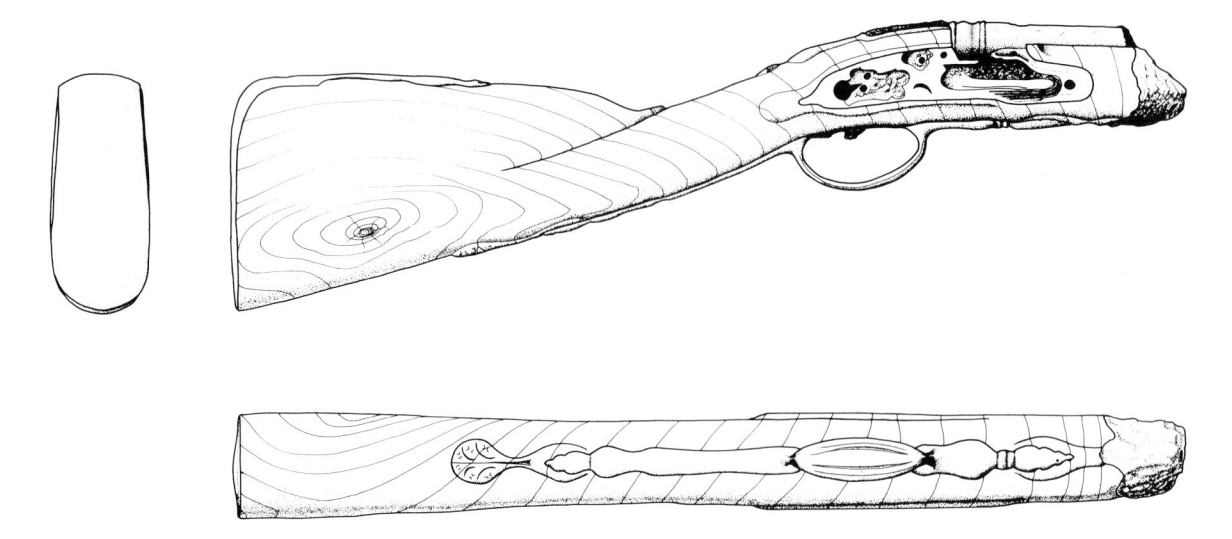

Fig. 3. One of the two muskets (length 515 mm) manufactured in The Netherlands. From the J. Betsema collection, Oudeschild, Texel. (Drawing: P. Kleij).

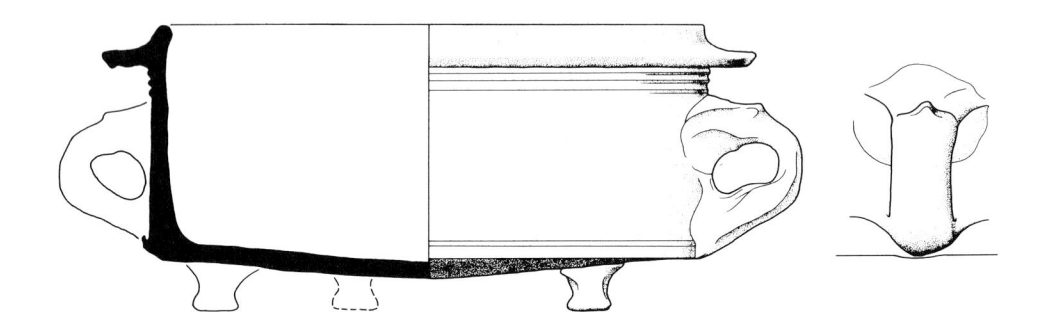

Fig. 4. Red earthenware pan (diameter 314 mm) made in West-Brabant, The Netherlands. From the G.J. Betsema collection, Oosterend, Texel.
(Drawing: P. Kleij)

away during cleaning, and the maker or town of origin can no longer be traced: *The Netherlands*.
Furniture: nothing in this category was found.
Victuals: two objects were brought up: one bone of unknown origin, and a brass tap or spigot paralleled by an example from Amsterdam: *The Netherlands*.
Heavy military equipment: nothing in this category was present at the findspot.
Cargo: the cargo also produced valuable information. Of the objects with an identifiable origin, some were manufactured in *The Netherlands*, such as clay pipes from Gouda, the red earthenware pans and bowls from West-Brabant (Fig. 4), a fragment of half-finished (biscuit-fired) pottery plate from Delft (Fig. 5), and a biscuit-fired Dutch or Frisian *maiolica* plate. Objects made *outside* The Netherlands, but whose

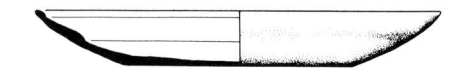

Fig. 5. Fragment of biscuit-fired tin-glazed earthenware (maiolica) plate (diameter about 220 mm) manufactured at Delft, The Netherlands. From the F. Duinker collection, Oudeschild, Texel. (drawing: P. Kleij).

distribution area included The Netherlands are the stoneware storage vessels filled with fat (Fig. 6), the stoneware jars, the stoneware pickling jars and the *Bartmänner* (Fig. 7), odd pieces belonging to one or more porcelain coffee- or teasets from *China* and the white pottery olive jars from *Spain* or *Portugal*. The only exceptions are the parts of one or more English clocks of a type that were fitted to cases in The Netherlands and subsequently sold in North Germany.
Ship: the ship was not investigated nor salvaged.

Clay pipes can assist in establishing the precise date of a particular archaeological complex, as demonstrated on Spitsbergen (Hacquebord 1984, 164–165).
A number of barrels of Gouda clay pipes were found among the cargo, and one of these was salvaged. A pipe with the brand *Spaarpot* bears the name *Jan van de Broek* (operating between 1731 and 1737) on its stem. This pipe indicates that the ship must have sunk in the third decade of the 18th century, and other artefacts support this. A clay pipe bowl with the brand *Gekroonde 32* first came into circulation in 1729. The moulded bottles date from after 1730. The parts of the clock date from the second quarter of the 18th century. The pot-

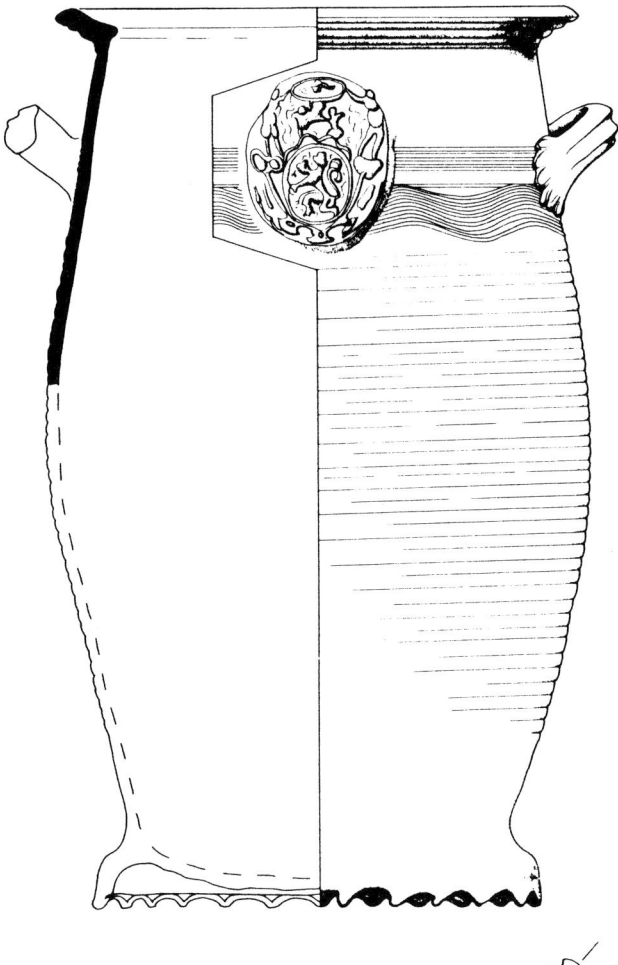

Fig. 6. Stoneware vessel filled with fat (height 512 mm) made at Langerwehe (Rheinland), Germany. From the G.J. Betsema collection, Oudeschild, Texel. (Drawing: P. Kleij)

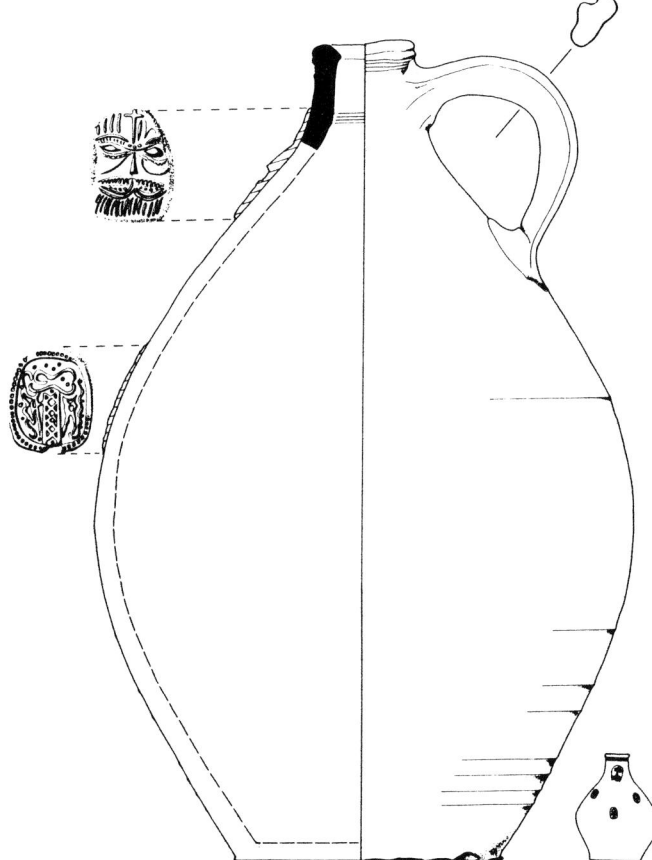

Fig. 7. Stoneware Bartmann jug (height 469 mm) made at Stadlohn, north-west Germany. From the G.J. Betsema collection, Oudeschild, Texel. (Drawing: P. Kleij)

tery objects are typical of the period up to 1740/1750, and mass-produced pottery, which was sold in bulk after 1750 by England to the Dutch market, is absent. Objects which can be definitely dated post-1740 are also absent. The ship therefore sank between 1731 and 1740.

The categories *personal belongings, galley utensils, light military equipment, eating and drinking equipment* and *victuals* all provided evidence pointing to *The Netherlands*. There is not one indication that this ship may perhaps have come from another country, and it may be concluded that TXS IV was a Dutch ship.

The cargo consisted partly of Dutch products, or products that were being conveyed in transit via The Netherlands. The parts of the English clocks may have been intended for the North German market, suggesting that the ship may have been *en route* to the Baltic. This is supported by the absence of heavy weapons. In the first half of the 18th century, the Baltic was one of the few regions where Dutch merchantmen sailed almost unarmed.

The above scheme produces the following picture: that TSX IV is the wreck of a Dutch ship which took on a cargo in The Netherlands. It set off from The Netherlands possibly for the Baltic. It never arrived, though, because it sank in the roads of Texel. The cause of the shipwreck is unknown. From the artefacts we may conclude that all this took place between 1731 and 1740. After sinking, the ship was covered by a layer of sand which protected it for some 250 years. In 1985 changing currents exposed the wreck; if erosion continues at the same rate, the wreck will have disappeared by the year 2010.

POSTSCRIPT

Both the archaeological and historical investigation of objects from shipwrecks and their function on board are still in their infancy. Within this discipline there are also great regional differences, and the scheme presented above is only a rough blueprint. Various matters still have to be solved. For example, as a result of insufficient knowledge of objects on board ship, one user of the scheme may place an artefact in one category, whereas another may allocate the same find to a completely different field, with consequences for the value of the reference to the place of origin derived from the object.

Moreover, no attention has been paid to regional differences in the scheme. It is quite possible that certain objects may have remained on board ship for several voyages in one country, whereas in another they were taken off the ship after every voyage. These differences can only be established by further research, so that they can be accounted for in the scheme.

The scheme is only a rough framework which, though already applicable, requires refining so that regional differences in the use of objects on board ship can be taken into account. For this reason it is important that shipwreck investigations focus attention not only on the construction and building methods and the more spectacular objects, but also on less obvious matters.

Notes

1. This classification in categories is based on the article by Reinders in Cederlund 1985, 81–100.
2. This includes all objects and tools needed to enable a ship to sail safely, such as sails, rigging, anchors and blocks.
3. This includes all tools and devices needed to enable a ship to function as a means of transport, e.g. tackles, hoisting apparatus and stowage timber.
4. The account of this excavation will be published shortly.
5. After being reported to the Underwater Archaeology Department of the Dutch Ministry of Culture, the findspot received the registration number TXS IV, Texelstroom IV.
6. Another pestle lay separately on the wreck.

References

Bass, G.F. 1983 'A Plea for Historical Particularism in Nautical Archaeology', *in* R.A. Gould, 91–104.
Boeles, P.C.J.A. 1951 *De geschiedenis van Friesland tot de elfde eeuw*, Den Haag.
Beylen, van J. 1970 *Schepen van de Nederlanden*, Amsterdam.
Cederlund, C. O.(ed.) 1985 'Postmedieval Boat and Ship Archaeology', Swedish National Maritime Museum, Stockholm Report No.20, BAR International Series 256, Oxford.
Childs, W.R. 1978, *Anglo-Castilian trade in the later Middle-Ages,* Manchester.
Dorsman, W. 1986 'FT 8423/8502 : een poging tot reconstructie van een kist met wijnflessen', *in* J.H.G. Gawronski (ed.) 1986, 77–79.
Gawronski, H.G. (ed.) 1986 *Amsterdam project : jaarraport van de stichting V.O.C. – Schip "Amsterdam" 1985.* Amsterdam.
Green, J. N. 1977 *The A-VOC Jacht VERGULDE DRAECK, wrecked Western Australia 1656*, Part I. BAR Supplementary Series 36, Oxford.
Gould, R.A. 1983 *Shipwreck Anthropology*, Albuquerque.
Hacquebord, L. 1984 *Smeerenburg. Het verblijf van Nederlandse walvisvaarders op de westkust van Spitsbergen in de 17e eeuw,* Proefschrift, Amsterdam-Groningen.
Ingelman-Sundberg, C. *1978 Relics from the Dutch East Indiaman Zeewijk. Foundered in 1727*, Perth.
Jankuhn, H. 1953 'Der fränkischer friesischer Händler zur Ostsee im früher Mittelälter', *Vierteljahrschrift für Sozial- und Wirtschaftsgeschichte* 64, 193–243.
Kleij, P. 1989 *Een methode om de herkomst te bepalen van scheepswrakken*, eindscriptie Universiteit van Amsterdam, IPP, Amsterdam.
Kleij, P. 1992 'Texelstroom IV – herkomst en bestemming van een onbekende koopvaarder', *in* R. Reinders 1992, 80–89.
Kleij, P. 1993 'Oostvoornsemeer Zuidoever: een Straatvaarder voor Rotterdam', *in* R.Reinders & Van Holk, 44–55.
Maritieme Geschiedenis der Nederlanden, deel II, Bussum 1976.
Maritieme Geschiedenis der Nederlanden, deel III, Bussum 1977.
McBride, P.W.J. 1973 'The Mary, Charles II's Yacht. Her history, importance and ordnance', *IJNA* 2, 61–70.
Muckelroy, K. 1978 *Maritime Archaeology*, Cambridge.
Murphy, L. 1983 'Shipwrecks as Data Base for Human Behavioural Studies', in R.A. Gould, 65–89.
Pernambuco de Mello, U. 1979 'The shipwreck of the galleon Sacramento – 1668 off Brazil', *IJNA* 8, 211–223.
Price, R. & Muckelroy, K. 1974 'The second season of work on the Kennemerland site, 1973. An interim report', *IJNA* 3, 257–268.
Reilly, K. 1984 'The Bones', *in* M. Redknap, *The Cattewater wreck. The investigation of an armed vessel of the early sixteenth century*, BAR British Series 131, 88–92
Reinders, R. 1985 'The inventory of a cargo vessel wrecked in 1888', *in* C.O. Cederlund, 81–100.
Reinders, R. 1992 *Scheepsuitrusting en inventaris,* Groningen.
Reinders, R. & A. van Holk 1993, *Scheepslading,* Groningen.
Renfew, C. 1968 'Obsidian and the origins of trade', *Scientific American* 218, 3, March, 38–56.
Sténuit, R. 1974 'Early relics of the VOC trade from Shetland. The wreck of the flute 'Lastdrager' lost off Yell 1653', *IJNA* 3, 213–256
Wignall, S. 1980 'Shipwreck and Boat archaeology in Welsh Waters', *in* J. Blanchard, blz. 263 – 273.
Zeiler, J.T. 1993 'Zes vaten rundvlees uit het scheepswrak SCHEURRAK SO1', *Tussentijdse Rapportage* 10.

16

Wreck de mer and dispersed wreck sites: the case of the *Ann Francis* (1583)

Mark Redknap and Edward Besly

INTRODUCTION

This paper aims to illustrate the potential of the systematic analysis of beach finds for identifying and unscrambling dispersed, non-sealed wreck sites.

Artefacts derived from wreck can be snatched up by tide and wave to be redeposited upon beaches whenever conducive conditions prevail. In many cases, such as the the Padre Island wrecks (Arnold and Weddle 1978), artefacts and ballast can migrate downwards through several metres of sand and silt to become scattered on top of a dense substratum. This material may be occasionally uncovered by storms from beneath tons of sand or pebbles, to be found by beach walkers or metal detectorists. In practice, such discoveries are rarely recorded centrally, and their cumulative potential to indicate the location of ancient wreck remains frequently unrealised.

BACKGROUND

Over the last twenty-five years, finds have periodically been made from Margam Sands, situated on the eastern side of Swansea Bay (south-east of Port Talbot) in South Wales. The discoveries have been made either by eye through beach walking or metal detecting, the finders bringing many items to the Department of Archaeology & Numismatics of the National Museums & Galleries of Wales for identification. The earliest recorded finds were made in the 1850s of three silver Spanish coins (in a private collection at Nottage) thought to be from the same area of beach. In 1972, several coins were found by Mr David B. Rees, and the late George Boon, then Keeper of Archaeology, suggested that these (copper 3-reais of John III of Portugal, 1521–57, silver thaler of Kempten, Bavaria, in name of Holy Roman Emperor Charles V, 1519–56) might derive from a 16th-century wreck.[1] Boon drew attention to the South Wales tradition that the orange trees at Margam had originally been sent as a gift from Philip II of Spain to Elizabeth, but that the vessel in which they were conveyed hither being wrecked on the coast of the Margam Estate, they became the property of one of the Mansell family, as lord of the manor, and since that time had been carefully preserved on this spot (Boon 1974, 324).[2] Since this discovery, the finds from Margam beach have grown in number to include about 200 silver coins, lead sounding weights, bronze dividers and at least one (possibly two) pewter bosun's pipes/calls, and the material has been associated with the wreck of the *Ann Francis*, lost in 1583 (Rees 1957, 178 f.; Rees 1977, 58–9; Blundell forthcoming).

THE *ANN FRANCIS*

The identification of the wreck site as that of the *Ann Francis* was first proposed by Mr A.L.Evans (Rees 1977, 59) and has been reiterated by John Blundell, who has published a historical account in issues of the newsletter of the Cardiff Naturalists' Society. The *Ann Francis* belonged to a King's Lynn merchant, Francis Shaxton. Francis Shaxton senior had become involved in the weaving industry, and was appointed as a searcher by the trade in King's Lynn, inspecting textiles. He appears to have moved to the export of grain (wheat for baking and barley for brewing), which was so successful that by the time his son took over the business in 1582, there were eight ships (Blundell 1994, 2). The *Ann Francis* left Lynn on 2 October 1583, and though no destination is recorded, she probably left for Spain (Cadiz or the coast of Portugal) with a cargo of wheat, a commodity much in demand in Spain at this time. The voyage from Cadiz to Lynn could take about four weeks, and Lynn to Cadiz about six weeks allowing for prevailing winds. Allowing for time to unload, find a return cargo and resupply, a return voyage could therefore take about twelve weeks.

WRECK AND AFTERMATH

In addition to their long experience of particular waters, mariners during the 16th century relied for navigation on a number of aids (particularly when in unfamiliar seas). The *rutter* was a small pocket book recording compass courses between ports and capes, the distances between them, the direction and flow of tidal streams, high water times, soundings and the nature of the sea-bed (Waters 1978, 11).[3] Instruments would have included lead and line for finding the depth

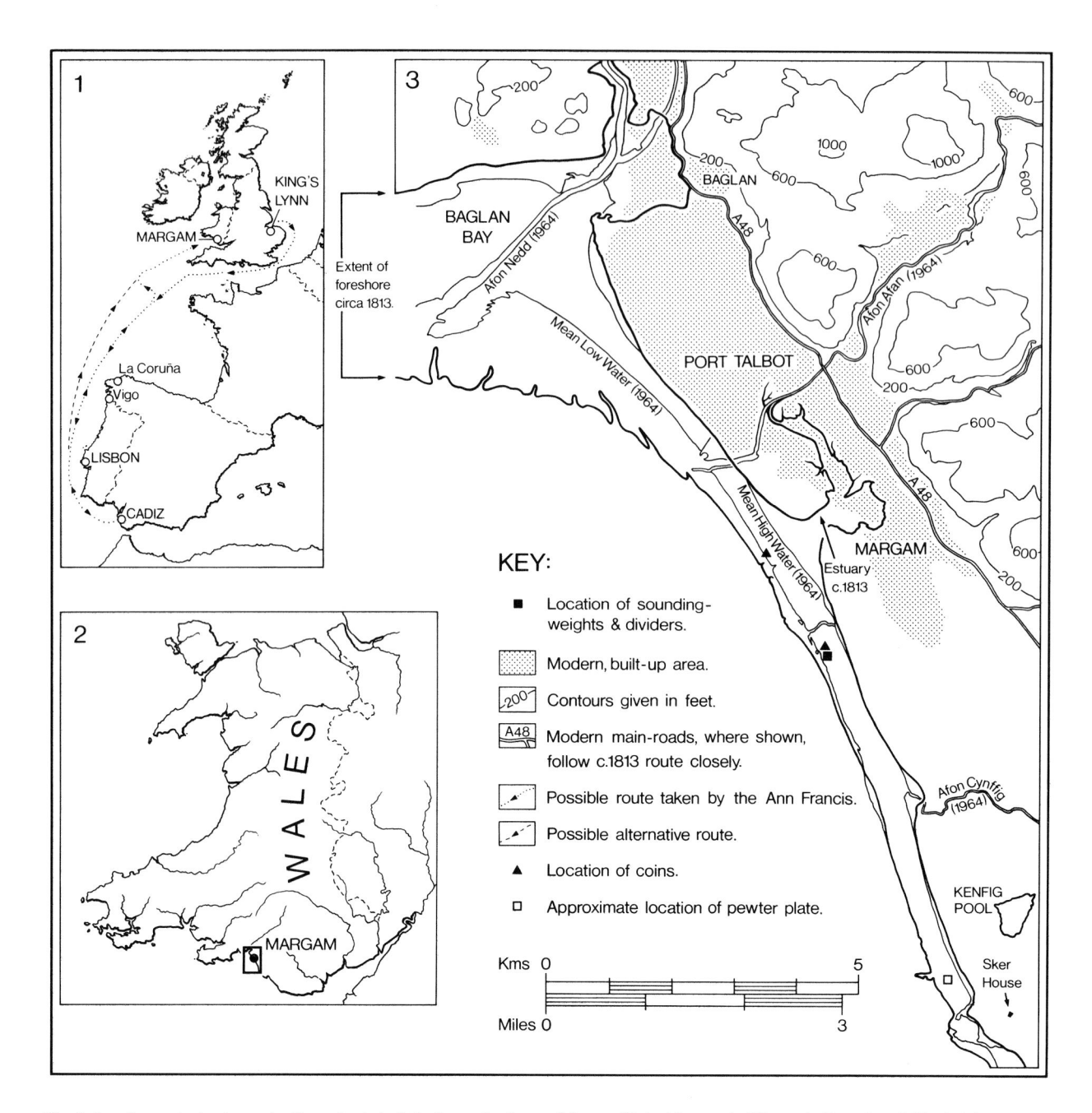

Fig. 1. Location map, showing main sites and extent of the former foreshore at Margam (derived from early OS maps). (Drawing: J.Chadwick, NMGW)

of water, sea-compass (whose degrees of accuracy varied widely), sand-glass for gauging the passage of the watches for relieving deck-hands and running the ship's routine, and (towards the later 16th-century) some form of chart (though distances on early charts were inaccurate).[4] When out of sight of land, such as on the voyage to Portugal, the ship-master had to keep a 'dead-reckoning' and record his estimate of the way his ship had gone, the effects of wind, tide, waves and of the waywardness of the ship. This course could be recorded on a traverse board. In fresh and strong winds, it is easy to underestimate speed through the water, and this common error may have resulted in a late change in course to starboard, into the Bristol rather than English Channel. Another con-

tributing factor may have been exceptional storms towards the end of her voyage sweeping her off course. Analysis of records of known casualties for the south coast of Cornwall and Devon by month of loss indicates that December and January are the heaviest periods of loss by sailing vessel (RCHME 1996), and the *Ann Francis* may have succumbed to such a storm, stranding on Margam Beach on 28 December 1583 (N.L.W. Penrice and Margam Mss 5728). Plundering of the wreck appears to have occurred fairly rapidly, with a confrontation on the beach of upwards of 100 persons, before George Williams, agent to Lord Pembroke (representing his Baglan estate) and Anthony Mansell, brother/son of Sir Edward Mansell of Penrice, Oxwich and Margam (Glamorgan), could muster escorts to exert law and order. Within this three to four hour period, sundry 'outrageous misdemeanors' were committed, and much wreckage spirited away (Star Chamber Proceedings in Glamorgan M.12/23 and P.51/39).

Six men were arrested in possession of money and sent to London for trial. Sir Edward Mansell was ordered by the Privy Council in June 1584 to re-arrest three of the men, who had escaped and returned to Glamorgan, and Mansell made an inventory of everything of value still on board (NLW Penrice and Margam Mss. 5728), which is reproduced below.

Both Williams and Mansell claimed the goods which had been impounded, and the dispute was contested in the Star Chamber court, ultimately turning in Pembroke's favour (Rees 1957, 178). However, by March, Francis Shaxton, who in February had acknowledged the loss of the ship '*by stresse of wether and the godes perished*' on a voyage to Hartlepool (Williams 1951; Exch.K.R.Port Books, 427/7), had received information about the Glamorgan wreck, which he successfully laid claim to. The *Ann Francis* (*Anne Frauncis*) was his newest (fifth) ship, built between 1580 and 1583. An agreement signed by Shaxton and Mansell required the latter to return the iron ordnance, two anchors, two of the best cables, four fowlers, and half of the money recovered from the six men. In late May 1584 he had to be reminded by letter from the Privy Council to carry out the terms of the agreement (Rees 1957, 179). The Star Chamber accounts record that the ship was estimated at 180 tons. Ship tonnage was often carelessly recorded in Port Books: Glamorgan and Monmouthshire were the only areas in Wales according to the State Paper records to harbour a few ships of 100 tons and above (Lewis 1927).

THE INVENTORY

Some of the finds reported here were generously donated to the National Museums & Galleries of Wales by the finders (accession nos given).

The Coins (see schedule below and Fig.3)

Of the two hundred or so coins said to have been recovered from the area of Margam and Aberavon beaches, only sixteen have been examined and recorded fully. Photographs of a further seventeen were shown in 1994 by John Blundell, who provided information regarding another four. There are three distinct groups of coins: Spanish and Spanish-American, Portuguese, and German states, together with a single Polish coin. In principle these should provide a good indication of the date of the wreck, were there not alternative sources of information.

The Spanish coins are all in the names of Ferdinand and Isabella (1474–1504), but it is well known that such coins continued to be struck after their deaths. The Mexico coins in the names of Juana and Carlos were in production by 1554: assayer L accounts for 84% of the Mexico coins from the Padre Island wrecks of that year (Arnold and Weddle 1978, 279). 'Spanish silver' to the value of £12–16–00d is confirmed from Mansell's inventory (N.L.W. Penrice and Margam Mss

5728), though the entry does not indicate whether it was coined or uncoined (or whether the term is a catch-all for 'foreign silver').

The four Portuguese coins – one gold and three copper – are all from late in the reign of John III, who died in 1557. The gold S. Vicente (see back cover) was introduced in 1555 and probably produced in John's name until January 1558 (Almeida do Amaral 1977, 486, 532). This specimen is unworn.

The silver coins from German states form the bulk of the finds which have been examined. They comprise Guldengroschen/Guldiner and Talers, mostly from the 1540s, the latest being a Taler of Batenburg (a free barony in the Low Countries) – undated, but struck in 1556. Where well preserved, they appear in general not to be worn.

THE ARTEFACTS

Objects of silver

1. Oval religious medallion (Fig.2; private collection, information and photograph courtesy of J. Blundell), bearing the legends:
(*obv*) EL SANTISSIM[O] SACRAN(M)EN[T]O A GANADO ' SSA ('The most sacred sacrament has triumphed. Spiritu Santo Amen?'), in oval around eucharistic motif of communion chalice with host, surmounted by halo, suspended above it. Two winged angels, one on either side venerate the host, hands uplifted in prayer. Below chalice, the legend ROMA.
(*rev*) M (Maria?)CONCEBIDA.SIN.PECADO.ORIGIN(AL) ('conceived without original sin', the Immaculate Conception), in oval around Blessed Virgin Mary, crescent at feet, with crown of seven stars (her 'joys') within rayed mandala. Length about 30 mm. The reference is to Revelations 12 v.1.

A similar oval gold version of the depiction of the Virgin with crown of eight stars enclosed by a rayed mandala was found as part of a gold and ebony rosary from the wreck of the *Nuestra Señora de Atocha* (1622; Christie's 1988, 152–3), and a brass medallion of similar size was found with rosary beads on the *Vergulde Draeck* (1656; Green 1973, Fig.17). The Margam

Fig. 2. Obverse and reverse of the silver medallion from Margam beach. Actual length about 30 mm. (Photograph: John Blundell).

Fig. 3. Spanish, Portuguese and German coins from Margam and Aberavon beaches. Scale 1:1. (Photographs: NMGW)

Schedule of coins from Margam/Aberavon Beach[5]

Spain
In the names of Ferdinand and Isabella:
1.	4–reales	Seville	P	C. & T. 181	12.99g	NMGW 77.54H/1
2.		Seville	P	C. & T. 181	13.16g	seen 1.ix.1988
3.	2–reales	Cuenca	R	C. & T. 209–10		from photo
4.	1–real	Granada	+/o – +/o	C. & T. 257		from photo
5.		Seville	* – S	C. & T. 281	2.02g	NMGW 77.54H/3
6.		Seville	* – S	C. & T. 281		from photo
7.		Seville	S	C. & T. 283	2.92g	NMGW 77.54H/2
8.		Seville	S – *	C. & T. 296	2.92g	NMGW 77.54H/4
9.	½–real	Seville	P	C. & T. 354		from photo
10.		Seville	P	C. & T. 354		from photo

Spanish America – Mexico
Juana and Carlos:
11.	4–reales		assayer L	C. & T. 94		from photo
12.	2–reales		assayer L	C. & T. 126		from photo

Portugal
John III (1521–57):
13.	S. Vicente	Lisbon	A. do A. 1524–5	7.55g	NMGW 77.54H/5
14.	3–reis	Lisbon	A. do A. 1724ff.	4.73g	NMGW 77.54H/6
15.		Lisbon	A. do A. 1724 ff.	3.21g	NMGW 77.54H/7
16.		Lisbon	A. do A. 1724 ff.	3.71g	NMGW 77.54H/8

German States
Brunswick-Wolfenbüttel, Duchy: Heinrich der Jüngere (1514–68):
17.	Guldengroschen	1547, Riechenberg		S.435	27.39g	Private possession*[6]

Halberstadt, Bishopric: Albrecht V of Brandenburg (1513–45):
18.	Taler	1544		S.1035	27.58g	NMGW 77.54H/10

Herford, Abbey and City:
19.	Taler	1552		S.1180		from photo

Kaufbeuren, City:
20.	Taler	1544		S.1557		from photo

Kempten, City:
21.	Taler	1541		S.1578	27.77g	NMGW 77.54H/9
22.	Taler	1543		S.1578		from photo

Köln (Cologne), City:
23.	Taler	1549		S.1692		from photo

Leuchtenberg, Landgraves: Georg III (1531–55):
24.	Taler	1547		S.1748		from photo

Lübeck, Imperial City:
25.	Taler	?undated 1549–54		S.1824?		coin not seen

Mansfeld, County: Coinage of Johann Georg I, Philipp II, Gebhard VII and Albrecht VII:
26.	Taler	1545?		S.2040	18.22g corr.	NMGW 77.54H/12

Mecklenburg-Güstrow, Duchy: Heinrich (1508–52):
27.	Guldengroschen	1540, Grevesmühlen		S.2097?		coin not seen

Münster, Bishopric:
28.	Taler	n.d. or 1541–6?		S.2306/7?		coin not seen

Öttingen, County: Karl Wolfgang, Ludwig XV, Martin (1534–46):
29.	Guldiner	1544		S.2617	27.68g	NMGW 77.54H/11

Saxony, Electoral: Moritz (1541–53):
30.	Taler	1547, Annaberg		S.3243	27.41g	NMGW 77.54H/13
31.	Taler	1548, Annaberg		S.3245		from photo

Stolberg, County: Coinage of Wolfgang, Ludwig II, Heinrich XXI, Albrecht Georg and Christoph I:
32.	Taler	1550, Wernigerode		S.3427		from photo

Wismar, City:
33.	Taler	1552		S.3620	27.96g	NMGW 77.54H/14

Habsburg Lands
Tirol, County: Ferdinand I (1522–64), with title Rex Romanorum (1531–47):
34.	Guldiner	n.d.		S.4517	28.22g	Private possession*
35.	Guldiner	n.d.		S.4517		from photo

Low Countries
Batenburg, Free Barony: William de Bronkhorst (1556–73):
36.	Taler	n.d., with titles of Charles V				from photo

Poland
Sigismund I (1506–48), or later:
37. 'Dreigroschen', no further details; the coin is mentioned by Blundell (forthcoming).

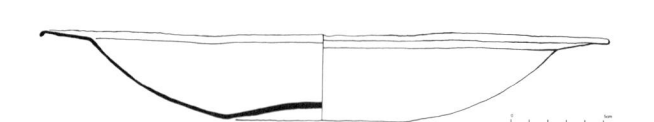

Fig. 4. Pewter bowl from Margam beach, and close up of mark. (Photograph: NMGW)

Fig. 5. Bosun's pipe from Margam beach. (Photograph: John Blundell)

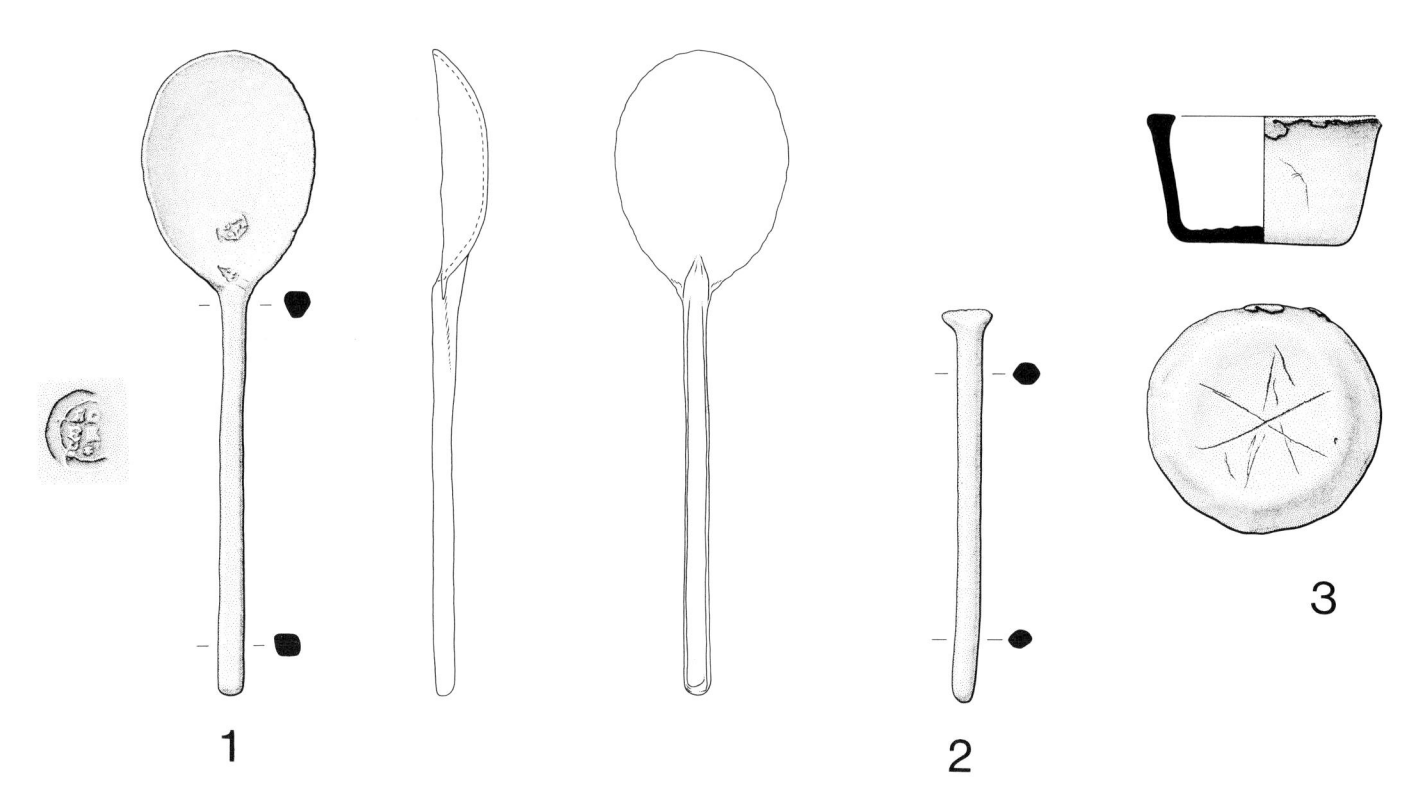

Fig. 6. Lead and lead-tin alloy objects from Margam beach. Nos 1–2, scale 1:2; no.3 and touch mark, scale 1:1. (Drawing: J.Chadwick, NMGW)

find may also have hung as a gaud from the base of a rosary. A pewter medallion of similar form, bearing the image of the Virgin Mary looking left, within a rayed mandala, was found on *El Gran Grifón* (1588), with string still knotted on its suspension loop, suggesting that it may have hung around the neck of a seaman or soldier (Martin 1975, Plate 8a). The stimulus provided by the Counter Reformation to the veneration of the Virgin led to an increase in Immaculate Conception *veneras*, peaking in the second decade of the 17th century. Medallions in pewter are known from the *Girona* (Flanagan 1988, 129–10) and *La Trinidad Valencera* (Crédit Communal 1985, 202–3), and may have been distributed wholesale. A religious medallion bearing the legend ROMA was also recovered from the early 17th-century Mombasa wreck (Piercy 1978). In 1619 medals were struck in Rome and sent to Spain bearing on one side chalice with host and legend *'Alabado sea el Smo.Sacramento'* and on reverse an image of the Immaculate Conception inscribed *'Concebida sin pecado original'*, both differing slightly from the Margam legends (for a discussion see Stratton 1994, 84). The Immaculate Conception occurs on one side of a silver medallion found on the *San Diego*, lost off Ile de Fortune near Manilla in 1600 (Provoyeur 1994, cat.54). The silver example from Margam was probably a personal possession, often carried by passengers or sailors as a symbol of commitment to Catholicism and God (but see below).

Objects of lead-tin alloy

2. Large bowl, English (Fig.4; private collection, information courtesy of J. Blundell). Worn lip edge to rim. Pewterer's touch mark on rim: Tudor Rose and initials ER (Edward Roe), who operated in London from 1560s to late 1580s (1588 elected to Office of Master of the London Company of Pewterers). Stamped on either side of the touch mark are the initals M N, presumably the original owner's mark. No sign of s'graffito personal marks of identification. Diameter 306 mm. Found on 30 December 1989, 'a couple of miles from the wreck site towards Sker' (Blundell 1994, 7). A similar bowl, also marked Edward Roe, was found on *La Trinidad Valencera* (lost 1588: Flanagan catalogue entry in Rodríguez-Salgado *et al* 1989, cat.10.8). Another bowl from *La Trinidad Valencera* had a diameter of 353 mm (*idem*, cat 10.6).

3. Boatswain's pipe or call with serpent-like creature (Fig.5; private collection; information and photograph courtesy of J. Blundell). Similar in silver with slightly different design to tube and serpent, from Armada wreck *Girona* (1588; Flanagan catalogue entry in Rodríguez-Salgado 1989 no.10.24). Another from the 16th-century Western Ledge Reef wreck (Watts 1993, Fig.21).

4. Fragment of another pipe or call (private collection; information provided by J. Blundell).

5. Pewter spoon with slip end (Fig.6 no.1; Fig.7). Indistinct and incomplete circular touch mark inside bowl below handle BO/ER? over mullet. Length 169 mm. Found by Mr D. Rees (NMGW 77.54H/46). For similar marks on 16th century spoons see Cotterell 1978, no. 5822.

6. Pewter spoon handle, with slip end (as above) and hexagonal stem (Fig.6 no.2). Length 103.5 mm. (NMGW 77.54H/51).

Fig. 8. Copper alloy spigot/tap from Margam beach. Scale 1:1.
(Photograph: NMGW)

Fig. 7. Spoon from Margam beach, and a detail of the touch mark.
(Photograph: NMGW)

Objects of Copper Alloy

7. Spigot/tap with handle in shape of a cockerel or hen (Fig.8; NMGW 77.54H/57). Similar 16th-century example from Amsterdam, Zwanenburgw./Moddermolenstraat (Baart *et al* 1977, cat.no.665).

8. Brass compasses or dividers (Fig.9, 2). Two tapering, straight legs, upper parts of which are decorated with pairs of 'M's. Length 117 mm (NMGW 77.54H/42). Similar from *La Trinidad Valencera* (1588; Crédit Communal 1985, 6.4) and the Barents expedition (1596), with similar mouldings on legs

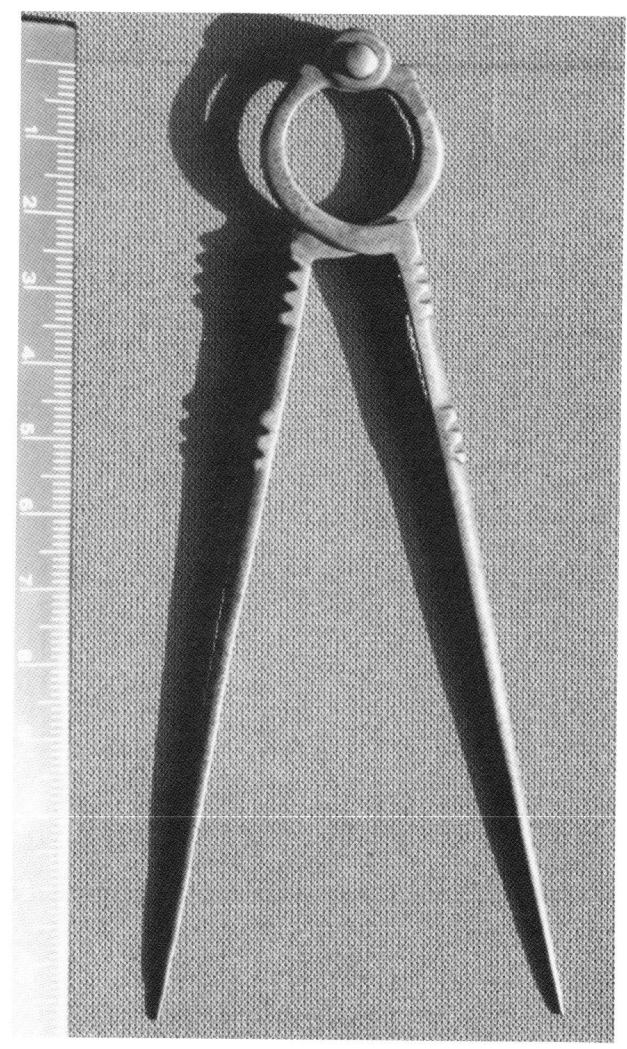

Fig. 10. Navigational dividers from Margam beach.
(Photograph: John Blundell)

(Rodríguez-Salgado 1989, cat no.12.19). These are chart compasses of 'bow-type' as defined by Price and Muckelroy (1974, 264). They were found 'some distance away' from the Talers and and copper 3-reais found by Rees.

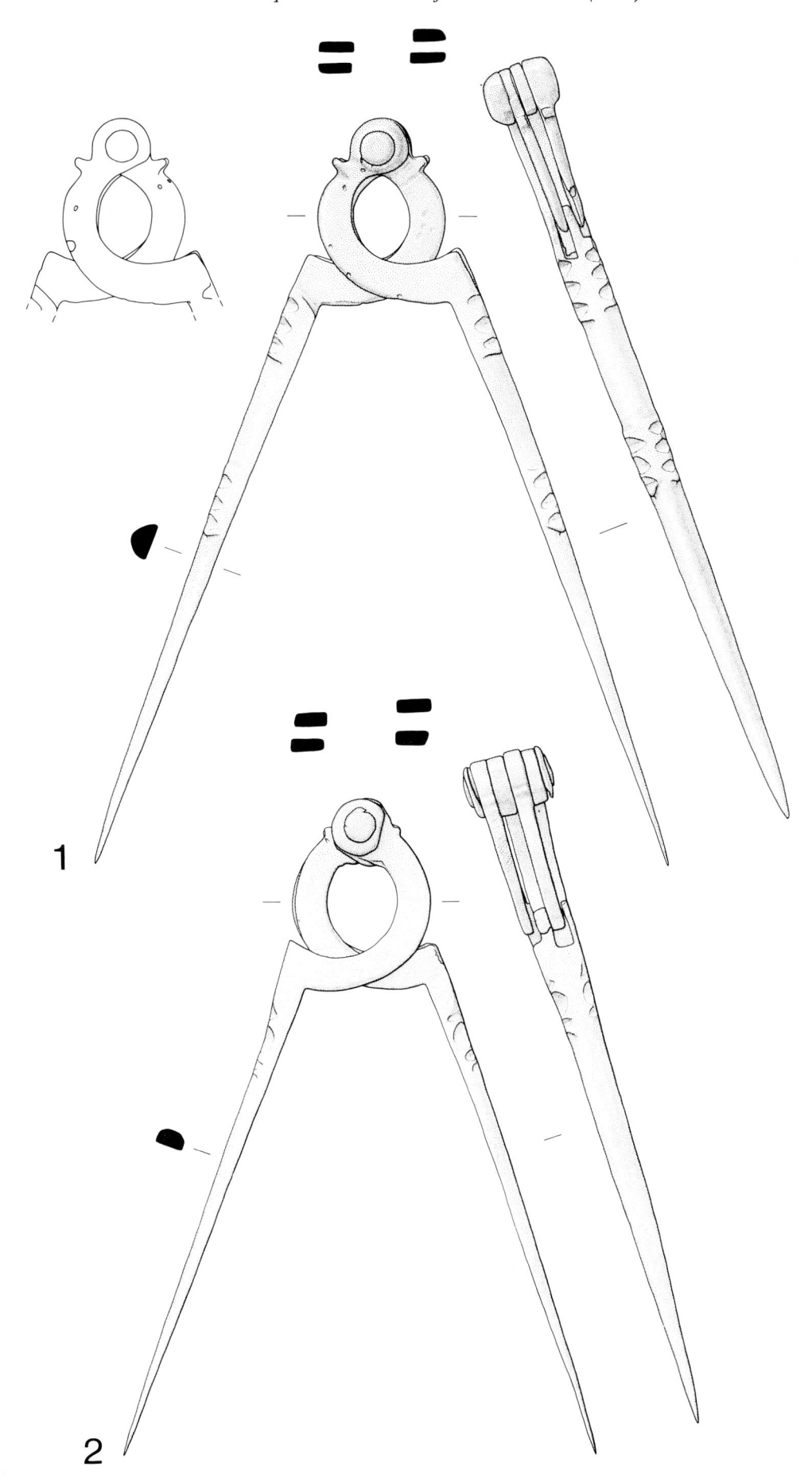

Fig. 9. Navigational dividers from Margam beach. Scale 1:1. (Drawing: J.Chadwick, NMGW)

9. Brass compasses or dividers, similar to no.7 (Fig.9, 1). Length 133 mm. Small indents in the tops of the 'G's may be casting flaws rather than ownership marks (NMGW 77.54H/41). Similar from the 16th-century Western Ledge Reef wreck (Watts 1993, Fig.20).

10. Brass compasses or dividers (Fig.10; private collection; information and photograph courtesy of J. Blundell). As above. Length about 147 mm.

Objects of lead

11. Flared lead vessel with flattened upper rim edge adorned with hammered sheet copper alloy (Fig.6, 3). The underside bears a scratched radial six spoked star motif. Concentric circles and moulded marks are visible on the inside of the base, as if hammered over a lathe-turned former. Maximum diameter 31 mm, weight 29.41g (5% short of a Troy ounce; NMGW 77.54H/49). This may perhaps be a cup weight, container of

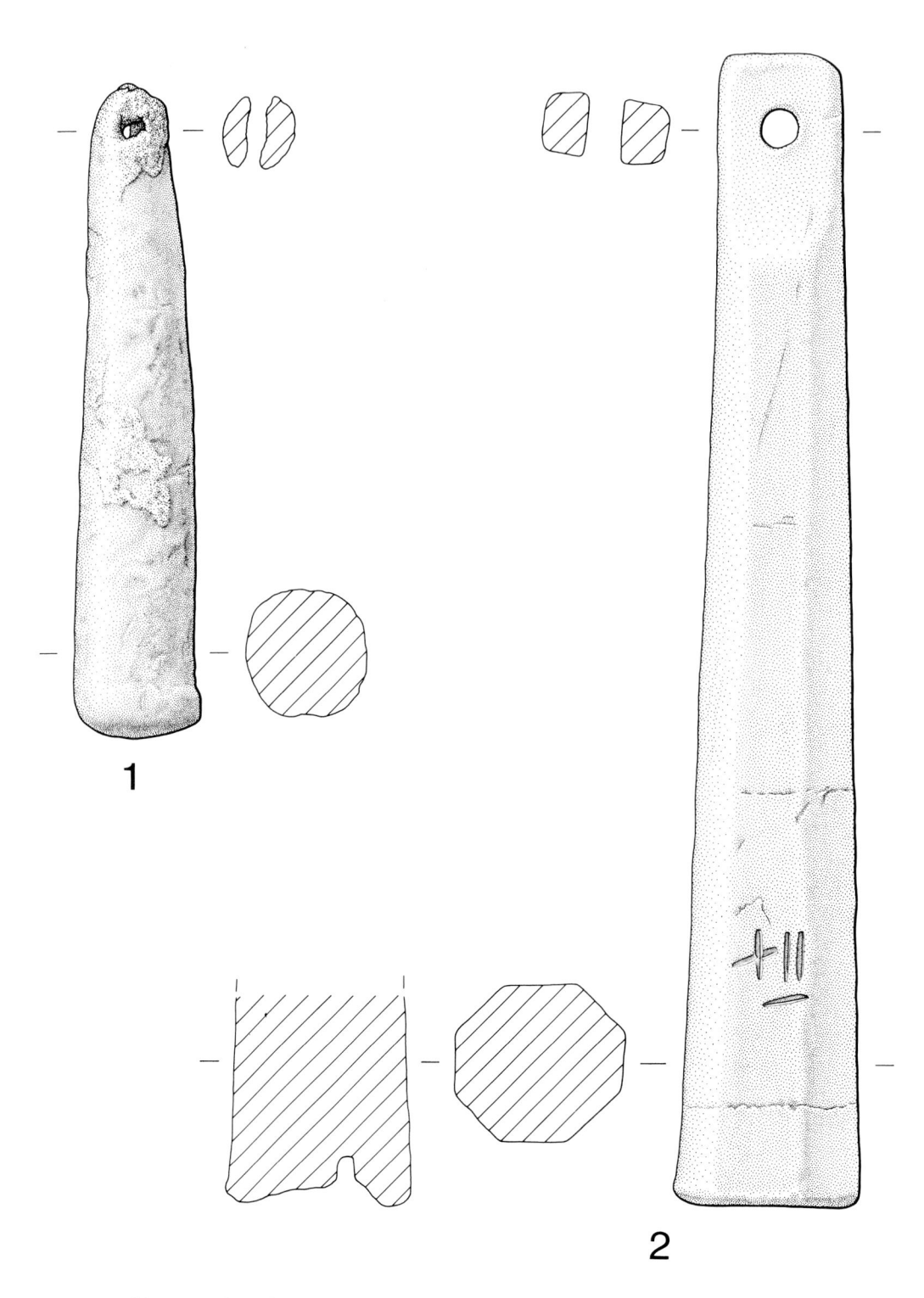

Fig. 11. Lead sounding weights from Margam beach. Scale 1:2. (Drawing: J.Chadwick, NMGW)

oil from a chrismatory or lead seal for a 'case' bottle (often gin). The mid-17th century wreck at Mullion Cove produced a similar object, identified as a bottle top (Larn, McBride and Davis 1974, Fig.14). External marks are known on lead cup weights (e.g. Winchester; Biddle 1990, cat.no.3197).

12. Plain sounding lead (commonly below 7 lb in weight) of circular cross-section, with a small mishapen circular hole to take a line (Fig.11, 1). Weight 4 lb 3.5 oz/ 1.96 kg; length 102.5 mm (NMGW 77.54H/43).

13. Sounding lead of octagonal cross-section. Lower end has a recess which could be armed with tallow. Punched with XIII at lower end, denoting lbs (Fig.11, 2). Weight 13 lb 4.5 oz/ 6.10 kg. Length 179 mm (NMGW 77.54H/44). Similar from Barents expedition (1596; Rodríguez-Salgado 1989, cat.no. 12.20), and 16th-century Rye barge (G. Hutchinson, *in litt.*). The weight indicates that the Margam find is a 'deep sea' lead (14lb common)

14. A collection of lead shot (Fig.12). Six examples of linked shot with square holes, and diameters between 17–18 mm (weight 32.2–36.8g); ten examples of shot with diameters between 16.5 – 17 mm (weight between 36.5g and 39.2g); four examples of shot between with diameters between 15.5–16 mm (weights 31.5–31.9g, one with sprue); seven examples with diameters between 13.5–14 mm (weights 23.2g and 25.2g); two examples with diameter of 13 mm (weights 19.6–19.7g), and one lead casting with five small scatter shot attached (NMGW 77.54H/47). Shot from *El Gran Grifón* had diameters of 20 mm, 13 mm and 3 mm (scatter shot; Martin 1972, 65); shot from the earlier Cattewater wreck measured 16 mm and 13 mm (Redknap 1984, 48). Linked shot of similar weight has been found on the *Kennemerland* (Price and Muckelroy 1974, 262–3) and the Mullion Cove wreck (Larn, McBride and Davis 1974, 78).

Fig. 12. Selection of lead shot from Margam beach. Scale 1:1. (Photograph: NMGW)

DISCUSSION

The recovery of stray artefacts from an 'open' site such as a beach does not constitute proof of origin from a dispersed wreck at all, let alone that of the *Ann Francis*. However, when one considers the overall chronological span and frequency of finds from such contexts, patterns may be discerned for which this shipwreck provides the most convincing explanation. The balance of probability, taking into account of topographic, historical and archaeological factors, suggests that in this case most (if not all) artefacts have been redistributed by a combination of currents, storms, drift along the coast and perhaps loss during the plundering and confrontation which followed the stranding. While some finds of Bronze Age and early medieval date, together with a handful of coins dating after 1680, have been made along this stretch of Margam beach, their numbers are insignificant when compared to the number of artefacts belonging to the 16th century.[7]

Charts provide information on the tidal zones between Mean High and Mean Low Water Springs. Early charts and maps contain inaccuracies, without clear conventions for calculating the line between sea and land. However, if sufficient 'landmark' control points exist, they can provide useful information on the relative changes to the coastline, and contribute to our understanding of former coastlines. The early maps by, for example, Speed at times ignored low-lying land, and often relied on earlier maps (such as Saxton's). Findspots have been plotted onto the OS map, which also shows the present coastline, superimposed over the earlier OS of *c.*1813 (Fig.1). The main roads on both maps can be matched fairly closely, providing an important record of the area prior to the canalising of the river Afan with the construction of the steel works at Port Talbot. Continual encroachment of sand along this beach is indicated by the so-called Theodoric's Grange, a former hermitage granted to Margam Abbey about 1188, recorded in Margam charters near the mouth of the Afan, and inundated by sand sometime after suppression. Dunes can impede drainage of land behind them: at Aberavon the dunes have formed a ridge in places over 17 m high which protects a flat alluvial tract behind them (North 1955, 79). The 1989 finds were made after a late winter of severe south-west and westerly gales and Spring Tides, which scoured large quantities of sand between St Davids and Nash Point, revealing underlying strata of pebbles, clay, peat and rock. The mobile beach deposits reworked sediments, sands and gravels which overlie Flandrian clays and peats. By comparing the earlier mean high and low water marks with those of today, it is possible to suggest the extent of the former Afan estuary prior to the alterations associated with the construction of the present day steel works.

It is clear that the above artefacts represent but a small fraction of the original vessel contents. The concentration of 16th-century artefacts on the beach may, in part, reflect a bias in the focus of metal detecting activity. Nevertheless, they do coincide with the recorded 16th-century distribution of wreck material *on both sides of the river Afan*, whose original form is clearly shown on the early maps by Saxton and Morris (Figs 13, 14). The pewter plate is described being found on peb-

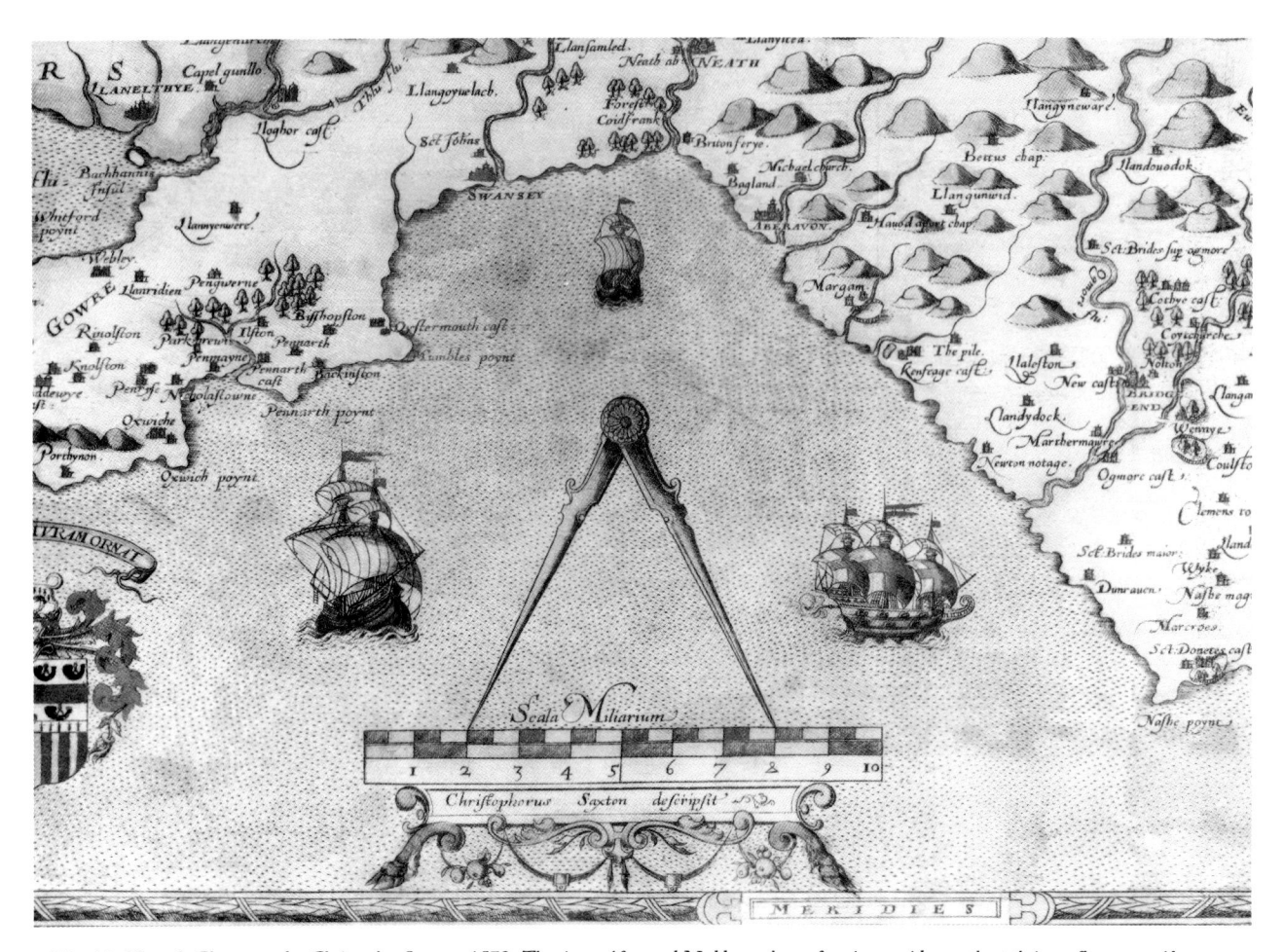

Fig. 13. Map of Glamorgan by Christopher Saxton, 1578. The rivers Afan and Nedd are shown forming a wide mouth at their confluence at Aberavon.
(Photograph: NMGW)

bles three and a half miles from the wreck site towards Sker (see Fig.1), and this position may be the result of a number of agencies, such as tidal drift or loss during the affray after the initial discovery and salvage of material from the wreck.

Do the finds corroborate the *Ann Francis* as source of the material? The *fowlers*, of importance in the contemporary inventories, confirm a date sometime in the second half of the 16th century: iron fowlers are included in the 1547 inventory of Henry VIII's armaments (Smith 1993, 7); they were slightly smaller than 'port-pieces', large calibre iron breech loaders. Blundell reports the finding of a second pewter plate, which neither he nor the authors have been able to see. He has examined the Norfolk ship-master's portion of the 1582 National Shipping Survey (PRO) and found no name to correspond with the initials on the plate, which may have been owned by several individuals (one possibility being transfer from father to son). Edward Roe appears to have traded abroad, for examples of his work have been found on the Armada wreck *La Trinidad Valencera*. This particular find supports identification of the scatter with the wreck of the *Ann Francis*. The spoons are very similar to three with crowned bowl touch marks from the Indschot/Zuidoostrak wreck near Texel (The Netherlands). This wreck also produced a brass barrel spigot, a lead balance weight and late 16th-century pottery, and a dendrochronological felling date from timber of not before 1586 +/- 6 (Maarleveld, Goudswaard and Oosting 1994). Similar spoons bearing the touchmark of a crown in sunburst have also found on the late 16th-century wreck believed to have been lost off Alderney in 1592. This site has also produced a sounding lead identical to the larger Margam example (15 lb/6.75k), also marked XIII (Davenport and Burns 1995, 35). The dividers are usually called 'single' or 'one-handed' dividers, and they were well adapted for use by navigators for chartwork and the solution of navigational problems on a sector, plane scale or Gunter's scale (for a discussion see Bryden 1968). The navigational dividers find close parallels on Armada period wrecks, and representations of them were often incorporated into the decorative title pages of navigational treatises, such as *Spieghel der Zeevaerdt* by the cartographer Lucas Janszoon Wagenaer (1585), and charts or maps (e.g. Fig.13). However, they change very little with time, and close stylistic dating of specific examples is not usually possible. If the silver religious medallion is from the *Ann Francis* and not a later loss, it is an early example of the unity of the *custodia* of the eucharist and Mary, symbolic of the Immaculate Conception as proclaimed by the early 17th-century confraternities in Spain.

Collectively, the coins have a consistent terminal production date of around 1556–8, with no firm evidence for extended circulation beyond that, though several of the smaller Spanish coins (the precise dates of which are not known) have been clipped. In the absence of other evidence, this might normally be taken to indicate a wreck towards 1560 (Boon 1974), a context perhaps being provided by the circumstances under which a French ship was wrecked at Oxwich (Gower) in 1557. However, there is no contemporary reference to such a wreck at Margam. On the other hand, there is the abundantly documented *Ann Francis* in 1583, which must be the source of most, if not all, of these coins – part of the £400 or more said to have been lost by Francis Shaxton (N.L.W. Penrice and Margam Mss L36). The *Ann Francis* appears to be the 'exception which proves the rule', since *termini post quos* for coin series from other post-medieval wrecks seem to lie very close in date to the wreck, where the ship has been identified (Besly, in this book). Is there an explanation?

The production of Talers had been suppressed by an Imperial Edict in 1551, in favour of Reichsguldiner and, from 1559, Reichsgulden, of different standards, as the normal large silver coins of the Holy Roman Empire. These moves were unpopular in northern Germany (source of much of the silver), where Talers had taken root. In 1566 Talers were readmitted as coins of the Empire, and proceeded to supplant the previous imperial coins. Earlier Talers therefore continued to circulate, as is evident, for instance, from the valuations for the Lower Saxon currency area (*Niedersächsischer Kreis*) printed in Leipzig in 1572 (Anon. 1572). In this, coins such as nos 30–31, or similar to nos 17 and 34–35, are '*guten Taler*' (and therefore current in Saxony at 24 groschen), while others such as nos 18 and 33 are non-standard and appropriate valuations are given (23gr 1pf and 22gr 10pf respectively). Plenty of pre-1551 Talers also feature in a merchants' coinage book published in Antwerp in 1580 (Anon. 1580). These coins were therefore widely available in Europe, as currency, at the time of the *Ann Francis* voyage in 1583. The absence of Reichsguldiner of the 1551 Edict and of the 1559 Reichsgulden could be explained by their removal from currency as the Talers took over: the first contained more, and the second considerably less silver than the Talers. Post-1566 Talers might, however, be expected in an assemblage from 1583: of twenty-three Talers and their fractions in the near-contemporary hoard from Walle, East Friesland (1585), seventeen were post-1566, for instance (Hagen-Jahnke and Walburg 1987). The silver coins as a whole therefore show every sign of having been assembled and put aside before *c*.1560, a possibility which their generally unworn state might support. At this point, too, the flood of Spanish silver from the new mints at Lima (1565) and Potosí (1575) was yet to reach Europe.

Blundell (forthcoming) has drawn attention to the contemporary use of bulk silver as bullion to pay for cargoes such as the grain the ship is presumed to have carried for export. The silver will have been of varying finenesses, the Spanish coins above sterling (925/1000), and the German coins below, but recoining it would have presented no problems for the assayers and melters at the Tower Mint.

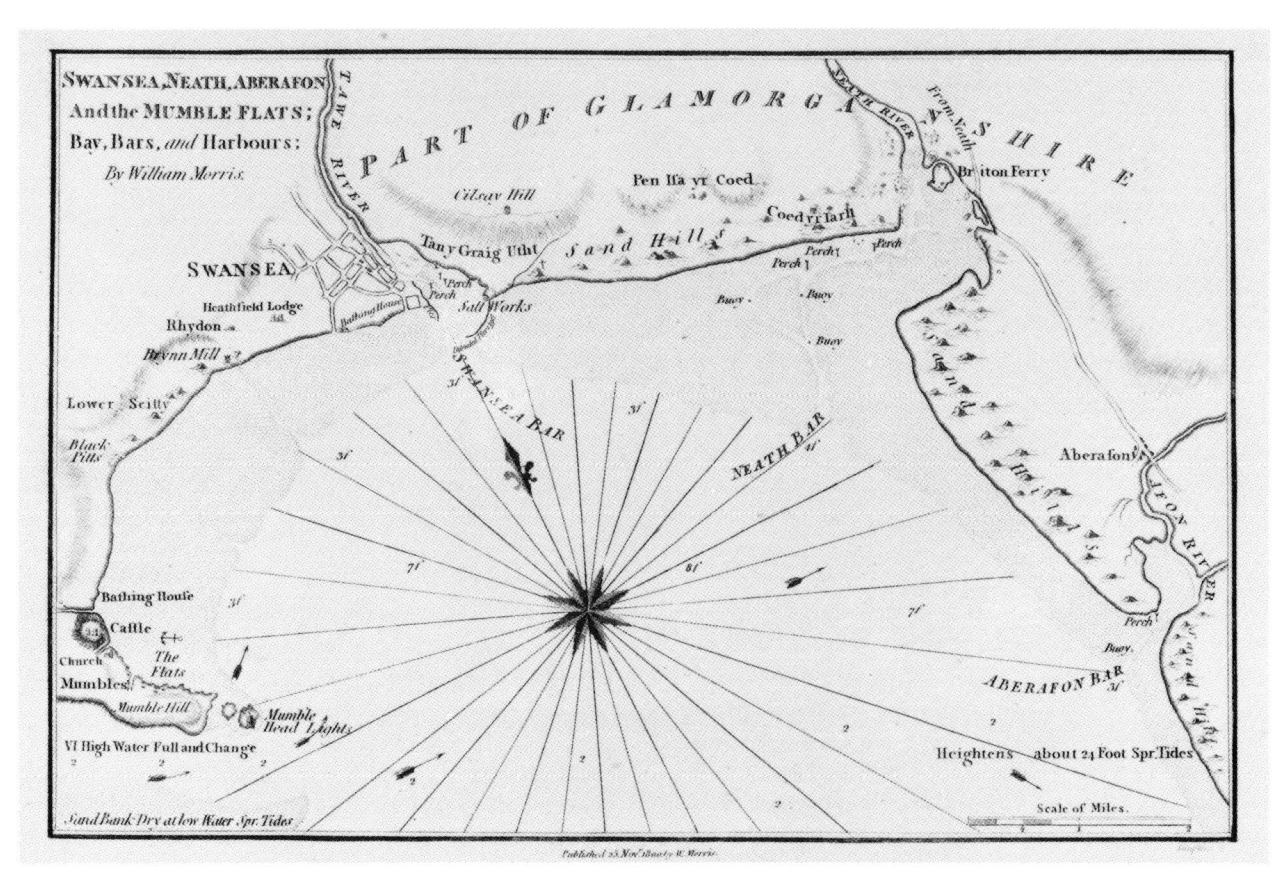

Fig. 14. Map of Swansea, Neath, Aberavon and the Mumbles Flats, by William Morris, 1800. (Photograph: NMGW)

There remain the Portuguese coins, of gold and copper, which fit the date, but not the overall pattern of the others. The presence of small change, in particular, might indicate a visit to Portugal: was this the *Ann Francis*'s original destination? However, the gold coin and the two reasonably well-preserved coppers, none later than 1557–8, do not show signs of anything like twenty-five or more years' circulation. Rather, allowing for the action of sea and sand, they appear to be virtually uncirculated. Other factors could be relevant, such as the nautical design of the gold San Vicente, which might have had a talismanic significance to its owner, but this little group, while perfectly consistent with a coin assemblage from the later 1550s, does not sit wholly comfortably with a batch of bullion silver acquired in 1583.

It is possible to construct a partial inventory of artefacts by combining the information on those items originally salvaged and those items lost to be relocated in recent times. *NLW Penrice and Margam Mss 5728* provides a valuable contemporary record of *wreck de mer* (transcribed with permission of the National Library of Wales):

A true Inventorye of all such goods as weare cast to land on both sides the river of Avan in the grainge of Lanvigelith pcell of the Lordshippe of Havorporth in the Com of Glamorgan on the night of the xxviijth of December last, 1583. which came to the hands of Edward Mansell, Knight.

First	in cast Iron peece named minions each wayinge 1200 §	2	
Itm	one other cast Iron peece wayinge 1300 §	1	
Itm	in cast Iron peeces each wayinge 700 §	2	
Itm	one cast Iron peece wayinge 620 §	1	
Itm	in fowlers §	4	
Itm	in chambers §	2	
Itm	a ladle§	1	
Itm	in Kalivers §	5	[hand guns]
Itm	in flaskes §	2	
Itm	in Anchors §	2	
Itm	a steele Targett §	1	
Itm	one little broken anchore for a Cocke §	1	[cock-boat]
Itm	one cable aboute 90 fathome longe §	1	
Itm	one other cable aboute 82 fathome longe §	1	
Itm	one hawser §	1	
Itm	two lesser ropes §	2	
Itm	peeces of the maine sayle torne & spoyled §		
Itm	small ropes therby §		
Itm	one stremor of Bulter §	1	[boltering; bolter cloth]
Itm	three peeaces of the main mast §	3	
Itm	a smaller mast cotaininge 30 foote §	1	
Itm	two sayle yards §	2	
Itm	a Cocke boate §	1	
Itm	a pipe half full of sacke brechd §		[damage to ms]
Itm	a barell wth some tarre §		[damage to ms]
Itm	one glasse bottle §		[damage to ms]
Itm	two emptie spruse cofers lockes brok[		[damage to ms]
Itm	one other emptie cofer of oke: locke broken §	1	
Itm	in cloves §	3 li	
Itm	two boxes of marmelade wayinge §	2 li	
Itm	in two peeces of Callicowe §	22 ells [plus]	
Itm	a silver whissell wth a peece of a chaine wayinge 4 ounces		
Itm	in Spanishe silver §	12–16–00	
Itm	v or vj emptye caskes §		
Itm	two ship cords §	2	
Itm	a walkinge staffe §		

Remarkably, this 16th-century inventory groups materials according to function, in a very similar format and order to an archaeological inventory of ship remains. In the table below, this information has been combined with the catalogue of artefacts to form a fuller list of ship contents:

	Salvaged	Found recently
Ship management:		
'ship's gear'	'washed ashore'	
6 iron guns	(2 minions, 4 iron peeces) into the hands of Mansell, returned to Shaxton	
4 fowlers[8]	into the hands of Mansell, returned to Shaxton	
2 breech chambers	into the hands of Mansell	
5 *kalivers*	into the hands of Mansell	
2 powder flasks	into the hands of Mansell	
lead shot		some found
1 steel *target* (shield)	into the hands of Mansell	
2 anchors	into the hands of Mansell, returned to Shaxton	
small broken anchor	into the hands of Mansell	
cables/hawsers/ropes	into the hands of Mansell (2 of the best cables returned to Shaxton)	
damaged sail (part)	into the hands of Mansell	
1 streamer	into the hands of Mansell	
1 barrel of tar	into the hands of Mansell	
ship's boat	into the hands of Mansell	
Navigational equipment:		
2 sounding leads		found
3 brass dividers		found
Galley utensils:		
brass cask tap		found
Eating/drinking utensils:		
a pewter cup	seized from looter by George Williams	
a pewter spoon	seized from looter by George Williams	
1 glass bottle	into the hands of Mansell	
2 pewter bowls		found
2 pewter spoons		found
Personal belongings:		
silver pendant		found
2 bosun's pipes		found
silver whistle (bosun's pipe) with section of chain into the hands of Mansell		
1 walking staff	into the hands of Mansell	
lead vessel		found
Cargo/victuals:		
2 spruce chests	into the hands of Mansell	
1 oak chest	into the hands of Mansell	
5–6 empty barrels	into the hands of Mansell	
£400 in silver bullion	£12 16s 0d into the hands of Mansell (*Spanishe money*), half returned to Shaxton.	some recovered recently
22 ells of calico[9]	into the hands of Mansell	
pipe of sack	into the hands of Mansell	
2 lb marmalade	2 boxes into the hands of Mansell	
3 lb cloves	into the hands of Mansell	
'diverse spices'	seized from looter by George Williams	
40 nutmegs	seized from looter by George Williams	

This table provides a fairly full account of the salvaged material and those goods declared, and an indication of some of the extraction processes which followed the wrecking. It excludes: i. perishables, ii. items which have not been preserved, iii. items which floated away, iv. items which are still buried (artefacts which cannot have floated away would include anchors (some recovered), ballast, guns, quern- or grindstones, iron, lead, nails, shot, jewellery, mercury, and a number of commodities and victuals. Blundell has pointed out that very little of the ship's domestic equipment was listed by

Mansell, other items appearing to have received prior attention.

The site may be regarded as a typical dispersed site: some hull structure may survive in the area, but has not yet been located; some organics and imperishables may remain, of which much will have been scattered along the coast.

After 1580 the number of English attacks on the New World and Spain itself grew, and English attempts to establish settlements in the New World provided a direct challenge to the Iberian Empire of Philip II. Elizabeth hoped to avoid open war and yet still curb Philip's power; as war became inevitable, Philip became more receptive to proposals such as those of the Marquis of Santa Cruz (1583) for an attack against England. However, open war did not occur for several more years, with the Treaty of Nonsuch of 1585. Such was the political stage to the voyages of the *Ann Francis*, possibly in evasion of customs duties (her voyage was not recorded in the Port Books).[10] According to Robert Daniell, searcher at King's Lynn, more corn was exported in the 1560s and 1570s abroad than had been licensed, and that the merchants '*used sometime at theire retorne from beyond sea to geve thofficers spices, sugar, lynnen cloth and such storre of housholds*' (Williams 1951). The loss came at a period of developing interest in the science of navigation, when many English ship masters frequently employed French and Portuguese pilots to assist them. It is ironic that from 1576, improvements in higher mathematics and navigation were made good by consultation with the famous mathematician and astronomer of Welsh descent, navigational advisor to the Muscovy Company, Dr John Dee, whose preface to the first English *Euclid* (1570) had stimulated interest in navigational problems (Waters 1978, 114).[11]

Acknowledgements

The authors are indebted to John Blundell for sharing the results of his research with us, and allowing the National Museums & Galleries of Wales to record the new finds; to David B. Rees for his valuable discussion of the site, and generously donating his finds for the National Museums & Galleries of Wales; the late Gerard Lahive, Andrew Spira and John Kenyon for information; Jacqueline Chadwick for the line drawings; to the Department of Photography for Figs 2, 4, 7, 8, 12; to the Department of Geology, National Museums & Galleries of Wales for permission to reproduce the maps by Saxton and Morris.

Notes

1. Boon reported the finds made by Mr David Rees between 1969 and 1975 to the Receiver of Wreck in June 1976, and they were delivered to the Museum for safekeeping.
2. Another tradition exists that the orange trees were part of Catherine of Braganza's dowry on her marriage to Charles II, carried in a convoy of three ships, one of which was wrecked on Margam beach
3. For example '*And coming out of Spain [steer the courses given] until you reach the Soundings [the 100-fathom line]. Then if you find 100 fathoms depth, or 90, sail north until you sound in 72 fathoms and bring up fair grey sand between Cape Clear (cape of SW Ireland) and the Scilly Is.*' (Waters 1978, 12 fn.2).
4. Charts based on Mercator's projection were not in common use before 1594. Astrolabes were used to measure position.
5. Standard references: A. do A. = Almeida do Amaral 1977; C. & T.= Calico, Calico & Trigo 1988; S. = Schulten 1974.
6. The two coins in private possession which are marked with asterisks (*) – nos 17 and 34 – are said to have been found on Aberavon Beach. They are at the time of writing on loan to, and displayed at, the National Museum & Gallery in Cardiff, alongside nos 1, 13, 18, 22, 29, 31, and 33 and two pairs of nautical dividers from the wreck site.
7. A number of other finds have been reported but not seen by the authors, including a bronze or brass pully block wheel with seven spokes, and a small finger ring.
8. Breech loading guns for small shot (stone) used for 'scouring our deckes'. They appear from c.1540, usually forged iron (Blackmore 1976, 230–1).
9. An ell = 45", and 22 ells therefore about 82' 6". Rolls of cloth appear to have formed a significant part of the cargo.
10. For the background to trade with Iberia at this period, see Williams 1951.
11. Since this paper went to press, fifteen coins found on Margam Beach have been shown to the writers. Eight are Talers already known from photographs (nos. 19, 22, 23, 24, 31, 32, 35 and 36). There are six new Talers, of Jülich-Cleve-Berg, Kempten (2), Saxony (2, of the Electors Moritz and August) and of Liège. The last is dated 1557, and unworn. There is also a copper 10-reis of John III of Portugal. The existing discussion is otherwise unaffected.

References

Almeida do Amaral, C.M. 1977 *Catálogo descritivo das moedas Portuguesas, Museu Numismático Português*, Lisbon.

Anon. 1572 *Valvation des Niedersächsischen Kreises* (Leipzig).

Anon. 1580 *De figueren van alle goude ende silvere penninghen ...* (Antwerp).

Arnold, J. Barto III & Weddle, R.S. 1978 *The Nautical Archaeology of Padre Island. The Spanish Shipwrecks of 1554*. Studies in Archaeology, New York.

Baart, J. et al. 1977 *Opgravingen in Amsterdam. 20 jaar stadskernonderzoek*, Amsterdam.

Biddle, M. 1990 'Weights and Measures', *in* M. Biddle (ed.), Object and Economy in Medieval Winchester, Winchester Studies 7ii, 908–928.

Blackmore, H.L. 1976 *The Armouries of the Tower of London. Vol.1: Ordnance*, London.

Blundell, J. 1994, 'A Tudor wreck near Aberavon in Glamorgan', *Cardiff Naturalists' Society Newsletter* 22, 1–3.

Blundell, J. forthcoming 'A Tudor wreck near Aberavon in Glamorgan', *Maritime Wales*.

Boon, G.C. 1974 'A sixteenth-century wreck off Margam?', *Bulletin of the Board of Celtic Studies* 25, 523–524.

Bryden, D.J. 1968 'Two Pairs of Dividers and the Mariner's Mirror', *The Mariner's Mirror* 54, 77–84.

Calico, F., Calico, X. & Trigo, J. 1988 *Monedas Españolas desde Fernando e Isabel a Juan Carlos I*, 7th ed., Barcelona.

Christie's 1988 'Gold and Silver of the *Atocha* and *Santa Margarita*. Sale catalogue 14–15 June, 1988. New York.

Cotterell, Howard Herschel 1978 *Old Pewter. Its Makers and Marks*, London.

Crédit Communal 1985, *Trésors de l'Armada*, Catalogue of Exhibition organised by Ulster Museum at Brussels, 30.10.85 – 26.1.86 (Crédit Communal).

Davenport, T.G. & Burns, R. 1995 'A sixteenth-century wreck off the Island of Alderney', *The Archaeology of Ships of War, International Maritime Archaeology Series* 1, 30–40.

Flanagan, L. 1988 *Ireland's Armada Legacy* (Alan Sutton), Gloucester.

Glamorgan County History IV, 183.

Green, J.N. 1973 'The wreck of the Dutch East Indiaman the *Vergulde Draeck*, 1656', *IJNA* 2, 267–89.

Hagen-Jahnke, U. & Walburg, R. 1987 *Coin Hoards: the Example of Walle*.

Larn, R., McBride, P.M. & Davis, R. 1974 'The mid-17th century merchant ship found near Mullion Cove, Cornwall. Second Interim Report', *IJNA* 3, 67–79.

Lewis, E.A. 1927 *Welsh Port Books 1550–1603*, Cymmrodorian Record Series, No. XII.

Maarleveld, T.J., Goudswaard, B & Oosting, R. 1994 'New data on early modern Dutch flush shipbuilding: Scheurrak T24 and Inschot/Zuidoostrak', *IJNA* 23, 13–25.

Martin, C. J. M. 1972, 'El Gran Grifon. An Armada wreck on Fair Isle', *IJNA* 1, 59–71.

Martin, C. J. M. 1975 *Full Fathom Five. Wrecks of the Spanish Armada*, London.

North, F.J. 1955 *The Evolution of the Bristol Channel, with special reference to the coast of South Wales*, National Museum of Wales, Cardiff.

Piercy, R. C. M. 1978 'Mombasa wreck excavation. Second preliminary report, 1978', *IJNA* 7, 301–319.

Price, R. & Muckelroy, K. 1974 'The second season of work on the Kennemerland site, 1973. An interim report', *IJNA* 3, 257–268.

Provoyeur, P. 1994 'Les arts de la table, les bijoux et les objets de dévotion' in *Le San Diego. Un trésor sous la mer*, Réunion des musées nationaux, 258–297.

Redknap, M. 1984. *The Cattewater Wreck, The investigation of an armed merchantman of the early sixteenth century*, BAR British Series 131, National Maritime Museum Archaeology Series no.8, Oxford.

RCHME 1996 The National Inventory of Maritime Archaeology for England, NMR.

Rees, D.B. 1977 'Interesting Finds at Morfa Beach, 1970–75', *Transactions of the Port Talbot Historical Society* III.1, 57–59.

Rees, W. 1957 '(III) Wreck de Mer: Rights of Foreshore in Glamorgan', *South Wales and Monmouth Record Society Publication* No.4, 178–80.

Rodríguez-Salgado, M.J. *et al* 1989 'Armada 1588–1988. The Official Catalogue'.

Schulten, W. 1974 *Deutsche Münzen aus der Zeit Karls V*, Frankfurt/M.

Smith, R.D. 1993 'Port-pieces. The use of Wrought Iron Guns in the Sixteenth Century', *Journal of the Ordnance Society* 5, 2–10.

Stratton, S.L. 1994 *The Immaculate Conception in Spanish Art*, Cambridge University Press.

Waters, David, 1978 *The Art of Navigation in England in Elizabethan and Early Stuart Times*, Modern Maritime Classics Reprint no.2.

Watts, G.P. 1993 'The Western Ledge Reef wreck: a preliminary report on the investigation of the remains of a 16th-century shipwreck in Bermuda', *IJNA* 22, 103–124.

Williams, N.J. 1951 'Francis Shaxton and the Elizabethan Port Books', *English Historical Review* 66.

17

Artefacts from the *Kronan* (1676): categories, preservation and social structure

Lars Einarsson

The Swedish Royal ship *Kronan* ('The Royal Crown') exploded and sank off the east coast of Öland in a battle with an allied Danish-Dutch fleet on 1 June 1676 (Fig.1). According to contemporary documentary records, she was one of the largest sailing vessels in Europe, with a displacement of 2,200 metric tons, carrying 126 guns[1] and a crew of 850 men (Zettersten 1903, 574). The *Kronan* constituted a floating society, both in terms of the crew number and its social structure, during a period when the distinction between military and civilian society was rarely clear.

Kronan is easily distinguished from its famous fellow-countryman *Vasa*, firstly because of her rich contents[2], and secondly for the different episode the vessel represents during Sweden's period as a 'Great Power'. The two sites are also fundamentally different in terms of their marine archaeological methodology: *Vasa* was first salvaged and then excavated, whereas *Kronan* is the subject of continuous underwater archaeological investigation.

In order to interpret the information from the shipwreck, it is of great importance to study the social, political and economic conditions of society during this period, and to examine under what specific conditions and objectives the vessel was built. Recent studies have shown the rapid development of technical and administrative competence by the European States during late 17th century, and their importance for handling the increasingly complex systems of the armies and navies (Glete 1985, 257). The navies developed from consisting of a great number of privateers into units with greater vessels, more heavily armed and built exclusively for military purposes. England led the way in the 1650s, The Netherlands in the 1660s.

From 1656, The Netherlands started to intervene militarily in the Baltic Sea, at that time their most important market area in their worldwide empire of trading. While Sweden's export depended on the Dutch trade, the Dutch policy of supporting Denmark undoubtedly meant a serious threat to Swedish

Fig. 1. The Battle of Öland, 1 June 1676: Kronan *explodes. Oilpainting by Claus Möinichen, Frederiksborg's Castle, Denmark.*

ambitions of controlling the trade in the Baltic area and maintaining connections with their provinces in the Baltic region.

Triggered off by these considerations, a Swedish shipbuilding programme was initiated in 1659, orientated towards great ships of 60–90 guns. The Swedish ambition is underlined by the extra support to the programme which was granted by the Crown in 1664. Three English shipwrights were to form the new core of know-how in shipbuilding: Thomas Day, Robert Turner and Francis Sheldon the elder. A total of ten ships of 1,200 to 1,700 tons were launched between 1662–1671. An eleventh exceptional ship, 500 tons larger than the others, was also launched during the period. It was *Kronan*, built on Skeppsholmen in Stockholm between 1665–68, and constructed by Francis Sheldon the elder (1610–1692).

THE CONCEPT OF MICROCOSMS AS SOCIETIES IN MINIATURE

Shipwrecks are often mentioned as 'microcosms', societies in miniature. But how adequate is this epithet? Does the wreck really have the characteristics to qualify for such an appellation? In order to determine the accuracy of the expression, it is important to first of all study the nature of the *ship*, and secondly the nature of the *wreck*. Thus, the basic purpose of the investigation is to close the gap between ship *and* wreck, by summing up and interpreting historical and archaeological data obtained. The interaction between documentary and physical records is a key to a successful investigation. Comparative studies may be fruitful regarding, for instance, how theory was practically applied on board. Research may focus on topics such as supplies, equipment and the location of the crew. A positive identification and dating of the wreck, as in the case of *Kronan*, naturally increases the value of the source.

The study of the wreck itself, should include one initial question: how representative is the *wreck* with its surviving material culture, in comparison with the original *ship*? The investigation should consider i) the affects of the loss, ii) the degredation of the wreck and the artefacts (which includes a study of the conditions for preservation on the site), iii) the distribution of finds – in other words the history of the wreck.

ASPECTS OF PRESERVATION

The following aspects from the examination of the *Kronan* should be the subject of thorough consideration during the study of material culture from a wreck:

– the nature of the sailing vessel.
– whether damage to the ship preceded the capsize. According to contemporary eyewitness reports *Kronan* was never involved in the battle.
– the violent shifting of the ship's contents from starboard to port, in connection with the capsize.
– the partial loss of contents from the ship, when drifting.
– the extent of loss and damage of objects, in connection with the explosion and opening of the ship's structure.
– the rapid sinking resulting from the loss of the vessel's buoyancy.
– the secondary deposition of objects vertically within the hull once the wreck came to rest on the seabed.
– the importance of the anaerobic sediments on the site.
– the effects of salvage operations on the site 1676–1686.
– the effects of natural erosion, minesweeping and fishing.
– the nature of the underwater archaeological investigation: methodology, excavation techniques, etc.

THE STRUCTURE'S IMPORTANCE REGARDING CONDITIONS FOR PRESERVATION

A study of the preserved wreck structure on the site may reveal a number of factors favourable for ship preservation. The considerable weight of the remaining contents of the ship, in particular the ordnance, probably compressed larger elements of the wreck into the protective sediments on the site shortly after the sinking (Fig.2).

The starboard side of the hull constituted a wall protecting the centre of the site, where the vast majority of the artefacts were deposited. Wooden sculpture which had originally been fastened by iron nails onto the ceiling planking on the port side of the upper deck was discovered *in situ*, despite its shallow position within the sediments (Einarsson 1990, 285). The carvings had clearly been protected from erosion by structural elements such as knees and stringers.

A separate part of the hull structure measuring about 10 m × 25 m, possibly a part of the starboard side, was found about 35 m south-west of the main wreck site. This section may have been connected with the main wreck for a considerable period of time, thus contributing to the protection of the interior of the wreck from degradation.

Data collected from the site over the years has shown that the ship came to rest on the seabed at an angle of about 45° from vertical. The forward third section of the ship had broken off as a result of the explosion. After a period of time, the upper part of the port side from the lower deck collapsed, causing a longitudinal fracture of that side. This fracture is visible at several locations inside the wreck, particularly close to the stern. Hitherto, no actual *separation* of the upper and lower part of the port side has been observed. The fact that the upper part of the port side used to lie at a 45° upright position is confirmed by the presence of large quantities of artefacts from the ship's interior found beneath the ship's side.

Athwartships-structure in the wreck is almost completely absent, making artefacts on board lower decks hard to distinguish. However, loose objects from the vessel's interior have been recovered, though often in secondary positions.

Several observations during excavation indicate that objects having various social and functional origins were used in the same compartments of the ship. This is the case in the most recently investigated area of the wreck – the borderline between hold and orlop, about twelve metres forward of the

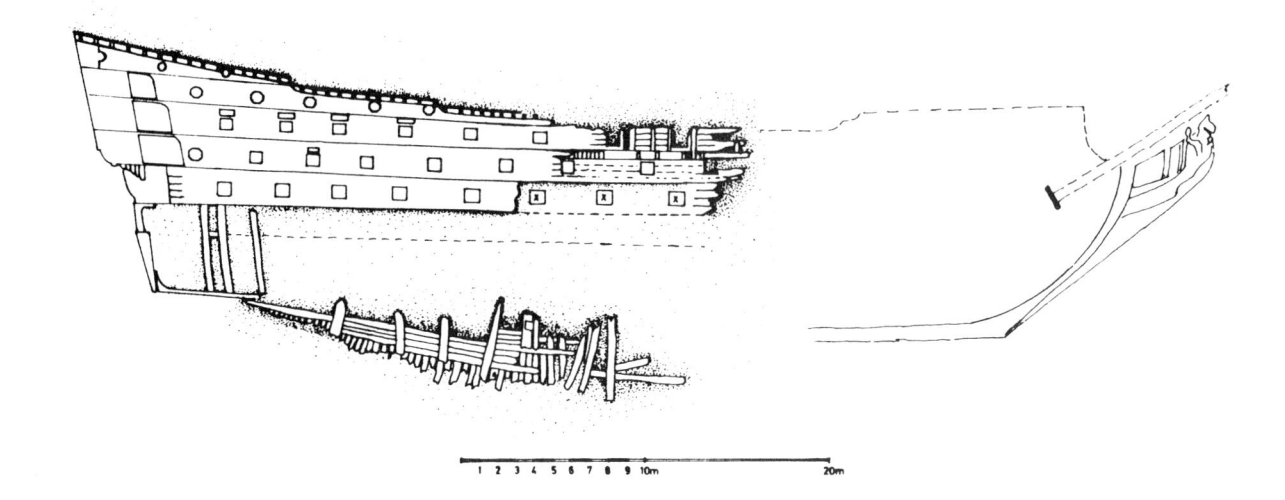

Fig. 2. Plan of Kronan. (Copyright: Kalmar läns museum/The Kronan-Project)

stern. Pewter plates and glass bottles belonging to officers on board were found on top of barrels and other containers, which were likely to be found in the area. At first, one would surmise that these objects were secondary depositions in the area resulting from vertical 'fallout' of heavier objects from compartments on decks above and astern. However, the same categories of relatively sophisticated objects were found deeper down in the layers of the storage rooms, in direct association with the barrels. In this case a likely explanation would be that both kinds of objects were originally used and stored in the same compartment, because of the lack of space caused by an exceptionally large crew, and possibly on either side of the deck.

THE CATEGORIES OF MATERIAL

In the case of the *Kronan*, three important characteristics regarding the material culture may be distinguished:

1) the great number of artefacts
2) the great variety of artefacts, both in terms of function and the material
3) the excellent state of preservation of the artefacts.

The objects from *Kronan* may be divided into four categories:

1) ship's equipment
2) objects of warlike nature (weapons and weapon-related objects)
3) common utensils
4) private belongings.

The distinction between the categories may at times be unclear (for example, instruments for navigation can both be private possessions as well as common utensils).

More than 22,000 objects have now been recovered from the *Kronan*. In percentages, the distribution of finds based upon material is as follows:

Material	%
Wood	51.5
Leather	9.1
Brass	7.5
Textile	6.4
Lead	4.5
Pewter	3.8
Copper	3.2
Glass	2.3
Clay	1.8
Silver	1.7
Iron	1.4
Ceramics	1.4
Horn	1.3
Hemp	1.1
Bronze	0.7
Gold	0.6
Stone	0.4
Bone	0.3
Others	1.0
Total	100.0

SOCIAL STRUCTURE

When discussing how representative *Kronan* is as a 17th-century 'cosmos'[3] in terms of her material culture, Professor Sten Carlsson's social structure of classes in Swedish late 17th-century society can be applied to the artefacts from the wreck (Carlsson 1971, 16). A fundamental problem is the definition of the specific classes to which each artefact should belong within this theoretical system. However, it may very well serve as a fruitful guideline in spite of its theoretical rigidity.

Social structure and classes in Swedish society during the late 17th century (based upon Carlsson 1971). Examples within brackets.

1. *High aristocracy* (nobility; counts, barons, squires, court dignitaries, high officials, generals, admirals, colonels).
2. *Lower aristocracy* (nobility; judges of appeal, deputy judges, majors, captains).
3. *Untitled gentry* (doctors, professors, wealthy artisans).
4. *Lower gentry* (non-commissioned officers, clerks, private teachers).

The above four classes consist of so-called persons of rank. They represented approximately 5% (75,000–100,000 persons) of the total Swedish-Finnish population (1.5–2.0 million) during the later part of the 17th century (Carlsson 1962, 17; Rystad 1977, 113).

5. *Independent farmers* (paying tax to the Crown).
6. *Leaseholding farmers* (under the Crown or aristocracy).
7. *Crofters, soldiers, factory workers.*
8. *Proletarian workers* (maids, farm-hands, sailors).
9. *Workshouse inmates, paupers.*
10. *Vagrants and an additional group of people outside proper society.*

The above six classes formed the remaining 95% of the Swedish-Finnish population during this period.

A similar social structure may be distinguished in the abundant osteological material from the site. Hitherto, the remains of between 200–300 individuals have been recovered from the site. Hypothetically, comparative studies of the structure of the ship and the osteological material from each deck-level could serve as basis of information regarding the hierarchy of the ship's society.

THE MATERIAL CULTURE

Great potential exists for getting as close as possible to the nature of the original object and its user. Although comparative or similar objects are often to be found in museums and private collections, these artefacts have undergone changes and modification, and the lack of context is often apparent. A concrete example from the *Kronan* material culture is a violin with all its parts preserved, recovered in 1993. It was discovered inside a wooden box, specially designed for the instrument. Unique original parts, which have been replaced and now are non-existent on preserved instruments on land, were found on the *Kronan* violin.

Documentary records provide us with information concerning the material status of certain categories of personnel. One example is a list of private belongings brought on board *Svärdet* – 'The Royal Sword' – by 1st Captain Olof Olofsson Nortman (Svärdet was a 1st-rate of 90 guns, lost together with 600 men, some six hours after the loss of *Kronan*. Nortman himself survived the battle, but lost all his belongings on board):

'Two sets of 'clothes', one coat, one raincoat, one brand new wolfskin coat, one pair of wolfskin gloves, two hats, twelve scarves, thirteen pairs of stockings, one pair of silk stockings, one gun, two rapiers, two pistols, one cartridge pouch, one cane, one brand new horse saddle with holsters and stirrups, linen, bedclothes, provisions, a service and a box containing twelve bottles'. (Zettersten 1903, 238) (Fig.3)

Fig. 3. A box containing twelve bottles, of the same type as that mentioned in a letter to the Admiralty from Captain Olof Nortman's widow, was recovered from Kronan *in 1981.* (Copyright: Kalmar läns museum/ The Kronan-Project)

The list of his valuables taken on board was found in a letter addressed to the Admiralty. It was written by Nortman's widow after her husband's death in 1679, in an attempt to obtain compensation from the Admiralty (which she never got). The stated value of the items (according to the widow a total of 890 daler silver coins) indicates that Nortman must have been rather well off. The sum exceeds two years' salary for a captain of Nortman's rank (Zettersten 1903, 217). The fact that Nortman brought so many of his private belongings on board is not at all surprising. The lack of standard equipment on ships at the time, in combination with the desire to display one's social and material position, must be regarded as a general behaviour of the era. This phenomenon is clearly visible on *Kronan*. Several wooden boxes have been recovered on the site, containing artefacts belonging to high ranked officers (Fig.4). The contents represent a wide spectrum of activities: musical instruments, books, brooches, weapons, clothes, spices, cutlery, pens, combs and brushes (Einarsson 1993, 9).

RANK AS A SYMBOL FOR SOCIAL IDENTIFICATION

Uniforms, in the full sense of the word, did not exist in the Navy during the 17th century. The first indication of the use of a uniform in the Swedish Navy appears in the 1740s (Ekman 1943, 446). However, other symbols of military rank did exist. On *Kronan*, two gorgets have been recovered (Fig.5).

Fig. 4. Several wooden chests were recovered from the orlop deck on Kronan *in 1993. They are perfect examples of closed finds with rich contents.*
(Copyright: Kalmar läns museum/The Kronan-Project)

Fig. 5. Two gorgets were found on Kronan. *The crowned back-to-back monogram stands for King Karl* (Carolus). *According to contemporary specifications, the gorget in the picture in gilded silver with the King's crowned monogram with palm fronds on each side, belonged to either a lieutenant-colonel or a major.*
(Copyright: Kalmar läns museum/The Kronan-Project)

Gorgets in the form of the examples from *Kronan* started to appear as a symbol of military rank during the reign of King Karl XI (1672–1697; Brandt 1947, 49). According to the instructions, a colonel's gorget should be in gilded silver with the King's crowned monogram and other ornament in enamel; those for a lieutenant-colonel and major were not as exquisitely decorated, but gilded with palm-fronds on either side of the King's crowned monogram. A captain's gorget should be in gilded silver but without palm-fronds and a lieutenant's and ensign's in polished silver with a gilded monogram below a Royal Crown of the same size and appearance as the captain's (Bellander 1973, 209).

Another find from the site indicative of rank is a jacket recovered in 1991. It was discovered during airlifting around a vertically standing 36-pounder gun, located close to the gunwale on the port side (Einarsson 1991, 11). Since all of *Kronan*'s 36–pounders (a total of twelve) were placed amidships on the lower deck, the gun with its context must originate from the starboard side of the same deck. When the ship capsized and exploded, the equipment dramatically shifted from one side to the other, allowing objects of great weight to fall down onto other decks within the opened-up hull. The remains of the owner was found inside the jacket. The lower part of his body was discovered on the opposite side of the gun. The context indicates that the gun pulled the carriage, ropes and the man with it, when it fell from the one side to the other. One interesting characteristic of the jacket, apart from its remarkable state of preservation is the occurrence of uniform-like attributes on the sleeves (Colour Plate 4A and front cover). The braided sleeves must have been intended as decoration.

Several artefacts from the wreck can be directly linked to specific persons. Thus, the material status of socially distinguishable persons can be defined. Let us take one example as a case study. One notable person on the ship was the General Admiral *pro tempore* Lorentz Creutz (Fig.6). Several of his personal belongings have been recovered in the wreck. One question to consider is whether is this was coincidental. Turning first to Creutz's social position in society, he belonged to a group of some twenty families which formed the high aristocracy. This group was in control of two-thirds of the Swedish land in the middle of the 17th century (Rystad 1977, 131). Lorentz Creutz held several important positions: privy-councillor, vice-president of the mining-authorities, associate judge of appeal, governor of two provinces (Elgenstierna 1926, 61). As a baron he belonged to the uppermost class of three within the nobility, a group of considerable difference in class within itself. Even though *Kronan* brought with her several members of the Swedish aristocracy, no one else in the crew could match Lorentz Creutz's social position.

The circumstances were not extremely favourable where Creutz's belongings were found, in the sense that the same natural conditions exist at several other locations on the site where objects of similar material might have been discovered. However, from an archaeological and historical point of view, the conditions for recovery of Creutz's artefacts were extremely favourable, since very few persons would have been in a social and economical position to own such objects in the first place. Members of the extreme upper class, like Creutz, were likely to bring a larger number of objects with them as a manifestation of their positions in society. In many cases, these objects were made of less degradable material. The conditions for the material culture recovered from the lower classes are generally the opposite. They were likely to bring fewer objects per capita and of a less resistant nature. The recovery of several of General Admiral Creutz's private belongings on the site must therefore be explained in the light of his rank in society.

The prospect of making a positive identification of the owner of a recovered artefact also increases the possibility of determining the person's social and economical 'radius of action'. Such is the case with the pewter plates bearing the initials of Creutz and his wife, which were recovered during 1994 and 1995 on the wreck (Einarsson 1994a, 20). They all bear four stamps and crowned-rose – an English symbol for supreme quality – attributed to the two London makers Nicholas Kelk and William Hulls the Elder, who were manufacturing around 1670 (Fig.7). The fact that the plates were made without doubt shortly before the sinking, indicates not only a short time between manufacturing and purchasing, but also in terms of the purchaser's distance from the market. In the case of Creutz, this is not at all surprising. The question

Fig. 6. The General Admiral pro tempore Baron Lorentz Creutz perished onboard Kronan. Creutz was one of the most powerful men during Sweden's period as a 'Great Power'. This painting shows Creutz dressed as Admiral. The features, however, are not those of the Admiral. The painting was finished after his death, using his oldest living son, Lorentz Creutz the younger, who posed as model.
(Copyright: Kalmar läns museum/The Kronan-Project)

Fig. 7. Pewter plates of the highest quality bearing the initials of Admiral Lorentz Creutz and his wife Elsa Duvall on the back side. The plates are made in London about 1670 by Nicholas Kelk. (Copyright: Kalmar läns museum/The Kronan-Project)

is rather how this relationship is reflected in the find material as one descends the hierarchy of the ship's society.

An example of one artefact's importance for shedding light upon aspects of social and economic conditions during the 17th century is a golden drinking spoon recovered on the site in 1994 (Colour Plate 4B). It was found inside a wooden chest together with fifteen square glass bottles with pewter lids, and probably had a sacramental function. The spoon was engraved with the initials 'P G' and the coat of arms of the noble family Golawitz. The spoon had originally belonged to Lieutenant-Colonel Peter Golawitz, a neighbour of Lorentz Creutz in Finland. When Peter Golawitz passed away in 1673, he disinherited his only son Johan, who had led a vicious life and (according to his father) was unworthy of being called his son. Golawitz's land and personal property was left to Lorentz Creutz and Creutz's daughter Britta. The situation resulted in a trial in which Johan Golawitz was accused of defaming Creutz and his unmarried daughter. Johan Golawitz was eventually sentenced to death, but the following year pardoned and instead forced to go into exile (Einarsson 1995, 101–109)[4]. The legal case of Creutz *vs.* Golawitz is a concrete example of how archaeology can draw attention to aspects of the material culture of the actual period of time.

CANNON, COINS AND EMBELLISHMENT

At the time of writing, forty-four cannon, all bronze, have been recovered from the wreck site (Fig.8). That 40 % comprise trophies reflects the contemporary naval ambition to equip capital ships with captured guns (Börjesson 1942, 252; 254). Of a total of between 124 and 128 cannon, sixty were salvaged during the 1680s (Einarsson 1994b, 63)[5]. There is great variety in the provenance of the recovered ordnance: twenty-six are Swedish, eight Spanish, six Danish and three (possibly four) German (The Holy Roman Empire). Most of the foreign cannon seem to be trophies from the latter part of the Thirty Years' War (1618–48). In size, the cannon range from 3- to 36-pounders. The oldest gun recovered is a German 30–pounder, cast in 1514; the youngest are three Swedish 36–pounders from 1661.

Most of the nine Swedish 24-pounders from *Kronan* were recovered from the middle deck, which exclusively carried thirty-six 24-pounders (Zettersten 1903, 327). They are all of the same type as the three cannon that were recovered from the *Vasa* after the discovery of the wreck in the mid-1950s (Clason 1964). The state of preservation of the majority of the cannon suggests that they had been exposed to previous corrosion. Indeed, some of the *Vasa*-type cannon, recovered from *Kronan*, might well have been salvaged from *Vasa* in 1664–65 by Hans Albrekt von Treileben and his men, and then put on board *Kronan*.

Of her complement of 124–128 cannon exclusively made of bronze (Einarsson 1994b, 62), 104 were recovered from *Kronan* before and after the discovery in 1980. Thus a maximum of twenty to twenty-four cannon remain to be found on the site. The locations on the site for two of these are known.

In 1982/83, the largest discovery of minted gold ever found in Sweden was made, comprising 255 coins together

Fig. 8. Forty-four bronze cannon have been recovered from the wreck site of Kronan. Eleven were discovered outside the hull structure. (Copyright: Kalmar läns museum/The Kronan-Project)

with coins of other metals, navigational instruments and a gold ring, in and around the remains of a wooden chest. The find clearly lay in a secondary position, close to the keelson on the starboard side. The majority of the coins originate from central Europe, though some were minted in remote places like Turkey and Egypt (Golabiewski-Lannby 1988, 20). Their date range runs from the early 16th century to 1676. The gold ring found among the coins, together with a unique 10-ducat piece, indicate that the valuables might have belonged to Admiral Creutz. This possibility of attributing the find to a specific person once again offers an opportunity to conduct a material survey of a socially distinguishable person. The results may define his position in the social hierachy and his status in relation to other classes. The gold treasure was valued at 1,191 dalers in silver. Creutz, in his post as councillor of the realm, received a salary of 3,000 daler in silver *per annum*. The value of the gold was equivalent to ten years of continuous labour for an average paid worker of the period.

Decoration on ships during the 17th century is still a field which is relatively unknown. *Vasa* is, of course, an exception, and a thorough study and analysis of her sculpture has been made (Soop 1986). Nevertheless, the absence of comparative material is obvious. The decoration on *Kronan* is later baroque, somewhat different to the period of the *Vasa* forty years earlier, particularly in the colour of the sculpture. While recent studies of colour-samples from *Vasa* show decorations painted in more naturalistic colours than previously thought (Tångeberg 1993, 7), *Kronan* apparently had more gilded features.

The earliest known English example of a painting contract is that for the *Henry* (originally named the *Dunbar*, but renamed at the Restoration) and the *London* in 1655 (Howard 1979, 125). In the contract, references are made to the colours of the *Naseby*, completed in 1655 (renamed *Royal Charles* at the Restoration; Fox 1980, 69). The information is of great interest, since Francis Sheldon may have been involved in build-

Fig. 9. In 1987 a wooden sculpture in the form of a Roman warrior bearing Royal attributes, was recovered from underneath the ship's port side. It still floated after being recovered, illustrating the preservative conditions on the site. (Copyright: Kalmar läns museum/The Kronan-Project)

Fig. 10. The same wooden sculpture in the form of a Roman warrior as in Figure 9 after recovery. (Copyright: Kalmar läns museum/The Kronan-Project)

ing both the *Naseby* and the *London* before commencing his service in Sweden (Anderson 1957, 102). Here, fruitful comparisons may be made between the documentary and physical records.

Rich finds of both exterior and interior wooden sculpture have been recovered on the site of the *Kronan*. The discovery of wooden sculpture *in situ* in the Admiral's cabin on the upper deck in the early 1980s was an important break-through in the investigation of *Kronan*. The possibility that more accurate information could help reconstruct the ship was suddenly far more likely. The sculpture also represented an important category of artefact, in terms of its *symbolic* value. Such is the case of the wooden sculpture in the form of a Roman warrior recovered in 1987 from the ship's exterior (Figs 9, 10). The sculpture carries Royal attributes, and is in all probability a depiction of the Swedish King Karl X (1622–1660) of the Palatinate Dynasty.

Comparisons can be made with the decoration on a ship-model in the National Maritime Museum in Stockholm. The model represents another ship designed by Francis Sheldon, *Postiljon* ('Post-Boy'). The ship, described as an English frigate, was launched at Gothenburg in 1664. Built as a Swedish 3rd-rate, she was converted to a fire-ship by 1676 (Zettersten 1903, 579). A wooden sculpture in the form of a Roman warrior, like that recovered from *Kronan*, can be seen on each stern counter of the model. The fashion of decorating the angles of the stern with large, carved figures (so-called quarterpieces) seems to have been predominant during the beginning of the second half of the 17th century (Lavery 1984, 51). It is possible that this was the original position of the sculpture found on the site.

In 1994 two test trenches were opened in connection with the gunwale of the port side, in order to determine the presence of exterior sculpture *in situ* on its underside. In both trenches wooden sculptures were uncovered *in situ* (Figs 11, 12), despite their relatively exposed position next to the gunwale (Einarsson 1994a, 8–10, 14–15). The discovery indicates that the ship came to rest in its capsized position shortly after the sinking. However, artefacts from the ship's interior recovered beneath the port side in both test trenches indicate that the ship's side had been projecting above the seabed for some time after the sinking. Eventually the hull structure collapsed, causing a longitudinal fracture along the border between the orlop and the lower deck (Einarsson 1990, 291). Objects from the ship's interior had found a place of refuge under the overhanging upper part of the port side, and were then trapped under the main hull structure. The presence of exterior sculpture and decoration *in situ* will have an important bearing on the future of the *Kronan* project and in the long term be an incentive to recover the ship's structure.

Fig. 11. Wooden carving tightly pressed beneath the gunwale on the border between the poop and quarter deck.
(Copyright: Kalmar läns museum/The Kronan-Project)

Fig. 12. The foot, calf and thigh of a sitting figure on the border between the quarter deck and the upper deck. Note the belaying pin in situ.
(Copyright: Kalmar läns museum/The Kronan-Project)

Notes

1 All bronze, weighing in total about 230 tons.
2 *Vasa* was only partially equipped for her maiden voyage when she sank.
3 Not a microcosm, since the number of men on board corresponds to the population of a medium-sized town in Sweden at the time.
4 The article is based on a study of the documents from the legal case *Lorentz Creutz vs. Johan Golawitz. Nedre Justitie Revisionen. Revisionsakt 8/6 1675* (the Swedish National Archives).
5 The specifications regarding the gun salvage operations on *Kronan* during the 1680s are to be found in *Amiralitetskollegii Skrivelser till Kungl. Maj:t.* Vol.8. 29/3 1686 (the Swedish National Archives). The specifications regarding the complement of cannon are found in *Amiralitetskollegium. Oordnade handlingar. Nya nummerserien. Avd.II. Nr.12. Förteckning 507* (The Swedish Military Record Office).

References

Anderson, R. C. 1957 'Francis Sheldon and his family', *The Mariner's Mirror* 43(2), 101–105.
Bellander, E. 1973 *Dräkt och uniform,* Stockholm.
Brandt, T. 1947 'Ringkragar', *Föreningen Armémusei Vänner Meddelanden* VIII, 48–60.
Börjesson, H. 1942 'Sjökrigsmaterial och skeppsbyggnad åren 1612–1679', *Svenska flottans historia* I, 233–294.
Carlsson, S. 1962 *Bonde-präst-ämbetsman,* Stockholm.
Carlsson, S. 1971 *Att byta samhällsklass,* Stockholm.
Clason, E. 1964 'Om *Vasas* bestyckning', *Tidskrift för Sjöväsendet* 1964, 762–779, 849–864.
Ekman, C. 1943 'Personalens klädsel', *Svenska flottans historia* II, 446–460.
Einarsson, L. 1990 'Kronan – underwater archaeological investigations of a 17th-century man-of-war. The nature, aims and development of a maritime cultural project', *IJNA* 19, 279–297.
Einarsson, L. 1991 *Rapport om 1991 års marinarkeologiska undersökningar av vraket efter regalskeppet Kronan,* Kalmar läns museum.
Einarsson, L. 1993 *Rapport om 1993 års marinarkeologiska undersökningar av vraket efter regalskeppet Kronan,* Kalmar läns museum.
Einarsson, L. 1994a *Rapport om 1994 års marinarkeologiska undersökningar av vraket efter regalskeppet Kronan,* Kalmar läns museum.
Einarsson, L. 1994b 'De marinarkeologiska undersökningarna av regalskeppet Kronan', *Sjöhistorisk årsbok 1994–1995,* 51–68.
Einarsson, L., 1995 'Svart som Golawitzen...', *Årsbok för Kalmar län. Kalmar läns museum 1995.*
Elgenstierna, G. 1926 *Den introducerade svenska adelns ättartavlor* II, Stockholm.
Fox, F. 1980 *Great Ships. The Battlefleet of King Charles II,* London.
Glete, J. 1985 'De statliga örlogsflottornas expansion. Kapprustningen till sjöss i Väst- och Nordeuropa 1650–1680', *Studier i äldre historia tillägnade Herman Schück.*
Golabiewski-Lannby, M.(ed.) 1988 *The gold treasure from the Royal ship Kronan.* The Royal Coin Cabinet Catalogue no.24, Kalmar.
Howard, F. 1979 *Sailing Ships of War 1400–1860.* London.
Lavery, B. 1984 *The Ship of the Line II,* London.
Rystad, G. 1977 *Svenskt 1600–tal,* Malmö.
Soop, H., 1986 *The Power and the Glory. The Sculptures of the Warship Vasa,* Uddevalla.
Tängeberg, P. 1993 *Rapport över färgundersökningar på regalskeppet Vasa 1990–1993.* Typewritten partial report regarding the determination of the original colour scheme of the *Vasa* sculptures, commissioned by the Vasa-Museum, Lästringe.
Zetterstén, A. 1903 *Svenska flottans historia. Åren 1635–1680,* Norrtelje.

18

Family life on board: the Dutch boat people between 1600 and 1900

André F. L. van Holk

INTRODUCTION

When I first became interested in maritime affairs, I happened to be living in the province of Groningen, in the northern part of The Netherlands. To my surprise, it appeared that in the middle of the 19th century most of the Dutch skippers (ship's masters or captains) were domiciled in Groningen, particularly in the inland peat digging area called the '*Veenkoloniëen*'. Vestiges of the erstwhile flourishing shipbuilding industry still survive, and many wharves are doing a remarkably good job of continuing the tradition. On almost all the photographs of the crews of these Groningen ships dating from about 1900, one can see that the skipper sailed with his family on board (Fig. 1). In fact, families could be found not only on board inland traders, but also aboard vessels engaged in the coastal and sea trade: for skipper, his wife and children, the ship formed their primary residence. This situation can best be described as a form of sea nomadism. Many interesting oral traditions exist about that period, some painting a lively picture of the difficulties of (the reproduction of) life on board: sometimes children were born at sea – '*born through the hawsehole*', as the saying goes.

How old was this phenomenon? Was it a common practice? This paper examines whether it is possible to find traces of the family in archaeological 'ship-inventories'.

Fig. 1. Skipper, wife and children on board a Dutch inland freighter. (Photograph private collection H.J. Smit, from Loomeijer 1980, 53)

Written sources seem to indicate that the kind of family to be encountered on board was similar in structure to the 'nuclear family'. The wife of the skipper and children above a certain age were, in fact, part of the crew. Apart from a social unit, the family was also an economic or productive unit. Consequently, the wife of the skipper was referred to in Dutch as *schipperse* – the female form of 'skipper'. Nineteenth-century probate inventories indicate that when a skipper died, his wife often continued the business and kept on sailing: such cases usually concern inland ships. This form of social and economic organisation can be compared to the traditional farm, where the family also formed both the social and productive unit.

That families also lived on board ships in earlier times can be deduced from several (mainly written) sources. On the basis of this evidence, this paper aims to outline where and when family life on board did occur, though it is not based on systematically collected data. As will become clear from the discussion of the archaeological remains of shipwrecks, it is, for several reasons, often difficult to interpret the meagre evidence.

WRITTEN EVIDENCE FOR THE FAMILY ON BOARD

It is generally thought that the family started to appear on board ships in the middle of the 19th century (i.c. Verrips 1991; Gerding 1995). Most scholars think that people gave up their land-bound residence because of the economic changes brought about by the Industrial Revolution. It is believed that the free transport market had a rather strong competitive character, and that costs had to be drastically reduced. The saving which resulted from having the family on board was two-fold. Firstly, the costs of housing on land were saved because the ship functioned as primary residence. Secondly, family members were the cheapest crew a skipper could ever have. By the same line of reasoning, it has been argued that the regulated shipping between two places (Dutch: *beurtvaart*) was replaced by tramp shipping (Dutch: *wilde vaart*). This is a second misunderstanding. The *beurtvaart* is relatively well documented and was organised to a high degree in guilds. Tramp shipping, however, was by its very nature under-represented in the written sources. Two misconceptions underlie the idea of a late date for the beginning of family life on board: i) the replacement of *beurtvaart* by tramp shipping, and ii) the connection of tramp shipping and families residing on board.

Genealogical studies of families active in the Rhine trade in Germany and The Netherlands suggest that certainly in the last quarter of the 17th century it had become customary for families to live on board ship (Heubes 1973). This is well illustrated by the places of birth of the children on board, each being registered in a different town along the Rhine. The oldest indication for family life on board in this area goes back to about 1625 (Van Loo 1989, 386). An etching by Reinier Nooms, dating to the second half of the 17th century, depicts two so-called *'Oberländer'*. On one vessel, two women can be seen at work (Fig. 2). It seems, however, that both ships were used as house-boats. On the other hand this ship type was described by Nicolaes Witsen in 1671, who wrote '*complete families lived on board of these Rhine ships*' (Witsen 1671, 170). In the 18th century, some of the Rhine skippers also sailed on the Zuiderzee with their families.

Fig. 2. Etching by Reinier Nooms, alias Zeeman (1623–1667), showing two Rhine ships. On the left-hand vessel, two women can be seen at work. These house-boats have erroneously been regarded as Rhine-freighters. (Taken from Greup 1952, 15)

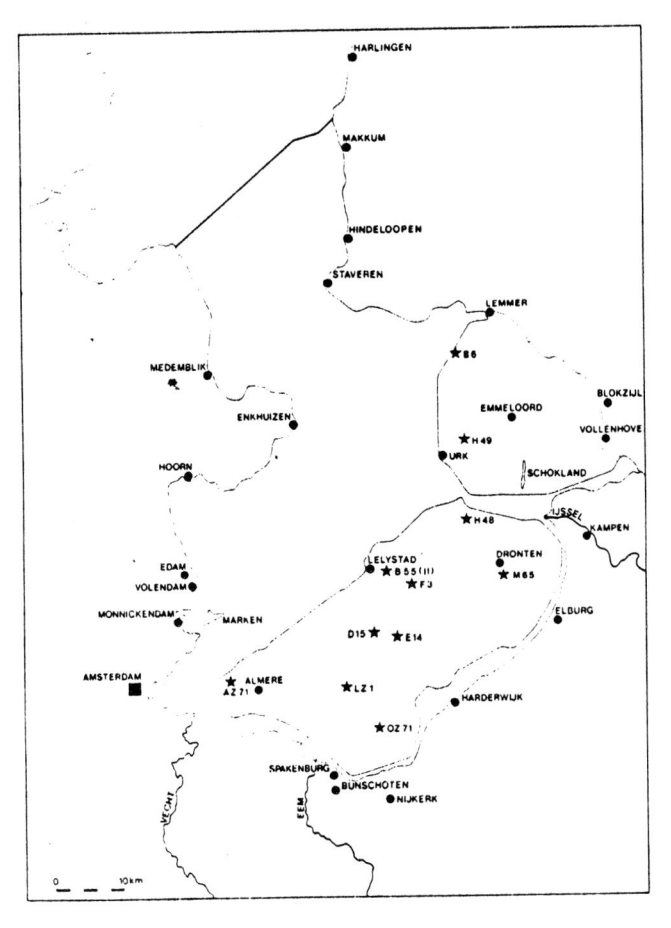

Fig. 3. Sites mentioned in the text.

Another rather early case of a family on board is found in the province of Groningen. A skipper got in trouble with other skippers so that his ship got stuck in a sluice. In the testimony concerning this case, it was stated that *'the noise of breaking timbers woke the wife and children of the skipper; terrified they came on deck, totally naked and screaming terribly'* (Coert 1983, 183). This dramatic event happened in the year 1668.

Some written evidence indicates the presence of families on board ships in the Zuiderzee area. Apart from the above-mentioned Rhine skippers who sailed on the Zuiderzee in the 18th century, the description of a *tjalk* wrecked on the Zuiderzee in 1779 states that on board were the skipper and his *housewife* (Van der Doe 1985). In a town like Blokzijl on the eastcoast of the Zuiderzee in the year 1880, 22 % of the tax paying heads of families lived on board ship (Prins 1969, 14).

Probate inventories which had to be drawn up when a parent died and left behind a minor, can be useful. A sample of 19th-century inventories of inland ships in the province of Groningen shows that all the families lived on board their ships (*Rijksarchief Groningen, Notarieel Archief*).[1]

Another area where, from about 1900 onwards, the wife of the skipper sailed with her husband is the Oderhaff and neighbouring rivers (Rudolph 1973, 329). This phenomenon started to become regular practice on the Weser and Elbe a little earlier (around 1850; Steppat 1987a, 212).

The first accounts of women occasionally accompanying their husbands to sea (sea-borne trade) date from about 1700 (Henningsen 1987, 17), but it has to be stressed that this never became regular practice, there being only occasional references during the 18th and 19th century.

To conclude, families lived on board ships in different areas. Written sources indicate that the earliest family occupation was among the Rhine skippers during the first quarter of the 17th century; by the last quarter of that century, this probably became normal practice. There are indications of families on board ships in the 18th and 19th century in the Zuiderzee area. More intensive research might bring more of these sources to the surface. There are early records of the family on board ship both on the Rhine and in the northern part of The Netherlands.

ARCHAEOLOGICAL EVIDENCE

This paper reviews the material culture of archaeological ship inventories from wrecks found in the IJsselmeerpolders dating approximately from 1600–1900 (Fig. 3). More or less 'complete' inventories have been selected for analysis at random. The ships can be described as small inland freighters, operating as carriers of bulk cargo (most being identified as '*tjalk*-like' and '*praam*-like' vessels). The ships, which range in length from 17 to 23 m, are coded according to the lot in which they were found: for example, Lz 1, D 15 and H 49.

Table 1. List of the ships included in this survey

Ship (lot)	Date of construction/loss	Type	Dimensions (l × br)
Lz 1	1586–1604	'*praam*-like'	20.2 × 4 m
Oz 71	1652–1685	'*tjalk*-like'	17 × 4.4 m
M 65	? –1697	'*tjalk*-like'	20 × 4.65 m
B 55(II)	? –1731	'*tjalk*-like'	19.5 × about 4 m
D 15	1702–1742	'*praam*-like'	18.80 × 4.7 m
Az 71	? –1750	'*praam*-like'	19.5 × 3.51 m
E 14	? –1783	'*praam*-like'	about 20 × about 4 m
B 6	1770–1786	'*tjalk*-like'	19.6 × 4.2 m
H 49	? –1850	'*praam*-like'	19.6 × 3.6 m
H 48	? –1888	*praam*/barge	20.32 × 4.52 m
F 3	1878–1886	*tjalk*	23.20 × 4.64 m

Of particular interest is the degree of change in the social structure and organisation of the crew on board, and how such changes might be detected in the archaeological record. The following questions will be addressed:

– how can family life on board be traced? What kind of artefacts are related to either women or children?
– at what moment in time did families move on board?
– what mechanism in society led to the decision to start to live permanently on board these inland freighters?

Rather than accepting the general belief that ship inventories are complete as an *a priori* assumption, this idea should be tested. Different natural and cultural factors influence the completeness of any inventory. One can compare the effect of these factors to that of a sieve. Only a fraction of the material culture on board will be tracable and be caught in the mesh.

It might appear an easy task to look for those components of material culture on board which are gender- or age- related: one just selects those items which fulfill one of these conditions. However, it is first necessary to interpret the available material culture, and secondly to interpret that material culture in the specific context of the ship-board community.

The ship inventories under consideration contain some artefacts which indicate the presence of women and children. Such objects have been divided into two classes (Table 2).

Table 2. Gender- and age-related objects found in ships from the IJsselmeerpolders. Some of the smaller objects are marked with an asterisk to indicate that in the case of an unclear archaeological context, the object might not belong to the ship inventory.

Class 1. Gender- and age-related objects		Class 2. Objects with uncertain gender association
A. female	B. child	
shoes	shoes	decorative plate
apron	glove	wooden carving
(perfume bottle) lid	chair & chamberpot	statuette
*pendant	spoon?	vase
*brooch	skate	knitting pin
bracelet	*marble	knitting case
*bead	*lion (toy?)	*hairpin?
*shell-shaped ornament	miniature pincers	
oval box	and claw hammer	
iron		
iron glass		
thimble		

This classification is still under discussion and it might be necessary to bring about a few changes or add or subtract items. *Class 1 A* contains those objects which are related to females, but even apparently obvious examples need close scrutiny. For example, the difference between women's or men's shoes can be minor, such as the overhanging heel of the lower mule (Fig. 4). Moreover, some shoe types might be the same for both sexes, in which case a family might be concealed within the artefactual evidence for a 'male' community. Relatively short and at the same time wide shoes or soles can be attributed to women; where the soles of shoes only survive, size can give a clue. It is therefore necessary to differentiate between adult male and female shoe sizes within the different periods.

The gender association of the apron in the past has been clearly female, and oral historical sources for the *tjalk* '*De Zeehond*' on which a little apron was found (Fig. 5), confirm that a family lived on board. The perfume bottle found on the same ship is also positively female related. In many probate inventories a perfume bottle (often with a golden lid) is listed together with the jewellery belonging to the wife of the skipper. Jewellery is seldom found on board inland ships; it is quite likely that such items were worn by the women at the time of sinking, and also possible that they did not own much jewellery. One problem concerning small objects in

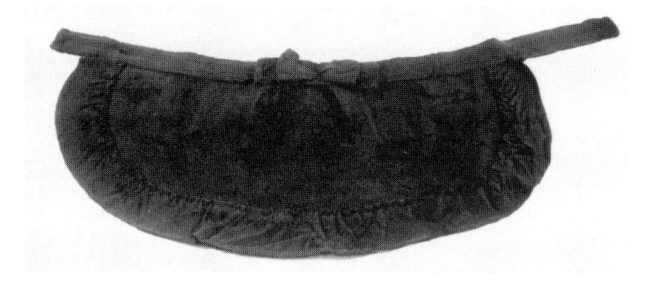

Fig. 5. The small apron found on board wreck F 3. (Photograph: N.I.S.A.).

Fig. 4. Woman's mule with overhanging heel. (Photograph: RUG)

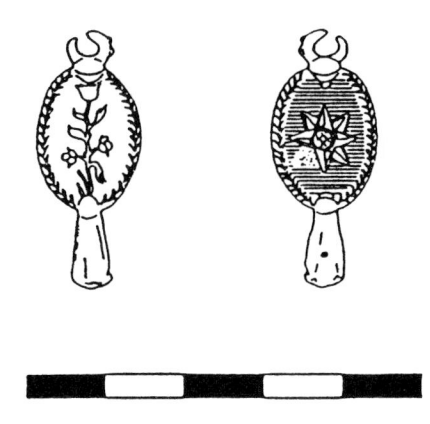

Fig. 6. Pewter pendant from wreck Az 71. Scale 1:1. (From McLaughlin 1992, 114)

general is that they might not belong to the ship inventory at all. One possible exception is the pewter pendant found on board wreck Az 71 (Fig. 6).

The inventories of two ships contained oval boxes (Fig. 7), often used by women to put away their traditional costumes, in particular hats (though it is possible that they were used to store other items). Also associated with female dress are the iron and smoothing glass (Fig. 8a & b). It appears that only certain pieces of women's clothing needed ironing. Women are always depicted in paintings handling irons, except in the special case where a tailor is involved. Caution is required because in the ship context it is possible that men also did the ironing.

Fig. 7. Oval box, presumably used by women to put away their costumes. (Photograph: RUG)

Fig. 8. (a)↑ 18th-century iron from wreck D 15 and 20th-century ironing/smoothing glass (Photograph: RUG); (b)↓ artefacts from wreck F 3 (De Zeehond, lost in 1886), including an iron. (Photograph: N.I.S.A.).

224   *André F. L. van Holk*

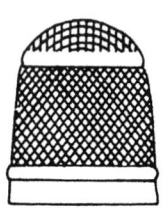

Fig. 9. Thimble found on board wreck D 15, which sank after 1742.

Fig. 12. Child's pewter chamber pot. Scale = 5 cm.

Fig. 10. Child's shoes (on right) among other shoes from wreck F 3.
(Photograph: N.I.S.A.)

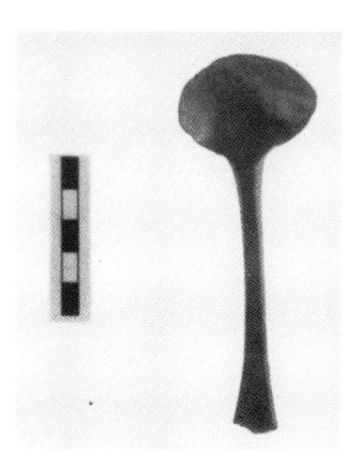

Fig. 13. Pewter spoon, possibly for a child. Scale = 5 cm.
(Photograph: N.I.S.A.)

Fig. 11. Child's shoe, wooden shoe (clog) and glove found on board wreck H 49, lost about 1850. (Photograph: RUG)

The thimble is attributed to a woman because of its size (Fig. 9). Nevertheless, it is known that men on board did sew, and generally speaking a thimble might be a typical *Class 2* object, though in the case given it indicates a female presence.

The next class of objects (*Class 1B*) is taken to represent children: first and foremost toys, but also other artefacts. Sometimes their shoes are easily recognised. Only when shoe size is sufficiently small (for example, under 20 cm) can it be interpreted as belonging to a child (Fig. 10). Apart from the child's shoe, a child's wooden shoe (clog) and child's glove were found on board wreck H 49 (Fig. 11). A child's skate was recovered from ship B 55(II), wrecked about 1730.

One of the ships that probably operated in both inland and coastal waters was that discovered on lot B 6. A pewter vessel found on board could not initially be identified (Fig. 12). It was discovered, according to a newspaper article about the excavation, in a child's chair (Van der Heide 1956); the location provided a clue to its function as a child's chamber pot.

A peculiar pewter spoon was found on board wreck A 71(Fig. 13), its form suggesting that it had been for a child (McLaughlin 1992, 112), perhaps acting also as a tool of some kind.

Some artefacts may be interpreted as toys. Marbles, found on several ships, were also used as toys on the street, and it is possible that they ended up in the ship's hold along with street sweepings which were often transported by inland ships active in the peat trade. Adults also used marbles for games, so the marble has an uncertain age association. A small pipe-clay lion found on board a wreck on lot E 14 may have been a toy, if not purely decorative (Fig. 14).

The miniature pincers and claw hammer found on board

Fig. 14. Moulded pipe-clay lion, possibly a toy. Scale 1:1. (Drawing from McLaughlin 1992, 75)

the '*Lutina*' (H 48) have been interpreted as toys, but oral and written sources about this ship indicate that at the time of sinking only the skipper and a barge-hand were on board. The wife of the skipper lived onshore with their children, but it seems possible that at an earlier stage the skipper lived on board with his family. Two brooches found in the wreck may be further signs of a previous arrangement.

Class 2 encompasses those objects with an uncertain gender- and age-association, including items with a decorative function. Some researchers believe that when the skipper's wife came on board, a more 'homely' atmosphere was created. On the other hand, the '*Lutina*', with only skipper and mate as crew, had one vase. Other decorative items include a group of plates on board wreck D 15, a porcelain statuette and a piece of woodcarving on board wreck F 3 (Figs 15 a-c).

Table 3. Artefacts discussed in this paper arranged by ship

Lz 1	OZ 71	M 65
marble	marble	marble
		woman's shoe
		knitting case

B 55 (II)	D 15A	Az 71
children's skate	woman's shoe	pendant
	iron	child's spoon
	thimble	
	decorative plate	

E 14	B 6	H 49
bead	oval box	oval box
hairpin?	child's chair	iron glass
shell-shaped ornament(?)	and chamber pot	child's shoe/(clog?)
lion (toy?)	marble	wooden shoe
		child's glove
		knitting needle

H 48	F 3
bead	woman's shoe
bracelet	little apron
brooch	(perfume bottle) lid
marble	iron
miniature pincers	child's shoe
and claw hammer	knitting needle
wooden carving	wooden carving
vase	decorative plate
statuette	

A knitting needle was found on board of wreck H 49 and a knitting case was found on board wreck M 65 (Fig. 16). Knitting was an activity that was also performed by men, in particular by skippers and herdsmen. The presence of a woman cannot therefore be inferred from knitting equipment, though the frequently decorated knitting case (*breischede*) used to place the knitting needle in was often given as a wedding present from husband to wife.

When gender- and age-related objects are examined by ship, it becomes clear how meagre are the indicators for women and children (Table 3). On the other hand, the number of ships containing such evidence is surprisingly high. During the 18th century, between one to four items can possibly be attributed to women or children for each ship, and a family may have lived on some vessels; on others this is less certain. The wreck found at lot D 15 may be the oldest ship found in The Netherlands with evidence for a family on board. Its crew composition is supported by the use of space on board. A hearth was present both fore and aft, creating two clearly segregated living spaces. Wreck B 55 (II) showed the same spatial arangement, but the discovery of only one child's skate seems too slender a basis for a family presence. The woman's shoe and knitting case on board wreck M 65 may indicate the presence of the skipper's wife, but it is uncertain whether the

226   *André F. L. van Holk*

A

B   C

Fig. 15. (a) Decorated tin-glazed earthenware plates found on board wreck D 15 (scale 1:5) (Photograph: RUG); (b) woodcarving (scale 1:6; from Oosting & Vlierman 1990, 59); (c) statuette (scale 1:3; taken from Oosting & Vlierman 1990, 58). (b) and (c) are from wreck F 3.

Fig. 16. Decorated knitting case from wreck M 65. Scale = 5 cm. (Photograph: RUG)

small objects on wrecks Az 71 and E 14 belong to the inventory and indicate a family presence. Wrecks B 6 and H 49 display more positive proof. The *'Lutina'* (lot H 48) is a very confusing case, with eight objects that can be classified as belonging to women and children. It is known that only the skipper and his mate were on board, and consequently great care needs to be taken when interpreting material culture in this manner. In this particular case, it is possible that the skipper lived with his family on board at an earlier period, the objects representing 'fall-out' from that situation. The presence of a family crew on board the *Zeehond* (lot F 3) is based on the interpretation of the material culture, supported by oral and written evidence. The date of families first appearing on board inland ships sailing on the Zuiderzee would on the basis of the above evidence be about 1700.

CONCLUSION

Apart from the problem of the gender- or age-association of the artefacts themselves, a question arises of whether it is legitimate to conclude on the basis of only a few finds that a family was present or even lived on board? The correct answer must be i) that written sources indicate that families were actually on board; ii) that the archaeological record in turn provides but a glimpse of family life. The scarcity of family indicators in the archaeological record can be explained by the fact that people owned few personal possessions. The composition of the material culture of crews, be they families or not, on board small inland freighters, was modest and frugal. Members of the crew have almost never been found on board ships wrecked on the Zuiderzee; if a person owned just one pair of shoes, then no trace of him/her might be found. In some cases it is possible that crew members tried to take their valuables with them before abandoning the sinking ship.

Another factor not yet touched upon is the age of a ship when she sank. If we suppose that vessel had one skipper throughout its life, we would hardly expect to find evidence of children on board a ship that is over forty years old (this could, in some cases, explain the absence of toys). The life-cycle of ship and crew should be kept in mind when interpreting material culture on board.

According to documentary evidence, families lived on board ships in the Zuiderzee area from the last quarter of the 18th century. According to the archaeological evidence, this could start about 1700. Further research may reveal that this became normal practice by the beginning of the 18th century, but the oldest documentary evidence indicates that families were living on board boats on the rivers Rhine and Meuse by the first quarter of the 17th century.

Many different explanations have been proposed for the process which resulted in family life on board vessels. Steppat (1987a; 1987b) and Rudolph (1973) follow the same line of reasoning for different areas (the Rhine and Weser around 1850, and the Oderhaff around 1900), that the changing competitive position of independent skippers, resulting from

Fig. 17. Crew and guests on board a 'Grey Devil'. (Photograph: Loomeijer 1987, 133)

economic and technical changes of the Industrial Revolution, caused families to live on board. This view has also been articulated by Verrips in connection with Dutch inland navigation (1991, 23), who believes that in the period before 1850 this practice was an exception rather than a rule, and also that it was restricted to navigation on rivers. There seems, therefore, to be disagreement about the beginnings of family residence on board ships: archaeological and historical evidence indicates a much earlier date, and consequently that the Industrial Revolution cannot provide an adequate explanation (though it is possible that more families started to live on board post-1850).

Conditions of ownership also deserve some consideration. When part of, or even the whole, ship were owned by a skipper, it was easier for him to take along his wife and children. Another factor, mentioned above, is the kind of shipping involved. According to Verrips (1991, 16) the replacement of the regular service shipping (Dutch: *beurtvaart*) by tramp shipping was one of the reasons for the skipper giving up his house on the shore and taking wife and children on board. This proposal is seriously undermined by the fact that most of the Rhine skippers who had their families on board were active in regular service shipping (let alone the fact that the replacement of regular service shipping by tramp shipping never took place).

In conclusion, different reasons existed in different areas for families settling on board. All these reasons have an economic basis in common. It was far cheaper to have only one residence and your family as unpaid or low paid labourers. It is suggested that the early economic rise in the 17th century of the Dutch Republic could have had an effect on crew composition on the Zuiderzee.

Even in the 1920s captains from the province of Groningen engaging in coastal trade took their families with them. These skippers were engaged among other things in the English home trade. They were accused by the English of false competition, which was to some degree true, because, as Loomeijer (1987, 133) wrote: '*father was captain, mother cook, the eldest son first mate and the youngest mate*'. As a result, English skippers referred to the Dutch ships as '*Grey Devils*'. The devil part might be clear – the colour referred to the colour of the ships. This situation is ably illustrated in one family picture (Fig. 17), in which captain, wife and son were members of the crew (the other people in this photograph sailed with the ship as guests). However, the first mate and mates who were not on the ship were indeed paid labourers.

One of the reasons for the success of those *Groninger* shippers in the English home trade was the composition of the crew. The roots of this kind of social organisation go back to the Zuiderzee, possibly to about 1700 (and still earlier for the Rhine trade).

Note
1   In most inventories the ship is given as the only residence.

References

Coert, G.A. 1983 'Het schuitenschuiversgilde en de vrije vaart naar de Oostermoerse venen', *in* P. Brood, G.A. Coert, F Keverling Buisman & A.J.M. den Teuling (eds), *Vergezichten op Drenthe. Opstellen over Drentse geschiedenis* (Boom, Meppel), 165–186.

Doe, E. van der, 1985 *Verscholen schepen*. Verslag van een archiefonderzoek naar enige op de Zuiderzee en op de Waddenzee vergane schepen, 1600–1800 (State University of Leiden, June 1985).

Gerding, M.A.W. 1995 *Vier eeuwen turfwinning: de ververingen in Groningen, Friesland, Drenthe en Overijssel tussen 1550 en 1950*. Afdeling Agrarische Geschiedenis, Landbouwuniversiteit, Wageningen.

Greup, G.M. 1952 *De Rijnverbinding van Amsterdam en haar geschiedenis*. Becht, Amsterdam.

Heide, G.D. van der 1956 'Nieuwe scheepsopgravingen (I). Plavuizen uit in de 18e eeuw gezonken schip voor vloer in museum Lelystad', *Het Nieuwe Land, 29 september 1956*.

Henningsen, H. 1987 *Der Seeman und die Frau*, Koehlers, Herford.

Heubes, H. 1973 *Knipscheer-Knipschaar, 400 Jahre niederrheinisch-holländische schiffer*, Veröffentlichungen der Westdeutschen Gesellschaft für Familienkunde e. V., Neue Folge Nr. 7, Köln und Düsseldorf.

Loo, J. van 1989 'Johan Aeldersz. de Veer 'de Jonge', 'kannecooper/ beytelschipper' uit Dordrecht in de zeventiende eeuw', *Antiek 23, no. 7*, 383–390.

Loomeijer, F.R. 1980 *Met zeil en treil. De tjalk in binnen- en buitenvaart*, De Alk, Alkmaar.

Loomeijer, F.R. 1987 *Water over dek en luiken*, De Alk, Alkmaar.

McLaughlin, K. 1992 *Two eighteenth-century prams from the Ijsselmeerpolders*. Unpublished Master's thesis, Department of Anthropology, Texas A&M University.

Oosting, R. & Vlierman, K. 1990 *"De Zeehond". Een groninger tjalk gebouwd in 1878, vergaan in 1886*. Flevobericht 323. Rijksdienst voor de IJsselmeerpolders. Lelystad.

Prins, A.H.J. 1969 'Schippers van Blokzijl. Een maritieme maatschappij in miniatuur', *Uit het Peperhuis, jaargang 1969, no. 1*, Zuiderzeemuseum, Enkhuizen.

Rudolph, W. 1973 'Frauenbezatsung auf Schiffsfahrzeugen im Oderhaff', *Greifswald-Stralsunder Jahrbuch 10*, 325–341.

Steppat, S. 1987a 'Der Alltag auf dem Binnenschiff im Wandel der Zeit', in J. Bachman & H. Hartmann, *Schiffahrt, Handel, Häfen. Beitrage zur Geschichte der Schiffarht auf Weser und Mittellandkanal*, Minden, 211–229.

Steppat, S. 1987b *Schifferfrauen auf dem Rhein. Die familiäre und soziale Lage der Frauen von Binnenschiffern. Studien zur Volkskultur in Rheinland-Pfalz. Bd. 2*, Mainz.

Verrips, J. 1991 *Als het tij verloopt.... Over binnenschippers en hun bonden 1898–1975*, Het Spinhuis, Amsterdam.

Witsen, N. 1671 *Aeloude en hedendaegsche scheepsbouw en bestier*, Amsterdam.

Archives
Rijksarchief of the province of Groningen, Notarieel archief.

19

Artefacts from wrecks: an endnote

Alan Aberg

The papers presented at Cardiff during the *Artefacts from Wrecks* conference demonstrate the significance of the results of archaeological investigations on wreck sites, both in the United Kingdom and overseas. They reinforce the position of the need for a critical archaeological approach and appropriate standards for research on historic wrecks, and provide a reminder, as expressed by Bob Thompson in the presentation on the late 16th-century Alderney wreck (not published here), that land and maritime cultures are integrated not separate, and need to be studied as a whole: that they are a single expression of history, not fragments of the past.

The importance of wrecks lies firstly in providing a closed context for dating objects, and the use of the words 'time capsule' have familiarised us and the public with events, often catastrophic, that created the unique deposits associated with the loss of a ship, crew and cargo. As an additional source of evidence for the typologies created from the painstaking interpretation of stratification during excavation on land, wreck sites provide a range of contemporary artefacts that assist the confirmation of evidence that is at the core of dating methods. When the wreck is soundly dated, as in the case of the *Mary Rose*, the finds are of durable value, and even when the date of loss and identification of the ship remain doubtful, these papers demonstrate the significance of the associated material found at such sites.

Preservation of the organic materials – wood, leather, textiles etc – is an obvious bonus to the study of artefacts. The contribution to studies from the preservation of gun carriages on 16th-century warships is widely seen as one achievement of underwater archaeology, because it has provided examples of carriage types little known or inadequately described by documents, and proved the provision of a variety of types in one ship. The study of navigational instruments has similarly benefited from finds such as those at Duart Point, and the technical information to be gleaned on furnishings, equipment and personal possessions is demonstrated from sites in The Netherlands and Baltic. For example the shipboard literature preserved in the books discovered on board the Swedish warship *Kronan* extends the range of organic materials in new directions, and throws unexpected light on the reading habits of mariners of the period.

On land, archaeological investigation has particular difficulty in revealing the extent of the personal possessions of those who lived and worked in the countryside and towns. It is recognised that survival is often selective as a result of the processes of deposit and corrosion, and even the discovery of rich funeral groups does not provide more than an insight into the customs and possessions of the more prosperous social groups. Artefacts from shipwrecks have helped to redress this balance, and the finds from the *Invincible*, *Mary Rose* and other sites have provided an insight into the clothing and possessions of the common sailor and passengers of different social classes. The excavations on vessels in The Netherlands also demonstrate how this insight can be extended to family groups for the Dutch boat people, and provide new evidence on the gender, age and family status of those who made a living on the inland waterways. The closed contexts of wrecks give an opportunity with careful excavation to compare the private possessions of those on board, and the study of the artefacts also reveals detail on the length of use, wear and the techniques available to repair them. The commonplace is, as emphasised by Colin Martin, the most significant element in understanding reality, and the evidence from wrecks is one means of redressing the imbalance from other sources.

The technological benefits from the study of artefacts recovered from shipwrecks was a repeated theme during the conference. Of particular importance is the opportunity provided by cargoes which provide the quantities necessary to analyse manufacturing techniques, packaging and contemporary practice in marketing. As was pointed out in the paper on ingots from shipwrecks, this applies also to the raw materials that constitute cargo as much as the finished goods, since the technology represented in the metals can provide details of smelting and casting processes as well as the origin of the ingots, if not already known. The study of the 200 bundles of footwear from the 16th-century Spanish Basque Galleon thought to be the *San Juan* is another example of how technical research allowed the identification of the styles and frequency of different shoe types, while the excavation of the *Machault* provided an illustration of contemporary perception of the trade goods thought to be marketable in the 18th-century colonies: pottery, footwear, metal vessels, shoe buckles and other supplies.

Finally, there is the ship itself as a representative of the technical skills, culture and investment of the society that built and equipped it. One may argue over the archaeological status of the vessel as a portable object or a site with an associated impact zone and debris field, but the growing evidence provided by systematic investigation can now claim to have improved our understanding of ship construction and building techniques, particularly during that vital period of change in the 16th century. The trade patterns and evidence for life on board as demonstrated by the artefacts substantiate and expand our limited documentary evidence, and the papers presented at this meeting will be appreciated by both underwater or land archaeologists interested in the wider discipline and philosophy of the subject.

Index of wrecks

Ships:
Adelaar, VOC (1728)   8–9
Adgillus (1874)   131, 132
Admiral Gardner, EIC (1809)   137, 149, 153 n.1 & n.14
Albion, EIC (1765)   149, 153
Amsterdam, VOC (1749)   105, 126, 187
Ann Francis (1583)   138, 140, 191 f.
'*Armada*'   1, 4, 5, 105, 137
Association (1707)   106
Assurance, HMS (1753)   138, 140
Batavia, VOC (1629)   v., 8, 11, 35, 101, 102, 104, 124, 125, 126, 127, 175, 177
Benamain, SS (1889)   152, 153
Benvrackie, SS (1942)   137
Bredenhof, VOC (1753)   147, 153 n.1
Buitenzorg, VOC (1760)   21, 26, 35, 187
Campen, VOC (1627)   145
Carnbrae Castle, EIC (1829)   149, 151, 152
Cheerful, SS (1885)   151
Dartmouth, HMS (1690)   1 f., 11, 133, 135, 171, 176
DeBraak, HMS (1798)   140
Doddington, EIC (1755)   107
Douro (1843)   143
Earl of Abergavenny, EIC (1805)   146, 149, 153
Fanny, EIC (1792)   144
Feversham, HMS (1711)   138, 140
Fowey, HMS (1748)   102
Geldermalsen, VOC ('The Nanking wreck';1752)   8, 126
Girona (1588)   140, 197
Göteborg (1745)   147, 153 n.9
El Gran Grifón (1588)   199, 201
'*Great Bark*' (1531)   84
Henry Addington, EIC (1798)   145, 153
Hindostan, EIC (1803)   149
Hollandia, VOC (1743)   v., 126, 137, 139, 140, 145
Invincible, HMS (1758)   108, 229
John (1573)   85 n.17
Kennemerland, VOC (1664)   v., 9, 11, 125, 127, 132, 175, 201
Kronan (1676)   101, 104, 126, 157, 173, 211 f., 229
Lastdrager, VOC (1653)   v., 124–5, 127
Leonidas (1832)   137
Lutina (1888) Lot H 48, Oostelijk Flevoland   27, 29, 31, 32, 221, 225, 227
Machault (1760)   37–48, 106, 111, 120 n.1, 132, 133, 230
Maravillas (1656)   147

Mary, Royal Yacht (1675)   138, 139, 140
Mary Rose (1545)   9, 51 f., 76, 82, 87 f., 102, 104–8, 123, 127, 138, 140, 157, 229
Mauritius, VOC (1609)   104, 105, 146
N.S. de Atocha (1622)   137, 138, 140, 193
N.S. de la Luz (1752)   137, 139, 140
N.S. de la Pura y Limpia Concepción (1641)   135
Olive Branch (1699)   133, 135
Pandora, HMS (1791)   177
Pomone, HMS (1811)   138, 140
Prince de Conty (1746)   144, 147
Sacramento (South Africa, 1647)   106
Sacramento (Brazil coast, 1668)   185 f.
St Anthony (1527)   150
St Bartholomew (1597)   153 n.4
San Diego (1600)   197
San Juan ('Red Bay wreck'; mid-16th-century)   10, 76, 82, 85 n.11 & 12, 111 f., 229
San Martin (1618)   84 n.9
Santa Margarita (1622)   84 n.9
Santa Maria de la Rosa (1588)   10
Sea Venture (1609)   123
Slot ter Hoog, VOC (1724)   147
Svärdet (1676)   212
La Trinidad Valencera (1588)   4 f., 76, 104, 105, 197–8, 202
Vasa (1628)   104, 105, 126, 132, 138, 140, 157, 173, 209, 215, 216
Vergulde Draeck, VOC (1656)   11, 125, 126, 127, 131, 133, 134, 175, 187
Waddingsveen, VOC (1697)   150, 151, 153
Whydah (1717)   140
Witte Leeuw, VOC (1613)   123, 124, 146, 147, 153
Winterton, EIC (1792)   148, 149
De Zeehond (*tjalk*,F 3, 1886)   31, 33, 35, 221, 222, 224–5, 227
Zeewijk (1727)   187
De Zeven Provinciën (17th century)   35, 132, 157

Wreck sites:
Aber Wrac'h (15th-century)   76
Alderney (1592)   83, 130, 134, 202, 229
Almere cog (1420/40)   31, 127, 140
Anholt II (17th-century)   106
Barra (Outer Hebrides) (1728)   1
Bermuda Channel (16th-century)   147
Blackfriars, London (Roman)   137
Boudeuse Cay, Seychelles (16th-century)   123

231

Index of wrecks

Calvi I (late 16th-century) 82
Cattewater (early 16th-century) 73f., 123, 201
Cayo Nuevo 108
Dover bronze Age boat (Kent, England) 1
Duart Point, Mull (?possibly the *Swan*, 1653) 11, 102, 103, 123, 133, 167 f., 229
Erne Bay, Devon 108
Highborn Cay (16th century) 76, 82, 105, 108
Indonesia 132

Ijsselmeer wrecks:
Oostelijk Flevoland:
lot B 19: mud barge (17th-century) 25
lot B 55: *tjalk* (mid-18th-century/*c.*1731) 24, 26, 221, 225
lot B 71: *beurtschip* (early 17th-century) 15, 19
lot D15 (*praam*-like, *c.*1742) 221, 223, 224, 225, 226
lot E14 (*praam*-like, *c.*1783) 31, 221, 227
lot F 34: *boyer* (late 18th-century) 24
lot F 60: *botter* (mid-19th-century) 25
lot H 41: *ventjager* (*c.*1700) 15, 17, 21
lot H 107: cargo vessel (late 17th-century) 20
lot K 45 armed *tjalk* (1673) 102, 104, 127, 157f.,
lot K 73/74 (15th-century) 138, 139, 140
lot K 84: *waterschip* (early 16th-century) 23
lot L 79: ship (late 18th-century) 28
lot M 65 (*tjalk*-like, *c.*1697) 221, 225, 226
lot S 19: vessel (17th-century) 17
lot U 34: *hulk* (*c.*1500) 19, 21, 26

Zuidelijk Flevoland:
lot Az 71: *praam*-like (*c.*1750) 28, 221, 223, 227

lot Kz 47: *waterschip* (late 16th-century) 23
lot Lz 1: *praam*-like (*c.* 1604) 24, 221
lot Lz 8: punt (18th-century) 25
lot Mz 66 (cargo-vessel, 15th-century) 162
lot Oz 36: Kampen cog (late 13th/early 14th-century) 21, 22
lot Oz 71 (*tjalk*, *c.*1685) 221

Nordoostpolder:
lot B 6 (*tjalk*-like, *c.*1786) 221
lot E 81: merchantman (mid-17th-century) 15, 16, 26, 29, 30
lot H49 (*praam*-like, *c.*1850) 221, 224, 225, 227
lot K 7: cargo ship (19th-century) 17

Kattegat (16th-century) 76
Kvitsøy galliot (1677) 126, 127
Mollases Reef (early 16th-century/1500–50) 82, 85 n.14, 103, 108
Mombasa wreck (early 17th-century) 197
Monte Cristi 'Pipe wreck'(*c.*1651–4) 132, 133, 134
Mullion Cove wreck (mid-17th-century) 201
Oxwich Bay (1557) 140
Padre Island (1554) 102, 103, 108, 123, 139
Riddarholmen, Stockholm 76
Rye Vessel A (16th-century) 82, 201
Studland Bay (16th-century) 83, 84 n.5 & 6, 85 n.12
Tal-y-bont, Cardigan Bay ('Bronze Bell') 105, 108
Texel TXS IV (*c.*1731–40) 186 f.
Vejby cog (late 14th-century) 137, 139
Villefranche (?*Lomellina* 1516) 82, 103, 140
Western Ledge Reef (16th-century) 197, 200
Yarmouth Roads, Isle of Wight (16th-century) 76
Yassi Ada (16th-century) 82

Colour Plate 1

Colour Plate 1A. Wrought iron portpiece on a reproduction carriage, set within the hull of the Mary Rose *(1509–1545) at the gun station where it was found.* (Copyright: The Mary Rose Trust)

Colour Plate 1B. Diver excavating contents from a chest on the Mary Rose. (Copyright: The Mary Rose Trust)

Colour Plate 1C. Selection of treen and domestic artefacts from the Mary Rose *(1509–1545).* (Copyright: The Mary Rose Trust)

COLOUR PLATE 2

Colour Plate 2A. Chest from the Mary Rose *with decorative spandrels.* (Copyright: The Mary Rose Trust)

Colour Plate 2B. Chest from the Mary Rose *with decoratively carved front panel.* (Copyright: The Mary Rose Trust)

Colour Plate 2C. A gimballed compass, plotting board and dividers recovered from the pilot's cabin on the Mary Rose. *The sundial in the leather case was found inside the carpenter's cabin.* (Copyright: The Mary Rose Trust)

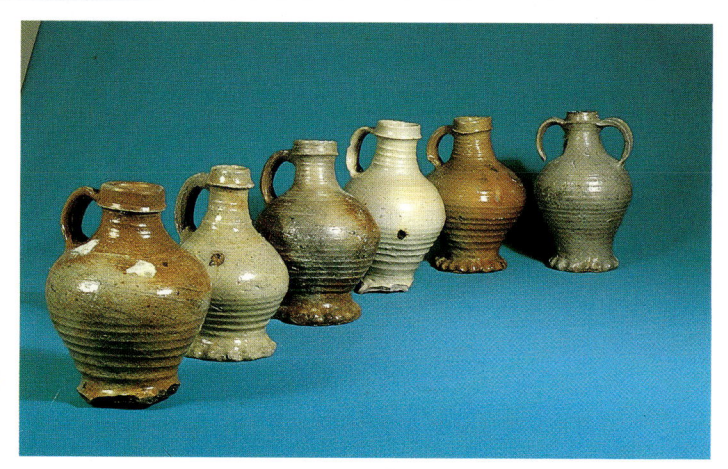

Colour Plate 2D. Raeren stoneware bottles of the period c.1475–1525 from the barber surgeon's chest of the Mary Rose, *lost off Portsmouth, 1545.* (Copyright: The Mary Rose Trust)

Colour Plate 3

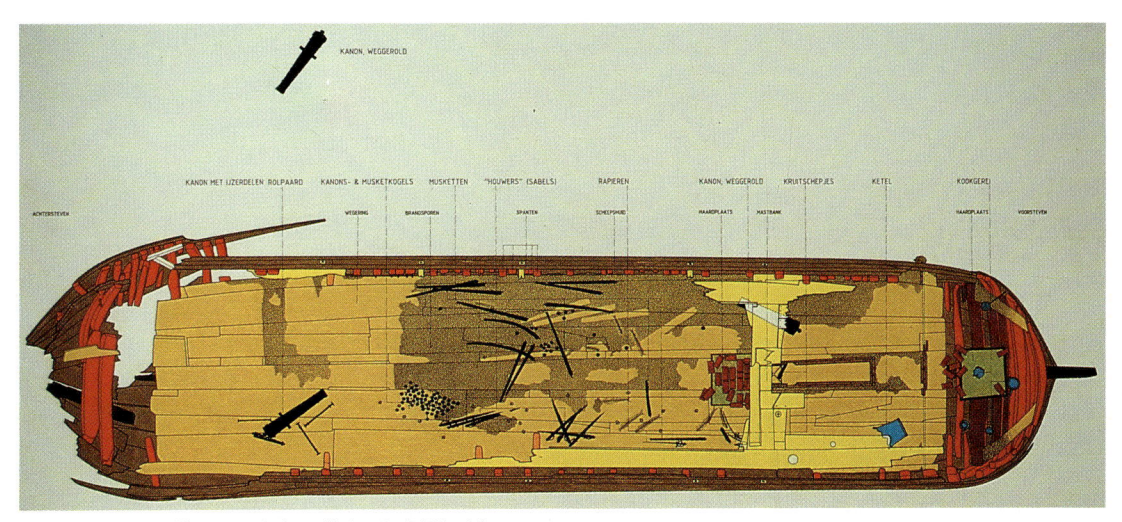

Colour Plate 3A. Top view of the tjalk lost in 1673 with scorch marks on the ceiling planking, showing the distribution of the guns and other weaponry.

Colour Plate 3B. The three different copper kettles and two skimmers, some redware cooking pots and stoneware jugs ('Bartmanner') from K 45.

Colour Plate 3C. All the galley utensils and cooking, eating and drinking equipment from K 45.

Colour Plate 4

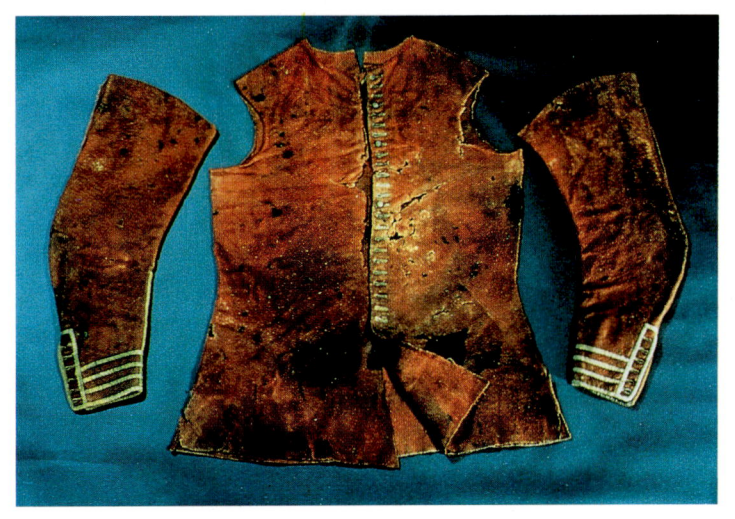

Colour Plate 4A. This scarlet jacket was found on its owner next to a 36–pounder gun on the Kronan. *It is made of wool and dyed with madder.* (Copyright: Kalmar läns Museum/The Kronan-Project)

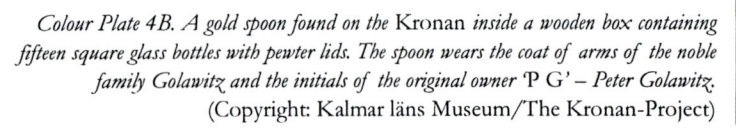

Colour Plate 4B. A gold spoon found on the Kronan *inside a wooden box containing fifteen square glass bottles with pewter lids. The spoon wears the coat of arms of the noble family Golawitz and the initials of the original owner 'P G' – Peter Golawitz.* (Copyright: Kalmar läns Museum/The Kronan-Project)

Colour Plate 4C. Distribution of pottery and location of wooden bowl on the Cattewater *wreck.* (Photograph: National Museums & Galleries of Wales)

Colour Plate 4D. Knife handle from Cattewater wreck (see Fig.8, 2). (Photograph: M. Redknap)